A Student's Guide to Relevance, Character, Habit, and Impeachment

A Student's Guide to Relevance, Character, Habit, and Impeachment

Clifford S. Fishman
Emeritus Professor of Law
Catholic University of America
Columbus School of Law

Carolina Academic Press
Durham, North Carolina

Library of Congress Cataloging-in-Publication Data

Names: Fishman, Clifford S., author.
Title: A student's guide to relevance, character, habit, and impeachment / by Clifford Fishman.
Description: Durham, North Carolina : Carolina Academic Press, LLC, [2021] | Series: The student's guide series
Identifiers: LCCN 2021049192 (print) | LCCN 2021049193 (ebook) | ISBN 9781531022365 (paperback) | ISBN 9781531022372 (ebook)
Subjects: LCSH: Examination of witnesses--United States.
Classification: LCC KF8950 .F57 2021 (print) | LCC KF8950 (ebook) | DDC 347.73/66--dc23/eng/2021122
LC record available at https://lccn.loc.gov/2021049192
LC ebook record available at https://lccn.loc.gov/2021049193

Carolina Academic Press
700 Kent Street
Durham, NC 27701
(919) 489-7486
www.cap-press.com

Printed in the United States of America

I dedicate this book to the thousands of students to whom I had the honor and privilege of teaching evidence. They helped me learn how to teach, and, over the years, taught me so much more.

I also dedicate this book to the students who will use it (and will use A Student's Guide to Hearsay*) to learn challenging and difficult aspects of evidence law. (May they number in the thousands each year!)*

Finally—rather, I should say, first, last, and always—I dedicate this book to Betty, my Editor for Life.

—CSF

Contents

Table of FRE Provisions

Statutes

Table of Cases

Preface: Short Important Comments[1] You Should Read First

§ P.1 Fishman Rule of Evidence 001

The law of evidence is not a precise science. Conscientious and diligent pursuers and transmitters of knowledge on the subject may disagree on one point or another. If your evidence professor should disagree about something I say in this book, apply the following:

> **Fishman Rule of Evidence 001.**
>
> If at any time and under any circumstance your evidence professor disagrees with something I have said in this book, your evidence professor is always right.
>
> Until after the exam.

§ P.2 How to learn the law *and* get a good grade in evidence

You are using this book for two main reasons: to help you learn a challenging and important aspect of evidence law, and to help you get a good grade in your evidence course. The two are related, of course, but learning the law does not always guarantee a good grade in a course. It also helps to learn how to "read" your professor. This book from time to time provides suggestions how to do so.

Here's the first gold nugget: we law professors crave positive feedback from students. We may seem self-assured and all-knowing, but in reality we are seething blobs of uncertainty and self-doubt. (Well, most of us are, and those who aren't, should be.) So in class, on quizzes, and on exams, it's important, yes, to demonstrate that you know the law, but it's also important to demonstrate that it was your professor's exceptional teaching that helped you learn it.

1. Well, most of the comments are important, anyhow.

This does *not* mean that your answer to every essay question should contain everything your professor ever said in class on any subject, in the hope that your prof will pick out the relevant parts.

More generally, remember that in evidence law, as in every other law course you take, there is often no "right answer."[2] Quite often in classroom discussions and on essay questions, there are issues with plausible arguments on both sides.

And remember that while every *substantive* course (like evidence) you take in law school is dedicated to teaching you a particular aspect of the law, *every* course in law school—not just the "skills" courses—is also dedicated to teaching you "how to lawyer": how to analyze the facts and applicable law in a case from both sides, come up with the best argument each party can make, and only then decide who should win and why. That's what professors look for in class discussion.

For example, in each of my courses, if a student tended to be defense-oriented, I would call on that student to give the prosecutor's argument, and vice versa. My goal was not to aggravate and annoy those students (although that was sometimes a fringe benefit); it was to force them to look at the question from "the other side," so they would learn the law better—and be better able to represent their "own side," having anticipated their opponent's arguments.

The odds are that a law professor grading a high-point-value essay question will likewise look for a discussion of each side's argument; an answer which fails to do so will receive fewer points. The answers to the practice questions throughout this book provide numerous examples of how to do so.

§ P.3 Another reason to use this book

When I was a law student back in the ~~19th~~ 20th Century, I recall one professor used his own book for a course he taught—nothing inherently wrong with that, of course, but that book was the best cure for insomnia I've ever encountered: it put me to sleep before I'd read five pages.[3] Most law books—in particular, books written for law students—are better than that, but let's face it, they are not an easy read. This one isn't, either—the topic is too complex and challenging to be easy. But I think this book will be more fun to read than most books about the law.[4] It includes dozens of amusing[5] and entertaining[6] historical, cultural, and artistic references, puns, and useful nuggets of professional and personal advice. In fact, in § P.8, I provide a scavenger hunt-type list of them for you to search for, if you've the time and inclina-

---

2. Exception: on a well-written multiple-choice question, there is a single correct answer.

3. That mirrored his classroom performance, too. I managed a B-minus in the course—I'm still not sure how.

4. Off-hand, I can think of only one law book that can compare to it in the fun-to-learning ratio: *A Student's Guide to Hearsay* (5th ed. 2019).

5. To me, anyhow.

6. I hope.

tion. Some of these are easy to spot; other clues are cryptic. Have fun searching for them (or don't bother, if that's your preference).

§ P.4 What to read in this book... and what you can skip

To properly teach everything you need to know about evidence would require a six-credit course. Most law schools allot only three or four credits, which means that most professors have to pick and choose what to omit or give a very light once-over, and what to emphasize. Since I have no way of knowing what your professor will emphasize, skim or omit, I've written this book assuming that each law professor will stress each rule or topic I cover in it. Read and skip accordingly.

§ P.5. Vocabulary: Parts of a question

The basic fact pattern in a question—the part that gives you the information (facts and law) you need—is called the "stem."

The part of the question that tells you what you are asked to do is the "call." Sometimes the call is quite specific, instructing you to apply specific provisions of the FRE, or asking how a particular litigant might respond to what has been set out in the stem. Sometimes the call is quite general: "Discuss the issues thus presented." In that case, the applicable law includes any provision of the FRE which has been covered in the book so far. In answering such questions, as a rule, you should discuss how each side in the case might plausibly argue for or against the admissibility of the evidence or the propriety of a lawyer's question, before deciding how the judge should rule.

In a multiple-choice question, the answer choices are called "options."

§ P.6 Historical perspective; progress; and vocabulary

My law school class (Columbia, 1969) had 270 students. Twenty-three were women. The class was overwhelmingly White. My law school yearbook included photographs of fifty-seven members of the full-time and adjunct faculty. All fifty-seven were White men.

In 1969, I was one of fifteen new Assistant D.A.s hired by the New York County (i.e., Manhattan) D.A.'s Office. All of us were White, and twelve of us were men. The three women were immediately assigned to the Appeals Bureau, because the men who ran the office "knew" that women did not have what it took to survive in the combative atmosphere of a courtroom or the fortitude to work with cops and informants in an investigations bureau.

I cite these facts not (I assure you) out of nostalgia for the "good old days," but to give a bit of historical perspective: our profession and our nation have a long, long way to go before they truly exemplify the ideals expressed in our founding documents, but we have made considerable progress in the past fifty years. As Dr. King was fond of saying, "The moral arc of the universe is long, but it bends toward justice."[7] That arc is not constant; it suffers periodic setbacks; but the law is an essential tool in the struggle to achieve a just society.

Our use of language reflects that progress, but that progress often poses challenges. Anyone who speaks or writes for public consumption must (or at least should) try to balance several sometimes-conflicting goals: to write clearly; to write with some degree of style or flair (for self-satisfaction, and to keep the reader engaged, or, at least, awake); to reflect reality; to avoid negative stereotypes and offending usages.[8] I have tried my best to strike the right balance in this book.

§ P.7 A brief bio

I was born in New York City in 1945. In 1953, my family was among the first to move from the city to the suburbs (Long Island). I attended public schools K-12. I got my BA (and more importantly, met and fell in love with Betty, my Editor-for-Life) at the University of Rochester (1966).

I received my JD at Columbia University Law School in 1969. I graduated with a B average; I did not make law review. By then I was so sick of being a student all my life that I vowed I'd never set foot on a college campus again (well, at any rate not until my children, if I ever had any, would be applying to colleges). I became an Assistant D.A. in Manhattan; after three years there, I was assigned to the city's Special Narcotics Prosecutor's Office, where I tried dozens of cases, oversaw all our investigations (including the most expensive purchase of a kilogram of pancake mix in the history of law enforcement), and helped put some pretty bad people away for a long time.

In 1976, I set up an informal program to teach our first- and second-year A.D.A.s the basics—how to conduct direct examination, the basics of cross, how to work with cops on investigations. That became the most enjoyable aspect of my job; that's what prompted me to think about teaching law. And I wanted to spend more time with Betty and our (first) daughter. In addition, almost by accident, I become the office specialist on electronic surveillance, and wrote an office manual on the subject, and thought: hey, maybe I should write a book on it.

I interviewed at a number of law schools. Catholic University of America was the best school to offer me a job, and it was in the most interesting city (Washington DC). I had a few qualms—"will Catholic be a good place for a 'nice Jewish boy from

---

7. This phrase is derived from comments by Theodore Parker, a 19th century Transcendentalist, Abolitionist and Unitarian minister whose works also inspired the closing sentence of President Lincoln's Gettysburg Address.

8. See, e.g., § 9.2. Also consider the current debate over the use of gender-specific pronouns.

New York?'" Turned out, it was an excellent place to be. It has been a pleasure being at a school that takes religion seriously and respects all religions. CUA has gone out of its way to support me and other Jewish faculty members to bring Jewish speakers and programs to the law school.

I was on the faculty at CUA for 42½ years. I taught evidence, criminal law, and criminal procedure to thousands of students. I've written 11 law books by myself—the five editions of *A Student's Guide to Hearsay,* the one-volume first edition of *Wiretapping and Eavesdropping,* and the first five volumes of the 7th edition of *Jones on Evidence.* Anne T. McKenna—my former student, and my professional partner and friend since 1994—and I have written an additional eight books—the second and third editions of *Wiretapping and Eavesdropping: Surveillance in the Internet Age,* and volumes 6 and 7 of *Jones.*[9] These 19 books and annual supplements, and my 20 scholarly articles, take up 47 inches of shelf space.

If Carolina Academic Press prints this book on thick enough paper, it will bring my shelf-space total to an even four feet.

Will this be my last law book? As I write this, I think so. But then again that's how I felt after each of the previous 19, too, so who knows?

§ P.8 The "scavenger hunt"

Here is the list of the puns, obscure references to history, music, art, sports, etc. This list does not include where they appear, but I will give you two hints. First, this is the order in which they appear in the book. And in the Afterword at the end of the book, I tell you where each is, and explain each, if an explanation is necessary.

The cosmic significance of 9:37 p.m., October 30, 2019.

---

9. The two treatises are published by another company whose name must not be mentioned here, but its initials are the same as those of the only twentieth century President enshrined on Mount Rushmore.

Don't it make that brown eye blue? No, it don't.

Why it is good to have a friend with a short attention span who knows nothing about the law.

"Could this be magic?"

Blake Shelton's 2004 hit song "Some Beach."

"Could this be magic?" (again).

Twenties questions.

Holodecks.

Professional advice: where not to interview a client.

Professional advice: where not to discuss a case.

Tissues and country and western music.

A business model you should *not* recommend to a client.

L. Frank Baum and Judy Garland.

Sir William S. Gilbert.

What Oliver Wendell Holmes, Eleanor Roosevelt, Linus Van Pelt, and Confucius have in common.

Charles Lutwidge Dodgson.

Lin-Manuel Miranda.

When would history buffs and lovers of Shakespeare make poor jurors?

Professor Fishman favorably compares himself to one of the greatest writers and statesmen in world history.

A vehicle pulled by three horses abreast.

Shar-peis.

Dog poop.

The official definition of "elderly."

Dog poop.

Professor Fishman favorably compares himself to the Bible.

A defensive tackle for the Dallas Cowboys.

Judy Garland.

Sainthood in everyday life.

What Rudolph does the rest of the year.

What "kemosabe" means in various Native American languages.

Charles Dickens.

Taking three wickets from three consecutive balls. Or else, an octopus.

Weather in the Heights.

A particularly bad way to pick up some extra cash fast.

Professor Fishman's pre-law school employment history.

Professor Fishman's efforts to insure domestic tranquility.

Eschewing pellucidity.

What Hollywood and Kansas City, Missouri, have in common.

Or well that ends well. (Or: the weather in April.).

The professor channels his inner Roger Ebert.

Longfellow Deeds and the pixies; or, the professor again channels his inner Roger Ebert.

Roger Ebert, 3.0.

What do a Jabberwock, Mad Magazine and a witch doctor have in common?

The difference between beef wellington and beef stroganoff.

What the Dickens?

Pulitzer Prize for fiction.

A-B-C, easy as 1-2-3-4-5.

We don't care how miserable you feel, Victor: you go first.

Weather in the Heights.

Volleyball and Einstein's theory of special relativity.

Before you leave home …

The prof quotes the Bard (but doesn't use quotation marks).

How not to apologize.

"Just when you thought it was safe to get back in the shower. …"

Albert King (not the basketball player), Jimi Hendrix, Pat Travers, Cream.

"Sunrise, sunset; sunrise, sunset; swiftly fly the days…"

When would someone from, say, the Rockies, be referred to as a "Flatlander"?

Happy hunting.

Acknowledgments

Some people have likened having a book published to giving birth. I have not, myself, had the latter experience, although I was present on three occasions when a new child entered the world. (I have clear memories of the latter two; the first time, I was too young to appreciate the experience.) I doubt if anyone who has given birth would endorse the comparison. Still, there are similarities—the first stage of the process is often joyful and a cause for celebration; what follows is lengthy, awkward and uncomfortable; the last stage often involves so much hard labor that it sometimes seems amazing that anyone who has experienced it the first time would voluntarily go through it again. But people do! This is my twentieth. (Law book, not child.)

Another similarity: In each act of creation, the prolonged parts of the process are much, much easier if the creator has help, as I have for each of my books. So: my thanks to the Columbus School of Law, the Catholic University of America, for its continued support of my work, even after I ascended to the exalted status of Professor Emeritus. My thanks as well to Kathleen Soriano-Taylor and her staff at Carolina Academic Press for their work on the book (and their continued patience even after I missed the "nth" deadline). And of course, to Betty, my Editor for Life.

The Columbus School of Law, The Catholic University of America, has been my professional home since the summer of 1977. I taught there under a dozen deans and with several dozen faculty colleagues. We have worked, debated, laughed, celebrated and mourned together, and, occasionally, disagreed, vigorously but respectfully. We brought different backgrounds, beliefs and approaches to what we taught and how we taught, and these differences strengthened and enriched our lives and our community.

The law school's administrative and support staffs contributed beyond measure to make the school a warm, welcoming and inclusive place to study, learn, teach, research and write about the law. It is impossible to name everyone to whom praise and thanks are due, but I will mention four special people here:

Joan Vorrasi, who for four decades was at the center of student life at the law school. I will always cherish our conversations about Judaism and Catholicism, and the energy and loving attention she gave to every aspect of student activities and events at the school. May her memory always be for a blessing.

Law school librarian Steve Young, for whom no reference is too obscure and no source is too daunting to track down. Steve not only found whatever I was looking for; often he anticipated what I would need before I realized that I needed it. If a law professor asked Steve to find the Lost Ark, I'm sure Steve would locate it in a day or two without any of that Indiana Jones fuss and bother.

Georgia Niedzielko received her JD from Catholic in 1981. Between 1988 and her retirement in 2021, Georgia served as our director of legal career services, as an assistant to the dean, as the assistant dean for academic affairs, and as the assistant dean for administration. Georgia and I worked together on the drafting and administration of the law school's honor code and on several other projects. We have all benefitted from her dedication to our students and to the quality and integrity of our educational program, and from her decency and honor and wisdom and sense of humor.

Julie Kendrick's years as my administrative assistant were my best years as a teacher and my most productive years as a scholar, and that was no coincidence. Julie created and administered a record-keeping system that enabled me to give multiple anonymously graded quizzes each semester; she reached out to students who missed classes or who did poorly on the quizzes. My students quickly recognized that they could trust and confide in her—as did I.

Thanks to you all.

A Student's Guide to Relevance, Character, Habit, and Impeachment

Chapter 1

Relevance—FRE 401, 402, 104(b), and 106

A. Relevance: FRE 401–402

§ 1.1 The centrality of "relevance" in the law of evidence: FRE 402

Relevance is the fundamental component of the law of evidence. Evidence that is irrelevant should not be admitted at trial. Evidence that is relevant should be admitted, unless barred by some other rule. FRE 402 enunciates this basic principle:

> **Rule 402. General Admissibility of Relevant Evidence**
>
> Relevant evidence is admissible unless any of the following provides otherwise:
>
> - the United States Constitution;
> - a federal statute;
> - these rules; or
> - other rules prescribed by the Supreme Court.

So the basic rule is: "Relevant evidence is admissible—unless..." This book will help you learn what "relevant evidence" is—and also help you learn when the "unless" kicks in.

The opposite is also true: "Evidence that is not relevant is not admissible."[1]

§ 1.2 Relevance defined; FRE 401

FRE 401 provides:

> **Rule 401. Test for Relevant Evidence**
>
> Evidence is relevant if:
>
> (a) it has any tendency to make a fact more or less probable than it would be without the evidence; and
>
> (b) the fact is of consequence in determining the action.

In other words, evidence is relevant only to the extent that it helps prove or disprove a fact which itself is important to the resolution of a case.

Suppose cars driven by WNF and PPF collide in a suburb just outside Washington, D.C. The issue: which driver ran a stop sign. WNF was wearing a red hat with a

1. Evidence which starts out irrelevant may become relevant during the trial. We'll explore examples of this later on.

white curly "W"; he was also wearing a red shirt with a similar W on the front, and "Scherzer 31" on the back. If you are a baseball fan, you may know that the "curly W" appears on Washington Nationals uniforms, and that Max Scherzer, who was a pitcher for the Washington Nationals at the time, wore uniform number 31.[2] If we need to know what team WNF roots for, WNF's hat and shirt are clearly relevant as making it more probable—in fact, a lot more!—than it would be without the evidence that WNF is a Washington Nationals fan.[3]

But is *that* fact "of consequence" in determining who ran the stop sign?

Almost certainly not, if the collision occurred, say, in February.[4] Who WNF roots for is just a random fact which has nothing to do with the collision.

But if the collision occurred on October 30, 2019, at 9:37 p.m. and WNF's car radio was tuned to seventh and final game of the 2019 World Series between the Washington Nationals and Houston Astros, the fact that WNF is a Nationals fan *is* a fact "of consequence." Why? Because that's when Howie Kendrick hit a two-run home run to give the Nats a 3–2 lead in game 7 of the World Series—a moment, I can assure you, that no Nats fan will ever forget,[5] and supports the inference that WNF was paying more attention to the game on the radio than he was to traffic signs, which in turn makes it more probable than it would be without the evidence that WNF ran the stop sign.[6]

"Wait-a-minute," you might be thinking. "Just because he was wearing that stuff, it doesn't necessarily follow that he was a Nationals fan. And even if he was a fan, it doesn't automatically mean he wasn't paying attention to traffic signs!" And you'd be right on both accounts. But to be relevant, evidence doesn't have to "automatically mean" something, and the desired inference does not have to "necessarily follow" from the evidence. That's not the test of relevance.

Read the definition again. To be relevant, evidence doesn't have to "prove" a fact, if by "prove" you mean, "establish to a certainty." To be relevant, the evidence only has to "*have any tendency*" to make a fact of consequence—in this case, that WNF ran the stop sign—"more probable than it would be without the evidence." WNF's Nationals gear, plus what was going on in the ball game (and on the radio) at the time of the collision, has at least a slight tendency to make it more probable than it would be without the evidence that WNF was distracted and didn't notice the stop sign.

2. Besides being an excellent pitcher, Scherzer is best known for having one blue eye and one brown eye. (I am not making this up.)

3. The fact that I am using this hypothetical also makes it more probable than it would be without this hypothetical that I am a Washington Nationals fan, too.—CSF

4. The major league baseball season usually begins in April and ends in late October or (good grief!) early November.

5. You have perhaps noticed that the inference in note 3 is getting stronger. (In case you forgot—the Nats won the game, 6–2.) The series was remarkable (among other reasons) because it was the first time that all seven games in a World Series were won by the visiting team.

6. This fact pattern is not autobiographical. My wife and I were watching the game on TV.

To put it differently: WNF's Nationals gear supports the inference that he is a Nationals fan; and that fact, in the time and circumstances, supports the further inference that he was distracted by the game and didn't see the stop sign.

Conclusion: in the World Series hypothetical, the evidence is relevant, and the judge should admit it (unless it violates some other rule[7]). Then, it is up the jury to decide how much weight to give it.

§ 1.3 How relevance "fits" with the rest of evidence law: an outline

This section may be useful as a brief outline of the entire evidence course.

Determining whether evidence is admissible is a multi-step process. The steps are as follows:

1. ***Determining relevancy.*** FRE 402 directs that evidence which is not relevant is not admissible; evidence which is relevant is admissible (unless barred by another rule of evidence, the Constitution, an Act of Congress, or some other rule promulgated by the Supreme Court).[8] FRE 401 defines relevance; FRE 104(b) must also be considered.[9]

It is not enough, however, to decide *whether* evidence is relevant; it is also necessary to determine *how* and *why* it is relevant, because only after you have defined how the evidence is relevant are you in a position to determine whether other rules of evidence may affect its admissibility. At a trial, the judge will expect the offering party to explain how and why the evidence is relevant. Similarly, in your evidence course, your professor will expect you to do so with regard to each offer of evidence.

Once it has been determined whether (and how and why) an offer of evidence is relevant, the next step is to consider whether there is another specific rule within the FRE that affects its admissibility. Such rules may be roughly categorized in steps 2–5 as follows.

2. ***Substantive exclusionary and inclusionary rules.*** Some FRE rules direct that certain kinds of evidence shall not be admitted; others specify that certain kinds of evidence shall be admitted; others, that certain kinds of evidence may be admitted,

---

7. I cannot think of any plausible argument to exclude it.

8. This book focuses primarily on the Federal Rules of Evidence. However, other legal principles also affect the admissibility of evidence. For example, in criminal trials, evidence which is highly relevant to a defendant's guilt may be suppressed if it was obtained in violation of a defendant's Fourth Amendment right against unreasonable searches and seizures. Statements obtained from a defendant during custodial interrogation not preceded by proper Miranda warnings and a valid waiver are likewise inadmissible. And so on.

9. See § 1.13, discussing conditional relevancy. And see § 1.14, which briefly discusses authentication and identification, which are subcategories of relevance.

assuming they are not barred by another rule. See, e.g., FRE 404–415; Article V; FRE Rules 601–610.

3. Rules that speak to the *form* of the evidence (e.g., FRE Articles VIII, X).

4. Rules regulating the ***procedure*** whereby evidence is offered (e.g., FRE 104(a), 611–614).

5. Assuming the evidence appears to be admissible after these analytical steps have been taken, the next step is to determine whether, despite its relevancy, the evidence should be excluded because it is unfairly prejudicial, or is confusing, misleading, too time consuming, or cumulative; in other words, ***apply FRE 403***.

6. ***Damage control; protecting the record.*** Once the judge has ruled, at least one party will be disappointed and disadvantaged by the ruling. What should that party do to minimize the damage, or to protect the trial record for a potential appeal? This requires consideration of FRE 103, 105 and 106.

This chapter introduces you to the first step just mentioned: determining relevancy (Rule 401). Subsequent chapters will cover several of the rules that fall into the five remaining steps.

§ 1.4 "Material"; "fact of consequence"; "element"

"Relevancy" does not exist in a vacuum. Under traditional definitions, to be relevant, a fact must be "material," a term which Rule 401 replaces with the phrase, "fact that is of consequence in determining the action." To determine whether a fact is "material" or "consequential," it is necessary to examine the issues in the case, as defined by the underlying substantive law, the pleadings,[10] applicable pretrial orders, and events that develop during the trial. As a rule, evidence is relevant only if, directly or indirectly, it helps a party prove or disprove an element of the crime, cause of action or defense.

The connection to an element need not be direct, so long as it exists.[11] Once a witness has testified to certain facts, for example, the accuracy of his testimony (sometimes confusingly referred to as his "credibility") is "a fact that is of consequence to the determination of the action," and evidence relating to the accuracy of his testimony is therefore relevant—but only if the facts the witness has already testified about are themselves relevant.

---

10. "Relevancy is not an inherent characteristic of any item of evidence but exists only as a relation between an item of evidence and a matter properly provable in the case." Advisory Committee Note to the Federal Rules of Evidence, 56 FRD 183, 215. In criminal cases, "pleadings" include the formal charging document—which may be called the complaint, or the indictment, or the information—and a defendant's formal notice that he or she is asserting particular defenses, where a jurisdiction requires such formal notice.

11. See the Advisory Committee Note, supra: "The fact to be proved may be ultimate, intermediate, or evidentiary; it matters not, so long as it is of consequence in the determination of the action."

Question 1.

How can I tell what the "elements" are in a case or problem?

Answer:

In the real world, you would find the statute the defendant is accused of violating, or the case law which spells out the jurisdiction's substantive law defining the crime, claim, or defense. Maybe you would research how other jurisdictions handle the issues, check out treatises and law reviews, etc.

In all likelihood, your evidence professor will not require you to do any of this. She may expect you to know the basic elements of, say, a simple breach of contract action or a tort negligence action. (She's assuming you retained at least that much from your first-year torts and contracts courses—particularly if she taught one of those courses.) But the odds are, each evidence problem will tell you what the elements of a crime, claim or defense are—if you read the problem carefully. Similarly, a case in the casebook will quote the statute, or the controlling court decision, or a Restatement of Law, that spells out the elements of a crime, claim or defense.

Question 2.

P, an employee of GoodFoods Supermarket, claimed that he slipped and fell on corn silk that was on the floor of the produce department while he was walking from the company lunchroom to the cash register where he was about to resume his shift. P brought a workman's compensation action to recover damages for medical expenses and lost wages while he was recuperating from his injuries. Under workman's compensation law, an employee is entitled to certain specified compensation so long as (a) the employee was injured while engaged in job-related activities, and (b) the employee suffered medical expenses and lost income as a result.

GoodFoods contests P's claim. At the proceeding, GoodFoods seeks to offer evidence that the corn silk had been dropped onto the floor by a customer no more than five seconds before P slipped on it—and that therefore GoodFoods had had no opportunity to clean the floor, and thus was not negligent with regard to the corn silk on the floor. GoodFoods also offers evidence that P was contributorily negligent—he was looking over his shoulder at an attractive customer as he walked toward the front of the store, instead of looking where he was going. P objects that both items of evidence are irrelevant. Ruling?

Answer:

Objections sustained. Read the last sentence of the first paragraph of this question: "Under workman's compensation law, an employee is entitled to certain specified compensation so long as (a) the employee was injured while engaged in job-related activities, and (b) the employee suffered medical expenses and lost income as a result." Those are the *only* elements in a workman's comp case. Negligence simply is not an issue in workman's comp cases. It is not an element of the claim; and contributory negligence is not a defense.

Question 3.

"Wait a minute—aren't negligence and contributorily negligence always issues in a personal injury lawsuit?"

Answer:

"Always"? Maybe; I don't know. Ask your Torts professor. But this is not a personal injury lawsuit, it is a workman's comp case. The last sentence of the first paragraph of Question 2 told you what you needed to know about such cases. Negligence is simply not a "fact of consequence" in a workman's comp suit. This means that evidence that GoodFoods was or was not negligent, or that P was or was not contributorily negligent, is not relevant in P's workman's comp action, and since it is not relevant, it is not admissible.

Question 4.

Federal law prohibits employers from discriminating in hiring and promoting on the basis of sex, age, race, religion, or national origin. When a company or organization is sued for employment discrimination, the defense often offers evidence that it denied plaintiff the job or the promotion, not as an act of discrimination, but for a different, valid reason.

Plaintiff sues XYZ Co., a local supermarket, alleging that XYZ refused to promote him because he was born in country "T." Plaintiff presents his case and rests; XYZ moves for a directed verdict, which the judge denies.[12] During the defense case, XYZ offers evidence that it refused to promote plaintiff, not because of where he was born, but because he is not a Christian. Is this evidence relevant?

Answer:

No.

Why? Read the first sentence of the question again: "Federal law prohibits employers from discriminating in hiring and promoting on the basis of sex, age, race, religion or national origin." Now read the second sentence again: "Typically a defendant who is sued for job discrimination will offer evidence that it denied plaintiff the job or the promotion, not as an act of discrimination, but for a different, *valid* reason."

As a matter of substantive law, XYZ's "defense" is not a *valid* defense. Discrimination on the basis of religion is unlawful; therefore, it cannot be a "valid" defense against a claim of discrimination on the basis of national origin.[13]

As I said earlier, as a rule, an evidence problem will tell you the elements of a crime, claim or defense—if you read the problem carefully.

12. We will review motions for directed verdict in § 2.12.

13. If this happened in an actual case, Plaintiff might not object—he might *want* the jury to hear this evidence, because XYZ is admitting that it did in fact discriminate against him on an unlawful basis, albeit a different basis than Plaintiff alleges. But if Plaintiff moved to exclude or strike the evidence, the judge would grant the motion.

§ 1.5 "More probable or less probable"

The second element of the definition of relevance is that the evidence must in fact have, as the second sentence of FRE 401 puts it, some "tendency to make the existence of any fact that is of consequence to the determination of the action more probable or less probable than it would be without the evidence." The offering party should be prepared to articulate the inferences which connect the evidence to a fact of consequence, or explain how the evidence will assist the factfinder in evaluating other evidence. Assessing whether the evidence has the required tendency depends upon "principles evolved by experience or science, applied logically to the situation at hand." In other words, it depends on common sense—and on how well a lawyer can argue for or against the relevance of an item of evidence.

Question 1.

D is charged with assault in the second degree, defined as follows.

> 120.05 Assault in the second degree
>
> A person is guilty of assault in the second degree when:
>
> 1. With intent to cause serious physical injury to another person, he causes such injury to such person or to a third person;...[14]

The state offers evidence that on the evening in question, D, in a bar, threw a heavy glass beer pitcher at X, intending to seriously injure X; X ducked, but the pitcher hit Y in the head that caused recurrent headaches, as a result of which Y had to miss a week of work.

What are the elements of the crime?

Answer:

The statute spells them out:

1. D engaged in the conduct (which is sometimes referred to as the "actus reus")—i.e., he threw the pitcher at X.
2. He intended to cause serious physical injury to X.
3. In fact, he caused serious physical injury to Y.

Let's start with the first element. What did D do? The prosecutor has to offer evidence that tends to prove that D threw the pitcher.

14. New York Penal Law § 120.05 subd. 1. The statute's reference to "a third person" incorporates the common-law principle of "transferred intent": if a defendant acted with criminal intent toward X, but his effort went awry and he injured Y instead, even though the defendant had absolutely no intent to injure Y, the law "transfers" D's unlawful intent against X and applies it to the charges against Y. (You learned this in your criminal law course; I'm simply reminding you, at no extra charge.)

D, on the other hand, is permitted to offer evidence that *he* did not throw it, someone else did. Or perhaps D will offer evidence that he did not *throw* it; he picked it up and it slipped out of his hand. All of this is relevant to make it less probable that D threw the pitcher.

Question 2.

How might the prosecutor attempt to prove (i.e., attempt to persuade the jury beyond a reasonable doubt) that D intended to cause serious physical injury to X?

Answer:

To begin with, we have the act itself. Throwing a fairly heavy object at a person certainly supports the conclusion that the intent was to seriously injure that person. Jurors do not have to accept that conclusion, but they certainly could.

The prosecutor might also offer evidence of the prior relationship between D and X. Were they rivals at work? Were they both romantically interested in the same person? Did something happen between D and X earlier that week, that day, or just a few seconds before the pitcher flew through the air, that angered D? All this may be relevant to show that D had (in his own mind, anyway) a motive to want to hurt X. Evidence that D had a motive to hurt X also tends to disprove D's claim that someone else threw the pitcher, or that it slipped out of D's hand by accident.

D, on the other hand, can offer evidence that he and X got along pretty well and he had no motive to hate or want to injure X. Such evidence is relevant because it would make it less probable that D intentionally threw the pitcher at X.

Question 3.

Now consider the third element: that Y suffered a "serious physical injury" from being hit by the pitcher. Y testifies that getting hit in the head by the pitcher caused recurrent headaches as a result of which he had to miss a week of work, and that even now, months later, he gets debilitating headaches from time to time. The prosecutor offers medical records documenting Y's trip to the emergency room and follow-up visits to his doctors. This evidence is relevant to show the severity of the injury.

Suppose, during the defense case, D offers a clip from a broadcast of a Washington Nationals baseball game which took place three days after Y was hit on the head by the pitcher—a day when Y would normally be at work. The clip shows Y, at the ball game, wearing a Nationals hat and shirt, jumping up and down and high-fiving everyone within reach after Nationals outfielder Juan Soto hit a three-run homer. Is this evidence relevant?

Answer:

It is *not* relevant, if offered to disprove that D threw the beer pitcher.

It is *not* relevant, if offered to disprove that D intended to seriously injure X.

It *is* relevant, if offered to disprove the prosecutor's allegation that Y suffered a serious physical injury, because Y's presence and conduct at the ball game tend to make it less probable than it would be without that evidence that Y suffered such bad headaches that he was unable to go to work.

The point here is that to be relevant, it is not necessary that evidence tend to prove or disprove *every* element in a case; it need only have "any tendency" to prove or disprove *any* element in the case.

If this was a civil case—if Y was suing D for monetary damages for pain, suffering and lost income—the clip from the ball game would be relevant for essentially the same reason: to make it less likely that Y's injury was as serious as Y claims.

§ 1.6 Relevancy distinguished from admissibility; sufficiency and weight of the evidence; witness credibility; the judge's role

As already noted, relevancy is a precondition to the admissibility of evidence, but is not its equivalent: a substantial portion of the law of evidence, and portions of this book, focus on the various reasons that relevant evidence might be excluded. The six-step process suggested in § 1.3 outlines various reasons why relevant evidence may be excluded.

It is also important to distinguish between relevance and sufficiency. By the close of its case in chief, a party must satisfy its burden of production, or suffer a directed verdict (see § 2.12, infra); but it is not required to meet the test of sufficiency with each offer of evidence. An individual item of evidence is not required to prove that a "consequential fact" is "more probable than not"; It need only have "*any* tendency to make [that fact] more probable... *than it would be without the evidence.*"[15] Or, if a party is trying to disprove an alleged fact, an item of evidence need only have "any tendency to make [that fact] less probable... than it would be without the evidence."

This means that the standard to apply in assessing relevance should be liberal, generous and relatively undemanding.

And because the jury, not the judge, is the ultimate arbiter of the credibility and weight to be given to witness W's testimony or other evidence, it follows that, so long as W and W's testimony or other evidence meet the minimal standards of competency, a judge may not consider credibility in assessing relevance.

This means the judge's role in determining relevance is quite limited. She cannot exclude the evidence as irrelevant simply because she disbelieves W. She cannot exclude the evidence as irrelevant simply because she is not convinced that the evidence supports what its proponent offers it to prove. If a rational jury *might* be

15. FRE 401 (emphasis added).

convinced that the testimony (or other evidence) has "*any* tendency" to make the proponent's case stronger (or the other side's case weaker) than it would be without the evidence, the evidence is relevant and, barring some other objection, the judge should admit the evidence and let the jury consider it.

§ 1.7 Inferences; testimonial inferences

Inferences. An inference is a factual conclusion that can rationally be drawn from other facts. If fact *A* rationally supports the conclusion that fact *B* is also true, then *B* may be *inferred* from *A*. This process, drawing inferences based on a rough assessment of probabilities, is what makes indirect or circumstantial evidence relevant at trial. If the inference (fact *B* from fact *A*) is strong enough, then fact *A* is relevant to prove fact *B*.

Inferences are by their nature permissive, not mandatory: although the fact proved (fact A) rationally supports the inferred fact (fact B), the factfinder is free to accept or reject the inference.[16] In the collision between WNF and PPF, the fact that WNF was wearing a Washington Nationals cap and shirt supports the inference that WNF is a Nationals fan; but the jury is entitled to reject that inference. And if the collision occurred while WNF was listening to a crucial point in the 2019 World Series, that supports the further inference that he was distracted by the game and not paying attention to road signs. A jury does not have to accept that inference; but it certainly can do so.

Testimonial inferences. A witness's testimony can be relevant to an issue in a trial only if we make four basic testimonial inferences, involving perception, memory, narration and veracity (sometimes referred to as '"sincerity" or "bias" or "motive to lie"). To say the same thing more elaborately, testimony has probative value on the point for which it is offered only if the fact-finder is satisfied (1) that witness W accurately perceived the objects, events or conditions about which W is testifying; (2) that W remembers those objects or events or conditions accurately; (3) that W is communicating accurately what W perceived and remembers, i.e., that the words W uses while testifying mean the same to W as they do to the fact-finder; and (4) that W is not consciously lying or subconsciously shading the truth.[17]

Logically, therefore, any evidence which supports any of the four inferences is relevant; likewise, any evidence that undermines any of the four elements is relevant.

---

16. Some inferences are so powerful that they *are* mandatory unless the adverse party rebuts them. Such inferences are called presumptions. That subject is beyond the scope of this book.

17. These same testimonial inferences underlie much documentary evidence. More precisely, the testimonial inferences underlie any documentary evidence that is offered to prove the truth of the matter asserted in the document, i.e., that is offered for a hearsay purpose. (If you want help understanding hearsay, consider obtaining my other Student's Guide, *A Student's Guide to Hearsay* (5th edition, Carolina Academic Press, 2019), available (I hope) at a bookstore near you. (If not, you can buy it online.) If you do buy one, be sure you get the 5th edition. (End of commercial.)

Suppose witness M testifies that she saw the collision between WNF and PPF discussed in §1.2, and testifies that she saw WNF come to a complete stop, but that PPF "sped through the intersection at a very fast speed." Her testimony is obviously relevant—assuming the four testimonial inferences are accurate in this case. This means that any evidence that bolsters (or undercuts) the accuracy of M's testimony is also relevant, because such testimony has a tendency to make the accuracy of M's testimony more probable than it would be without the evidence (or less probable, if it casts doubt on M's perception, or memory, or narration, or sincerity/veracity).

Perception. Had M consumed any alcohol or perception-altering drugs (legal or not) shortly before she saw the accident? Was she wearing her glasses? Was it raining? If so, were her glasses wet? Was it foggy out? Was M alone or with others, and if with others, what if anything were they doing or discussing which might have divided M's attention when the collision occurred?

Memory. How long ago did the accident occur? In the time between the accident and when M testified, had M made any statements about what she saw that are consistent or inconsistent with her testimony? Had M witnessed any other collisions or near collisions at around the same time, or since, that might have caused her to confuse this collision with another?

Narration. M testified that PPF entered the intersection "at a very fast speed." What does M consider a "very fast speed"—15 MPH over the speed limit? 10 MPH? Or might she even consider 5 MPH a "very fast speed" at an intersection regulated by 4-way stop signs?

Veracity. Is there a reason why M might deliberately lie, or subconsciously shade her testimony for some reason? For example, suppose PPF offers evidence that M and WNF were good friends; or that M and PPF intensely disliked each other. Or suppose that PPF had a bumper sticker on his car supporting a candidate or organization that M despises. Or suppose PPF was a teenager and several people have told PPF's attorney that M frequently complains that all teenage drivers should be kept off the road because "they all drive crazy." Each fact discussed in this paragraph would be relevant, because each tends to make it less probable than it would be without the evidence that M's testimony is accurate.

On the other hand, WNF might offer evidence that M and PPF are good friends, or that M and WNF have never gotten along. (Here's how WNF's lawyer might use this in his closing argument: "M is testifying *against* a friend; she is testifying *in favor* of someone she doesn't like. What better guarantee could you ask for, that she is testifying truthfully?")

I'm not saying that all the evidence in the previous five paragraphs would necessarily be *admissible.* Much of it would be; some of it might not be. But all of it would be *relevant,* because each item has some "tendency" to make it more likely than it would be without the evidence that M's testimony *is* accurate; or it has some tendency "to make it less likely than it would be without the evidence" that M's testimony is accurate.

§ 1.8 Direct and circumstantial evidence

Evidence can be divided into two categories.

Direct evidence is evidence that is relevant to prove a particular fact without the need to draw any inferences other than the testimonial inferences.

Circumstantial evidence, to be relevant to prove a particular fact, requires one or more inferences to be drawn in addition to the testimonial inferences.

PO, a police officer, testifies that when he got to the intersection where WNF and PPF had collided only moments earlier, he noticed that WNF was wearing a Nationals hat and shirt. That testimony is *direct* evidence that WNF was wearing a Nationals hat and shirt. If the officer is testifying accurately, we need draw no further inferences to accept that testimony as an accurate description of what WNF was wearing.

But PO's testimony is *circumstantial* evidence that WNF was a Nationals fan, because to reach that conclusion, we have to draw the inference: someone wearing a particular team's cap and shirt probably roots for that team. That is a rather obvious and in all likelihood an accurate inference to draw, but it still requires that additional step.

If PO testifies that when he arrived, WNF's radio was playing the 2019 World Series, that is direct evidence of what WNF's radio was turned do when the officer arrived. It is also circumstantial evidence that WNF was listening to the game while he was driving. In turn, that fact is circumstantial evidence that WNF was distracted by the game and paying less attention than he should have to traffic signs, and therefore is also circumstantial evidence that he failed to stop at the stop sign. PPF's lawyer will certainly argue this theory to the jury, and the jury rationally could accept it, but it is not required to accept it.

Here is how you might spell out the chain of inferences:

Consequential fact: WNF did not stop at the stop sign.

Direct evidence: WNF was wearing Washington Nationals shirt and cap.

Direct evidence: WNF's car radio was playing the seventh game of the 2019 World Series, Nationals vs. Astros. The collision occurred just seconds after Howie Kendrick hit a two-run home run to give the Nationals a lead in the seventh inning of the seventh game.

(1) Inference: WNF is a Nationals fan.

(2) Inference: WNF was listening to the game.

(3) Inference: WNF was so excited about Kendricks' home run that it is more probable than it would be without the evidence that he was paying less attention to road signs than he should have.

(4) Inference: Therefore, it is more probable than it would be without the evidence that he failed to notice the stop sign, and, therefore, that he failed to stop at the stop sign.

It is axiomatic that circumstantial evidence can suffice to sustain a verdict with either side, both in civil and in criminal actions.

Here is another scenario that illustrates the difference between the direct and circumstantial evidence. Assume V, a pedestrian, was struck and killed at 1 a.m. on February 1 by a car driven by D. D is charged with driving while intoxicated and with manslaughter for causing V's death. D denies being intoxicated, and insists that V walked directly into D's path and it was impossible for D to stop or swerve around V before striking him with his car.

At trial, W1, a police officer, testifies that, moments after V was killed, D blew 0.15% on a breath-alcohol test.[18] For this evidence to be relevant on the question whether D was intoxicated, the only inferences we need draw are:

(1) the device functioned properly,[19]

(2) the officer used it correctly;

(3) the officer perceived the test and its results accurately;

(4) the officer accurately recalls the results;

(5) the officer is accurately communicating the test results to the jury, and

(6) the officer is not deliberately or subconsciously shading his testimony.

(Inferences (3)–(6) are the four "testimonial inferences" described in § 1.7.) Hence, this is direct evidence that there was a concentration of alcohol in D's blood of 0.15%; since that concentration of alcohol fits the legal definition of intoxication, it is also direct evidence that (a) D was intoxicated at the time, which makes it more likely than it would be without the evidence that (b) D committed vehicular manslaughter when his car struck and killed V.

Suppose, instead, D is not apprehended until 4 a.m., in his home, three hours after V was struck and killed by D's car. Several witnesses testify that between 1:30

18. This is generally considered per se evidence that D was legally intoxicated. In fact, many state statutes directly provide that a driver with a blood-alcohol content of 0.15 or more is guilty of driving while intoxicated. (Some jurisdictions may set even a lower concentration—e.g., 0.08%—as intoxicated as a matter of law.)

19. Note, however, that questions have arisen as to the accuracy of such tests, whether conducted at the accident scene or back at the police station.

a.m. (when he arrived home) and 4 a.m., D consumed several alcoholic beverages.[20] Officer W1's testimony that D blew 0.15% at 4 a.m. is direct evidence of D's intoxication at 4 a.m., but that fact casts no light on whether he was under the influence three hours earlier.

So instead of calling W1, the prosecutor calls W2, who testifies that he is D's neighbor; that he saw D in a local bar that evening from 11:30 p.m. to 12:45 a.m.; and that during that time, he saw D consume three glasses of a pale brown liquid. This is direct evidence that D did what W2 claims to have seen. For it to be relevant on the question of whether D was intoxicated as he drove home, however, we have to draw two additional inferences: (1) that each glass contained alcohol as opposed to, say, ginger ale or apple juice, and (2) D consumed enough alcohol to significantly impair his ability to drive safely.

The first inference is fairly strong, because common sense and experience tell us that most people who consume beverages in a bar at that hour of the night are drinking alcohol. So is the second inference: experts agree that although some people can "hold their liquor" better than others, three alcoholic beverages in 75 minutes will definitely affect a person's judgment, ability to perceive, and ability to react quickly. Still, W2's testimony is relevant only if the jury accepts both of these inferences. Therefore, W2's testimony is only circumstantial, rather than direct, evidence that D was intoxicated at 1 a.m. Nevertheless, W2's testimony still makes it more probable than it would be without the evidence that (a) D was intoxicated when his car struck and killed V, that (b) his intoxication was a reason why his car struck V, and therefore, that (c) D is guilty of manslaughter.

Suppose the prosecutor also calls W3, who will testify that he saw D enter that local bar at about 11 p.m., but that since W3 was not inside the bar, he has no direct knowledge of what D did once he entered. For this testimony to be relevant on the question of whether D was intoxicated at 1 a.m., we have to infer (1) that D consumed one or more beverages while in the bar, (2) that those beverages contained alcohol, and (3) he drank enough to become intoxicated. W3's testimony is a lot less probative than W2's because it provides no direct evidence that D drank anything (perhaps he went there to use the phone or men's room or just to schmooze with friends)—we must instead infer it; and the need to draw this additional inference weakens the inferential chain. W3's testimony is nevertheless relevant on the question whether D was intoxicated at the time of the accident, because it has "*any* tendency" to make the fact of his intoxication more probable than it would be without his testimony. But the tendency is a lot weaker than it is with W2's testimony. Is that tendency so weak that the judge should exclude the evidence as irrelevant?

No. Even if W3 testified after W2 had testified, W3's testimony is clearly relevant, because W3's testimony partially corroborates W2, by placing D in the bar that

20. Why were all these witnesses awake and at D's house so early that morning? I don't know, but the prosecutor might ask them that question on cross-examination.

night. In addition, by placing D in the bar as early as 11 p.m. (half an hour earlier than W2 saw him there), W3's testimony supports the inference that D may have had one or more alcoholic beverages between 11 a.m. and 11:30 (which is when W2 first noticed D), which enhances the inference that D consumed enough alcohol by 12:45 a.m. to seriously impair his ability to drive safely.

§ 1.9 Questions: "U.S. v. Penn and Teller"[21]

Teller was arrested the day after he stole 20 bonds from the bank where he worked. Teller confessed and told the police that he was planning to give them to Penn, who would forge various names on the bonds and cash them at other banks; then they would split the proceeds. In fact, Teller insists, the whole idea was Penn's. Based on Teller's statements and his agreement to testify against Penn, Penn was also arrested. Penn and Teller were charged with conspiring to embezzle, forge and fraudulently cash the bonds.[22]

Prior to trial, Teller pleaded guilty and, as promised, testifies against Penn at trial, claiming that the idea was Penn's. Penn, of course, claims that Teller is lying, and that Penn had no knowledge of, and did not participate in, the scheme.

<u>Question 1.</u>

Suppose someone who knew nothing about the law asked you, "What is this case about?" How would you answer? Or to put it another way: *without using any legal terminology at all*, what is the one basic issue the jury will have to decide to resolve this case?

<u>Answer:</u>

"Is Teller telling the truth about Penn, or is he lying?" That's really what this case boils down to, isn't it? If Teller is telling the truth, Penn is guilty; if not, he's not.

<u>By the way</u>: It is a good idea, whenever you read a case or are assigned a problem—not only in this course, but in any law course you take— to ask yourself: "How can I explain what this case (or casebook question) is about, to a friend who knows nothing about the law and has a short attention span?" Answering that question will often help you see the legal issues better.

---

21. This sequence of questions is based on U.S. v. Craft, 407 F.2d 1065 (6th Cir. 1969).

22. I "borrowed" the names of two much-beloved entertainers because their names so perfectly fit the roles of the two actual criminals in the Craft case—the bank employee ("Teller") and the forger ("Penn")—who conspired to deceive people by using false IDs to cash stolen bonds. I certainly do not mean to suggest that the real Penn and Teller would do such a thing. I am quite sure the real Penn and Teller are good, honest men who would never attempt to deceive anyone.

Question 2.

After Teller is cross-examined, the prosecutor calls Detective DET1, who will testify that when he arrested and searched Penn, Penn had a blank check in his wallet from Teller's personal checking account. Penn objects that this is irrelevant. Is it?

Answer:

Objection overruled. The fact that Penn had a blank check from Teller's checking account suggests that they knew each other—and that they were more than casual acquaintances. That has some tendency to make it more probable than it would be without the evidence that they were also conspirators in the scheme to steal and cash bonds—just as Teller claims.

Think about it: how often in your life have people given you a blank, unsigned check to their bank account? How often have you given someone such a check? Barring a special relationship with that person, I doubt that this has happened very often.

Of course, Penn's possession of a blank check from Teller's personal checking account does not "prove" Penn's guilt. But it does nudge the case at least slightly in the prosecutor's favor. To be relevant, that is all an item of evidence needs to do.

Question 3.

Suppose DET1 testifies that when Penn was arrested, Penn had eight items of stolen or forged identification in his pocket, each with a different name. Penn objects: irrelevant! Ruling? Is this direct or circumstantial evidence? And how should the judge rule on the objection?

Answer:

DET1's testimony is direct evidence that Penn possessed these items, because we don't have to draw any inferences (other than that DET1 is testifying accurately that Penn had them in his pocket) to accept that conclusion.

It is also circumstantial evidence of Penn's guilt, so Penn's objection should be overruled. Why?

Possessing eight items of forged or stolen IDs is highly unusual. (How often have *you* possessed eight items of forged or stolen identification?) Those items have no plausible *lawful* use. They would be extremely useful, however, to someone who planned to cash stolen bonds without using his own name—which is exactly what the Government, and Teller, accuse Penn of conspiring to do. Therefore, Penn's possession of these items has a substantial tendency to make Penn's participation in the scheme more likely than it would be without the evidence. (At trial, the prosecutor would elicit testimony, from DET1 or some other law enforcement official with knowledge and experience in such matters, explaining why these items would be useful in such a scheme.)[23]

23. This should be categorized as expert testimony governed by FRE 702–704, but some courts might admit it as lay witness testimony per FRE 701. I'll leave it for your evidence professor to sort

Here is the chain of inferences:[24]

"Consequential fact:" Penn participated with Teller in a conspiracy to steal bonds from Teller's bank and to cash them and split the proceeds.

Direct evidence: Penn had eight forged or stolen IDs in his pocket.

(1) Inference: those items would be extremely useful to someone planning to cash stolen bonds without using his own name or ID.

(2) Inference: therefore, it is more likely than it would be without the evidence that Penn was, as the Government claims and Teller testified, a participant in the scheme.

Question 4.

Without going back and checking, how is the stem (the basic fact statement) of question 3 worded? Which of the two following options is correct?

(a) "When Penn was arrested, he had eight items of stolen or forged identification in his pocket, each with a different name."

or

(b) "DET1 testifies that when Penn was arrested, Penn had eight items of stolen or forged identification in his pocket, each with a different name."

(c) What is the difference between (a) and (b)? Does it matter?

Answer:

The answer is (b), and in the context of an exam question, it may matter a great deal. Version (a) tells you (the student), "You can accept this fact as true." Version (b) tells you, "This fact may be true, but it may not be; the other side has the right to try to challenge it, impeach it, and so on."

Maybe your evidence professor won't expect you to see the difference, but maybe she will. Learning to read questions carefully is good training for the careful attention to detail that your clients will expect of you when you are in practice.

Question 5.

Suppose instead DET1 testifies that when he arrested Penn, Penn was sitting alone on a park bench and that a small green cloth bag was on the bench next to

---

all this out.

24. Don't get the impression that there is only one "correct" way of articulating a chain of inferences. Your chain might articulate the connection between the evidence and the consequential fact to which it relates somewhat differently. So long as you show the inferences that must be drawn showing that connection, you've done what an evidence professor—or a judge—expects.

Penn. When DET1 arrested him, he asked, "Is that your bag?" Penn replied, "No, it was here on the bench when I sat down." DET1 searched the bag and found the eight items of stolen or forged identification. Is this direct or circumstantial evidence? Is this information relevant?

Answer:

It is direct evidence that the eight items of ID were in the green bag next to Penn on the bench. It is circumstantial evidence that Penn was, as Teller testified, part of the scheme to steal and cash the bonds.

The only difference between Question 3 and this question is that before we reach that conclusion, we have to draw an additional inference:

Consequential fact. Penn participated with Teller in a conspiracy to steal U.S. bonds from Teller's bank and to cash them and split the proceeds.

Direct evidence: there were eight items of stolen or forged IDs in a small green cloth bag on the bench where Penn was sitting when he was arrested.

(1) Inference: Penn was the person who put the bag there, i.e., he possessed the bag and its contents.

(2) Inference: those items would be extremely useful to someone planning to cash stolen bonds without using his own name or ID.

(3) Inference: therefore, it is more likely than it would be without the evidence that Penn was, as the Government claims and Teller testified, a participant on the scheme.

The probative value of an item of circumstantial evidence (i.e., its weight in proving the proposition of fact for which it is offered) depends upon two factors: the number of inferences that must be drawn to show the connection, and the strength of each inference. (As the saying goes, "A chain is only as strong as its weakest link.") The additional (first) inference makes this chain of inferences one link longer than in the previous question. So how strong is that inference?

As to the new, first inference—that Penn possessed the bag and its contents—there are only two possibilities. (1) Some time before Penn sat on that bench, someone else sat there, put the bag on the bench, then got up and left, forgetting the bag and leaving it behind. Or (2) Penn was carrying the bag with him and put it on the bench when he sat down, then denied that it was his when he was arrested. Which is the more likely?

The second, for two reasons.

The first reason is common sense and experience. It is fairly rare for someone to put something on a park bench, and then forget to take it with him when he gets up to go. Oh, sure, it happens—lots of times, probably—but those times are no doubt a tiny fraction compared to how often a person does remember to take an item with him.

The second reason is the bag's contents: items uniquely useful to do what Teller claimed Penn planned to do. Which is more likely—that someone *else* forgetfully left the green bag containing precisely what Penn would need if he was conspiring with Teller; or that it was Penn's bag?

Note that in the previous paragraph, the prosecutor has used the ultimate fact that she wants to prove—that Teller's testimony is true—to establish the relevance of a piece of evidence that the prosecutor will use to corroborate Teller's testimony. There is nothing improper about that: relevance can be shown by arguing from the evidence to the conclusion, or from the desired conclusion back to the evidence, or both. In assessing whether any particular item of evidence is relevant, the judge should consider *all* of the evidence in the case, not just the evidence that directly relates to that item.[25] And so should you, in discussing relevance in an evidence problem.

But wait a minute, you may be thinking: Penn denied that the bag was his! Doesn't that make the evidence irrelevant?

That depends on the jury. A juror who believes Penn's testimony will reject the government's chain of inferences. But a juror could disbelieve Penn's denial and accept the inferences. It is up to each juror, and the jury as a whole, to evaluate who and what to believe. The same is true if Penn claims that DET1 is lying, i.e., that there was no bag with phony IDs on the bench. The jury, not the judge, gets to decide who is telling the truth and who isn't.

Question 6.

Next, the prosecutor wants to offer evidence that the bag and the stolen or forged IDs were tested for fingerprints and DNA, but no usable prints or identifiable DNA could be obtained from them. Penn objects, arguing that this evidence proves absolutely nothing—it is neither evidence of Penn's guilt, nor of his innocence; hence it is irrelevant and inadmissible. Ruling?

Answer:

In one sense, Penn's objection is valid: this testimony neither adds to nor subtracts from the rest of the evidence; therefore, it is irrelevant.

But in another sense, it is relevant, because it addresses expectations that jurors may bring with them: crime novels, TV shows and movies often give the impression that fingerprints or DNA or other forensic evidence will show up in almost every case.[26] (This is sometimes referred to as the "CSI effect.") If the prosecutor fails to produce such evidence and also fails to explain why, jurors may assume either that the prosecutor and police were too lazy to test the items, or that they are hiding

25. The Supreme Court said as much in Huddleston v. U.S., 485 U.S. 681 (1988), discussed extensively in § 7.11.

26. In Old Chief v. U.S., 519 US 172 (1997), the Supreme Court, in applying Fed R Evid 403, acknowledged that a prosecutor has an important and sometimes compelling interest in satisfying juror expectations about evidence. *Old Chief* is covered in § 3.6 & § 3.7.

something; if so, they may give the state's actual evidence less weight than it merits. Thus, testimony that no forensic evidence was obtainable is relevant because it helps the jury evaluate the rest of the evidence accurately.[27]

Question 7.

When DET1 arrested Penn, he filed a report describing the arrest, but the report does not mention finding the green bag or the forged or stolen IDs. Penn's attorney wants to introduce that report and cross-examine DET1 about it.[28] The prosecutor objects that this is irrelevant. Ruling?

Answer:

Here is how the cross-examination might proceed. (I have numbered each exchange between the defense counsel and the witness or judge, so I can refer back to particular Q&As later in this section.)

Q1 Detective, was this the first case you ever had involving stolen securities or checks or the like?

A No, as a member of the financial fraud squad I've had dozens of them.

Q2 And you've explained on direct examination how useful it would be for a participant in a scheme to forge and cash stolen bonds to have stolen or fraudulent IDs when cashing those items. Do you recall that testimony?[29]

A Yes.

Q3 And you knew, on March 2, 2019, when you arrested Mr. Penn, that finding such items would strengthen your case, right?

A Yes.

Q4 Is it fair to say you were hoping to find such items when you arrested Mr. Penn?

A You always hope to find useful evidence.

Q5 Thank you. Detective, whenever you take a significant action in an investigation, you are required to file a report spelling out what you saw, what you heard, what you did—correct?

---

27. I've researched this issue for my evidence treatise, and although I have not taken a count, it's my impression that most courts (in reported opinions, anyhow) agree that such testimony—that no fingerprints or DNA evidence could be obtained—is relevant and admissible.

28. Under federal law (the "Jencks Act," 18 USC § 3500), in a criminal trial, once a government witness completes direct examination, a prosecutor must provide defense counsel access to any "statement or report in possession of the [government]" which the witness prepared or participated in preparing that relates to the subject of the witness's direct examination. This rule comes into play most often regarding police officers' reports. Most states have roughly equivalent laws. For a more detailed discussion of the Jencks Act, see *A Student's Guide to Hearsay* § 9.5 (5th ed. 2019).

29. See the answer to question 2.

A Yes.

Q6 What is that form or report called?

A It's a DD-5.[30]

Q7 Why are detectives required to fill out DD-5s?

A Several reasons. It helps the detective remember the details which may be important later in the investigation, or to prepare to testify at trial. It helps other investigators keep up to date as to what's happened in the case. It helps the prosecutor prepare for trial.

Q8 Thank you. Detective, do you consider the arrest of a suspect a "significant step in an investigation"?

A Yes.

Q9 Do you consider seizing incriminating evidence a "significant step in an investigation"?

A Yes.

Q10 (Removing a document from his briefcase): Your honor may I have this document market as defense exhibit 1 for identification?

J You may.

[Defense counsel gives the "document" to the court clerk, who stamps it "Def. Exh. 1 for ID."]

Q11 Your honor, may I show it to DET1?

J You may.

Q12 Detective, please look at Defense Exhibit 1 for identification. Do you recognize this? Can you tell us what that is?

A Yes. That's a photocopy of the DD-5 I filled out after arresting defendant Penn on March 2, 2019.

Q13 Your honor, I offer exhibit 1 in evidence.

Judge "It is so received." [Defense counsel hands the DD-5 back to the court clerk, who scratches out the "for ID." Defense counsel hands a photocopy of the DD-5 to the judge and the prosecutor.][31]

---

30. In the 1970s, when I was a prosecutor in New York City, NYPD detectives' reports were called "DD-5s" (DD meaning "Detective Division"). Back then, they were done in ink with quill pens on parchment.—No, actually, detectives typed them on sheets of paper, with carbon copies. I suspect the process—and maybe the name of the form—have changed somewhat since then. (If you don't know what a "carbon copy" is, look it up on Wikipedia.)

31. Q&A 10 through Q&A 13 provide an example of how to identify and authenticate a document, per FRE 901(a) and 901(b)(1).

Q14 (After handing it back to DET1) Detective, please read aloud where in your DD-5 you reported seizing a green cloth bag containing all those stolen or forged IDs.

A It's not—I didn't include that information in the DD-5.

Q15 You didn't include it? Why-ever not?

A I thought I had. I guess I just forgot to include it.

Q16 You *forgot to include it?*

A I guess I must have.

Q17 You "guess you must have forgot to." I suppose that's one possible explanation. Tell me, detective, when did you write up this DD-5?

A It's dated March 3, 2019.

Q18 The day following the arrest?

A That's right.

Q19 Were the events of the arrest fresh in your mind?

A Yes.

Q20 Is it fair to say that your memory of those events was better back on March 3, 2019, than it is today, so many months later?

A I remember seizing the cloth bag and finding the forged and stolen IDs.

Q21 That's not what I asked you, but never mind. Tell me, detective, in the, oh, let's say 6 months before you arrested Mr. Penn, did you conduct any other arrests and searches in fraud cases?

A Sure.

Q22 How many?

A Half a dozen, a dozen—somewhere along those lines.

Q23 And in the months since March 2, 2019, roughly how many?

A More, probably.

Q24 Did you seize evidence during any of those searches?

A Yes.

Q25 In how many—half?

A Probably something like that.

Q26 In some of those cases, did you seize forged or stolen IDs?

A Yes.

Q27 And did you describe what you seized in each of those DD-5s?

A I expect so. I hope so.

Q28 If we went back and checked them all, how many would be like this case—in which you "probably forgot" to include that significant information?

A None, I hope.

Q29 Just in this case?

A Yes, sir.

Q30 Did you re-read all those DD-5s in all those other cases, before coming to court today?

A No, why should I?

Q31 Because maybe you are confused—maybe you are confusing what you seized in one of those other cases with this one, in which, according to your DD-5, you seized nothing?

A No sir. I seized that bag and those IDs from the bench where Penn was sitting, and I sent them to the property office the same day. All I forgot was to put that in my DD-5.

Now do you see the relevance of the DD-5?

A couple of final comments about this cross-examination.

1. Defense counsel pretty much knows the answers that DET1 is likely to give to most of these questions, and in all probability, none of this cross-examination comes as a surprise to DET1. After all, if the prosecutor properly prepared for trial, she read over all the DD-5s in the case and noticed that DET1's DD-5 failed to mention the search and seizure of the bag and the IDs. If so, she told DET1 what to expect during cross-examination, and instructed him to give straightforward answers, even though the answers may make him look bad, because if the detective tried to outwit the defense counsel, it will only make DET1—and the state's case—look even worse.
2. This cross-examination is an example of how to use a "prior inconsistent statement" to impeach a witness's testimony. DET1's DD-5 is a "statement" by him about the arrest which he made prior to testifying, and which is inconsistent with his direct testimony because it omits a significant fact he mentioned in his testimony. Fed. R. Evid. 613 regulates such cross-examination.[32]
3. Notice how, in Q1-Q9, defense counsel built up the importance of the inconsistency before springing the "trap" in Q10-Q16. The rest of the cross-examination is basically icing on the cake, and some judges may not allow defense

32. That rule is covered briefly in § 12.13, *infra*, and more extensively in §§ 4:6 and 4:7 of C. Fishman, *A Student's Guide to Hearsay* (5th edition, Carolina Academic Press, 2019). (End of commercial.)

counsel to go that far. I wrote this cross to show how an attorney can maximize the impact of what, after all, was probably only a minor misstep by an honest police officer.

4. The overt thrust of this cross-examination is to suggest flaws in DET1's memory: he is confusing this case with another case in which forged and stolen IDs were seized.
5. But counsel is also subtly challenging the officer's veracity, too. The comment in Q17 ("I suppose that's one possible explanation") and other aspects of the cross subtly suggest that DET1 could have supplied the 8 forged or phony IDs from other cases and claimed that Penn possessed them. But counsel never directly accused the officer of doing that. (Some attorneys might flat-out accuse the detective of doing so; I think it is more effective to let the suggestion linger in the air without explicitly accusing the officer of it, and then suggesting it more directly in closing argument.)
6. A trial judge has discretion to cut defense counsel off at some point, and not every judge would indulge counsel this far.
7. It is unlikely your evidence professor will expect you to conduct a cross-examination this elaborate in class (or write one on a quiz or exam). But if you are called upon to do so and can pull it off, your professor will be impressed by your brilliance.[33]

Here is the chain of inferences:

Consequential fact: Did Penn possess the stolen and forged IDs?

Direct evidence: If Penn had possessed the stolen and forged IDs, DET1's DD-5 should have mentioned this. DET1's DD-5 did not mention finding the cloth bag with the IDs.

(1) Inference: There was no cloth bag containing the IDs next to Penn when DET1 arrested Penn.

(2) Inference: Therefore, it is less probable than it would be without the DD-5 that Penn conspired with Teller to steal, forge and cash the bonds.

§ 1.10 Comment about "possession"

As you may have learned in criminal law or elsewhere, the law recognizes two types of possession: physical possession—what I am holding in my hands or in my pockets, for example—and constructive possession. Constructive possession exists

33. Or else she'll figure, "This student must have used Fishman's book!" Which also demonstrates your brilliance, so it's pretty much the same thing, right?

when a person exercises some degree of dominion or control over an item, even though he or she does not physically possess it.

I "possess" what is in my home or car, or my wife's car, or my office, or in the cubbyhole in my synagogue where I keep certain objects, even if I am not in any of those places. And this is so even if I do not exercise *exclusive* dominion or control. For example, my wife also possesses what's in our house, or her car, or my car.

And the inference of possession exists even if I cannot necessarily exclude others. University employees clean faculty offices overnight, and occasionally enter to make repairs, etc. An employee could put something in my office without my knowledge. Similarly, anyone could remove something from my synagogue cubbyhole, or put something there that I did not want or know about. Still, evidence that something was found in my synagogue cubbyhole supports the inference that I knowingly possessed it. And testimony from W1 that he saw an object in my office or in my synagogue cubbyhole on Tuesday, May 1, supports the inference that I probably possessed it there on, say, April 27, and still possessed that object there on, say, Monday, May 7.

Similarly, if I lend something to a friend, or ask her to let me store it in her house, I still constructively possess those items, because I have the right to have them returned—even though my friend also "possesses" them.

That I do not have exclusive or *absolute* dominion or control over the items weakens the inference that I control them, but that inference still exists, and a jury is entitled to accept that inference if they find it persuasive.

§ 1.11 Back to "U.S. v. Penn and Teller": more questions

Question 1.

Suppose instead DET1 arrested Penn in a house with three bedrooms. There were four other persons in the house at the time. DET1 testifies that he searched a bedroom in which he found (a) Penn's wallet; (b) clothes in the closet that fit Penn's tall, thin body, and two pairs of shoes that were the same size as the shoes he was wearing when arrested; (c) a hairbrush with Penn's fingerprints on it; (d) a book with Penn's name written on the inside cover; (e) in a dresser drawer, underwear and socks that fit Penn; and (f) in an otherwise empty drawer in a night table, DET1 found eight stolen and forged IDs. DET1 also testifies that Penn's fingerprints were found in numerous places in the bedroom.[34] Should the IDs be admitted?

34. In real life, the prosecutor would probably have to call at least one or two other witnesses to introduce the fingerprint evidence: the officer who lifted the prints from the bedroom, and the forensic examiner who compared the prints lifted from the room and the objects to Penn's prints. But that doesn't change our assessment of the relevance of the IDs, so let's assume DET1 could testify about the fingerprints.

Answer:

Here is the chain of inferences:

Consequential fact: Penn participated in the scheme to steal, forge and cash stolen bonds.

Direct evidence: there were eight items of stolen or forged ID in an otherwise empty night table drawer in a room containing several items belonging or apparently belonging to Penn, a room in which Penn's fingerprints were found on several items and surfaces.

(1) Inference: therefore, Penn was living in that room, or at least was using it at around the time of his arrest in that house.

(2) Inference: therefore, Penn possessed the eight stolen or forged IDs.

(3) Inference: those items would be extremely useful to someone planning to cash stolen bonds without using his own name or ID.

(4) Inference: therefore, it is more likely than it would be without the evidence that Penn was, as the Government claims and Teller testified, a participant in the scheme to steal, forge and cash the bonds.

Note that this chain has an extra inference—the first one. And in this chain, the first two inferences are certainly weaker than they were in § 1.9 question 3, where the IDs were in Penn's pocket, or in § 1.9 question 5, where the IDs were in the green cloth bag next to him on the park bench. While cross-examining DET1, Penn's lawyer will stress the weakness of the evidence connecting Penn to the IDs found in the night table drawer. During their closing arguments, the prosecutor will dwell on the strengths and the defense attorney will stress the weaknesses of the connection. The bottom line, though, is that each inference in the prosecutor's relevance chain logically follows from what precedes it, and each is plausible enough; none of them require mere speculation. Therefore the eight IDs are still relevant, even though the jury might give less weight to the IDs in this question than they would have in § 1.9 question 3 or question 5.

Question 2.

The judge admits the testimony and IDs DET1 says he found in the night table. On cross-examination, Penn's attorney seeks to elicit the following information: (a) The bedroom also contained clothing of a man much shorter and heavier than Penn. (b) The bedroom also contained several dresses and women's pants suits, and a pair of women's shoes. (c) In addition to Penn's fingerprints, the police found dozens of prints in that bedroom that clearly were not Penn's, including the prints of one of the other men who was in the house when Penn was arrested.[35]

35. It is generally not possible to tell how "old" a fingerprint is.

How is this relevant?

Answer:

The cross-examination is relevant because it suggests that other people instead of or in addition to Penn may have lived in that room from time to time. It also establishes that many, many people have had access to that room. The evidence therefore makes inferences (1) and (2) less likely than they would be without the evidence elicited by Penn's attorney, and therefore makes the rest of the inferential chain less likely, too.

Question 3.

In light of this evidence, Penn's attorney argues that the IDs are no longer relevant, and (1) moves to strike them and DET1's testimony about them from the record, and (2) requests the judge to instruct the jury to disregard them.[36] How should the judge rule?

Answer:

Motions denied. Each link in the chain of inferences is still plausible, even though the information elicited on cross weakens the chain. The jury should still be quite capable of assessing the strength or weakness of the evidence connecting Penn to the IDs.

§ 1.12 Twenties Questions

Question 1.

Early on the morning of June 3, Jackson Zwanzig went to a store to purchase a $1.50 pack of gum and gave the cashier a $20 bill. The cashier asked if he had anything smaller; Zwanzig said he didn't. The bill didn't look quite right to the cashier, who called the manager, who came with a security guard, who escorted Zwanzig to the manager's office. The officer told Zwanzig the manager would be back in a few minutes, and waited outside. Zwanzig was alone in the office for two or three minutes. The manager entered with a detective who told Zwanzig that the bill was counterfeit, and arrested Zwanzig. The charge: knowingly presenting counterfeit money with intent to defraud.

The detective searched Zwanzig. In his wallet, he found fourteen other $20 bills. They were also counterfeit—in fact, they had the same (bogus) serial number as the counterfeit $20 bill Zwanzig had attempted to use to buy the gum. Are the additional bills relevant, and if so, how?

36. In fact, Penn's attorney might even move for a mistrial, arguing that the jury would not be able to disregard the evidence and that its impact would unduly prejudice Penn's right to a fair trial.

Answer:

There are only three elements to the crime:

(1) Zwanzig presented the $20 bill to someone to buy something.

(2) The bill was counterfeit.

(3) Zwanzig knew the bill was counterfeit when he attempted to use it to make a purchase and receive change.

Which of these issues is contested? Only the third. The prosecutor has to persuade the jury beyond a reasonable doubt that Zwanzig intended to defraud, i.e., that Zwanzig knew the $20 was counterfeit. Does Zwanzig's possession of fourteen more identical counterfeit 20s help support the inference that he knew that the 15th—the one he tried to use in the store—was counterfeit?

Yes. Common sense and the law of averages say so. Anybody might innocently come into possession of a bogus $20 and innocently try to spend it. (That is not a crime.) But what is the likelihood that someone might innocently possess fifteen identical counterfeit bills?[37] That would be a remarkable coincidence, wouldn't it? And really, the only alternative to Zwanzig's innocently possessing fifteen identical counterfeit 20s is that he knew they were all counterfeit. Which is more likely? That Zwanzig knew.

Consequential fact: Zwanzig offered a counterfeit $20 to the cashier, knowing it was counterfeit.

Direct evidence: Zwanzig had 14 more identical counterfeit $20s in his wallet.

(1) Inference: it is unlikely a person would lawfully and innocently come into possession of 15 identical counterfeit $20 bills.

(2) Inference: Therefore, it is more likely than it would be without the evidence that Zwanzig knew the $20 he gave the cashier was counterfeit.

The jury doesn't have to accept that inference, of course; but certainly, it could quite logically and rationally accept it. Hence the fourteen bogus $20s in Zwanzig's wallet are relevant.

Question 2.

After the government rests, during the defense case, Zwanzig calls Venti, who testifies that he and Zwanzig and several other men were in a poker game on June 2; the game ended shortly after midnight on June 3. Zwanzig was the big winner:

37. We can reasonably assume he didn't get them from a bank or an ATM machine, since banks carefully check the currency they dispense or put in ATMs.

when he cashed in his chips, the man running the game paid him in 15 $20 bills. Is this relevant?

Answer:

Yes, because (assuming Venti is testifying truthfully), this makes it much less likely that Zwanzig knew the $20 he gave to the cashier was counterfeit:

Consequential fact: Zwanzig did not know the $20 was counterfeit.

Direct evidence: early on the morning of June 3 (shortly before arriving at the store), Zwanzig received $300 in $20 bills as payment for $300 he was owed.

(1) Inference: Zwanzig did not know the $20s were counterfeit when he accepted them. (After all, who in his right mind would accept counterfeit money to settle a debt he was owed?)

(2) Inference: Nothing happened between his receiving the bills, and stopping at the store, that would have informed Zwanzig the bills were counterfeit.[38]

(3) Inference: Therefore, Zwanzig did not know the $20 he gave to the cashier was counterfeit.

Question 3.

Suppose, instead, that when the detective arrested and searched Zwanzig, Zwanzig had no additional counterfeit currency on him. However, two days later, a store employee dusting the manager's office discovered fourteen other $20 bills concealed under a lamp. They were also counterfeit and had the same (bogus) serial number as the $20 bill Zwanzig had attempted to use to buy the gum. At trial, the prosecutor seeks to have that employee testify, and to introduce the additional fourteen counterfeit 20s.

Are they relevant?

Answer:

Yes, for the same reason they were in the previous problem—except now we must first articulate an additional inference.

---

38. You might wonder: why call Venti? Why didn't Zwanzig simply testify to these facts himself? That way, it wouldn't be necessary to draw any inferences. If Zwanzig's testimony was true, he didn't know the $20 was counterfeit; verdict, not guilty!

I can think of two reasons why Zwanzig might not testify. (1) A jury might tend to disbelieve Zwanzig simply because such testimony is so self-serving. Calling another person to establish the key facts (poker game, etc.) might be more persuasive. (2) Zwanzig might have been particularly vulnerable to impeachment if he testified. Suppose, for example, he had several previous felony convictions, which the prosecutor could have brought out on cross-examination if Zwanzig testified. (See §13.10 to §13.29.) Zwanzig's attorney might decide it was too risky to put Zwanzig on the stand.

Consequential fact: Zwanzig offered a counterfeit $20 to the cashier, knowing it was counterfeit.

Direct evidence: (1) Zwanzig knew he was under suspicion of using a counterfeit $20. (2) He was alone in the manager's office for a few minutes. (3) A few days later, 14 identical counterfeit $20s were found under a lamp in the manager's office.

Let's think about this for a minute. Someone hid what appeared to be $280 in an office and never returned to retrieve it. That is rather unusual conduct, isn't it? How many times have you done that? Can you think of anyone you know who has done that? What possible reason could a person have to do that?

(1) Inference: Only someone with a powerful motive not to be found with those $20s would hide what appeared to be $280 in an office he'd probably never be able to go back to.

(2) Inference: Zwanzig, knowing that he was suspected of trying to spend a counterfeit $20, was afraid he would be searched and that the other identical counterfeit $20s would be found on him. He also had a brief opportunity to hide the bills before the manager came back with a policeman.

(3) Inference: Therefore, it was Zwanzig, and not anyone else, who hid the $20s under the lamp.

(4) Inference: Since Zwanzig knew the 14 $20s were counterfeit, it is more likely than it would be without the evidence that when he tried to use the other $20 to buy gum, he knew that $20 was also counterfeit.

Zwanzig's attorney can point out that dozens of people probably had access to that office both before and after Zwanzig was left alone there for a few minutes; any of those others could have hidden the bills there. And maybe some of them were afraid to get searched, too.

To which the prosecutor and judge would respond: defense counsel is certainly entitled to explore those possibilities while cross-examining the state's witnesses, and to present such evidence during the defense case. But given Zwanzig's brief opportunity to hide the bills and his powerful motive to do so, a jury could reasonably infer that it was Zwanzig, not anyone else, who hid them; and infer from that that he knew they were counterfeit, and infer further that therefore he knew the $20 he used to buy gum was also counterfeit.[39]

---

39. Zwanzig might claim that he didn't know the bills were counterfeit until he was taken to the office; then, when left alone, he looked at the other bills, saw they all had the same serial number, panicked, and hid the bills. If this testimony prevents the jury from being satisfied beyond a

Question 4.

Suppose when the officer searched Zwanzig, he found no counterfeit currency. In fact, let's also assume that no additional counterfeit bills were found, period. But in Zwanzig's pocket he found several folded "sets" of bills. One set consisted of a $10, a $5 and two $1s. Another set consisted of three $5s and a $1. A third set was a $10 and 6 $1s. A fourth was a $10 and 4 $1s. How is this relevant?

Answer:

If you are having difficulty coming up with an answer, re-read the first three sentences in problem question 1 in this section.

***

***

***

(I'm waiting while you re-read them.)

***

***

Ok, so he lied. Why is *that* relevant to make it more probable than it would be without the evidence, that Zwanzig knew the $20 was counterfeit?

If you still don't see it, I'll give you a hint: Zwanzig didn't care about the gum. Didn't want it, didn't need it, never chews it; he planned to throw it away unopened before he got home. So why did he buy it? What was he *really* interested in receiving in making that purchase?

Have you figured that out? If so, good. Now apply what you've figured out to the "sets" of currently he had in his pocket. How would a prosecutor most effectively use that evidence?

The prosecutor would call a law enforcement officer—say a U.S. Secret Service agent[40]—as an expert witness.[41] Direct examination might proceed as follows:

> Q. Agent Secret, suppose I was a counterfeiter, and I made, say, a large quantity of counterfeit $20 dollar bills. What would the typical counterfeiter do with them? Would I walk into a store to buy a pair of slacks and a shirt for $100, and pay with 5 of my 20's?

---

reasonable doubt that he knew the first $20 was counterfeit, then they will find him not guilty. But that goes to the weight the jury gives to the fourteen $20s under the lamp, not to their admissibility.

40. The Secret Service is best known these days at the agency that protects the President and other major federal officials. But its original responsibility, which is still a major focus of the agency, is to protect our financial system from certain fraudulent activities—and in particular, to investigate counterfeiting.

41. Expert witnesses and expert testimony are regulated by FRE 702–707.

A. No, absolutely not.

Q. Why not?

A. Because if you use several bills in the same purchase, that increases the risk that the cashier will notice that something is "off" about them; it also increases the risk the cashier might remember you, since these days, so many people use a credit card for amounts like $100. In fact, the person who manufactures counterfeit money almost never actually spends it directly, to avoid being caught with it.

Q. Then what would I do with it?

A. You would sell it to someone for, say, ten or twenty cents on the dollar.

Q. OK, now say I am the person who buys counterfeit money from the guy who makes it. What would I do with it? Would I go to the store and buy that pair of pants and a shirt for $100 using 5 of the $20s I bought from the counterfeiter?

A. Again, no, for the same reason. More important, the buyer isn't really interested in buying things with the counterfeit money.

Q. No? Why does he buy it, then?

A. To turn it into real money.

Q. How would he do that?

A. He uses each counterfeit $20 to buy something cheap—a buck or two or three—and getting real money as change.

OK, *now*—if you hadn't gotten it already—explain the relevance of the various "sets" of folded currently the officer seized from Zwanzig. What inference do they support?

Don't peek at the answer. Identify and articulate the answer for yourself first.

***

Finished? No? OK, I'll wait. I've got time. I'm retired. Like the song says, "I've got no place to go and all day long to get there."[42]

***

Finished now?

<u>Answer</u>: The evidence supports the inference that Zwanzig used what appeared to be $20 bills to buy inexpensive items and received $17 change for one purchase, $16 change for two additional purchases, and $14 for yet another purchase. Therefore, based on Agent Secret's testimony, it is probable that Zwanzig knew those other $20

---

42. Actually, the song—*Some Beach,* by Rory Feek and Paul Overstreet, recorded by American country music artist Blake Shelton in 2004—doesn't quite say that, but close enough.

bills were counterfeit, which makes it more probable than it would be without the evidence that he knew the $20 bill he tried to buy gum with was also counterfeit.

B. Conditional Relevance: FRE 104(b)

§ 1.13 Conditional relevance; "sufficient to support a finding"; order of proof: FRE 104(b)

Another rule, besides FRE 401 and 402, must be considered in assessing whether and how evidence is relevant: FRE 104(b). It provides:

> **Rule 104. Preliminary Questions**
>
> **(b) Relevance That Depends on a Fact.** When the relevance of evidence depends on whether a fact exists, proof must be introduced sufficient to support a finding that the fact does exist. The court may admit the proposed evidence on the condition that the proof be introduced later.

This rule covers three issues: what is "conditional relevance"; what must the offering party do to satisfy the "condition"; and at what point in the trial must the "condition" be satisfied.

Conditional relevance

"Conditional relevance" arises when there is a factual gap between an item of evidence—let's call that "*fact a*"—and the fact it is being offered to prove or disprove[43]—"*fact c.*" The situation often arises when a party offers circumstantial evidence; in fact, we have encountered it several times already.

Consider, for example, the questions in § 1.8: the prosecution of driver D for driving while intoxicated and killing pedestrian V at 1 a.m. Witness W2 testifies that he is D's neighbor; that he saw D in a local bar that evening from 11:30 p.m. to 12:45 a.m.; and that during that time, he saw D consume three glasses of a pale brown liquid.

The relevance of that testimony to show that D was intoxicated depends on the fact that what D consumed contained alcohol. In other words:

Fact (a) D was in the bar that evening from 11:30 p.m. to 12:45 a.m., and consumed three glasses of a pale brown liquid. (W2's testimony is direct evidence of this fact; hence no inferences need be drawn other than that W2's testimony is accurate.)

43. I use the phrase "to prove or disprove" as shorthand for "has any tendency to make a [fact that is of consequence to the action] more probable or less probable than it would be without the evidence."

Fact (b) Those beverages consisted of, or included, alcohol.

Fact (c) D was intoxicated at 1 a.m. when his car struck and killed V.

But the prosecutor has offered no direct evidence of fact (b)—that those beverages contained alcohol. Thus, the relevance of fact (a) to prove fact (c) depends, as Rule 104(b) puts it, "on whether [fact (b)] exists."

Burden of proof: "sufficient to support a finding"

How persuasive must P's evidence be, that the beverages D consumed contained alcohol? Again, Rule 104(b) provides the answer: the evidence in the case must be "sufficient to support a finding" that the beverages contained alcohol.

So what does "sufficient to support a finding" mean?

> Evidence is "sufficient to support a finding" when a rational jury could conclude, by a preponderance of the evidence, that the fact is true.[44]

This language may seem simple enough—by now you are familiar with the "preponderance of the evidence" standard. A preponderance of the evidence exists when a fact is more likely true than untrue, right?[45]

But to admit W2's testimony, the prosecutor does not have to satisfy the judge by a preponderance of the evidence that those beverages contained alcohol. The prosecution only has to offer sufficient evidence that a rational jury *could* (might) find that fact by a preponderance.

In other words, in ruling on D's relevancy objection, the judge does *not* ask herself, "Am *I* convinced by a preponderance of the evidence that those drinks contained alcohol?" Rather, she must ask herself, "Could a rational jury reach that conclusion based on this (and on the other evidence) in the case?" In this hypothetical, the answer to that question is, "Yes." Common sense and experience tell us that if a person enters a bar shortly before midnight and consumes three beverages over a 75-minute period, it's likely those beverages contained alcohol.

The jury is not required to accept this conclusion, but it rationally could accept it; and that is all that relevancy requires. Therefore W2's testimony is relevant evidence, because it tends to make it more probable that D was intoxicated when his car struck V at 1 a.m.

---

44. The Supreme Court elaborated on this standard in U.S. v Huddleston, 485 U.S. 649 (1988). This aspect of *Huddleston* is discussed in some detail in § 7.11.

45. There *are* times when admissibility of evidence *does* depend on whether a litigant has satisfied the judge by a preponderance that certain facts are true. I call this situation "conditional admissibility." See § 2.10.

Question 1.

Let's change the facts. Suppose the state's first witness is W3, not W2. W3 testifies that he saw D enter the bar at 11 p.m. That's all W3 saw. He does not know how long D remained in the bar. He does not know what D did while it was inside.

The relevance of this evidence, to show that D was intoxicated while driving at 1 a.m., depends on the fact that D consumed enough alcohol to render him intoxicated. In other words:

Fact (a)	D entered a bar at 11 p.m. (W3's testimony satisfies the prosecutor's burden to prove this fact.)
Fact (b)	D consumed a quantity of alcohol while in the bar.
Fact (c)	D was intoxicated at 1 a.m.

Is W3's testimony—remember, in this hypothetical, he is the state's first witness—by itself, sufficient to support a finding that D consumed enough alcohol while in the bar to be intoxicated at 1 a.m.? If not, and D objects, should the judge exclude the testimony?

Answer:

No; and no, not necessarily.

Has the prosecutor offered enough evidence, at this point in the trial, "sufficient to support a finding" that D got drunk while in the bar? No. Fact (b) (that D got drunk) is a possibility, of course, but there is simply not enough evidence entitle a rational jury to accept it by a preponderance.

D's attorney therefore objects that W3's testimony is irrelevant. Should the judge sustain the objection and preclude W3 from testifying? (Or, if W3 has testified, should the judge strike his testimony from the record and tell the jury to disregard it, which is more-or-less the same thing?[46])

Order of proof

Not necessarily. Now we must consider the "order of proof," i.e., the sequence in which evidence is presented. The last sentence of FRE 104(b) reads: "The court may admit the proposed evidence on the condition that the proof be introduced later." Here's the sequence:

1. W3 testifies on direct.
2. D's attorney objects that it is irrelevant.

46. "More or less the same thing"? Maybe a better way of putting it is "kind of sort of the same thing, but not really." We'll discuss that in § 2.11.

3. The judge looks quizzically at the prosecutor, who responds, "Your honor, please take this subject to connection, per Rule 104(b)."
4. The judge says, "Objection overruled—for now."

Step 3 is courtroom code: the prosecutor is saying, "Judge, I know I haven't satisfied Rule 104(b) yet, but I will; take my word for it for the time being." Step 4 is the judge saying, "OK, I'll take your word for it—for now."

Next, the prosecutor calls W2, who testifies about seeing D drink those three beverages between 11:30 p.m. and 12:45 a.m. W2's testimony is not only relevant in and of itself to show that D was intoxicated at 1 a.m.; it also satisfies the prosecutor's burden with regard to W3's testimony, because now the jury does not have to speculate about how long D was in the bar or what he did there; W2's testimony supplies the missing link (fact (b)).

Note also that W3's testimony is not only (now) relevant to suggest that D was drunk at 1 a.m.; it is also relevant to corroborate W2's testimony, by putting D in that bar that night.

§ 1.14 Authentication and Identification: a brief introduction

V was stabbed several times and bled to death. D is charged with murder. At trial, the prosecutor cannot simply open up her brief case and say, "Your honor, I offer into evidence the knife that was found in a dumpster two blocks from the crime scene."

Similarly, an attorney in a contracts case cannot simply remove a document from a folder and say, "Your honor, I offer into evidence the contract containing the plaintiff's and the defendant's signatures."

Before any physical object is admitted into evidence, the attorney party must produce evidence tending to establish that it is what he or she claims it is. This is called "authenticating" the evidence.

Similarly, witness W in an obstruction of justice case, *U.S. v. Bully*, cannot simply testify, "I received a phone call from Mr. Bully, and he threatened to have me beat up if I testified against him." W must testify how W knew it was Bully who placed the call. This is called "identifying" the source of the evidence.

Authentication and identification are covered in Article IX of the FRE. The general rule is stated in FRE 901(a):

Rule 901. Authenticating or Identifying Evidence

(a) In General. To satisfy the requirement of authenticating or identifying an item of evidence, the proponent must produce evidence sufficient to support a finding that the item is what the proponent claims it is.

Does that language sound familiar? It should, because it basically restates FRE 104(b), set out in the previous section:

> "When the relevance of evidence depends on whether a fact exists, proof must be introduced sufficient to support a finding that the fact does exist..."

In other words, the process of authenticating or identifying evidence is simply a specialized application of FRE 104(b). Which makes sense: the relevance of the knife in the murder case "depends" (is conditioned) in part on where it was found.[47] The relevance of the document in the contract case depends on (is "conditioned on") whether the offering party can show that it is in fact the contract signed by both parties. The phone call in the obstruction case is relevant only if the prosecutor can show that the call did in fact come from Bully.

How strong must the evidence be, identifying the knife, or the contract, or Bully's voice? The evidence must be "sufficient to support a finding."

FRE 901(b) gives ten different "illustrations" of evidence which satisfies this standard. Rule 901(b)(1) provides:

> **(b) Examples.** The following are examples only—not a complete list—of evidence that satisfies the requirement:
>
> (1) Testimony of a Witness with Knowledge. Testimony that an item is what it is claimed to be.

In other words, witness W can authenticate or identify a physical object, or can identify a voice, simply by explaining how W has first-hand knowledge about it. A homicide detective can identify and authenticate the knife by saying "I recognize it as the knife I found in a dumpster 2 blocks from the crime scene because I recognize the crack in the handle and the little indentation halfway down the blade."[48] A witness can authenticate and identify the document as the contract by testifying, "I remember signing it and I saw defendant sign it, and I kept it in my filing cabinet until coming to court today." The witness in the extortion case can identify the caller as Bully by testifying, "A week before I received the phone call, Bully walked into my store and threatened me if I testified; I recognized his voice over the phone from that conversation."

---

47. The prosecutor will also have to introduce evidence tending to prove that this knife is the murder weapon and evidence connecting the defendant to the knife.

48. Although this is enough to identify the knife per FRE 901(a) and FRE 901(b)(1), the prosecutor will also offer evidence of the chain of custody from the time the officer found the knife to the time it was brought to the courtroom. Such testimony, though not technically necessary to satisfy Article IX in this case, certainly strengthens the evidence establishing that it is in fact that knife.

The rest of Rule 901(b) provides examples of common situations that often arise and the kinds of evidence that satisfy the "sufficient to support a finding" standard. I'll let your evidence professor cover those.

C. The "Rule of Completeness"; FRE 106; Other General Relevance Principles

§ 1.15 The Rule of Completeness: *Beech Aircraft Corporation v. Rainey*[49]

Beech Aircraft v. Rainey is undoubtedly in your casebook, but here is a brief review. A Navy training aircraft crashed, killing Lieutenant Commander Mrs. Rainey (the pilot-instructor) and her student. Lieutenant Commander Morgan was assigned to investigate the crash, and issued a report concluding that the most probable cause was pilot error.

Mr. Rainey, who like his late wife was a Lieutenant Commander and a Naval flight instructor,[50] conducted his own investigation and then wrote a letter to Commander Morgan. In it, Mr. Rainey conceded two facts on which Morgan had relied—that Mrs. Rainey had tried unsuccessfully to postpone the flight because her student was mentally exhausted, and that their plane turned prematurely during maneuvers, which initiated the sequence that ended with the fatal crash. But most of the letter—and its entire purpose—was to show that a defect in the plane—a power failure, not pilot error—caused the crash.

Mr. Rainey sued Beech Aircraft. The key issue at trial was whether pilot error or a defect in the plane caused the crash. Mr. Rainey's attorney did not call Mr. Rainey as a witness, but during the defense case, Beech called Mr. Rainey. On direct, Beech's attorney elicited that Mr. Rainey wrote to Commander Morgan and that, in his letter, Mr. Rainey acknowledged Mrs. Rainey's attempt to cancel her flight and conceded that pilot error set the fatal events in motion.[51] On cross-examination, Mr. Rainey's attorney sought to bring out that the entire thrust of Mr. Rainey's letter was to establish that a power failure in the plane, not pilot error, caused the crash. Beech's attorney objected. The judge sustained the objection, and did not allow Mr. Rainey to testify further about the contents of his letter.

The Supreme Court, dividing 7–2, held that "the District Court erred in refusing to permit Rainey to present a more complete picture of what he had written to

---

49. 488 U.S. 153, 109 S.Ct. 439, 102 L.Ed.2d 445 (1988).

50. Except where I quote from the Supreme Court decision, henceforth I will refer to the plaintiff as "Mr. Rainey" (the plaintiff) and the deceased as "Mrs. Rainey."

51. It was entirely proper for Beech's lawyer to do so.

Morgan." This, the Court held, violated the common law "rule of completeness": "[W]hen one party has made use of a portion of a document, such that misunderstanding or distortion can be averted only through presentation of another portion, the material required for completeness is ipso facto relevant and therefore admissible under Rules 401 and 402." Rainey, 488 US at 182. Because Rainey was prevented from describing his letter more fully during cross-examination, "the jury was given a distorted and prejudicial impression of Rainey's letter. It is plausible that a jury would have concluded from this information that Rainey did not believe in his theory of power failure and had developed it only later for purposes of litigation. Because the court sustained defense counsel's objection, Rainey's counsel was unable to counteract this prejudicial impression by presenting additional information about the letter on cross examination." Rainey, 488 US at 170–171.

Don't be misled by the name of the "rule of completeness." That Beech offered part of Mr. Rainey's letter did not necessarily entitle Rainey to introduce his "complete" (i.e., his entire) letter into evidence. The rule of completeness entitled Mr. Rainey to introduce (or testify about) enough of his letter to give the jury a more accurate understanding of what the letter contained and what Mr. Rainey intended to communicate to Commander Morgan. Ultimately, the trial judge, not Rainey's lawyer, would have the final say as to what would be enough to counter the misimpression created by Beech Aircraft's careful selection of the portions of the letter it introduced on direct examination.

§ 1.16 Digression: the evidentiary "backstory" to *Beech v. Rainey*

This section explains a bit more of the evidentiary background of the Court's ruling in *Rainey.* It isn't essential to your understanding of the "rule of completeness" and FRE 106, so skip over it if you are rushed for time, but it gives you some useful context.

1. Beech Aircraft could have called Commander Morgan as an expert witness to give his opinion as to what caused the crash. Instead, Beech introduced Morgan's report into evidence. His report's conclusion—that the crash was caused by pilot error—is hearsay, because he made that statement ("I therefore conclude that the most probable cause for the crash was pilot error"[52]) out-of-court, and Beech offered it evidence to prove that in fact pilot error was what caused the crash. Although this conclusion was hearsay, the trial court ruled, and the Supreme Court agreed, that it satisfied the "public record" exception for "factual findings," per what was then FRE 803(8)(C) and is now FRE 803(8)(A)(iii). See *A Student's Guide to Hearsay*, § 9.46.

2. Mr. Rainey conducted his own investigation and stated his conclusions, and the reasons for them, in his letter to Commander Morgan. It is possible that Mr. Rainey also could have qualified as an expert, in which case he could have testified

52. This is a paraphrase—not a direct quote—of Morgan's conclusion.

at trial and expressed his conclusions ("rollback, power failure, defective design or manufacture"[53]) as to what caused the plane to crash. But Mr. Rainey's attorney decided—wisely, I think—not to go that route. Let's assume the jury had a lot of sympathy for Mr. Rainey. Still, it is hard to imagine the jury would rely on his opinion—after all, he was trying to exonerate his late wife's reputation and sought monetary damages for her death. Mr. Rainey's lawyer presumably presented a good deal of evidence supporting the "power failure" theory, perhaps including an expert witness of his own.

3. Mr. Rainey could not introduce his report into evidence, because it did not satisfy any hearsay exception. It would not qualify as a public record, because that exception applies only when the investigation and resultant report were "legally authorized," i.e., conducted by someone with an official duty to investigate and report. Commander Morgan had such a duty: he was assigned to do so by his superiors in the Navy. Mr. Rainey had no legal duty to investigate. Therefore, his report did not qualify under any hearsay exception.

4. Beech Aircraft, on the other hand, introduced parts of Mr. Rainey's letter under a different hearsay exception: FRE 801(d)(2)(A). That provision holds that a party's own statement can be introduced against that party simply because the party made it. See *A Student's Guide to Hearsay*, § 5.2 to § 5.11.

5. But by introducing the parts of Mr. Rainey's letter that helped Beech Aircraft's case, the Supreme Court held, Beech opened the door to other portions of the letter that were necessary to correct the misleading impression that Beech created by cherry-picking the two passages in the report that helped Beech's case.

6. "But wait a minute, Prof," you might be thinking, "didn't you just say, in ¶ 3, that Mr. Rainey could not introduce his letter, because if he offered it, it would be inadmissible hearsay?" Yes, I said that and yes, it would be inadmissible hearsay—*if Mr. Rainey offered it top prove that rollback and engine failure caused the crash.* But once Beech offered part of the letter into evidence, Mr. Rainey had a different theory of relevance: to make sure the jury was not left with an inaccurate idea about what Rainey said in his letter. This is an example of FRE 105: evidence that is inadmissible for one purpose may be admissible if offered for another purpose. (I discuss FRE 105 in § 2.8.)

7. One other point. Two Justices dissented—not because they disagreed with the majority's conclusions, but because, in their opinion, Mr. Rainey's attorney had failed to preserve the issue because he did not adequately explain his theory of relevance to the trial judge. If your casebook coverage of *Rainey* includes footnote 3 of the Court's opinion in that case, you'll notice that Mr. Rainey's lawyer tried to do so, but the judge didn't even let the lawyer finish a sentence; after hearing all of twenty-five words from Mr. Rainey's lawyer, the judge sustained Beech's objections.

---

53. This is a paraphrase—not a direct quote—of Rainey's conclusion.

Why? Well, sometimes a judge thinks, "I know what Lawyer X is trying to say, and what Lawyer X is trying to say is bogus, so I'll just rule against X now, instead of wasting time listening to X." Sometimes the judge is right. This time, the judge was wrong. But this side issue illustrates a point: when arguing a point to a judge, don't bury the lede;[54] tell the judge your main point as quickly and succinctly as possible.

Question 1.

How could Rainey's lawyer have made his basic point clear in 5 words or less, assuming the first two words are "Your Honor"?

Answer:

"Your Honor, rule of completeness." Or: "Your Honor, Rule 106."

Moral of story: Rule numbers and catch phrases do not constitute a valid legal argument (and are likely to be inadequate as an answer to an essay question). But they are a convenient way to immediately alert a judge—or a law professor—to the basic thrust of your argument.

§ 1.17 FRE 106

In *Rainey*, the Supreme Court commented: "The Federal Rules of Evidence have partially codified the doctrine of completeness in Rule 106," but concluded the case did not actually involve FRE 106.

FRE 106 provides:

> **Rule 106. Remainder of or Related Writings or Recorded Statements**
>
> If a party introduces all or part of a writing or recorded statement, an adverse party may require the introduction, at that time, of any other part—or any other writing or recorded statement—that in fairness ought to be considered at the same time.

But isn't that what Mr. Rainey's lawyer tried to do? Didn't the Supreme Court rule that it was reversible error for the trial judge to disallow it? So why did the Court comment that FRE 106 didn't apply?

To answer these questions, I first have to tell you one more aspect of the "rule of completeness": it says that if Party A introduces part of an oral, written, or recorded statement, another party (Party B) may introduce other aspects of that oral, written, or recorded statement that are necessary to give the jury a fairer and more complete

54. To "bury the lede" is to fail to emphasize the most important part of a story from the start. It was a term coined by journalists to describe a shortcoming in a news report. Supposedly journalists spelled the term "lede" instead of "lead" to prevent confusion back in the day when printing was done with lead print.

understanding of the statement as a whole. But the common law "rule of completeness" does not specify *when* Party B is entitled to do so.

The "when" aspect of the common law rule didn't really present any problem in the Rainey case, because Beech called Mr. Rainey as a witness and used him to introduce the two short portions of his letter to Commander Morgan that helped Beech's case. Since Mr. Rainey was already on the stand, under the rule of completeness Mr. Rainey's lawyer should have been allowed to elicit testimony from Mr. Rainey to give the jury a more complete understanding of the letter's content ant thrust.

But suppose instead of calling Mr. Rainey, Beech had called BWx, who testified, "Mr. Rainey showed me a copy of the letter he sent to Commander Morgan. I clearly remember that Mr. Rainey's letter admitted that Mrs. Rainey tried to cancel the training exercise because the pupil was exhausted, and it admitted that the pilot made an unsafe maneuver shortly before the plane crashed." On cross-examination, BWx insisted that this was all BWx could recall from Mr. Rainey's letter. After Mr. Rainey's lawyer finished cross-examining BWx, Beech then proceeded to present the rest of its case. It introduced Commander Morgan's report concluding that the cause of the crash was pilot error, and any other evidence Beech had to support that conclusion. That might have taken several days. Under the rule of completeness, only then, after Beech rested, could Mr. Rainey's lawyer, in rebuttal, call Rainey on the stand to give the jury a more complete and accurate understanding of his letter. By then, the misimpression the jury initially received (from BWx's testimony during the defense case) might have become so ingrained in the jurors' minds that Rainey's testimony might come far too late to do much good.

FRE 106 introduces a procedural wrinkle: if the statement was in writing or recorded, FRE 106 permits "[t]he adverse party [in this case, Mr. Rainey] to "introdu[ce], at that time,... any other part—or any other writing or recorded statement—that in fairness ought to be considered at the same time." (Emphasis added.) In other words, Mr. Rainey's lawyer would not have to wait until the defense rested. Rule 106 says (subject to trial judge discretion) that Mr. Rainey's lawyer could authenticate the letter and introduce appropriate portions of it during cross-examination of BWx or immediately after BWx finished testifying.

§ 1.18 Other general relevance principles

1. "Evaluative" relevance. Evidence is relevant if it assists the factfinder in evaluating other evidence. As the Advisory Committee Note to FRE 401 explains, that rule follows previous prevailing practice in admitting "[e]vidence which is essentially background in nature,... offered as an aid to understanding."

For example, a witness might testify about the standards and practices in a particular profession or business, to help the jury evaluate the events or behavior in question. Thus, in a prosecution of an attorney for participating in a criminal scheme where the defense is that the attorney simply gave legal advice to a client, the state and the defense should both be permitted to offer evidence relating to an attorney's professional and ethical responsibilities. Such testimony is relevant to assist a jury in deciding whether an attorney acted with criminal intent. Similarly, in complex business litigation, a judge might admit evidence about business practices as background information to help the jury assess the evidence in the case.

Somewhat more problematically, courts sometimes admit and sometimes exclude "background" information that explains why the police targeted the defendant for investigation. If such information is excluded, the jury may get the impression that the prosecution is presenting an incomplete or artificial story; yet, the information itself often consists of otherwise inadmissible hearsay evidence of other criminal acts.[55]

2. <u>Rebut a negative inference</u>. Evidence also may be relevant to rebut a negative inference that might be drawn in the absence of the evidence. For example, see § 1.9, question 6, relating to the absence of fingerprint and DNA evidence.

3. <u>"Spoliation" evidence.</u> Where a litigant destroyed evidence under circumstances suggesting bad faith, the adverse party is entitled to argue that the destruction supports the inference that the evidence would have been damaging to the party who destroyed it; indeed, in some jurisdictions, the adverse party may be entitled to a jury instruction to that effect.

4. <u>Other party misconduct.</u> That a litigant bribed or threatened a witness, or attempted to fabricate evidence, likewise triggers an inference of consciousness of guilt or wrongdoing, on the theory that a party who was innocent, or who had a valid civil claim or defense, would not stoop to such tactics.

5. <u>Criminal defendant's lack of funds before a crime; possession of unexplained wealth after the crime</u>. Prosecutors sometimes offer evidence that a defendant was impoverished or in debt at the time a crime was committed, on the theory that the defendant's lack of resources gave the defendant a motive to commit the crime. Courts should, and generally do, reject such evidence because of its negligible relevance. After all, such evidence would be equally relevant against *anyone* in financial difficulty. Moreover, such evidence has a dangerous tendency to put a poor person under unfair suspicion merely because he or she is poor.

On the other hand, this is not an absolute ban. "If a man is notoriously broke and cannot buy a pack of cigarettes Tuesday, and that night a laundromat is burglarized, and on Wednesday the man buys a carton of cigarettes and a $40 bottle of scotch, all with quarters, the man's financial circumstances have obvious and significant probative value."[56] And possession of large and unexplained quantities of cash is often admitted in prosecutions for extensive conspiracy to traffic in drugs.

---

55. See *A Student's Guide to Hearsay* § 2.34 (5th ed. 2019). (End of commercial.)

56. U.S. v. Mitchell, 172 F.3d 1104 (9th Cir. 1999). That assumes that customers in the laundromat had to insert quarters into the washers and dryers to use the machines.

6. Evidence made relevant by other evidence. Here's an example. Tony is accused of killing Nardo. During the state's case in chief, the prosecutor offers evidence that Tony and Maria are in love. The defense objects: irrelevant! The prosecutor concedes to the judge that Maria was not at the scene where Nardo was killed, that she had nothing to do with his death, and that the prosecutor does not intend to call Maria as a witness. Hearing this, the judge sustains the objection. Then, during the defense case, Maria testifies as an alibi witness: she swears that when Nardo was killed, she was with Tony several miles away from the crime scene. Now the romantic attachment between Tony and Maria clearly is relevant, because it supports the inference that Maria may be lying to keep the person she loves from being convicted of murder.

Question 1.

Why do these names sound familiar?

Answer:

They are important characters in *West Side Story.*

7. Remote or abstract relevance; "equivocal" evidence; "inference on inference." Although evidence is relevant so long as it has *"any tendency"* to make a fact of consequence more probable or less probable (FRE 401), courts nevertheless occasionally exclude the evidence because it has only remote, or abstract, but not "legal" relevance, or because it lacks sufficient connection to the key events or individuals, or because its theory of relevance is too speculative or tenuous. Sometimes the term "remote" is used in an attempt to assess quantifiable factors such as time and distance. The situation arises with some frequency in automobile collision cases, in which one party ("X") seeks to introduce evidence that the other party ("Y") was seen to be speeding or committing another moving violation on the same day, some time and distance prior to the collision, to support the inference that Y continued to drive in the same unsafe manner until he reached the intersection where the collision occurred. Suffice it to say that courts do not follow any consistent pattern in such cases.

Courts occasionally exclude evidence because it is equivocal or ambiguous, i.e., it could be interpreted to support either side on an issue, but the better approach is to admit such evidence and allow the jury to assess its probative worth; in any event, it is difficult to see what harm or prejudice could result.

Occasionally, a court rejects evidence as "irrelevant" because other evidence directly contradicts the inference the offered evidence supports. This is an inappropriate theory of exclusion that may improperly pre-empt the jury's role as factfinder.

Occasionally, one may still come across a statement in a judicial opinion that evidence is inadmissible because it is impermissible to base an inference upon an inference. Adherence to such a rule would eliminate most circumstantial evidence; such expressions should be taken as poorly worded attempts to express the principle that an inferential chain may be so weak or tenuous that it fails to be sufficient to support a finding.

Chapter 2

Procedural Matters

§ 2.1 Introduction

This chapter discusses how evidence issues are litigated in the courtroom; what the party whose objection is overruled can do to challenge the evidence the judge has admitted; and the motions a party should make when the other side rests.

§ 2.2 Objections in general; motion in limine

When one party offers evidence at a trial, a party who wants to challenge its admissibility must object.[1] FRE 103(a) spells out the requirements for a valid objec-

1. Any party in a trial may object. Usually this is the opponent of the party offering the evidence, but not always. Suppose a civil action: P is suing D1 and D2. D1 offers evidence that would harm D2.

tion: (1) it must be timely; and (2) it must specify the specific grounds for the objection, unless that is apparent from the context.[2] I always required my students to include the rule number—including subdivisions—in their objections: Example: "Objection. Hearsay, Rule 801(c)," or "Objection: beyond the scope of cross-examination, Rule 611(b)." That way, the rule numbers become part of the classroom's organic vocabulary.

Once the objection is made, the judge may resolve the issue prior to trial (assuming the issue was raised before trial); or at a **motion in limine** hearing during the trial, out of the jury's presence; or during the normal course of taking testimony and receiving evidence in the jury's presence. The Federal Rules of Evidence leave it pretty much up to the judge how to proceed, although FRE 104(c) directs that the judge *must* conduct the hearing out of the jury's presence in two very specific situations and one general circumstance. The specific situations set out in FRE 104(c)(1) and FRE 104(c)(2) arise only in criminal trials.[3] FRE 104(c)(3) directs that as a general principle, the hearing must be out of the jury's presence if "justice so requires."

How many objections may an attorney make to an offer of evidence? As many as he or she can plausibly argue. I can imagine a situation in which an attorney might argue that a particular offer of evidence is irrelevant; and violates Rule 408 (offer to compromise or settle); and is inadmissible hearsay; and has not been properly authenticated; and violates the "best evidence rule" (Article X); and should be excluded per Rule 403; and perhaps a few others besides.[4]

Consider the previous paragraph as a reminder: whenever you read a question in this book or consider a question or problem in your casebook or in class, sure—start off with the rule of evidence that the class is currently studying. But also give some thought to every other rule that has already been covered. Questions on quizzes and on the exam will not be labeled: "This is only a hearsay question," or "This requires you apply Rule 408 and no other rule." In real life, a single item of evidence may raise issues involving several separate rules. Similarly, questions you encounter during your evidence course will sometimes involve previously-covered material, as well as—or instead of—the material you are currently covering.

Even though D1 and D2 are not formally opposing parties, D2 can still object to its admissibility.

2. If the judge excludes the evidence, the adverse party must make an offer of proof—in essence, must describe the excluded evidence for the trial record, and state the reasons why (in the offering party's opinion) the evidence should have been admitted. See § 2.6.

3. FRE 104(c)(1) requires that if a hearing is held to resolve whether a defendant's statement to law enforcement officials was obtained in violation of the Fifth Amendment, that hearing should be held while the jury is not in the courtroom. Rule 104(c)(2) mandates that a hearing on the admissibility of evidence in a criminal case should be held outside the jury's presence if the defendant is going to testify on that narrow issue. Each provision is designed to protect a defendant's Fifth Amendment rights.

4. I never actually wrote a quiz or exam question quite that brutal, which helps explain how I taught law for 42½ years without even once being challenged to a duel.

You might protest: "You mean, we have to review the entire course to date each time we get a question?" Yes, that *is* what I mean, because that's the best way to learn and relearn the rules as a coherent whole, rather than as isolated bits.

One more preliminary point about objections: how to respond to them. Most often, an objection must be answered in its own terms. If the adverse party (the party against whom the evidence is offered) objects that evidence is hearsay, the offering party cannot respond, "Your Honor, the evidence is relevant, and it is properly authenticated and satisfies the best evidence rule and it is proper lay witness opinion testimony." It may be all these things, but none of them respond to the hearsay objection. Rather, the offering party must persuade the judge, (a) that it is not hearsay, or (b) even though it is hearsay, it fits within this or that exception to the hearsay rule. So a proper response might be: "Your Honor, the statement satisfies the co-conspirator exception, Rule 801(d)(2(E)."

This means that if the adverse party makes all of the objections I mentioned in the third paragraph of this section, the offering party has to address each of those objections—and has to win the evidence argument on every one of them—in order to get the evidence admitted. To keep the evidence out, the objector only has to succeed on one objection; to get the evidence in, the offering party has to convince the judge on all of them.[5]

Another point about objecting: Once a judge overrules an objection and concludes that the evidence is admissible, in order to preserve the right to appeal that ruling, does the lawyer who lost the motion still have to object when the other side offers the evidence at trial? And on the flip side: if the judge excludes evidence a lawyer sought to offer, does that lawyer need to do anything else (other than make an offer or proof, see § 2.6) to preserve the right to appeal the judge's ruling?

FRE 103(b) directs:

> **(b) Not Needing to Renew an Objection or Offer of Proof.** Once the court rules definitively on the record—either before or at trial—a party need not renew an objection or offer of proof to preserve a claim of error for appeal.

In a typical trial scenario, during the trial, attorney A asks a question, attorney B objects to the question (or the answer). If the judge overrules the objection, B need not make an additional objection. But if the objection is litigated prior to trial or at a hearing out of the jury's presence, must B make an objection once the trial begins (or once the jury is back in the courtroom listening to evidence) and A offers the evidence or asks the question?

---

5. This paragraph overstates the case somewhat, because evidence that is inadmissible on one theory of relevance may nevertheless be admissible on a different theory or for a different purpose. See FRE 105, discussed in § 2.8.

FRE 103(b) says, in essence, that B must object when A offers the evidence or asks the question at trial, unless the judge's ruling overruling B's earlier objection is "definitive." How is B to know whether the ruling is "definitive"?

The best way is for B to ask the judge, on the record (i.e., while the court stenographer is taking down what's being said): "Your Honor, is that a definitive ruling?" If the judge says "Yes," then B need not object again when A offers the evidence at trial. But if the judge says pretty much anything else—such as "Well, counselor, that's my current position, depending on what else happens"—then B should object again when A offers the evidence at trial, or else risk losing the right to appeal the judge's ruling.

But even if the judge says that his ruling is "definitive," that doesn't mean it is carved into stone tablets. Things often happen in a trial that open the door to evidence the judge had previously excluded. It is attorney B's responsibility to renew the objection, even though the judge's ruling was "definitive," if events during the trial provide a new basis to object.

Similarly, if the judge has excluded evidence B wanted to introduce, but during-the-trial events or newly discovered evidence give B another—or a stronger—basis to argue for admission, it is B's responsibility to ask the judge to reconsider his or her ruling.

Suppose, for example, prior to trial, B moves for a ruling that W1 should be permitted to testify about the events of June 12. At the hearing, B explains that she anticipates that A will offer testimony about June 13th, and that therefore, out of fairness, evidence about the 12th is necessary to put what happened on the 13th into context. In response, A tells the judge he will not offer evidence about or refer in any way to the events of the 13th. On that basis, the judge rules that B's evidence about June 12th is inadmissible. But during B's case-in-chief, A asks B's witnesses a series of questions on cross-examination which clearly allude to the events of the 13th. At this point, B should renew his motion to allow W1 to testify about June 12th, and the judge might very properly conclude that A has opened the door to B's evidence about the 12th.

§ 2.3 Litigating admissibility of evidence

P is suing Megacorp. P alleges that he bought a holodeck[6] manufactured by Megacorp; that the holodeck was defective; and that the defect caused a fire in P's home. At trial, P wants to call W to testify that a woman named DL said, "That holodeck was defective when it left the factory and never should have been sold to P or anyone else." DL's statement is clearly relevant, because it has some tendency to make it more probable than it would be without the evidence that the holodeck

6. This is a Star Trek reference. For more information, type "holodeck star trek" into your search engine. (Mine produced 137,000 "hits.")

was defective. But Megacorp objects: "DL's statement is hearsay, because its relevance depends on whether what DL said is true and accurate.[7] Your Honor therefore should exclude it!"

"Not so fast," P responds. "DL's statement satisfies an exception to the hearsay rule, because when DL made the statement, she was an authorized spokesperson for Megacorp." P makes a good point: FRE 801(d)(2)(C) says that a statement made by a party's "authorized spokesperson"[8] is admissible against that party over a hearsay objection.[9] Therefore, the judge should admit the statement.

"Except for one little detail," Megacorp's attorney responds. "DL was *not* our 'authorized spokesperson' when she made that statement."

Now what? One thing is clear: since P seeks to invoke FRE 801(d)(2)(C) (the "authorized spokesperson" rule), P has the burden of establishing that DL was an authorized spokesperson for Megacorp when she made the statement. Unless P can do so, Megacorp's hearsay objection must be sustained. W will not be allowed to testify about what DL said.

This raises three questions. (1) Who gets to decide whether DL was Megacorp's authorized spokesperson? (2) What kinds of evidence may P and Megacorp use to show that DL was, or was not, Megacorp's spokesperson? (3) What is P's burden of proof on the issue?

By now the Megacorp scenario may raise a fourth question: "Um, . . . Fishman *does* realize this is not his *hearsay* book, doesn't he?" Yes, I do. But I use the Megacorp scenario here and in a few subsequent sections of this chapter because it works so well to illustrate the procedural issues that are likely to arise in a wide variety of situations, regardless of the particular rule(s) of evidence that apply.

§ 2.4 Who decides on admissibility? What kinds of evidence may be considered? FRE 104(a)

These issues require us to consider FRE 104(a).

> **Rule 104. Preliminary questions**
>
> **(a) In General.** The court must decide any preliminary question about whether . . . evidence is admissible. In so deciding, the court is not bound by evidence rules, . . .

---

7. See *A Student's Guide to Hearsay*, § 2.20. (End of commercial.)

8. "Authorized spokesperson" can cover a wide range of activities within a company. It includes the CEO and the chairman of the board of directors; perhaps each individual member of the board; the VP in charge of public relations; people in charge of advertising; and individual salesmen who speak to customers about the product or services the company sells. It also includes in-house attorneys and outside counsel who represent the company in various matters.

9. See *A Student's Guide to Hearsay* §§ 5.19–5.22. (End of commercial.)

In the Megacorp scenario, who gets to decide whether DL's statement is admissible? Rule 104(a) tells us: "The court [i.e., the judge, not the jury] must decide... whether... evidence is admissible." That certainly makes sense: whether to admit evidence is a question of law; resolving questions of law is the judge's job, not the jury's.

What kind of evidence is P permitted to use to satisfy its burden of proof? The rule answers that question, too: "In so deciding, the court is not bound by evidence rules,..." In other words, when P tries to persuade the judge that DL was authorized by Megacorp to speak for it, *P may rely on evidence that would not be admissible at trial.*

Let's assume that the judge holds a hearing, either before trial or out-of-the-jury's hearing during the trial, on whether DL was an authorized spokesperson for Megacorp. Each side presents evidence and argues the issue to the judge. P has the burden of proof. What is that burden?

§ 2.5 Burden of proof

The Federal Rules of Evidence do not explicitly answer that question. Happily, however, the Supreme Court gave us the answer in *United States v. Bourjaily*:

> [D]ecisions regarding admissibility determinations [often] hinge on preliminary factual questions. We have traditionally required that these matters be established by a preponderance of proof.... The inquiry made by a court concerned with these matters is not whether the proponent of the evidence wins or loses his case on the merits, but whether the evidentiary Rules have been satisfied.... The preponderance standard ensures that before admitting evidence, the court will have found it more likely than not that the technical issues and policy concerns addressed by the Federal Rules of Evidence have been afforded due consideration.[10]

In other words, as a rule, the party making an objection has the burden to persuade the judge, by a preponderance of the evidence, that the factual basis for the objection exists. Similarly, the party seeking to invoke an exception to a rule has the burden to persuade the judge, by a preponderance of the evidence, that the factual basis for the exception exists.[11]

"But wait a minute," you may be thinking, "(1) Didn't you just tell us, in § 1:13, that the test was *not* 'a preponderance of the evidence'; it was 'sufficient to support a find-

10. United States v. Bourjaily, 483 U.S. 171, 175 (1987). For a more detailed discussion and analysis, see *A Student's Guide to Hearsay* §§ 5.33–5.35. (End of commercial.)

11. That's how I understand it, anyway. But cf. Fishman Rule of Evidence 001, in § P.1 of the Preface, *supra*.

ing'? (2) And didn't you tell us in § 1:13 that the judge *cannot* exclude evidence even if she is not convinced by a preponderance, so long as a rational jury might be convinced by a preponderance? (3) And aren't you now telling us the exact opposite?"

Well, now that you mention it, (1), Yes, I did. And (2), Yes, I did. And (3) Actually, no, I'm not.

The "sufficient to support a finding" standard set out in FRE 104(b) and 901(a) and discussed in §§ 1.13 to 1.14 apply when the issue is whether the evidence is *relevant,* and its relevance depends on the existence of an intermediate fact.

But when other rules come into play—rules which by their explicit language are based on whether or not certain specified facts exist—the judge's role is more substantial: the party seeking to invoke the rule must persuade the judge by a preponderance that those facts exist—such as whether DL was an authorized spokesperson for Megacorp when she made the statement.

Question 1.

How can a person know, in any given problem, whether to apply the "preponderance of the evidence" standard, or the "sufficient to support a finding" standard?

Answer:

If the *relevance* of the evidence requires a factual finding, apply the "sufficient to support a finding" standard, per FRE 104(b) and FRE 901(a). If the evidence is obviously relevant—like DL's statement about the holodeck that P purchased—and an objection is made other than relevance, apply the "preponderance of the evidence" standard.

Question 2.

Suppose, at the hearing to determine whether DL's statement is admissible, after W testifies for P that DL made the statement, DL testifies for Megacorp and insists that she did *not* make the statement. What then?

Answer:

Now there are two issues of fact and law for the judge to consider. (1) Did DL make the statement, i.e., whose testimony is accurate, W's or DL's? (2) Assuming DL did make the statement, was she an authorized spokesperson for Megacorp when she said it? In deciding Megacorp's hearsay objection, the judge should consider each issue separately—and, as you will see, should apply a different standard to those issues.

Issue (1): Suppose DL was Megacorp's Vice President for Quality Control and Public Relations, in which case, she clearly was an authorized spokesperson for Megacorp, and Megacorp conceded that fact. But DL denies making the statement! Would W's testimony, "I heard DL say that the holodeck was defective and never should have left the factory," be admissible?

Of course! Whether DL made the statement is simply an issue of fact. What's more, it's an issue of witness credibility—whose testimony is more accurate, W's ("that's what DL said") or DL's ("I never said that"). Who—judge or jury—has the responsibility of deciding whether a witness's testimony is accurate? The jury.

W's testimony—"I heard DL say that the holodeck was defective when it left the factory"—is relevant only if the jury concludes that W's testimony is accurate. Or to express the issues in FRE 104(b) terms, "When the relevance of evidence [W's testimony that DL made the statement] depends on whether a fact [that DL said what W claims] exists, proof must be introduced sufficient to support a finding that the fact does exist [i.e., that DL said it]."

Was P's proof—W's testimony—"sufficient to support a finding" that DL said it, despite DL's denial?

Yes. A witness's direct testimony that she had first-hand knowledge about a specific fact ("I heard DL say it") is always sufficient to support a finding, because it is up to the jury, not the judge, to assess the credibility and accuracy of a witness's testimony.[12]

The same is true in our actual problem: in deciding whether to admit DL's alleged statement, the judge must assume that W's testimony—that DL made the statement—is true.

Issue (2): Was DL an authorized spokesperson for Megacorp when she said it? That is *not* an issue of conditional *relevancy*, because DL's statement (that the holodeck was defective) clearly is relevant, if true. Rather, DL's status and responsibilities at Megacorp are, as the Supreme Court put it in *Bourjaily*, a "preliminary factual question," i.e., a "technical requirement of [an] evidentiary Rule[], which embod[ies] certain legal and policy determinations." Accordingly, the judge should apply the "preponderance standard." And if there is a conflict in testimony—DL claims her duties included being a spokesperson for the company, her supervisor claims the contrary—then the judge, not the jury, has to decide whom to believe.

To repeat once more: if the issue is conditional relevancy, including a question of whom to believe, the judge applies the "sufficient to support a finding" standard, which means the judge must assume that the witnesses for the party seeking to introduce the evidence are testifying accurately and truthfully. But a party seeking to invoke an evidence rule other than relevancy has the burden of persuading the judge by a preponderance of the evidence that the "preliminary factual... requirements" of the rule have been satisfied; and that means the judge makes his or her

12. Well, *almost* always. If the witness's testimony is so incredibly implausible that no rational person could possibly believe it, then it would not be sufficient to support a finding. For example, suppose W claims that while sitting in the centerfield bleachers at Yankee Stadium during a Yankee-Red Sox game, she heard DL make the statement while DL was sitting in her office Rochester, New York—a distance of about 338 driving miles (perhaps 250 miles as the crow flies)—without use of any electronic devices. No rational jury could believe such testimony.

own determination about which testimony to credit and which testimony to discount.

§ 2.6 An objection is sustained. What is the offering party's next move? An offer of proof; FRE 103(a)(2)

If a judge grants an objection and excludes an item of evidence, the offering party should at least assure that it can argue the issue on appeal. FRE 103(a)(2) spells out what that party must do:

> **Rule 103. Rulings on evidence**
>
> **(a) Preserving a Claim of Error.** A party may claim error in a ruling to admit or exclude evidence only if the error affects a substantial right of the party and:
>
> . . .
>
> (2) if the ruling excludes evidence, a party informs the court of its substance by an offer of proof, unless the substance was apparent from the context.

A proper offer of proof must do two things: it must inform the trial judge of the substance of the evidence being excluded, and explain to the judge the offering party's theory of relevance and admissibility. Doing so serves two purposes: (1) It gives the judge information that the judge might not have known when she excluded the evidence, and—who knows?—might persuade her to reverse her ruling. (2) It places the offering party's arguments on the trial record, thereby preserving the issue on appeal.[13]

There are exceptions to the offer of proof requirement—see FRE 103(b)—and it is up to the judge to decide when and how the party should make its offer of proof, see FRE 103(c). Your evidence professor will tell you what you need to know about these issues.

§ 2.7 An objection is overruled. What comes next? (a) Move to redact

If a judge overrules an objection, the adverse party should consider asking the judge to redact some aspects of the evidence because it violates

13. Failure to preserve the record does not completely preclude an attorney from pursuing the issue on appeal, but the attorney would have to argue that excluding the evidence was plain error. Appellate courts rarely grant "plain error" reversals.

some other rule, or is not relevant, or because the jury may misuse it, or because it is unduly prejudicial.

Question 1.

In the drunk driving case in § 1.8, the prosecutor wants W3 to testify that, a few days after D's car struck and killed V (the pedestrian), D (who made bail following his arrest) had a conversation at a local strip club with W3, during which D told W3, "I was so drunk that night I don't even remember driving home after I killed that woman." W3 is an attorney, so D's trial attorney objects that the conversation is inadmissible because it was protected by the attorney-client privilege, but the judge rules that no attorney-client relationship existed at that time between D and W3 and, therefore, the privilege did not apply and W3 has to testify. What further motion might D's attorney make?

Answer:

D's attorney should move to preclude any mention that the conversation occurred at a strip club. That fact is irrelevant as to whether it was D's fault that he killed the pedestrian, yet the jury is likely to draw negative inferences about D from the location of the conversation. The judge should grant the request and order the prosecutor and W3 not to refer to where the conversation occurred.[14]

§ 2.8 Objection overruled? (b) Request a limiting instruction per FRE 105; redaction

Rule 105 is another way an attorney can seek to limit the damage when evidence is admitted against a client:

> **Rule 105. Limiting Evidence That Is Not Admissible Against Other Parties or for Other Purposes**
>
> If the court admits evidence that is admissible against a party or for a purpose—but not against another party or for another purpose—the court, on timely request, must restrict the evidence to its proper scope and instruct the jury accordingly.

The rule covers two situations.

(1) An item of evidence may be admissible on one theory of relevance, but for a variety of reasons, not admissible on another theory of relevance. If the judge admits

14. For a more detailed discussion of when the attorney-client privilege might preclude testimony about a conversation, see § 2.13. But while we're on the subject, here's some free advice for after you graduate and pass the bar: it is generally not a good idea for an attorney to interview a client at a strip club.

the evidence, the adverse party is entitled to have the judge explain to the jury how it may use the evidence and how it should not use it.

Many in the legal profession express skepticism that this does any good, reasoning that once a jury hears evidence, it will use it as it sees fit, regardless of an instruction limiting how the jury should consider it. (And how to word the instruction is also problematic—the judge often has to choose between wording the instruction so vaguely that the jury may have to guess at what the instruction means, or wording it so explicitly that it hammers home the very inference the instruction intends to steer the jury away from.) Still, appellate courts emphasize the importance of such instructions, and professors expect students to assert the rule where such an instruction is appropriate. (I always insisted that it is not enough for a student to say "X's attorney should ask for a limiting instruction"; rather, the student must spell out what the judge should say to the jury. That forces a student to really wrestle with the issue until he or she can articulate both the permissible and impermissible inferences the evidence supports.)

We will encounter this situation frequently in subsequent chapters.

(2) An item of evidence may be admissible against one party—for example, one of several defendants in a civil or criminal case—but not admissible against another party—e.g., another defendant—even though the evidence is apparently relevant against the second defendant as well as the first. If the judge admits the evidence, Rule 105 entitles the second defendant to have the judge instruct the jury against whom it should consider the evidence, and against whom it should not.

As per § 2.7, where possible, rather than admit an entire item of evidence that would be covered by Rule 105 and then give a limiting instruction, it is preferable to *redact* (i.e., edit) the evidence to delete the inadmissible reference or material. For example, in a two-defendant criminal trial, D1, after arrest, *Miranda* warnings and a waiver, told police, "D2 and I committed the crime." This statement is admissible against D1, but is inadmissible against D2, per the hearsay rule and the Sixth Amendment Confrontation Clause.[15] Therefore, if D1 and D2 are being tried together, the officer would be instructed by the court to testify that D1 said "I committed the crime," without referring to any other person.

Needless to say, what should be redacted in a particular situation, and how it should be redacted, are often contentious issues. That issue will arise in a later chapter, but a detailed discussion of it is beyond the scope of this book.

§ 2.9 Objection overruled. (c) How can the adverse party challenge the evidence? FRE 104(e)

Let's assume that in *P v. Megacorp*, the judge holds a hearing to determine whether DL's statement is admissible against Megacorp. (It doesn't matter whether

15. See generally Fishman, *A Student's Guide to Hearsay* (5th ed.), chapter 6. (End of commercial.)

the hearing was held prior to trial, or during trial while the jury was out of the courtroom.) At that hearing, P offers evidence tending to show that DL was an authorized spokesperson for Megacorp when she made the statement; Megacorp offers evidence tending to show that DL was not its authorized spokesperson. Each side cross-examines the other's witnesses, and the court hears oral argument from each. The judge rules that she is satisfied that P has established, by a preponderance of the evidence, that DL was an authorized spokesperson for Megacorp when DL made the statement and that DL's statement is therefore admissible against Megacorp.

The jury is *not* told that the judge concluded by a preponderance that DL was an authorized spokesperson for Megacorp. And the jury is not informed at this point about any of the evidence P introduced on that topic at the hearing; nor about Megacorp's contrary evidence. At most, if the motion in limine was held during the trial, the jury knows that (1) P called W as a witness; (2) Megacorp objected to a question P's attorney asked or to an answer that W gave; (3) the judge and lawyers did something in the courtroom while the jury waited in the jury room; and (4) now P's lawyer has resumed his or her questioning of W.

With the jury back in the courtroom hearing evidence, P continues his direct examination of W, who testifies that he heard DL make the statement. After Megacorp's lawyer cross-examines W, P offers whatever *admissible* evidence he has to show that DL was an authorized spokesperson for Megacorp.[16] This will probably include the evidence P introduced at the hearing that does not violate any evidence rule.

How can Megacorp respond to this evidence?

(1) Despite the judge's ruling, Megacorp wants to try to impeach P's evidence that DL was an authorized spokesperson for Megacorp.[17] (2) After P rests, Megacorp wants to offer evidence which (it hopes) will persuade the jury that DL was *not* an authorized spokesperson. (3) Finally, during closing arguments, Megacorp wants to urge the jury not to consider DL's statement against it, because DL was not an authorized spokesperson for the company. Is Megacorp allowed to do any of these things, and if so, which?

FRE 104(e) makes it clear that Megacorp is allowed to do all three.

---

16. I italicize "*admissible*" to remind you that although P was allowed to offer inadmissible evidence to the judge at the motion in limine (per FRE 104(a), see § 2.4), he can only offer admissible evidence at trial. P will offer such evidence because DL's relationship with Megacorp probably tends to make her statement more persuasive to the jury.

17. Even though the judge has overruled Megacorp's objection, DL's connection with Megacorp, and the scope of her responsibilities with the corporation, may be relevant in helping the jury assess how much weight to give to her statement. Presumably, the jury would weigh her testimony more heavily if she was an authorized spokesperson than if she was, say, a truck driver for the company, or a clerk in the accounting department.

> **Rule 104. Preliminary questions...**
>
> **(e) Evidence Relevant to Weight and Credibility.** This rule does not limit a party's right to introduce before the jury evidence that is relevant to the weight or credibility of other evidence.

This provision entitles Megacorp to attack the "weight or credibility" of W's testimony that DL made the statement, and to attack the "weight or credibility" of P's evidence that that DL was an authorized spokesperson for Megacorp, and entitles Megacorp to argue those positions to the jury in its closing argument.

Doesn't this fly in the face of the judge's conclusion that DL was Megacorp's authorized spokesperson? Not really. *The judge's ruling on the hearsay issue only resolved whether P would be allowed to have W testify about DL's statement to the jury.* But the jury must decide for itself which witnesses or documents are truthful and accurate, and the weight it will give to any given piece of evidence.

This is why the jury should not be told that the judge concluded that DL was an authorized spokesperson for Megacorp, because if they were told, they likely would accept the judge's conclusion rather than making their own decision on the matter in the course of their deliberations.

§ 2.10 Conditional admissibility; order of proof

In § 1.13, I explained that, with regard to "conditional *relevance*," a judge can permit a party to offer evidence (let's call it "item a") conditionally, i.e., on condition that later on during its case, the party will offer additional evidence ("item b") firming up the relevance of item a.

The same is true with regard to what I call "conditional *admissibility*." A judge may allow a party to offer "item a" in evidence before offering other evidence necessary to show that "item a" satisfies an evidence rule or that "item a" overcomes an opposing party's objection, on the condition that the party will provide this other evidence before he, she or it rests.

So, when and how do we find out whether the party satisfied the "condition"?

§ 2.11 Motion to strike

Assume in the Megacorp case neither party had raised the issue about DL's statement prior to trial. At trial, P calls W to testify about DL's statement and Megacorp objects that DL's statement is hearsay. P responds (at the bench, out of the hearing of the jury), "Your honor, I ask you to admit conditionally; I will introduce evidence later on establishing that DL was an authorized spokesperson for Megacorp at the time she made the statement." The judge responds, "Objection overruled—conditionally." P presents the rest of his admissible evidence at trial, then rests.

When P rests, the judge will send the jury out of the courtroom. Once they are gone, Megacorp should make a **motion to strike** W's testimony about DL's statement, on the ground that P has not satisfied the "condition," i.e., that P has not established, by a preponderance, that DL was an authorized spokesperson for Megacorp. P's attorney responds to the motion. At this point, the judge rules on the issue. If the judge grants the motion, once the jury returns to the courtroom, the judge tells the jury that it should disregard and ignore DL's statement, because it is no longer evidence in the case.[18]

If the judge denies the motion—i.e., if the judge is satisfied by a preponderance that DL was an authorized spokesperson for Megacorp, and her statement is therefore admissible—there is no need to tell the jury anything about the motion to strike. After all, the jury has already heard P's evidence about DL's statement and evidence of DL's relationship to Megacorp.

The same is true regarding evidence admitted as conditionally relevant. For example, in the murder case described in § 1.14, the prosecutor offered evidence sufficient to identify the knife as the one found in the dumpster two blocks from the murder scene, but that only satisfies Article IX. The knife is relevant in the murder trial only if and when the prosecutor offers evidence connecting the knife to the murder and to the defendant. So after the officer identifies the knife, D should object that the prosecutor has not yet shown that the knife is relevant. Let's assume the judge granted the prosecutor's request to admit the knife as conditionally relevant. The prosecutor presents the rest of the state's evidence, and rests. At this point, the defense attorney should move to strike the knife and have the jury instructed to disregard it. The judge then decides whether the prosecutor has offered evidence sufficient to support a finding that the knife was the murder weapon and that the defendant had owned the knife or at least had had access to it at the time of the crime.

Note that in each case, it is up to the party against whom the evidence was conditionally admitted—Megacorp in the civil case, D in the murder case—to move to strike each item of evidence which the judge allowed the other side to admit conditionally. Once the offering party rests, if the adverse party's lawyer forgets to move to strike a conditionally admitted item of evidence, the judge is not required to assess or decide whether the offering party satisfied the condition, and the objection is deemed to have been waived.

If you become a trial lawyer, once your opponent rests his, her, their or its case, you should always move to strike any evidence the judge conditionally admitted against you—even if it is beyond debate that your opponent has met the conditions.

18. Megacorp may move for a mistrial, arguing that DL's statement is so impactful that the jury would be incapable of disregarding it despite the judge's instruction, and is likely to decide the case against Megacorp based on DL's statement. If the judge grants the motion, the case will have to be tried again in front of a different jury.

Make the motion anyway, because that gives your client the impression that you are fighting on your client's behalf; and it reassures the judge—and any lawyers in the courtroom who happen to be watching—that you know what you are doing.

Now let's look again at the Penn and Teller case, involving the stolen bonds and the stolen and fraudulent IDs. In § 1.11 question 1, DET1 testifies that he searched a bedroom in which he found (a) Penn's wallet; (b) clothes in the closet that fit Penn's tall, thin body, and two pairs of shoes that were the same size as the shoes he was wearing when arrested; (c) a hairbrush with Penn's fingerprints on it; (d) a book with Penn's name written on the inside cover; (e) in a dresser drawer, underwear and socks that fit Penn; and (f) in an otherwise empty drawer in a night table, DET1 found eight stolen and bogus IDs. DET1 also testifies that Penn's fingerprints were found in numerous places in the bedroom. Remember the chain of inferences:

> Consequential fact: Penn participated in the scheme with Teller to steal, forge and cash stolen bonds.
>
> Direct evidence: there were eight items of stolen or bogus ID in an otherwise empty night table drawer in a room containing several items belonging to Penn, a room in which Penn's fingerprints were found on several items and surfaces.

(1) Inference: therefore, Penn was living in that room (at least temporarily).

(2) Inference: therefore, Penn possessed the eight stolen or bogus IDs.

(3) Inference: those items would be extremely useful to someone planning to cash stolen bonds without using his own name or ID.

(4) Inference: therefore, it is more likely than it would be without the evidence that Penn was, as the Government claims and Teller testified, a participant in the scheme to steal, forge and cash the bonds.

In terms of conditional relevance:

Fact (a)	The IDs were found in that drawer, in that room.
Fact (b)	Penn possessed (exercised dominion and control over) the IDs.
Fact (c)	Penn planned to use those IDs to further the conspiracy.

Fact (a) is relevant to help the prosecutor prove fact (c), only if the state has offered evidence "sufficient to support a finding" that fact (b)—that P possessed those IDs—is true. Given all the evidence—the fact that Penn was arrested in the house, plus the other evidence connecting him to that room, plus Teller's testimony about the scheme—could a rational jury accept fact (b) by a preponderance? Clearly, yes.

Question 1.

But suppose no IDs were seized when Penn was arrested. Rather, the prosecutor calls PO2, who had nothing to do with the Penn-Teller investigation. PO2 testifies that two weeks after Penn and Teller were arrested, he and several other officers searched a three-story apartment building (with two apartments on each floor) two blocks away from the building where Penn lived. That building was condemned and boarded up; nevertheless, it is still frequently used by homeless people to get out of the rain, by drug addicts to use drugs, and by prostitutes. PO2 testifies that under the floorboards in a second-floor apartment, he found numerous stolen and forged IDs.

D's attorney moves to strike the testimony as irrelevant. The prosecutor, invoking Rule 104(b), persuades the judge to admit it conditionally. Later in the trial, the prosecutor calls a witness who testifies that, a few days before Teller and Penn were arrested, he saw Penn on the same block as that boarded-up building.

At the end of the trial, D moves again to strike PO2's testimony and to exclude the IDs. How should the judge rule?

Answer.

Consider the chain of inferences now:

Consequential fact: Penn participated in the scheme with Teller to steal, forge and cash stolen bonds.

Direct evidence: Two weeks after Penn and Teller were arrested, eight items of stolen or bogus ID were found hidden under the floorboards in an apartment in a boarded-up six-apartment building two blocks from where Penn lived—a building frequently used by drug users and homeless people and prostitutes.

Direct evidence: A few days before Penn and Teller were arrested, Penn was seen on the same block as the boarded-up building.

(1) Inference: Penn was the person who hid the IDs in that building.

(2) Inference: those items would be extremely useful to someone planning to cash stolen bonds without using his own name or ID.

(3) Inference: therefore, it is more likely than it would be without the evidence that Penn was, as the Government claims and Teller testified, a participant on the scheme to steal, forge and cash the bonds.

Here, the evidence actually linking Penn to the IDs—inference (1)—is extraordinarily weak. True, the IDs are precisely what Penn would need to participate in the scheme, as Teller and the government allege. But there is no direct evidence that Penn was ever in the building. Not only that, the building was frequented by an unknown number of people, including many who used it to break the law, both before and after Penn was arrested, which raises a distinct possibility that someone else might have hidden the IDs there.

The judge should grant Penn's motion to strike the IDs and tell the jury to disregard them.

§ 2.12 Motion for a directed verdict

After the plaintiff or prosecutor rests and the judge has ruled on the defendant's motion to strike any evidence presented by the plaintiff or prosecutor that was admitted conditionally, the defense should move for a directed verdict.[19]

i. Motion for a directed verdict: civil cases

In essence, a motion for a directed verdict asks the judge to dismiss the case because P has failed to offer adequate evidence as to one or more elements of its cause of action. The judge should grant the motion only if she concludes that, <u>viewing all of the evidence in the light most favorable[20] to P, no rational jury could find for P by a preponderance of the evidence</u>. Only then should the judge take the case away from the jury and render a directed verdict for Megacorp.[21]

If this motion is denied, Megacorp proceeds to present its case. When Megacorp rests, P makes a motion to strike any evidence Megacorp was allowed to introduce conditionally. Once the judge has ruled on that motion, P moves for a directed verdict. The judge should grant the motion only if she concludes that, even <u>after viewing all of the evidence in the light most favorable to Megacorp</u>, a rational jury would *have to* find that P has proven all the elements of its cause of action by a preponderance of the evidence.[22]

If this motion is denied, then the plaintiff gets to present rebuttal evidence; the defense gets to present evidence rebutting the plaintiff's rebuttal; and so on. Eventually both sides rest, and each makes a motion for a directed verdict. Assuming both motions are denied, the attorneys make their closing arguments to the jury, the judge instructs the jury on the law, and then everybody waits to see what the jury decides.

There are two important wrinkles to remember here. (1) A party should always move to strike an opponent's conditionally admitted evidence before moving for a directed verdict. (2) In ruling on a party's motion for a directed verdict, the judge must view the evidence in the light most favorable to the nonmoving party, i.e., in the light most favorable to the party against whom the motion was made. What this means is discussed in § 2.12–iii.

---

19. The discussion that follows assumes the case is a jury trial; in a non-jury trial, the basics are the same, although the vocabulary and procedures vary slightly.

20. I discuss this term in § 2.12–iii.

21. If P has brought several claims against Megacorp, the judge must assess the adequacy of P's evidence as to each claim, and might grant a directed verdict for Megacorp on some claims but deny it on others.

22. Things get a bit more confusing if Megacorp has pleaded and introduced evidence supporting an affirmative defense—such as contributory negligence—on which Megacorp has the burden of proof. I'll leave it up to your evidence professor to decide whether to cover that subject.

ii. Motion for a directed verdict: criminal cases

The pattern is similar in criminal cases, but with a few critical differences.

1. When the prosecutor rests, after the judge rules on the defense motion to strike, the defense makes a motion for a directed verdict (sometimes called a motion for a judgment of acquittal). The judge, viewing the evidence in the light most favorable the prosecution (there is no "presumption of innocence" at this stage of a criminal trial), must assess whether a rational jury *could* find the defendant guilty beyond a reasonable doubt. If the answer is yes, the judge denies the motion, and the jury will decide the case.

The difference between civil and criminal litigation is that in civil litigation, the judge applies the "could a rational jury find for the plaintiff by a *preponderance of the evidence*" standard; in a criminal trial, the standard is, "could a rational jury find for the prosecutor *beyond a reasonable doubt*."[23]

2. In a criminal case, the prosecutor cannot move for a directed verdict of guilty. No matter how rock-solid and air-tight the prosecutor's case may be, a judge cannot take the case away from the jury and enter a verdict of guilty.[24]

iii. "Light most favorable"

Note that when ruling on a party's motion for a directed verdict, the judge must always view the evidence in a light most favorable to the non-moving party. In doing so, the judge must assume that the jury will resolve all credibility issues in favor of the non-moving party—that is, the judge must assume that the jury will believe the non-moving party's evidence and will disbelieve the moving party's evidence.

§ 2.13 Question

Question 1.

In a criminal trial, *US v. D*, the prosecutor calls Juris, an attorney, as a witness. The prosecutor asks Juris; "On March 1, 2021, did you have a conversation with D regarding D's activities on February 26, 2021?" D's trial attorney DAT objects that the conversation between D and Juris is protected by the attorney-client privilege.

As a matter of law, that privilege applies only if (1) Juris was in fact an attorney; (2) D was Juris's client; (3) the conversation related to matters on which Juris was acting as D's attorney; and (4) D and Juris intended the conversation to be confidential and took reasonable precautions to avoid being overheard.[25] The judge cannot rule on the objection without first deciding whether these four conditions existed.

23. If D has pleaded and introduced evidence supporting an affirmative defense on which D has the burden of persuasion, see footnote 24.

24. But the prosecutor can move to dismiss certain affirmative defenses, on which the defendant has either the burden of production or the burden of persuasion.

25. Sometimes the issues are more complex than that, but those are the basic requirements.

How should the judge proceed, and who has the burden of persuading the judge on those four requirements, and what is that burden?

Answer:

To resolve this issue, the judge should hold a factual hearing (out of the jury's presence) at which both sides are permitted to call witnesses, cross-examine the other side's witnesses, offer documents, etc.

D, the party who made the objection, has the burden to persuade the judge, by a preponderance of the evidence, that the factual basis for the objection exists. Thus, DAT, D's trial attorney, will have to persuade the judge by a preponderance that Juris is in fact an attorney; that D was Juris's client on March 1, 2021; that the conversation related to a matter on which Juris was acting as D's attorney; and that D and Juris intended the conversation to be confidential and took reasonable precautions to avoid being overheard.

At the hearing, each side may introduce evidence on the issue, including evidence that would not be admissible at trial.

If at the close of the hearing, DAT has persuaded the judge by a preponderance of the evidence that these four requirements have been satisfied, the conversation is protected by the privilege, and Juris will not be required or permitted to testify. But if D's lawyer *fails* to persuade the judge by a preponderance that one or more of the requirements was satisfied, the conversation was not privileged, and Juris will be required to testify.[26]

---

26. For example, if Juris was an attorney but the only relationship between D and Juris is that they played golf in the same foursome each week, the conversation is unprivileged. And even if D was Juris's client and the conversation related to the matter on which Juris was acting as D's attorney, the conversation is not privileged if they were speaking in the presence of the others—say, in an elevator. (I specifically mention elevators because in my days as a prosecutor, I was present and overheard an astonishing number of courthouse elevator conversations between lawyers and clients—or between lawyers and lawyers, or between prosecutors and witnesses—about the cases that brought them to the courthouse. Perhaps the lawyers (who should have known better) thought it was safe to talk because they assumed that nobody else in the elevator would know what case they were talking about. Making that assumption is a good way to lose a case, a client, a job, and maybe your license.)

Chapter 3

FRE 403

§ 3.1 The rule

An attorney might legitimately object to an opponent's evidence on a wide variety of grounds, including the substance of the evidence, the form in which it is offered, and the procedure the other side's lawyer has used to offer it. § 1.3 provides a general overview of these categories and the rules to consider with regard to each. When you encounter an offer of evidence in this course, you should always assess whether an objection to that evidence may be made on the basis of specific provisions in the FRE regulating substance, form or procedure. After you have done that, you should assess whether the adverse party can (also) make a plausible objection based on FRE 403.

Why should you always look for other bases to object first,[1] before turning to Rule 403? The short-term answer is that your professor will expect you to. The medi-

1. To be more precise: you should always consider whether an objection can be made based on what you have covered thus far in your evidence course. For example, would be unwise to raise

um-term answer is, doing so will help you learn the law. The long-term answer is, that is what good lawyers do. See §1.3.

That being said, Rule 403 is important: aside from Rule 401, it is probably the most frequently cited provision of the Federal Rules of Evidence. It provides as follows:

> **Rule 403. Excluding Relevant Evidence for Prejudice, Confusion, Waste of Time, or Other Reasons**
>
> The court may exclude relevant evidence if its probative value is substantially outweighed by a danger of one or more of the following: unfair prejudice, confusing the issues, misleading the jury, undue delay, wasting time, or needlessly presenting cumulative evidence.

If an offer of evidence is relevant and survives any challenges that might be brought with regard to substance, form and procedure, "[t]he court *may* [nevertheless] exclude [it] if its probative value is *substantially* outweighed by the danger of one or more of the following: *unfair* prejudice, confusing the issues, misleading the *jury*, undue delay, wasting time, or needlessly presenting cumulative evidence." Rule 403 (emphasis added). The language of the rule should be examined in some detail.

The use of the word "may" serves as a reminder that considerable discretion is vested in the trial judge, and it is rare that a judge will be reversed for excluding, or refusing to exclude, evidence on Rule 403 grounds.

The six bases for exclusion included in the rule are divisible into two parts. The first three grounds—that the "probative value" of the evidence is "*substantially* outweighed" by the danger of unfair prejudice, or may confuse the issues or mislead the jury—appear to be applicable only if the case is being tried before a jury. The law assumes that judges, unlike juries, are not susceptible to becoming confused, misled, or unduly unfairly prejudiced by an item of evidence.

The second part of Rule 403 permits exclusion of otherwise admissible relevant evidence if its probative value "is *substantially* outweighed... by a danger of... undue delay, wasting time, or needlessly presenting cumulative evidence." These three grounds apply whether the case is being tried before a jury or before a judge alone.

§3.2 "Probative value"

FRE 403 introduces a new term not included in Rules 401–402: "probative value." That term is related to relevance, but is not synonymous with it. To determine whether evidence is relevant, we ask only whether it has "any tendency" to make

and discuss a hearsay objection in an assignment or in classroom discussion if the professor hasn't covered hearsay yet. Doing so would be unwise for two reasons. First, it would probably annoy your professor, who has arranged the syllabus to cover the rules in the order in which she can teach the course most effectively. Second, if you attempt to apply a rule that has not yet been covered in class, you will probably apply it incorrectly.

a consequential fact more probable, or less probable, than it would be without the evidence. To measure the "probative value" of an item of relevant evidence, we ask several additional questions:

1. How important is the "consequential fact" the evidence is being offered to make more probable or less probable?
2. How strong is the evidence's "tendency" to make that fact more, or less, probable?
3. How important is this item of evidence to prove or disprove the "consequential fact" at issue, in light of all the other evidence that the offering party has introduced or could introduce?
4. Are there steps the judge can take to afford the offering party the most probative value the evidence merits, while protecting the adverse party from the 403 risks to the extent possible?

§ 3.3 "Undue delay, wasting time, or needlessly presenting cumulative evidence"

These Rule 403 risks apply to both jury trials and non-jury trials. They are basically self-explanatory.

"Undue delay" might arise where, say, party X wants to call witness W who will not be available for several days, and asks that the trial be postponed or suspended until then. Judges tend to be reluctant to grant delays or mid-trial suspensions, and for good reasons, but this does not automatically justify denying the request; a judge would have to consider a variety of factors: how important is W's testimony to X's case, what other evidence is available to X on the same issue, and, perhaps most important, whether W's current unavailability can be attributed to sloppy planning by X's lawyer (or former lawyer).

The "needlessly presenting cumulative evidence" clause gives the judge discretion to say "enough is enough." This does not mean that a judge has the right to restrict a party to the minimum amount of evidence required to support a finding as to a particular fact. A party has the right—within reasonable limits—to prove an important fact several different ways and with several different witnesses.

Question 1.

Derma is on trial for knocking an elderly woman down and stealing her purse. The prosecutor plays a video of the crime retrieved from a surveillance camera mounted in front of a store. The video is in black and white and of less than movie-studio quality, but the assailant bears a striking resemblance to Derma. Next the prosecutor calls Vladina, the victim, who identifies Derma as the woman who assaulted and robbed her.

Next, the prosecutor calls PW1, who will testify that she has known Derma for several years; that they live in the same neighborhood and see each other frequently; that she was at the scene when the crime happened; and that she recognized Derma as the woman who assaulted the victim and stole her purse.

Derma's attorney objects that, given the video and Vladina's testimony, PW1's testimony is no longer relevant. How should the judge rule?

Answer:

Objection overruled. The relevance of PW1's testimony is measured by whether the evidence has any tendency to make it more likely than it would be without the evidence that Derma was the robber. An eyewitness's testimony—"I saw what happened, here's what I saw"—is always relevant.

Question 2.

Instead, Derma's attorney objects that, given the video and Vladina's testimony, PW1's testimony would constitute needless presentation of cumulative evidence. Ruling?

Answer:

Objection overruled. The video is enough to support a conviction—if the jury is convinced that Derma is in fact the person recorded in the video. The same is true of Vladina's testimony. But who knows? Videos can be deceiving. And a crime victim's testimony identifying a stranger in a brief and distressing encounter is notoriously unreliable. W1's testimony adds significant weight to the state's case.

Question 3.

The prosecutor wants to call PW2, PW3, PW4, PW5, PW6, PW7 and PW8, each of whom will also testify that he or she knew Derma before the crime, that he or she witnessed the crime, and that he or she recognized Derma as the perpetrator. Objection: needless presentation of cumulative evidence. Ruling?

Answer:

The judge could quite reasonably say to the prosecutor, "You've already had Vladina testify, and you've shown the video, and PW1 has made an eye-witness ID of Derma. I'll give you three more witnesses to testify; that's enough." (But if, later in the trial, Derma calls several alibi witnesses who testify that Derma was with them far away from the scene of the crime when it was committed, the judge might allow the prosecutor to call some of the other witnesses as rebuttal witnesses.)

Question 4.

Suppose there were no eyewitnesses (other than Vladina), but the prosecutor wants to call three witnesses (PW1, PW2, and PW3). Each will (a) testify that he or she knows Derma well, and explain how they know her; (b) testify that at the prosecutor's request, he or she viewed the video of the crime; and (c) testify that he or she recognizes Derma as the person who committed the crime. Derma's attorney objects: "Judge, this is a waste of time—the jury can look at the video and look at Derma and make its own decision whether that's her." Ruling?

Answer:

Objection overruled. It is not a waste of time, because someone who knows Derma well is able to do more than merely compare body shapes and facial features; presumably, such witnesses will be able to recognize how Derma stands, how she moves, what she is capable of physically, how she reacts to certain situations. Thus PW1, PW2 and PW3 each probably bring something to the witness stand which the jury cannot itself duplicate.

§ 3.4 "Confusing the issues or misleading the jury"

These are two of the bases to exclude evidence per Rule 403 in jury trials. They do not arise very often. In essence, they give the judge discretion to exclude evidence that adds little legitimate substance to the case but might distract the jury from the key factual issues they were empaneled to decide.

§ 3.5 "Unfair prejudice"

Of the three jury-trial related grounds for exclusion listed in Rule 403, the one most frequently cited is the risk of unfair prejudice.

In everyday language, the word "prejudice" is often associated with discrimination based on an improper and invalid basis—race, religion, national origin, sexual preference, etc. That kind of prejudice is inherently unfair. But that is not how the word "prejudice" is used in FRE 403. Rather, in Rule 403, the word "prejudice" itself is value-neutral; it merely means "evidence that favors one side and disadvantages the other." Used that way, nearly all evidence introduced at a trial is "prejudicial." P's attorney offers evidence that will favor her client and therefore "prejudice" D's chances of winning the lawsuit, and vice versa.

That is why Rule 403 specifies *unfair* prejudice. In *Old Chief v. U.S.*, the Supreme Court has defined "unfair prejudice" as follows:

> The term "unfair prejudice," as to a criminal defendant, speaks to the capacity of some obviously relevant evidence to lure the factfinder into declaring guilt on a ground different from proof specific to the offense charged.... So, the [Advisory] Committee Notes to Rule 403 explain, "'Unfair prejudice' within its context means an undue tendency to suggest decision on an improper basis, commonly, though not necessarily, an emotional one."[2]

2. Old Chief v. U.S., 519 U.S. 172, 180 (1997), quoting the Advisory Committee's Notes on FRE 403, 28 U.S.C. App., p. 860.

This definition of "unfair prejudice" has pretty much the same meaning in civil cases.

One frequently cited example: in a prosecution for murder, the state offers numerous gruesome photographs showing the injuries on the victim's body, or the state of decay of the body when it was found, or photographs taken during the autopsy. Such photos may have significant relevance, such as showing cause of death, or the presence or absence of defensive wounds, or the angle from which the fatal bullet, stab or blow came; but they also are likely to arouse strong emotions among jurors that could prompt them to convict despite only thin evidence tending to prove the defendant's guilt. Similarly, in a prosecution for pornographic exploitation of children, the question is how much of the video (or how many photographs) the prosecutor should be permitted to show to the jury.

Another fairly common situation arises where an item of evidence is relevant for two purposes, one permitted, and one not. A Iimiting instruction per FRE 105 is one solution. See § 2.8. Redacting some of the more unfairly prejudicial aspects of the evidence is another. See § 2.7. Excluding the evidence altogether is the least preferred option, but a judge has discretion to exclude evidence entirely if the risk of unfair prejudice substantially outweighs the legitimate probative value of the evidence.

Unfair prejudice can occur in civil litigation as well, whenever a substantial risk exists that an item of evidence, although relevant, might prompt a jury to decide a case on an improper basis. The risk of unfair prejudice is considered greater in criminal cases because, for the defendant, the stakes—potential loss of liberty—are higher; on the other hand, the prosecutor's need for the evidence may be greater, since the state has to prove its case beyond a reasonable doubt, not merely by the civil preponderance of the evidence standard. Still, the Rule 403 "unfair prejudice" analysis is basically the same for criminal and civil cases.

§ 3.6 Balancing probative value vs. risk of unfair prejudice: *Old Chief v. U.S.*

Keep in mind that even in a jury trial, the mere fact that evidence may create a risk of unfair prejudice or might involve one or more other Rule 403 risks does not justify exclusion. The judge can exclude on 403 grounds only if the judge concludes that the probative value of the evidence "is *substantially* outweighed by a danger of... *unfair* prejudice, [or the danger of] confusing the issues, [or the danger of] misleading the jury...." Federal courts begin with a strong assumption that relevant evidence should be admitted despite the risk of unfair prejudice, and exclusion on Rule 403 grounds should be granted only where the 403 risk is much, much higher than the probative value.

Which brings us to the *Old Chief*[3] decision. I'm sure your professor has covered this case in class. Here's my brief summary.

---

3. Old Chief v. U.S., 519 U.S. 172 (1997).

In 1993, Old Chief was "arrested after a fracas involving at least one gunshot." He was charged with three crimes: assault with a dangerous weapon; using a firearm in relation to a crime of violence; and violation of 18 U.S.C. § 922(g)(1), which makes it a felony for a person who was previously convicted of any felony to possess a firearm (hereinafter: "FPF," i.e. being a felon in possession of a firearm). To prove the "felon" element of § 922(g)(1), the government sought to introduce documentary evidence that five years earlier, Old Chief was convicted of the felony of assaulting and seriously injuring a man. At his 1993 trial, Old Chief's attorney offered to stipulate that Old Chief had a previous felony conviction, and moved per FRE 403 to exclude the nature of the felony. The government declined to accept the stipulation, and the judge permitted the prosecutor to inform the jury, not merely that Old Chief had a previous felony conviction, but that the prior conviction was for assaulting and seriously injuring someone.

The Supreme Court reversed, voting 5-to-4 that the judge should have excluded the nature of the conviction (thereby in essence forcing the prosecutor to accept the stipulation). In so holding, however, the majority went on at great length to emphasize that its holding is based primarily on the technical nature of § 922(g)(1). The Court held that since any felony conviction would do, all felony convictions had equal probative value in satisfying that factual element of § 922(g)(1); but since Old Chief was on trial for a crime of violence and his prior conviction was for a crime of violence, the name or the nature of the prior conviction—felonious assault—created a strong risk that the jury might use that information in deciding that Old Chief in fact had committed the assault with a deadly weapon for which he was now on trial.

Question 1.

Was Old Chief's prior conviction for felonious assault relevant evidence that he also committed the crimes for which he was now on trial?

Answer:

Yes. Evidence that he previously committed a serious crime of violence has some tendency to make it more probable than it would be without the evidence, that he also committed the violent crime for which he was currently being tried—"if he did it before, he probably did it this time, too."

Question 2.

Then why all the fuss? If his conviction for prior felonious assault was relevant to prove that Old Chief committed the assault for which he was on trial, why not admit it for that purpose as well as to prove the prior conviction requirement in the FPF charge?

Answer:

Because the reasoning by which the prior conviction is relevant to prove that Old Chief also committed the current assault—"if he did it before, he probably did it this time, too"—though logical and reasonable, is not one a jury is allowed to consider, per FRE 404(b)(1). The basic rule is that when a person is charged with a crime, his guilt or innocence should be based on the evidence that he committed it, not on what he may have done on one or more unrelated occasions in the past.[4]

Question 3.

So: what's the solution?

Answer:

Think of this as an FRE 105 situation. The prosecutor points out that Chief's prior felony assault conviction is not merely relevant and admissible on the FPF charge, it is fundamentally essential: as a matter of law, the government could not obtain a conviction on the FPF charge without proving that Old Chief had previously been convicted of a felony. Ergo, the prosecutor argues, allow the prosecutor to introduce the conviction, following which the judge instructs the jury to consider the conviction only in deciding whether the prosecutor had proved the "prior felony conviction" element of the FPF charge, but not to consider it in deciding whether Old Chief in fact committed the assault with a deadly weapon for which he is now on trial.

Realistically, though, that's not much of a solution. Asking a jury to disregard the fact that Old Chief was previously convicted of assault as a felony while they decide whether he committed the assault for which he was on trial, may be asking the impossible. Even if the jury tried to disregard it, there is considerable risk that it will nonetheless influence them.

In essence, the Court held, the solution is to redact the information creating the 403 risk. In the highly narrow and unusual circumstances of a § 922(g)(1) FPF case, Old Chief's offer to stipulate that he was previously convicted of a felony gives the government absolutely everything to which it was properly entitled. The nature (or name) of that prior felony adds nothing regarding the FPF charge; yet it carries a considerable Rule 403/Rule 404(b) risk of unfair prejudice. Given the stipulation, the Court held, the trial judge should have excluded the title of the felony for which Old Chief had previously been convicted.

Question 4.

Suppose Old Chief's prior felony had been for forging a check for $1,000. You represent Old Chief. Do you offer to stipulate that D was convicted of a prior felony, thereby preventing the prosecutor from informing the jury of the nature of the prior felony?

---

4. FRE 404(b) is one of the most challenging and complex rules you will encounter in law school; I devote an entire rather lengthy chapter to it. For now, just take it as given that it applies here. (But at least FRE 404(b) is not quite as complex as the hearsay rule and all its exceptions.—By the way, have I mentioned that my *A Student's Guide to Hearsay,* now in its 5th edition, is available for purchase? I have? Oh, good.)

Answer:

Absolutely not. Forging a check is a relatively benign felony—no one was hurt physically, no one was threatened, and the victim was a bank, not a person who desperately needed the money. Therefore, the conviction carries little risk of unfair prejudice—the jury is unlikely to think, "Because Old Chief forged a check several years ago, it's likely D attacked people with a firearm this time." As D's attorney, I would want the jury to know the nature of the prior conviction, so they won't speculate that maybe it was for a violent crime.

§ 3.7 *Old Chief*, continued: more on balancing probative value vs. risk of unfair prejudice

Although the Court ruled that the trial judge erred in not requiring the prosecutor to accept the defendant's stipulation (a conclusion which prompted a blistering dissent by four justices), the majority went out of its way to discuss how probative value and the risk of unfair prejudice should be balanced, and to stress the narrow scope of its decision. Here are key passages:

> [W]hat counts as the Rule 403 "probative value" of an item of evidence, as distinct from its Rule 401 "relevance," may be calculated by comparing evidentiary alternatives.[5]
>
> [I]n deciding whether the danger substantially outweighs the value and whether the evidence ought to be excluded[, the trial judge must] take account of the full evidentiary context of the case as the court understands it when the ruling must be made.... On objection, the court would decide whether a particular item of evidence raised a danger of unfair prejudice. If it did, the judge would go on to evaluate the degrees of probative value and unfair prejudice not only for the item in question but for any actually available substitutes as well. If an alternative were found to have substantially the same or greater probative value but a lower danger of unfair prejudice, sound judicial discretion would discount the value of the item first offered and exclude it if its discounted probative value were substantially outweighed by unfairly prejudicial risk.... [T] he judge would have to make these calculations with an appreciation of the offering party's need for evidentiary richness and narrative integrity in presenting a case, and the mere fact that two pieces of evidence might go to the same point would not, of course,

5. Old Chief v. U.S., 519 US 172, 184 (1997).

> necessarily mean that only one of them might come in. It would only mean that a judge applying Rule 403 could reasonably apply some discount to the probative value of an item of evidence when faced with less risky alternative proof going to the same point. [U]nder this... approach, a defendant's Rule 403 objection offering to concede a point generally cannot prevail over the Government's choice to offer evidence showing guilt and all the circumstances surrounding the offense.[6]

When determining the admissibility of evidence under Rule 403, courts tend to "employ a sliding scale approach: as the probative value increases, so does our tolerance of the risk of prejudice."[7] As the Advisory Committee Note states, in assessing "whether to exclude on grounds of unfair prejudice, consideration should be given to the probable effectiveness or lack of effectiveness of a limiting instruction [see FRE 105]. The availability of other means of proof may also be an appropriate factor."

Question 1.

True or false: "If evidence creates a high risk of unfair prejudice, it should be excluded."

Answer:

False. It should be excluded only if, after

(1) weighing its probative value (see § 3.2)

(2) against the risk of unfair prejudice, and

(3) considering the degree to which redaction or a limiting instruction or both will allow the offering party to retain the legitimate probative value of the evidence while reducing the risk of unfair prejudice,

the judge nevertheless concludes that the risk of unfair prejudice "substantially outweighs" its probative value.

Question 2.

Consider the following passage from *Old Chief* and an accompanying footnote:

> [I]n deciding whether the danger substantially outweighs the value and whether the evidence ought to be excluded[, the trial judge must] take account of the full evidentiary context of the case as the court understands it when the ruling must be made.

6. *Old Chief*, 519 U.S. 172, 182–183.

7. Whitehead v. Bond, 680 F.3d 919, 930 (7th Cir. 2012).

In the footnote, it added:

> It is important that a reviewing court evaluate the trial court's decision from its perspective when it had to rule and not indulge in review by hindsight.[8]

Why did the Court include the passage? Why did it include the footnote? What perhaps unfair advantage might that give the offering party, and how might opposing counsel and the judge prevent that unfair advantage?

Answer:

The sentence in the text ("full evidentiary context") serves to remind us (and the trial judge) that probative value depends in part on what other evidence is available to the offering party to prove the same fact or facts. The footnote reminds *appellate* courts to judge the trial judge's decision on what the trial judge knew about the case at the time she decided whether to admit the evidence. At that point, the judge may not know what other evidence the offering party might present to prove the same fact or facts.

This, however, suggests a perhaps an unfair tactic on the part of the offering party: Offer probative evidence which carries a high risk of unfair prejudice first. The judge, assuming that's all the offering party has to prove a fact, admits it. Then the offering party offers its additional non-prejudicial evidence.

Opposing counsel can attempt to frustrate this tactic by bringing a motion in limine—preferably prior to trial. In considering the motion, the trial court can ask the offering party: "What other evidence do you have to prove the fact(s) in question?" This gives the judge a better idea of the "full evidentiary context" into which the evidence in question appears.

Question 3.

True or false: "If a party offers to stipulate that a particular fact is true, the judge must order the offering party to accept the stipulation rather than attempt to prove that fact by evidence."

Answer:

False! Re-read the lengthy passage quoted near the beginning of this section.

Question 4.

P fell while on D's property and brought a personal injury action, alleging D negligently allowed a dangerous condition to exist which proximately caused the fall and that she suffered serious injuries as a result. D denies all aspects of P's claim. During P's case-in-chief, her attorney seeks to play a lengthy video recording of a

8. *Old Chief*, 519 U.S. 172, 182 n 6.

physical therapy session. The recording captures P's expressions of pain and discomfort during the session. P also offers a second lengthy video recording showing P attempting to do various things in her home—make or eat breakfast, manipulate her computer mouse, put on makeup, etc. It shows how limited and restricted P's life is (and perhaps may always be) as a result of her injuries.

Are the videos relevant, and if so, how? What Rule 403 risks, it any, might they trigger? What options are available to the trial judge?

Answer:

The videos are irrelevant as to whether D was negligent and, assuming he was, whether that negligence proximately caused P's injuries. Yet, the video might create so much sympathy for P that the jury might hold D liable regardless of whether P's injury was truly D's fault. But the scenes portrayed in the videos do have considerable probative value as to the degree of pain and suffering P experienced as a result of her fall, and the impact it has on her life, and therefore constitute powerful evidence as to the amount she should receive in damages if D is found liable.

Perhaps the best option is to bifurcate the trial. First the jury decides whether D is liable for plaintiff's injuries. At the liability stage, the videos are inadmissible because they are irrelevant on whether D was negligent and if so, whether D's negligence was a proximate cause of P's injuries. Doing so reduces the risk that the jury will find D liable simply because they feel sorry for P. If the jury finds D liable, then the trial proceeds with the damages phase, at which the videos, or whatever portion of them the judge thinks is fair, would be admissible.

This isn't a perfect solution. If the effects of P's injuries are visible in the courtroom, the jury may be moved out of sympathy to find D liable just so they can have the opportunity to vote monetary damages for P. But the alternative is to try both liability and damages at once, and either allow P to play the videos (or portions of them), which would be unfair to D on the issue of liability; or exclude the videos altogether, which would deprive P of what might be the best, most convincing evidence on the issue of the amount of damages P should receive.

§ 3.8 Questions: "where there's a will, ..."

P, decedent F's only child, is suing to contest a will in which F, a widower, left his entire multi-million-dollar estate to ABC Charity. The will was executed with all the appropriate formalities. F died two weeks after he executed the will. P claims that F lacked testamentary capacity when the will was executed. At trial, P introduces a prior will which F executed when the son was 17 (he's now 27), leaving 90% of his estate to P. P calls witnesses who testify that F and P always had a good relationship. P offers further evidence that although he now lives several hundred miles away from where F lived, he visited him several times a year.[9]

---

9. Assume the case involves events prior to the Covid-19 pandemic.

P also calls witnesses who had known F for decades, and others who participated in taking care of F during those last months, who testify that during those last months, F's mental condition deteriorated rapidly; that sometimes F did not recognize people he'd known for decades; and that on two occasions, F confused P with F's brother B, who died when F was 19 and B was 26. P also offers testimony that during F's last few months, executives of the defendant charity "practically moved in with" F, and arranged for F's new will, which was executed only two weeks before F died. Assume all this evidence is properly admitted. P rests.

When P rests, ABC moves for a directed verdict. Assume this motion is properly denied. ABC then presents evidence tending to show that, at the time F executed the will, he was aware that P was his only son and knew he was signing a will leaving all his property to ABC. Assume this evidence was properly admitted.

Question 1.

Next, ABC Charity introduces evidence that F had long supported the charity and served on its board for several years, stepping down only five years before he died.

Is this evidence relevant? How? Should it be admitted, over a Rule 403 objection by P?

Answer:

It supports the inference that F had a logical reason to be generous to ABC in his will, which in turn makes it more probable than it would be without the evidence that he knew what he was doing when he signed the new will. There is no plausible argument in favor of excluding it.

Question 2.

Now ABC seeks to introduce evidence that P is himself a millionaire. Is this relevant? If so, how?

Before formulating your answer, ask yourself another question. Is there anything about the facts in this case that might strike the jury as unusual, perhaps even shocking?

I'll wait a few more seconds for you to consider the question.

* * *

Have you figured it out yet?

Answer:

A father cut his only child out of his will, leaving him *nothing!* That is so shockingly unusual, so different from normal behavior, that unless ABC can provide a persuasive reason why F would do so, the jury quite properly will be highly skeptical of the validity of the will.[10]

---

10. General suggestion: in this course, in all your other courses, and in your legal practice after you are admitted to the bar, always ask yourself if there is something unusual or out of the ordinary

Given this, ABC has a compelling need to provide an explanation why F would logically and plausibly do so. Evidence that P is already quite wealthy provides an explanation: F, knowing of his son's wealth, could have logically concluded that P did not need any more, and decided to give the money to charity instead.

Question 3.

Is there a "missing link" between the evidence ABC is offering, and the fact that it is offering it to prove? Consider:

> Consequential fact: F had a plausible and logical reason to leave his entire estate to ABC charity, rather than to his son P.
>
> Direct evidence: P was already independently wealthy.
>
> Inference: Therefore, it is more probable than it would be without the evidence that F had testamentary capacity when he signed the will giving his entire estate to ABC.

What inference must the jury draw, in order to accept the inference ABC wants them to draw? What is the missing link?

Answer:

The missing link is that F *knew* P was already independently wealthy. If F did not know, evidence of P's wealth is irrelevant on the issue of the validity of the will.

Perhaps a jury might simply infer that F knew, but ABC should offer evidence that F knew—for example, that F frequently visited P in P's obviously expensive home, or that P sometimes drove F in P's expensive car, or that F spoke proudly to friends about P's successful career, etc.

Question 4

Does this evidence present any of the Rule 403 risks?

Answer:

Yes. The main risk here is unfair prejudice. The jury's job in this case is quite simple: decide whether F had testamentary capacity when he signed the will. The risk is that, hearing that P is already quite wealthy, the jury might decide: "P is already rich. He doesn't need any more money. Let's give the money to the charity, where *we* think it will do the most good."

---

about the case, or about an item of evidence being offered. The odds are that the unusual fact or evidence is important to the case. In the *Penn & Teller* case, §1.9 & §1.11, Penn's possession of several sets of stolen or forged IDs was highly unusual. Here, it is the fact that F left P nothing in the will he signed shortly before he died.

Perhaps in the larger scheme of things, it would do more "good" to give F's money to ABC. But that is not the jury's job. If the jury used evidence of P's wealth in this fashion, that would unfairly prejudice P's right to a fair trial on the issues the jury was empaneled to decide, i.e., whether F had testamentary capacity when he signed the will.

Question 5

How should the judge rule?

Answer:

Assuming ABC offered evidence that F was aware of P's wealth, I would admit evidence that P was wealthy, although I might limit the details of precisely how wealthy; and if asked to do so by P, I would instruct the jury that they can only consider that information in deciding whether F knew what he was doing when he signed the will.

Question 6.

Suppose, instead, ABC offers evidence that in the five years preceding F's death, P was arrested four times, and convicted twice, for exposing himself to children in a school yard near P's home. What objection should P make; how should ABC respond; how should the judge rule?

Answer:

P objects: FRE 403. The risk of unfair prejudice is obvious: if the jury hears that P has exposed himself to elementary school children, there is a strong possibility that they will render a verdict for ABC on that ground alone, regardless of how strong a case he has that F lacked testamentary capacity when F signed the will shortly before his death. Clearly, the Rule 403 risk is much greater here than in questions 2–5.

But the probative value is also potentially greater. P's behavior might well drive a father to disinherit his son out of shame for the son's conduct and concern over the harm it might have done to the children who observed it.[11] But the probative value of this evidence depends, even more heavily than in questions 2–5, on the "missing link," i.e., on evidence that F knew of P's arrests and convictions. (Did you notice, in the "stem" of the question, that P lives several hundred miles from where F lived and died? That fact makes it less likely that F would have heard about it from neighbors or the local newspapers.) Per FRE 104(b), the judge should admit the evidence only if ABC introduces evidence sufficient to support finding that F was aware of P's arrests and convictions.

---

11. Some experts argue that such conduct is a the product of mental illness which should be treated, rather than deliberately malicious and evil behavior that merits punishment. See, e.g., https://www.psychologytoday.com/us/conditions/exhibitionism. Nevertheless, it might plausibly prompt a father to disown a son who engages in it.

By the way: if you have taken Trusts and Estates (or Gratuitous Transfers or whatever your school calls the course), you've learned that when a testator wants to cut someone out of a will who would normally be a major recipient, it is wise to include in the will an explanation of why the testator is doing that. This doesn't completely prove that F was aware—if he lacked testamentary capacity, he might have had no idea of what he was signing or what it said—but it is at least some evidence of F's awareness.

§ 3.9 Evidence of a third person's guilt: *Holmes v. South Carolina*

Note: if your professor does not cover Holmes in class, it is probably safe to skip this section.

In *Holmes v. South Carolina*, 547 U.S. 319 (2006), the Supreme Court gave another lesson on what can, and what cannot, be considered in a Rule 403 analysis. The issue in *Holmes* involved the defendant's attempt to offer evidence that someone else, not he, committed the crime for which Holmes was on trial.

The general rule is that a defendant should be allowed to offer evidence suggesting that someone else (not the defendant) committed the crime if the evidence of that third person's[12] guilt raises a reasonable inference as to the defendant's innocence, but should be excluded if it merely "cast[s] a bare suspicion upon another" or "raise[s] a conjectural inference as to the commission of the crime by another." Stated more specifically, there must be evidence showing that the third person had a motive and the opportunity or means to commit the crime.

The Court acknowledged the general validity of the principle that a court may exclude evidence of another person's guilt if the legitimate probative value of the evidence is substantially outweighed by the risk of unfair prejudice, confusion of the issues, or the potential to mislead the jury, or the evidence is repetitive or only marginally relevant. The Court unanimously held, however, that a South Carolina variation on the doctrine, which excluded evidence of another's guilt if the state's case was perceived to be particularly strong, was unconstitutional. Exclusion, the Court insisted, could only be based on an evaluation of the evidence the defendant offered, not on the supposed strength of the evidence it was offered to counter.

i. Facts

Holmes was charged with robbing, raping, and beating an elderly woman so severely that she died of her injuries. The state's case was apparently a strong one. Witnesses testified that they saw the defendant near the victim's home within an hour of the time when, according to the state's evidence, she was killed. Moreover, the state offered substantial forensic evidence connecting him with the crime. In

12. The phrase "third person" is often used in this context, because the victim and the defendant are the first and second people in the equation.

response, Holmes introduced evidence suggesting that some of the forensic evidence had been mishandled by the police, and other forensic evidence had been planted by them to frame him. In addition, Holmes sought to have witnesses testify that they had seen another man, White, near the scene at the time of the crime, and that White had made numerous statements afterward either acknowledging his own guilt or asserting Holmes' innocence.

ii. State court action

The trial judge excluded this evidence, citing a 1941 state supreme court decision, *State v. Gregory,* 198 S.C. 98, 16 S.E.2d 532 (1941). *Gregory* held that evidence of a third person's guilt is admissible if it "raise[s] a reasonable inference or presumption as to [the defendant's] own innocence,'" but should be excluded if it merely "cast[s] a bare suspicion upon another" or "raise[s] a conjectural inference as to the commission of the crime by another." On appeal, South Carolina's Supreme Court upheld exclusion of Holmes' evidence suggesting that White was the perpetrator. In so doing, the state court cited *Gregory* and a 2001 decision, *State v. Gay,* 343 S.C. 543, 541 S.E.2d 541 (2001), in which that court held that "where there is strong evidence of an appellant's guilt, especially where there is strong forensic evidence, the proffered evidence about a third party's alleged guilt does not raise a reasonable inference as to the appellant's own innocence." The state court held that Holmes failed to satisfy the *Gay* standard, i.e., did not "overcome the forensic evidence against him to raise a reasonable inference of his own innocence."

iii. Holding

The U.S. Supreme Court unanimously reversed, concluding that the *Gay* rule violated the defendant's due process right to present a defense. The primary failing of the *Gay* rule was that it basically ignored the nature and quality of the evidence proffered by the defense:

> Under this rule, the trial judge does not focus on the probative value or the potential adverse effects of admitting the defense evidence of third-party guilt. Instead, the critical inquiry concerns the strength of the prosecution's case: If the prosecution's case is strong enough, the evidence of third-party guilt is excluded even if that evidence, if viewed independently, would have great probative value and even if it would not pose an undue risk of harassment, prejudice, or confusion of the issues.

Id. at 329. This approach, the Court held, deprived the defendant of his right to have the jury evaluate the strength of the state's case in light of all of the probative evidence on the issue:

> The rule applied in this case appears to be based on the following logic: Where (1) it is clear that only one person was involved in the commission of a particular crime and (2) there is strong evidence that the defendant was

> the perpetrator, it follows that evidence of third-party guilt must be weak. But this logic depends on an accurate evaluation of the prosecution's proof, and the true strength of the prosecution's proof cannot be assessed without considering challenges to the reliability of the prosecution's evidence. Just because the prosecution's evidence, *if credited,* would provide strong support for a guilty verdict, it does not follow that evidence of third-party guilt has only a weak logical connection to the central issues in the case. And where the credibility of the prosecution's witnesses or the reliability of its evidence is not conceded, the strength of the prosecution's case cannot be assessed without making the sort of factual findings that have traditionally been reserved for the trier of fact and that the South Carolina courts did not purport to make in this case.

Id. (Emphasis in original). Ultimately, therefore, the *Gay* rule was impermissibly "arbitrary" because it did not "rationally serve the end that the *Gregory* rule and other similar third-party guilt rules were designed to further." *Id.* at 330. Thus, the rule applied in this case deprived Holmes of his constitutional right to have a "meaningful opportunity to present a complete defense." *Id.* (Cites and internal quotation marks omitted).

<u>Question.</u>

In *Holmes,* why did the Court reject the South Carolina *State v. Gay* rule banning evidence of third-party guilt so long as the state's evidence was particularly strong?

<u>Answer</u>

For two reasons. First, *Gay* required the judge to assess the strength of the state's case. But (so long as the state's case is strong enough to survive a motion for a directed verdict, see § 2.12), assessing the strength of the state's case is the jury's job, not the judge's. Second, if the judge decided the state's case was strong enough, the *Gay* rule allowed a judge to reject the defendant's third-party evidence without ever assessing the strength of that evidence.

§ 3.10 Balancing, continued

It bears repeating: FRE 403 authorizes judges to edit or tailor evidence to give the offering party (in civil as well as criminal cases) as much of the legitimate probative value of its evidence as possible, while protecting the adverse party, to the extent possible, from the risk of unfair prejudice. But the court should do so only after assessing the legitimate probative value of the contested evidence, which includes the offering party's need for it.

§ 3.11 Questions: "Six years in the pen but I'm gonna make it home tonight."[13]

X, Y and Z are charged with racketeering. The indictment alleges that between 2018 and 2021, the three men extorted money from legitimate trucking companies and set up a sham trucking corporation (STC) as part of the scheme.[14] The government offers evidence that during the entire period in question, X was listed as the president of STC—even though at the time, X was in a state prison, serving a sentence for manslaughter.

Question 1.

Defendant X objects that this evidence is irrelevant. How should the prosecutor respond; how should the judge rule?

Answer:

The prosecutor has a legitimate need to establish that STC was a sham corporation. Evidence that its supposed president was in prison is powerful evidence establishing that fact. The judge should overrule the objection.

Question 2.

X offers to stipulate that during STC's entire existence, X performed no duties for STC and in fact was unavailable to do so. X argues that, given the offered stipulation, the judge should per Rule 403 exclude evidence that X was in state prison. How should the judge rule?

Answer:

Motion to exclude denied. Based on the stipulation, the jury might assume that X's unavailability was for any one of several innocent reasons—that X was busy with other businesses, that he was ill, etc. The government sought to show more than X's unavailability; it needed to show that the corporation was a complete *sham*. Evidence that, while X was STC's "president," he was doing time in a state prison establishes that far more persuasively than a mere stipulation of his "unavailability." (See *United States v. Provenzano*, 620 F.2d 985 (3d Cir. 1980).)

---

13. Cf. Earl Green & Carl Montgomery, *Six Days on the Road,* a country and western song which, according to Wikipedia, has been "hailed as the definitive celebration of the American truck driver." For another good song about truck-driving, check out Alan Jackson's *Where I Come From*. And for maybe the best song ever written about trucks, or driving, or, for that matter, about being a parent or a child, listen to Jackson's song *Drive*. (Have a box of tissues handy.)

14. Example: The Honest Trucking Co. obtains a contract to haul products from a manufacturer to regional retail stores. Someone from STC goes to the owner of Honest and demands a payoff, or else Honest's trucks would be vandalized, its drivers would be beaten up, etc. The payoff would be disguised payments to STC for doing some of the trucking, even though STC owned no trucks, employed no drivers, and never had any contact with the manufacturer or its products. (Free advice to students: this *not* a business model you should suggest to a potential client.)

Question 3.

Is there any other motion X's attorney might make regarding the evidence described in the question stem?

Answer:

Yes. X's attorney should move to exclude the fact that the crime X was doing time for was manslaughter; rather, the jury should merely be told he was serving a sentence after being convicted of a felony. The judge should grant this motion. The fact that X was serving a multi-year prison sentence has enough legitimate probative value that STC was a sham to overcome the unfair prejudice that inherently flows from evidence that a defendant has a prior felony conviction serious enough to warrant a several-years prison sentence. But the added fact that the prior conviction was for manslaughter—i.e., for unlawfully killing someone—itself as little or no legitimate probative value, while the risk of unfair prejudice is extremely high.

X's attorney should also ask the judge for a limiting instruction, per FRE 105, that they should draw no inferences about X's guilt in the racketeering case from the fact that he had prior felony conviction. The judge should give such an instruction.

§ 3.12 Questions: "You can bank on that."

Federal law requires that banks must be managed to ensure the solvency of the bank and to protect the interests of its depositors. D, an officer in B Bank, is charged with the crime of knowing misapplication of bank funds for arranging for the bank to lend money to friends and relatives at little or no interest. The government presents its evidence and rests. D moves for a directed verdict, which is denied.

D now seeks to introduce evidence that (a) former officials of the same bank had engaged in similar transactions, (b) those transactions were investigated by the Federal Deposit and Insurance Corporation (FDIC), a civil branch of the federal government, and (c) those officials were not prosecuted or civilly sanctioned.

Question 1.

The prosecutor objects that this evidence is irrelevant. How should D respond; how should the judge rule?

Answer:

What are the elements of the crime? There are three.

The first element is that D in fact arranged for loans to friends and relatives. (The prosecutor quite plausibly argues that what other officers of the bank did for other people on other occasions is not relevant to prove that D arranged the loans charged in the indictment.)

The second element is that the loans D arranged for his friends and relatives were improper: they violated federal laws governing the circumstances under which a bank may make loans. (The prosecutor quite plausibly argues that what other bank officials did on different occasions is not really relevant to determine the propriety or impropriety of what D did with regard to the loans he arranged.)

The third element of the crime is its mens rea (culpable mental state). What is that mens rea? If you are not sure, re-read the first paragraph of the question stem.

The first paragraph tells you that "D is charged with *knowing misapplication* of bank funds." This means that the government must prove, not only that D arranged for the loans and that the loans were unlawful, but that D *knew they were unlawful.*

Are the prior bank officers' loans, and the FDIC investigation and decision not to take action, relevant as to whether D knew that the loans he arranged were unlawful?

Yes, because they support D's claim that, since the FDIC took no action against those officials for their loans, he believed that it was lawful for him to make similar loans to his own relatives and friends.

Question 2.

Does the prosecutor have a valid FRE 403 objection to the evidence?

Answer:

Yes. Although in criminal cases, a defendant will make a Rule 403 objection far more often than a prosecutor will, a prosecutor can also assert the rule.

The prosecutor can plausibly argue that the evidence might confuse and mislead the jury, because the jury might assume that the FDIC's decision in the previous case means that there was nothing wrong with what D did—i.e., the jurors might assume that D's loans did not violate the law at all. This relates to the second element of the crime.

To use the contested evidence in assessing whether D's loans were improper is confusing and misleading, because there might be many factual differences between the prior cases and D's case. For example, FDIC officials might have decided that the prior cases involved only a few small loans; by contrast, D arranged for much larger loans for a larger number of his own friends and relatives. The evidence available to the FDIC in those cases might have been weaker than the Justice Department's evidence in D's case. If the prior loans were ultimately repaid, that would understandably diminish the FDIC's zeal to press the case. Or the FDIC simply may not have had the resources to pursue the earlier case. And so on. If the judge admits D's evidence, the prosecutor argues, the government would have to present evidence illustrating the differences between the other cases and D's case, to explain why the jury should not assume based on the prior cases that D's loans were in fact lawful. This would prolong the trial and confuse the issues.

These are legitimate points: there is a serious risk the jury will misuse the evidence regarding the second element.

Question 3.

How should the judge rule?

Answer:

This is basically a Rule 105 issue. The evidence is relevant and admissible on the third element; it is (less) relevant, and inadmissible, on the second element. The judge should rule that the risk of unfair prejudice on the second element (were D's loans illegal) does not substantially outweigh the legitimate probative value to the defendant on the third issue (did D know his loans were illegal).

Moreover, the judge can reduce the risk of unfair prejudice by instructing the jury that it should not consider the prior case in assessing whether D's loans violated federal law, but only on whether D knew his loans were illegal.

§ 3.13 More questions

Question 1.

Police searched D's home computer and found nine videos ranging in length from several seconds to forty-five minutes, each showing graphic and explicit sexual exploitation of children. D denied downloading the videos and insisted he did not know how they got on his computer. Prior to trial, D offers to stipulate that each of the nine clips satisfies the statutory definition of child pornography, and moves, per FRE 403, to preclude the prosecutor from playing any portion of any of the videos. How should the judge rule?

Answer:

In the vast majority of such cases, courts permit the prosecution to play clips from at least a few of the videos despite a defendant's offer to stipulate. Some courts base this result on the theory that it goes to show that the defendant had knowledge of what was on the clips, even if the defendant denied knowing the videos were on his computer at all. A better argument for allowing the clips to be shown, per *Old Chief*, is that the prosecutor should be permitted to show at least brief excerpts to demonstrate to the jury the nature of the crime and to avoid the impression that the prosecutor is attempting to hide evidence from the jury.

Question 2.

Decedent, age 37, died when an XYZ Company truck, driven by an employee, smashed into decedent's car and killed her. Plaintiff, decedent's mother, who is 67 years old, brought a wrongful death action against XYZ, claiming that the accident occurred because the truck driver ran a stop sign.

During the defense case in chief, XYZ seeks to offer evidence that plaintiff frequently physically abused the decedent when decedent was a child. Plaintiff objects that the evidence is irrelevant and, even if relevant, violates Rule 403. How should the judge rule?

Answer:

The typical student reaction is: The judge should sustain the objection! How the plaintiff treated decedent while decedent was a child cannot possibly be relevant on whether the truck driver ran a stop sign!

And that reaction is correct: plaintiff's alleged abuse of her daughter is completely irrelevant regarding whose fault it was that her daughter is dead.

But the judge should overrule plaintiff's objection.

How? Why?

There are three elements to a wrongful death action.

First: plaintiff has to persuade the jury that the defendant caused the decedent's death.

Second, plaintiff has to persuade the jury that the defendant's *wrongdoing* (in this case, the driver's negligence) caused the death. (If the XYZ driver was driving lawfully, and decedent ran into the truck's path, and it was not possible for the driver to stop in time, the truck caused decedent's death as a matter of fact, but its driver and owner are not legally culpable for doing so.)

Third,...

Stop and think. What is the third element in a wrongful death action? For that matter what is the final element in almost every civil cause of action? Why is plaintiff bothering to sue? What does she hope to gain?

Monetary damages.

The purpose of a wrongful death action is to require a defendant who wrongfully caused the decedent's death to compensate the plaintiff financially (to the extent that this is possible) for the hole the decedent's death creates in the plaintiff's life.

The decedent was 37 when she was killed. What might a 67-year-old parent expect to "get" from a 37-year-old child? Love. Affection. Emotional support. Perhaps financial support. In the years to come, help facing the inevitable complications of old age (trips to the doctor, help paying bills, choosing a retirement community, etc.).[15]

Why is the evidence of plaintiff's physical and emotional abuse during decedent's childhood relevant?

---

15. This assumes that the decedent lived close enough to the plaintiff to be able to provide such hands-on assistance.

Because it makes it much less likely that decedent, had she lived, would have felt any love or affection for her mother, or any emotional or moral obligation to help her mother deal with the challenges and indignities of aging. Thus, the evidence makes it less likely that the mother is entitled to monetary compensation for her daughter's death.

Question 3.

In an assault prosecution in which the victim was knocked unconscious by a blow to the head with a blunt object, the prosecutor wants to introduce into evidence a piece of plumbing pipe which has hair and a bloodstain that matches the victim's DNA. Defendant objects that the prosecutor has failed to show that the defendant possessed the pipe prior to the assault. Which of the following standards of admissibility should be applied by the court to an item of evidence connecting the defendant to the pipe?

(a) Whether the evidence could satisfy a reasonable juror beyond a reasonable doubt that the defendant possessed the pipe.

(b) Whether the evidence has any tendency to make it more probable than it would be without the evidence that the defendant possessed the pipe.

(c) Whether the evidence is sufficient to prove, absent contrary evidence, that the defendant possessed the pipe.

(d) Whether the evidence makes it more likely than not that the defendant possessed the pipe.

Answer:

(b). This question is one of conditional relevancy. Each item of evidence tending to connect the pipe to the defendant need only "have any tendency" to make that connection more probable than it would be without the evidence. See § 1.2. Ultimately, the admissibility of the pipe depends on whether, considering all of the evidence, a rational jury could find by a preponderance that the defendant possessed the pipe. See § 1.10.

You may be wondering: what does this question have to do with Rule 403? Answer: it doesn't. But it doesn't hurt, from time to time, to review material we've covered in earlier chapters.

§ 3.14 Miscellaneous FRE 403 issues

A party may sometimes "open the door" to evidence from the other side that otherwise would have been excluded per 403 or other rules. As general proposition, for example, when a defendant is charged with a specific crime, a prosecutor is not permitted to offer evidence of other, uncharged crimes. See FRE 404(b)(1), covered extensively in Chapter 7, *infra*. Consider, for example, *United States v. Catano,* 65 F.3d 219, 225–226 (1st Cir. 1995). At defendant's trial on drug charges, the defense, on cross-examination, attempted to undermine a prosecution witness' credibility by suggesting that he barely knew the defendant. Held: it was no abuse of discretion to permit the prosecutor, on redirect, to elicit testimony that the witness knew the defendant from prior drug transactions; the cross-examination had opened the door by suggesting (inaccurately) that a meeting between the witness and the defendant had been an isolated event.

"Surprise." As the Advisory Committee Note to Rule 403 states, otherwise relevant evidence is not to be excluded merely because it surprises an opponent who is unprepared to meet or rebut it. Rule 403 does, however, authorize a judge to exclude evidence if presentation of that evidence would result in "undue delay [or] waste of time." Evidence that *unfairly* surprises the adverse party—because, for example, it introduces new issues not addressed in the pleadings, or involves information which should have been disclosed during pretrial discovery—may therefore be excluded if the adverse party would require a lengthy mid-trial continuance in order to obtain and present counter-evidence. See, e.g., *Lease America Corp. v. Insurance Company of North America*, 276 N.W.2d 767 (1979).

Chapter 4

An Introduction to Rules 404 and 405

§ 4.1 "Toto, I've a feeling we're not in Kansas anymore."

In the 1939 movie *The Wizard of Oz,* the opening sequence (which runs 17 minutes and 34 seconds) introduces us to Dorothy Gale, a young girl living on a farm in Kansas. It ends when Dorothy gets conked on the head as a tornado tosses her house about. This sequence—as all movies were up to that point—was filmed in black and white. When Dorothy comes to, she opens the door—and the world is in technicolor! (Imagine how startling and miraculous this must have seemed to movie audiences who had never before seen a moving picture in technicolor.) That's when Dorothy says to her dog, "Toto, I've a feeling we're not in Kansas anymore." Dorothy soon learns how right she is: nothing is the same. The logic and order which governed her life in Kansas are gone; she is now in a world where weird things happen and logic and common sense are often irrelevant or, worse, completely misleading.

Law students experience something along those lines (minus the technicolor) when they make the transition from any other aspect of evidence law to character evidence and evidence of "extrinsic acts."

Most provisions of the Federal Rules of Evidence are well-written, and there is an underlying logic that helps a student to learn, and an attorney to apply, this or that rule. That is not the case with Rules 404 and 405. I tell you this at the outset because as you begin your study of this subject, you may find yourself thinking, "This stuff doesn't make any sense!" Once you realize that, it will be easier to learn the law governing "character evidence" and "extrinsic act" evidence.

§ 4.2 What is "character evidence"? What is "extrinsic act" evidence?

The typical lawsuit focuses on the conduct and/or state of mind of one or more individuals at a particular time in the past. Who ran the stop sign when two cars collided, driver A or driver B? Is this the contact P and D signed? Did Dr. MD deviate from sound medical practice in treating patient L, and if so, is that what caused L's loss of health? Was it X who broke into a gas station at 2 a.m. and stole several items that were inside? When Z walked out of a clothing store with several unpaid-for items, did Z intend to steal them, or was it just an absent-minded oversight?

Rules 404 and 405 regulate when and how two closely related kinds of evidence can be used as a basis to infer what person "X" did on that particular occasion, or why X did it. The following example will illustrate what these forms of evidence consist of, and how a litigant might attempt to use them. (I'm numbering the paragraphs to make it easier to refer to them in the discussion that follows.)

> ¶1. P is an investor. He sought the advice of D, an investment counselor. D advised P to invest in the stock of ABC Mining Corporation. P followed D's advice; ABC went bankrupt; P lost his investment. P sues D, seeking to make D compensate him for his loss. P's complaint makes the following allegations:
>
> 1. P sought D's professional advice to find a safe, conservative investment.
> 2. D persuaded P to invest in ABC by advising P that ABC was a safe, conservative investment.
> 3. D was aware at the time that ABC was a wildly speculative, risky venture.
> 4. D did not inform P that D had invested heavily in ABC, that ABC was in severe financial difficulties, and that D feared he would lose his own investment unless others could be persuaded to shore up the company by investing additional funds.
>
> ¶2. D's response contains the following allegations:
>
> 1. When P came to D for advice, P said he was looking for an investment that could double or maybe even triple his money in a year.
> 2. D told P that such investments were inherently risky and speculative. P said he was willing to take risks.

3. When D told P about ABC, he said: "I've put quite a bit of money into it myself. I think it's a good gamble. Of course, I may lose my shirt!" P responded: "If you're willing to gamble your money on it, I'm willing to gamble mine."

¶ 3. Thus, factual issues in the lawsuit include: what kind of investment was P looking for; what did D tell P about ABC; and why did D advise P to invest in ABC. At trial, each litigant will testify to his own version of the facts; each will introduce correspondence and other documentary evidence that bolsters his version of what each said to the other when they discussed whether P should invest in ABC. Evidence that focuses on what P and D said and did during their meetings and dealings with each other is not "character evidence"; nor is it "extrinsic act" evidence; none of it implicates FRE 404 or 405.

¶ 4. In addition, P would like to call other investment counselors with whom he has done business; these counselors will testify that in their opinion, P has always been a cautious, conservative investor.

¶ 5. P further wants to introduce evidence that D's reputation among investment counselors is that of a man who would lie to a client to further his own financial position.

¶ 6. D, on the other hand, wants to offer evidence of his excellent reputation for honesty in the financial community.

¶ 7. Further, D seeks to prove that a few days before P came to D for investment counseling, P had rejected the advice of another counselor as "too cautious and stodgy," complaining, "I wouldn't make money fast enough with him."

Discussion

The evidence described in ¶¶ 4–6 are examples of what FRE 404(a) calls "character evidence," i.e., "[e]vidence of a person's character or character trait:"

In ¶ 4, P hopes to offer evidence of a trait of his own character—that he is a cautious investor. P hopes that if the jury hears this evidence, it will infer that since P has always been a cautious investor in the past, he probably sought the same kind of investment from D on this occasion.

In ¶ 5, P hopes to offer evidence of a trait of D's character—that D lies to clients. P hopes that if the jury hears this testimony, it will infer that since D has the reputation of lying to clients, he probably lied to P when P sought investment advice from him.

In ¶ 6, D hopes to offer evidence of a trait of his own character—that D deals honestly and truthfully with his clients. D hopes that the jury will infer from this that he was honest and truthful in his dealings with P.

The first sentence of FRE 405(a) defines how such evidence might be offered: "When evidence of a person's character or character trait is admissible, it may be proved by testimony about the person's reputation or by testimony in the form of an opinion." This is precisely what P and D attempt to offer in ¶¶4–6. Note that the first sentence of FRE 405(a) does *not* say that such evidence is admissible; it says that *if* such evidence is substantively admissible, it can be either in the form of reputation testimony or opinion testimony.

¶7 is an example of what FRE 404(b) refers to as evidence of a "crime, wrong or other act." This is often referred to as "extrinsic act" evidence, because P's conversations with the other investment counselor are extrinsic to—i.e., not directly related to or a part of—P's dealings with D.[1] D hopes that the jury will infer from this that since P sought a speculative, "get rich quick" investment from the other counselor, he also sought a similarly speculative investment from D.

Here is a useful way to differentiate "character evidence" from "extrinsic act" evidence. Character evidence is a *general description* of an aspect of a person (X)'s character—is X moody or cheerful; thrifty or a big spender; emotional or stoic; respectful of members of the opposite sex or sexual orientation, or disdainful of them; patient with children or rigid and demanding. As a supervisor, is X supportive or demeaning? Is X open to opinions that differ from his or her own, or does X view differing opinions as a personal attack or as showing a lack of intelligence? Does X consume alcohol in moderation, or does X overindulge? Is X a careful driver, or a reckless or negligent one?

"Extrinsic act" evidence, on the other hand, relates to how that person acted on a particular situation that is not directly related to the facts of the lawsuit.

The relevance of character evidence and extrinsic act evidence is based on the theorem, "Tell me what others think of a person, tell me how he has behaved in similar situations in the past, and I'll be able to infer what he did this time and why he did it." That theorem is not always accurate, but it is logical; it makes sense. We use it every day. Should you trust teenager L to walk your dog twice a day while you are on a trip? Should you trust teenager T to babysit your children? Should you let law student Z join your study group? M, who works in the same office as you do and who lives just a few blocks from your apartment, offered you a ride home. Should you accept, or decline? Should you take a course from Professor A? Professor B asked you to be his research assistant on a project. What should you say? In each of these situations, your decision may be based, at least in part, on what others have said about L or T or Z or M or A or B; or your own previous contacts with them; and with how those individuals have conducted themselves on other occasions in the past.

---

1. "Extrinsic" is defined in pertinent part as "not part of the essential nature of something; coming or operating from outside."

Reminder: all we have done so far is analyze whether an offer of evidence consists of character evidence or extrinsic act evidence. We have not yet discussed whether any of this evidence would be admissible if offered about X at a trial.

§ 4.3 Questions

Question 1.

X applies for a job as a cashier with S Supermarket. He lists his minister, Reverend R, as a reference, and the DEF Department Store (supervisor: Ms. G) and H's Restaurant as his two most recent employers. PM, the personnel manager for the supermarket, phones Reverend R, introduces herself, explains why she is calling, and asks: "What can you tell me about X?"

Reverend R replies, "Everyone says he's a trustworthy, dependable fellow."

If Reverend R said this during trial testimony, would it constitute character evidence (and if so, which kind—reputation or opinion), extrinsic act evidence; both; or neither?

Answer:

This is character evidence in the form of reputation—what "everybody says" about X.

Question 2.

Reverend R continues, "He is a fine, decent, honest young man." If Reverend R said this during trial testimony, would it constitute character evidence (and if so, which kind—reputation or opinion), extrinsic act evidence; both; or neither?

Answer:

This is character evidence in the form of opinion testimony: Reverend R is giving his own personal opinion of X's character.

Question 3.

Next, PM calls H's Restaurant and asks H about X. H responds that X worked for him as a waiter, and that "all my customers say he is a nice, polite, courteous young man." If H said this during trial testimony, would it constitute character evidence (and if so, which kind—reputation or opinion), extrinsic act evidence; both; or neither?

Answer:

This is character evidence in the form of reputation—what all H's customers say about X.

Question 4.

PM asks: "Is he honest? Can I trust him at the cash register?"

"Let me put it this way," H answers. "Shortly after X came to work for us, a customer left X a ten-dollar bill as a tip on a six-dollar meal. X realized the customer must have made a mistake, so he ran after the customer and returned the ten to him." If H said this during trial testimony, would it constitute character evidence (and if so, which kind—reputation or opinion), extrinsic act evidence; both; or neither?

Answer:

This is extrinsic act testimony. H is relating how X acted on one specific occasion in the past, as an example of X's honesty and trustworthiness.

Question 5.

Finally, PM phones Ms. G, who had been X's supervisor at the DEF Department Store. Ms. G relates that X had worked for a month as a stock boy in the store's warehouse while the regular stock boy was out sick. She adds: "I wouldn't trust him if I were you. We took inventory just before his month was over, and fourteen digital cameras were missing. We never had that problem when our regular stock boy was with us." If Ms. G said this during trial testimony, would it constitute character evidence (and if so, which kind—reputation or opinion), extrinsic act evidence; both; or neither?

Answer:

Ms. G's comments include both character evidence (her opinion, "I wouldn't trust him") and testimony about an extrinsic act (information from which PM could infer that X stole fourteen cameras).

These questions do not address whether any of this evidence is admissible; they only give you an exercise in distinguishing between character (reputation or opinion) testimony on one hand, and evidence relating to extrinsic acts, on the other.

§ 4.4 Rules 404 and 405, divided by form

It is tempting to say that Rule 404(a) regulates when character evidence is admissible, Rule 404(b) regulates when extrinsic act evidence is admissible, and Rule 405 merely sets out rules governing the form and procedure governing both kinds of evidence. And that is true to an extent, but is actually misleading. All told, FRE 404–405 set out eleven different rules dealing with character evidence and extrinsic act evidence. Your first major challenge is figuring out which rule or rules apply to the evidence that is being offered. The more provisions you can eliminate quickly, the easier that task.

The following chart divides these eleven provisions into character evidence and extrinsic act evidence.

Character evidence

404(a) unwritten sentence:
Char. as Essential
Element (CEE)

404(a)(1) general prohibition

Exceptions:

404(a)(2)(A)	(about D)
404(a)(2)(B)	(by D about V/AV)
404(a)(2)(B)(i)	(by Pr about V/AV)
404(a)(2)(B)(ii)	(by Pr about D)
405(a)(1st sent.)	(re D or V/AV)

Extrinsic act evidence

404(b)(1): about anyone: rule of exclusion
404(b)(2): about anyone: rule of inclusion
405(a)(2nd sent.) (re D, V/AV)
405(b) Char. as Essential Element

Abbreviations:

CEE	Character as essential element
D	Defendant
Pr	Prosecutor
V	Victim
AV	Alleged victim

The provisions in the left column apply to character evidence, i.e., where witness W testifies as to X's reputation in the community, or where W gives his or her own opinion about an aspect of X's character. The provisions in the right column apply to extrinsic act evidence, such as W's testimony describing what he saw X say or do on a specific instance in the past (other than what X did that is directly relevant to the central facts in dispute).

How to use this chart. Read the facts carefully to determine whether the evidence is character evidence, or extrinsic act evidence. If it is character evidence, you should ignore all of the rules in the right-hand column, and examine each of the rules in the left-hand column to determine whether each rule governs this particular offer of general character evidence, and if so, whether it admits or excludes it.

The opposite is also true: if the evidence is extrinsic act evidence, ignore all of the provisions in the left column, and apply each of the rules in the right column to determine whether each rule governs this particular offer of specific-act character evidence, and if so, whether it admits the evidence or excludes it.

Note that these provisions are listed in the numerical order in which they appear in Rules 404 and 405. They are not listed in order of importance. The chart works only vertically, not horizontally: you can't go from left to right. This chart has one purpose, and one purpose only: once you recognize which form (character or extrinsic act) evidence is being offered at a trial, it tells you which rules you can ignore, and which rules might apply to the evidence.

I'm not going to explain anything more about this chart until we consider various kinds of character evidence in the context of civil or criminal trials, starting in the next chapter.

§ 4.5. Theories of relevancy (purpose)

A litigant may seek to offer character evidence or extrinsic act evidence (or both) on any of three distinct theories of relevancy:

1. to prove an essential element of a claim, charge (crime) or defense to a claim or charge. (*Abbreviation:* CEE—"character as essential element.") This is covered in Chapter 5.
2. as circumstantial evidence of how a person acted on a particular occasion. (*Abbreviation:* CIRCOND—"character as ***cir***cumstantial evidence of ***con-d***uct.") See Chapter 6.
3. "other purposes." (*Abbreviation:* FASPRELIPI—"***fa***ctually ***sp***ecific ***rel***evance ***i***ndependent of the ***p***ropensity ***i***nference.") This is covered in Chapter 7.

This list includes abbreviations which I've developed in the 40+ years I taught evidence; my students found them useful, so I offer them to you at no extra charge. Be patient; I'll explain them, too.

§ 4.6. "Character evidence": reputation and opinion testimony; general rule of exclusion

FRE 404(a) regulates the admissibility of general (reputation or opinion) character evidence. Rule 404(a)(1) provides:

> **Rule 404. Character Evidence; Crimes or Other Acts**
>
> **(a) Character Evidence.**
>
> **(1) Prohibited Uses.** Evidence of a person's character or character trait is not admissible to prove that on a particular occasion the person acted in accordance with the character or trait.

The first question that comes to mind might well be: what does the phrase "evidence of a person's character or character trait" mean? To answer that question, we turn to the first sentence of FRE 405(a):

> **Rule 405. Methods of Proving Character**
>
> **(a) By Reputation or Opinion.** When evidence of a person's character or character trait is admissible, it may be proved by testimony about the person's reputation or by testimony in the form of an opinion....

In other words, "character evidence" about X means "reputation or opinion testimony" about X. Rule 404(a) precludes the use of reputation and opinion evidence, if that evidence is offered "to prove that on a particular occasion [X] acted in accordance with the character or trait"—unless the case falls into one of the written, or the unwritten, exceptions to the rule.[2]

This means that in a lawsuit between A and B to determine which motorist ran a stop sign and caused a collision, reputation and opinion evidence about how good or bad a driver A is would not be admissible to prove or disprove that he ran the stop sign. Nor would such evidence be admissible regarding B. In a medical malpractice suit against MD, reputation or opinion evidence about her skill and competence as a doctor would not be admissible as evidence of whether she did, or did not, follow acceptable medical practice in diagnosing and treating patient L. And so on.

§ 4.7. Specific extrinsic act evidence; "propensity inference"; general rule of exclusion

FRE 404(b) regulates the admissibility of specific-act character evidence. Rule 404(b)(1) provides:

> **(b) Crimes, Wrongs, or Other Acts.**
>
> **(1) Prohibited Uses.** Evidence of a crime, wrong, or other act is not admissible to prove a person's character in order to show that on a particular occasion the person acted in accordance with the character.

This rule excludes extrinsic act evidence whose relevance is based on what is often called the "propensity inference." Evidence that X has behaved in a certain way on specific occasions in the past is not admissible to suggest, (a) X has a propensity to behave that way, and therefore, (b) X probably behaved that way on the occasion that is the focus of the current litigation.

---

2. The unwritten exception to the FRE 404(a)(1) rule excluding such evidence is covered in Chapter 5. The written exceptions are covered in Chapter 6.

The first thing to understand is that the exclusionary rule in Rule 404(b)(1) only applies to evidence of extrinsic specific acts. It does not apply to evidence about how X acted on the occasion in question. Thus, in the lawsuit that arose between A and B after they collided in an intersection, evidence about what each motorist was doing as his or her car approached the intersection is not regulated by this rule. Evidence that A was arguing about politics with his front-seat passenger would not be excluded, because that evidence relates directly to whether A was paying attention to the road when the cars collided. Similarly, evidence that B was a Nationals fan and was listening to the 7th game of the 2019 World Series is not extrinsic act evidence, for the same reason.

But evidence that A caused three other collisions in the eighteen months preceding the A-B collision is "extrinsic" to the A-B collision because those other collisions were not part of the A-B collision itself, nor part of the immediate sequence of events which led to the A-B collision. Thus, Rule 404(b)(1) says that evidence would not be admissible to suggest that A has a propensity to be an inattentive or careless driver, and therefore, was probably inattentive or careless on October 30, 2019, and therefore probably caused this collision, too.

In a medical malpractice suit against MD, Rule 404(b)(1) directs that evidence that MD treated 14 other patients with similar conditions similar to patient L's and did so in full compliance with medical standards would not be admissible to suggest that she has a propensity to follow proper standards, and that, therefore, she probably followed standard medical practice when she diagnosed and treated L. The converse is also true: evidence that she failed to follow standards in treating another patient would not be admissible to suggest she has a propensity to deviate from proper standards, and therefore, failed to follow standards with regard to L.[3]

This rule of general exclusion applies equally in criminal cases.[4] Thus, for example, if X is charged with selling cocaine on June 1st, evidence that he also sold cocaine in February and April is not admissible to suggest that he has a propensity to sell cocaine, and therefore probably also sold cocaine on June 1st.

§ 4.8 Why the law excludes character and extrinsic act evidence—except when it doesn't

Why does the law, as a general rule, ban such evidence? For several reasons. First: if we routinely admitted such evidence, trials would take much longer—each side might call a parade of witnesses saying nice things about one litigant and nasty things about the other litigant, and each litigant might then offer additional witnesses to rebut the nice-or-nasty things the other litigant's witnesses said—none of which directly relates to the central issue in the case—who ran the stop sign, or

3. Depending on circumstances, however, such evidence may be admitted per Rule 406.
4. In fact, Rule 404(b) is cited far more often in criminal litigation than in civil litigation.

whether Dr. MD fail to comply with acceptable medical practice (or whatever the key factual issues may be in a lawsuit).

Similarly, each side might call witnesses to testify about how each of the litigants behaved in situations not directly related to the collision, or to MD's treatment of patient L.

Second: Whether X should win or lose a lawsuit, or whether X should be convicted or acquitted of a crime, should be based on the facts and evidence directly relating to the case at hand, not on how X acted on other, unrelated occasions in the past; and not on something as vague and amorphous as what other people think about X (i.e., reputation or opinion evidence about his or her character). A person's reputation might be worse, or better, than he or she deserves. And people often act "uncharacteristically." "Good" people sometimes do "bad" things, and vice-versa. Smart people sometimes do dumb things. People who are normally careful sometimes act rashly. A person who has been a sleazebag most of his or her life might, for once in his or her life, do the right, decent, honorable thing—might even act heroically.[5]

Third, the law as a general rule bans extrinsic act evidence, despite its relevance, because a jury might give it far more weight than it actually deserves, i.e., its legitimate probative value is all too often substantially outweighed by the risk of unfair prejudice. In other words, FRE 404(b)(1) can be seen a specialized application of Rule 403.

So Rules 404(a)(1) and 404(b)(1) are both exclusionary rules: such evidence, despite its relevance, is not admissible.

If these general rules were all you had to know about character evidence, your life (or at least this semester) would be a lot easier, and instead of writing this book, I could be hanging out with my wife and playing with my grandchildren and hiking and writing unpublished fiction. But guess what: there *are* a few exceptions to these general rules. No, that's not quite right; there are a few *dozen* exceptions to these rules. (And some of those exceptions might even apply to lawsuit *A v. B*, or to lawsuit *L v. MD*.)

In a sense, that's what most this book is about: the exceptions, in Rules 404 and 405 and 406, and 412–415, and 608 and 609, to these general rules of exclusion.

§ 4.9 Whose character are we talking about?

To apply Rules 404 and 405, it is necessary to categorize the person whose character the evidence relates to and the role in which he or she appears in the lawsuit. These rules are applicable when a litigant seeks to introduce character evidence (good or bad) about *any* person ("X"), whether or not X is a party in the lawsuit, as a basis to infer what X did or why he or she did it during the events that are at issue in the trial.

5. Oskar Schindler is a prime example.

It is important to keep in mind, however, that Rules 404 and 405 do *not* apply when evidence about X falls into a narrow category of behavior called "habit evidence," which is regulated in FRE 406. Nor do FRE 404–405 apply to evidence relating to the prior sexual behavior of either the complainant or defendant in sex offense cases; those cases are regulated by Rules 412–415. Nor do rules 404–405 regulate the uses of character or extrinsic act evidence regarding the *credibility of a witness* who has given testimony at trial; use of such evidence to impeach or rehabilitate a witness is covered in Rules 608-609.[6]

There are similarities and interrelationships between all of these rules—and the rules governing impeachment generally. In § 11.23 to § 11.31, I divide the courtroom scenarios in which any of these rules might apply into eight "litigation situations," and list the rules that you should consider in each litigation situation. The litigation situation sections are a useful brief summary and review of each situation after we have covered each in depth. But let's nail down Rules 404-405 first.

§ 4.10 How Rules 404 and 405 fit with other rules and issues

In § 1.3, I offered a basic outline of evidence law that may prove useful in helping you see where each rule fits in the overall picture. Here is how Rules 404 and 405 fit within that outline.

1. *Relevance.* What is the purpose for which the character evidence is offered, i.e., how is it relevant to the factual or legal issues in dispute? See § 4.5, *supra*.
2. *Applicability of exclusionary or inclusionary rules to evidence offered for that purpose.* Rule 404(a) and Rule 404(b) each contain both exclusionary and inclusionary provisions.
3. *Form and procedure.* Rules 404 and 405 each regulate aspects of both character evidence and extrinsic act evidence and procedures governing the offer of such evidence. See the chart in § 4.4. (In the next few chapters, we will examine each of the provisions listed on that chart.)
4. *Prejudice; interests of justice.* If the evidence appears admissible under the first three steps, should it nevertheless be excluded under Rule 403 or 102? If the evidence appears to be inadmissible under the first three steps, should it nevertheless be admitted under Rule 102 or 106?
5. *Making a record.* Finally, once the trial judge has ruled, what (if anything) should the adversely affected party do under Rule 103 or 105 to preserve the issue for appeal?

---

6. Occasionally, a non-testifying hearsay declarant is regarded as a witness for purposes of Rules 607–609. See Rule 806, covered in § 7.5 of *A Student's Guide to Hearsay*. (End of commercial.)

Chapter 5

Character as "Essential Element" of a Claim, Charge or Defense

§ 5.1 When is character an "essential element" ("CEE")?

Character is an "essential element" of a claim, charge (crime), or defense to a claim or charge only when a litigant *must* introduce evidence of a person's ("X") character or suffer a directed verdict on at least some issues in the lawsuit. This occurs when the substantive law underlying the lawsuit explicitly or implicitly includes a person's character as an element of the claim, charge, or defense. In such cases, a litigant is entitled to offer both character evidence and extrinsic act evidence that is relevant to X's character.

In certain types of lawsuits, character is often an essential element of a civil claim or defense to a claim. The main ones are as follows.

1. Negligent entrustment
2. Child custody litigation
3. Personal injury suits (sometimes) relating to damages
4. Wrongful death actions (sometimes) relating to damages
5. Defamation suits (sometimes)

This chapter discusses each of these situations. Other instances arise from time to time, but those at the main ones, so I wouldn't worry about others unless your professor makes a point of specifying others. And if your professor doesn't cover "character as an essential element," you can skip this chapter altogether.

But before we look at these five categories, let's take a first look that the provisions of Rules 404 and 405 that govern character evidence and evidence of extrinsic acts in such cases.

§ 5.2 FRE 404(a), unwritten sentence; FRE 405(b)

What do Rules 404 and 405 say about character evidence and evidence of extrinsic act evidence, where character is an essential element of a claim or defense? Consider once again the chart from § 4.4:

Character evidence

404(a) unwritten sentence:
Char. as Essential Element (CEE)

404(a)(1) general prohibition

Exceptions:

404(a)(2)(A)	(about D)
404(a)(2)(B)	(by D about V/AV)
404(a)(2)(B)(i)	(by Pr about V/AV)
404(a)(2)(B)(ii)	(by Pr about D)
405(a)(1st sent.)	(re D or V/AV)

Extrinsic act evidence

404(b)(1): about anyone: rule of exclusion

404(b)(2): about anyone: rule of inclusion

405(a)(2nd sent.) (re D, V/AV)

405(b) Char. as Essential Element

Abbreviations:

CEE	Character as essential element
D	Defendant
V	Victim
AV	Alleged victim
Pr	Prosecutor

First, let's look at the extrinsic act column. The first rule there is 404(b). Rule 404(b)(1) states that as a rule, evidence of extrinsic acts "is not admissible to show that on a particular occasion the person acted in accordance with the character," i.e., evidence of extrinsic acts is not admissible to prove propensity.[1] Since showing propensity is the whole purpose of evidence when character is an essential element,

1. Let's ignore Rule 404(b)(2) for the present.

it would seem that Rule 404(b) bans extrinsic act evidence in such cases. But don't underline or highlight this sentence just yet.[2]

The second rule is FRE 405(a), second sentence:

> **Rule 405. Methods of Proving Character**
>
> **(a) By Reputation or Opinion....**
>
> ... On cross-examination of the character witness [who has testified to a person's reputation, or has expressed an opinion as to that person's character], the court may allow an inquiry into relevant specific instances of the person's conduct.

Does it apply to this situation? Clearly not. That rule regulates cross-examination of a character witness after the witness has testified on direct examination. We are not there yet; we're still trying to figure out whether a party can call any of these witnesses in the first place.

The third provision is FRE 405(b):

> **Rule 405. Methods of Proving Character**
>
> ...
>
> **(b) By Specific Instances of Conduct.** When a person's character or character trait is an essential element of a charge, claim, or defense, the character or trait may also be proved by relevant specific instances of the person's conduct.

This rule says quite explicitly that in CEE cases, i.e., when someone's character or character trait is an essential element of a charge, claim or defense, specific instances of conduct that are relevant to illustrate the person's character are admissible. And although the rule does not explicitly use the term "extrinsic," clearly that must be what is meant; no special rule is required to admit evidence that directly relates to the key facts that gave rise to the lawsuit.

Thus, even though the Rule 404(b)(1) general rule bans extrinsic specific act evidence if offered to support the propensity inference, in CEE cases, Rule 405(b) is an exception to that rule.

---

2. Remember:

Things are seldom what they seem,
Skim milk masquerades as cream;
Highlows pass as patent leathers;
Jackdaws strut in peacock's feathers.

William S. Gilbert, *HMS Pinafore* Act II (1978).

But there is something curious about the wording of Rule 405(b): it says that when a person's character is an essential element of a claim, charge or defense, that person's character "may also" be proven by evidence of specific extrinsic acts. Huh? "May also"? What does *that* mean? Well, since 405(b) regulates extrinsic-act evidence, "may also" implies that where "a person's character or character trait is an essential element of a charge, claim or defense," character evidence must "also" be admissible, right? Right! So somewhere in Rules 404 or 405, there is a provision saying so. Right?

Wrong. Rule 405(b) is the only provision in either rule that refers to cases in which character is an essential element.

Examine the Rule 404–405 chart again. Notice the first item listed on the "general" side of the chart: the "unwritten sentence"—something you've been wondering about since you first read the chart in § 4.4.

The unwritten sentence, if the drafters of the Federal Rules had bothered to write it, would read:

> *RULE 404: "Unwritten sentence" (character as "essential element")*
>
> "When a person's character is an essential element of a claim or defense, a party may offer reputation or opinion evidence about that person's character, as provided by Rule 405(a) first sentence, or evidence of extrinsic acts that illustrate that person's character, as provided by Rule 405(b)."

Instead of putting this in the rule, which would have brought useful clarity to a murky subject, the experts who drafted the FRE buried it in the second paragraph of the Advisory Committee Note to Rule 404(a) with the cryptic remark that when character is an element, "No problem of the general relevancy is involved, and the present rule has no provision on the subject. The only question relates to allowable methods of proof, as to which see Rule 405...." There are so many wrong things about this passage that it would take several hundred words to discuss them all, but in essence, it is as if the Advisory Committee was saying, "*We*, who drafted these rules, understand this arcane little corner of evidence law, so *we* don't need to put anything in Rule 404 to explain it. The rest of you will just have to grope in the dark."

To which I reply: "It is better to light one candle than grope in the darkness."[3] And you, wise reader, need not even light the candle; this section has done it for you.

3. This paraphrases the expression, "It is better to light one candle than curse the darkness," an aphorism apparently coined in 1907 by an American minister in a sermon but since attributed to Oliver Wendell Holmes; various other clergymen and educators; Eleanor Roosevelt; Linus Van Pelt (from the *Peanuts* comic strip); and Confucius.

§ 5.3 Character as essential element: summarizing the law

Putting together the unwritten sentence in Rule 404(a) and relevant provisions of Rule 405, here is what these rules say about character evidence and evidence of extrinsic acts when character is an essential element:

a. Rule 404(a): "unwritten sentence": "When a person's character is an essential element of a claim or defense, a party may offer evidence of a pertinent trait of that person's character, as provided by Rule 405."

b. 405(a): first sentence regulates use of character evidence in this situation: reputation and opinion evidence are both admissible (assuming the trait testified to is "pertinent" and a proper foundation has been laid).

c. 405(a): second sentence regulates cross-examination of a witness who has been called to give reputation or opinion evidence. (I am deferring discussion of FRE 405(a)(2nd sentence) until Chapter Six.)

d. 405(b): when character is an essential element, the litigants may also offer evidence of that person's relevant specific extrinsic acts.

Note: the rules covered in Chapters 4 through 13 apply in eight different courtroom scenarios, which I refer to as "litigation situations." In § 11.23 to § 11.31, I summarize each litigation situation and list the rules that apply in that litigation situation. The litigation situation sections of this book provide you with a brief review of each situation after we have covered each in depth. The scenario here—civil cases in which character is an essential element of claim or defense—is litigation situation A; see § 11.24.

We will now discuss each of the five most common situations in which a person's character (or trait of character) is an essential element of a claim or defense.

§ 5.4 Negligent entrustment

A negligent entrustment action arises in either of two situations.

1. D provides X with a dangerous item (a car, a firearm, etc.). X, using that item, injures P or damages P's property. P sues D, alleging that it was negligent of D to provide that instrument to X.
2. D appoints X to a position of authority. While exercising that authority, X injures P. P sues D, alleging that it was negligent of D to give X that authority.

The first kind of negligent entrustment action arises sometimes in suits against an employer. D company employs Driver. Driver collides with P. P sues both Driver and D Company, alleging Driver's negligence. CEE is not an issue in such cases. But suppose P seeks not only actual damages, but also seeks punitive damages against D Company, alleging that it was negligent of D Company to have hired Driver in the first place, because D Company knew or should have known that Driver frequently drove while intoxicated. That makes Driver's character for intoxicated driving an essential element of P's punitive damages claim, not against Driver, but against D Company.

Similarly, suppose Homeowner hires C, a contractor, to completely redo the master bathroom in Homeowner's house. C assigns Leake, a plumber, to handle the plumbing. Shortly after the job is finished, a main connecting pipe comes loose, flooding a substantial portion of the house. Homeowner sues C, alleging that Leake negligently failed to install the connection properly, thus causing the flood. Character is not an essential element in the case.

But suppose Homeowner discovers that during a three-year period before C assigned Leake to work on his house, Leake had been fired by two other contractors for incompetence, and had lost his certification as a licensed plumber. Based on this information, Homeowner adds a punitive damages claim against C, alleging that it was negligent of C to hire Leake in the first place, because C knew, or should have known, that C was not competent to do the job C assigned Leake to do. Leake's incompetence as a plumber is an essential element of Homeowner's punitive damages claim against C, and reputation and opinion testimony about Leake's competence or incompetence as a plumber, and extrinsic acts illustrating that competence or incompetence, would be admissible at trial against C.

Here's an example of a negligent entrustment suit unrelated to an employer-employee context. FC is a firearm collector. Buyer asks to purchase one of FC's handguns—let's say a SW .32 caliber revolver. FC agrees to sell it to Buyer. (Assume this is entirely lawful.) X is friendly with both FC and Buyer, so on March 1, FC asks X to deliver the (unloaded) revolver and a box of ammunition to Buyer. X agrees.

While driving to Buyer's house to deliver the revolver and ammunition, X collides with V, another motorist. Both men get out of their cars to inspect the damage, which is slight, but things do not go well: the incident ends when X loads the revolver and shoots and injures V.

V sues X for assault. There are three elements to V's claim:

(1) X shot V.

(2) X had no legal justification or excuse for doing so.

(3) V suffered damages (medical expenses, lost income, pain and suffering, and perhaps permanent disability) for which X should be required to compensate him.

X responds that he shot V in self-defense because V threatened to beat him with a tire iron. V says that this is completely untrue; that X began cursing at V, who responded, "Here's my insurance information; just give me yours and we can be on our way." According to V, X got back into his car, got out again, pointed a gun at V, said "Here's my insurance information," and shot V in the thigh, then drove off.

V's attorney discovers:

(a) X has a reputation in the neighborhood for losing his temper and getting into fights.

(b) In separate incidents, X was convicted of feloniously assaulting Black and was convicted of a misdemeanor assault of Blue.

(c) A civil suit is pending against X for destroying a neighbor's (N's) fence with an axe after the neighbor complained that a bush on X's side of the fence was growing through the fence into the neighbor's yard.

Notice that (a) consists of general character evidence (about X's character for losing his temper and violence); (b) and (c) each constitute evidence of extrinsic acts that illustrate X's character for losing his temper and responding violently.

All of the evidence that V's attorney discovered about X (a), (b), (c) is *relevant* as tending to prove that X lost his temper and shot V with no justification. Item (a) suggests that it was "in character" for X to act as V claims he did on their March 1 encounter. Similarly, (b) consists of two extrinsic instances in which X committed acts of violence, and (c) is an additional extrinsic instance when X lost his temper and committed a violent act. These incidents, individually and collectively, support the inference X has a propensity to lose his temper and become violent, which in turn supports the inference that he acted in conformity with that propensity on March 1st.

But <u>none of that evidence would be admissible in V's civil action against X.</u> The reputation evidence is barred by FRE 404(a)(1). The extrinsic specific-act evidence is excluded by FRE 404(b)(1).[4]

<u>But suppose V also sues FC for negligent entrustment</u>, alleging that FC was negligent (or, worse, reckless) in giving a handgun and ammunition to X, because FC knew or should have known that X frequently lost his temper and had a propensity for violence. Then (a), (b) and (c)—all of which is <u>in</u>admissible against <u>X</u>—<u>is</u> admissible against <u>FC</u>, because X's tendency to lose his temper and act violently is an essential element of V's suit—not against X, but against FC. To make out this claim against FC, V is required to produce evidence supporting the following elements:

---

4. Nor, if X is prosecuted for felonious assault, would a prosecutor be permitted to offer (a), (b) or (c) against X, unless X opened the door to such evidence. See § 6.13.

(1) FC gave a firearm and ammunition to X.

(2) FC knew or should have known that X had a violent temper and had committed numerous acts of violence when angered.

(3) Therefore, it was negligent for FC to give X possession of the firearm and ammunition.

(4) X shot V.

(5) X had no legal justification or excuse for doing so.

(6) V suffered damages for which FC should be required to compensate him.

The second element of V's action against FC *requires* him to prove aspects of X's character—that he often lost his temper and responded violently—or suffer a directed verdict in his negligent entrustment claim against FC.

As we saw in § 5.3, the relevant provisions in CEE cases are the unwritten sentence in Rule 404(a), which governs the admissibility of character evidence where character is an essential element of a claim or defense, and Rule 405(b), which governs evidence of extrinsic acts in such cases.

Evidence of X's reputation for losing his temper and acting violently certainly satisfies the Rule 404(a) unwritten requirement that the trait be "pertinent" to the cause of action.

Similarly, FRE 405(b) admits "relevant specific instances of conduct"—i.e., extrinsic acts (b) and (c)—that support the inference that X has a propensity to lose his temper and act violently.

So, in V's negligent entrustment suit against FC, all of the evidence V's attorney discovered about X, which is inadmissible against X, <u>is</u> admissible against FC.

If V sues X as well as FC, this raises an obvious problem: (a), (b) and (c) are all admissible against FC as proof of X's character for losing his temper and responding violently, but they are inadmissible—and highly prejudicial—against X. A judge could handle this in a variety of ways. She could sever the two trials, but that would prove very costly and time-consuming. She could let the evidence in, and instruct the jury not to consider it in deciding whose version (X's or V's) of the incident to believe, but only to consider it against FC—which would be absurd and impossible. Or she could bifurcate the trial: exclude the evidence until the jury reaches a verdict in V's suit against X, and if the jury finds for V, then allow V to offer the additional evidence against FC.

<u>Question 1.</u>

OK, so Rule 405(b) allows V to offer evidence of (b), X's two prior assaults (each of which resulted in a conviction). How, precisely, could V offer such evidence?

Answer:

Your first reaction might be, simply introduce court records of the convictions. Well, perhaps you can, but it depends. A court record such as a conviction is hearsay when offered to prove that X in fact committed those assaults. Thus, to determine whether such records are admissible, we would have to consult FRE 803(22).[5] Per that rule, the admissibility of a court record documenting a conviction depends on whether the convictions were for felonies or misdemeanors. The conviction for assaulting Black was a felony, so the court record of that conviction is admissible to prove that X committed the assault.[6] But the conviction for assaulting Blue was a misdemeanor, so the court record is not admissible. To offer evidence of the Blue assault, V would have to call Blue, or someone who witnessed it, to testify about it.

Question 2.

How could V offer evidence of (c), i.e., that a civil suit is pending regarding the bush and the fence?

Answer:

V could not offer evidence about the pending lawsuit.[7] But he could call the neighbor as a witness to testify about the facts—the fence, the bush, and X's chopping up the fence.

Two more points merit mention here briefly; we'll cover them in greater detail later.

First: reputation, opinion and specific extrinsic act evidence is admissible only where that evidence relates to a *pertinent* character trait. Evidence that X has been convicted three times for shoplifting would not be admissible, because shoplifting is a non-violent crime which tells us nothing about the likelihood that he acted violently after the fender-bender with V.

Second, since X's supposed character for losing his temper and for violence is an essential element of V's claim against FC, FC is entitled to offer reputation, opinion, or specific extrinsic act evidence suggesting that X is *not* hot-tempered and does *not* have a propensity toward violence. This

5. Have I mentioned that I am also the author of *A Student's Guide to Hearsay*? I have? Oh, good. FRE 803(22) is discussed in § 10.13 of that book.

6. If one of X's assault convictions was for a felony, X committed a federal felony merely taking possession of the handgun to deliver it to Buyer. If FC knew that X had a prior felony conviction, giving the handgun to X to deliver it was also a felony. See the discussion of *Old Chief v. U.S.*, § 3.6, *supra*.

7. The fact that someone is suing is not admissible to suggest that the facts alleged in the complaint are true, because such use would violate the rule against hearsay.

aspect of character evidence law occurs more often in criminal cases, so I am deferring discussion of it until then. See § 6.2 to § 6.13.

At the beginning of this section, I mentioned that there are two kinds of negligent entrustment actions: the first, illustrated above, arises when D gave something dangerous to someone, who used or misused it in a way that injured the plaintiff.

The second negligent entrustment situation arises when D appoints X to a position of authority. While exercising that authority, X injures P. P sues D, alleging that it was negligent of D to give X that authority. Example: D School hires X as a teacher or teacher's helper. X physically abuses several children in the school. Their parents discover that D never checked X's references before hiring X, and that X was fired from two other schools for abusing children. The parents have a negligent entrustment suit against D School, because D was negligent in failing to check X's references before giving X access to and authority over the children at the school.

§ 5.5 Child custody litigation

Character is also an essential element in child custody litigation. Ostensibly, the issue in such litigation is which parent will be the better custodian for the child. In practice, the trial often deteriorates into a mudslinging contest, each side trying to prove that the other is worse. Since virtually every trait of character is pertinent to being a good (or bad) parent, such suits will rarely give the observer an exalted view of humanity.

And sometimes, traits of character that are good in some contexts may be not-so-much in family court. Suppose X and Y are divorcing, and each wants to be the primary custodial parent for their 4-year-old. X works for a marketing firm. At the child-custody trial or hearing, Y offers in evidence a properly authenticated copy of an employee evaluation form filled out about X by X's supervisor.[8] The supervisor wrote:

> X's dedication to the company is exemplary. X is a perfectionist determined to make the best possible impression for us. Weeks before a recent presentation to potential clients, X was in the office at 7 a.m. and frequently did not leave until 7:30 p.m. or later. X has earned a significant year-end bonus and should be fast-tracked for greater and greater responsibilities.

This contains both opinion evidence of X's value as an employee ("exemplary ... determined ... earned significant bonus ... should be fast-tracked") and examples of extrinsic conduct ("in the office at 7 a.m.... until 7:30 p.m. or later").

---

8. Assume that it qualifies as a business record per FRE 803(6), which is covered in *A Student's Guide to Hearsay*, § 9.20–9.37.

If you were a family court judge charged with deciding whether X or Y should have primary custody of a 4-year-old, would this trait of X's character weigh in favor of X, or against X? If I were the judge, I'd wonder: if X is this career-obsessed, who is going to get the kid up and breakfasted and ready for pre-school in the morning? Who is going to make the kid dinner and play with the kid and tuck him in at night?

§ 5.6 Personal injury and wrongful death actions—damages

In personal injury actions where plaintiff seeks to recover compensation for loss of ability to earn an income, a factfinder must estimate what that income would have been but for the injury. This necessarily requires consideration of aspects of plaintiff's character and habits that would have affected plaintiff's earning power.

Please understand: the plaintiff's character is <u>not</u> an essential element with regard to whether or not the defendant was culpable in causing plaintiff's injury. Reputation and opinion evidence about the plaintiff would not be admissible in the liability stage of the trial; nor would evidence of extrinsic specific acts by the plaintiff (unless the case comes within FRE 404(b)(2), which is covered in Chapter 7).

Similarly, in assessing damages in a wrongful death action, the jury attempts to put a dollar figure on the value of decedent's life to the plaintiffs. This has two components: financial, and non-financial. Evidence of decedent's character, and extrinsic acts demonstrating the decedent's earning power, are therefore admissible. Similarly, reputation and opinion evidence about what kind of wife X was—loving and supportive, or suspicious and angry—and specific acts illustrating character as a wife and mother (if she was a mother), are therefore admissible on that issue. Defendants as well as plaintiffs are permitted to offer relevant evidence about the decedent with regard to the decedent's character as an earner, and as a wife, mother, and loving child of her parents (if they are still alive).

§ 5.7 Defamation

Dill and JD, a lawyer, became embroiled in a bitter dispute (unrelated to legal matters). Trying to hurt JD, Dill tells several people that "JD is a crooked lawyer. She bribes witnesses, and she steals money from her clients!" JD learns what Dill has been saying about her, and sues Dill for defamation of character. To prevail, JD must prove the following:

1. That Dill uttered the words in question and communicated them to others. Witnesses will testify that they heard Dill make these statements.
2. That the words were not true.
3. That JD had a good reputation before Dill slandered her. JD will call witnesses to testify about what others said and thought about her before Dill's accusation.

4. That Dill's slander damaged JD's reputation.

Focus on the second element. Dill's accusations are a direct attack on JD's character: he accuses JD of being "crooked," of bribing and stealing. Thus, JD's character for honesty and truthfulness are essential elements of JD's claim against Dill. Therefore, per the unwritten sentence in Rule 404, she is entitled to offer reputation and opinion testimony about her honesty and integrity. Per Rule 405(b), JD can also call former clients to testify about how meticulous and scrupulous JD was in handling their assets.

Dill can defend the suit by calling witnesses who would give negative reputation or opinion testimony about JD's character for honesty, and who would testify about instances in which JD allegedly cheated clients and stole their money.

Change the facts. The original dispute involved Pickle and Dill. The case went to trial, and Pickle won. Furious, Dill tells people, "It's because JD, Pickle's lawyer, bribed the key witness and also bribed two jurors." When JD learns what Dill said, she sues for defamation. To prevail, JD must prove the following:

1. That Dill uttered the words in question and communicated them to others. Witnesses will testify that they heard Dill make these statement.
2. That the words were not true.
3. That JD had a good reputation before Dill slandered her. JD will call witnesses to testify about what others said and thought about her before Dill's accusation.
4. That Dill's slander damaged JD's reputation.

As far as issues and evidence is concerned, is this case any different from the first one?

Yes.

Here's where it gets tricky, and unless your evidence professor discusses defamation as an example of character-as-essential-element in some detail, it is probably safe to skip the rest of this section.

Focus again on the second element of JD's defamation action. In some jurisdictions, at least, Dill's accusation—that JD bribed a witness and two jurors in one particular lawsuit—is not considered a general attack on JD's character;[9] it is merely an accusation that in one particular case, JD committed three dishonest and unlawful acts of bribery. Therefore, the argument goes, JD is not entitled to call reputation and opinion witnesses to testify as to JD's good character, as evidence that JD did

9. Realistically, of course, it *is* an attack on her character, but at least in some jurisdictions, the law does not consider it as such.

not engage in the specific wrongdoing that Dill alleged. Nor can JD offer testimony about specific instances of JD's honesty and integrity.

Similarly, Dill is also precluded from offering reputation or opinion testimony about JD's general character, nor may he offer evidence of specific extrinsic acts by JD that would reflect negatively on her character.

But, assuming the jury (without considering reputation or opinion testimony about JD's character) decides that Dill's accusations were false, both sides still can offer reputation and opinion evidence about JD's reputation before and after Dill's statements, because that is one way a jury measures damages in defamation cases.

As I said a few paragraphs ago, this intersection between defamation and evidence law is quite tricky, and unless your evidence professor dwells on it, I wouldn't spend too much time on it.

§ 5.8 FRE 405(a)(2nd sentence): cross-examining a character witness

The second sentence of FRE 405(a) provides that after a character witness has given reputation or opinion testimony about X, "On cross-examination of the character witness, the court may allow an inquiry into relevant specific instances of the person's conduct." This would be a logical place to discuss that provision, but I am deferring that discussion to § 6.14 to § 6.24, in the context of character evidence in criminal cases.

§ 5.9 Character as "Essential Element": criminal cases

As a practical matter, a defendant's character is *never* an essential element of a crime or a defense to a crime. A prosecutor is never legally required to offer reputation or opinion evidence about a defendant's character. To establish the defendant's guilt, the prosecutor need only prove that the defendant engaged in the specific acts charged in the indictment, and did so with the requisite mental state. Similarly, a defendant is never obliged to prove his good character to make out a defense. All that is required is that the jury be left with a reasonable doubt as to whether he engaged in the conduct charged, or whether he did so with the requisite mental state.

Similarly, the victim or complainant's character is never an essential element of a crime or defense to a crime.[10]

---

10. Theoretically, of course, a crime could be defined in a way that made someone's character an essential element. The Advisory Committee Note offers the illustration of "the chastity of the victim under a statute specifying her chastity as an element in the crime of seduction." I doubt if anyone has been prosecuted for that "crime" for many decades, or even if it is still on the books. (It *is* a crime to have sex with someone who lacks the mental ability to give lawful consent, but that

Entrapment. When a defendant asserts the defense of entrapment, he concedes that he engaged in the conduct in question, but claims he did so only after unfair and improper inducement by law enforcement authorities. It is sometimes said that character is an essential element in the defense of entrapment. This is incorrect. Under the subjective approach to entrapment followed by the federal courts and in a substantial number of states, to establish entrapment, the defendant must establish that, until the government began its campaign of inducement, the defendant had no *predisposition* to commit that type of crime. *Jacobson v. United States,* 503 U.S. 540 (1992). Clearly, evidence of prior *specific* acts similar to those currently charged is highly probative of the defendant's predisposition, and such evidence is unquestionably admissible. Thus, for example, where a defendant is accused of selling narcotics to a government informant, evidence that he sold drugs on other prior unrelated occasions is admissible to rebut his entrapment defense.[11] But some courts hold that a prosecutor should not be permitted to offer general character evidence (e.g., a witness who would testify that the defendant has the reputation of being a drug pusher) as evidence of the defendant's predisposition to sell drugs.

§ 5.10 Questions

Questions 1–5 relate to the investor-investment counselor litigation described in § 4.2, *supra.*

Question 1.

a. Is P's character an essential element of P's claim against D?

b. Is D's character an essential element of P's claim against D?

c. Is P's character an essential element of D's defense to P's claim?

d. Is D's character an essential element of D's defense to P's claim?

Answer:

No; no; no; and no.

The elements of P's claim against D are set out in ¶ 1 in § 4.2. Each element relates to what P said to D and how D responded; and what D knew at the time about ABC.

---

lack of capacity is considered an aspect of the complainant/victim's mental or medical "condition" or status, not "character.")

11. The degree to which the extrinsic acts must resemble the charged act can sometimes raise problems. Consider *People v. Placek,* 184 Ill. 2d 370, 704 N.E.2d 393 (1998). At defendant's trial for selling cocaine, the state introduced evidence that (a) he also had marijuana in his possession, and (b) he regularly trafficked in stolen auto parts. The court held that possession of marijuana is similar enough to selling cocaine to be admissible to show a predisposition to commit the latter crime (a conclusion with which many would plausibly disagree); but that trafficking in stolen auto parts is not: it shows only a predisposition to commit crimes in general, which is not a valid theory of relevance to disprove entrapment.

The substantive law governing that lawsuit does not require P to prove anything about his own character; nor does it require P to prove anything about D's character.

Similarly, D's defense is, simply, that P's version of what P and D said to each other about investing and about ABC is untrue. That defense does not require D to prove anything about his character, or about P's.

Therefore, neither party's character is an element of P's claim or D's defense.

Question 2.

P wishes to call W1, who will testify that D's reputation among investment counselors is that of a man who would lie to a client to further his own financial position.

a. Is the offer character evidence or extrinsic act evidence?

b. Based on the discussion of Rules 404 and 405 up to this point, is the evidence admissible?

Answer:

This is character evidence (i.e., reputation testimony), and because D's character for dishonesty is not an essential element of P's cause of action against D, this evidence is excluded by Rule 404(a)(1).

Question 3.

P seeks to call W2, an investment counselor with whom P has done business. W2 will, if permitted, testify that P has always been a cautious, conservative investor.

a. Is the offer character evidence or extrinsic act evidence?

b. Based on the discussion of Rules 404 and 405 up to this point, is the evidence admissible?

Answer:

This is character evidence: W2 is being asked to give his opinion about an aspect of P's character (what kind of investor P is). Even though W2's opinion is probably based on several extrinsic acts (i.e., on several occasions where P and W2 discussed investment strategy, and on investments P did or did not make), W2 is not being asked to describe one or more instances in which P sought or accepted investment advice from W2; rather, W2 is summarizing his experience with P's investment strategy by expressing an opinion of that aspect of P's character or a trait of that character.

Because P's character for cautious investing is not an essential element of P's cause of action against D, this evidence is excluded by Rule 404(a)(1).

Question 4.

After P rests his case, D seeks to call W3, who will, if permitted, testify as to D's excellent reputation for honesty in the financial community.

a. Is the offer character evidence or extrinsic act evidence?

b. Based on the discussion of Rules 404 and 405 up to this point, is the evidence admissible?

Answer:

This is character evidence in the form of reputation testimony. Because D's character for honesty is not an essential element of D's defense, the testimony is excluded by Rule 404(a)(1).

Question 5.

In addition, D seeks to elicit testimony from W4, another investment counselor, who will, if permitted, testify that a few days before P went to D for investment advice, P had sought investment advice from W4 but then rejected that advice, telling W4, "You're too cautious and stodgy; I'm looking to make a big killing quickly."

a. Is the offer character evidence or extrinsic act evidence?

b. Based on the discussion of Rules 404 and 405 up to this point, is the evidence admissible?

Answer:

This is extrinsic act evidence, i.e., it tells how P acted on one specific occasion. Based on the discussion of Rules 404 and 405 up to this point, is appears that it would be excluded by Rule 404(b)(1). But we haven't covered Rule 404(b)(2) yet, so let's not jump to conclusions.

Question 6.

Dribble belongs to the same social group as Turnover, who, on several occasions, became noticeably intoxicated at social events attended by Dribble. Turnover was involved in two prior auto collisions within the last fourteen months while under the influence of alcohol. On March 1, Dribble loaned his car to Turnover. Turnover got drunk and collided with Pointguard. Turnover is unemployed and uninsured (i.e., Turnover would not be able to pay a judgment against him in favor of Pointguard), so Pointguard files an action against Dribble. What cause of action should Pointguard bring?

Answer:

Pointguard should sue Dribble for negligently entrusting his car to Turnover (see § 5.4), asserting that Dribble knew or should have known that Turnover frequently drove while under the influence of alcohol.

Question 7.

How would Pointguard attempt to prove the underlying facts in support of the cause-of-action? What Federal Rule of Evidence would Pointguard rely on for admission of the supporting evidence?

Answer:

Pointguard could call witnesses who observed Turnover's conduct at the social events mentioned earlier, and ask those witnesses to describe how much alcohol Turnover drank and how Turnover behaved after consuming several drinks. Pointguard would also ask these witnesses whether Dribble was present on occasions when Turnover was visibly intoxicated. This testimony would be admissible per Rule 405(b), because the testimony relates extrinsic specific instances of Turnover's conduct which demonstrated Turnover's propensity to drink too much, and also show that Dribble was aware, or should have been aware, of this aspect of Turnover's character.

Pointguard could also call witnesses who know Turnover and ask their opinion as to whether Turnover had a drinking problem and whether that was obvious to people who attended parties and other events with Turnover. These witnesses could also testify that Turnover had a reputation of being someone who drank too much and could not "hold his liquor."[12]

Regarding Turnover's two prior DUI collisions: Pointguard would have to call the other motorists or other eyewitnesses to testify about how the collisions occurred and how Turnover's post-collision behavior demonstrated that he was under the influence. If a police officer came to the scene and administered a blood-alcohol content test, the officer could testify as to the results. Police reports about the incident would be admissible only if those reports overcame a hearsay objection.[13]

Question 8.

On March 10, 2021, Pencil and Drawback are involved in an automobile collision on Coolidge Road, and Pencil sues, alleging negligence. At trial, Pencil calls W1, who will testify that on October 1, 2020, Drawback sideswiped W1's car on Harding Avenue. What does P hope to prove with this testimony? Is W1's testimony admissible? Why?

Answer:

Pencil is hoping to prove that Drawback has a propensity to drive negligently on roads named after post-World War I Republican presidents. W1's testimony should be excluded per Rule 404(b)(1).

Question 9.

X was killed in an auto collision, and H, her husband, brought a wrongful death action against D, the other driver. D asserts that the collision was X's fault, not D's.

---

12. In case you are unfamiliar with the expression, a person ("X") is able to "hold his (or her) liquor" if X is able to consume alcohol but without it substantially changing X's behavior or judgment or overtly impairing X physically.

13. For a discussion of the admissibility of public records (including police reports) in civil litigation, see *A Student's Guide to Hearsay* § 9.39-§ 9.48). (End of commercial.)

During H's case in chief, H calls HW1, who will, if permitted, testify that he was X's supervisor at work, and that X, who had joined HW1's marketing firm a few months before the collision, "was a real hard worker and had a great feel and talent for marketing."

During D's case in chief, D calls DW1, who will, if permitted, testify that he knew X for many years, and that "although X was a lovely person, she was a lousy driver—she often failed to pay attention to where she was going, missing stop signs and so on."

Assuming each witness establishes a proper foundation for his testimony,

A) HW1's testimony should be admitted, but DW1's testimony should not.

B) DW1's testimony should be admitted, but HW1's testimony should not.

C) Both DW1's testimony and HW1's testimony should be admitted.

D) Neither DW1's testimony nor HW1's testimony should be admitted.

Answer:

HW1's testimony is not even relevant, let alone admissible, as to which motorist, X or D, was at fault. But a suit for wrongful death seeks compensation for (among other things) the monetary loss the plaintiff suffers from the death of the decedent. HW1's testimony consists of HW1's opinion of X's professional skills and, inferentially, her potential earning power which is now lost to H and H and X's children, if any. Since X's earning potential is an important component as to the damages element of a wrongful death action, H is required to offer evidence on that issue. Therefore HW1's testimony comes within the "unwritten sentence" in Rule 404(a), and is admissible.

DW1's testimony is highly relevant as to whether X or D was at fault in causing the fatal collision. But X's character as a careful or careless driver is not an essential element of H's claim or D's defense. Neither H nor D is *required* by law to offer evidence of a trait of X's "character" of being a careful or inattentive driver. Hence, DW1's testimony falls squarely within the prohibition of Rule 404(a)(1), and must be excluded.

Therefore, the correct answer is A.

Chapter 6

Rules 404(a) and 405(a): Character as Circumstantial Evidence of Conduct

§ 6.1 Overview

In § 4:6, we saw that FRE 404(a)(1) states a general rule of exclusion: "Evidence of a person's character or character trait is not admissible to prove that on a particular occasion the person acted in accordance with that character or trait." That is why in civil litigation, except where a person's character is an essential element of a claim or defense, reputation or opinion evidence about that person's character is never admissible.

Rule 404(a)(2), however, creates two exceptions in *criminal* cases: the defendant has the option to unlock the otherwise locked doors to character evidence.

i. The defendant's character

Rule 404(a)(2)(A) and Rule 405(a)(1st sentence) entitle the defendant (D) to offer character evidence about himself, herself or theirself: D may call witnesses to give favorable reputation or opinion testimony (or both) about a pertinent trait of D's character, as evidence that D is not the kind of person who would commit the crime for which D is on trial. Such testimony is relevant, because it has some tendency to make it less probable that D committed the conduct D is charged with. Or, if D concedes having engaged in the conduct in question, D may offer reputation or opinion testimony that tends to make it less probable that D did so with the criminal intent (mens rea) specified in the definition of the crime.

If D offers such evidence, the prosecutor may respond in two ways. First, Rule 405(a)(2nd sentence) entitles the prosecutor to cross-examine D's character witnesses about "relevant specific instances of [D's] conduct." Second, after D rests, in rebuttal, Rule 404(a)(2)(A) and 405(a) (1st sentence) permit the prosecutor to call witnesses to give negative reputation or opinion testimony about the same trait of D's character. Defense counsel can then cross-examine the prosecution's negative character witnesses about "relevant specific instances of [D's] conduct."

ii. The alleged victim's character

Similarly, Rule 404(a)(2)(B) and Rule 405(a)(1st sentence) allow the defendant to offer reputation or opinion evidence about a pertinent trait of the alleged victim's character. The prosecutor's options and the defense response to what the prosecutor does follows the same pattern as described in the previous paragraph, but with certain restrictions and complications.

iii. Defendant alone holds the keys

It is important to remember that in each case (the defendant's character and the alleged victim's character), the prosecutor is not allowed to offer such evidence unless the defense first opens the door. When the defense calls a witness to give reputation or opinion testimony about D or about the victim or alleged victim, that automatically opens the door to the prosecutor's right to respond. As to what other trial tactics or mistakes might open the door, see § 6.13.

A. The Defendant's Character

---

§ 6.2 *Michelson v. U.S.*

Michelson v. United States, 335 U.S. 469, 69 S.Ct. 213, 93 L.Ed. 168 (1948), is still the leading case. If *Michelson* is in the casebook your professor uses, you have already read the lengthy passage from that opinion that constitutes the bulk of this section. It is worth careful reading again.

Background: Charged in 1947 with offering a bribe to an Internal Revenue Service agent, Michelson asserted the defense of entrapment, and called several character witnesses in support, each of whom testified that Michelson's reputation for honesty was good. On cross-examination, the prosecutor asked each of these witnesses whether he or she had heard "that on October 11th, 1920, the defendant, Solomon Michelson, was arrested for receiving stolen goods?" None of the witnesses had heard about this arrest. Following his conviction, Michelson appealed, claiming that allowing this cross-examination of those witnesses constituted reversible error.

The Supreme Court denied Michelson's appeal and upheld his conviction. In so doing, the Court summarized and explained the "logic" underlying the law.[1] That passage is reproduced below, with the following caveats:

First caveat: when *Michelson* was decided, the law permitted character evidence only in the form of reputation testimony. I have edited the passage to incorporate opinion testimony as well, and to insert references to FRE 404(a)(2)(A) and FRE

---

1. "'Curiouser and curiouser,' cried Alice." Lewis Carroll, *The Adventures of Alice in Wonderland* chapter 2.

405(a), which were not enacted until 25 years after *Michelson* was decided. These inserts and revisions in the passage from *Michelson* are clearly offset by the use of [brackets].

Second caveat: I have broken up the passage into numbered paragraphs to make it easier for me to refer back to the case in later sections of this chapter. For the same reason, I have broken some paragraphs in the opinion into several paragraphs. So do *not* quote the passage as it appears here in an exam answer or brief. Note: The bracketed numbers do *not* correspond to a certain Other Publisher's headnotes. They are my own insertions. I will refer to them hereinafter as Cliffnotes.—What? Yet another publisher has trademarked that term? Drat! All right, then; I'll call them "fishnotes."

Here is the passage:

> [1] Courts... disallow resort by the prosecution to [introduce] any kind of evidence of a defendant's evil character to establish a probability of his guilt. [This principle is now codified in Rule 404(a)(2)(A), which precludes the prosecutor from being the first to offer character evidence about a defendant, and by Rule 404(b)(1), which precludes a litigant from offering evidence of a person's extrinsic acts to support the inference that the person has a propensity to act that way.]
>
> [2] The inquiry is not rejected because character is irrelevant; on the contrary, it is said to weigh too much with the jury and to so over-persuade them as to prejudge one with a bad general record and deny him a fair opportunity to defend against a particular charge. The overriding policy of excluding such evidence, despite its admitted probative value, is the practical experience that its disallowance tends to prevent confusion of issues, unfair surprise and undue prejudice.
>
> [3] But this line of inquiry firmly denied to the State is opened to the defendant because character is relevant in resolving probabilities of guilt. He may introduce affirmative testimony that [his character is so good] that the jury may infer that he would not be likely to commit the offense charged....
>
> [4] [The court discussed the limits on and the required foundation for such testimony. FRE 404(a)(2)(A) and FRE 405(a)(1st sentence) limit such testimony to reputation or opinion testimony. The foundational requirements for reputation testimony are set out in § 6.8; for opinion testimony, see § 6.9.]
>
> [5] ... [T]he witness must qualify to give an opinion by showing such acquaintance with the defendant, the community in which he has lived and the circles in which he has moved, as to speak with authority of the terms in which generally he is regarded. [The foundation required to entitle

a witness to testify about the defendant's reputation is discussed in § 6.8. The foundation for opinion testimony is discussed in § 6.9. A single witness can give both types of testimony, so long as defense counsel first elicits testimony from the witness that satisfies the foundation for both.]

[6] [The character witness is permitted to say] that he has "heard nothing against defendant" ... upon assumption that, if no ill is reported of one, his reputation must be good. But this answer is accepted only from a witness whose knowledge of defendant's habitat and surroundings is intimate enough so that his failure to hear of any relevant ill repute is an assurance that no ugly rumors were about.

[7] Thus the law extends helpful but illogical options to a defendant. Experience taught a necessity that they be counterweighted with equally illogical conditions to keep the advantage from becoming an unfair and unreasonable one. The price a defendant must pay for attempting to prove his good [character] is to throw open the entire subject which the law has kept closed for his benefit and to make himself vulnerable where the law otherwise shields him.

[8] The prosecution may pursue the inquiry with contradictory witnesses [as per FRE 404(a)(2)(A)(final clause)].

[9] It may test the sufficiency of [the defense character witness's] knowledge by asking what stories were circulating concerning events, such as [the defendant's arrest on unrelated matters], about which people normally comment and speculate. [This principle is now codified in FRE 405(a)(2nd sentence).]

[10] Thus, while the law gives defendant the option to show as a fact that his [character] reflects a life and habit incompatible with commission of the offense charged, it subjects his proof to tests of credibility designed to prevent him from profiting by a mere parade of partisans.

[11] To thus digress from evidence as to the offense to hear a contest as to the standing of the accused, at its best opens a tricky line of inquiry as to a shapeless and elusive subject matter....

[12] Wide discretion is accompanied by heavy responsibility on trial courts to protect the practice from any misuse. The trial judge [in *Michelson*] was scrupulous to so guard it in the case before us. He took pains to ascertain, out of presence of the jury, that the target of the question [Michelson's arrest in a matter unrelated to the current charge] was an actual event, which would probably result in some comment among acquaintances if not injury to defendant's reputation. He satisfied himself that counsel was not merely taking a random shot at a reputation imprudently exposed or asking a groundless question to waft an unwarranted innuendo into the jury box.

[13] [In a footnote, the Court added:] [The] law on this subject has evolved from pragmatic considerations rather than from theoretical consistency. The relevant information that it is permissible to lay before the jury is talk or conversation about the defendant's being arrested. That is admissible whether or not an actual arrest had taken place; it might even be more significant of repute if his neighbors were ready to arrest him in rumor when the authorities were not in fact. But before this relevant and proper inquiry can be made, [the prosecutor] must demonstrate privately to the court an irrelevant and possibly unprovable [I think the Court meant "inadmissible"] fact—the reality of arrest. From this permissible inquiry about reports of arrest, the jury is pretty certain to infer that defendant had in fact been arrested and to draw its own conclusions as to character from that fact.... [Requiring the prosecutor to establish to the judge that Michelson had been arrested in the past] limits legally relevant inquiries to those based on legally irrelevant facts in order that the legally irrelevant conclusion which the jury probably will draw from the relevant questions will not be based on unsupported or untrue innuendo. It illustrates Judge [Learned] Hand's suggestion that the system may work best when explained least. [D]espite its theoretical paradoxes and deficiencies, we approve the procedure as calculated in practice to hold the inquiry within decent bounds.

[14] The question permitted by the trial court, however, involves several features that may be worthy of comment. Its form invited hearsay; it asked about an arrest, not conviction, and for an offense not closely similar to the one on trial; and it concerned an occurrence many years past.

[15] [The Court noted the then-prevailing view that the prosecution could word the question, "Have you heard?" but not "Do you know?" That distinction made sense when the witness could only testify as to the defendant's reputation, but not give his own opinion of the defendant's character. Because FRE 405(a) permits opinion testimony as well, "Did you know" is now also a permissible way to ask the question.]

[16] A character witness may be cross-examined as to an arrest whether or not it culminated in a conviction, according to the overwhelming weight of authority.[2]

---

2. The Court added: "This rule is sometimes confused with that which prohibits cross-examination to credibility by asking a witness whether he himself has been arrested." Cross-examining a witness about his or her own convictions is regulated by FRE 609. That rule is covered in § 13.10 to § 13.29.—Cross-examining a witness about his or her own prior alleged wrongdoings that did not result in conviction is regulated by FRE 608(b). See § 13.2 to § 13.9.

> [17] Arrest without more does not, in law any more than in reason, impeach the integrity or impair the credibility of a witness. It happens to the innocent as well as the guilty. Only a conviction, therefore, may be inquired about to undermine the trustworthiness of a witness.
>
> [18] Arrest without more may nevertheless impair or cloud one's reputation. False arrest may do that. Even to be acquitted may damage one's good name if the community receives the verdict with a wink and chooses to remember defendant as one who ought to have been convicted. A conviction, on the other hand, may be accepted as a misfortune or an injustice, and even enhance the standing of one who mends his ways and lives it down. Reputation is the net balance of so many debits and credits that the law does not attach the finality to a conviction when the issue is reputation, that is given to it when the issue is the credibility of the convict.
>
> [19] The inquiry as to an arrest is permissible also because the prosecution has a right to test the qualifications of the witness to bespeak the community opinion. If one never heard the speculations and rumors in which even one's friends indulge upon his arrest, the jury may doubt whether he is capable of giving any very reliable conclusions as to his reputation [or as to the witness's own opinion about the defendant's character].

The Court also observed that while receiving stolen goods did not have all that much in common with bribing an IRS agent, that did not render the cross-examination improper:

> [20] The good character which the defendant had sought to establish was broader than the crime charged and included the traits of "honesty and truthfulness" and "being a law-abiding citizen." Possession of these characteristics would seem as incompatible with offering a bribe to a revenue agent as with receiving stolen goods. The crimes may be unlike, but both alike proceed from the same defects of character which the witnesses said this defendant was reputed not to exhibit. It is not only by comparison with the crime on trial but by comparison with the reputation asserted that a court may judge whether the prior arrest should be made subject of inquiry. By this test the inquiry was permissible. It was proper cross-examination because reports of his arrest for receiving stolen goods, if admitted, would tend to weaken the assertion that he was known as an honest and law-abiding citizen.

Our next step is to examine how FRE 404–405 have revised and codified the law set out in this passage.

1. Defense evidence: restrictions and requirements

§ 6.3 Rules 404(a)(2)(A); 405(a)

Here is the text of the rules that apply when a defendant offers character evidence:

> **Rule 404. Character Evidence; Other Crimes, Wrongs or Acts**
>
> (a) **Character Evidence.**
>
> (1) **Prohibited Uses.** Evidence of a person's character or character trait is not admissible to prove that on a particular occasion the person acted in accordance with the character or trait.
>
> (2) **Exceptions for a Defendant or Victim in a Criminal Case.** The following exceptions apply in a criminal case:
>
> (A) a defendant may offer evidence of the defendant's pertinent trait, and if the evidence is admitted, the prosecutor may offer evidence to rebut it; ...
>
> **Rule 405. Methods of Proving Character**
>
> (a) **By Reputation or Opinion.** When evidence of a person's character or character trait is admissible, it may be proved by testimony about the person's reputation or by testimony in the form of an opinion. On cross-examination of the character witness, the court may allow an inquiry into relevant specific instances of the person's conduct.

Here is the by-now-familiar chart dividing Rules 404 and 405 into provisions governing character evidence, and provisions governing evidence of extrinsic acts. I have underlined the provisions that apply when a defendant offers evidence about his own character.

Character evidence

~~404a unwritten sentence: CEE~~	
404a1	general prohibition
Exceptions:	
404a2A	(about D)
404a2B	(by D about V/AV)
404a2B(i)	(by Pr about V/AV)
404a2B(ii)	(by Pr about D)
404aC	(by Pr about D in homicide cases)

Extrinsic act evidence

404b(1):	general rule of exclusion
404(b)(2):	rule of inclusion
405a(1st sent.)	(re D or V/AV)
405a(2nd sent.)	(re D or V/AV)
~~405b CEE~~	

Abbreviations:

CEE	character as essential element (not applicable in criminal cases)
D	Defendant
V/AV	Victim or alleged victim
Pr	Prosecutor

The following chart may also prove helpful:

> *Character as "circumstantial evidence of conduct": **defendant's character** (criminal cases)*
>
> a. Character evidence
>
> (1) Rule 404(a)(2)(A): D can offer general evidence of a "pertinent" trait of D's character. If D does so, so may P.
>
> (2) Rule 405(a)(1st sentence): such evidence may be offered through either reputation or opinion testimony (or both).
>
> b. Extrinsic act evidence:
>
> (1) Rule 404(b)(1) says evidence of D's extrinsic acts may not be offered for this purpose.
>
> (2) Rule 404(b)(2) ("other purposes": see chapter 7).
>
> (3) 405(a)(2nd sentence) regulates cross-examination of a witness who has been called to give character evidence about D: on XX only, W may be asked about "relevant specific instances of [D's] conduct."
>
> (4) Rule 405(b) is inapplicable, because D's character is not an "essential element" of the crime or defense.

I have underlined the rules that govern evidence about a defendant's character or a trait of his character.

Note: the rules covered in Chapters 4 through 13 apply in eight different courtroom scenarios, which I refer to as "litigation situations." In § 11.23 to § 11.31, I summarize each litigation situation and list the rules that apply in that litigation situation. The litigation situation sections of this book provide you with a brief review of each situation after we have covered each in depth. The scenario here—D offering evidence of his or her good character—is litigation situation B; see § 11.25.

§ 6.4 Impact of character evidence; jury instruction

For a time, there was uncertainty about how a judge should instruct the jury as to the impact of character testimony. Some argued that a judge should instruct a jury that evidence of the defendant's good character, standing alone, may be sufficient to create a reasonable doubt. But if that was once the law, it no longer is. The following instruction, published by the Third Circuit, is typical:

> **4.39 Defendant's Character Evidence**
>
> You have heard (reputation)(opinion)(reputation and opinion) evidence about whether the defendant has a character trait for (name trait, such as truthfulness, peacefulness, honesty, being a law-abiding citizen, etc.).

> You should consider this character evidence together with and in the same way as all the other evidence in the case in deciding whether the government has proved the charge(s) beyond a reasonable doubt.[3]

In other words, good character is not a defense, per se; rather, evidence of the defendant's character is simply that: evidence that has some tendency to make the defendant's guilt less probable than it would be without the evidence.

Instructing a jury about a prosecutor's cross-examination of a character witness is more complicated. That subject is covered in § 6.23.

§ 6.5 Rule 404(a)(2)(A): procedure and requirements

D is charged with a crime. After each attorney makes an opening statement, the prosecutor presents the state's "case in chief." The prosecutor is not allowed to present any "character evidence" about the defendant during its case-in-chief, i.e., cannot call witnesses to testify about the defendant's reputation, nor call witnesses to express an opinion about the defendant's character.[4]

In every criminal trial, once the prosecutor rests, the defendant moves for a directed verdict (sometimes called a motion for a judgment of acquittal). This requires the judge to decide whether, based on the state's evidence, a rational jury could find that the prosecutor has proved every element of the crime beyond a reasonable doubt.

If the judge denies the defendant's motion, the defense may present evidence that challenges the state's evidence. This includes character evidence.

A defendant's right to offer character evidence is subject to the following restrictions.

1. It must be about a <u>pertinent trait</u> of the defendant's character. See § 6.6.
2. It must be restricted to <u>reputation or opinion testimony</u>, not evidence of the defendant's extrinsic acts. See § 6.7.
3. Before a witness can testify about the defendant's <u>reputation</u>, he or she must lay a <u>foundation</u> establishing that the witness is qualified to give such testimony. See § 6.8.

---

3. Mod. Crim. Jury Instr. 3d Cir. 4.39 (2020).

4. It is sometimes argued that if the defense informs the jury (during jury selection or in an opening statement) that the defense will present character evidence, the prosecutor may offer negative character (i.e., reputation or opinion) testimony about the defendant during the government's case-in-chief. Unless your professor mentions this, ignore that arcane wrinkle. Whether the prosecutor may offer evidence of extrinsic acts depends on whether the evidence falls within FRE 404(b)(1) or FRE 404(b)(2), covered in Chapter 7.

4. Before a witness can give his or her own <u>opinion</u> about the defendant's character, he or she must lay a <u>foundation</u> establishing that the witness is qualified to give such testimony. See § 6.9.
5. A defendant can also offer <u>expert testimony</u> about a defendant's character. See § 6.10.

§ 6.6 "Pertinent" trait

Rule 404(a)(2)(A) requires that the character trait to be testified about must be "pertinent" to the crime charged. For example, a defendant (D) charged with aggravated assault would be permitted to elicit testimony that D is a peaceful, non-violent person, because evidence that D is peaceful and non-violent tends to make it less probable that D committed a violent crime. But if D is charged with assault, D would not be permitted to elicit testimony concerning D's honesty with other people's money, since that is not "pertinent" to rebut an accusation of aggravated assault.

There is no one officially approved list of acceptable character traits, so defense counsel can be somewhat creative. For example, a man charged with sexually assaulting a woman could offer reputation or opinion evidence of his non-violent character, and could also elicit testimony about his respect for women.

Character evidence can be "pertinent" on the issue of identity, as evidence that the defendant did not commit the crime he is accused of. The reasoning is: "D is a peaceful, non-violent person, therefore it must have been someone else, not D, who assaulted the complainant."

Character evidence can also be "pertinent" where identity is not an issue, i.e., D acknowledges that he was involved or at the scene, but did not commit the act. Here, the reasoning is: "Yes, D was a guest in AV's home that afternoon, but AV is mistaken or lying when he accuses D of stealing silver candlesticks from AV's house. D's character for honesty demonstrates that he is not the kind of person who would do that."

Character evidence can also be "pertinent" where D acknowledges engaging in the conduct, but insists he or she did so without criminal content. Suppose, for example, D, an officer in a company, is indicted for inducing V to invest heavily in the company by deliberately lying to V about the company's financial situation. Her defense might be: "Yes, I told V that the company's finances were sound, because that's what I believed; I did not know at the time that higher-ups in the company had 'cooked the books' to hide how much money it owed." Evidence of D's character for honesty and truthfulness would be "pertinent" to rebut the mens rea element (that she said what she said with intent to defraud).[5]

---

5. But in a *civil* action against D (or against the company) for fraud, neither D nor the company could offer character testimony about D's honesty. Her character is not an "essential element" of V's

Usually, the character witness will testify about a positive trait of defendant's character—non-violence, peacefulness, truthfulness, sobriety, honesty. But less flattering traits might also be "pertinent" to a defense. A defendant charged with starting a fight might call a witness to testify about the defendant's "timidity and fear of conflict or confrontation."

Sometimes a character witness will testify about the defendant's character for being "law-abiding." That is broad enough to be pertinent against virtually any criminal charge, from homicide to littering. But it runs a risk: the broader the trait the witness ascribes to the defendant, the broader the scope of a prosecutor's cross-examination of the witness about the defendant, per Rule 405(a)(2nd sentence). See § 6.2, *Michelson* fishnote [20]. This is discussed in § 6.15, *infra*.

§ 6.7 Character evidence, yes; extrinsic acts, no (except, sometimes, indirectly)

If the defense attorney in a criminal case chooses to offer evidence to prove D's good character, FRE 404(a)(2)(A) and FRE 405(a)(1st) sentence) permit a defense character witness to do so via reputation or opinion testimony. FRE 404(b)(1), by contrast, precludes the defense from offering evidence of instances of D's specific conduct to illustrate D's good character.[6] Thus, witness DCW1[7] may testify to D's reputation for peacefulness and non-violence (if that trait is "pertinent" to the charges being tried). DCW1 may also express his or her own opinion that D is a peaceful and non-violent person. DCW1 may not, however, testify about specific instances during which D displayed his or her peaceful, non-violent character. Similarly, in a prosecution for submitting false statements to a government agency, defense witnesses may give reputation or opinion testimony concerning the defendant's character for truthfulness, but may not testify about other specific instances (unrelated to the events for which D is on trial) in which D was truthful even when such statements were contrary to D's own self-interest.

But sometimes, while laying the foundation for reputation or opinion testimony about the defendant's character, defense counsel can indirectly refer to favorable extrinsic acts. See § 6.8, *infra*.

claim, nor D's defense, nor the company's defense, and Rule 404(a)(2)(A) allows character evidence only in criminal cases, not in civil litigation.

6. A defendant is permitted to offer evidence of specific acts if that evidence has sufficient "other" factually specific relevance to be admissible per FRE 404(b)(2). That rule is covered in Chapter 7.

7. Defense character witness #1.

§ 6.8 Foundation for reputation testimony

A person's reputation is, in essence, what a group of people think or say about that person. Before a witness (W) is allowed to testify about defendant D's reputation in the community, defense counsel must establish that W is qualified to give such testimony. By means of structured direct examination, the witness must first satisfy these requirements.

1. W personally knows D.
2. W and D belong to the same "community" where the defendant is well-known. Traditionally, the "community" was restricted to the neighborhood in which the defendant lived. More recently, scholars have argued that a witness should also be permitted to testify about D's reputation in other "communities" in which D is well known, such as D's place of employment, where D worships, attends school, etc.
3. The community must be large enough and stable enough, and D must have been part of that community long enough, for that community's assessment of D's character to have probative value. If D works at a gas station with four employees, only two of whom have been there more than a few months, a judge might reasonably preclude testimony about D's reputation in that "community."
4. The testimony must relate to specific pertinent traits of D's character.
5. W must testify that he has in fact spoken to others in the community about that aspect of D's character.
6. W's testimony about D's reputation should relate to D's reputation at, roughly, the time D allegedly committed the crime for which D is on trial.

Direct examination of a reputation witness (DCW1) in an assault case, where the defense is mistaken identity, might go like this:

Q Please tell the court and jury your name, where you live, and your occupation.

A I am the minister of the [name of church].

Q Do you know my client, D?

A Yes, I've known him for about 15 years.

Q In what capacity do you know him?

A He was a member of the church when I became the minister there 15 years ago. He is a regular at sabbath services, we've served together on—oh, let's see, the social action committee, the neighborhood outreach committee, the building committee. Our families socialize frequently. Until my knee went bad, D and I used to go bike-riding together.

Q How large is the church? How many families belong?

A Oh, roughly 150 families.

Q Is D well-known to church members?

A Yes. As I said, he's regular on Sundays; he's served on lots of church committees besides the ones I already mentioned. He played on the church softball team for several years. When I'm away, D sometimes leads our worship.

Q Are you familiar with D's reputation for peacefulness and non-violence among the church membership?

A Yes, I am.

Q And what is that reputation?

A Excellent. He is known to be a peaceful, non-violent man.

Q On what do you base your conclusion?

A Well, first of all, I've had lots of conversations over the years with the members, and when D's name came up, nobody ever said anything to suggest that D might fly off the handle and hurt somebody like what happened to the victim in this case. And when we heard that D was arrested, it was like a total shock to everyone. People said things like, no, that can't be that's not D, he would never do such a thing. And then when you asked me to be a witness and to ask people about what they thought about D, was he a violent guy or not, everyone I spoke to said basically the same thing: "D couldn't have done it, he's such a peaceful, non-violent guy, there must be some mistake."

This direct examination is a bit more elaborate than most, and scores pretty much all the points the law allows.

Note that DCW1 has attested to D's good reputation in two different ways: by testifying to what "everybody says" about D, and by testifying (more persuasively, perhaps) that he has never heard anyone say anything bad about D's character for peacefulness. In *Michelson*, the Court explained why this is permitted. See § 6.2, *Michelson* fishnotes [6]–[7].

§ 6.9 Foundation for opinion testimony

Prior to enactment of the Federal Rules, only reputation testimony was permitted; a witness was not allowed to express his own opinion as to the defendant's character. Rule 405(a) rejects this restriction: opinion testimony is now permitted, provided that the witness demonstrates that he has a valid basis for his opinion.

As a rule, a witness would have to establish that he is well-acquainted with the defendant for a fairly lengthy period of time, and has had ample opportunity to observe the defendant display the character trait in question. The witness may not, however, testify to specific occasions on which the defendant demonstrated that character trait.

Assume, for example, that D is on trial for forging a check, and calls W, his employer, as a character witness. W would be permitted to testify that D has worked as a cashier in W's store for several years (thereby laying a foundation establishing that W is "qualified" to give opinion testimony about D's character), and that "in my opinion, D would never do anything dishonest," or that "in my opinion, D's character for honesty is good." W would not be permitted, however, to add that "on several occasions, when a customer forgot to take his change after making a purchase, D ran after the customer to give him his change."

By choosing the right witness and preparing the witness how to respond to certain questions, counsel can at least hint at or suggest extrinsic acts. In describing the community, for example, a witness may say "Yes, we both belong to the same church and are active in the committee to provide food and shelter to the poor," or "we volunteer together at the shelter for homeless women and children."

Note: when a character witness (CW) is testifying as to CW's opinion about D's character, the size or stability of a community is not relevant; what matters is whether CW has had sufficient contact with the defendant to have a basis to have an informed opinion about the defendant's character.

§ 6.10 Expert opinion testimony

Rule 405(a)(1st sentence) also permits a defendant to offer expert opinion testimony (usually that of a psychiatrist or psychologist) concerning pertinent traits of defendant's character. To lay a proper foundation, the witness ("XW") would have to establish his or her credentials as an expert (see FRE Article VII) and also establish that he or she has had sufficient exposure to the defendant (through interviews, testing and the like) to be knowledgeable about the defendant's character. For example, where a defendant pleads entrapment to a charge of selling drugs to an undercover officer, a psychiatrist should be permitted to testify concerning the defendant's unusual susceptibility to suggestion or manipulation.

But courts reject expert testimony as to whether a defendant fits within a "profile" of people who are, or are not, likely to commit particular kinds of crimes.[8]

---

8. In appropriate cases, an expert may testify that specific acts by D are consistent with how criminals prepare to commit a particular type of crime. For example, where D is charged with sexually molesting a child, courts generally permit an exert to testify that D's behavior toward and with that child during the weeks or months prior to the alleged molestation was consistent with the "grooming" process by which sexual predators gradually seduce children into acquiescing to the molestation. But "profile" evidence is quite different. A prosecutor should not be permitted to elicit expert testimony that sexual abusers of children frequently have certain common characteristics, and then offer evidence that D fits that profile. Nor should a defense attorney be permitted to elicit

§ 6.11 Questions

Question 1.

D is charged with the murder of V. At trial, the prosecutor calls PW1 who will testify that D has a reputation for being a wild and assaultive person.

a. What is the relevance of this testimony?

b. Is PW1's testimony admissible? Apply Rules 404(a), 404(b), 405(a), and 405(b).

Answer:

a. Relevance

To some extent, its relevance depends on the factual issue at trial. If the issue is who killed V, the evidence is relevant on the theory that, if D has a reputation for being "wild and assaultive," that makes it more probable than it would be without that evidence that D in fact is "wild and assaultive," which makes it more probable than it would be without the evidence that it was D, and not someone else, who killed V.

If D acknowledges that he killed V, but claims he did so in self-defense,[9] then the evidence is relevant to make it more probable that D was the initial aggressor and therefore did not act in self-defense.

So, the evidence is, in fact relevant. Not very, perhaps, but it has "some tendency" to make the ultimate fact of consequence—D's guilt—more probable than it would be without the evidence. See § 6.2, *Michelson* fishnote [2].

b. Admissibility

Is it admissible, per Rules 404(a), 404(b), 405(a), and 405(b)?

Reputation evidence is character evidence, so we can ignore Rules 404(b) and 405(b) and the second sentence of Rule 405(a), each of which deal with evidence of extrinsic acts.

Reputation is an acceptable form of character testimony, per Rule 405(a)(1st sentence), assuming PW1 has given testimony which satisfies the foundation for reputation testimony (see § 6.8). And the trait of being "wild and assaultive" is certainly a pertinent trait where D is charged with murder. But Rule 404(a)(2)(A) states:

> (A) a defendant may offer evidence of the defendant's pertinent trait, and if the evidence is admitted, the prosecutor may offer evidence to rebut it;...

---

such testimony and then offer evidence that D does not fit the profile. A "perpetrator profile" may be useful as an investigative tool; perhaps it may be considered—although never sufficient in and of itself—in determining whether an officer had probable cause to arrest or search. But "profile" testimony should not be admitted at a criminal trial as evidence of a defendant's guilt or innocence.

9. As you no doubt learned in your criminal law course, a person is justified in using deadly force to defend himself or a third person if he or she reasonably believed it was necessary to do so to protect him- or herself or the third person from the use of deadly force.

Remember: the door to evidence of the defendant's character is locked, and only the defendant has a key. The prosecutor cannot offer such evidence about a defendant unless the defendant has first unlocked the door. The usual way for a defendant to open the door is by calling one or more favorable character witnesses during the defense case-in-chief. That entitles the prosecutor to cross-examine the character witness, per Rule 405(a)(2nd sentence)—see § 6.14 to § 6.23, *infra*. Moreover, once a defendant has introduced favorable character evidence (i.e., reputation or opinion testimony), the prosecutor may offer negative character evidence about the defendant during the state's rebuttal (see § 6.24, *infra*). But unless and until a defendant first opens the door to evidence of his or her good character, the prosecutor may not pass through that doorway.

By the way, on an exam or quiz, it is probably enough to simply say "The evidence is inadmissible because Rule 404(a)(2)(A) does not permit the prosecutor to offer character evidence about D unless D has first offered such evidence." But this question, and others in this chapter, will ask you to apply all of the sub-provisions of FRE 404 and 405 as a way of helping you to become familiar with all aspects of those rules.

Question 2.

In the same trial, after the prosecution rests, D calls DCW1, who will testify that D has a reputation in his residential community for being a peaceful, non-assaultive person.

a. What does D hope to prove with this testimony, i.e., how is it relevant?
b. Is DCW1's testimony admissible? Apply FRE 404(a), FRE 404(b), FRE 405(a), and FRE 405(b).

Answer:

a. Relevance

If the issue is, who killed V, the evidence is relevant on the theory that, if D has a reputation for being "peaceful and non-assaultive," that makes it more probable than it would be without that evidence that D in fact is "peaceful and non-assaultive," which makes it less probable than it would be without the evidence that D killed V.

If D acknowledges that he killed V, but claims he did so in self-defense, then the evidence is relevant on the theory that, if D has a reputation for being "peaceful and non-assaultive," that makes it more probable than it would be without that evidence that D in fact is "peaceful and non-assaultive," which makes it more probable than it would be without the evidence that D did not start the fight and acted in the reasonable belief that he had to use deadly force to defend himself from deadly force.

b. Admissibility

Once again we can ignore FRE 404(b), FRE 405(a)(2nd sentence) and FRE 405(b), which deal with evidence of extrinsic acts.

Rule 404(a)(2)(A) allows defendants to offer evidence of a "pertinent trait" of their character. Being peaceful and non-assaultive is pertinent to defend against an accusation of murder. And reputation evidence is an acceptable form of character evidence. Thus, DCW1's testimony is admissible, assuming defense counsel first elicited testimony from DCW1 showing that DCW1 had an adequate foundation to give such testimony.

Question 3.

At the same trial, D calls DCW2 who will testify that in her opinion, D is an "honest, honorable man." Is DCW2's testimony admissible? Apply Rules 404(a), 404(b), 405(a), and 405(b).

Answer:

Once again we can ignore Rules 404(b), 404(a)(2nd sentence) and 405(b), which deal with evidence of extrinsic acts.

Regarding Rule 404(a)(2)(A), is being "honest and honorable" a trait that is "pertinent" in a murder trial? Probably not. First off, what does "honest" mean? Most often, it is probably used to describe someone who does not steal or cheat people. Sometimes "honest" is used as a synonym for "truthful." But not stealing and being truthful are not considered "pertinent" to rebut a charge of murder.

The definition of "honorable" is even more vague than "honest." In essence, an "honorable" person is someone who believes in truth and in doing the right thing, and who tries to live up to that standard. It is a dangerous word to use in describing a defendant's character because, even more than testimony indicating that the defendant has good character for being "law-abiding," it broadens the scope of the defendant's conduct behavior against which a prosecutor can use Rule 405(a)(2nd sentence) while cross-examining the character witness about the defendant's past conduct that tends to contradict the witness's claim that the defendant is "honorable." For example, an "honorable" people would not cheat on a spouse or claim credit for someone else's ideas. Such conduct is not "relevant" to rebut a witness's testimony about the defendant's peaceful or non-violent character or reputation, behavior, but is relevant to rebut testimony that the defendant is "honorable."[10]

---

10. Besides, not so long ago, if one man insulted another man's "honor," the offended man might feel obligated to challenge the offender to a duel. Do the names Aaron Burr and Alexander Hamilton ring a bell? As recently as the Civil War, instances arose when Union generals challenged each other to duels over a real or imagined slight. So, if you are defending a murder case and plan to offer character testimony about how "honorable" your client is, make sure there are no history buffs on the jury.

And in Shakespeare's play *Julius Caesar,* Marc Antony, in his funeral oration, several times sarcastically praises Caesar's assassins as "honourable men"—all the while stirring the mob to violence against them. So if you represent an "honorable" (or "honourable") client, it would be best to avoid Bardophiles on the jury, too.

2. Prosecutor's response

§ 6.12 The prosecutor's options

Once the defendant opens the door by calling a character witness, the prosecutor is entitled to respond. The prosecutor has five options.

The first three options arise while the prosecutor is cross-examining that witness:

1. Impeach the witness. The prosecutor may seek to show that the witness has a motive to lie, or that for some other reason his testimony about the defendant is unreliable. This subject is covered in Chapters 12 and 13.
2. Attack the foundation. The prosecutor may seek to show that the witness never discussed the defendant's reputation with anyone, or that the "community" in question is too small or too transient to matter much, or that the witness has had insufficient contact with the defendant for his opinion to be significant. See § 6.8 and § 6.9.
3. Explore the witness's knowledge about prior bad acts by defendant, per the second sentence of Rule 405(a). We will cover that in § 6.14 to § 6.23.
4. After the defense rests, the prosecution is entitled to present rebuttal evidence: the prosecutor can call a witness to give negative character testimony about the defendant, per the final clause of FRE 404(a)(2)(A). See § 6.24.
5. Finally, if the defense has managed to put information to the jury in violation of Rules 404 and 405, the judge has the option of permitting the prosecutor to respond in kind, a concept known as "fighting fire with fire." See § 6.25.

§ 6.13 What constitutes "opening the door"?

The next several sections discuss the ways a prosecutor may respond once the defendant has "opened the door" regarding his or her character. The obvious and formal way for a defendant to open the door is to call a character witness during the defense case in chief, after the prosecutor has rested. But a foolish defendant can open the door inadvertently. This can happen in a variety of ways.

Variation 1. D is charged with selling heroin to an undercover officer on May 1. He has also been indicted and is pending trial on five other, unrelated drug cases in nearby counties.

At trial for the May 1 sale, after the state rests its case, D takes the stand and testifies he was nowhere near the area where the officer said he purchased drugs. Seeking to emphasize D's denial, defense counsel concludes his direct examination by asking: "And so, Mr. D, under oath and as God is your witness, are you telling this jury that you did not sell drugs to Officer X on May 1?" D replies with the rehearsed answer, "Yes, sir, as God is my witness, it wasn't me." Then, carried away by the drama of the moment, the defendant adds: "I would never have anything to do with illegal drugs!"

By ad-libbing that last sentence, D has testified as to his good character with regard to illegal drugs. A judge might reasonably conclude that this entitles the prosecutor to pursue the options listed in § 6.12 and discussed in § 6.14 to § 6.23.

Variation 2. Suppose instead D ended his direct testimony with "It wasn't me; I didn't do it; I was with my friends Smack and Horse several miles away at the time." On cross, the prosecutor asks, "Have you ever possessed or sold illegal drugs?" The question is, arguably, improper. But suppose defense counsel fails to object, or the judge overrules the objection, and the defendant answers, "No, I have not." Does this entitle the prosecutor, in rebuttal, to cross-examine the defendant, per Rule 405(a)(2nd sentence), about his prior arrests for drug offenses?

No. If D, on direct examination, testified only to facts relating to the crime he is charged with, the prosecutor cannot "convert" a defense fact witness—i.e., a witness (including D him- or herself) who has been called to testify to facts relevant to the current charge—into a character witness, and thereby open the door to Rule 405(a) (2nd sentence) cross-examination. Nor would the prosecutor be entitled to call a negative character witness during the state's rebuttal evidence per Rule 404(a)(2)(A).

Variation 3. The prosecutor conducts a proper cross-examination, challenging D's testimony about his whereabouts when the crime was committed, etc., but asks no questions directly or indirectly about any prior involvement D might have had with illegal drugs on other occasions.[11] In answer to one such question, the defendant says: "Look, let's cut to the chase. I didn't do it. I would never have anything to do with illegal drugs!" Does this open the door?

I think the answer should be, yes. Even though this comes on cross-examination, not on direct, in this variation, the prosecutor did not deliberately or inadvertently ask a question calling for such a response. This situation should be treated the same as variation 1: D has opened the door to prosecutorial use of the techniques covered in § 6.14 to § 6.23.

Variation 4. Let's assume instead that Smack is the first defense witness. He testifies that D was with him and Horse several miles away when the undercover officer bought the heroin. On cross-examination, the prosecutor asks: "Do you think D is the kind of person who would buy, sell or use heroin?" Smack says, "Absolutely not!"

Does this open the door to prosecutorial use of the techniques covered in § 6.14 to § 6.23? No, for the same reasons I discussed in variation 2. D called Smack as a *fact* witness—to support D's alibi, to establish D's whereabouts on the day and at the time of the crime. The prosecutor cannot, on cross-examination, "convert" Smack

---

11. If D has previous felony convictions for drug offenses, FRE 609 directs that the prosecutor may (subject to trial judge discretion) impeach D by cross-examining D about those convictions regardless of whether D "opened the door" to character evidence. See generally § 13.11 to § 13.29.

into a character witness and then employ the techniques discussed in the next several sections to rebut Smack's "character testimony."

Variation 5. But suppose, after testifying that D was with him and Horse at the time of the crime, Smack adds, "Besides, D would never do such a thing! He's absolutely opposed to everything involving illegal drugs!" Does that open the door and allow the prosecutor to respond per Rule 405(a)(2nd sentence) or Rule 404(a)(2)(A)?

Probably not. The door to evidence about the defendant's character should stay locked unless (a) the defense attorney opens it by calling a witness to testify to defendant's supposed good character, or (b) the *defendant himself or herself* opens the door by testifying to his good character during direct examination (variation 1), or testifying to his good character gratuitously and non-responsively during cross-examination (variation 3). If defense counsel calls a character witness, the law assumes that defense counsel was aware of the risks of opening the door and made a strategic decision to do so anyway.[12] In variations 1 and 3, the law has little sympathy for a defendant who hurts his case by his own folly.[13] But what lies beyond that door is often so prejudicial to the defendant that an innocent mistake by a defense witness should not unlock the door.

I began the previous paragraph with the words "probably not," because I can imagine a situation where a judge might reasonably conclude that defense counsel instructed the defense witness to "blurt out" his endorsement of D's character even though counsel has not explicitly asked the witness a question which would call for such an answer. Suppose, for example, JD, D's lawyer, regularly represents people charged with drug offenses,[14] and in several of JD's recent trials, defense fact witnesses "inadvertently blurted out" praise of JD's clients' character during cross-examination, even though, as in the current trial, the prosecutor's question did not seek or logically call for an answer relating to D's character. The trial judge could reasonably conclude that this was a deliberate tactical ploy by JD to introduce evidence of D's good character without opening the door to a prosecutorial response, and conclude that JD had opened the door.[15]

---

12. A defense counsel who did not realize that calling a character witness opened the door to Rule 405(a)(2nd sentence) cross-examination has rendered ineffective assistance of counsel.

13. Indeed, a good defense attorney will explicitly instruct such a client *not* to "spontaneously" blurt out such an assertion, and explain why.

14. Please understand: I do not say this disparagingly. There is nothing wrong with developing such a practice. People facing drug charges are entitled to competent, zealous representation (so long as the lawyer obeys the rules), as is anyone else charged with a crime. Our system of justice works well only when all defendants, guilty as well as innocent, receive competent legal representation. And this is true even though most people charged with a crime are probably guilty. A defense attorney who only represents clients whom he or she believes to be innocent either (a) has other sources of income, or (b) is naïve, or (c) has difficulty paying for luxuries like food and rent.

15. Cf. FRE 404(b)(2), covered in Chapter 7.

a. Cross-examining the character witness

§ 6.14 Rule 405(a)(2nd sentence): cross-examining the character witness about the defendant

FRE 405(a)(2nd sentence) provides that when a defendant has called a character witness (CW), on cross examination, "the court *may allow* inquiry into relevant specific instances of [the defendant's] conduct." This entitles the prosecutor (subject to the judge's discretion) to ask CW whether CW knows, or has heard, that D committed certain acts. But Rule 405(a)(2nd sentence) forbids the prosecutor from offering evidence that the defendant in fact committed the extrinsic act; the prosecutor is only allowed to ask CW whether CW knows about, or has heard, about D committing the extrinsic act.

I italicized the words "may allow" in the previous paragraph to emphasize that a prosecutor does not have an absolute right to ask such questions; the judge retains discretion to preclude this or that question. But the judge's discretion to preclude is limited. The Rule assumes that such questioning is proper and has legitimate probative value. A judge cannot say "I think allowing such questions jeopardizes a defendant's right to a fair trial, so in my courtroom, Rule 405(a)(2nd sentence) questioning is prohibited."

Several issues arise regarding this rule.

1. The "specific instance of [D's] conduct" must be "relevant." See § 6.15.
2. The prosecutor must have a good-faith basis to believe that D did in fact engage in the extrinsic act. See § 6.16.
3. The extrinsic act must have been one which the community, or the opinion character witness, is likely to have heard about.[16] See § 6.17.
3. Issues arise as to how the question must be worded. See § 6.18 to § 6.21.
4. What can the prosecutor do if the witness denies knowing, or hearing, about the extrinsic act? See § 6.22.
5. Once the question is asked and answered, how should the judge instruct the jury about the Q&A? See § 6.23.

---

16. Yes, I know: there is a "rule" against ending a sentence with a preposition. Legend has it that a copy editor once accordingly corrected a sentence on one of Winston Churchill's manuscripts, to which Churchill allegedly wrote, "This is the sort of impertinence, up with which I will not put!" If one of the greatest writers in the history of the English language (who also did as much to save Western civilization as any single human being in history) can break this rule, why can't I?

§ 6.15 "Relevant"

The "specific instance" of X's conduct must be "relevant." In the context of Rule 405(a)(2nd sentence) cross-examination, the relevance of an extrinsic act by a defendant depends primarily on two factors: the kind of act, and when it was committed.

A defendant's specific extrinsic act is "relevant" if it is inconsistent with the trait of the defendant's character the character witness testified about on direct. It is not necessary that the extrinsic act closely resemble the crime for which D is now on trial; what matters is whether the extrinsic act is inconsistent with the trait of good character the character witness ascribed to D. Suppose D is charged with mail fraud, for offering N95 respirator masks for sale but after receiving payment, sending much cheaper, much less protective paper masks instead. At trial, D calls DCW1 to testify that D has a good reputation for honesty and truthfulness. On cross, the prosecutor asks: "Have you heard that 'X' years ago, D used a stolen credit card to buy $2,000 worth of clothing?"

Using a stolen credit card is a different type crime than the mail fraud for which D is now on trial, but it is "relevant" nonetheless, because using a stolen credit card is clearly inconsistent with being honest and truthful. (See § 6.2, *Michelson* fishnote [20].) On the other hand, the prosecutor could not ask whether DCW1 had heard (or knew) that three years ago D was arrested for aggravated assault, because that "specific act" is not "relevant" enough to rebut having good character for "honesty and truthfulness." (But if DCW1 had instead testified about D's character for "law-abidingness," D's prior assault arguably would be a "relevant" to challenge such testimony.)

But the relevance of the credit card incident also depends on when that happened. People sometimes change a great deal (for better or worse) with the passage of time. D's use of the stolen credit card is clearly "relevant" per FRE 405(a)(2)(2nd sentence) if it happened, say, five or six years prior to the mask sale mail fraud for which he is now on trial. If it occurred twenty-five years ago, its relevance is dubious at best. Your professor will probably give you guidance as to what is recent enough to be relevant vs. what is too old to matter.[17]

§ 6.16 Good-faith basis

The prosecutor must have a good-faith basis to believe that the defendant actually committed the "relevant specific instance[] of [the defendant's] conduct" (to quote Rule 405(b)(2nd sentence). It is, obviously, impermissible for the prosecutor to make something up and then ask whether DCW1 had heard about it. See § 6.2, *Michelson* fishnote [12].

---

17. FRE 609(b) sets a guideline of ten years for impeaching a witness with a prior conviction. See § 13.26. FRE 405(a)(2)(2nd sentence) is somewhat analogous to that situation, so I told my students to apply a ten-year period in assessing the "relevance" of FRE 405(a)(2)(2nd sentence) cross-examination.

A "good-faith basis" can exist even if there was no conviction. An arrest can provide a good-faith basis. See §6.2, *Michelson* fishnotes [13]–[19]. So can an indictment. So can a civil claim filed against the defendant. A good-faith basis can exist even if the alleged "specific instance" never resulted in a formal charge; even if the "specific instance" was not a crime. All that is required is that the prosecutor have a plausible reason to believe the allegation is true.

If defense counsel doubts the validity of a "specific instance" of D's conduct the prosecutor asks DCW1 about, counsel should rise and ask, "Your Honor, may we approach the bench?" At the bench (out of the jury's hearing), counsel then asks the judge to require the prosecutor to establish that there is a good-faith basis for the question. The judge can do so at the bench; or, if it appears that it might take more than a minute or two to resolve the issue, the judge can send the jury to the jury room while the judge and attorneys argue and resolve the question.

§6.17 Known or knowable

The purpose of Rule 405(a)(2nd sentence) is to test the witness's knowledge of the defendant's conduct, and if the witness is testifying to the defendant's reputation, to test the community's knowledge. Accordingly, several courts have held that a prosecutor may question a character witness about the witness's (and the community's) knowledge about a specific extrinsic act by the defendant, only if the act was one that the witness, or the community, is likely to have learned about. Acts committed locally and in public, or which receive wide publicity, or (even if committed in private) whose repercussions are public (such as an arrest, or being fired or suspended), generally satisfy this requirement.

But if the "specific instance of [the defendant's extrinsic] conduct" was committed under circumstances where the community or character witness could not possibly have known or heard about it, then it could not possibly have affected the community's, or the witness's, assessment of the defendant's character. In that case, some courts reason, the specific instance of the defendant's conduct is not "relevant" to rebut the character witness's reputation or opinion testimony about the defendant.

<u>Question 1.</u>

Four years ago, a federal grand jury investigated whether executives of Bolshie Enterprises committed securities fraud for lying about the company's indebtedness to persuade potential investors to invest in the company. V testified that X, an employee of Bolshie, persuaded V to invest in the company by telling V the company carried only minimum debt. The grand jury subpoenaed X, who asserted her Fifth Amendment privilege not to testify. The grand jury granted her immunity,[18] and questioned

18. In federal courts and grand juries, "immunity" does not mean she cannot be prosecuted. She can still be prosecuted, but the government's evidence at trial cannot use her testimony against her

her[19] about whether, when she made the pitch to V, she was aware that the company's indebtedness was ten times worse than what she told V. X testified that she didn't know. After she finished testifying, the prosecutor confronted X and her attorney with hard evidence proving she did know. She admitted that she had lied to the grand jury. Her attorney worked out a deal: if she cooperated with the government's investigation against company higherups, she might escape prosecution. And in fact, X gave the prosecutor so much evidence incriminating Leon, Joseph and Vladimir, the troika[20] that ran the company, that they all pleaded guilty without going to trial, and the prosecutor decided not to prosecute X for perjury after all.

Three years later, X is on trial for mail fraud—totally unrelated to the Bolshie case—which X allegedly committed last year. XCW testifies as a defense character witness that X's reputation for truthfulness in the residential community is excellent. (Truthfulness is a pertinent trait in fraud cases.) On cross-examination, the prosecutor asks: "Had you heard [or: did you know] that X lied to a federal grand jury three years ago?" Is the question proper per FRE 405(a)(2nd sentence)?

Answer:

Lying to a grand jury is certainly inconsistent with X's supposed character for truthfulness, and the prosecutor obviously has a good-faith basis to ask the question. But X's grand jury testimony was given in secret (see footnote 19) and was never made public. Therefore, in a jurisdiction that requires that a "specific instance of [the defendant's extrinsic] conduct" be known or knowable to the character witness or to community, X's lies to the grand jury are not "relevant" to challenge the witness's, or the community's, assessment of X's character for truthfulness.

Note.

This is a somewhat arcane wrinkle in an area of law with enough other wrinkles as to make a Chinese shar pei's face look smooth by comparison. So, if your professor doesn't mention it, you shouldn't, either.

directly, nor use any evidence her testimony led them to. (This is known as "use and derivative use immunity.") And if the witness lies, she can be prosecuted for perjury and her perjurious testimony can be used against her.

19. Grand jury testimony is given in secret and does not become public unless the witness testifies at trial or a judge orders that it be released.

20. The literal definition of troika is a Russian sled pulled by a team of three horses abreast.

§ 6.18 Wording the question: "Have you heard" vs. "Did you know"

Prior to enactment of the Federal Rules, many courts had held that while it was permissible for the prosecutor to ask a character witness, "Have you heard [about a specific extrinsic act by the defendant]," it was improper to ask the witness, "Did you know [about the specific extrinsic act]?" Rule 405(a) eliminates this distinction; either form of the question may be used.[21]

§ 6.19 Wording the question: "intrinsic" vs. "extrinsic" wording

There is another way to divide questions into two categories, which I call intrinsically worded and extrinsically worded. An intrinsically worded question takes this form: "Did you know that [describe X's conduct]?" No outside source of information is explicitly invoked. In the context of FRE 405(a)(2nd sentence) cross-examination, the question, "Did you know that seven years ago, D knocked his neighbor N to the ground because N complained that D's dog frequently pooped on N's lawn?" is considered intrinsic, because the question does not explicitly name any source of information. (The odds are, of course, that N is the one who told the police or prosecutor about the incident, but the question is considered intrinsically worded because the prosecutor did not explicitly invoke N as the source of information.)

An extrinsically worded question is one which explicitly includes a reference to another person or group, and often informs the jury that this other person or group reached a conclusion, e.g., "Did you know [or: "Have you heard] that D was arrested two years ago for knocking N down during an argument about dog poop?" The words "was arrested for" explicitly informs the jury that a police officer came to the conclusion that D committed the "specific extrinsic act" of knocking the neighbor down, and arrested D for doing so.

Other phrases that involve extrinsic wording include:

(1) Did you know [or: Have you heard] that D was indicted for...

(2) Did you know [or: Have you heard] that D was convicted of...

(3) Did you know [or: Have you heard] that D was charged with...

(4) Did you know [or: Have you heard] that D was sued for...

(5) Did you know [or: Have you heard] that D was fired for...

(6) Did you know [or: Have you heard] that D was suspended for...

---

21. See Advisory Committee Note to Rule 405, fourth paragraph.

(7) Did you know [or: Have you heard] that D was disciplined for...

Each of these questions are extrinsic in form:

Example (1) Informs the jury that a grand jury formally charged D with committing the specific act.

Example (2) Informs the jury that a trial jury formally concluded beyond a reasonable doubt that D committed the extrinsic act—or that D pleaded guilty to committing the extrinsic act.

Example (3) informs the jury that someone formally accused D of committing the extrinsic act.

Example (4) informs the jury that someone filed a formal lawsuit against D for committing the extrinsic act.

Example (5) informs the jury that an employer concluded that D committed the extrinsic act, and fired D for it.

Example (6) informs the jury that an employer, a school, or an organization of some kind, came to the conclusion that D committed the extrinsic act, and suspended D for doing so.

Example (7) informs the jury that an employer, a school, or an organization of some kind, came to the conclusion that D committed the extrinsic act, and took disciplinary action against D for doing so.

In *Michelson v. U.S.*, the Supreme Court held that it is permissible to ask a defense character witness about a defendant's prior arrests. See § 6.2, *Michelson* fishnotes [16]–[19] regarding the use of the word "arrested." Neither Rule 405(a)(2nd sentence) nor the legislative history of that rule make any reference to whether the rule permits such questions, but the Advisory Committee cited *Michelson* broadly in its discussion of the rule, and courts continue to allow extrinsically worded questions. See also § 6.21 questions 7–15.

You might reasonably wonder: If courts allow extrinsically worded questions, why did I bother discussing the distinction? Answer: because, although extrinsically worded questions are permitted in the 405(a)(2nd sentence) context, in other litigation situations, they are not permitted. I'm introducing you to the distinction here to prepare you for what is to come.

§ 6.20 Wording the question: questions assuming the defendant's guilt

Most courts hold that it is improper for the prosecutor to ask a character witness, "Would your opinion of the defendant's character change if you learned [or heard] that defendant had [engaged in the conduct for which the defendant is now on trial]?"

§ 6.21 Questions

D and V argued about a parking space; D is on trial for ending the argument by assaulting V with a baseball bat. Charged with aggravated assault and assault with a deadly weapon, D insists V is mistaken: it was someone else, not D, who argued with and then beat V.

During her pretrial investigation, the prosecutor has learned:

(1) D was arrested seven years ago for pushing a neighbor (N) to the ground when N complained that D's dog had on several occasions relieved itself on N's lawn. The prosecutor has a copy of the arrest report. (The case was dismissed after D completed a course on anger management.)

(2) Four years ago, D was convicted of assault for punching a man during an argument about political lawn signs. The prosecutor has a certified copy of the judgment of conviction in her case folder.

(3) EM, an elderly man,[22] hearing about D's arrest in the present case, came to the prosecutor's office and told her that two years ago, D, angry that EM's slow pace prevented D from catching an office building elevator, grabbed EM by the front of his shirt and threatened to "break a few bones" if EM ever got in his way again. (EM quickly identified D's picture when showed a series of photographs of men who were of the same basic physical shape and skin coloring as D.)

The trial begins, and V, the prosecutor's first witness, testifies about the parking-space argument and getting beaten, and identifies D as his assailant. The prosecutor introduces medical testimony and records detailing V's injuries. Assume all this evidence was properly admitted and raises no legal issues.

<u>Question 1.</u>

Next, the prosecutor offers the dog poop assault arrest report (paragraph (1), *supra*) in evidence. What objections should defense counsel make? How should the trial judge rule?

<u>Answer:</u>

D has two objections. First: this is inadmissible extrinsic act evidence, per FRE 404(b)(1): its only relevance is to show that D has a propensity for violence, to suggest that his alleged assault on V is consistent with that propensity. Objection sustained.

Counsel can also object that the police report is inadmissible hearsay and violates the Confrontation Clause. Objection sustained. An arrest report, if offered as evidence that the arrestee actually committed the crime for which he was arrested, is

22. The official definition of "elderly" is "Five years older than Professor Fishman." As of this book's publication date, therefore, "elderly" is defined as "age 83 or older."

inadmissible hearsay—and violates the Confrontation Clause, too, if the person in question is the defendant in a criminal case.[23]

Question 2.

Next, the prosecutor offers the certificate of defendant's conviction in the lawn sign assault (paragraph (2)). Objections? Rulings?

Answer:

First objection: the evidence violates FRE 404(b)(1), because its only relevance in the current case is to show Defendant's propensity for violence. Objection sustained. In this context, there is no difference between an assault arrest which did not result in a conviction, and an assault arrest that did.

Counsel can also object that the certificate of conviction is hearsay: it is, after all, a piece of paper asserting the fact that D was convicted of committing the lawn sign assault. But FRE 803(22) admits proof of certain convictions over a hearsay objection. Let's assume that this conviction satisfies FRE 803(22).

Question 3.

The judge sustained one objection to the evidence, but overruled another objection. So which is the answer: is the lawn sign assault conviction evidence admissible, or not?

Answer:

Not. As a general rule, the party offering the evidence has to satisfy every objection the other side can plausibly make; failure to overcome any one objection requires excluding the evidence.

This general rule does not apply when evidence has more than one theory of relevance, and the evidence is admissible under one theory but not on the other. In that case, the judge decides whether, per FRE 403, the risk of unfair prejudice—that the jury will rely on the evidence for the impermissible purpose—substantially outweighs the legitimate probative value of the evidence on the proper purpose, factoring in the degree to which the Rule 403 risk can be mitigated by redaction or a limiting instruction per FRE 105. See § 3.6, § 3.10, and § 3.11.

But here, there is only one theory on which the evidence is relevant—the propensity inference—which, per FRE 404(b)(1), is not a permissible inference. (Besides, FRE 803(22) does not render the conviction admissible; it only overcomes a hearsay objection; it cannot overcome an objection based on any other rule—such as FRE 404(b)(1).) D's conviction for the lawn sign assault is not admissible during the prosecutor's case-in-chief.

23. See the fifth edition of my *A Student's Guide to Hearsay,* § 9.45 to § 9.47. (Oh, good—I've kept my streak alive—so far I've mentioned by hearsay book at least once in every chapter.) If you haven't covered hearsay yet, ignore the hearsay aspects of these questions.

Question 4.

What about FRE 405(b)? That admits evidence of extrinsic acts, too.

Yes, it does—but only in civil litigation where someone's character is an essential element of a claim or defense. This is a criminal trial.[24]

Question 5.

Next, the prosecutor seeks to have EM, the elderly man (paragraph (3)), testify about what D did to him two years ago. Objections? Ruling?

Answer:

Objection, FRE 404(b)(1); objection sustained.

There is no hearsay issue here, because EM is himself testifying to facts about which he has first-hand knowledge. But the other objection is the same—what D did to EM is relevant only to show D's propensity for violence, and if offered for that purpose, it is banned by FRE 404(b)(1).

Question 6.

At trial, D calls DCW1, who testifies that he and D have lived in the same neighborhood and belonged to the same country club for 11 years, that during that time, he has had many conversations about D with others who live in that neighborhood and are members of that country club, and that "No one was ever said anything to suggest that D is violent or non-peaceful." Is this evidence admissible?

Answer:

Yes. Peacefulness and non-violence are clearly pertinent traits at a trial for aggravated assault and assault with a deadly weapon, see § 6.6, and DCW1's testimony satisfies the foundation requirements for reputation testimony, because it is reasonable to assume that the residential neighborhood and the country club are both large and stable enough to qualify as "communities" for purposes of FRE 404(a)(2)(a). See § 6.8. And[25] even though DCW1's testimony is expressed in negative terms—"I've never heard anyone say anything bad about Defendant in that regard"—rather than in positive terms—"His reputation for peacefulness and non-violence is good"—this is an acceptable form of reputation testimony. See § 6.2, *Michelson* fishnote [6].

Question 7.

On cross-examination, the prosecutor wants to ask DCW1 about the dog poop incident (paragraph (1)). How would she do so, wording the question intrinsically?

---

24. It is theoretically possible for a crime to be defined in such a way as to make someone's character an essential element, but as a practical matter, character is never an "essential element" of a crime or a defense to a crime. See § 5.9.

25. I know: there is a "rule" that one should never begin a sentence with the words "and" or "but." But the Bible begins hundreds of sentences with "and." And good luck to whoever wants to argue with the Bible about that.

Answer:

"Have you heard [or: Did you know] that seven years ago, D pushed a neighbor to the ground in an argument over dog poop?"

Question 8.

How would the prosecutor ask DCW1 regarding the dog poop incident, wording the question extrinsically?

Answer:

"Have you heard [or: Did you know] that D was arrested seven years ago for pushing a neighbor to the ground in an argument about dog poop?"

Question 9.

Is it permissible to ask about the dog poop incident, and word the question extrinsically?

Answer:

Yes, per FRE 405(a)(2nd sentence): "On cross-examination of the character witness, the court may allow an inquiry into relevant specific instances of the person's conduct."

The "person" the rule refers to is the person about whom the character witness has testified on direct. Here, the "person" is D. DCW1 gave direct testimony about D's reputation, as a way of establishing D's character for peacefulness and non-violence. The dog poop incident is "relevant," because pushing someone to the ground is inconsistent with being peaceful and non-violent.

Rule 405(a)(2nd sentence) does not say whether the "inquiry" permits extrinsically worded questions. But federal courts allow extrinsic wording when cross-examining a character witness—including mentioning an arrest even if the arrest did not result in a conviction—because an arrest, by itself, is likely to affect a person's reputation, and because that is the sort of thing that neighbors and friends are likely to talk about. If DCW1 did not know about D's arrest, this calls into question how well DCW1—and the people in the neighborhood and in the country club he spoke to—actually knew D. Thus, their lack of knowledge about the arrest has some tendency to make the neighbors' and country club members' assessment of D's character somewhat less reliable than it would be without the evidence. See § 6.2, *Michelson* fishnotes [13], [16]–[19].

And if DCW1 and the two "communities" *did* know about the dog poop incident and nevertheless consider D to be peaceful and non-violent, this suggests that their definition of "peaceful and non-violent" is somewhat different than most people's, which in turn makes their assessment of D's character less reliable than it would be without the evidence.

Question 10.

Continuing on cross-examination, the prosecutor wants to question DCW1 regarding the lawn sign assault. How would she word the question intrinsically?

Answer:

"Had you heard [or: Did you know] that seven years ago D punched a man during an argument about lawn signs?"

Question 11.

How would the prosecutor word the question extrinsically?

Answer:

"Did you know that four years ago, D was convicted of assault for punching a man during an argument about political lawn signs?"

Question 12.

Is extrinsic wording permissible?

Answer:

Yes, for the same reasons, and via the same reasoning, as applied regarding the dog poop incident.

Question 13.

Next, the prosecutor asks: "Had you heard that two years ago, D threatened to break an elderly man's bones because the man couldn't walk fast enough to let D catch an elevator?" Is this question worded intrinsically or extrinsically?

Answer:

This is intrinsic. It does not explicitly invoke any source of information—it does not contain phrases like "arrested for" or "charged with." It simply asks, "Had you heard [or: Did you know] that D did this relevant specific extrinsic act?"

Question 14.

Is this question permissible?

Answer:

Yes. Even though there was no conviction or arrest, EM's statement to the prosecutor (or to a police officer, who in turn informed the prosecutor) about the incident provides the prosecutor with a good-faith basis to believe the incident happened. And while this incident isn't as violent as the first two, D's conduct is still clearly inconsistent with being peaceful and non-violent.

In a "known or knowable" jurisdiction (see § 6.17), admissibility might be challenged if no one else saw it and EM didn't tell anybody, or if it happened somewhere pretty far from D's residential community and the country club.

Even if the EM incident is otherwise admissible, however, at this point, D might plausibly object per FRE 403—needless presentation of cumulative evidence, because the prosecutor has already questioned DCW1 about two other "specific instances of [D's extrinsic] conduct." A judge might agree that two such incidents are enough. But the prosecutor might plausibly argue that he needs all three to show that these are not rare and isolated instances, and that D hadn't mellowed much with the passage of time.

Question 15.

Since neither the arrest report, or the certificate of conviction, or EM's testimony, is admissible, is there any practical reason for the prosecutor to have the documents in her trial folder, or have EM present in the courtroom?

Answer:

Yes. If defense counsel (or the judge) asks the prosecutor whether she has a good-faith basis for the question, she can prove that she does.

Besides, having EM—and the victims of the dog poop and lawn sign assaults—sitting in the courtroom might upset and unnerve D, and the jury might notice. Lawyers sometimes play mind games on parties and witnesses and each other, and that's okay, so long as the tactic doesn't violate the rules and is not morally objectionable.

§ 6.22 Suppose the witness hasn't heard and doesn't know

Suppose, in the assault trial discussed in § 6.21, DCW1 replies each time to the prosecutor that he hadn't heard or didn't know about the arrest, the conviction, and the threat to EM. The prosecutor has the arrest report and the certification of conviction in her trial folder, and EM is sitting just outside the courtroom, ready and eager to testify. Can the prosecutor introduce the documents, or call EM to testify?

No.

Why not?

Because the documents and EM's testimony are just as inadmissible now, per FRE 404(b)(1), as they were when the prosecutor offered them during the state's case-in-chief (§ 6.21, questions 1–5).

Think of it this way. The dog poop arrest, the lawn sign conviction, and the EM threat are relevant on two separate theories.

1. Each incident demonstrates D's propensity for violence; each, and all 3 together, make it more probable than it would be without the evidence that D, as charged, assaulted V with a baseball bat over a parking space. But FRE 404(b)(1) says these specific extrinsic acts are not admissible to show propensity.
2. These three incidents are also relevant to test a community's, or a character witness's, knowledge about them, and therefore are relevant in helping a jury decide how much weight to give to the character witness's testimony. That it why FRE 405(a)(2nd sentence) says "the court may allow inquiry into relevant specific instances of [D's extrinsic] conduct."

In other words, once a defendant calls a character witness, FRE 405(a)(2nd sentence) says the prosecutor can ask the character witness if he or she has heard (or knows) about specific relevant instances in the defendant's extrinsic conduct (assuming, as is the case here, that the prosecutor has a good-faith basis that they actually happened), but FRE 404(b)(1) says the prosecutor is not permitted to prove that they actually happened.

Question 1.

"A question by itself is not evidence; only the question and answer together is evidence." Isn't this a fundamental, basic rule?

Answer:

Yes, that is a fundamental rule of evidence, and the judge should instruct the jury of that rule wherever it is appropriate.

Question 2.

So, when a prosecutor asks DCW1, "Did you know that D was arrested for the dog poop assault and was convicted of the lawn sign assault, and that D threatened EM in the elevator incident," and DCW1 says he's never heard about any of them, in essence no evidence has been introduced that any of those incidents actually occurred. Right?

Answer:

Right.

Question 3.

But isn't the jury going to assume that they happened?

Answer:

Yup.

Question 4.

Even though no evidence has actually been introduced that they happened?

Question 5.

Yup.

Question 6.

And the law allows this?

Question 7.

Yup.

Question 8.

But that doesn't make any sense at all!

Answer:

Correct! See, you 're getting it! Once you accept that common sense sometimes gets in the way of understanding this body of the law, it becomes easier—not easy, but at least easier—to learn. (I warned you about that back in § 4.1.)

The Supreme Court, in *Michelson*, explicitly acknowledged and endorsed this feature of character evidence law. See § 6.2, fishnote [13].

§ 6.23 Instructing the jury about Rule 405(a)(2nd sentence) cross-examination

Here is the Third Circuit's model jury instruction, which is typical of federal instructions in other Circuits as well:

> 4.40 Impeachment of Defendant's Character Witness
>
> If character witness testified to reputation: You heard (name of witness) testify about the defendant's reputation for (insert character trait covered by testimony). On cross-examination of (name of witness), the prosecutor asked (him)(her) some questions about whether (he)(she) had heard that (briefly describe the subject of the cross-examination on the character trait, e.g., defendant was convicted of fraud on an earlier occasion). The prosecutor was allowed to ask these questions only to test whether (name of witness) was familiar with the reputation of the defendant in the community. This is not evidence that the acts described in these questions actually occurred.
>
> You may not use the information developed by the prosecutor on this subject for any other purpose. Specifically, you may not use this information to conclude that the defendant committed the act(s) charged in the indictment or as proof that the defendant has a bad character or any propensity to commit crimes.
>
> If character witness testified to opinion: You heard (name of witness) testify about the defendant's character for (insert character trait covered by testimony). On cross-examination of (name of witness), the prosecutor asked (him)(her) some questions about whether (he)(she) knew that (briefly describe the subject of the cross-examination on the character trait, e.g., defendant was convicted of fraud on an earlier occasion). The prosecutor was allowed to ask these questions only to test whether (name of witness) had a good basis for (his)(her) opinion of the defendant's character. This is not evidence that the acts described in these questions actually occurred.
>
> You may not use the information developed by the prosecutor on this subject for any other purpose. Specifically, you may not use this information to conclude that the defendant committed the act(s) charged in the indictment

> or as proof that the defendant has a bad character or any propensity to commit crimes.[26]

As the Supreme Court commented in *Michelson* (§ 6.2, fishnote [13], "the system may work best when explained least." (But the judge should still give a limiting instruction, because otherwise an appellate court might conclude that not giving it was reversible error.)

b. Negative character witness

§ 6.24 FRE 404(a)(2)(A): "... and if the evidence is admitted, the prosecutor may offer evidence to rebut it."

The final clause of Rule 404(a)(2)(A) directs that if the defendant calls a character witness to give reputation or opinion testimony about a pertinent trait of his character, "the prosecutor may offer evidence to rebut it." This means that, in addition to or instead of cross-examining the defense character witness as discussed in §§ 6.14–6.23, the prosecutor can rebut defense character testimony by calling witnesses, to testify about the defendant's bad character for the same pertinent trait.

The prosecutor's witness would have to satisfy the same foundational requirements discussed in § 6.8 and § 6.9. Defense counsel could cross-examine these witnesses about specific relevant good acts ("Have you heard that my client turned the other cheek when...").

This option is rarely used. I suspect the situation arises more often on law school exams than in real life.

c. "Fighting fire with fire"

§ 6.25 "Two can play that game!"

As a general matter, that one party broke a rule by presenting inadmissible evidence to the jury does not entitle the other party to retaliate in kind. The law presumes that a judge can undo or limit the unfair advantage by sustaining an objection and instructing the jury to disregard the improperly produced testimony. But where the judge is convinced that these measures are not enough to protect the other side's

26. Mod. Crim. Jury Instr. 3d Cir. 4.40 (2020). FEDCRIM-JI3C 4.40 Federal Jury Practice and Instructions. The comment to the instruction adds:

> If the prosecutor is permitted to cross-examine the defendant's character witness, the court should make a ruling as to what the prosecutor may ask a character witness on cross-examination. The court should consider making a preliminary ruling on the content of the cross examination of defense character witnesses to ensure that questions of such witnesses are based on accurate information and are not substantially more prejudicial than probative.

Id.

right to a fair trial, the judge has other options. The most extreme is to declare a mistrial. Another is to publicly chastise the offending attorney, either with the jury outside the courtroom, or inside. In a criminal case, if the judge chastises defense counsel in the jury's presence, the judge should immediately tell the jury not to hold the attorney's shenanigans against the defendant.

Another option is to allow the other party to admit otherwise inadmissible evidence to offset the unfair advantage the first party sought to gain by its improper conduct. For example, if a defense character witness testifies (in violation of Rule 405(a)(1st sentence) about a specific wonderful good deed the defendant did, the judge might allow the prosecutor to call a witness to contradict the inadmissible testimony by testifying that the defendant's conduct on that occasion was very different than the way the defense character witness described it. There are no hard and fast rules governing this situation; the best solution probably lies in a judicious application of Rules 102 and 401–403.

§ 6.26 Questions

Question 1.

D is charged with the murder of V. At trial, D calls DCW1 who testifies that D has a reputation in D's residential community for being a peaceful, non-violent person. What does defense counsel hope to accomplish with this testimony? Set out the chain of inferences.

Answer:

a. Relevance

The evidence is relevant via the following chain of inferences.

(1) If D has a reputation for being peaceful and non-violent, that makes it more likely than it would be without the evidence that D is in fact a peaceful, non-violent person.

(2) If D denies killing V, and If D is in fact a peaceful, non-violent person, that makes it less probable than it would be without the evidence that D killed V.

Or if D admits killing V but pleads self-defense, D's good character for peacefulness and non-violence makes it more probable that D was not the initial aggressor; rather, it makes it more probable that D killed V while reasonably believing that it was necessary to use deadly force to defend himself or herself against the imminent use of deadly force by V.

Question 2.

The prosecutor objects that this is not valid character evidence. Is DCW1's testimony admissible? Apply rules 404(a), 404(b), 405(a), and 405(b).

Answer:

Rules 404(b), 405(a)(2nd sentence) and 405(b) do not apply to DCW1's direct testimony, because those rules govern evidence of specific acts, not character evidence.

FRE 404(a)(2)(A) allows a defendant to offer evidence of a "pertinent" trait of his character. Being peaceful and non-violent is obviously pertinent defense evidence in a murder trial.

FRE 405(a)(1st sentence) permits character evidence to be in the form of reputation testimony. Therefore DCW1's testimony is relevant if D's attorney has elicited from DCW1 the information necessary to establish a proper foundation: that D and DCW1 live in the same residential community, and have done so for a considerable amount of time; and that DCW1 has spoken to others in that community about D's character for peacefulness and non-violence. See § 6.8.

Comment: I required my students to spell out the foundational requirements for reputation and opinion testimony, rather than ignore those requirements or merely say "assume a proper foundation has been established." On the other hand, none of the MBE questions I have reviewed refer in any way to the required foundation for character evidence. Take your lead from your evidence professor as to what he or she expects from you.

Question 3.

Let's assume that DCW1 testified that he and D lived in the same residential neighborhood for several years; that DCW1 explains how well he knows D; and that DCW1 has spoken to others in the community about D's character for peacefulness and non-violence.

On cross-examination of DCW1, the prosecutor asks: "Name the people you spoke to about DCW1's character." Does defense counsel have a valid objection to this question?

Answer:

No. It is a valid question, because it tests whether there is in fact an adequate foundation for DCW1's testimony per FRE 404(a)(2)(A). See § 6.8.

Question 4.

If DCW1 is unable to name anyone, what should the prosecutor do next?

Answer:

The prosecutor should ask the judge to strike DCW1's testimony from the record and instruct the jury to disregard it. That's what happens when a witness gives testimony without a proper foundation. The fault, of course, belongs to the attorney who called the witness, for failing to assure that the witness in fact has a proper foundation. Having testimony stricken like this is embarrassing to the witness and to the attorney. It also tends to reduce the defendant's faith in his or her attorney, and suggests to the judge and jury that the defense attorney might not be the brightest bulb in the chandelier.

Question 5.

Is there something the prosecutor might have done that could have prevented DCW1 from testifying about D's reputation in the first place?

Answer:

Yes. Once a witness has testified to facts establishing an apparently adequate basis for his or her testimony, but before getting to the actual substance of the testimony, opposing counsel can ask permission to conduct a "voir dire" regarding the foundation. In this context, "voir dire" means "a limited mini-cross-examination testing whether the witness's foundation is truly adequate." Once DCW1 admits he has not actually asked anyone about their opinion of D's character for peacefulness and nonviolence, the prosecutor can ask the judge to disqualify the witness from testifying before the witness even gets to say that D's reputation is "good."

Question 6.

In the same trial, D calls DCW2 who will testify that he and D work for the same employer, and DCW2 has never heard anyone in the workplace say anything to suggest that D was a violent person. Is this testimony admissible?

Answer:

The relevance of this testimony is the same as DCW1's, but DCW2's testimony differs from DCW1's testimony in two respects.

First, it refers to D's reputation in the workplace. The prosecutor should object that the witness has not established an adequate foundation for his testimony and therefore does not satisfy FRE 404(a)(2)(A) or FRE 405(a)(1st sentence). Before asking DCW2 the "what is D's reputation in the workplace," or "what have you heard from your fellow employees about D's character for peacefulness and non-violence," D's attorney should ask DCW2 questions that will satisfy the foundation requirements: that the workforce at that workplace is large enough and stable enough, and that enough people work there and interact with D often enough, for D's reputation there to be sufficiently relevant.[27]

Second, instead of saying that D's reputation for peacefulness and non-violence is "good," DCW2 testified that he has never heard anyone say anything bad about D's character for peacefulness. If this were a quiz or exam question, it would be worth mentioning in your answer that in *Michelson*, the Court held that this was an acceptable form of character testimony. See § 6.2, *Michelson* fishnote [6].

27. For example, if D works for a large company with a stable workforce, but D works remotely from home, query whether D's co-workers have a basis to judge how D interacts with others in person.

Question 7.

In the same trial, D calls DCW3 who will testify that D's reputation in the residential community is that he is a truthful person. Is this testimony admissible? Is there an objection the prosecutor should make, and if so, based on what rule?

Answer:

"Objection, your honor, Per FRE 404(a)(2)(A): being 'truthful' is not a 'pertinent' trait in a murder trial."

Objection sustained.

You might be thinking: well, D pleaded not guilty, which means he says he didn't do it, and he probably denied his guilt to the police when they arrested him. So isn't his truthfulness relevant? And you are right, of course, to an extent, but the term "pertinent" as used in FRE 404(a)(2)(A) means, more precisely, "pertinent to directly rebut an element of the crime for which D is on trial." Acting untruthfully *is* an element in several crimes—perjury, fraud, forgery, etc. But it is not an element in homicides, assaults, robbery, weapons or controlled substance violations, etc.

If D testifies at trial (or succeeds in admitting his own hearsay statement), then his *credibility as a witness* (or as a hearsay declarant) becomes an issue in the case. FRE 608–609 regulate when parties in a case can offer evidence attacking or defending a witness's credibility. We will cover those rules in Chapters 12 and 13.

Question 8.

Once the judge has sustained the objection, what should the prosecutor do next?

Answer:

She should ask the judge to strike DCW3's testimony from the record and instruct the jury that they should disregard it.

Question 9.

In the same trial, D calls DCW4. She is asked: "What is your opinion of D's character for peacefulness and non-violence." DCW4 responds, "He is one of the gentlest, most peaceful people I've ever known. He wouldn't hurt a fly!" Is this testimony admissible?

Answer:

Not unless D's attorney has first elicited from DCW4 testimony sufficient to establish that DCW4 has an adequate basis for her testimony. How long has she known D? In what context (work, neighborhood, worship, social action, the goth milieu, on-line chess, etc.)? How frequently does she interact with D?

If DCW4 satisfies the foundation requirements, opinion character testimony is admissible. Her description of D's character is much more colorful than if she simply said "D's character for peacefulness and non-violence is good," but there is nothing wrong with that.

Question 10.

On cross-examination of DCW4 in the previous problem, the prosecutor asks: "Have you heard that D was indicted for embezzlement last year?" Is the question proper? What rule should defense counsel cite in objecting?

Answer:

This is cross-examination of a defense character witness, per FRE 405(a)(2nd sentence). That rule permits "inquiry into *relevant* specific [extrinsic] instances of [D's] conduct." Embezzlement is not "relevant" to rebut testimony about D's character for peacefulness and non violence. Objection sustained.

Question 11.

After the defense rests, the prosecutor calls PCW1. She will testify that she has lived in the same neighborhood as D for the past nine years and has had numerous conversations about D with others in that neighborhood. (Assume this testimony satisfies the foundation for reputation testimony.) The prosecutor asks: "Are you familiar with D's reputation in the community for being peaceful and non-violent?"

PCW1 responds, "Everybody says watch out for D, he's a bully and a brute and a liar. If he gets mad at you, he'll take a swing at you, and he gets mad a lot. From what I hear, he knocked somebody down who complained D's dog dumped on his lawn. Another time he beat up a guy because he didn't like the guy's lawn sign. He even threatened an old man in a building lobby who wouldn't get out of his way."

Is this testimony admissible? Apply rules 404(a), 404(b), 405(a) and 405(b).

Answer:

Some of this testimony is admissible, some not.

a. "Everybody says watch out for D, he's a bully and a brute and a liar. If he gets mad at you he'll take a swing at you, and he gets mad a lot."

FRE 404(a)(2)(A) directs that "if the [defendant's] evidence [about the defendant's pertinent trait] is admitted, the prosecutor may offer evidence to rebut it." DCW1 and DCW4 each gave testimony that D's reputation for peacefulness and non-violence is good. Therefore, the prosecutor can offer character evidence to rebut their testimony. Most of the first two sentences of PCW1's testimony relates to D's reputation for violence, is therefore admissible per FRE 405(a)(1st sentence). PCW1's description of D's reputation is vivid and colorful, but there is nothing objectionable about that.

But D was permitted to offer evidence only relating to D's reputation for peacefulness and non-violence. Therefore PCW1's testimony that "everybody says D is a liar" is not admissible. In Q7, the judge sustained the prosecutor's objection to DCW3's testimony about D's character for truthfulness because truthfulness is not a "pertinent" trait in a murder case. For the same reason, the prosecutor cannot offer evidence about that trait, either.

Well, what about "fighting fire with fire"? The jury heard DCW3's testimony about D's reputation for truthfulness, even though it clearly was improper. Shouldn't the prosecutor be able to respond in kind?

D's attempt to offer such evidence was improper and rather blatantly so, but the judge promptly instructed the jury to ignore it. Granted, jurors may not be able to completely ignore evidence once they have heard it, but it is highly unlikely that DCW3's improper testimony would have much impact on the jury. I don't think the "fighting fire" principle applies here.

b. "From what I hear, he knocked somebody down who complained D's dog dumped on his lawn. Another time he beat up a guy because he didn't like the guy's lawn sign. He even threatened an old man in a building lobby who wouldn't get out of his way."

This testimony does not satisfy FRE 405(a)(1st sentence), because it is not in the form or reputation or opinion evidence; it relates to specific instances of D's extrinsic conduct. Therefore, we must look to FRE 404(b), 405(a)(2nd sentence) and 405(b).

FRE 404(b)(1) does not permit evidence of extrinsic conduct to show a person's propensity to act in a certain way, and ultimately, showing D's propensity for violence is the only relevance this evidence has.

But wait, you might protest, it is also relevant to corroborate PCW1's testimony about D's reputation!

Nice try, but that won't work, because it corroborates PCW1's testimony only via the propensity inference.

FRE 405(a)(2nd sentence) doesn't work, either. That rule allows "inquiry into relevant specific instances of [D's] conduct," but only "on cross-examination of the witness." PCW1 offered that testimony during her direct examination. Therefore Rule 405(a)(2nd sentence) does not admit this testimony, either.

If D's attorney were foolish enough to ask PCW1, "Have you heard about any specific situations in which my client supposedly acted violently," then, of course, PCW1 can testify about them, because the defense literally asked for it. But that's a question a competent attorney is unlikely to ask.

And FRE 405(b) does not admit PCW1's testimony about the three incidents, because this is a criminal case, and character is never an essential element of a crime or defense in a criminal case.

Question 12.

On cross-examination, D's attorney asks:

Q Is it fair to say that you and D are both politically active? Just yes or no, please.

A Yes.

Q Is it also fair to say that you and he disagree vehemently about whether abortion should be legal?

A Yes.

Q Is it fair to say that you and he disagree vehemently about affirmative action to redress prior unequal treatment of minority groups?

A Yes.

Q Is it fair to say that you and he disagree vehemently about whether global warming is a fact or a myth?

A Yes.

Q Is it also fair to say that you and he were on opposite sides in the recent presidential election?

A Absolutely.

Is this cross-examination relevant? Is it permissible?

Answer:

It has nothing to do with character evidence, but it is relevant, because it suggests that PCW1 has a strong antipathy toward D (which is lawyer-talk for "She hates his guts"),[28] which therefore suggests that PCW1 may have a motive to lie or exaggerate about D's reputation. Showing that a witness is biased or has a motive to lie is almost always relevant to impeach a witness's testimony. (We will cover that topic in greater detail in §12.7 to §12.9, but I'm raising it here as a "sneak preview.") And unfortunately, many people these days tend to stereotype and demonize those on the "other side" of controversial issues.[29]

Question 13.

On cross, D's attorney asks PCW1: "Have you heard that nine months ago, when D was wearing a brand-new light tan suit, a young man in a bar accidentally spilled two glasses of red wine all over D, and D calmly told the young man not to worry and even paid for two more glasses of wine for the man?" Is this proper cross-examination?

---

28. Of course, it does not necessarily follow that people on the opposite sides of these issues hate each other. I have good, decent, intelligent friends with whom I disagree on all these issues. I respect their right to be wrong; they respect my right to believe what they mistakenly think is wrong. But vehement disagreement on these issues has some tendency to make it more probable than it would be without this evidence that PCW1 had a strong dislike for D, and therefore it is relevant to suggest PCW1's potential bias against D.

29. Oh, and by the way: if you automatically assumed that you know which side of those issues PCW1 and D were on, you just did some stereotyping and demonizing.

Answer:

Yes, assuming counsel has a good-faith basis for the question. It falls squarely within Rule 405(a)(2nd sentence), because it is a "relevant specific instance of D's [extrinsic] conduct" which undercuts PCW1's testimony.

Question 14.

Would it be permissible for PCW1 to answer, "Yes, I heard that, and I also heard that the 'young man in the bar' plays defensive tackle for the Dallas Cowboys."

Answer:

Yes. Assuming the witness has a good-faith basis for the answer. (If you don't understand why: the Dallas Cowboys are a professional football team. Professional football is a sport in which aggressive and violent acts are not only tolerated, but expected and celebrated, within certain specific limits; and defensive tackles tend to be among the largest, most muscular and aggressive players. This circumstance could explain why D reacted so calmly, non-violently—and uncharacteristically—on this occasion.)

B. The Victim's Character

§ 6.27 FRE 404(a)(2)(B)

FRE 404(a)(2)(B) and 404(a)(2)(C) regulate evidence concerning the character of the victim (or alleged victim) of the crime being tried. The issue is most likely to arise in homicide cases, but may occasionally arise in a non-homicide trial.

These provisions don't come into play very often. For example, a search for federal court decisions in cases containing FRE 404(a)(2)(B) within the same paragraph as "evidence" produced only 24 cases, of which only half a dozen were officially reported in F. Supp., F. Supp. 2d, F.2d or F.3d. Some evidence professors may skip these provisions on the reasonable theory that the time they would take to cover would be better spent on other rules that are cited more frequently. If your professor skips over these provisions, you can skip this section and § 6.28.

FRE 404(a)(2)(B) and 404(a)(2)(C) provide:

> **(a) Character Evidence.**
>
> **(1) Prohibited Uses.** Evidence of a person's character or character trait is not admissible to prove that on a particular occasion the person acted in accordance with the character or trait.
>
> **(2) Exceptions for a Defendant or Victim in a Criminal Case.** The following exceptions apply in a criminal case:

. . .

(B) subject to the limitations in Rule 412, a defendant may offer evidence of an alleged victim's pertinent trait, and if the evidence is admitted, the prosecutor may:

(i) offer evidence to rebut it; and

(ii) offer evidence of the defendant's same trait; and

(C) in a homicide case, the prosecutor may offer evidence of the alleged victim's trait of peacefulness to rebut evidence that the victim was the first aggressor.

§ 6.28 How this rule works

In essence, the restrictions and procedures governing evidence of the defendant's character in FRE 404(a)(2)(A) and FRE 405(a) apply the same way to evidence of the alleged victim's character. The defendant owns the only key to the door of the alleged victim's character, and the defendant unlocks that door by offering reputation or opinion evidence about a pertinent trait of the alleged victim's character. Once defendant does so, the prosecutor has a number of options. But there are a few additional wrinkles and complexities in FRE 404(a)(2)(B) and 404(a)(2)(C) beyond those in FRE 404(a)(2)(A).

The first wrinkle is that these rules do not apply when the defendant is charged with sexual assault. Evidence of the alleged victim's character in such cases is regulated by FRE 412, covered in Chapter 9..

The second wrinkle is that if the defendant offers evidence of the alleged victim's character by calling a witness (DNCW)[30] to give negative reputation or opinion testimony about a pertinent trait of V/AV's character, the prosecutor has an option not available with regard to FRE 404(a)(2)(A). Here are the prosecutor's options:

1. Impeach the witness. The prosecutor may seek to show that DNCW has a motive to lie, or that for some other reason DNCW's testimony about V/AV is unreliable. Impeaching a witness is covered extensively in Chapters 12 and 13.
2. Attack the foundation. The prosecutor may challenge whether DNCW has a valid foundation for his testimony about AV. This corresponds to the discussion in §§ 6.8 and 6.9.
3. Per FRE 405(a)(2nd sentence), the prosecutor can explore DNCW's knowledge about prior specific extrinsic acts by AV which are inconsistent with the negative reputation or opinion testimony DNCW testified to on direct examination. This corresponds to the discussion in §§ 6.14–6.23.

30. "Defendant's negative character witness."

4. Per FRE 404(a)(2)(B)(i), the prosecutor can rebut DNCW's negative testimony about AV's character by calling a witness to offer favorable character (reputation or opinion) testimony about AV.

So far, 404(a)(2)(B) follows the 404(a)(2)(A) pattern: once D opens the door to evidence about V/AV's character, the prosecutor may respond by attacking DNCW's testimony (options 1 and 2) or by offering favorable information about V/AV (options 3 and 4). But once D has opened the door on the issue of V/AV's character, the prosecutor has a fifth option:

5. Per FRE 404(a)(2)(B)(ii), the prosecutor <u>can offer negative reputation or opinion testimony about the same trait of the defendant's character</u>.

In other words, by opening the door to evidence about V/AV's character, D also opens the door to evidence about his or her own character.

The following chart outlines how these provisions work:

4. *Character as "circumstantial evidence of conduct":* ***alleged victim's character*** *(criminal cases)*
   a. Character evidence
      (1) Rule 404(a)(2)(B): D can offer character testimony about a "pertinent" trait of V/AV's character.
      (2) Rule 405(a)(1st sentence): such evidence regarding a pertinent trait of V/AV's character may be offered by reputation testimony, opinion testimony, or both.
      (3) If D invokes FRE 404(a)(2)(B) by calling a negative witness to attack the V/AV's character, the prosecutor may:
         - call a character witness to testify favorably about V/AV, per FRE 404(a)(2)(B)(i); and
         - call a character witness to testify negatively about the same trait of D's character, per 404(a)(2)(B)(ii).
      (4) Moreover, in a homicide case, if D offers evidence that V/AV was the initial aggressor, the prosecutor may offer general character evidence about V/AV's peacefulness. FRE 404(a)(2)(C).[31]
   b. Specific extrinsic act character evidence:
      (1) Rule 404(b)(1) says specific extrinsic act character evidence may not be offered for this purpose.
      (2) 405(a)(2nd sentence) regulates cross-examination of a witness who has been called to give general character evidence about AV: on cross-examination only, DNCW may be asked about "relevant specific instances of [V/AV's] conduct" that are inconsistent with the negative testimony DNCW gave about V/AV on direct.
      (3) Rule 405(b) is inapplicable, because V/AV's character is not an "essential element" of the crime or defense.

<u>Abbreviations:</u>

D	defendant
DNCW	defendant's negative character witness about V/AV
V/AV	victim or alleged victim

31. I cover this provision in § 6.29.

Question 1.

Dangle and Vapid get into a fight. Dangle wins the fight, Vapid goes to the hospital, and Dangle is arrested and charged with assault. At trial, Vapid testifies for the state that she and Dangle bumped shopping carts in a supermarket parking lot and Dangle knocked her down and kicked her several times before someone grabbed Dangle and made her stop. On cross, Dangle's attorney challenges this version of events, but, not surprisingly, Vapid does not retract her accusation. The prosecutor offers medical evidence of Vapid's injuries, and rests.

During the defense case, Dangle testifies and insists that Vapid started it and Dangle merely used reasonable force to defend herself. Next, Dangle calls DNCW to testify, per FRE 404(a)(2)(B) and FRE 405(a), that Vapid's reputation in the neighborhood is that she is a turbulent, violent woman who often starts fights.

How is DNCW's testimony relevant?

Answer:

The testimony makes it more probable than it would be without the evidence that Vapid is in fact a turbulent, violent woman who often starts fights, which makes it more probable than it would be without the evidence that Vapid started this fight and that Dangle used reasonable force to defend herself.

Question 2.

Is DNCW's testimony admissible?

Answer:

Yes, assuming defense counsel elicited from DNCW the necessary testimony to satisfy the foundational requirements for reputation testimony.

Question 3.

How can the prosecutor respond?

Answer:

The prosecutor can use any one or more of the following options.

First, the prosecutor can attempt to impeach DNCW is a variety of ways, such as showing DNCW's long-time friendship with Dangle or his animosity toward Vapid. See generally §§ 12.7–12.9, *infra*.

Second, the prosecutor can attack the foundation for DNCW's testimony by cross-examining DNCW about whom he spoke to about Vapid, etc.

Third, the prosecutor can cross-examine DNCW per Rule 405(a)(2nd sentence) by asking whether he knows of (or has hear about) specific instances when Vapid responded calmly and non-violently to offensive or provocative behavior.

Fourth, after the defense rests, in the state's rebuttal case, the prosecutor can call PCW per FRE 404(a)(2)(B)(i) to testify that, in his opinion, Vapid is a very peaceful, non-violent person.

Fifth, still in the state's rebuttal case, the prosecutor can call PNCW, to testify, per FRE 404(a)(2)(B)(ii), that Dangle has the reputation in the neighborhood of a woman who frequently starts fights when someone annoys her. Note that even though Dangle did not present evidence of her own character per FRE 404(a(2)(A), when Dangle presented negative character testimony about Vapid per FRE 404(a(2)(B), this entitles the prosecutor, not only to defend Vapid's character per FRE 404(a)(2)(B)(i); it also entitles the prosecutor to present negative character testimony about Dangle's character per FRE 404(a)(2)(B)(ii)—so long as the attack focuses solely on the same character trait as the trait of Vapid's that Dangle had attacked.

Rule 404(a)(2)(B) can be invoked in other types of crimes as well. Suppose D is charged with defrauding V. D defends: "I wasn't the defrauder, AV was—he gulled me into giving him money and then created a false paper trail to make it look like it was the other way around." To support that defense, D might offer character (reputation or opinion) testimony that portrays AV as a lying, deceitful person. This would entitle the prosecutor to (i) offer reputation or opinion testimony that AV is an honest, truthful person, and (ii) offer reputation or opinion testimony that D is dishonest and deceitful.

Evidence attacking the character of an alleged victim in sex offense cases is regulated by FRE 412, covered in Chapter 9.

§ 6.29 FRE 404(a)(2)(C): homicide cases

In a homicide case, if the defendant claims that the alleged victim was the initial aggressor—"He pulled a knife on me! I had to defend myself!"—then, even if the defense has offered no negative character evidence about the defendant, the prosecutor, per FRE 404(a)(2)(C), may nevertheless offer reputation or opinion testimony about the victim's peacefulness. After all, in a homicide case, the prosecutor cannot call the victim to rebut the defendant's claim that the victim started it; this rule gives the prosecutor an opportunity to defend the victim (and the state's case) somewhat against that claim.

§ 6.30 Questions

Question 1.

On July 1, D shot and killed V, and is indicted for murder. D and V were roughly the same age. D is 5'8" and weighs 160 pounds. V was 6'4" and weighed 240, played football in college, and stayed in shape since graduating. At trial, D's attorney, in his opening statement, tells the jury: "The evidence will show that D acted in the reasonable belief that it was necessary to use deadly force to protect himself from the imminent use of deadly force against him by V." The government calls witnesses who testify that they saw D and V appear to argue briefly at a dance, which ended when D pulled a revolver and shot and killed V. The state then rests.

As his first witness, D calls DW1, who will testify that V had a reputation in the community of being "wild, assaultive and turbulent."

a. What does D hope to prove with this testimony?

b. Is the testimony admissible? What rule provides the answer?

Answer:

This testimony makes it more likely than it would be without the evidence that V was the initial aggressor and that D acted in self-defense. It is admissible per FRE 404(a)(2)(B).

Question 2.

In the same trial, D calls DW2, who will, if permitted, testify:

> Back in January, I had just finished parking my car when V came running out of his house screaming, "Nobody parks in front of my house but me!" I told him, "You don't own the street, buddy," and he said, "Yeah? Well I own this baseball bat!" And he whomped me with it and broke my collar bone.

a. What does D hope to prove with this testimony?

b. Is the testimony admissible? What rule provides the answer?

Answer:

This is an extrinsic act of violence by V. It is relevant to show that V had a propensity to act violently when angered.

Because it is an extrinsic act, we look at the rules in the right column of the chart in § 6.3. FRE 404(b)(1) says that evidence of specific extrinsic acts is not admissible to show a person's propensity to act in a particular way. Rule 405(a)(2nd sentence) does not apply, since this is direct testimony by a defense witness, not cross-examination of a witness who has given reputation or opinion testimony. V's character is not an essential element of the crime or defense, so Rule 405(b) does not apply.

Thus, the evidence is excluded per FRE 404(b)(1).

Question 3.

Assume D has not called DW2 as a witness. In the same trial, D takes the stand and testifies that late in June he attended a dance, met a very nice young woman, and danced several times with her.

Q. And then what happened?

A. DW2 walked over to me and said, "Don't you know that she is V's girlfriend?" I asked him, "Who is V?" DW2 said, "V is a guy it's a good idea to stay away from," and then DW2 told me about how V broke DW2's collar bone with a baseball bat just for parking in front of V's house.

a. What is the relevance of this testimony?

b. What objections can the prosecution make to this testimony? How should the defense attorney respond; how should the trial judge rule; on what Rules should the judge rely? If the judge rules the testimony is admissible, what option is available to the prosecutor?

Answer:

At first glance, this testimony is virtually identical to that in the previous question: the parking spot/baseball bat incident is a specific instance of V's extrinsic conduct, relevant only to show his propensity for violence, and therefore inadmissible per FRE 404(b)(1).

But there is also a second theory on which D's testimony is highly relevant—and admissible. Do you see it?

If not, re-read the opening paragraph of question 1 again, and ask yourself three questions:

(1) What is D's defense in this case?

(2) How does the law define that defense, as per defense counsel's opening statement?

(3) What is the second theory on which D's testimony is relevant?

A person is not guilty of homicide if he acted in the *reasonable belief* that deadly force was necessary to protect him/herself from the imminent use of deadly force. (Deadly force is defined as force which creates a substantial risk of causing death or serious physical injury.)

If you had been in D's situation when V came walking toward D with an unpleasant look on his face—just after hearing what DW2 had said—what would be your state of mind toward V? Considerable fear, right?[32] "If this guy breaks somebody's collarbone over a parking space, what's he gonna do to me for dancing with his girlfriend?" DW2's statement to D is highly relevant to show that D was in considerable fear when V came toward him. And DW2's statement to D is relevant to show that fear, *even if DW2 was lying to D; even if the broken collarbone incident never actually happened.*[33]

The evidence is relevant on two theories—to show V's propensity for violence, and as evidence supporting D's claim of reasonable fear. It is inadmissible on the

32. Remember, you're 5'8", 160 pounds; D is 6'4" and weighs 240 and works out a lot.

33. I do not mean to suggest that this evidence entitles D to be acquitted. Whether D's fear of death or serious injury was reasonable enough to justify shooting V would be up to the jury. But DW2's story is certainly relevant on whether D reasonably feared a violent attack from V.

first theory per Rule 404(b)(1), but since the second theory is not dependent on the truth of what DW2 said, Rule 404(b)(1) does not apply to this theory.

The judge must admit the testimony, and if the prosecutor requests, give a limiting instruction: "You may consider D's testimony (if you believe it) about what DW2 allegedly told him solely in deciding whether D acted in reasonable fear of imminent death or serious physical injury when he shot and killed V. You are not to assume that V in fact broke DW2's collarbone; you can consider the story only as something DW2 told D, not something that actually happened."

Incidentally, if you have already covered hearsay in your evidence course and you had the brilliance and foresight to buy the fifth edition of my *A Student's Guide to Hearsay,* this sequence of questions may sound familiar, because I used the same scenario in § 2.33 of that book, questions 4–7.

Question 4.

(Ignore this question if you haven't covered hearsay yet.) Speaking about hearsay... if the prosecutor objects that D's testimony about what DW2 told him is hearsay, how should D respond and how should the judge rule?

Answer:

DW2's statement to D is not hearsay because it is not being offered to prove the truth of the matter asserted in the statement; it is being offered to show the impact that hearing the statement (even if DW2 was lying) had on D's state of mind just before his encounter with V.

Question 5.

The judge permits D's testimony about what DW2 told him. D now seeks to offer into evidence a certified copy of a court record showing that V had been convicted by guilty plea of the crime of felonious assault for breaking DW2's collar bone. Does the prosecutor have a plausible objection? If so, what is it, and how should the judge rule?

Answer:

"Objection, impermissible evidence of extrinsic acts, Rule 404(b)(1)."

"Objection sustained." The conviction is relevant solely to prove that V in fact broke DW2's collarbone; and since that relevance relies exclusively on the propensity inference, it is banned by Rule 404(b)(1). In other words, evidence that D *heard* about V's parking space assault is admissible; evidence proving that V *actually committed* that assault is not.

Question 6.

What evidence might the prosecutor consider offering in rebuttal, after D rests?

Answer:

The prosecutor could offer character (reputation or opinion) about V's peaceful, non-violent character. Such testimony would be admissible per FRE 404(a)(2)(B)(i) to rebut the testimony D elicited from DW1 back in Question 1.

If D has produced any evidence (including his own testimony) that V actually hit or threatened or attempted to hit D before D shot V, evidence of V's peaceful, non-violent character would also be admissible per FRE 404(a)(2)(C).

Since D has introduced DW1's testimony about V's supposed violent character, the prosecutor could also call a witness to give reputation or opinion evidence about D's character for violence, per FRE 404(a)(2)(B)(ii).

Chapter 7

"Other Acts" Evidence: FRE 404(b)—Propensity Inference; Factually Specific Relevance

A. The Rule

§ 7.1 Introduction

FRE 404(b) regulates the use of evidence of "crimes, wrongs or other acts" that are not an intrinsic part of the events which are the primary focus of the trial. Except for FRE 403, FRE 404(b) may well be the FRE provision cited most frequently in federal court decisions. It applies in civil as well as criminal litigation. It can apply regardless of the party who offers the evidence: by a prosecutor in a criminal case, or by a defendant; or by a litigant in a civil action. It can be about a party, a witness, a victim, or someone who fits none of these categories. But it is cited most often when a prosecutor offers evidence of a defendant's extrinsic "crimes or wrongs or other acts" in a criminal trial, so I will use that scenario most of the time.

This provision applies only to *extrinsic* acts, i.e., to conduct that is not directly related to the conduct, acts or events that are the focus of the trial. Whether an act is (a) "intrinsic" (i.e., a part of or intimately connected) to the events that are the focus of the trial), or is (b) "extrinsic" (neither part of nor intimately connected) to those events, is sometimes a hotly contested issue. If the conduct in question is "intrinsic" to the charged crimes, FRE 404(b) does not apply, and the evidence comes in, so long as it is relevant and does not violate some other rule. See § 7.4 to § 7.6.

In analyzing any case or question, always begin by assuming the party against whom the evidence is offered will object that the evidence is excluded by FRE 404(b)(1). The next step is to think like the offering party (most often, the prosecutor): "How can I get this evidence in, over, under, or around or through an FRE 404(b)(1) objection? How can I persuade the judge, either that it is not 404(b) evidence at all (see § 7.4 to § 7.6), or that it falls within FRE 404(b)(2) not FRE 404(b)(1)?"

Then switch hats: as the objecting party, ask yourself, "How can I persuade the judge that the offering party's arguments are specious and the evidence should be excluded per FRE 404(b)(1) or some other rule (for example, FRE 801 (hearsay) or FRE 403)?"

Finally, put on the black robe and decide how the judge should rule.

In § 7.8 I provide a 5-step process outlining how to perform this analysis.

Before you read any further, let me acknowledge the obvious: this chapter is quite lengthy. You might quite reasonably wonder: "Do I really need to read and master the whole chapter?"

That depends. If you want a deep, nuanced understanding of the rule, studying the entire chapter will give you that. But if your immediate concern is learning the basics well enough to handle quiz and exam questions about Rule 404(b)—which is a completely reasonable goal, given everything else law school and life are throwing at you—read through § 7.14 (and § 7.23, if your prof covers the *Huddleston* case), and the questions in § 7.36, and then pick and choose among the rest of the sections depending on what your professor seems to emphasize.

§ 7.2 The text of the rule and how to read it

Effective December 1, 2020, FRE 404(b) provides:

Rule 404. Character Evidence; Other Crimes, Wrongs or Acts

. . .

(b) Other Crimes, Wrongs, or Acts.

(1) Prohibited Uses. Evidence of any other crime, wrong, or act is not admissible to prove a person's character in order to show that on a particular occasion the person acted in accordance with the character.

(2) Permitted Uses. This evidence may be admissible for another purpose, such as proving motive, opportunity, intent, preparation, plan, knowledge, identity, absence of mistake, or lack of accident.

(3) Notice in a Criminal Case. In a criminal case, the prosecutor must:

(A) provide reasonable notice of any such evidence that the prosecutor intends to offer at trial, so that the defendant has a fair opportunity to meet it;

(B) articulate in the notice the permitted purpose for which the prosecutor intends to offer the evidence and the reasoning that supports the purpose; and

(C) do so in writing before trial—or in any form during trial if the court, for good cause, excuses lack of pretrial notice.

The 2020 amendment revised the notice requirement, which we will examine in §7.7.

FRE 404(b)(1) is an *exclusionary rule:* evidence of other specific acts is not admissible to prove a trait of character for the purpose of showing a person acted in accordance with that character on a particular occasion. In other words, if its relevance relies on the propensity inference, FRE 404(b)(1) requires its exclusion—unless it is admissible via another rule.[1] This forbidden "propensity inference" is sometimes referred to as the "bad man" or "bad person" inference (although the rule also applies to "good" prior acts, too—see §7.4–iii.

Here are two examples.

(1) On May 1, cars driven by P and D collide. Each claims the other entered the intersection against a red light. In litigation between the two, P wants to offer evidence that in the previous 18 months, D twice was ticketed for running red lights.

(2) S is charged with selling drugs to an undercover agent on June 1. The prosecutor also wants to offer evidence that on May 15 and June 15, S also sold drugs to other people.

FRE 404(b)(1) mandates that in example (1), P cannot introduce evidence concerning D's two prior red-light violations to support P's claim that D ran the light on the occasion that resulted in the collision. Likewise, in example (2), evidence of S's

1. See §7.3 for a list of other rules under which evidence of extrinsic acts may be admissible.

prior and subsequent sales of drugs is not admissible as evidence that S sold drugs to an undercover officer on May 1.[2]

FRE 404(b)(1) excludes such evidence for two reasons. First, it may be too prejudicial: in deciding the defendant's guilt or innocence or a civil litigant's claim or defense in the case being tried, a jury is likely to rely too heavily on what someone did on other, unrelated occasions. The second reason is that allowing such evidence is likely to make trials much longer. If a litigant is permitted to offer evidence of X's[3] extrinsic conduct to show X's propensity, then the other litigant must be permitted to offer evidence (assuming it exists) that X did not engage in the extrinsic act, or that the circumstances surrounding X's extrinsic conduct were so different than the circumstances at issue in the trial that the jury should not accept that the extrinsic conduct establishes a propensity in the first place. This would prolong the trial and distract the jury from the issues they were empaneled to decide.

404(b)(2), by contrast, is an *inclusionary rule:* such evidence "may be admissible for another purpose [i.e., for a purpose other than showing propensity], such as proving motive, opportunity, intent, preparation, plan, knowledge, identity, absence of mistake or lack of accident." If the party offering X's extrinsic act can convince the judge that that evidence is relevant on a theory or for a purpose other than the propensity ("bad person" or "good person") inference forbidden by FRE 404(b)(1), it should be admitted—unless it is banned by some other rule.[4] To put it differently, if the evidence has what I call "factually specific relevance independent of the propensity inference," the default assumption is that the evidence should be admitted.

Note that I did not say that, to satisfy rule 404(b)(2), the evidence must have factually specific relevance "instead of" the propensity inference. FRE 404(b)(2) evidence of extrinsic "crimes or wrongs or other acts" quite often carries a propensity inference with it—sometimes a very strong propensity inference. But that does not require exclusion, so long as (a) the evidence has sufficient factually specific relevance to give it probative value independent of the propensity inference, and (b) that factually specific relevance is not substantially outweighed by the risk of unfair prejudice, waste of time, confusing the jury, etc. Thus, FRE 404(b) is in essence a specialized version of FRE 403.

One final comment. In Chapter 6, I emphasized several times that Rule 404(a)(2) prohibits a prosecutor from presenting character evidence (i.e., reputation or opinion testimony) about the defendant or about the victim or alleged victim, unless the defendant first opened the door. FRE 404(**b**)(2) contains no such restriction. In

2. Under some circumstances, a prosecutor could charge all three sales in the same trial, but often that is not practicable.

3. Remember: "X" could be a defendant, a victim or alleged victim, a plaintiff, a witness, a police officer, or some other person whose crime-or-claim-specific conduct is an issue at the trial.

4. For example, if the only evidence available to prove that X committed an extrinsic act is inadmissible hearsay, the evidence would be excluded on that ground, even if it satisfied FRE 404(b)(2).

a criminal case, the prosecutor may—and very often does—offer evidence of the defendant's extrinsic acts during the state's case-in-chief.

Circumstances do arise when evidence that should be excluded per Rule 404(b)(1) at the beginning of the trial may become admissible per Rule 404(b)(2) based on what the defense did during the trial, but those circumstances do not create a general rule regarding Rule 404(b); rather, such cases merely reflect a much more general rule that what happens during a trial may affect what evidence can be admitted later in the trial. To repeat: there is no general rule precluding a prosecutor from offering extrinsic act evidence unless the defense first opens the door; the only precondition is that the prosecutor's extrinsic act evidence must satisfy FRE 404(b)(2) and survive any other objections that the defense may make.

§ 7.3 FRE 404(b) in context

This chart may help you distinguish between FRE 404(b), and the other rules we have covered (so far) dealing with extrinsic act evidence.

Evidence of extrinsic acts: propensity; "other purposes"

a. FRE 404(b)(1) is an exclusionary rule: it directs that specific character evidence is not admissible to prove the "propensity inference."
b. FRE 404(b)(2) is an inclusionary rule: such evidence may be admissible for "other" purposes, so long as it has factually specific relevance *independent of* the forbidden 404(b)(1) propensity inference.
c. FRE 405(a)(1st sentence) is inapplicable, as that governs only witnesses who give reputation or opinion testimony about someone's character.
d. FRE 405(a)(2nd sentence) is inapplicable; that rule applies only to cross-examination of witnesses who give reputation or opinion testimony about someone's character.
e. FRE 405(b) is inapplicable: that provision applies only in civil litigation where someone's character is an "essential element" of a claim or defense. See generally Chapter 5.

Note: the rules covered in Chapters 4 through 13 apply in eight different courtroom scenarios, which I refer to as "litigation situations." In § 11.23 to § 11.31, I summarize each litigation situation and list the rules that apply in that litigation situation. The litigation situation in which FRE 404(b) applies most often is in a criminal trial, during the prosecutor's case-in-chief, which is litigation situation E; see § 11.28. But FRE 404(b) might apply in virtually any of these litigation situations. (For now, ignore this paragraph; I include it here as a cross-reference that may be helpful later.).

But several other provisions also apply to extrinsic act evidence. Here is a more complete list:

- FRE 406, relating to habit evidence. See Chapter 8.
- FRE 412, relating to the complainant in a sex offense prosecution. See Chapter 9.
- FRE 413–415, relating to the defendant in sex offense prosecutions. See Chapter 10.
- Impeachment of a witness's perception, memory, narration or bias/motive to lie. See Chapter 12.
- FRE 608(b) and, very occasionally, on cross-examination, FRE 608(a). See § 13.2 to § 13.9.
- FRE 609. See § 13.10 to § 13.29.
- Any other rule that might be applicable—hearsay, authentication, subsequent remedial measures, etc.
- FRE 403, which should be considered with regard to virtually every offer of evidence.

B. When FRE 404(b) Applies—and When It Doesn't

§ 7.4 What are "crimes, wrongs, or other acts"?

i. "Crimes"

We pretty much know what a "crime" is: conduct that fits the description of a crime defined in the penal code. Evidence that X committed a crime that is extrinsic to the central facts of the current case may be direct or indirect. Direct evidence that X committed the extrinsic crime can take a variety of forms. (1) A party might offer in evidence a court document certifying that X was convicted of the extrinsic crime. (2) One or more witnesses might testify that they saw X commit the extrinsic crime. (3) One or more witnesses might testify that they heard X admit to committing the extrinsic crime. (4) A party might introduce a handwritten note or text message or email in which X acknowledges committing the extrinsic crime. (5) A party might introduce a video which captured X committing the extrinsic crime. And so on. Whatever the form of evidence, a litigant opposing the evidence should object, citing FRE 404(b)(1) and FRE 403. That party should also raise any other objection to the evidence that might apply. For example, examples (1), (3) and (4) raise hearsay issues. Example (4) also raises authentication issues: can the offering party offer adequate evidence that X is the person who wrote the note, text message or email. Example (5) also raises authentication issues.

Some courts have held that evidence that *indirectly* suggests that "X" has committed prior crimes or wrongs also implicates FRE 404(b)(1). Consider, for example, testimony that police showed X's "mugshot" to a witness, or had X's fingerprints on file, or that X's DNA profile was in a government data base. Some courts reason that this implicates FRE 404(b)(1), because a jury might assume that X must have been in trouble with the law at some point in his or her life—otherwise, why would X's prints, photograph or DNA be in a government data base? Other courts reason that because the evidence does not refer to a specific crime or wrong, admissibility is governed only by FRE 401 and 403.

Follow your professor's lead as to whether to apply Rule 404(b) in such cases. But whether we apply Rule 404(b), or Rules 401 and 403, X's attorney should object to references to the fact that X's mugshot or fingerprints or DNA profile were already available to police; the judge should assess whether the evidence has factually specific relevance, and if so, whether the risk of unfair prejudice can be mitigated. Regarding the mugshot situation, for example, the judge should instruct the witness that he identified "a photo" of X without specifying it was a mugshot.[5] And if the judge does allow in evidence that police already had copies of X's mugshot or fingerprints or DNA profile, the judge should instruct the jury that they should draw no inference about defendant's character from that fact; nor should it infer that the defendant was previously convicted of a crime.

A party might similarly object to indirect evidence that X committed other "wrongs" or "acts."

ii. "Wrongs"

A "wrong," on the other hand, is not a crime, but it is nevertheless conduct which carries a stigma of impropriety or misbehavior.

Question 1.

P and D were business partners. The business went bankrupt, and P sued D, alleging that D diverted business funds to his own use and cheated P out of a considerable amount of money. D denies doing anything of the kind. At trial, P wants to introduce evidence that during the period in question, D spent a good deal of money entertaining and buying expensive presents for XGF, D's girlfriend at the time. D objects that the evidence is irrelevant and also violates FRE 404(b)(1).

---

5. If the defendant claims mistaken identity and challenges the accuracy of the photo ID, the judge should allow the prosecutor to show the photos to the jury so the jury can assess the fairness of the photo array for itself.

Answer:

Assuming D had no source of income other than the P-D partnership, the evidence of lavish spending on XGF is relevant to suggest a motive for diverting business funds and to show where the money went. And while spending lavishly to impress a woman may indicate bad judgment, it is not a crime; nor is it necessarily a "wrong." Nor does the relevance of the evidence depend on a propensity inference. Hence, Rule 404(b)(1) provides no basis to exclude the evidence.

Question 2.

P also wants to offer evidence that D was spending lavishly on XGF while D was married and living with his wife. D objects: irrelevant, FRE 401; unduly prejudicial; FRE 403; and inadmissible per FRE 404(b)(1).

Is the evidence relevant for any legitimate reason; and if so, does FRE 404(b)(1) nevertheless exclude it?

Answer:

Now we arguably in FRE 404(b)(1) territory. Cheating on one's spouse is not a crime, but it most people would agree it is morally wrong. And it raises a propensity inference: the fact that D was cheating on his wife suggests that he would cheat his business partner, too.[6]

So should the judge exclude the fact that D was committing adultery? Does that evidence have factually specific relevance, independent of the propensity inference? See if you can devise a plausible argument. We will return to this fact pattern in a later section.

Evidence that X is affiliated with a street gang or organized crime family creates a strong inference of bad character, and a powerful inference of guilt by association. Here, too, some courts might apply FRE 404(b) and 403 to such evidence; other courts might skip Rule 404(b) and apply FRE 401 and 403. Under either approach, evidence of X's affiliation should be excluded unless there was a clear connection between the crime X is being tried for and X's affiliation with the organization, or unless for some other reason X's affiliation has factually specific relevance.

iii. "Other acts"

Most often, X's extrinsic acts are "crimes or wrongs," and evidence of them is offered as a basis to infer that because X committed one or more particular crimes or wrongs on one or more other, unrelated occasions, X

6. Adultery and stealing from a partnership are very different forms of "cheating," but they do indicate a propensity for betraying intimate relationships—one personal, one professional.

has a propensity to commit such crimes or wrongs, and therefore X probably committed the same kind of crime or wrong in the events that are the focus of the current trial. In other words, most 404(b) evidence is negative in nature.

But evidence of acts other than crimes or wrongs may also be relevant to suggest propensity to behave in a particular way—including proper, even admirable behavior. The phrase "other act" means "any other extrinsic act, even if it is neither a crime or a wrong, if offered to prove propensity."

Example: Cars driven by L and Z collide at an intersection with stop signs at all four corners. Each sues the other, claiming the other failed to stop. Z wants to call T, a teenager, who will testify, "Z's daughter Zinnia and another kid and I carpool to school and back, and Z drives us to school two mornings a week. Z always stops at every stop sign. Even if there's nobody in sight—no cars, no walkers, nobody riding a bike—nobody in sight! Z. Still. Stops. And I mean full, complete stops. At. Every. Stop sign. No matter what. Even if we are running late. He stops. At. Every. Stop sign. Every. Single. Time."[7]

Z's consistency at stop signs is not a "crimes or wrongs"; in fact, it is praiseworthy.[8] But each stop at a stop sign is an extrinsic act. Why does Z offer such testimony? "[I]n order to show that on a particular occasion [i.e., just before Z and L collided], the person [Z] acted in accordance with the character [i.e., that Z stopped at that stop sign on that occasion]." This language requires the judge to sustain L's Rule 404(b)(1) objection to this testimony, because its relevance depends exclusively on the propensity inference.

<u>Question 3.</u>

JD, an attorney, represents UM, a union member, in a civil lawsuit. One benefit of union membership is that in certain kinds of cases, the union pays members' lawyers' fees. JD is charged with trying to bribe a witness to testify in favor of UM. At trial, the prosecutor offers evidence that the union in fact paid JD to represent UM in that lawsuit. JD objected, arguing that this violates FRE 404(b)(1) and 403. How should the judge rule?

<u>Answer:</u>

Objection overruled. Receiving payment from UM's union is relevant to show that JD in fact represented UM, but carries no stigma or risk of unfair prejudice, since there is nothing illegal or morally wrong about receiving a fee for services rendered. And Rule 404(b)(1) does not apply, because its relevance does not rely on a propensity inference.

---

7. Assume this testimony is accompanied by typical teenage eye-rolling.

8. In fact, as anyone who has driven a carful of teenagers will attest, the urge to get them to their destination and out of the car as quickly as possible is sometimes so strong that Z's persistence at stopping at every stop sign (thereby prolonging the drive to school) may approach sainthood.

§ 7.5 "Extrinsic" vs. "intrinsic" acts; conspiracy; scheme or plan

i. Overview

FRE 404(b) applies only to acts that are "extrinsic" to—i.e., not part of—the events that are the subject-matter of the case being tried. Admissibility of evidence concerning acts which are "intrinsic" to, i.e., part of, the events in question is regulated by FRE 401 and 403 without reference to FRE 404(b).

Here's an example of the difference between an intrinsic and an extrinsic act. D is charged with criminally negligent homicide because he struck and killed a pedestrian on March 22 during his drive home from work. Evidence that D frequently stopped at a bar for a couple of drinks on his way home from work would be extrinsic act evidence, and should be excluded if D objects citing FRE 404(b)(1). Its relevance depends on the suggestion that he has a propensity to drink on the way home and therefore probably did so, and therefore was probably under the influence, on March 22. But evidence that he stopped in a bar for a couple of drinks on his way home from work on March 22 is not "extrinsic act" evidence, because it is *directly* relevant to the key issue in the case, i.e., whether D was intoxicated on the evening of March 22 and therefore was more likely criminally negligent in the way he drove.

ii. Common situations

In some common situations, most courts agree that evidence should be considered intrinsic to a crime, rather than extrinsic. Here are two examples:

Where certain physical objects are connected with a crime, evidence that the defendant possessed those objects sometime before the crime or sometime after the crime is admissible to suggest that the defendant also possessed those items at the time of the crime, which makes it more probable than it would be without the evidence that the defendant committed the crime. Thus evidence that the defendant possessed them before or after the crime (or both before and after) is considered intrinsic, rather than extrinsic, to the crime.

When a defendant coerces a victim into complying with his demands by threatening to do to the victim what he (claims he) has done to others, the threats themselves should not be considered extrinsic acts, because they are part of the underlying crime.

iii. What is the defendant charged with?

Whether a "crime, wrong or act" is intrinsic or extrinsic to the charges being tried may depend on what the defendant is charged with.

Suppose, for example, police lawfully search D's home in County A, and find dozens of items that were stolen in seven separate home burglaries committed in a three-county area: two In County A, three years apart; two in County B, four years apart; and three in and C, five years apart. In other words, these items have only two things in common: they were all stolen in home burglaries, and they were all in

D's home when police searched it. D claims he bought the items from the County A burglaries at yard sales and flea markets, and had no knowledge they were stolen.

If, in County A, D is charged only with burglary, a judge should exclude evidence of the items that had been stolen in Counties B and C, because that evidence, and the burglaries in County B and County C, are extrinsic to the County A burglaries, and are relevant only to show D's propensity to commit burglaries.

But if, in addition to the County A burglaries, D is also charged in County A with criminal possession of all the stolen property seized from his home when the police searched it, then all those items, including those stolen from County B and County C, are intrinsic to the possession of the stolen property charges.

Question 1.

How could the County A prosecutor establish that each of the items was stolen?

Answer:

D's attorney might stipulate that all the items in question were in fact stolen in home burglaries. If D does not stipulate, the prosecutor cannot simply introduce lists of items prepared by the police or by the various burglary victims, because those lists are inadmissible hearsay. After a police officer points out each item found in D's home, the prosecutor must call the owner of each item to testify, "My home was broken into on [such-and-such a date], and several things were taken," then identify each item that had been taken from that owner's home. (In fact the prosecutor might opt to do this even if D does stipulate. Testimony from the burglary victims is far more compelling to a jury than merely a stipulated list of items.)

iv. Conspiracy

You learned in your criminal law course that a conspiracy is an agreement between two or more people to commit a crime or a series of crimes. By including a conspiracy count in an indictment, a prosecutor may be able to admit evidence of uncharged crimes that otherwise would be considered extrinsic.

On May 1, CI-1, an informant, introduced UC, an undercover officer, to D1. UC told D1 she was looking for someone to supply seller-quantities of heroin. On May 5th, D1 introduced UC to "my partner, D2." On May 10th, D1 and D2 sold a quantity of heroin to UC. On May 15th, D2 and UC met to negotiate another sale, which culminated on May 25th. On June 15, D1 and D2 were arrested and indicted.

While preparing for trial, police officers acquire additional information about D1 and D2.

PW1 is willing to testify that on May 8th, D2 sold him a small quantity of heroin.

PW2 is willing to testify that on May 12th, he overheard D1 telling someone that "me and my partner are expecting a big package soon; we'll let you know when we've got it."

PW3 is willing to testify that on May 28th, she and D1 were in D2's apartment and saw a scale, packages of quinine and starch, and heat-sealable bags stored on a shelf together.

If the indictment merely charged D1 and D2 with selling heroin to UC on May 10th and May 25th, many courts would exclude PW1's testimony because it has only propensity relevance; likewise, PW2's testimony; likewise PW3's.

But if the indictment also charged that "From on or about May 1 to on or about May 25, D1 and D2 conspired with each other to distribute heroin," all three witnesses' testimony would be admissible, because each witness's testimony is relevant to prove that during the period alleged in the indictment, D1 and D2 were in fact conspiring with each other to sell heroin.[9]

v. Scheme or plan

If a defendant is charged with a crime that is the culmination of a scheme or plan, preliminary crimes designed to further the scheme are sometimes classified as intrinsic to the overall scheme, and therefore beyond the scope of FRE 404(b), or are classified as falling within FRE 404(b)(2), rather than FRE 404(b)(1). See § 7.32, infra.

Question 2.

V was robbed at gunpoint on March 1 by a man wearing a bright red polo shirt wielding what V described as "a small handgun." D was arrested for the robbery in August. At trial, D's neighbor N perhaps reluctantly testifies that sometime early in June, he and his wife had dinner at D's house, that D was wearing a bright red polo shirt, and after dinner, D showed N a small .22 caliber pistol. D objects that the evidence is irrelevant because his wife gave him the polo shirt as a birthday present in April—after the robbery was committed. D also claims that he did not obtain the pistol until June, and that evidence that he owned a pistol violated FRE 404(b)(1). (D's wife is prepared to testify to these facts.) How should the prosecutor respond; how should the judge rule?

Answer:

Objections overruled.

Regarding relevance: that D possessed a bright red polo shirt and a small handgun three months after the robbery makes it more probable than it would be without the evidence that D possessed both items back on March 1, which makes it more probable than it would be without the evidence that he was the robber. And this is true even though V's description of the polo shirt and handgun was rather generic

9. PW3's testimony is relevant because an expert witness would explain that quinine, starch and heat-sealable bags are frequently used by heroin dealers to dilute and package heroin for sale. And even though PW3's testimony relates to events after May 25th, they should still be admissible on the conspiracy charge, because May 28th comes within the "or about" phrase of the conspiracy charge.

and so was N's. Ditto the fact lots of people probably possess either or both of those items.[10] Surely defense counsel, on cross and in summation, will stress the generic descriptions and the widespread possession of a small handguns and a red polo shirts. The jury will evaluate the significance of D's possession of them.

D's wife's testimony that D obtained both items after the robbery eliminates the probative value of N's testimony—BUT only if the jury believes D's wife's testimony. Her testimony goes to the weight of the evidence, but not its admissibility.

Finally, query whether this evidence carries any "bad man inference" at all. Possession of most firearms in one's home is now lawful throughout the United States,[11] and possession of a red polo shirt is neither a crime nor a wrong.

Question 3.

Suppose the dinner get-together happened three months before the robbery, rather than three months after it. Would that change the outcome?

Answer:

It shouldn't. D's possession of those items three months before the robbery makes it more probable than it would be without the evidence that he still possessed them on the day of the robbery, which makes it more probable than it would be without the evidence that he was the robber. Thus, possession of these items before and/or after the crime is still "intrinsic" to the robbery, and not covered by FRE 404(b).

If you are not convinced, think of all the things that you possessed three months ago—clothing, furniture, athletic gear, electronic gear, books, dishes, flatware, cookware, appliances, etc.—not including perishables (no fair including the bag of salad or the apples). How many of those things do you still possess today? Unless you have undergone a dramatic change of circumstances, you still possess most of them. Now ask yourself: how many of those things do you expect to get rid of in the next three months? Barring unusual circumstances, three months from now, you will still possess most of what you now possess.

---

10. The evidence would be far more probative if the weapon was a sawed-off shotgun and the shirt depicted, say, two reindeer mating, one of which had a bright red nose. But although the lack of distinguishing characteristics other than "red" and "small" diminishes the probative value of N's testimony, it doesn't erase it.

11. District of Columbia v. Heller, 554 U.S. 570 (2008).

§7.6 "Arising from same transaction"; "inextricably intertwined"; "necessary to complete the story"; "part of the 'res gestae'"

The four phrases set in quotes in the title of this section appear frequently in Rule 404(b) case law.[12] Some courts rely on one or more of these phrases as reasons why a Rule 404(b)(1) objection should be overruled.[13]

Their use is a source of considerable confusion. First, although different definitions of each phrase[14] can be found in court decisions, these labels are often used interchangeably, so it is often difficult to truly distinguish one from the other.

Second, courts differ as to why evidence fitting into one of these labels should be admitted over an FRE 404(b)(1) objection. Some courts seem to say that in such cases, a "crime, wrong or act" fitting within one of these labels is automatically intrinsic to the charged crime, and therefore not subject to Rule 404(b). In some jurisdictions, courts seem to say that crimes, wrong or acts fitting within one of these labels are exempt from Rule 404(b), regardless of whether they are intrinsic or extrinsic to the charged crime. Still others apparently hold that a crime, wrong or act that fits one of these labels automatically satisfies FRE 404(b)(2).

Here are a few examples:

Courts frequently admit such evidence where the uncharged conduct is an integral part of the events in question. For example: D is charged with selling drugs. When arrested, he possessed a loaded handgun. Courts generally have held that evidence of weapon possession is admissible in prosecutions involving substantial quantities of drugs, even if D did not use or display a weapon when he made the sale for which D is now on trial.

Where a defendant is charged with committing a violent crime, acts of violence that immediately preceded or followed the charged act are often admitted to place the charged acts in context or to "complete the story."

Along the same lines, some courts hold that evidence of uncharged crimes should be admitted if they were apparently part of the same "crime spree." Suppose on Monday, a couple—let's call them Bonnie and Clyde—break into a house in Maine and steal a gun and a car. Tuesday, in New Hampshire, they use the gun and car to rob a bank. On Wednesday, they abandon the first car and steal a car parked at a

12. The phrase "scheme or plan" is also often used in this context. See §7.32, *infra*.

13. I do not recall any court decision using any of these phrases in a civil case, although there may be some.

14. "Res gestae" is a Latin term which (I am informed) means, more or less, "the thing itself." It is used in the law in about as many different situations as a switch-hitting utility infielder-outfielder in baseball.

train station in Massachusetts, then rob a grocery store in Rhode Island. Thursday, in Connecticut, they break into a home and force the occupant to turn over several hundred dollars in cash. Friday, they rob a liquor store in New York and are apprehended after a short chase.

At their trials in each state for the crimes committed in that state, a plausible argument can be made why at least some evidence of crimes committed in other states should be admitted over a Rule 404(b)(1) objection.[15] But the prosecutor should be required to make that argument, and the judge should be required to rule on the issue without simply citing one of the labels. Accordingly, some courts reject these labels altogether, complaining that they have become only convenient excuses to admit the evidence without even considering whether the evidence should be excluded by FRE 404(b)(1).

It is particularly important that, before relying on one of these labels, a court should determine whether the "crime, wrong or act" is an intrinsic part of, or is extrinsic to it. Why? Because if the "crime, wrong or act" is extrinsic, the prosecutor is obliged to give the defense pretrial notice of it, per FRE 404(b)(3). See § 7.7, *infra*.

§ 7.7 The notice requirement

If the prosecutor plans to offer extrinsic act evidence per FRE 404(b)(2), FRE 404(b)(3) requires her to give advance notice to the defense in writing.[16]

FRE 404(b)(3)(A) and FRE 404(b)(3)(C) require the prosecutor to give "reasonable notice of any such evidence," in writing, before trial. Presumably, that means she must specify, in the notice, the specific extrinsic acts she plans to offer, and, perhaps, the precise nature of the evidence she plans to use to prove that the defendant committed the extrinsic acts. And the prosecutor must notify the defense far enough in advance of the trial to give "the defendant... a fair opportunity to meet" the evidence.

FRE404(b)(3)(B) requires the prosecutor to "articulate in the notice the permitted purpose for which the prosecutor intends to offer the evidence and the reasoning that supports the purpose...." That means the notice must, at least, specify the 404(b)(2) purpose or purposes the prosecutor relies on. Moreover, the prosecutor must also set out how the evidence has factually specific relevance independent of the propensity inference.

If the prosecutor fails to provide the required notice, the judge may exclude the evidence; or suspend the trial for a period of time to give the defense attorney an opportunity to investigate it; or declare a mistrial.

---

15. For example, in the Massachusetts car-theft trial, evidence that they possessed and used the car in the New York liquor store robbery a few days later should be admissible to help identify them as the car thieves.

16. The text of FRE 404(b)(3) is set out in § 7.2.

C. An Analytical Model

§ 7.8 The five step process; "fasprelipi"

This section sets out a five-step process for analyzing whether extrinsic act evidence is admissible, i.e., whether it is banned by the FRE 404(b)(1) exclusionary rule, or whether it is admissible per the FRE 404(b)(2) inclusionary rule. Sometimes applying this process will point clearly to one result or the other. Quite often, however, at the end of the process, you will have to make a judgment call whether to admit or exclude—just as a judge often must during a trial. The goal of the process is not to guarantee you will reach the right conclusion; it is to make sure you carefully analyze the evidence and don't fall into the trap of merely relying on a convenient label without any analysis.

This process has worked well for me in the classroom, and I required my students to apply it in class and on quizzes and the exams. I am confident that it helped them apply FRE 404(b), and I am confident it will help you, too. (But if your professor has developed his or her own analytical model and expects you to apply it, remember Fishman Rule of Evidence 001.)

Keep in mind that you should apply this process only after analyzing whether the evidence involves an extrinsic act, or whether the conduct is intrinsic to the crime, cause of action or defense that is at issue in the current trial. If you conclude that the evidence is intrinsic, then, logically, there is no need to apply this process at all.

But also keep in mind that although *you* might think the "crime, wrong or act" is intrinsic to the central issues in the current trial, your professor may not. If you are answering an essay question that carries a high point total, the safest bet might be to explain why you think the evidence is intrinsic, and then say, "Assuming the judge rules this is extrinsic act evidence, however," and then apply this process (or your professor's own preferred approach).

Once you've concluded that the evidence might be considered extrinsic, the first step is to apply this process from the perspective of the offering party—most often, the prosecutor in a criminal case.

1. Issue/purpose/theory of relevance. Articulate the purpose for which the evidence is offered, i.e., what factual/legal issue in the case is the evidence being offered to address. Initially, this step involves choosing one or more of the "purposes" listed in FRE 404(b)(2), although that list of purposes is not an exclusive list. See § 7.9.
2. Need. Looking at all of the evidence that is has been or is likely to be offered, determine whether there is a need for evidence to accomplish the specified purpose. Does the evidence address a hotly contested issue, or an issue which

the other side more or less concedes, or on which the offering side already has overwhelming evidence? Would excluding the evidence disappoint the jury's expectation as to what evidence the offering party would present? Would a jury suspect that the offering party is hiding something if the evidence is not admitted? See § 7.10.

3. Proof that X committed the extrinsic act. Analyze how, and how persuasively, the offering party (usually, the prosecutor in a criminal case) can prove that "X" (usually, the defendant in a criminal case) committed the extrinsic act. See § 7.11.
4. "Fasprelipi." Combining the first three steps, assess the *legitimate* probative value of the evidence on issues that are legitimately in the case. To put it differently, does the evidence have **fa**ctually **s**pecific **rel**evance **i**ndependent of the **p**ropensity **i**nference? For the rest of this book, I will refer to this as "fasprelipi."[17] If the evidence lacks fasprelipi, it is inadmissible. See § 7.12 & § 7.13.
5. FRE 403 and 105. Once this assessment is made, apply Rule 403, and any provision of Article I that might apply, including, most often, FRE 105 (limiting instruction). See § 7.14.

The next several sections examine each step in detail.

§ 7.9 Purpose/issue/theory of relevance

The offering party (most often a prosecutor in a criminal case) has the initial burden of specifying the purpose (other than the forbidden propensity or "bad person" or "good person" inference) for which the evidence is offered. It is not enough merely to select at random one of the purposes enunciated in the rule. Rather, the prosecutor should be required to identify the ultimate trial issue—i.e., the *element of the crime, cause of action or defense*—toward which the evidence is offered.

With only slight oversimplification, it is fair to say that the prosecutor in a criminal case ultimately must prove three (and often, only three) things beyond a reasonable doubt: *conduct*—that a criminal act was committed; *identity*—that it was the defendant, not someone else, who committed it;[18] and *mental state*—that the act was committed with the mental state specified in the statute.[19] With the same risk

17. I will do so for several reasons. First, it gets tiresome to type out "factually significant relevance independent of the propensity inference" several times in each section. (But I will spell out the entire phrase from time to time, to remind you what it means.) Second, using the mnemonic will help you remember the phrase. Third... well, I just get a kick out of inventing ridiculous mnemonics.

18. The distinction between "identity" and "conduct" is a subtle and somewhat slippery one. I discuss that question a little further into this section, and again in § 7.21.

19. Some crimes require the prosecutor to prove some additional fact or facts. The degree (severity) of theft-related crimes may depend on the value of the item the defendant stole or attempted

of slight oversimplification, the same can be said with regard to most civil litigation: ultimately, the issues are conduct, identity and mental state (plus damages).

If you have read the rule carefully, you have noticed that FRE 404(b)(2) lists nine possible "other purposes"—"motive, opportunity, intent, preparation, plan, knowledge, identity, absence of mistake, lack of accident." And true enough, the evidence satisfying FRE 404(b)(2) will almost always fall within one of these categories.[20] But merely finding a convenient "label" within FRE 404(b)(2) will satisfy neither the law nor your professor. Each of these "labels" (except identity) is a way of connecting the evidence to one of the three ultimate purposes or theories of relevance: identity, conduct, mental state. Your job is to figure out how (if at all) the offering party can logically argue from the evidence to the ultimate purpose or theory of relevance without relying on the propensity inference.

The following chart will ultimately be helpful when you have to analyze fact patterns to determine whether evidence satisfies FRE 404(b)(2):

Identity	Conduct	Mental State
Motive	Motive	Knowledge
Opportunity	Intent	Intent
Preparation	Lack of accident	Absence of mistake
Plan	Preparation	Lack of accident
Knowledge	Plan	Motive
	Knowledge	Preparation
		Plan

Later sections will reproduce this chart when we discuss each of the three ultimate facts of consequence.

to steal. The degree of burglary may depend on whether the premises was a dwelling. Some crimes require the prosecutor to prove some fact about the complainant or victim—his or her age or mental capacity or occupation, for example, or in hate crimes, the victim's age, race, religion, nationality, sexual orientation. And the definition of some crimes requires the prosecutor to prove the defendant's relationship to another person's conduct, as in conspiracy charges and cases involving accomplice (accessorial) liability. But a prosecutor is always required to offer satisfactory evidence regarding the perpetrator's identity, conduct and mental state.

20. The purposes listed in FRE 404(b)(2) are not an exclusive list, rather, the rule speaks of "another purpose such as" the nine purposes listed in the rule. But in virtually every case, directly or indirectly, any evidence that satisfies FRE 404(b)(2) can ultimately be traced back to one of these three purposes—identity, conduct or mental state.

In the typical criminal case—a theft, robbery, sale of a controlled substance, burglary or homicide—the defendant does not challenge the prosecutor's allegation that *someone* committed the crime; rather the defendant denies that he or she was the one who committed it, that the case is one of mistaken identity. Accordingly, *the default assumption is that the key issue in a criminal case is "identity."* This should be where you start, unless the facts—or a cleverly crafted argument—require or enable a party to cite a different purpose.

Sometimes, however, a defendant makes it clear that he or she *is* challenging whether the *conduct* in question was committed. Example: on June 15, M and W went to dinner and a movie. M took W back to her home, stayed awhile, and left. She accuses him of raping her after he brought her home, using brute strength and threats to overcome her physical resistance. (a) If he denies intercourse ever occurred, the issue is not *identity*—he acknowledges he was with her in her home for a while that night. Rather, the issue is *conduct*—he denies having intercourse with her at all. (b) If he acknowledges that they had intercourse, but insists that she consented, the case is likely to present a mixed issue of *conduct* and *mental state* (*mens rea*): he will deny that she resisted physically or that he used force *(conduct)*, and will testify that she consented, or, at least, he reasonably believed that she consented (*mens rea*).

Sometimes the prosecution and defense may disagree as to whether the key issue in the case is identity, conduct, or mental state. Remember: neither side in a lawsuit views the case from an abstract, neutral perspective. Each wants to win. Where the prosecutor offers a defendant's extrinsic conduct, she starts where she wants to end up—getting the evidence admitted—and works backwards from there: "What purpose (identity, conduct or mental state) can I plausibly cite that gives me the best chance of persuading the judge to admit the evidence? If it would be inadmissible to prove identity, for example, can I make a plausible argument that the evidence is admissible to show the defendant's mental state, which would give me a better chance to persuade the judge to admit the evidence?"

The defense attorney, of course, does the same thing: "I want to keep the evidence out. So I have to challenge the prosecutor's 'purpose.' If I can convince the judge that the real issue in the case is something else, not what the prosecutor argues, I have a better chance of a ruling excluding the evidence." I'll explain this further in §7.24 et seq.

Then put on the black robe and decide the motion.

Sometimes, of course, the evidence stacks up so much in favor of one side that the other side lacks a plausible argument. Such cases make pretty good multiple-choice questions. But sometimes arguments exist for both sides. Make a point of looking for both sides' arguments; don't just assume that the most obvious purpose is the only one worth discussing.

§ 7.10 Need for the evidence

Once the purpose has been identified, the next step is to evaluate whether the evidence is really necessary. How much evidence besides the extrinsic act evidence does the prosecutor have on the issue? Is the issue truly contested, or is it virtually conceded? If there is no compelling need for the evidence, its probative value is reduced to the point where it might be outweighed by its prejudicial impact.

Sometimes the need for "other acts" evidence does not emerge until late in the trial, when it becomes clear what issues are really in dispute.[21] Some courts emphasize this factor, which may make it more difficult for a prosecutor to secure admission of the evidence; other courts significantly discount this factor, which often makes it easier for the prosecutor to admit the evidence.

Once you have looked at the other evidence in the case and identified where the prosecutor has the greatest need for the evidence (identity, conduct or mental state), you might go back to step one and revise the purpose the prosecutor might specify.

§ 7.11 Proof that D committed the extrinsic act; *Huddleston v. U.S.*

i. *Huddleston*

For the extrinsic act to be relevant to prove D's identity, conduct or mental state in the charge now being tried, the prosecutor must first offer evidence that D in fact committed that extrinsic act. FRE 404(b) considerations aside, the prosecutor's evidence that D committed the extrinsic act must be *admissible.* If the evidence of the defendant's extrinsic act is inadmissible for some reason other than Rule 404(b)(1) (for example, if it is inadmissible hearsay), it will be excluded on that ground.

In *Huddleston v. United States,* 485 U.S. 681 (1988), the Supreme Court enunciated the standard against which proof of the extrinsic act is to be measured. That aspect of *Huddleston* is covered here. *Huddleston* also discussed the use of extrinsic act evidence to prove a defendant's mental state. That aspect of *Huddleston* is covered in § 7.23.

Huddleston was charged with selling 5,000 stolen blank Memorex video cassette tapes in April 1985, knowing them to be stolen. Huddleston did not contest the government's evidence that the tapes had been stolen a few days earlier from an

---

21. In civil litigation, each side often has to state its theory in its pleadings, and in a criminal case, the state must do so in the indictment and in the prosecutor's opening statement. In criminal cases, a jurisdiction's rules of criminal procedure may require the defense to give advance notice of certain defenses—e.g., insanity or alibi. But defense attorneys in criminal cases generally are not required to announce their theory of defense to a jury, because until the state has rested its case, the attorney does not know what defense provides the best chance to win an acquittal.

interstate shipment, nor that Huddleston had sold them at about 60% of the manufacturing cost. Rather, Huddlestson denied he knew they were stolen. Thus, the only real issue at trial was whether Huddleston knew the tapes were stolen.

On the issue of knowledge, the government offered evidence of two extrinsic acts.

First, a record store owner testified that in February of 1985, Huddleston told him he could supply several thousand 12" black and white television sets at $28 each,[22] and in fact sold him 38 of the sets. The government was unable to offer any direct evidence that the tv sets were stolen.

Second, an FBI agent testified that in May of 1985, Huddleston offered to sell him a large quantity of Amana appliances—28 refrigerators, two ranges, and 40 ice-makers—for $8,000,[23] roughly 40% of their value. The appliances, which were seized when Huddleston and a confederate named Wesby were arrested, were part of a shipment that had been stolen. (Huddleston testified that Wesby had supplied him with the appliances, the tv sets and the Memorex tapes.)

The judge admitted evidence regarding both the tv sets and the appliances, accepting the government's reasoning that Huddleston's sales of three different kinds of stolen merchandise from the same source (Wesby) was strong circumstantial evidence that he was aware that each of these items, including the Memorex tapes, was stolen.

Huddleston was convicted. On appeal, Huddleston asserted that admitting the tv set evidence was error, because the government failed to prove that the tv sets were stolen;[24] thus, he argued, the tv evidence was not relevant for the purpose the government offered it. Moreover, he argued, extrinsic act evidence was inadmissible under FRE 404(b) unless the prosecutor proved that a defendant committed the extrinsic act by a preponderance of the evidence. The Sixth Circuit agreed and reversed the conviction. The government appealed to the Supreme Court.

The Supreme Court reversed, reinstating Huddleston's conviction. The Court emphasized that nothing in the language of FRE 404(b)[25] or its legislative history specified the burden of proof the offering party must meet in establishing that a defendant committed the extrinsic act. Therefore, the Federal Rules of Evidence govern the question. The issue, the Court emphasized, was one of conditional relevancy: the relevance of the tv set evidence depended on the condition that the tv sets were stolen. FRE 104(b) articulates the applicable standard:

> **(b) Relevance That Depends on a Fact.** When the relevance of evidence depends on whether a fact exists, proof must be introduced sufficient to

22. That's the equivalent of roughly $73 in 2022.
23. That's the equivalent of roughly $21,100 in 2022.
24. On appeal, he did not contest the admission of evidence relating to the stolen appliances.
25. At the time, FRE 404(b) was not divided into subsections.

> support a finding that the fact does exist. The court may admit the proposed evidence on the condition that the proof be introduced later.[26]

Thus, to satisfy this aspect of rule 404(b), the government need only offer evidence "sufficient to support a finding" that the defendant committed the extrinsic act.

The Court emphasized that in assessing the sufficiency of the evidence under Rule 104(b), the trial court must consider all evidence presented to the jury. "[I]ndividual pieces of evidence, insufficient in themselves to prove a point, may in cumulation prove it. The sum of an evidentiary presentation may well be greater than its constituent parts." Applying that test to the facts of the case, the Court observed:

> In assessing whether the evidence was sufficient to support a finding that the televisions were stolen, the court here was required to consider not only the direct evidence on that point—the low price of the televisions, the large quantity offered for sale, and petitioner's inability to produce a bill of sale—but also the evidence concerning petitioner's involvement in the sales of other stolen merchandise obtained from Wesby, such as the Memorex tapes and the Amana appliances. Given this evidence, the jury reasonably could have concluded that the televisions were stolen, and the trial court therefore properly allowed the evidence to go to the jury. (485 U.S. at 691.)

Note what the Court says here: in deciding whether evidence of the defendant's commission of the extrinsic act meets the "sufficient to support a finding" standard, the trial judge must consider, not only the circumstances surrounding the extrinsic act and inferences that can be drawn from those circumstances; the judge should also consider all the other evidence in the case which is relevant on that issue, including evidence relating to the very crime (the Memorex tapes) for which the defendant was on trial.

ii. Additional comments on "sufficient to support a finding"

The FRE 104(b) "sufficient to support a finding" standard, and the related question of order of proof, are is discussed in some detail in § 1.13. If the concept is a bit vague in your mind, it would be useful to re-read that section. This subsection discusses that standard in the context of FRE 404(b).

In applying the "sufficient to support a finding standard," a judge—or a law student—must keep in mind the basic rule that the jury, not the judge, is responsible to assess the credibility of any witness's testimony. Thus, if a witness testifies, "I saw the defendant [commit the extrinsic act]," or "The defendant told me he [committed the extrinsic act]," this automatically satisfies the *Huddleston* standard, because (unless

26. This is the current text of the rule; it was revised in 2011 as part of the Advisory Committee's restyling project to make the rules more user-friendly.

the witness's testimony is inherently unbelievable) a rational jury could decide to believe the testimony.[27]

But satisfying this minimal requirement does not necessarily mean that the evidence is admissible. Satisfying *Huddleston* only satisfies the third step in the five-step process. The judge must still assess whether the evidence's fasprelipi[28] is sufficient to overcome the risk of unfair prejudice and the other FRE 403 risks.

Moreover, the strength of the evidence that the defendant committed the extrinsic act is a significant factor in assessing the evidence's fasprelipi. If the prosecutor can offer only weak circumstantial evidence that the defendant committed the extrinsic act, such evidence cannot have much probative value on the issue (identity, conduct or mental state) for which it is being offered. Thus, for example, if the prosecutor would have to call several witnesses to establish a tenuous circumstantial case that the defendant committed the extrinsic act, the probative value of that act diminishes, while increasing the Rule 403 risks of misleading, confusing or distracting the jury, and the additional expenditure of time. On the other hand, if the prosecutor can call a seemingly credible witness who will testify that he saw the defendant commit the extrinsic act, the probative value of that evidence is strengthened.

The easiest, and perhaps most persuasive, way of proving that the defendant committed the extrinsic act is to prove that D was convicted of committing it. Suppose, for example, in 2021, D1, D2 and D3, each of whom runs a construction company, are charged with conspiring with each other between 2015 and 2020 to bribe public officials and rig bids for public works contracts. In 2016, D1 was convicted of offering a bribe to the chairman of the county legislature committee on infrastructure. Now, in the 2021 trial, the prosecutor wants to offer evidence of the 2016 bribe, as an overt act in furtherance of the conspiracy.[29] To do so, the prosecutor need only present documentary proof—a court record certifying that D1 was convicted.[30]

iii. Suppose the defendant was acquitted of committing the extrinsic offense?

Okay, that makes sense, but what if D1 was *acquitted* of bribery in that 2016 case? You might logically think, well, in that case the prosecutor *cannot* use evidence about the 2016 bribe in the current conspiracy trial. Right?

---

27. Reminder: I'm using the "use against a defendant in a criminal case" context here, but this discussion applies regardless of what kind of trial it is or who the person is. It applies whenever any party in a case (criminal or civil) offers evidence about anybody—any party, any witness, any victim, etc.

28. "Factually significant relevance independent of the propensity inference."

29. The use of a defendant's prior conviction as evidence in a trial for other crimes does not implicate the defendant's double jeopardy protection so long as the 2021 jury is not asked to convict D1 again of that prior crime.

30. The certificate of conviction is hearsay, but is admissible, assuming it satisfies FRE 803(22). That provision is covered in §§10.13-10.14 of my *A Student's Guide to Hearsay* (5th ed. 2019).

You might logically think that, but you would be wrong. In *Dowling v. United States,* 493 U.S. 342 (1990), and *United States v. Felix,* 503 U.S. 378 (1992), the Supreme Court held that a prosecutor may use evidence of a prior crime, even if the defendant was acquitted of it, so long as the evidence satisfies the requirements of FRE 404(b) and is not barred by FRE 403. The Court reasoned that an acquittal does not represent a finding that the defendant was innocent or did not commit the crime; it represents a finding only that the prosecutor failed to persuade the jury of defendant's guilt beyond a reasonable doubt.

§ 7.12 Fasprelipi

The fourth step in the process is to determine if the extrinsic act has fasprelipi,[31] and if so, how much. This involves a combination of the first three steps—is the prosecutor's purported purpose or theory of relevancy (identity, conduct, mental state) in fact at issue; how great is the prosecutor's need for the extrinsic act evidence compared to the other evidence on that issue available to the state; and how strong is the evidence that the defendant in fact committed the extrinsic act. The challenge is to assess the probative force of the evidence *independent* of the propensity or "bad person" (or "good person") inference.

This is the most difficult and challenging part of the process, because it requires the offering party—usually, in the real world, the prosecutor; in your evidence class, you, the law student—to spell out the chain of inferences connecting the evidence to an ultimate fact of consequence (identity, conduct, mental state) without relying on the propensity inference. Sometimes it is fairly easy—one word (such as, in an appropriate case, "motive" or "knowledge") will do it. Sometimes it is impossible, because propensity is the only way the evidence is relevant. But often creative thinking and careful articulation are necessary. The rest of this chapter is devoted to helping you learn how to do this—first as the offering party, then as the opponent.

§ 7.13 Prior and subsequent extrinsic acts

Most extrinsic act evidence involves "crimes, wrong or acts" committed *prior* to the events involved in the current trial. In fact, you will find courts and scholars occasionally using "prior acts evidence" as a synonym for FRE 404(b) evidence. Sometimes, however, "other acts" committed *after* the conduct in question will be highly probative. See *Huddleston v. U.S.,* discussed in § 7.23, infra. See also the CVS robbery hypotheticals, § 7.17 & § 7.20, *infra*. In other circumstances, acts done after the conduct in question will be totally irrelevant. The only generalization that applies here is: the relevance of subsequent acts depends on the particular facts of each case—and on the ingenuity of the attorney arguing the point.

---

31. "Factually significant relevance independent of the propensity inference."

§ 7.14 Applying FRE 403 and Article I

i. FRE 403

Quite often, extrinsic act evidence creates a propensity inference.[32] If the extrinsic act evidence has no relevance other than via the propensity ("bad person") inference, it is excluded per FRE 404(b)(1). But if it has "fasprelipi"—factually significant relevance independent of the propensity inference—then FRE 403 must be considered.

The greater the similarity between the extrinsic acts and the crime charged, the greater the risk that the jury, despite a limiting instruction (see § 7.14-iv), will use the evidence for its propensity value: "if D robbed banks (or sold drugs, or forged a check, or assaulted other people, or drove inattentively, or misled customers, etc.) on other occasions," a jury might logically but improperly reason, "he probably robbed the bank (sold the drugs, forged the check, committed the assault, etc.) he's accused of or being sued for this time." While this reasoning is entirely plausible, and is consistent with human behavior generally, it is banned by Rules 404(b)(1) and 403.[33] If the risk that the jury will use the evidence this way substantially outweighs the fasprelipi of the evidence, the judge should exclude the evidence.

Application of Rule 403 in this context may require careful and subtle analysis, particularly where the ultimate purpose for the evidence is to identify the defendant as the perpetrator of a crime. Identity is a legitimate "other" purpose; yet the evidence should be excluded if its probative value to prove identity rests solely or primarily on the forbidden "bad person" inference.

This does not mean that extrinsic act evidence is automatically excluded if the extrinsic act or acts are similar to the one for which a defendant is on trial. Quite often, courts admit such evidence—even to prove identity—even though the extrinsic acts are similar to the charged acts. But in an essay answer, be sure to mention the similarity as a negative factor—albeit not necessarily a controlling factor—in your Rule 403 analysis.

Even if the evidence carries no significant propensity risk, it still may have considerable potential for unfair prejudice. For example, if a defendant is charged with embezzlement from the company he works for and the "other" act involves, say, an act of attempted murder which is extrinsic to the embezzlement, the propensity inference really doesn't apply—the charged crime (embezzlement) and the extrinsic acts (attempted murder) are very much unalike. A jury is unlikely to reason,

---

32. Usually, this is a negative inference—"if X did bad things like this in the past he probably did it this time, too." Much less often, it will create a risk of unfair prejudice because it creates a "good person" propensity inference.

33. The same is true if X—the person whose extrinsic act is offered in evidence—is an alleged victim, or a civil litigant, or any witness in a case. Evidence whose relevance is based on a propensity inference is generally inadmissible unless a specialized rule, such as FRE 405(b), FRE 413, FRE 608(b) or FRE 609, explicitly allows admission of evidence based on the propensity inference.

"Because D tried to kill someone several years ago, it is likely he cooked the books to steal money from his employer this time." But evidence that the defendant attempted to kill someone in the past might greatly prejudice the jury against him in ways that have nothing to do with the central facts in the embezzlement case.

Remember that Rule 403 is not an all-or-nothing rule; it gives the judge considerable flexibility. Assuming the extrinsic act has fasprelipi, can the risk of unfair prejudice be reduced or eliminated by redacting some details? Suppose D is on trial for knocking down an elderly man and stealing his attache case at 2:30 p.m. on August 12. The government wants to call PW to testify that she is a parole officer and that she met with D—who was on parole after serving four years of an eight-year sentence for armed robbery—that afternoon between 1:30 and 2:15. This evidence has considerable relevance, because the parole office was located only a block or so away from where the victim was knocked down and robbed, but also it carries considerable risk for unfair prejudice. Assuming D moves to exclude her testimony, the judge should allow PW to testify that she works for a "government agency" and met with D that day from 1:30 to 2:15, but should instruct her not mention that she is a parole officer.[34]

Also keep in mind that a judge's decision to exclude evidence per FRE 403 is not irreversible. The judge might exclude such evidence at one point in the trial, then later admit it because of other evidence that has been admitted in the meantime.

ii. Specificity of objection: FRE 103(a)(1)(B)

In applying FRE 404(b), as with any other rule, remember that an objection must "state the specific ground, unless it was apparent from the context[.]"An objection that evidence is "irrelevant" is not enough to preserve error[35] for evidence whose relevance is based on propensity; nor is it enough to preserve error regarding evidence carrying a heavy risk of unfair prejudice. The best way to preserve error here is: "Objection, Your Honor: Rules 404(b)(1) and 403."

iii. FRE 104(b) (conditional relevance) and order of proof

Keep in mind that FRE 104(b) applies here—as the Supreme Court explained in *Huddleston* (§ 7.11); and that FRE 404(b) issues often raise questions about the order of proof (see § 1.13).

---

34. The jury may wonder why the "agency" was never named; jurors may speculate that the witness was probably a parole or probation officer, from which they might infer that D has been convicted of some crime in the past. On the other hand, since the witness was called by the prosecutor, the jury might think, because the agency wasn't specified, that the prosecutor is deliberately hiding information from them. There is not much anyone can do to prevent that. Either side could request the judge to instruct the jury not to speculate what agency the witness worked for, but that might make jurors all the more curious.

35. "Preserve error" means, "to preserve the right to appeal a trial judge's decision without having to claim plain error."

iv. Limiting instruction: FRE 105

If the judge overrules a 404(b) objection, the objecting party should request the judge give an immediate limiting instruction, and should again request such an instruction in the judge's final instructions to the jury immediately before the jury begins to deliberate. The Seventh Circuit's instruction is typical:

> 3.11 Evidence of Other Acts by Defendant
>
> You have heard *[testimony; evidence]* that the defendant committed acts other than the ones charged in the indictment. Before using this evidence, you must decide whether it is more likely than not that the defendant took the actions that are not charged in the indictment. If you decide that he did, then you may consider that evidence to help you decide *[describe with particularity the purpose for which other act evidence was admitted, e.g., the defendant's intent to distribute narcotics, absence of mistake in dealing with the alleged victim, etc.]*. You may not consider this evidence for any other purpose. To be more specific, you may not assume that, because the defendant committed an act in the past, he is more likely to have committed the crime[s] charged in the indictment. The reason is that the defendant is not on trial for these other acts. Rather, he is on trial for *[list charges alleged in the indictment]*. The government has the burden to prove beyond a reasonable doubt the elements of the crime[s] charged in the indictment. This burden cannot be met with an inference that the defendant is a person whose past acts suggest bad character or a willingness or tendency to commit crimes.[36]

It is probably safe to assume your professor will not expect you to draft an instruction like that in answering an exam question. But if asked to draft an instruction, include the following:

1. D is not on trial for the [specified extrinsic crime, wrong or other act].
2. Before considering that evidence, you have to decide whether it is more likely than not that D committed that [extrinsic act].
3. If you conclude that it is more likely than not, you may consider it in deciding whether [a criminal act was committed] [the defendant did the acts alleged in the indictment] [the defendant acted with the mens rea specified in the crime]. But you may not assume that, because the defendant committed an act in the past, he is more likely to have committed the crime[s] charged in the indictment.

---

36. FEDCRIM-JI7C 3.11

D. Offered to Prove Identity

§ 7.15 Introduction

In § 7.9, I listed several of the Rule 404(b)(2) "purposes" under identity:

Identity
Motive
Opportunity
Preparation
Plan
Knowledge

Each of these, depending on circumstances, can help a prosecutor identify the defendant as the person who committed the crime.

A defendant's extrinsic act that shows he or she had a motive to commit the crime for which he is charged often has fasprelipi[37] because it makes it more probable than it would be without the evidence that the defendant committed it; and this is so even if many people might have the same motive.

An extrinsic act which places the defendant near the scene near the time of the crime has fasprelipi because it shows that the defendant had the opportunity to commit the crime, which makes it more probable than it would be without the evidence that the defendant was the person who committed the crime for which the defendant is being tried. Similarly, an extrinsic act which proves that the defendant possessed an object of the same kind that was used to commit the crime has fasprelipi because it shows the defendant had the opportunity to commit the crime for which he or she is on trial,[38] which makes it more probable than it would be without the evidence that the defendant committed the crime.

Preparation, plan. Evidence that the defendant committed extrinsic acts which appear designed to culminate in the charged crime has fasprelipi because it makes it more probable than it would be without the evidence that the defendant is the person who committed the charged crime.

Evidence that the defendant committed crimes in the past which in several ways were similar to the charged crime may have fasprelipi because it may make it more

37. "Factually significant relevance independent of the propensity inference."

38. The better view is that evidence the defendant possessed the item before or after the crime should be considered intrinsic to rather than extrinsic from the crime. See § 7.6. But if a judge rules that evidence of prior or subsequent possession of such an item is extrinsic to the crime, such possession nevertheless comes within the "opportunity" purpose in Rule 404(b)(2).

probable than it would be without the evidence that the defendant committed the crime for which he is now on trial. See § 7.17 and § 7.18.

Knowledge. Extrinsic acts by the defendant which prove he or she possessed certain information that would be extremely helpful or essential in committing the crime may have fasprelipi because it makes it more probable than it would be without the evidence that the defendant committed it.

§ 7.16 General rule of exclusion: "fungibly similar" extrinsic act

In most criminal cases, no one contests that a crime was committed; the main, or only, issue is whether the defendant was the perpetrator. This assumption applies unless something in the evidence or the prosecutor's or defense attorney's tactics make it clear that conduct or mental state is a contested issue.

True or false: FRE 404(b)(1) says other-act evidence is not admissible to prove a person's character, but FRE 404(b)(2) says other acts evidence "may be admissible for another purpose, such as proving... identity..." Therefore, whenever identity (i.e., "was it the defendant who committed the crime") is the issue, other acts evidence is admissible.

False. Keep in mind that evidence of one or more extrinsic "crimes, wrongs or acts" is not admissible if its relevance depends on the propensity inference.

Evidence that the defendant committed any prior "crime, wrong or act" carries the risk of unfair prejudice: informing the jury that a defendant did something (unrelated to the charged crime) that was illegal, unethical, immoral, or just plain nasty, may cause the jury to distrust him or want to punish him even if the case against him regarding the actual charges is a weak one. The risk of unfair prejudice is particularly acute if the extrinsic act was similar to the one he is now charged with, because that suggests that the defendant has a propensity to commit such crimes—the bad man (or woman) inference.

A general rule has emerged that most courts recognize and apply, in most situations: an extrinsic act which has only what I call "*fungible similarity*" to the charged act is *not admissible* to prove identity (i.e., as evidence that the defendant committed the charged act), because its only relevance regarding identity is the propensity inference. By "fungible" similarity, I mean crimes that are similar in kind, and are committed in a non-distinct, "routine" way.

Suppose Quickfingers is charged with robbing a grocery store in Fairfax on January 3rd. His defense: "It wasn't me. I was home with GF, my girlfriend." The evidence shows that the Fairfax robber entered the store, pretended to browse for several minutes until there were no other customers inside, then pulled a gun and forced the employee to give him all the bills in the cash register. Four years earlier, Quickfingers was convicted of committing the same kind of crime in Arlington, about fifteen miles from Fairfax. In that robbery, he waited until there were no other customers before pulling the gun and taking the money.

The Arlington robbery is only generically or fungibly similar to the Fairfax robbery—using a gun to rob a store clerk, and waiting until the only witness is the victim, are fairly routine features of store robberies. Therefore, the only relevance of the Arlington robbery is to show that Quickfingers has a propensity to commit store robberies; hence, it should not be admitted at the current trial to prove that Quickfingers committed the Fairfax robbery.

You may wonder: "How am I supposed to know what are 'fungibly similar ways' of committing certain crimes?" Well, one way would be to spend several years interacting with criminals who specialize various kinds of crimes. But my guess is that very few people with that kind of experience will read this book.[39] So here are some examples:

Bank robbery: A person walks into a bank and hands a teller a note which says, "I have a gun [or a bomb], put all your money into this paper bag."

Importing drugs into the U.S.: D hires a "mule" to body-smuggle the drugs, e.g., by swallowing balloons of drugs, crossing the border, and meeting D (or an associate of D) and then excreting the balloons.

Selling drugs on the street: D1 stands in front of a building, screening would-be buyers. After D1 negotiates with a buyer, D1 signals to D2, who is several feet away, to inform D2 the quantity D2 should give the buyer.

Theft:

(a) Someone jimmies open the door to a locked car, or climbs through a window into a home or apartment, and steals something inside.

(b) D1 bumps into the victim; while the victim is distracted by D1, D2 picks the victim's pocket or purse.

(c) D obtains a check drawn on X's account, and forges X's signature, or alters the amount on the check, then cashes it.

(d) Someone hotwires a car and steals it.

(e) D waits outside a bar at night until an apparently inebriated patron leaves the bar, follows the patron, then robs the patron.

If D is charged with a crime on this list, the fact that D previously committed the same kind of crime on the list should not be admitted as evidence that D was the perpetrator this time, too, unless other evidence gives the prior similar crime fasprelipi.

39. I actually *did* spend the first eight years of my professional career "interacting with criminals who specialize in certain types of crime." But my "interaction" with them was to prosecute them or to use them as informants.

§ 7.17 "Signaturesque" similarity ("m.o." or modus operandi)

If both the charged crime and the extrinsic crime have unusual or unique features in common—features that might be likened to a perpetrator's "signature," or "m.o."—these similarities may have sufficient fasprelipi[40] to justify admitting the evidence despite the heightened risk of unfair prejudice.

Suppose, for example, a man in a gorilla mask[41] and wielding a machete robbed a CVS pharmacy in Bethesda, Md., at 4 p.m. on June 1st. On June 3rd, at about 3:30 p.m., a man fitting the same general description (height, weight), wearing a gorilla mask and wielding a machete, robbed a CVS in Friendship Heights in Washington, D.C. (hereinafter: FH-DC). Doppelganger is charged with both crimes. (Because they were committed in different jurisdictions, they cannot be tried together.)

The two crimes are similar in many ways. They were similar in nature: both were committed in CVS pharmacies, they were committed only two days apart in the same general area[42] at roughly the same time of day, and, in particular, the two crimes had unusual features in common (mask, machete). Thus, evidence that Doppelganger committed the FH-DC crime would be admissible at the Bethesda trial per FRE 404(b)(2), and vice versa rather than excluded per FRE 404(b)(1) (assuming there is no other bar to its admissibility).

Here's how it might work: at the Bethesda trial, after the prosecutor offers evidence of the Bethesda robbery, she will then call the CVS store clerk in the FH-DC robbery. The FH-DC clerk will testify that at about 3:30 on June 3, a man in a gorilla mask wielding a machete forced her to give him all the cash in her register drawer. (Because the robber wore a mask, the Friendship Heights clerk cannot identify Doppelganger as the robber.) Next, the prosecutor will call PW3, who will, if permitted, testify: "On June 3, around 3:30 p.m., I was across the street from the CVS in Friendship Heights, and I saw a man wearing some kind of weird mask run out of the store! As soon as he got outside, he took off the mask, and I recognized him immediately. It was Doppelganger! I know it was him because we lived in apartments across the hall from each other in Woodley Park for about two years." PW3's testimony that Doppelganger committed the FH-DCs robbery[43] has factually specific relevance

40. "Factually significant relevance independent of the propensity inference."

41. I wrote this hypothetical before the pandemic which made wearing masks in public commonplace. But even at the height of Covid-prompted mask-wearing, I bet you didn't see too many people wandering around in gorilla masks. And I fervently hope that by the time this book is published, or soon thereafter, regular mask-wearing in public will be no more than an unpleasant memory.

42. Bethesda and Friendship Heights are adjacent to each other, separated only by the border between Maryland and D.C.

43. PW3 did not actually see Doppelganger commit the Friendship Heights robbery, but once the store clerk testifies that she was robbed by a man in a gorilla mask at about 3:30 that day (and that, so far as she knew, the robber was the only person in the store wearing any kind of mask),

tending to prove that Doppelganger also committed the Bethesda robbery for which he is being tried in Montgomery County, Maryland.

That conclusion does not end the analysis, of course; we still have to apply the fifth step (FRE 403 and Article I). Allowing the prosecutor at the trial of the Bethesda robbery to offer evidence that Doppelganger committed the Friendship Heights robbery clearly creates the risk of propensity-inference unfair prejudice: the jury might reason, "If he's robbed other stores, he probably robbed this one, too." But the relevance of the Friendship Heights robbery does not *depend* on the propensity inference: the unusual, "signaturesque" similarities between the two robberies gives the latter robbery fasprelipi.

How much similarity is required? That depends. If the Friendship Heights case involved a Rite-Aid store or a Safeway Supermarket, instead of a CVS, or occurred at a different time of day instead of mid-afternoon, the outcome would still be the same. The proximity of the two crimes in time and location, and the truly unusual features (gorilla mask, machete) of the two crimes, still would make a compelling case for admissibility.

What if the Friendship Heights robber wore a gorilla mask, but used a gun instead of a machete? Or suppose the Friendship Heights robber used a machete, but wore a Richard Nixon mask instead? Would the Friendship Heights evidence still be admissible at the trial of the Bethesda robbery? The case for admissibility would be much less of a slam dunk in either of these two cases, but I think the trial judge would still have discretion to admit it. But if the Friendship Heights robber used a gun and a Richard Nixon mask,[44] I think this would reduce the similarities between the two crimes from signaturesque to fairly fungible, and if I were the judge, I'd probably exclude the Friendship Heights evidence. But some judges might nevertheless admit the FH-DC evidence, and some appellate courts might agree.

Once the judge overrules defendant's FRE 404(b)(1)-403 objection, we turn to FRE 105: counsel asks for a limiting instruction, as soon as the FH-DC evidence is admitted, and again when the judge gives his or her final instructions before sending the case to the jury. The instruction would be worded something like: "Doppelganger is not on trial for the Friendship Heights robbery, and you may not consider evidence of that crime as a basis to judge his general character. But if you are persuaded that Doppelganger committed the Friendship Heights robbery, you may consider that in deciding whether Doppelganger is the man who robbed the CVS in Bethesda."[45]

PW3's testimony that she saw Doppelganger run from the store and take off a mask at about 3:30 strongly identifies Doppelganger as the Friendship Heights robber.

44. In posing this hypothetical, I intend no disparagement of President Nixon. Nor of gorillas, for that matter.

45. For a more elaborate instruction, see § 7.14–iv. You might well question whether an instruction like this really helps the defendant much—or, for that matter, whether it would help or confuse

But suppose the FH-DC case is tried first. After the store clerk and PW3 testify, can the prosecutor offer evidence of the Bethesda robbery? Yes—if there is evidence that Doppledanger committed the Bethesda robbery. But if there is no evidence identifying Doppledanger as the Bethesda robber, then the Bethesda robbery has no legitimate relevance and must be excluded.

§ 7.18 Sufficient common features

Even where the charged and extrinsic crimes do not share signaturesque or idiosyncratic similarities, if there are sufficient common features, this can be enough to give the extrinsic crimes factually specific relevance independent of the propensity inference. Cases fitting into this category generally involve fairly elaborate fact patterns—more elaborate than appear on a law school exam question, so the odds are probably against being tested on this. Still, it can't hurt to give you an example.

Suppose over a six-month period, in eight separate incidents, men were assaulted after leaving gay bars after 11 p.m. in three adjoining jurisdictions (Washington County, Adams County and Jefferson County). Brutus is charged with committing all of the assaults—let's say, three in Washington County, three in Adams County and two in Jefferson County. In many of the cases, evidence identifying Brutus as the assailant is weak—it was late at night, the lighting wasn't all that great, many of the victims and other witnesses were somewhat inebriated or high or both, and their descriptions of the robber were rather generic ("white guy, late twenties or early thirties, between 5'10" and 6'2", muscular, wore jeans and a hoodie"). If a prosecutor in one case tried to introduce evidence of the other assaults, the judge should exclude it, because the similarities between these crimes are too generic or fungible to overcome the propensity inference.

But suppose the prosecutor has the following additional evidence:

- In three of the cases, street surveillance photos show that Brutus's car was parked within three blocks of the bar from which that night's victim emerged.
- In another three cases, Brutus's smart phone was used to pay for a parking spot within a few blocks of that night's targeted gay bar.[46]

---

the jury. When you are a defense attorney in the real world, you will be free to make a tactical decision not to ask for such an instruction. But right now, you are a law student, whose job it is to learn the rules (and equally important, to demonstrate to your professor how brilliantly he or she has taught you the rules), so any time a party is entitled to a limiting instruction, you should be prepared to spell out how the judge should word the instruction.

46. Brutus may claim that he allowed someone else to use his car or his smart phone those evenings, or that he had been invited to parties within a few blocks of where he parked his car. Should this eliminate the car/smart phone evidence from the trial judge's special relevance calculus? Basically, no. Brutus can testify, and if he has evidence backing up his explanations, he can introduce that evidence as well. Ultimately the jury will decide whether to believe his evidence or not.

- Brutus lives and works in Madison County, within 50 miles of each of the robberies.
- Each of the assaults was committed on a night before Brutus had the day off from his job.

While none of the similarities between the assaults is unique or signaturesque, the sheer number of the similarities make it unlikely that they are all random coincidences. This very unlikelihood suggests that Brutus has a violent animosity toward gay men, and has been periodically seeking out and assaulting them. A trial judge would have discretion to admit, at a trial of an assault in, say, Washington County, evidence of other assaults committed in all three counties—assuming there was evidence in the extrinsic Adams or Jefferson assaults identifying Brutus as the assailant in those cases.

§ 7.19 Other situations

An extrinsic act can have fasprelipi—factually specific relevance to show identity, independent of the propensity inference—even if the extrinsic act is very *different* from the charged act. Suppose three masked men robbed a bank on September 30. The robbers escaped in a late-model Honda Civic, license plate ABC-123. Dillinger, Sutton and James[47] are charged.

Culling through crime reports, a detective discovers that on September 28, a man named Jackson Quinto reported that his car (a Honda Civic, plate ABC-123) was stolen from a parking garage elsewhere in the city. The surveillance videos from the garage on September 28 reveal that the car thief bears a striking resemblance to Sutton, and several people who know Sutton and who have viewed the video will, if permitted, testify that Sutton is in fact the person who stole the car. Stealing a car from a parking garage is very different than committing an armed robbery of a bank; but evidence that Sutton stole a car on the 28th that was used as the getaway car in a bank robbery two days later has substantial fasprelipi to show that Sutton was one of the robbers.

§ 7.20 Questions

As to each of the following, be prepared to apply the five-step process. If you conclude the judge should admit the evidence, state how the judge should word the

47. John Dillinger (1903–1934) was a professional bank robber—he was accused of robbing 24 banks and, just for variety, 4 police stations. He also escaped from prison twice. He was shot and killed by FBI agents. Willie Sutton (1901–1980) also was a bank robber who, during his 40-year career, stole an estimated $2 million and spent roughly half of his life in prison. Supposedly, when asked why he robbed banks, he replied, "because that's where the money is." Jesse James (1847–1882) robbed numerous trains and banks, and killed several people during his robberies.

limiting instruction. And recall that back in §7.9, I listed several of the FRE 404(b)(2) "purposes" under the heading of identity: motive; opportunity; knowledge; plan; preparation. Consider with regard to each problem whether the prosecutor might usefully cite one or more of these to best argue in favor of admissibility.

Question 1.

D is charged with murdering V on June 1, 2020. The prosecutor introduces evidence, to which no objection was or could be made, that establishes that V was shot three times in the chest from close range. Next, P calls PW1, who will testify that on May 24, 2020, D assaulted PW1. Apply the five-step process.

Answer:

1. Purpose/issue/theory of relevance. Apparently the only issue in this case is who killed V. (The circumstances of V's death clearly rule out accident or suicide, and D has done nothing to remove the default assumption that the issue is identity.)
2. Need. The stem of the question does not tell us what evidence the prosecutor has identifying D as the killer. Let's assume the state's case is not overwhelming and there is a need for additional evidence on the issue.
3. Proof of the extrinsic act. PW1's testimony satisfies *Huddleston.*
4. Fasprelipi. The assault on PW1 involves an extrinsic act—a physical assault on someone other than the homicide victim, with no known connection between V and PW1. The two acts are fungibly similar: each involves a violent act by D. Since the attack on PW1 is relevant only insofar as it shows that D has a propensity for violence, it is inadmissible per FRE 404(b)(1). So to answer this question, we really don't have to go to step 5.

Question 2.

In the same trial, P calls PW2, who will testify that twice in May, 2020, he saw D assault V. Apply the five-step process.

Answer:

1. Purpose/issue/theory of relevance: Identity—who killed V.
2. Need: The question stem hasn't told us what other evidence is available to the prosecutor to show that it was D who killed V. But unless the evidence identifying D as the killer is extremely strong, there is at least some need for additional evidence indicating D was the killer.
3. Proof of the extrinsic act: PW2's testimony clearly satisfies the *Huddleston* "sufficient to support a finding" standard: he witnessed D's two extrinsic assaults on V first-hand.

4. Fasprelipi. PW2's testimony, like PW1's, shows that D is a "bad man"—i.e., that he has a propensity for violence. It would not be admissible on that theory. But PW2's testimony also has fasprelipi—factually specific relevance independent of the propensity inference. Here's how:
   a. The circumstances of V's death—three shots to the chest at close range—make it clear that whoever killed V intended to do so. The circumstance also strongly suggests that the killer had a significant personal animosity toward V.
   b. That D physically attacked V twice in the month before V was shot strongly supports the inference that D had an intense dislike for or animosity toward V.
   c. Therefore, the evidence has a powerful tendency to make it more probable than it would be without the evidence—independent of the propensity inference—that it was D who shot V.

The propensity inference is still there, of course; D's prior attacks on V clearly support the inference that V has a propensity for violence. But the reasoning spelled out in subparagraphs a, b and c does not *rely* on the propensity inference; it is independent of the propensity inference.

5. Rules 403 and 105: This evidence has substantial fasprelipi; hence the risk that the jury would convict merely because they assume D is a violent person is comparatively small. That risk certainly does not "substantially outweigh" the factually specific relevance of the evidence.

Conclusion: the judge should, without a doubt, admit PW2's testimony. This question isn't close; it's a slam dunk for the prosecutor. If D's attorney requests, the judge should instruct the jury along these lines: "You can consider PW2's testimony in weighing whether it was D who shot V. However, you should not use PW2's testimony as evidence of D's general character."[48] That's not much help to D, is it? But that's all he is entitled to. As a defense attorney, I'd request the instruction if only to assure the judge (and an appellate court) that I wasn't asleep when PW2 testified.

Question 3.

In the Bethesda gorilla mask trial (§ 7.17), the first witness is the Bethesda CVS cashier who relates how a man wearing a gorilla-mask with a machete forced her to empty her cash register on June 1. The robber was masked, so the cashier is unable to make an identification.

48. For a more elaborate instruction, see § 7.14–iv.

The second witness is M, who testifies: "I was walking toward the CVS store in Bethesda on June 1 at around 3:30 p.m. and saw Doppledanger walking toward me. I recognized him because he used to date my sister for a year or so before she broke it off. As he neared the store he pulled out a gorilla mask. I thought that was weird, but I was late for an appointment, so I just kept walking." Assume this evidence is admitted without objection. (Don't be confused: this witness is testifying at the Bethesda trial about what he saw in Bethesda on the day of that robbery.)

Next, the prosecutor offers evidence about the Friendship Heights-DC robbery. The FH-DC clerk will testify that at about 3:30 on June 3, a man in a gorilla mask wielding a machete forced her to give him all the cash in her register drawer. (Because the robber wore a mask, the Friendship Heights clerk cannot identify Doppelganger as the robber.) Next, the prosecutor will call W1, who will, if permitted, testify: "On June 3, around 3:30 p.m., I was across the street from the CVS in Friendship Heights, and I saw a man wearing some kind of weird mask run out of the store! As soon as he got outside, he took off the mask, and I recognized him immediately. It was Doppelganger! I know it was him because we lived in apartments across the hall from each other in Woodley Park for about two years."

Discuss the issues presented.

<u>Answer:</u>

D objects to the FH-DC evidence: FRE 404(b)(1) and 403. Response: FRE 404(b)(2).

1. <u>Purpose/issue/theory of relevance:</u> the key issue—the only issue, really—is identity: "Who was that masked man?"[49]

---

49. Regarding "who was that masked man": I was born in January of 1945—that makes me even older than the baby-boomers—and during the infancy of television (1949-1954), my favorite TV show was The Lone Ranger, who always wore a mask—even though he was the Good Guy. The show's intro went:

> A fiery horse with the speed of light. A cloud of dust, and a hearty "Hi-yo, Silver!" The Lone Ranger! With his faithful Indian companion, Tonto, the daring and resourceful masked rider of the plains led the fight for law and order in the early West. Return with us now to those thrilling days of yesteryear. The Lone Ranger rides again!

In each episode (half an hour, minus time for commercials), the Lone Ranger and Tonto solved a crime and brought a villain to justice; and as he and Tonto rode off into the sunset, someone would ask, "Who was that masked man?" Someone else would say, "He's the Lone Ranger!" The episode would end as the Lone Ranger would call out to his horse, "Hi-yo Silver, away!" followed by the closing notes of the William Tell Overture.

For sure, I would not want to "return with us now to those early days of television." Tonto (which, by the way, means "fool" or "stupid" in Spanish) spoke pidgin-English ("Me no understand") and regarded the Lone Ranger—whom he called "Kemosabe," Apache for "friend"—with almost slave-like devotion. On the other hand, the Lone Ranger regarded Tonto as a friend and partner, not as a servant, and Tonto was brave and resourceful and (if I recall correctly) saved the Lone Ranger's life in more than one episode. Moreover, Tonto was portrayed by the actor Jay Silverheels (a member

2. Need: D can argue that M's testimony already identifies D as the Bethesda robber, so there is no need for W1's testimony about the Friendship Heights robbery; its only real impact, therefore, is the propensity inference banned by FRE 404(b)(1). And this argument is plausible: the more direct evidence the prosecutor has of identity, the less need there is for extrinsic act evidence (with its propensity inference baggage).
3. How to prove the extrinsic act: W1's testimony certainly satisfies *Huddleston*. It is up to the jury to decide whether it believes W1's testimony about the FH robbery.
4. Fasprelipi: Despite D's argument regarding need, the judge should overrule D's objection and admit W1's testimony about the Friendship Heights robbery. A case based on the testimony of a single eyewitness is notoriously weak, and M's testimony may have been impeached on cross in a variety of ways. The state needs to strengthen its identification of D as the Bethesda robber. Identifying D as the person who committed the nearby, nearly identical Friendship Heights robbery just a few days after the Bethesda robbery has considerable fasprelipi.
5. Rules 403/105: If the state has little more than M's testimony directly tying D to the Bethesda robbery, W's extrinsic act testimony about the Friendship Heights robbery has more than enough factually specific relevance to overcome D's FRE 403 objection.

The instruction would be along the lines of: "D is not on trial for committing the Friendship Heights robbery, and you should not make any judgments about D's character from testimony about that robbery. But if you may consider evidence relating to that robbery in deciding whether the evidence has persuaded you beyond a reasonable doubt that D committed the Bethesda robbery."[50]

Question 4.

Associate is charged with murdering Partner, his supervisor. At trial, the prosecutor offers evidence that Associate had been embezzling funds from the firm for which he and Partner worked, and that Partner caught him at it and was about to alert the managing partner and the police. The charged crime is murder; the extrinsic act is embezzlement. Apply the five-part process.

---

of the Mohawk tribe) with gravitas and dignity, and some episodes portrayed Tonto quite sympathetically as the victim of racial hatred. So despite the racist aspects of the character, Tonto created a positive rather than a negative impression of Native Americans; at least, that was my impression as a seven-or eight-year-old. (And according to something I read on the Internet—which means it must be true, right?—"Kemosabe," in Navajo, means "soggy bush." Did the writers know that? If so, Tonto was "getting back" at the Lone Ranger for calling him "Tonto.")

50. For a more elaborate instruction, see § 7.14-iv.

Answer:

1. Purpose/issue/theory of relevance: Once again, in the absence of any indication to the contrary, we assume that the key issue in the trial is identity: who killed Partner.
2. Need: In the absence of evidence to the contrary, let us assume that the state's case is not airtight.
3. How prove that D committed the extrinsic act: (the embezzlement). The question doesn't tell us, so let's assume the prosecutor can do so adequately.
4. Fasprelipi: Associate's embezzlement and Partner's discovery of it gives Associate a ***motive*** to kill Partner, i.e., to prevent Partner from alerting the firm and the police.
5. FRE 403: There's not that much Rule 403 risk. Evidence that Associate embezzled from the firm does not carry any real propensity taint. (It is unlikely for a jury to generalize about Associate "Once an embezzler, always a murderer.")

Admit the evidence. Instruction: "Associate is not on trial for embezzlement, but you may consider evidence concerning Associate's alleged embezzlement in deciding whether the evidence persuades you beyond a reasonable doubt he is the person who killed Partner."[51]

Question 5.

In the bank robbery case (Sutton, Dillinger, James), how should the judge word the limiting instruction regarding the theft of the car?

Answer:

The instruction would go something like this: "You have heard evidence which, if you are persuaded by it, indicates that Sutton stole the car that was used in the robbery. You should not use that evidence to make any judgments about Sutton's character. But if the evidence convinces you that Sutton stole the car that was used in the robbery, you may consider that in deciding whether, based on all the evidence, you are convinced beyond a reasonable doubt that Sutton was one of the robbers."[52]

Question 6.

Seller was arrested in December 2020, for attempting to sell Ancestral Pueblo[53] artifacts to an undercover officer, and was charged with violating a federal statute which makes it a crime to sell archaeological effects taken from federal land

51. For a more elaborate instruction, see § 7.14–iv.

52. For a more elaborate instruction, see § 7.14–iv.

53. Ancestral Puebloans are often referred to as Anasazi, but according to the current Wikipedia article, that term is not preferred by contemporary Puebloans.

or from reservations belonging to Native American tribes. (Native Americans, and archaeologists working with the tribes, search for such artifacts, which are scattered throughout undeveloped and largely unoccupied land throughout an area covering thousands of square miles in the American Southwest, but they are not easy to find.) As part of a plea bargain, Seller told federal agents that in July of 2020, he obtained the relics from Digger. Digger is charged with digging up the relics, removing them from the reservation, and selling them to Seller. He denies doing so, in essence claiming that Seller is lying.

At Digger's trial, putting aside all technical legal issues, what is the key issue? The jury is going to have to decide one question and one question only. What is that question?

<u>Answer:</u>

The only issue, from the jury's point of view, is whether Seller is telling the truth. If the jury is satisfied beyond a reasonable doubt that Seller is telling the truth, they will find Digger guilty. If the jury has a reasonable doubt about the truthfulness of Seller's testimony inculpating Digger, they will return a not guilty verdict.

<u>Question 7.</u>

In 2017, Digger had been arrested for reckless driving—doing 105 MPH in an 80 MPH zone—as he left Navajo Nation territory in Arizona. When police (lawfully) searched his truck, they found several Ancestral Pueblo artifacts in the car, together with camping gear and shovels and other tools. He refused to answer any questions about the artifacts. He was convicted of removing the relics from archaeological sites on the reservation.

A government expert is prepared to testify that the artifacts in the current (2020) case closely resemble those in the 2017 case—made at roughly the same time, from the same materials, and several were decorated with a pattern indicating they were made by members of the same clan.

The prosecutor wants to offer evidence of the 2017 arrest and seizure (and the expert's testimony). Apply the 5-part process.

<u>Answer:</u>

1. <u>Purpose/issue:</u> Identity: was it Digger who sold the artifacts to Seller?
2. <u>Need:</u> The only direct evidence is Seller's testimony. That's enough to convict—if the jury believes Seller's testimony beyond a reasonable doubt. But Seller's credibility is vulnerable, since he is accusing Digger to catch a break in his own case, so the government has a legitimate need for additional evidence against Digger.
3. <u>How to prove Digger committed the extrinsic (2017) act:</u> The fact that he was convicted of removing the artifacts from the Navajo Nation certainly satisfies *Huddleston.*

4. Fasprelipi: The evidence has propensity relevance: "He committed crimes involving Ancient Pueblo artifacts in the past, so he probably did it this time, too." But a person can't just pick such items up off the ground. They are difficult to find. The expert's testimony supports the inference that the 2017 relics and the 2020 relics were taken from the same location, or at least a closely related location. Evidence that Digger knew where to find the artifacts he was convicted of in 2017 therefore has fasprelipi that he had the knowledge necessary to obtain more artifacts in 2020.
5. FRE 403: The judge should admit the evidence to show that Digger had the knowledge necessary to find the 2020 artifacts, thereby strengthening the government's case that Digger was in fact Seller's source for the 2020 artifacts.

Question 8. "What the Dickens!"

A man snatched Nancy's purse at the corner of Seventh Avenue and 5th Street of a mid-size city (population 400,000 or so), at about 1:15 p.m. on August 2. The next day, Nancy picked Dodger's photo out of a book of mugshots at the police station. Although officers looked for Dodger on and off, they did not find him until October 17, when he was arrested. When arrested, he had no property belonging to Nancy in his possession.

At trial, Nancy testifies about the mugging and the photograph, and identifies Dodger as the perpetrator. You may assume that there is nothing objectionable about this testimony.

Next, P calls Olivia, who will testify that she was window-shopping along 6th Avenue between 6th and 7th Streets sometime between 1 and 1:30 on August 2, as she does once a week or so, and as she turned away from the window, she accidentally bumped into a man (whom she had never seen before in her life) as he was walking down the sidewalk. She apologized, but he cursed at her, used several racial epithets, and threatened to "punch her lights out" if she didn't watch where she was going. Olivia testifies that August 2nd was her wedding anniversary, and the incident "really ruined the whole day for me." Two months later, Olivia happened to be in court on another matter, when Dodger's purse-snatching case was on the calendar, and she recognized Dodger as the man she'd bumped into, so she notified the prosecutor.

In compliance with Rule 404(b)(3)'s discovery/disclosure provision (see § 7.7 *supra*), prior to trial, the prosecutor informs defense counsel of her intent to call Olivia as a witness. Dodger's attorney brings a motion in limine, challenging the admissibility of Olivia's testimony per FRE 404(b) and FRE 403. Apply the five-step process.

Answer:

1. Purpose/issue/relevance: The only issue at trial, really, is identity: was it Dodger who snatched Nancy's purse? Olivia's testimony is relevant to show

that Dodger was near the scene of the crime at the time of the crime, which means he had the *opportunity* to commit the purse snatch, which makes it more probable than it would be without the evidence that it was indeed Dodger who committed the crime.

2. Need: The prosecutor has a considerable need for Olivia's testimony; without it, all the prosecutor has against Dodger is Nancy's testimony, with nothing to corroborate her identification of Dodger as the purse snatcher.
3. How to prove the extrinsic act: Olivia's testimony clearly satisfies *Huddleston.*
4. Fasprelipi: Considerable. It puts Dodger near the scene near the time of the crime.
5. FRE 403 risk: Dodger's attorney will argue that the details of Dodger's encounter with Olivia are unduly prejudicial—if the jury hears that he cursed her and used racial epithets and threatened her, they might convict Dodger of snatching Nancy's purse just to punish him for that. Counsel asks the judge to order the prosecutor to redact portions of Olivia's testimony—to have her testify that she had an "encounter" with Dodger at that time and place, without the details. And in particular, the fact that August 2 was her wedding anniversary and the encounter with Dodger "ruined" the occasion has no relevance, yet would undoubtedly prejudice Dodger.

How should the prosecutor respond to counsel's Rule 403 motion?

Stripping away the details would render Olivia's testimony wildly implausible; she could only say, "On August second, around 1:15 in the afternoon, I had a brief encounter with a man on 6th Avenue between 6th and 7th Streets. Two months later, I happened to be in the courthouse on another matter, and I saw the man again. It's that man, there" (pointing at Dodger).[54] The jury would have several reasons to doubt this testimony. First, what was the nature of the "encounter"? Jurors might well assume that Olivia, or the prosecutor, is deliberately trying to hide something. Second, how does she remember so precisely that it was August 2nd, as opposed to any other date? Third, pedestrians in the center of downtown during lunchtime "encounter" lots of people. How could she remember Dodger, two or more months later?

The frightening, upsetting nature of the "encounter" are precisely what make it plausible that she would be able to remember and recognize Dodger two months later, and the fact that August 2nd was her anniversary explains why she remembers the date so clearly.

54. Prior to trial, when the prosecutor met with Olivia again to go over her testimony, Olivia asked, "When you ask me to point the man out, where in the courtroom should I look?" The prosecutor replied, "I don't blame you for asking that question, but it's not proper that I answer it, Olivia. Twist your head around from side to side and look at everyone's face, and I'm sure you'll recognize him." (Do not refer to this footnote in answering this question.)

Question 9.

Beetle Bumble, a detective in the Midtown Anti-Street Crime Unit, has informed the prosecutor that Dodger is often seen in the company of two older men, Fagin and Sykes, who run a gang of young men who pick pockets and snatch purses and swipe merchandise. Should Det. Bumble be permitted to testify?

Answer:

No. Bumble's information suggests that Dodger was a member of a conspiracy which included Fagin and Sykes and others, and that Snatching Nancy's purse was committed as part of the conspiracy. But the information is far too vague and speculative to be admissible. (But give yourself a bonus point if you thought about the possibility.)

E. Offered to Prove Conduct

§ 7.21 In general

Where a defendant admits that he is the person the complainant or witness means to accuse, but asserts, in essence, that the alleged crime never occurred—for example that the complainant or witness is lying, or that there is an innocent explanation for circumstantial evidence that suggests that the alleged act was committed—the key issue is not *identity*, but *conduct*—what some commentators refer to as the "corpus delicti" ("body of the crime") issue. As a general rule, a similar extrinsic act should not be admissible to rebut the defendant's denial that he engaged in the alleged conduct. FRE 404(b)(1) is explicit: evidence of extrinsic acts "is not admissible to prove the character of a person in order to prove that on a particular occasion the person *acted* in accordance with the character."

Such evidence may be admissible to prove that the defendant engaged in the alleged conduct, however, where its relevance, and the need for the evidence, are particularly compelling and its relevance is based on a theory other than propensity.

The following "purposes" might each be relevant to prove that the defendant engaged in the conduct alleged in the indictment, and evidence of the defendant's extrinsic acts may therefore be admissible.

Conduct
Motive
Intent
Lack of accident
Preparation
Plan
Knowledge

Here is an example. Sochat, a federal meat inspector for the USDA FSIS,[55] was indicted for extorting bribes from a meat processor (Basar) in the Eastern District of the State of Confusion. At trial, Sochat acknowledged that he was the inspector assigned to conduct the inspection of Basar's plant on the dates in question during the past eighteen months. (He had little choice, really, since his agency's records clearly listed him as the inspector.) Rather, he testified that he never asked for or received a bribe from any meat processors. Therefore, the issue in the case is not identity; it is conduct.

In rebuttal, the government seeks to call four meat processors from the Western District of Confusion, to testify that Sochat had extorted bribes from them, too.[56]

Should the Western District witnesses be allowed to testify? No, because the relevance of their testimony is based solely on Sochat's propensity to extract bribes.

As this example illustrates, usually there is little difference between how FRE 404(b) applies to conduct and how it applies when the issue is identity: evidence of extrinsic acts that are only fungibly similar is not admissible to prove either identity or conduct, because the relevance of such acts is based solely on the propensity inference.

<u>Question 1.</u>

Suppose Basar, the Eastern District complainant, testified that Sochat insisted that he pay the bribes in an unusual way: on the last Friday of each month—a day which never coincided with Sochat's official inspection visits—Sochat would come to the processing plant at 4:30 in the afternoon and purchase two pounds of their best quality ground beef, which he would pay for at their standard rate. Basar testified that he had to enclose $100 in a plastic baggie inside the meat. Sochat was arrested after walking out of the processing plant with a two-pound package of ground beef containing $100 in a sandwich baggie. (In other words, Basar notified FBI agents that Sochat had been extorting him, and the agents instructed Basar to prepare the usual package for Sochat so they could catch him with the bribe.)

When arrested, Sochat acknowledged his monthly purchases, but denies extorting bribes and insists that there had never been money in any of his prior purchases; he is the victim of a set-up, because two weeks earlier, he warned Basar that if he did not do extensive repairs and improvements in the plant before the next inspection, Sochat would submit a report citing Basar for violations.

Sochat was charged with nine counts of extortion—one count for each of the nine monthly bribe payments which (according to Basar) he received. (The only direct evidence the government has as to any of these counts is Basar's testimony, plus the money that was in the ground beef when Sochat was arrested.)

---

55. United States Department of Agriculture Food Safety Inspection Service.

56. The Eastern and Western District cases cannot be tried together because the alleged crimes occurred in different federal districts.

Mayor, the prosecutor, per FRE 404(b)(3), informs Patty Rindfleisch, Sochat's defense attorney, that he plans to call witnesses from four meat processing plants in the Western District who will, if permitted, testify that a few years earlier, when Sochat was assigned to inspect their facilities, he collected $100 a month from each of them, too, and required them to pay him in the same way. (In case you wonder how the government found out: After Sochat was arrested, FBI agents checked USDA FSIS records to find out what other plants Sochat had been assigned to inspect, and interviewed personnel at each of those plants.) Each would also testify that he or she had not discussed making payments to anyone until questioned by the FBI.

In this scenario, should the Western District witnesses be allowed to testify? Apply the 5-part process.

<u>Answer:</u>

1. <u>Purpose/issue/theory of relevance:</u> Conduct.
2. <u>Need:</u> Conduct clearly is a contested issue.
3. <u>Proving the extrinsic acts:</u> The Western District witnesses' testimony clearly satisfies *Huddleston.*
4. <u>Fasprelipi:</u> If the issue had been identity, clearly, the answer would be, "yes," because this is a highly usual way to collect a bribe—so unusual as to be "signaturesque."

   But the issue isn't identity, it is conduct. Should signaturesque similarity open the door when conduct is the issue, or is this still merely propensity inference?

   The prosecutor will argue that the only real issue in this case is whether Basar is telling the truth or not; that Basar had no way of knowing that Sochat had used the same unusual bribe-receiving technique elsewhere; and that fact, therefore, strongly corroborates Basar's testimony that Sochat did in fact engage in the conduct of extorting bribes from him. If I were the judge, I'd admit the testimony on that theory. But if the prosecutor had argued that the Western District witnesses' testimony was admissible to prove identity, I would have excluded the evidence because identity simply was not an issue in the case.
5. <u>FRE 403; Rule 105:</u> The Western District witnesses' testimony's fasprelipi is not substantially outweighed by the 403 risk that the jury will rely on the propensity interest. On the other hand, each Western District witness's testimony tends to prolong the trial and distract the jury's attention from the Eastern District charges they have been empaneled to hear. I would restrict the prosecutor to at most two witnesses from the Western District.

The limiting instruction: "Sochat is not on trial here for what he allegedly did in the Western District, and you should not use testimony relating to the Western District as a basis to assess Sochat's general character. But you may consider the testimony of the witnesses from the Western District processing plants in deciding whether Sochat in fact solicited bribes from Basar in the Eastern District."[57]

F. Offered to Prove Mental State

§ 7.22 Introduction

Nearly every crime defined in American law requires the prosecutor to prove that the defendant acted with mental culpability.[58] The law uses a wide range of terms to define (or at least label) the degree of mental and moral culpability. Putting aside the various forms of homicide, most crimes require the prosecutor to prove that the defendant in fact intended, not only to commit the *conduct*, but did so with the purpose or intention of committing the *crime*, or *knowing* that the conduct constituted a crime. Thus, if D is charged with shoplifting, it is not enough to prove that D walked out of a store with unpaid-for merchandise; the state's evidence must persuade the jury beyond a reasonable doubt that D did so intending to steal, rather than simply forgetting to pay for it.

Other crimes require the prosecutor to persuade the jury beyond a reasonable doubt that the defendant was aware of certain facts when he acted. If police find an unlawful weapon (such as a sawed-off shotgun) in D's house, the state's evidence must persuade the jury beyond a reasonable doubt that D knew it was there and exercised some dominion or control over it. If D is charged with selling stolen property, the state must persuade the jury, not only that D sold the property and that it was stolen, but also that D knew it was stolen. And so on.

To convict a person of, say, recklessly killing or injuring or endangering someone, a prosecutor must prove that the defendant was aware of circumstances that made his conduct unreasonably dangerous.

How can you "prove" what someone knew, or what someone intended, or what someone's purpose was when he or she acted?

Sometimes the inference of knowledge or purpose flows naturally from the act. If X shot Y three times while Y was asleep in bed, no sophisticated analysis is required to conclude that X intended to kill Y. If the shoplifter is wearing two blouses from a store clothing rack under her sweater as she leaves the store, her intent to steal is rather clear. If a witness testifies that the defendant showed him

57. For a more elaborate instruction, see § 7.14–iv.

58. The exceptions are, for our purposes, not important.

the sawed-off shotgun in his home (or better yet, if the defendant posted a picture of himself on Facebook brandishing the sawed-off in his living room) a few days before the police seized the weapon in his home, this constitutes direct evidence of his knowledge.

And, of course, the defendant's own words can establish mens rea. "I'm going to steal some blouses tomorrow from Fashonista Threads." "Congressman, I will arrange for you and your family to have an all-expenses paid vacation in Acapulco if you promise to use your influence in getting my company a multi-million-dollar contract with the government." "I can sell you these new appliances at less than half the manufacturing cost, because they were stolen off a truck last week." If a witness comes forward to testify that he or she heard the defendant say something along these lines, or if, after arrest, the defendant admitted to the police what he knew or what he intended, then the state's proof of the defendant's knowledge or intent or purpose is direct and solid (assuming the jury believes the witness).

But often the prosecutor does not have direct evidence of the defendant's intent or knowledge, and the defendant's conduct can plausibly be interpreted to support the either the inference of criminal intent or innocence, of guilty knowledge or ignorance. Or the government witnesses who supply the direct evidence of defendant's intent or knowledge may be highly impeachable. In such cases, the prosecutor must rely on circumstantial evidence—to establish the culpable mental state specified in the statute, or to corroborate the testimony of its direct-evidence witnesses. Quite often, extrinsic act evidence is offered for this purpose; and quite often it is admitted.

In § 7.9, I listed several of Rule 404(b)'s "other purposes" as ways in which extrinsic act evidence can help prove the mental state with which a person acted on the occasion that is the focus of the case being tried:

Mental State
Knowledge
Intent
Absence of mistake
Lack of accident
Motive
Preparation
Plan

Intent is itself a mental state and is an element of most crimes and many civil actions. The same is true of knowledge. In addition, showing that X knew a certain fact is often highly relevant to prove the intent with which he acted.

The same is true regarding absence of mistake, which is another way of describing knowledge, as a way of showing intent. Likewise, lack of accident: in criminal cases, "lack of accident" is a way of saying, "D didn't bring about a result accidentally or unintentionally; D intended to create a certain result."

Evidence of an extrinsic act which indicates D had a motive to do something or to cause a certain result is likewise relevant to show that D's conduct was intentional.

Ditto extrinsic acts which indicate the defendant had taken previous steps in preparation for the crime he is on trial for.

And so on. The label is not important; what matters is whether the prosecutor can articulate how, without relying on the propensity inference, the extrinsic acts help prove that D had a specific mental state when D engaged in the conduct for which D is now on trial.

The following sections explore this issue.

§ 7.23 *Huddleston v. U.S.*[59]

Huddleston was charged with selling 5,000 stolen blank Memorex video cassette tapes in April 1985, knowing them to be stolen. He acknowledged that he had sold them but denied that he knew they were stolen; he insisted that Welby, the person he had gotten them from, assured him they were not. As evidence that Huddleston had known that the tapes were stolen, the government offered evidence that in February of 1985, he sold large quantities of (probably) stolen tv sets, and in May 1985, he arranged to sell 70 stolen Amana appliances.

On appeal, Huddleston did not object to the relevance of extrinsic acts generally to prove intent or knowledge.[60] Nevertheless, the Court made a point of endorsing such use: "Extrinsic acts evidence may be critical to the establishment of the truth as to a disputed issue, especially when that issue involves the actor's state of mind and the only means of ascertaining that mental state is by drawing inferences from conduct."[61]

In other words: "he sold stolen property on three occasions; therefore, he probably knew all three collections of merchandise were stolen, including the one he is charged with possessing and selling."[62]

You might plausibly make two objections to this reasoning. First, even though all three sets of merchandise were stolen, that doesn't prove that Huddleston knew they were stolen. Second, doesn't the Court's reasoning basically accept the propensity theory?

---

59. Huddleston v. U.S., 485 U.S. 681 (1988).

60. For a more detailed statement of the facts in this case, and the Supreme Court's discussion of another aspect of Rule 404(b), see § 7.11.

61. *Huddleston*, 485 U.S. at 685. The Court added: "The actor in the instant case was a criminal defendant, and the act in question was 'similar' to the one with which he was charged. Our use of these terms is not meant to suggest that our analysis is limited to such circumstances." *Id.* at 685–86.

62. These are my words, not the Court's.

As to the first objection, going three-for-three with stolen property from the same source over a four-month period doesn't "prove" Huddleston knew, if by proof you mean "air-tight, indisputable and irrebuttable." But that is not the prosecutor's burden. The prosecutor was burdened with persuading the jury beyond a reasonable doubt that Huddleston knew the Memorex tapes were stolen. The Wesby-Huddleston hat-trick[63] basically asks the jury to make a common-sense judgment: "That much merchandise? All of it involving popular, sought-after items, that he could sell for Wesby at prices so far below manufacturer's cost, take a commission on the sales, and still leave Wesby with a profit? Come on! Huddleston would have to have chopped liver for brains[64] not to know."

As to the second objection: yes, this resembles the propensity inference. But courts traditionally treat extrinsic act evidence differently when offered to prove mental state, for precisely the reason the Supreme Court specified: often there is no direct evidence of what the defendant knew or thought or intended; it has to be inferred from conduct. Remember that the second factor in assessing admissibility of extrinsic act evidence is the degree to which the prosecutor needs to use the evidence to prove a fact.

§ 7.24 General rule

Most courts tend to agree that fungibly similar extrinsic acts which are not admissible to prove identity or conduct often are admissible to prove mental state, so long as mental state is a contested issue.[65]

As a result, where the extrinsic act has only fungible similarity to the charged act, a prosecutor may try to argue that evidence of the extrinsic act is offered to prove the defendant's mental state, because that is the prosecutor's best chance to get the evidence admitted. The defense attorney, of course, will argue the opposite: that the issue in the case is identity or conduct, not mental state, and therefore since the extrinsic act is only fungibly similar to what the defendant is now being tried for, evidence of the extrinsic act should be excluded.

---

63. "Hat-trick" is a sports expression: if a player scores three goals in a single game, that's called a "hat-trick." According to Wikipedia, the expression derives from a cricket game in 1858 "when a bowler took three wickets from three consecutive balls." I have no idea what that means, but apparently it was a good thing, because the bowler's teammates took up a collection and bought the bowler a hat with the proceeds. The expression has been adopted in a wide variety of sports—in hockey, it is customary for fans to throw their hats on the ice when a home team player scores three goals in a game. This is unrelated to the curious and cruel practice among some Detroit Redwings fans of throwing octopuses on the ice to celebrate particularly skillful plays. (By the way, octopuses are extremely intelligent animals—they have nine brains, use tools to solve problems, etc.)

64. For readers who are vegetarians or vegans, make that "shredded cauliflower."

65. The Court said so in *Huddleston*. In that case, given the closeness in time, the quantity of items in each separate instance, and the fact that the same person supplied all three groups of merchandise, the facts in *Huddleston* satisfy the fasprelipi standard.

Sometimes the prosecutor has no real argument that the issue is mental state; sometimes the defense has no real argument that the issue is not mental state. But sometimes each side has a plausible argument. The attorney who persuades the judge to see the case his or her way wins the battle over whether the evidence is admitted or excluded. That decision, in turn, may determine how the jury finally decides the case.

The preceding paragraph is true, not only relating to FRE 404(b), but to evidence issues generally. That is why it is so important that you approach each evidence problem, not as a neutral observer, but from three perspectives:

(1) "I am the offering party. How can I describe the case and frame the issues in a way that gives me the best chance to persuade the judge to admit the evidence?"

(2) "I am the opponent. How can I describe the case and frame the issues in a way that gives me the best chance to persuade the judge to exclude the evidence?"

(3) "I am the judge. Which of these two brilliant trial lawyers has persuaded me this time, and why?"

The first paragraph of this section raises the following issues. First: "How do I tell whether 'mental state is a contested issue' in a case?" Second, "How do I tell whether a particular case is one in which 'fungibly similar extrinsic act evidence is admissible, from one where it is not admissible?'"

As a general guideline, where X's conduct itself is ambiguous—if it can be interpreted as innocent or culpable—X's extrinsic acts of a similar nature are likely to be admissible to assist the jury in determining what motivated X to engage in the conduct that comprises the charges for which X is on trial.

<u>Question.</u>

Police Officers PO1 and PO2, sitting in their police car waiting for a light to change, noticed two people, Caldwell and JR, walking toward them. According to the officers, Caldwell looked at their marked police car and dropped a black handgun from his waistband to the ground. Caldwell had two prior felony convictions involving handguns, and therefore was charged in federal court with violating 18 U.S.C. § 922(g)(1) ("felon in knowing possession of a firearm"). Prior to trial, Caldwell stipulated to the fact that he had previously been convicted of a felony. Accordingly, the judge ruled, per *Old Chief v. U.S.*, that because of the stipulation, the government could not inform the jury that the prior convictions involved firearms. (See §§ 3.6–3.7.)

After the government rests, Caldwell testifies that it was JR—a juvenile with no criminal record—who possessed, and dropped, the gun. On cross, the prosecutor, citing FRE 404(b)(2), seeks to cross-examine Caldwell about his prior gun possession conviction. The prosecutor argues that the prior conviction is relevant to show Caldwell's knowledge that what he dropped was a gun. How should Caldwell's attorney respond; how should the judge rule?

Answer:

Defense counsel should argue that knowledge is not an issue here; the issue here is identity—who dropped the gun, Caldwell or JR. The likelihood that anyone who physically possesses a gun would not know what it was is absurd. The issue is identity, and since Caldwell's prior gun conviction is relevant only on a propensity theory, the judge should not allow the prosecutor to mention the prior gun conviction during cross-examination.

This problem is based on *U.S. v. Caldwell*, 760 F.3d 267 (3d Cir. 2014). The trial judge bought the prosecutor's argument—even though defense counsel offered to stipulate that whoever possessed the gun knew it was a gun. The Third Circuit reversed Caldwell's conviction and remanded for a new trial.

§ 7.25 Questions: Weather in the Heights[66]

Question 1.

Heathcliff, Lockwood and the Bronte sisters traveled together from the U.S. to Colombia and back again. U.S. ICE[67] officials noticed that Lockwood seemed extremely nervous and uncomfortable, so they detained and questioned him. He admitted that he had swallowed several balloons containing high-purity cocaine. He consented to take a laxative and excreted the balloons, which contained several ounces of the drug.

Lockwood's attorney worked out a deal: Lockwood pleaded guilty and testified for the government that Heathcliff had planned and paid for the trip, the real purpose of which was to smuggle cocaine back into the U.S. Originally, the Bronte sisters were supposed to swallow the balloons to get the cocaine into the U.S., but when they balked, Heathcliff persuaded Lockwood to do so instead.

Heathcliff is charged with smuggling cocaine into the U.S., and of conspiring with Lockwood to do so. At trial, Heathcliff's attorney tells the jury in her opening statement that Heathcliff and Lockwood and the sisters went to Colombia to vacation together, that Heathcliff had nothing to do with the cocaine, and that Lockwood's accusation is a lie he told to get a break in his own case.

---

66. If you majored in English literature in college, you should be able to figure out the name of this section.

67. Immigration and Customs Enforcement, a branch of the U.S. Department of Homeland Security.

Legal technicalities aside, and from the *jury's* perspective, what is likely to be the single key issue in the case?

Answer:

From the jury's perspective, the issue is: is Lockwood telling the truth or lying?

Comment: it is often useful to take a step away from the rules-of-evidence issues in a case, and imagine you are on the jury and have never studied law.[68] From that perspective, what would be the primary focus of your attention and deliberations? Doing so often will help you see issues—or aspects of issues—you might otherwise overlook.

Question 2.

The prosecutor, in compliance with the disclosure requirements of FRE 404(b)(3), informs Heathcliff's defense counsel that he intends to call a witness named Edward, who will testify that six years earlier, he accompanied Heathcliff to Colombia, and that Heathcliff offered him $1,000 to swallow several balloons containing cocaine. Edward will testify that he and Heathcliff made it through ICE without difficulties, that he excreted the balloons, and that Heathcliff paid him the $1,000.[69]

How should the defense attorney define the key issue in the case, in her motion in limine to exclude Edward's testimony, and why should she define it that way? Apply the 5-step process.

Answer:

Defense counsel objects that the issue is identity—who obtained the cocaine Lockwood had swallowed? Edward's testimony involves an alleged extrinsic act by Heathcliff that was only fungibly similar to what Heathcliff is currently charged with. (See § 7.16.) Therefore, the evidence must be excluded per FRE 404(b)(1). Here is Heathcliff's attorney's argument, as per the five-step process:

1. Purpose/relevance/issue: Identity. Who obtained and paid for the cocaine in Colombia?
2. Need: That is indeed *the* contested issue in the case.

---

68. That's difficult, I know. You are in at least your third semester of law school by now, and your professors have beaten the "think like a lawyer" drum from your first day at school, so putting that process aside—particularly while studying law—is a real challenge; in fact, it is a challenge in activities unrelated to law school. When I was a law student, my girlfriend was particularly good at nudging and teasing me out of the" law-is-everything" mode, and if nudging and teasing didn't work, dragging me out kicking and screaming. She still has to do that from time to time. (In 2022 we celebrated our 54th wedding anniversary.)

69. On the wild off-chance possibility that someone reading this is tempted to swallow a balloon or two to make a quick profit, consider this: if a balloon breaks inside the courier, the result is instant death.

3. How to prove the extrinsic act: Defense counsel concedes that Edward's testimony satisfies *Huddleston*.[70]
4. Fasprelipi:[71] Defense counsel argues that the evidence has virtually no fasprelipi. The relevance of Edward's testimony lies exclusively on the propensity inference: Heathcliff used Edward to smuggle cocaine into the U.S. last time, therefore, he probably used Lockwood to do so this time. This is a very common, non-unique, non-signaturesque way for an importer to get drugs through ICE while giving the actual importer plausible deniability if anything goes wrong.
5. We don't have to address FRE 403 and 105, because the evidence flunks FRE 404(b)(1).

Question 3.

How should the prosecutor define the key issue in the case, and why?

Answer:

"Your honor, the issue is mental state: why did Heathcliff go to Colombia with Lockwood and the Bronte sisters? Was it to vacation and party, like Heathcliff's lawyer claims, or was that just a cover to smuggle cocaine back into the U.S.? That's the issue the jury will have to resolve. Heathcliff's prior trip to Colombia with Edward provides the answer and confirms that Lockwood is telling the truth."

The prosecutor argues:

1. Purpose/relevance/issue: Mental state: why did Heathcliff go to Colombia with Lockwood and the Bronte sisters?
2. Need: That is indeed *the* contested issue in the case.
3. How to prove the extrinsic act: Edward's testimony satisfies *Huddleston*.
4. Fasprelipi: Considerable. Aside from Lockwood's testimony, there is no direct evidence as to Heathcliff's purpose or motive or intent in making the trip; that can only be shown by circumstantial evidence. And the circumstances line up: the only differences between the Edward importation and the current one is that this time, two women came along. Signaturesque similarity is not required when the extrinsic act is offered as evidence of the defendant's mental state.
5. FRE 403 and 105: The evidence has considerable fasprelipi which is not substantially outweighed by any of the Rule 403 risks.

70. The prosecutor probably will be able to provide circumstantial corroboration of aspects of Edward's testimony, e.g., that he and Heathcliff left the U.S. for Colombia on the same flight, stayed in the same hotel in Cali, Colombia, and came back on the same flight.

71. "Factually significant relevance independent of the propensity inference."

<u>Question 4.</u>

Who is right? How should the judge rule?

<u>Answer:</u>

The judge could reasonably go either way. If I were the judge, I'd admit the evidence, and issue a limiting instruction: "Heathcliff is not on trial for anything related to his trip with Edward to Colombia several years ago. But you may consider Edward's testimony and related evidence in deciding why Heathcliff went to Colombia with Lockwood and the Bronte sisters, and whether Heathcliff intended to bring the cocaine, ingested by Lockwood, back into this country."

<u>Question 5.</u>

Suppose Heathcliff had not accompanied Lockwood and the Bronte sisters to Colombia. Instead, according to Lockwood's testimony, Heathcliff had financed the venture, instructed Lockwood and the Brontes where and from whom to purchase the cocaine, and advised them how to bring it back to the United States undetected. How (if at all) would this change in the facts affect the admissibility of Edward's testimony?

<u>Answer:</u>

Edward's testimony should be excluded, because under this version of the facts, the prosecutor's "mental state" argument does not stand up.

Why?

In the original version of the case, the prosecutor had objectively verifiable evidence that Heathcliff engaged in conduct that plausibly connected him to the cocaine in Lockwood's digestive tract: airline reservations, ICE records of Heathcliff, Lockwood and the sisters leaving together and returning together, probably hotel records in Cali (or whatever city in Colombia the four of them visited), plus, probably, videos of them together in the airports in the U.S. and Colombia, videos of them together in the hotel, cell phone and email traffic back and forth, etc.

In this version, by contrast, other than Lockwood's testimony, there is no evidence that Heathcliff engaged in any conduct whatsoever relating to Lockwood and the sisters' trip or the cocaine. Therefore, the issue in this version is strictly identity/conduct: did Heathcliff do what Lockwood claims he did, or not? Fungibly similar extrinsic conduct is not admissible under FRE 404(b) when the only theory of relevance is, "He did it before, so he probably did it this time, too."

<u>Question 6.</u>

Suppose, in question 5, in addition to Lockwood's testimony, the government has acquired records showing that phones registered to or frequently used by Heathcliff were used to make calls to and receive calls from Cali, Colombia in the weeks preceding Lockwood and the sisters' trip; and additional calls were made to those same numbers while Lockwood and the sisters were in Cali. Moreover, Heathcliff made several withdrawals from various bank accounts prior to Lockwood and the sisters' departure; the amount withdrawn was enough to pay for three people to fly to and from Columbia, rent rooms in the hotel Lockwood and the sisters stayed in, and pay for the quantity of cocaine Lockwood brought back inside himself.

Does this change in the facts affect the admissibility of Edward's testimony?

Answer:

This version is about half-way between the original version and the scenario in question 5. Here, like the original version, we have objectively verifiable evidence of conduct by Heathcliff which circumstantially corroborates Lockwood's testimony to some extent. This gives the government a plausible argument that the issue is mental state: what was Heathcliff's intent, reason, purpose in making those calls and withdrawing that money. Still, this "objective" corroboration of Lockwood's testimony against Heathcliff is far less direct than in the first version, when Heathcliff actually accompanied Lockwood—and also less similar to what (according to Edward) he and Edward did six years earlier. So the fasprelipi of the Edward incident is less compelling, and the risk that the jury will rely on the propensity inference is greater.

The judge could rule either way.

§ 7.26 Knowledge

Evidence that a defendant had knowledge of certain facts is often relevant to prove mental state. Showing that a defendant knew a particular company's stock was worthless, for example, is relevant to prove that he knew his representations to the contrary were inaccurate, thus showing intent to defraud. On occasion, however, "knowledge" may also help prove identity. Evidence that defendant was one of only a few people who knew where a particularly valuable item could be found, for example, lends support to the inference that he is the one who stole it.

Somewhat more controversial is using evidence that a defendant committed a prior crime to prove that he knew how to commit the charged crime and therefore was the perpetrator. This is a proper use of extrinsic act evidence, where "knowledge" has special relevance—where, for example, the knowledge is something that few people possess and is particularly pertinent under the circumstances.

But "knowledge" should not be used as a mask for what in essence is propensity evidence.

Question 1.

In 2021, Driver was arrested while driving a car which Owner (who was not in the car) had allowed him to borrow. Passenger was next to Driver. Searching the trunk, the officers found a gym bag containing a clean towel and a pair of sweat socks. Inside the socks, they found a plastic food bag containing 85 grams (about three ounces) of cocaine. No fingerprints could be obtained from the gym bag or its contents. According to various web sites, the street value of cocaine is roughly $100 a gram.[72] Driver denied any knowledge of the cocaine's presence; so did Owner; so did Passenger. Owner and Passenger had no prior criminal record. Six years earlier, Driver had been arrested with 39 individually wrapped packages of cocaine and a scale in his car, and was convicted in that case of possession with intent to distribute.

Driver is charged with possessing the 85 grams with intent to sell. The prosecutor has notified defense counsel that she intends to offer evidence of Driver's prior conviction; Driver's attorney brings a motion in limine to exclude the evidence. Apply the five-step process.

Answer:

1. Purpose/issue/theory of relevance: P argues that the issue is knowledge: did Driver know the cocaine was in the trunk. D argues the issue is identity: was it Driver or someone else who put the drugs there.
2. Need: both are key issues in the case.
3. Proof of extrinsic act: Testimony by the officers in the prior case, plus documentary evidence of Driver's conviction, is convincing and persuasive.
4. Fasprelipi:[73] Even if we accept the prosecutor's argument that the key issue is knowledge, the prior case has *no* relevance to the current case, except to show propensity to possess seller-quantities of cocaine.[74]
5. FRE 403 and 105: Since the evidence fails step 4, we don't need to discuss step 5.

Comment: If the cocaine had been in a clear plastic bag on the console between Driver and Passenger, then Driver's prior experience with cocaine would have fasprelipi to show that he was familiar with cocaine's appearance,[75] which would in turn make it more probable than it would be without the evidence that he was knowingly transporting cocaine.[76]

---

72. Prices vary widely depending on circumstances, but clearly this is *not* a quantity an occasional user of cocaine would possess.

73. Factually specific relevance independent of the propensity inference.

74. This case is based on *U.S. v. Eggleston*, 165 F.3d 624, 625-26 (8th Cir. 1999).

75. This assumes the cocaine six years ago and the cocaine in the current case were both in powder form. If the cocaine in either case was crack cocaine, which is usually baked into pebbles, the inference of knowledge would be weaker.

76. This would be sufficient evidence to convict Driver of possession—even if the cocaine belonged to Passenger or Owner. See § 1.10. "Possession" need not be exclusive, and the law defines "possession" as having dominion or control over an item. Since Driver controlled the car, a jury

Question 2.

Reconsider the meat inspector case in § 17.21 Question 1. There, I concluded that although the prosecutor could not realistically claim that the extrinsic acts in the Western District had any fasprelipi to show identity, the prosecutor did have a plausible argument to show conduct.

Is there another "purpose" (theory of relevance), in addition to conduct, that the government should assert in its FRE 404(b)(3) notice? If so, how should the prosecutor satisfy FRE 404(b)(3)(B), which requires the prosecutor to notify the defense, in advance of trial, of "the reasoning that supports the purpose"?

Answer:

1. Purpose/issue/theory of relevance: Knowledge, i.e., that Sochat knew that the 2 pounds of ground beef he had purchased contained a plastic baggie with $100 in it.
2. Need: Based on Sochat's statement to the FBI agents, this is clearly a contested issue, and the only non-404(b)(2) evidence available to the government as to whether Sochat knew the money was in the meat was Basar's trial testimony.
3. Proof of the extrinsic acts: Testimony by the Western District witnesses clearly satisfies *Huddleston.*
4. Fasprelipi: Basar and the two Western District witnesses each will testify that he or she had never disclosed Sochat's extortion or unusual method of payment to anyone. By denying that he knew there would be $100 hidden in the package of ground beef, Sochat is accusing Basar of inventing that scheme to frame Sochat. What are the odds that Basar would invent the precise scheme that Sochat used with two other meat processing plants?
5. Rules 403 and 105: The fasprelipi of the Western District witnesses' testimony is compelling and easily overcomes a Rule 403 objection.

The limiting instruction would go something like: "Sochat is not on trial for any of his conduct in the Western district, and you must not consider the testimony of the [Western District] witnesses as a basis to judge his character. But you may consider their testimony in deciding whether Sochat knew there would be $100 hidden in the package of ground beef with which he was arrested on [date], and in evaluating the testimony of Basar regarding whether Sochat is guilty of extorting money from him."

---

could rationally conclude that he exercised control over whether he would transport the package of whitish power on the console.

§ 7.27 Degree to which mental state must be contested; stipulations

Virtually every crime contains within its definition a culpable mental state: in addition to proof that the defendant committed certain acts, the prosecutor must also prove he acted purposefully, or intentionally, or with the intent to rape, kill, defraud, distribute, etc.; or acted with malice; or acted with knowledge of certain facts (e.g. that certain items were stolen or consisted of controlled substances); or acted recklessly or negligently, to name just a few of the terms the criminal law uses to define (or at least label) the mental element of various crimes. (The same is true in many civil cases.)

If the current charge against the defendant has a similar mens rea as defendant's extrinsic acts, the latter may be highly relevant to prove that he or she engaged in the conduct in the current charge with the same mens rea. *Huddleston* provides a good example: at his trial for selling stolen videocassettes, the prosecutor had to prove, not only that he sold them (the actus reus) and that they were stolen (the attendant circumstance), but also that he knew they were stolen (the mens rea). Evidence that he sold other large quantities of stolen goods before and after he sold the videotapes, the Court correctly held, is relevant and admissible to prove that he knew all three items—including the videocassettes—were stolen. Why? Because direct evidence that "X" knew a certain fact is often not available, so a litigant often has to resort to circumstantial evidence supporting the inference that X knew that fact. And the greater the need for evidence to prove something (step 2 in the 5-step process), the greater its legitimate probative value is likely to be (step 4). See § 7.23.

The same is true of other mental states, as well. Example: possession with intent crimes—possession of a controlled substance with intent to sell, possession of burglar's tools (which can consist of a simple screwdriver or credit card, if the surrounding facts support the inference that that's why the defendant possessed them), etc. Example: transporting a female across a state line for purposes of prostitution, or crossing a state line to have sex with a minor. There is nothing illegal about bringing a 12-year-old child from, say, Maryland to D.C.—if the purpose is to take the child to a show at the Kennedy Center, or to the zoo, or the National Museum of African American History and Culture, or a Washington Nationals game. How do we prove that the intent behind this particular trip was not for entirely permissible and praiseworthy purposes, but to victimize the child sexually? Evidence that the defendant has done the latter in the past (or attempted to) certainly provides a strong inference that the defendant had the same purpose this time.

But if we applied this principle too broadly—if we always admitted similar extrinsic acts to prove the intent with which the defendant allegedly acted on this occasion—the "mental state" exception would swallow the exclusionary principle of FRE 404(b)(1). So when should the law allow similar extrinsic acts into evidence to prove mental state, and when not?

Where the defendant admits the *conduct* he is currently charged with but denies having the *culpable mental state,* the general rule is that evidence of his prior similar acts, committed with the same culpable mental state, are admissible as a basis to infer that the defendant had the same mental state this time, too. That's *Huddleston* in a nutshell. He admitted he sold the videocassettes, but denied knowing they were stolen. Therefore, evidence of prior or subsequent similar acts (the tv sets and Amana appliances), under circumstances supporting the inference that he knew *they* were stolen, is admissible to support the inference that he also knew the videocassettes were stolen. To repeat the general rule: *where a defendant admits engaging in the conduct he is charged with, but denies he did so with criminal mens rea*, evidence of the defendant's other, extrinsic acts of similar conduct, committed with the required mens rea, is admissible to prove that the defendant had that mens rea this time, too.

When the defendant denies engaging in the conduct in the first place, it gets a bit murky. If the alleged conduct (such as the Caldwell question in §7.24, possession of the dropped black handgun) pretty much also proves the requisite mental state (knowledge that it was a firearm), should the prosecutor nonetheless be permitted to offer prior unlawful possession of a handgun, to prove Caldwell's knowledge this time? Some courts say, "No, period." Some courts say "No, if the defendant affirmatively takes knowledge out of the case," for example, by stipulating that "whoever possessed the gun knew it was a gun." But some courts, at least in some situations, say that even a stipulation as to knowledge (or intent) does not preclude the prosecutor from offering evidence of fungibly similar extrinsic acts to prove intent this time.

Which of these three approaches should you take? I prefer the hybrid approach: where the conduct itself also establishes the mens rea, as in the dropped gun problem, and the defendant agrees to stipulate as to the mental element, the extrinsic act is not admissible. The stipulation must be unequivocal: "Your honor, we stipulate that whoever possessed the black handgun knew it was in fact a real firearm, and you may so instruct the jury." Or even more explicit, "Your Honor, we stipulate that if the jury finds beyond a reasonable doubt that the defendant possessed the handgun, we stipulate that on that basis, they may return a verdict of guilty of knowingly possessing it." But if your professor prefers the first or third approach ... Remember Fishman Rule of Evidence 001.

Problems arise, of course, where the conduct is itself ambiguous as to intent. Example 1: D possesses, let's say, six or eight individually wrapped user-quantity packages of cocaine. Did D possess them for his own personal use, a misdemeanor? Or with intent to distribute, a felony? If D denies he possessed the packages at all, does this open the door to prior instances of distribution on his part? To preclude use of evidence of extrinsic drug possessions or distributions, should D be forced to stipulate that "whoever possessed these packages of drugs did so with the intent to sell"—thereby elevating what might in fact have been a misdemeanor into a felony conviction?

Example 2. A client sues PT, a personal trainer, alleging that on several occasions PT touched the client's genital area or buttocks. PT insists: "I did not touch the client there." Although PT denies the conduct, mental state is still an issue, because a jury might reason, "I don't think the client is lying, maybe the trainer touched the client there accidentally and the plaintiff is blowing it out of proportion." Should this open the door to evidence that PT had done the same to other clients?

The quandary is simple to state and difficult to resolve, because admitting evidence of the prior acts to prove intent will inevitably be taken by the jury as proof that the defendant also engaged in the conduct—i.e., that he or she did in fact possess the drugs (which itself is a crime) or did touch the client.

If presented with an essay question with this sort of situation, your answer should state:

(1) The extrinsic acts are not admissible to prove conduct (e.g., possession, or improper physical contact); but

(2) A plausible argument exists that the extrinsic acts (possession with intent, or improper touching) have fasprelipi as to the defendant's intent in the current case.

(3) Therefore, a court might permissibly admit the evidence to show the defendant's intent, provided the judge (if requested) gives a limiting instruction.

In the drug case, the instruction would include: (1) The defendant is not on trial for the other occasions on which he allegedly sold drugs. (2) The jury should not consider those other occasions in deciding whether the defendant in fact possessed the drugs in this case, nor to make any general assessment about defendant's character. (3) But if the jury concludes beyond a reasonable doubt that the defendant did possess the drugs in this case, it may consider the evidence concerning the other sales in deciding whether he possessed the drugs in this case for personal use or with the intent to sell.

In the improper touching case, the instruction would include: (1) PT is not on trial for the other occasions on which he allegedly touched other clients' genital areas or buttocks. (2) The jury should not consider those other occasions in deciding whether the defendant in fact did what the plaintiff accuses PT of doing, nor to make any general assessment about defendant's character. (3) But if the jury concludes beyond a reasonable doubt that the defendant did touch the plaintiff's genital area or buttocks in this case, it may consider the evidence concerning the other clients in deciding whether he did so intentionally in this case.[77]

77. If Client sued PT in federal court (assuming a federal court had jurisdiction), the other incidents might well be admissible to prove conduct as well as mental state, per FRE 415. See Chapter 10.

§ 7.28 "Absence of mistake"

Extrinsic acts can disprove a defendant's claim that the defendant made an innocent mistake and acted without criminal or other improper intent.

In a crowded, standing-room-only subway train, defendant heads toward the door carrying an expensive attache case that belonged to another passenger. Arrested for theft, his defense is, "It was a mistake; I thought it was mine." And in fact, the defendant did have an attache case with him that vaguely resembled the one he was caught leaving with—roughly the same size and color, only old and somewhat battered and filled with the day's newspapers and a few tattered magazines. Evidence that on two prior occasions the defendant was caught making the same "mistake" on a crowded subway car or bus should be admitted as evidence that he did not mistake the other bag for his own; rather, that he intended to steal the other bag.

§ 7.29 "Lack of accident"

The use of extrinsic evidence to prove "lack of accident" can occur in a variety of circumstances. It can arise when a defendant denies engaging in any specific conduct. (1) The lawsuit against PT the personal trainer in § 7.27 is one example. (2) Several people have mysteriously gotten ill or died while under a defendant's care—see "doctrine of chances," § 7.31, *infra*.

"Lack of accident" can also arise where the defendant admits engaging in the conduct that caused, or could have caused, injury, damage or death, but claims it was accidental, not intentional. Doppledanger's gun goes off, killing or injuring or narrowly missing Vivacious, and Doppledanger is charged with murder or attempted murder or assault with a deadly weapon. His defense: it was unintentional—he dropped the gun and it went off unexpectedly. Sometimes an extrinsic act will have fasprelipi to disprove that defense.

"Lack of accident" is also applied sometimes where a defendant claims he did not know that a package contained drugs, or that certain items of property were stolen (see *Huddleston,* § 7.23), and the like.

G. Miscellaneous Extrinsic Act Issues

§ 7.30 Introduction

The next several sections discuss a variety of issues that arise governing the use of extrinsic act evidence per FRE 404(b)(2). If your professor doesn't cover these issues, it is probably safe to skip them.

§ 7.31 "Doctrine of chances"

A person in the defendant's care is injured or killed; or property in the defendant's possession is damaged or destroyed by fire. The evidence that the defendant caused the injury, death or damage is primarily or exclusively circumstantial, and defendant claims the event was an accident with which he had nothing to do. To rebut this claim and as circumstantial proof that the defendant's conduct caused the injury, death or damage, the prosecutor offers evidence of similar incidents in the defendant's past. The use of such evidence invokes the "doctrine of chances."

United States v. Woods, 484 F.2d 127, 132 (4th Cir. 1973), is perhaps the most-often cited example of the doctrine. Ms. Woods was charged with the death by suffocation of her infant foster son Paul. She denied having done anything to cause Paul's death. An expert testified for the state that there was a 75% likelihood that the death was a homicide, but could not reasonably rule out accident or unknown natural causes as possibilities—testimony which, by itself, would be insufficient to sustain a conviction. In addition, the state introduced evidence that, beginning some 15 years before, Ms. Woods had custody of or access to nine children who suffered at least twenty cyanotic (deprivation of oxygen) episodes, resulting in seven deaths. The Fourth Circuit held, correctly, that the evidence was admissible to support the inference that the defendant engaged in conduct causing Paul's death. The court reasoned that, while a reasonable doubt might necessarily exist as to any single episode involving a child, "the probability that some or all of the other deaths, cyanotic seizures, and respiratory deficiencies were accidental or attributable to natural causes was so remote, the truth must be that Paul and some or all of the other children died at the hands of the defendant." *Id.* at 132. The court observed that "when the crime is one of infanticide or child abuse, evidence of repeated incidents is especially relevant because it may be the only evidence to prove the crime." *Id.*

A prosecutor might also invoke the "doctrine of chances" in the possession of stolen property problems in § 7.5–iii. If I enjoy shopping at and collecting things from flea markets and yard sales, it is quite possible that I might have innocently purchased a few items that had been stolen in burglaries. But what are the chances that someone could innocently purchase dozens of separate items stolen in seven separate burglaries?

§ 7.32 "Scheme or plan"

The phrase "scheme or plan" has been used to describe rather different situations.

The first arises where a series of extrinsic acts are committed as part of a larger scheme to commit a culminating crime. Example: A , B and C plan to rob a bank. A steals a car to be used by the robbers, B commits a burglary to steal a homeowner's weapons, and C shoplifts masks from a store. Together, A, B and C use these stolen items to commit the robbery. Evidence of the extrinsic acts committed by A, B and C are admissible to prove that they were the robbers. (Sometimes a prosecutor might use the FRE 404(b)(2) label "preparation" instead of "scheme or plan.")[78]

The second category of "scheme or plan" arises where a perpetrator uses a particular technique again and again. This need not be a signaturesque "m.o." Examples:

a. An insurance salesman sold various policies to plaintiffs, promising that after only a few years, the policies would become "self-supporting"—i.e., it would no longer be necessary to pay premiums. Plaintiffs alleged that the salesman never told them that the premiums were being paid by loans against the policy, which, over time, substantially reduced the face value of the policy. The salesman, of course, insisted that he had fully informed plaintiffs of this fact. The key issue, therefore, was conduct: did the salesman inform the plaintiffs, or deliberately avoid telling them. To bolster their claim that the salesman had not informed them, plaintiffs elicited testimony from four other policy holders who testified that the salesman had misled them the same way. Held: no error; the evidence was properly admitted as circumstantial evidence that what the salesman had done to the other witnesses, he had also done to the plaintiffs. *Cartwright v. Equitable Life Assur. Soc.*, 914 P.2d 976, 989 (Mont. 1996).

b. At defendant's trial for slipping a drug into complainant's drink and then raping her after she passed out, held: evidence that he had similarly victimized other women was properly admitted to rebut his denial that he gave the complainant drugs and his claim that she consented to sex. *State v. Lough*, 125 Wash. 2d 847, 856, 889 P.2d 487, 492 (1995) (en banc).[79]

§ 7.33 Motive

We have already discussed how evidence of a defendant's motive to commit a crime may be relevant in several ways. First, showing motive may help establish that the defendant committed the crime—i.e., to prove identity or conduct. Second, motive may help establish that the defendant acted with the requisite mental culpability (purposefully, intentionally, knowingly, maliciously, etc.) or to negate a defense of accident or ignorance. Third, a jury in a criminal case may not be satisfied being shown who committed the crime, and how; it is likely to want to know why. Without evidence of motive, the jury may doubt the validity of the state's evidence or the credibility of the state's witnesses. Even where ample evidence exists to estab-

78. In such a case, the prosecutor could avoid Rule 404(b) issues altogether by charging A, B and C with conspiring together to rob the bank, and include each separate act as both a separate crime and an overt act in furtherance of the conspiracy.

79. In the prosecution of Bill Cosby in 2017 for victimizing a woman this way, the prosecutor had thirteen additional women prepared to testify that Cosby had done likewise to them. (The judge permitted the prosecutor to call only one such witness.) Cosby was convicted. The state supreme court later dismissed the charges against Cosby on a different ground.

lish identity and mental state, evidence of motive is nevertheless relevant to give the jury the complete story. Thus, evidence of an extrinsic act to prove a defendant's motive for a crime is often properly admissible.

But while evidence of motive may be important for a variety of reasons, a court should take care that "motive" does not become a back door to admit highly prejudicial evidence of little legitimate probative value.

a. Theft. As a rule, proof that the charged and extrinsic crimes both involved stealing money should not suffice to secure admissibility to prove the defendant committed both crimes. There is no great mystery why robbers rob, forgers forge, embezzlers embezzle, con artists defraud, "bribees" solicit bribes, or drug traffickers sell drugs, for example; they do it to obtain money.[80] Where defendant denies that he committed a theft of whatever kind, to admit evidence of a fungibly similar crime because each was motivated by a need or desire for money is simply a thinly disguised use of the propensity inference. Where, however, the extrinsic crime created a specific and immediate need for money, it may have fasprelipi with regard to the charged robbery or theft.

b. Drug addiction as motive. The issue often arises whether evidence that a defendant was a drug addict should be admitted as proof of her motive to commit a particular theft to suggest that she in fact committed the theft. Where defendant is charged with stealing the drugs themselves, evidence of her addiction is clearly relevant and should be admissible; likewise evidence of prior thefts of the drug. *United States v. Cunningham*, 103 F.3d 553 (7th Cir. 1996) (evidence of defendant nurse's prior addiction to and previous theft of Demerol was admissible to identify her, among the nurses with access to the drugs, as the probable thief). Likewise, when there is direct evidence (such as an accomplice's testimony) linking a theft to a defendant's need or desire to obtain drugs, such evidence ought to be admitted. But where evidence of addiction is relevant only on the general theory that addicts are motivated to steal in order to support their habits, this is merely a minor variation on the propensity inference ("because she is an addict, it is more likely that she stole"). Moreover, even as such, its relevance is dubious: although her addiction might provide the defendant with a greater motive than a non-addict would have, it does nothing to single her out from all other addicts who presumably had the identical "motive."

c. Motive in violent crimes. Where the extrinsic crime gives the defendant a particularized motive to commit the charged crime, evidence of the extrinsic crime has probative value independent of the propensity inference. The clearest example arises when a witness to the extrinsic crime is murdered prior to the trial of that charge. Evidence that the murder victim could have testified against the defendant at the trial of that charge is relevant to show that the defendant had a motive to

80. "Put money in thy purse." W. Shakespeare, *Othello*, Act I, Scene iii, line 345 (Iago).

kill the victim, thereby supporting the inference that the defendant is the killer. Similarly, where defendant's spouse or paramour has been murdered, evidence of prior assaults by the defendant on the victim suggests (a) the existence of an enmity toward the victim, which in turn suggests (b) that the defendant had a motive to kill the victim, which in turn suggests (c) that the defendant was the perpetrator. And evidence of the defendant's infidelity during the marriage is relevant to suggest a motive (i.e., a desire to be free of the marriage) and, therefore, to suggest the defendant was the killer.

d. Hate crimes; politically motivated crimes. Prior acts of racial or religious animosity toward a particular population subgroup may be admissible to show motive where a defendant is accused of physically assaulting a member of that group. Such evidence might be offered to prove identity or mental state (e.g., that the defendant injured or killed the victim intentionally, not inadvertently or accidentally). And, alas, the same situation may arise these days regarding political affiliation—a defendant's prior attacks on or threats against persons on a particular side of the political spectrum or a particular politically active organization may be relevant in a prosecution for assaulting or killing someone on that side or active in that organization.

§ 7.34 Use of extrinsic act evidence by defendant

Occasions arise where a defendant offers extrinsic act evidence. Rules 404(b)(1) and 404(b)(2) apply to defense-offered evidence, just as they do to extrinsic act evidence offered by a prosecutor. Some—but not all—courts have suggested that the law should lean a bit more toward admitting such evidence when offered by the defendant, or offered by a party in civil litigation.

Such evidence might be relevant on a variety of theories.

D may offer evidence of his or her own extrinsic conduct, as evidence of his or her innocence. Suppose D, the CEO of a large corporation, is charged with bribing X, the chief purchasing agent for the Metropolis City Public School System (MCPSS), in order to win a lucrative contract from MCPSS. The indictment alleges that the bribe was disguised as a charitable contribution:

(1) X is a member of the President's Council of the University of Erehwon, X's alma mater, an unpaid but prestigious position.

(2) D made a large contribution to Erehwon in X's honor.

(3) A week later Erehwon hired X's daughter to a well-paying position.

(4) A few weeks after that, X saw to it that D's company got the contract.

In other words, D contributed money to Erehwon to influence Erehwon to hire X's daughter, and in exchange, X arranged for D to obtain a lucrative contract from MCPSS.

Suppose D offers evidence that D regularly made large contributions to, say, Wobegon University, K.V. Shinayim School of Dentistry and Cacophony School of Music, to show that D regularly contributes money to institutions of higher learning, as a basis to infer that his donation to Erehwon was just another act of generosity. Such evidence should be excluded per FRE 404(b)(1), because its relevance is based on D's propensity to donate to other educational institutions. But evidence that D made sizable contributions to Erehwon years before D sought the contract might well be admissible as evidence that the contribution alleged in the indictment was not intended as an indirect bribe to benefit X's daughter in exchange for getting the contract from MCPSS.

Where D is charged with a crime that involved an unusual modus operandi, proof that someone else had committed similar crimes with that same modus operandi has probative value suggesting that the other individual, not D, committed the crime for which D is charged.

Similarly, where D and Z were involved in a scheme to defraud, evidence that Z had committed similar frauds in the past is relevant to show that Z did not need D's knowing cooperation to commit the fraud that is the subject of the current trial. This in turn suggests that D might have been an innocent dupe rather than an accomplice.

Where defendant D claims he was entrapped by police informant CI into committing the conduct with which D is charged, evidence that CI engaged in entrapment in other cases might be admissible to bolster D's claim that CI used the same entrapping tactics on D.

§ 7.35 Admissibility in civil litigation

I've said this a few times already, but it bears repeating: although FRE 404(b) is invoked in criminal cases far more often than in civil litigation, it applies in civil cases as well.

§ 7.36 Questions

Question 1.

Drab is charged with burglarizing CW's garage. At trial, CW will testify that on January 14, she saw Drab going through a tool chest in her garage; when she shouted: "You don't belong in here!" Drab ran off. PO, a police officer, will testify that after receiving CW's complaint and a description of the perpetrator, he cruised the neighborhood, and apprehended Drab a few minutes later a few blocks from CW's home. CW and PO1 each will testify that CW made an on-the-spot identification of Drab as the man in her garage.

What is the definition of burglary?

Answer:

Unlawful entry into a premises with the intent to commit a crime therein.

Question 2.

Four years earlier, PO2 had searched Drab's home and found the proceeds of several local burglaries. Drab pled guilty in that case of several counts of possession of stolen property. He was sentenced to three years' imprisonment, served 13 months, and was released on parole. Pursuant to FRE 404(b)(3), the prosecutor notified Drab prior to trial that she plans to elicit testimony from PO2 about what he found when he searched Drab's home four years ago, and to offer documentary proof that Drab was convicted by guilty plea of several counts of possession of stolen property.

Discuss the issues thus presented.

Answer:

Drab's attorney should bring a motion in limine, citing FRE 404(b)(1), seeking a ruling excluding PO2's testimony, evidence of Drab's prior conviction, and the fact that D is on parole.

1. Purpose/issue/theory of relevance. We begin with the default assumption that the issue is identity: was Drab in fact the person CW saw rummaging through the toolbox in her garage.
2. Need: Convictions are often obtained based on a single eyewitness's testimony, and assuming CW's description of Drab to PO1 closely matched Drab's actual appearance, that makes CW's subsequent identification of Drab somewhat stronger. Still, the state's case isn't exactly a top-of-the-tenth-inning grand slam home run.[81] The state has a legitimate need for additional evidence firming up CW's identification of Drab.
3. Proving the extrinsic acts: PO2's testimony, the transcript of Drab's guilty plea allocation, and documentary proof of the conviction and sentence clearly satisfy *Huddleston*—indeed, quickly, easily and convincingly establish Drab's involvement in the prior burglaries.
4. Fasprelipi: If the issue is identity, PO2's testimony, Drab's prior conviction and the fact that he is on probation are relevant only via the propensity evi-

81. Washington Nationals fans will long remember that in the fifth and final game of the first National League playoff round in 2019, Howie Kendrick—yup, the same guy (see § 1.2)—hit a grand slam in the top of the 10th, giving the Nats a 7-3 lead over the heavily favored Los Angeles Dodgers. It wasn't a walk-off—the Nats still had to retire the Dodgers in the bottom of the tenth without letting them score 4 or more runs—but a four-run lead over the home team in the final inning of a playoff game is pretty close to a sure thing. Dodger fans at the game certainly thought so—they started deserting Dodger Stadium by the thousands even before Kendrick finished circling the bases. Shame on them!

dence—he burgled (or received the proceeds of burglaries) before, now he burgled again. Therefore, the evidence should be excluded.

5. Rules 403 and 105: If the judge excludes per FRE 404(b)(1), there is no need to apply the fifth step in the process.

Can the prosecutor argue that mental state, as well as identity, are at issue in the case?

Mental state is technically an issue—to convict, the prosecutor has to persuade the jury that the defendant entered the garage with the intent to steal. And there is always the possibility that one or two jurors might refuse to convict of burglary because, "After all, Drab didn't actually steal anything." (The law doesn't require proof of actual theft, only the intent to steal, but some jurors may not understand that, or may refuse to follow the judge's instructions on that matter.)

But the conduct CW described leaves little reason to doubt that the intruder was looking for something to steal. Hence, the only real impact the extrinsic act evidence would be to convince the jury that it was in fact Drab whom CW saw rummaging through the toolbox in the garage, i.e., the propensity inference.

Question 3.

Suppose the judge ruled that Drab's prior possession of the proceeds of several burglaries, and his conviction, are admissible as evidence of his intent when he entered the garage. What might Drab's attorney do next?

Answer:

Drab could offer to stipulate that whoever was in CW's garage that day was there with the intent to steal, and that, therefore, if the jury concludes beyond a reasonable doubt that it was in fact Drab who was in CW's garage, they may convict him of burglary. Drab's attorney argues that this would so drastically reduce the need for evidence on mental state that the evidence relating to the other burglaries and stolen property no longer has enough factually specific relevance to overcome the unfair propensity inference regarding identity.

This has two risks: it may constitute a waiver of the right to appeal the judge's in limine ruling, and it gives up any realistic hope that the jury might convict Drab only of unlawful entry (or criminal trespass), a much less serious crime than burglary.[82]

Question 4.

Suppose instead that the judge ruled in limine that the state could *not* introduce evidence of Drab's prior possession of stolen property, nor refer to Drab's conviction. At trial, state calls CW, who testifies as to the man in her garage and what he was doing. She testifies about the description of the man she gave to PO1, and

82. For this reason, I think Drab's attorney should explain this to Drab, and offer the stipulation only if Drab concurs.

that she identified Drab as the man after PO1 arrested him. PO1 testifies about the description CW gave of the intruder, and her identification of Drab as the intruder after PO1 arrested Drab. Perhaps the state also calls a fingerprint expert to testify that there were fingerprints on the toolbox but they were too smudged to be of use. Assume all this evidence is properly admitted. Since the judge has excluded the extrinsic evidence about the prior burglaries, the state rests.

Drab decides to take the stand. He testifies that as he was passing CW's garage he noticed a strange flag on the wall and entered just to get a better look; he denies touching the toolbox.

Discuss the issues presented.

<u>Answer:</u>

Out of the jury's hearing, the prosecutor asks the judge to reconsider the in limine ruling excluding evidence of Drab's prior conviction for possession of stolen property. The prosecutor argues that Drab's testimony has changed the case entirely. The issue is no longer identification: Drab admits he was the man in the garage. Now the issue is mental state: *why*—with what intent—did Drab enter the garage? Evidence of Drab's involvement in prior burglaries now has fasprelipi[83] on a truly contested issue.

Drab counter-argues that the issue still is not mental state; it is conduct. CW claims Drab was rummaging through the toolbox; Drab denies doing so; he was simply looking at an unusual flag on the garage wall.[84] Drab's prior involvement with burglaries is only fungibly similar to what he is now on trial for, and fungibly similar extrinsic acts should not be admitted to prove conduct, as the relevance of such extrinsic acts relies exclusively on the propensity inference.

I think the judge could quite plausibly rule either way, but I would allow the cross-examination about his prior conviction, because Drab's testimony has placed his intent sufficiently at issue to give the extrinsic crimes fasprelipi.

<u>Question 6.</u>

Dillinger is charged with armed robbery committed on June 5 in Smalltown. Prior to trial, the prosecutor notifies defense counsel that he intends to offer evidence that on June 4, Dillinger escaped from a nearby federal penitentiary, where he was in the fifth year of a 12-year sentence for manslaughter; that Dillinger took a guard's handgun; and that he stole a car from a nearby parking garage. Discuss the issues thus presented.

---

83. "Factually significant relevance independent of the propensity inference."

84. Let's assume CW acknowledged, during cross-examination, that there was such a flag in the garage.

Answer:

1. Issue/purpose/theory of relevance: Our default assumption is that the key issue in any criminal case is identity: who committed the robbery.
2. Need: Let's assume there is no video of the robbery and only an eyewitness or two who can identify Dillinger as the robber.
3. How to prove the extrinsic act: Let's assume this poses no difficulty.
4. Fasprelipi: Does the fact that the day before the store robbery, Dillinger had escaped from a federal prison and stolen a gun and a car, have any relevance besides the "bad man" inference?

Do any of the "purposes" listed in FRE 404(b)(2) (other than identity itself) have resonance here? "Motive, opportunity, intent, preparation, plan, knowledge, identity, absence of mistake, lack of accident."

If you had just escaped from a—no, let me phrase that a little differently.[85] Try to put yourself in the position of someone who had just escaped from a federal penitentiary. What would be first and foremost on your mind?

Putting as much space as possible between the penitentiary and you.

What would you need to do so?

A means of travel and money to pay for it.

What's the quickest way to get money?

Steal it.

What would be quite helpful to someone who plans to steal money?

A handgun.

In other words, Dillinger's status as an escapee gives him a powerful *motive* to commit a robbery, and his theft of a gun gives him the means, i.e., the *opportunity*, to commit it.

But wait, professor! You said back in § 7.33 that the mere need for money should not be an excuse to admit evidence of a prejudicial extrinsic act.

Yes, I said that, but I also said that "Where, however, the extrinsic crime created a specific and immediate need for money, it may have fasprelipi with regard to the charged robbery or theft." Dillinger's situation creates a particularized and immediate need for money. His escape and theft of a gun and a car should be admitted.

85. If you had just escaped from a federal penitentiary, I doubt you'd be reading this book.

5. Rules 403 and 105: Query, though, whether the fact that he is serving a 12-year sentence for manslaughter has sufficient legitimate probative value to overcome the risk of unfair prejudice. That Dillinger was doing time in a federal penitentiary carries a considerable risk of unfair prejudice, but because that fact is critical to show Dillinger's motive to commit the robbery, the judge should allow the prosecutor to prove that fact. But the crime for which he was doing time—manslaughter—is less critical; and if the jury learns that he was serving a sentence for killing someone, there is a significant risk that the jury might convict him of the robbery almost as a reflex reaction.

The judge should redact the evidence to exclude the length of Dillinger's sentence and the crime for which he was serving it.

Chapter 8

Rule 406: Habit; Routine Practice

A. The Rule

§ 8.1 FRE 406

FRE 406 provides:

> **Rule 406. Habit; Routine Practice**
>
> Evidence of a person's habit or an organization's routine practice may be admitted to prove that on a particular occasion the person or organization acted in accordance with the habit or routine practice. The court may admit

> this evidence regardless of whether it is corroborated or whether there was an eyewitness.

Rule 406 covers two different, albeit somewhat related, subjects: "habit" evidence, and "routine practice" evidence. "Habit" evidence relates to an individual; "routine practice" relates to an organization.

Probably the rule is invoked most often to show a litigant's habit or routine practice. For example, a plaintiff might offer evidence of his or her own habit or its own routine practice, or of the defendant's habit or routine practice, and vice versa. But the rule also permits a litigant to offer evidence of a non-party's habit or routine practice. Thus, a party might seek to invoke it in several of the litigation situations discussed in Chapter 11.

B. Habit

§ 8.2 Introduction

Regarding habit, Rule 406 provides:

> Evidence of a person's habit ... may be admitted to prove that on a particular occasion the person ... acted in accordance with the habit ....

As we have seen in Chapters 6 and 7, evidence of a person's "character," in the form of reputation or opinion testimony, or evidence of that person's specific extrinsic acts, is generally not admissible as a basis to infer his or her conduct on a particular occasion. Exclusion is justified because such evidence often has uncertain probative value—people often do act inconsistently with their "character"—and is too likely to involve unfair prejudice, consumption of excessive time, and confusion of issues.

Evidence that a person frequently or regularly encounters a specific situation and consistently responds to it the same way, by contrast, has a much higher predictive value in assessing whether he acted the same way on a particular occasion. Thus, the law generally admits evidence that a person was in the "habit" of behaving in a certain way in response to a particular situation. FRE 406 codifies this principle.

Admissibility of evidence of a person's habit to prove action in conformity therewith raises numerous issues.

The first and most obvious is: where is the line to be drawn between (presumptively inadmissible) evidence of character and (admissible) evidence of habit? As courts readily acknowledge, it is often difficult to distinguish between the two. In assessing whether proffered evidence constitutes proof of character or of habit, four factors are particularly relevant:

1. The specificity or particularity of the situation.
2. The frequency with which the person in question encounters the situation.
3. The uniformity of the person's response to the situation.
4. The extent to which the conduct in question is reflexive rather than volitional.

Let's start with an example. On April 5th, cars driven by X and Y collided in the 4-way-stop-sign intersection of Avenue A and First Street. Evidence that motorist X is reputed to be an inattentive driver, or that X ran a different stop sign three months earlier, is not admissible to support the inference that X ran the stop sign at A and First on April 5th. The first is character evidence, banned by FRE 404(a)(1); the second is propensity-based extrinsic act evidence, banned by FRE 404(b)(1).

Similarly, S, who has often ridden with Y, might be willing to testify that, in his opinion, Y is a very careful, cautious driver, and Y might have documentary proof that Y has never been issued a traffic summons and was never involved in a collision before April 5th. Each is probative to suggest that the April 5th collision was not Y's fault. But S's testimony is barred by FRE 404(a)(1), and Y's documentation of his clean driving record would be banned by FRE 404(b)(1), since, in essence, Y is offering evidence of an absence of extrinsic acts that are relevant only on the propensity theory.

But suppose Y calls witness W, who testifies that X has regularly given W a lift to the commuter train each workday for the past two years; that X drove through that same intersection every day, five days a week, on the way to the station; and that, except when cars in front of X forced X to stop, X invariably rolled through that stop sign without stopping. Would such testimony qualify as evidence of X's "habit"?

1. <u>The specificity or particularity of the situation.</u> A stop sign in a specified intersection is a very precise and particular situation.
2. <u>The frequency with which the person in question encountered the situation.</u> If X drives through that intersection each day, we are talking about hundreds of instances a year.
3. <u>The uniformity of her response to the situation.</u> According to W, X "invariably" drove through the stop sign without stopping whenever it was physically possible for X to do so.
4. <u>The extent to which the conduct in question is reflexive rather than volitional</u>. When an experienced driver approaches an intersection regulated by a stop sign, he or she either stops at the sign, more or less automatically; or, if not, quickly glances both ways (at least we hope so!) and makes an almost instantaneous decision whether the road is clear enough to roll through the intersection without stopping. This is far more reflexive than volitional.

Thus, X's repeated conduct at that intersection is so "habitual" that it should be admissible per Rule 406 as a basis to infer that X ran the stop sign on April 5th.

Issues also arise with regard to *how* a litigant may seek to prove a person's habit. See § 8.6.

§ 8.3 Specificity or particularity of the situation

To qualify as habit, the evidence must relate to a fairly specific factual situation. The following examples illustrate the requirement.

1. Driving and pedestrian "habits."

Concerning evidence about a person's "habits" while driving, see the example discussed in § 8.2.

Similarly, evidence that a pedestrian "always looks both ways before crossing a street" would not be admissible as evidence that he looked this time (and therefore was not contributorily negligent), but testimony that he always crossed a particular street at a particular crosswalk and always looked both ways before crossing that street probably would qualify as "habit" and therefore would be admissible to support the inference that he did so on the occasion in question.

2. Intoxication and sobriety.

In the X-Y collision case, suppose Y had convincing evidence that X was intoxicated on many other occasions—perhaps even that X was habitually drunk--and offers that evidence a basis to infer that X was probably intoxicated at the time of the X-Y collision. The judge should exclude the evidence, because evidence of a person's supposed "habitual" drunkenness does not qualify as "habit" evidence per FRE 406. Likewise, evidence that a person has been under the influence of drugs (whether lawful or not) on other occasions does not qualify as "habit" evidence as a basis to infer that he was under the influence during the events giving rise to the lawsuit.

On the other hand, evidence that a motorist always stops at a certain bar on the way home from work for a boilermaker (a glass of beer mixed with a shot of whiskey) probably would qualify as evidence of a "habit," assuming the other requirements of Rule 406 are met, and therefore as a basis to infer that the motorist had done so on the occasion in question.[1]

---

1. This scenario, proposed in a leading evidence treatise (not mine), has been cited by courts as a good example of behavior which is sufficiently habitual to qualify under the rule. It is also a scenario with which I had first-hand experience. During the summer between my sophomore and junior years in college, I worked as a driver's helper for a liquor distributer: the driver would drive to various bars, restaurants, and liquor stores; I helped him unload the boxes of liquor. The workday was officially 8 a.m. to 4 p.m. My first day, we finished at about 2:45. Instead of returning to the distributor's warehouse, the driver stopped at a bar a few minutes' drive from the warehouse—where he met several other drivers and their helpers—and drank until 4 p.m. My driver explained that if we returned early, neither he nor I would get paid for the full day, so all the drivers stopped each day to

Courts are similarly reluctant to admit evidence of a person's sobriety, although cases can be found that allow evidence that a person never consumes alcohol at all.

3. Assaults.

Evidence of a person's prior assaults or violent behavior is generally characterized as character evidence, rather than habit: the varying circumstances of prior assaults necessarily precludes their use as evidence of habit or routine practice. Occasionally, however, the offering party is able to demonstrate sufficient particularity, similarity, and frequency to qualify as habit evidence.

4. Professional "habits."

Evidence that a person follows a routine practice on the job can qualify as habit evidence. The situation arises often in medical malpractice actions and the like: a doctor and/or the doctor's nurse testifies that the doctor always advises patients of the risks and benefits of the recommended course of treatment. Such testimony is admissible as evidence that the doctor did so on the occasion in question. Per the last sentence of Rule 406, such testimony is admissible even if the doctor and/or nurse testified that the doctor did in fact advise the patient in the case on trial.

A court has held that a police officer's testimony as to his routine in assuring it was after 7 a.m. before issuing parking tickets was admissible to establish that a particular ticket was in fact issued after 7 a.m.

A can of refrigerant exploded, injuring a mechanic while he was servicing an air conditioner, and the mechanic brought a products liability action against the manufacturer of the refrigerant. Held: evidence that the plaintiff mechanic had a habit of using an immersion heating coil to accelerate the flow of a refrigerant, despite warnings on the refrigerant container to not do this, should be admitted. The court found that when the circumstances involve "a deliberate and repetitive practice" which is unlikely to vary, evidence of habit should be admitted as evidence that the plaintiff had used an immersion coil on the occasion that led to his injuries.

X is injured on the job and brings a personal injury action against his or her employer. Evidence that X had suffered other injuries at work should not qualify to show X had a "habit" of carelessness, barring evidence that the circumstances of those other injuries closely resembled the current one.

Keep in mind, though, that evidence of X's frequent intoxication, or poor driving record, or evidence of prior assaults, etc., may be admissible in negligent entrustment actions against another party—such as X's employer, or the person who allowed X to drive his or her car, etc. See generally § 5.4.

"relax" until the clock struck four. I noticed a significant deterioration in my driver's attentiveness and judgment on the short ride from the bar to the warehouse. I quit the same day.

§ 8.4 Frequency of occurrence; uniformity of response

If a court concludes that the situation in question satisfies the specificity requirement, it must then determine whether the offering party has demonstrated that the situation occurred with sufficient frequency, and that the response to the situation was sufficiently uniform, to qualify as evidence of habit or routine practice. As the Advisory Committee Note to FRE 406 states, "adequacy of sampling and uniformity of response are key factors" in making the determination. One or two instances will not suffice; the minimum required number of instances varies with the type of conduct involved.

Once the offering party establishes that X has encountered the particular situation with sufficient frequency, it is then necessary to establish that X "always" or "invariably" responds to it the same way. Courts often require the offering party to make some showing of the "ratio of reactions to situations," i.e., the number of instances in which X encountered a specific situation compared to how often X responded with purportedly habitual behavior. Even a large number of specific instances of X's conduct may not suffice to establish habit if that number represents only a fraction of the times X has encountered the situation.

§ 8.5 Reflexive vs. volitional conduct

The Advisory Committee Note to FRE 406 speaks in terms of a "semi-automatic" response to specific stimuli. Accordingly, courts sometimes reject evidence if the behavior in question involves a "volitional," rather than a "semi-automatic," "reflexive," or "instinctive" reaction to a particular set of circumstances.

The problem, of course, is where to draw the line between volitional and nonvolitional response. The Advisory Committee note cites a case holding that a person's practice of attending a specific religious service on the same day at the same time every week was not sufficiently "reflexive" because it involved a certain degree of deliberation. Once a person deliberates a particular course of action, the court reasoned, that person's decision is influenced by legal, moral, and economic considerations that may depend on varying facts and circumstances; this type of volitional decision is not as probative as the semi-automatic nature of conduct governed by the "subliminal mind."

I'm not convinced that this reasoning is sound, but the Advisory Committee Note is fairly authoritative when it comes to interpreting and applying the Rule.

§ 8.6 Means of proof

i. Specific instances of conduct

To prove that a person "habitually" behaved in a specific way when confronting a specific situation, it is necessary to offer evidence—almost always, testimony—that satisfies the requirements of the rule. There is little difficulty where one or two witnesses can testify that they have observed numerous occasions in which X encountered a particular, specific situation, and that each time, X has responded and reacted in the same way. A frequently cited example arises when a doctor, or the doctor's nurse or office assistant, testifies that the doctor "always" follows an established routine when advising a patient about the risks of a particular medication or surgery or other course of treatment. Testimony by two or three people who have often ridden with X when X drove, that X always fastened his seat belt before putting the car in gear, suffices to establish that this was X's habit. And so on.

What about a litigant who wants to call, say, six or seven witnesses, each of whom will testify that he or she witnessed that X acted in the same way on one or two occasions? Depending on circumstances, a trial judge might have discretion to allow such testimony. For example, in a medical malpractice suit, where plaintiff alleges that a doctor failed to advise him of potential complications or side-effects from a prescribed medication, a judge might allow a doctor to call five former patients to testify that the doctor had carefully warned them of potential side effects concerning the same medication. But a judge would also have discretion to exclude these witnesses' testimony on the ground that a mere five instances does not satisfy the requirement of "adequacy of sampling and uniformity of response." (See § 8.4.)

ii. Opinion testimony

The original draft of FRE 406 contained a sub-rule (b): "Habit or routine practice may be proved by testimony in the form of an opinion or by specific instances of conduct...." The House Judiciary Committee deleted this provision, explaining that it was best to let courts decide what kinds of evidence should suffice, but added: "At the same time, the Committee does not intend that its action be construed as sanctioning a general authorization of opinion evidence in this area."

I have found no case in which a federal court, applying Rule 406, admitted opinion testimony about a person's habit, and I have difficulty imagining such testimony. So unless your professor specifically says otherwise, I think it is safe to assume that the *only* way to offer habit evidence that would satisfy FRE 406 is to offer testimony of a large enough number of instances in which X encountered a specific situation and responded the same way each time.

iii. Changes from prior practice

Prior to the enactment of the Federal Rules of Evidence, courts imposed a variety of restrictions on when habit evidence could be presented. Rule 406 abolishes the following restrictions. (Unless your professor makes a point of discussing these, it is probably safe to ignore this subsection.)

1. Prior to the FRE, some courts did not allow habit evidence when eyewitnesses to the event were available to testify to the actual facts. FRE 406 has abolished that restriction, and admits habit evidence regardless of the presence or absence of eye-

witness testimony. For example, in the medical malpractice scenario, a doctor could (1) testify that she warned the plaintiff of potential side-effects, (2) testify that she always warns all patients of potential side effects, (3) have her nurse testify that the doctor always warns all patients of potential side effects, and (4) call several other patients to whom the doctor prescribed the same medicine, each to testify that the doctor warned him or her of the potential side effects of the medication. (At least, the doctor could do so without violating Rule 406. At some point during this parade of witnesses, the judge should say "enough is enough" and, per FRE 403, preclude any further needless presentation of cumulative evidence.)

2. Prior to the FRE, some courts admitted evidence of habit or routine practice only if corroborated by evidence of the conduct on the occasion in question. FRE 406 has discarded this limitation on the theory that a failure to corroborate, like the presence or absence of eyewitnesses, affects the weight of the evidence before the factfinder, rather than its admissibility at trial.

C. Routine Practice of an Organization

§ 8.7 In general

FRE 406 provides, in pertinent part:

> Rule 406. Habit; Routine Practice
>
> Evidence of ... an organization's routine practice may be admitted to prove that on a particular occasion the organization acted in accordance with the routine practice. The court may admit this evidence regardless of whether it is corroborated or whether there was an eyewitness.

FRE 406 also admits evidence of the "routine practice" of organizations, as evidence that that practice was followed on the occasion in question. "Organization" covers a wide range of entities: government agencies, businesses, corporations, unions, religious institutions, charities, country clubs and other social organizations, etc.

Businesses and other organizations often develop routine, standard procedures and rules to handle a recurring kind of event or transaction. Courts generally admit evidence of such "routine practices" as probative of the actions taken by that organization on a particular occasion, because there is often no other way for a large organization to establish how it acted on a particular occasion, which may have taken place months or even years before trial. A frequent application of this principle involves proving that a particular item was mailed by showing how the organization routinely handles outgoing mail.

But the "routine practice" need not be a formal procedure; it need not be something that is specified in writing. Many organizations develop informal or unofficial routines as well. If a company's accounting department orders pizza from a local Italian restaurant for lunch every Wednesday, that might well qualify as a "routine practice" of that organization-within-an-organization.

An organization may offer evidence of its own routine practice, as evidence of how it conducted itself regarding the events that are the focus of the trial.

Evidence of an organization's routine practice may also be offered against that organization. For example, in a state action seeking to enjoin police officers from harassing or assaulting people or making arrests without probable cause, evidence of individual officers' practice of physically assaulting arrestees, coupled with a lack of disciplinary response from the police department, can establish a pattern of physical violence that was routine, systematic and likely to continue in the future, and would therefore be admissible as evidence of the department's routine practice.

The particularity of the situation and the frequency and uniformity of the organization's response to the situation apply to some extent to evidence of routine practice. ABC Corp. sues DEF Corp., alleging that DEF failed to deliver essential material on time as required by contract. DEF insist that its deliveries were timely. ABC wants to offer evidence that DEF regularly delivered late to other customers as well. Most courts would exclude this evidence, because how a company conducts business is likely to differ from customer to customer in a variety of ways. DEF's contracts with other companies may involve different materials or much larger or smaller quantities. A supplier like DEF may have different informal understandings with different customers as to the importance of timely delivery of certain items, and so on.

But courts sometimes apply the requirements of routine practice more liberally than they do for habit. For example, an organization's routine practice may be—often will and should be—volitional rather than reflexive. Large organizations in particular may have written directives or policies as to how employees should handle certain situations, including situations requiring evaluations and assessments. For example, a forensic laboratory will have specific rules as to how a particular examination of a substance is to be performed. The result of such an evaluation or assessment would not qualify under Rule 406, but the fact that employees were required to go through the specified steps that lead to a particular evaluation or assessment would be admissible as evidence that those steps were followed in the case at hand. (Evidence that the specified steps were routinely skipped or ignored would likewise be admissible to cast doubts on the validity or accuracy of the results.)

"Routine practice" evidence is admissible if it relates to the practices of a nonparty. For example, Sotweed is injured in an auto collision and is charged with driving while intoxicated. When she was taken to the hospital for treatment, a blood test revealed a high concentration of alcohol. Evidence that the hospital routinely takes such tests of admitted patients should be admitted to help show the trustworthiness of the test and its results.

Should evidence of the routine practice of an organization be admissible to suggest that an individual who was a member of that organization, and who is now on trial, acted in accordance with that routine practice? No. Mere membership in or employment by an organization (government agency, corporation, union, religious institution, charitable organization, etc.) should not be a basis to infer that the member or employee—who is the plaintiff or defendant in a civil case, or the defendant in a criminal case—behaved in accordance with that practice. Thus, for example, evidence that a police department routinely violated the rights of arrestees would be admissible in a suit against the department, or the city or county or state. But if Officers Smith and Jones are charged with assaulting prisoners White, Black and Green on April 30, evidence that the Police Department ignores and tolerates such behavior generally cannot be used to help prove that Smith and Jones assaulted White, Green and Black on April 30th.

§ 8.8 Means of proof

i. Written procedures, guidelines, etc.

The larger an organization or entity, the more likely it will have an employees' manual or other written guidelines spelling out how certain recurring situations should be handled. Such documents, which (barring unusual circumstances) will satisfy FRE 803(6) (the "business record" exception) or FRE 803(8) (the public record exception), are generally admissible as evidence—though certainly not as conclusive proof—that the organization or entity followed those procedures in the case being litigated.[2]

ii. Specific instances of conduct

This is the standard way of proving that an organization follows a routine practice in handling a particular, frequently recurring situation—particularly with regard to entities that do not have written standards governing that situation. An employee of a company could testify that outgoing mail is collected and taken to a mailbox or post office in the same standard way each day. Testimony by several accounting department employees that "The accounting department staff always sends out for lunch on Tuesdays" should also suffice to satisfy the rule.

iii. Opinion

Some courts have admitted opinion testimony that an organization had an unwritten or informal understanding that certain situations were to be handled in a certain way. But the witness must establish sufficient first-hand knowledge of the organization to satisfy the requirement for opinion testimony.

---

2. Concerning FRE 803(6), see *A Student's Guide to Hearsay* (5th ed.) §§ 9.20–9.38. Concerning FRE 803(8), see *id.*, §§ 9.39–9.57.

iv. Changes from prior practice

See § 8.6.

D. Questions

§ 8.9 Questions

Question 1.

On March 2, P was injured after falling on the staircase in the office building where he worked, and sued, alleging the steps were unsafe. Defendant Building Co. (DBC) denies the stairs were unsafe, and also asserts a defense of contributory negligence, alleging that P fell because he was dashing down the stairs in an unsafe manner. In a pretrial deposition, P denied having run down the stairs on the day in question and claims that there were several people who saw him fall, but that he did not know their names.

At trial, DBC seeks to have several people who work in the building testify that P was "always in a hurry from the minute he arrives in the morning to the time he leaves at night." Discuss the issues presented.

Answer:

Objection: inadmissible character evidence, per FRE 404(a)(1). This is opinion testimony about a trait of P's character, offered to prove that P acted in conformity with that trait on March 2.

DBC may respond that this is evidence of P's "habit" of hurrying, but the testimony does not address a specific enough situation; it is simply too general in nature. Objection sustained.

Question 2.

DBC also proffers W, who will, if permitted, testify as follows:

Q. How long have you and P worked for the same company?

A. About three years.

Q. Have you had occasion to be on the staircase at the DBC building at the same time as P?

A. Yes, many times—dozens. Maybe hundreds.

Q. And what is P's behavior on the stairs?

A. Usually he takes 'em two steps at a time, whether he's going up or down.

Q. You say "usually." Not always?

A. Well, no, not when there are too many people on the stairs. But otherwise.

Discuss the issues presented.

Answer:

This is admissible habit evidence.

1. The testimony describes a specific situation: P's behavior on a particular staircase.
2. Frequency: P presumably uses that staircase several times a day. W has witnessed P on the staircase "dozens, maybe hundreds of times." A judge could plausibly conclude that this is a large enough "sample" of P's behavior on that staircase.
3. Uniformity of P's behavior on that staircase: W testified that P "usually," but not always, took the steps two at a time. This may not appear to be "uniform" enough. But W's testimony actually describes a more specific situation than "how does P behave on that staircase." Rather, she is testifying: "Here is how P behaves on that staircase except when it is physically impossible to do so because too many other people are in his way."
4. Volitional vs. reflexive: How quickly a person goes up or down a flight of stairs doesn't involve much conscious thought: he or she sees the stairs, makes an instantaneous judgment about how fast to go, and then goes.

But wait, you might say, what about the other people who were on the staircase on March 2 when P fell? Doesn't that take us out of the "specific situation" that W testified about?

Perhaps. But how do we know that there were other people on the stairs that day? The only evidence is P's testimony that they were there. The judge, in deciding whether W's testimony satisfies FRE 406, is not obliged to accept P's testimony. If I were the judge, that's the conclusion I would reach. P was unable to name any of the "several people" he claimed were there. Beyond that: if several people who work in a building saw another person fall on a flight of stairs and seriously injure himself, surely some of them would have come to the injured person's aid, would have called for help, would have stayed with him until help arrived. Presumably, P's attorney would have attempted to locate such people to interview them and perhaps call them as witnesses. P's failure to produce, or even name, any such people casts doubt on the credibility of P's testimony.

Question 3.

As evidence that the staircase was safe if used correctly, DBC calls its resident manager to testify that no one had complained to her about the safety of the staircase. Should this testimony be admissible?

Answer:

This testimony is relevant: the lack of complaints about staircase safety makes it more probable than it would be without the evidence that no one perceived anything dangerous about the staircase, which makes it more probable than it would be without the evidence that the staircase was in fact safe.

Evidence about an absence of complaints is sometimes objected to as hearsay, but that objection should be overruled: silence is generally not considered a "statement" unless a person's failure to say something was intended by that person to be an "assertion." There is nothing about the facts that suggests stair users intended to assert anything about the staircase.[3]

Question 4.

Plaintiff was injured by a drunk motorist and sued a country club under the state's "dram act" law, which creates a cause of action against an individual or organization that serves alcohol to an obviously intoxicated guest or customer, if that individual, while still under the influence, injures someone. Plaintiff proffers the testimony of a local sheriff's deputy that he had observed bartenders at the country club sell alcohol to "visibly intoxicated" persons on numerous occasions. Discuss the issues thus presented.

Answer:

This qualifies as evidence of the "routine practice of an organization." We can assume that there was no formal "rule" requiring bartenders to keep serving alcohol to inebriated guests, but the deputy's observations strongly support the conclusion that there was a clear understanding that the bartenders were to keep the members happy and the cash registers full.

Question 5.

A tenant (T) sued her landlord LL (who owned and lived in another apartment in the building) for sexual harassment and sought to have four other tenants (W1, W2, W3, W4) testify that LL sexually harassed them, too. Discuss the issues thus presented.

Answer:

I think a good argument exists to admit their testimony per FRE 404(b)(2) or Rule 406 or both. (There is no need for T to prevail on both. To admit their testimony, she need only persuade the judge that it satisfies either rule.) First, Rule 404(b)(2):

1. Purpose/issue/theory of relevance: There are two factual issues in the case. (1) Conduct: did LL do and say the specific things T alleges, or not. (2) Assuming LL did so, do they constitute sexual harassment.
2. Need: Without the other tenants, it is a one-on-one case: she accuses, he denies.
3. Proving the extrinsic acts: Testimony by W1, W2, W3, W4, each describing what the landlord said and did to her, satisfies *Huddleston*.

---

3. See *A Student's Guide to Hearsay* (5th ed.) § 2.18.

4. Fasprelipi:[4] Testimony by W1, W2, W3, and W4 certainly shows that the landlord has a propensity to harass women. But its relevance is more specific than that: it shows that he has a plan: to harass a very specific category of women: those who live in his building to whose apartments he has ready access, and who necessarily rely on him to provide essential services. Their testimony also may rebut a claim by LL that T misinterpreted the landlord's innocent conduct or remarks, or that an occasional offensive act or expression was said or done by mistake.
5. Rules 403 and 105: The judge might reasonably conclude that four witnesses are too many, and limit T to, say, two or three witnesses. If requested, the judge would instruct the jury, in substance: "LL is not on trial for what he might have said or done to W1, W2, W3 and W4, and you must not use their testimony as a basis to draw conclusions about LL's general character. But you may consider their testimony in deciding whether LL did to T what T claims, and if so, whether the actions fit the legal definition of sexual harassment and whether they were said or done innocently or mistakenly, or intentionally."

Now, Rule 406:

1. The specificity or particularity of the situation. "Women living in his building" is a fairly specific situation.
2. The frequency with which the person in question encountered the situation. LL presumably had fairly frequent contact with T and W1-W4. Not daily, certainly, but probably a few times a month—contact ranging from passing each other in the hallway or lobby, to repairs in an apartment, to holding packages dropped off for tenants, etc.
3. The uniformity of LL's response to the situation. This may be a problem. Suppose six other women also lived in the building, and there is no evidence that LL harassed them. Does that defeat T's argument for admissibility per Rule 406? Maybe so—unless we can show that T, W1, W2, W3 and W4 have more in common than just their gender and street address. Is each of them within roughly the same age range (say, 20-40)? Is each single? Do they have physical similarities (race, body structure)? What about the other women, whom T did not call to testify? Are there specific reasons why LL might not have acted indecently to them? Are they married or living with someone? Do they have children or grandchildren?[5] And so on.[6]

---

4. Factually specific relevance independent of the propensity inference.

5. I do *not* mean to imply that grandmothers are unattractive. (I have been happily married for 54+ years to the grandmother of our five grandchildren, and hope to remain happily married to her for several decades more.)

6. In the case on which this problem was a based, the trial judge admitted the evidence per Rule 406, reasoning that the evidence satisfied Rule 406 simply because the landlord harassed all five

4. The extent to which the conduct in question is reflexive rather than volitional. I suppose there are some men for whom sexually harassing women is virtually a reflex; for others, it is a more evaluative and selective process. Most men, I hope and believe, try to avoid such conduct altogether.

women in the context of the landlord-tenant relationship. The appellate court affirmed, without discussing whether there were women tenants the defendant did not harass. Perhaps the defense never raised that argument in trying to exclude the testimony by W1-W4. Chomicki v. Wittekind, 128 Wis. 2d 188, 381 N.W.2d 561, 564 (Wis. App. 1985).

Chapter 9

Rule 412: Evidence of an Alleged Victim's Prior Sexual Behavior or Predisposition[1]

1. This chapter is based in part on Clifford S. Fishman & Anne T. McKenna, 3 *Jones on Evidence* (7th ed.) ch. 19.

A. Preliminary Matters

§ 9.1 Introduction

Rape is perhaps the most difficult aspect of criminal law to teach, to learn, even to discuss. Difficult legal questions inevitably intermix with strongly held beliefs, powerful emotions and, to some people, ghastly personal experience. This same controversy accompanies a key evidentiary question in many sexual assault cases: to what extent, if at all, should a defendant or prosecutor be permitted to offer evidence of the alleged victim's prior sexual history. "Rape shield" legislation, such as FRE 412, addresses that question.

Some criminal law professors skip the subject of sexual assault or cover it only superficially and do not test on it. Some evidence professors take the same minimalist approach to Rule 412. I covered each subject thoroughly in my criminal law and evidence classes, and tested on them accordingly. This chapter treats the evidence issue in depth. Read and study it to the extent that your professor's coverage of the subject indicates.

At the outset, I want to express my profound sympathy to any student who has been the victim of a sexual assault or is close to someone who has been a victim; and to anyone who has been falsely accused of sexual assault. I am convinced that false accusations are quite rare, but they do happen.

§ 9.2 Gender and vocabulary; abbreviations

Until a few decades ago, most statutes defined rape as a crime committed by a man against a woman or a girl. That reflected the reality that most perpetrators of sexual assaults are male, and most victims are female. But men and boys, and persons who are transgender and nonbinary, are also victimized by sexual assault. And people in each of these categories have committed sexual assaults.[2] In recognition of this more complete reality, statutes now are gender-neutral, which is a worthwhile development.

This poses a challenge to anyone who seeks to discuss the law defining rape and other sexual assaults and the law governing how such cases are tried. A general use of "he" and "his" when discussing defendants, and "she" or "her" when discussing victims, might be offensive to some on general principles. Some might see it as perpetuating gender stereotypes. Moreover, male victims of such assaults, and anyone who was sexually assaulted by a woman, may regard such use as dismissive of the humiliation and pain they have suffered.

Given all this, whenever possible I have avoided the use of pronouns altogether. As a result, some of the discussion may seem stilted and awkward. For example, in such discussions and in the questions, I use the word "defendant," or the letter D, over and over, rather than using a gender-specific pronoun.

The question also arises: how to refer to the accuser? FRE 412 uses the term "victim" throughout, then adds, as subrule (d): "In this rule, 'victim' includes an alleged victim." I have decided not to adopt this approach, because, despite Rule 412(d), the repeated use of the word "victim" may create a subconscious assumption that a rape or other sexual offense did in fact occur. Most of the time, this assumption is true: most accusations of rape or molestation are accurate and true. But as lawyers, we must not make that assumption about any specific case; we must always keep in mind that whether the physical act of intercourse was committed on an unwilling participant is a fact which the prosecutor (or, in a civil case, the plaintiff) must prove.

That is why I have chosen to used the term "alleged victim" in this chapter, as I have throughout this book. (When I quote Rule 412 directly, I will use the phrase "[alleged] victim.") Often in the discussion and in study questions, I will refer to the defendant as "D"; I refer to the alleged victim as "V/AV" ("victim or alleged victim").

2. For example, according to studies that seem to be credible, approximately one third of lesbians report that they have been raped, physically abused or stalked by another woman.

§ 9.3 Definition of rape; defenses; traditional view concerning the relevance of the alleged victim's "other sexual behavior"; the "yes/yes" inference

i. Definition of rape

Although the definition of rape varies from jurisdiction to jurisdiction, in essence the crime has three elements:

1. The defendant committed an act of sexual penetration on another person. (Most jurisdictions require that the defendant used force to do so.)
2. The other person did not consent to that act.
3. Either the defendant knew that the other person did not consent; or, under all of the circumstances, a reasonable person in the defendant's situation would have known that the other person did not consent.

Many jurisdictions now divide rape into several degrees, depending on the degree of force used, the existence of circumstances which reject consent as a defense (such as the alleged victim's age or lack of mental capacity), and other aggravating factors.

ii. Defenses

As a practical matter, four defenses are available to a defendant charged with a sexual offense.

1. The alleged victim has mistakenly identified the defendant as the perpetrator.
2. No sexual activity occurred; the alleged victim is either lying or confused.
3. The alleged victim consented to the sexual activity, and has since misremembered or is now lying about what happened.
4. If the alleged victim did not consent, the defendant nevertheless reasonably believed the alleged victim did.

iii. Traditional view concerning the relevance of the alleged victim's "other sexual behavior"; the "yes/yes" inference

Until the 1980s, it was routine for a defendant asserting any of the latter three defenses to offer evidence, assuming such evidence existed or could be manufactured, of the alleged victim's prior nonmarital or extramarital sexual activity. A defendant might do so by cross-examining the alleged victim about her prior sex life; or by calling one or more men to testify that they had had sex with her; or by calling witnesses to testify about the alleged victim's reputation for unchastity or promiscuity. (At least according to popular wisdom, perjury by defense witnesses was distressingly common in such cases.) Even if such evidence had no direct relevance to the specific facts of the case, it was considered relevant for the following reasons.

1. Credibility. It was considered "a matter of common knowledge that the bad character of a man for chastity does not even in the remotest degree affect his character for truth, while it does that of a woman."[3] Evidence that a woman was unchaste was thought relevant, in other words, to prove that she was also a liar.

2. Consent; the "yes/yes" inference. Evidence that the alleged victim engaged in other instances of nonmarital sex was considered relevant to support a defendant's claim that she consented to have sex with him on the occasion in question, because "common experience teaches us that the woman who has once departed from the paths of virtue is far more apt to consent to another lapse than is the one who has never stepped aside from that path."[4] In other words, the fact that the alleged victim consented to have sex with some men (other than her husband, if she is married) sometimes makes it more probable than it would be without the evidence that she would consent to have sex with any man at any time. This is occasionally referred to hereinafter as the "yes/yes" inference, i.e., the inference that "yes to some men sometimes means yes to any man any time." This view is reflected in the Advisory Committee Note to the 1975 version of FRE 404, which commented, "an accused may introduce pertinent evidence of the character of the victim, as in support of a claim of ... consent in a case of rape. ..."

3. Defendant's reasonable belief that the alleged victim consented. Even if the alleged victim did not in fact consent to intercourse, information concerning her prior sexual activity, *if known to the defendant* prior to the events giving rise to the rape accusation, was considered relevant on the question whether defendant reasonably believed that she consented.

§ 9.4 "Rape shield" legislation

Congress and most states have enacted "rape shield laws"[5] that restrict use of evidence of an alleged victim's prior[6] sexual conduct in prosecutions for sex offenses and related crimes. As a result, every American jurisdiction now rejects evidence of an alleged victim's prior sexual conduct if it is relevant only to attack the alleged victim's general credibility, or to support "yes/yes" inference, or to support a defendant's claim that he reasonably believed that the alleged victim consented—the three theories of relevance discussed in the previous section.

---

3. State v. Sibley, 131 Mo. 519, 531-32, 33 S.W. 167, 171 (1895).

4. State v. Wood, 59 Ariz. 48, 122 P.2d 416 (1942).

5. The phrase "rape shield law" reflects the fact that such legislation helps shield the alleged victim from the embarrassment of having her private life revealed (or lied about) during the trial.

6. By "prior sexual conduct" I mean "prior to the trial." Rape shield legislation regulates evidence of the alleged victim's sexual conduct *after* the alleged sexual assault rape as well as such conduct before the alleged assault. Usually, an alleged victim's conduct *subsequent* to the alleged rape or assault will be even less relevant than his or her conduct before it.

Why is such evidence excluded? In essence, because in most cases, the yes/yes inference is extremely weak, so the relevance of the evidence is minimal and is substantially outweighed by the social costs of admitting it. Allowing such evidence invades the privacy of the alleged victim and in essence puts the alleged victim on trial, thus discouraging victims from coming forward.

These statutes do allow evidence of an alleged victim's prior sexual conduct, but only if the evidence has factually specific relevance of certain kinds. Moreover, many of these statutes also require a defendant to give advance written notice of the intent to use such evidence, and provide for an in camera, pretrial hearing to determine its admissibility. FRE 412 is fairly typical of such statutes.

§ 9.5 FRE 412

i. The rule

FRE 412, effective Dec. 1, 2011, provides:

Rule 412. Sex-Offense Cases: The Victim's Sexual Behavior or Predisposition

(a) Prohibited Uses. The following evidence is not admissible in a civil or criminal proceeding involving alleged sexual misconduct:

(1) evidence offered to prove that a victim engaged in other sexual behavior; or

(2) evidence offered to prove a victim's sexual predisposition.

(b) Exceptions.

(1) Criminal Cases. The court may admit the following evidence in a criminal case:

(A) evidence of specific instances of a victim's sexual behavior, if offered to prove that someone other than the defendant was the source of semen, injury, or other physical evidence;

(B) evidence of specific instances of a victim's sexual behavior with respect to the person accused of the sexual misconduct, if offered by the defendant to prove consent or if offered by the prosecutor; and

(C) evidence whose exclusion would violate the defendant's constitutional rights.

(2) Civil Cases. In a civil case, the court may admit evidence offered to prove a victim's sexual behavior or sexual predisposition if its probative value substantially outweighs the danger of harm to any victim and of unfair prejudice to any party. The court may admit evidence of a victim's reputation only if the victim has placed it in controversy.

(c) Procedure to Determine Admissibility.

(1) **Motion.** If a party intends to offer evidence under Rule 412(b), the party must:

(A) file a motion that specifically describes the evidence and states the purpose for which it is to be offered;

(B) do so at least 14 days before trial unless the court, for good cause, sets a different time;

(C) serve the motion on all parties; and

(D) notify the victim or, when appropriate, the victim's guardian or representative.

(2) **Hearing.** Before admitting evidence under this rule, the court must conduct an in camera hearing and give the victim and parties a right to attend and be heard. Unless the court orders otherwise, the motion, related materials, and the record of the hearing must be and remain sealed.

(d) Definition of "Victim." In this rule, "victim" includes an alleged victim.

ii. Rape, sexual assault, sexual misconduct

Rape. The traditional definition of rape is outlined in § 9.3. Note, however, that FRE 412 does not use that term.

Sexual assault. Some jurisdictions no longer use the term "rape" in their penal codes. Rather, all sexual offenses are grouped together under the term "sexual assault," which is broken down into various degrees, depending on what the defendant is accused of doing to the alleged victim and other aggravating factors. Thus, "sexual assault" includes rape, but also includes sexual crimes which do not involve penetration.

"Sexual misconduct." Rule 412's title begins with the word "Sex-offense cases," but refers thereafter to "sexual misconduct," a term which it never defines. Nor does the Advisory Committee note. But in discussing the admissibility of evidence in civil cases, the Report comments: "Rule 412 applies in any civil case in which a person claims to be the victim of sexual misconduct, such as actions for sexual battery or sexual harassment."

I think we can take it as given that whenever D is charged with any sexual crime, FRE 412 excludes evidence of the alleged victim's prior sexual conduct unless D can persuade the judge that the evidence satisfies one of the exceptions set out in FRE 412(b)(1). In civil cases, the same is true even where the claim is for non-criminal sexual misconduct (such as sexual harassment).

iii. Relationship to other rules

The Committee Note to the 1994 amendment[7] specifies that "Evidence, which might otherwise be admissible under Rules 402, 404(b), 405, 607, 608, 609 or some other evidence rule, must be excluded if Rule 412 so requires." In essence, where evidence of an alleged victim's prior sexual behavior is concerned, Rule 412(a)'s exclusionary rule trumps all other rules. Thus, a defendant seeking to offer such evidence cannot argue for admissibility under any of those other rules, but must persuade the judge that the evidence falls within one of the subdivisions of Rule 412(b), each of which is discussed later in this chapter.

Other exclusionary provisions of the FRE still apply. For example, a document about the alleged victim which would satisfy one of the FRE 412(b) exceptions will still be excluded if the defendant fails to adequately authenticate it.

§ 9.6 Rule 412(a)(1): "other sexual behavior"

Rule 412(a)(1) directs that, unless the case falls within Rule 412(b), evidence of the alleged victim's "other sexual behavior" is not admissible. The Advisory Committee Note to the 1994 amendment to the Rule defines that term as follows: "Past sexual behavior connotes all activities that involve actual physical conduct, i.e., sexual intercourse or sexual contact." The Report endorses cases excluding evidence that the alleged victim used contraceptives, gave birth to a child out of wedlock, or had a venereal disease, since (barring unusual circumstances) such evidence is relevant only to imply that the alleged victim had engaged in "other sexual behavior." The report adds that "the word 'behavior' should be construed to include activities of the mind, such as fantasies or dreams."

Some courts consider viewing pornography as "other sexual behavior" and, therefore, evidence that the alleged victim did so on "other" occasions is presumptively inadmissible.

<u>"Intrinsic vs. extrinsic sexual behavior."</u> The Committee Note comments: "The word 'other' is used to suggest some flexibility in admitting evidence 'intrinsic' to the alleged sexual misconduct." "Intrinsic," when used in connection with FRE 412, has the same meaning as when used in connection with FRE 404(b).

§ 9.7 Rule 412(a)(2): "sexual predisposition"; reputation and opinion testimony

The Committee Note on the 1994 version of the rule explains the term "sexual predisposition":

7. The Rule was added to the Federal Rules by Congress in 1978, and was substantively amended in 1994. In 2011, it was amended stylistically, but no substantive changes were intended in the 2011 revisions.

> The rule has been amended to also exclude all other evidence relating to an alleged victim of sexual misconduct that is offered to prove a sexual predisposition. This amendment is designed to exclude evidence that does not directly refer to sexual activities or thoughts but that the proponent believes may have a sexual connotation for the factfinder. Admission of such evidence would contravene Rule 412's objectives of shielding the alleged victim from potential embarrassment and safeguarding the victim against stereotypical thinking. Consequently, unless the (b)(2) exception [relating to civil actions] is satisfied, evidence such as that relating to the alleged victim's mode of dress, speech, or lifestyle will not be admissible.

Although the Rule does not explicitly exclude reputation (or opinion) testimony about the alleged victim's sexual predisposition, the 1994 Amendment Committee Note to Rule 412(b) (second paragraph) explains that such evidence is excluded "in recognition of the limited probative value and dubious reliability of evidence of reputation or evidence in the form of an opinion." Although (prior to the rule) such evidence was frequently offered by a defendant charged with sexual assault, Rule 412 precludes its use by either side in a criminal trial. Thus, a defendant cannot offer testimony that the alleged victim was reputed to be "easy" or "promiscuous." The prosecutor cannot offer evidence that the alleged victim was reputed to be "virginal" or "chaste" or "monogamous." Neither side can offer evidence that the alleged victim was reputed to be straight, gay, bisexual or non-binary.

§ 9.8 Scope of the rule

Rule 412(b) applies in any criminal case, not just cases in which the defendant is accused of sexually assaulting the alleged victim. The 1994 Amendment Committee Note explains that "the need to protect the victim is equally great when a defendant is charged with kidnapping, and evidence is offered, either to prove motive or as background, that the defendant sexually assaulted the victim."

But such cases are rare: the vast majority of cases applying Rule 412 arise where the defendant is charged with raping or sexually assaulting the alleged victim, so that is the factual context used throughout this chapter.

Note: the rules covered in Chapters 4 through 13 might apply in eight different courtroom scenarios, which I refer to as "litigation situations." In § 11.23 to § 11.31, I summarize each litigation situation and list the rules that apply in that litigation situation. Evidence relating to an alleged sex assault victim's prior sexual behavior is likely to be offered either during the defendant's case-in-chief, <u>litigation situation C</u>, § 11.26, or while the defense attorney is cross-examining the alleged victim, litigation situation F, § 11.29. (For now, ignore this paragraph; I include it here as a cross-reference that may be helpful later.).

§ 9.9 Procedure; factual disputes

FRE 412(c)(1) mandates that if a "party" plans to offer evidence about an alleged victim's prior sexual conduct per Rule 412(b), that party—usually, the defendant in a criminal case; rarely, a prosecutor; occasionally, a civil litigant—must file a motion "that specifically describes the evidence and states the purpose for which it is to be offered." The motion must be served on all the parties in the litigation, and also on the alleged victim, if the alleged victim is not a party. (Keep in mind that victim or alleged victim in a criminal case is not a "party"; in all criminal cases, the parties are, on one side, the state or government or commonwealth, and on the other side, the defendant.)

FRE 412(c)(2) mandates that before admitting such evidence, the judge must conduct a hearing, not accessible to the public, at which all parties and the alleged victim may be heard. The rule does not require the judge to conduct a hearing in every case: if the motion is inadequate on its face, the judge may deny it without a hearing.

In many cases, a factual dispute may exist as to whether the alleged victim in fact engaged in the sexual conduct alleged in the motion. Example: D is charged with raping V/AV on May 10; D claims that V/AV consented. D files a motion per Rule 412(1)(B) alleging that he and V/AV engaged in consensual sex on several occasions prior to May 10. V/AV denies ever engaging in sexual behavior with D prior to May 10.

How is the judge to resolve the factual dispute? Rule 412 does not address this issue. Rather, we turn to *Huddleston v. U.S.* (see § 7.11) and FRE 104(b) (see § 1.13). The relevance of D's 412(b)(1)(B) evidence is conditioned on the fact that the prior, consensual sex actually occurred. Rule 104(b) directs that in such cases, D must offer evidence at the hearing "sufficient to support a finding" that D and V/AV in fact had consensual sex on those prior occasions. D's testimony, without any corroboration, will satisfy that standard, since it would be the jury's job, not the judge's, to decide who to believe, D or V/AV.

The same standard—sufficient to support a finding—applies if D seeks to offer evidence that V/AV engaged in consensual sex with other people on other occasions. If DW1 testifies at a hearing that DW1 and V/AV had consensual sex on a particular occasion, that satisfies that standard.

Thus, in deciding whether D's evidence satisfies FRE 412(b)(1), the judge is required to assume, for purposes of applying FRE 412, that D's testimony (or DW1's testimony) is true.[8]

---

8. If D's evidence about an alleged victim's other sexual behavior is inadmissible for another reason—e.g., if it consists of inadmissible hearsay—the judge can and should exclude it on that ground.

§ 9.10 "Relevance" vs. "prejudice"

If the judge concludes that evidence of the alleged victim's prior sexual behavior has sufficient special relevance per FRE 412(b)(1)(A), (B) or (C) to merit consideration, it becomes necessary to assess that relevance against the risk of unfair prejudice, embarrassment, humiliation, etc.

The application of the term "relevant" or "probative value" in this context needs no detailed explanation: a defendant should be required to specify the issue or issues the evidence is intended to address, and demonstrate how the evidence is truly probative on those issues exclusive of the forbidden "yes/yes" inference.

Application of the term "prejudice," however, is the source of some confusion in this context. Some scholarly commentary, some court decisions, and at least one statute speak of the "unfair prejudice [of such evidence] *to the victim*...." Traditionally, of course, the concept of "prejudice" is applied only to *parties*, not to a witness, however closely identified with a particular party the witness may be (as the alleged victim is to the prosecutor in such cases).

However, general principles of evidence require a judge to protect any witness against "harassment or undue embarrassment,"[9] and most rape shield statutes enhance those protections with numerous additional procedural and substantive protections. Assessment of "unfair prejudice" should therefore focus on the impact of the evidence on the state, not the alleged victim. The Supreme Court of Washington put it well:

> The issue is not whether evidence is prejudicial in the sense that it is detrimental to someone involved in the trial. Rather, the question is whether the evidence will [unduly] arouse the jury's emotions of prejudice, hostility, or sympathy. Arguments that sexual history evidence is inadmissible because of its prejudicial impact on the rape victim miss the point. Adverse psychological effects suffered by crime victims, although regrettable, are not grounds for excluding probative evidence.[10]

Thus, after assessing the legitimate probative value of the evidence, the court should "consider the effect of excluding such evidence on defendant's right to a fair trial" and balance that effect against "potential prejudice to the truthfinding process itself... to determine whether the introduction of the victim's past sexual conduct may confuse the issues, mislead the jury, or cause the jury to decide the case on an improper or emotional basis."[11]

---

9. FRE 611(a)(3): "The court shall exercise reasonable control over the mode and order of interrogating witnesses and presenting evidence so as to:... (3) protect witnesses from harassment or undue embarrassment."

10. State v, Hudlow, 99 Wash. 2d 1, 659 P.2d 514, 521 (1983).

11. *Id.*, 659 P.2d at 521.

The application of this standard will be discussed in connection with each of the subsections of Rule 412(b)(1).

§ 9.11 Questions

Question 1.

D, charged with sexual assault, concedes he had intercourse with V/AV but asserts the defense of consent. What is the state's burden of proof, with regard to V/AV's state of mind?

Answer:

The evidence must persuade the jury beyond a reasonable doubt, first, that D engaged in "sexual conduct" with V/AV; second, that V/AV did not consent to the sexual conduct.

Question 2.

Where D asserts the defense of consent, what must the state prove, beyond a reasonable doubt, with regard to D's state of mind?

Answer:

The law on this issue is somewhat murky in some jurisdictions, but in most jurisdictions, it suffices that the evidence persuades the jury beyond a reasonable doubt that D should have known that V/AV did not consent. In other words, if, given all the circumstances, a reasonable person would have realized that V/AV did not consent, D can be convicted of sexual assault even if D honestly (but incorrectly) believed that V/AV consented.

Question 3.

D seeks to call DW1, who will testify that V/AV had a reputation of being "ready and willing, any time, any place, any man." Would this have been admissible prior to the enactment of Rule 412?

Answer:

Yes, per what is now FRE 404(a)(2)(B), on the theory that, if that was V/AV's reputation, then it makes it more probable than it would be without the evidence that V/AV was "ready and willing" to have sex with D as well.[12]

Question 4.

Is it admissible per Rule 412?

12. In fact, the Advisory Committee Note to the original version of FRE 404(a) cites this as an example of admissible evidence about the alleged victim in a sex offense case.

Answer:

No. Reputation and opinion testimony about V/AV's character for sexual conduct is no longer admissible. Rule 412 rejects the validity of reputation (or opinion) evidence regarding an alleged victim's character or "predisposition." See § 9.7.

Question 5.

D further wishes to have DW1 testify, "When D told me he had a date with V/AV, I told him, 'You better take the *big* blue pill. Everybody says V/AV is ready and willing, any time, any place, any man.'" How, if at all, is this relevant? Does it differ in any way from the evidence offered in Q3? Is it admissible?

Answer:

It differs from question 3 in that it has a second theory of relevance: it is evidence that D was aware of V/AV's reputation, which, arguably, was relevant as to whether D reasonably believed that V/AV consented to sex (see § 9.3). So far as I know, no court has accepted such evidence on this theory of relevance.

Question 6.

D serves pretrial notice that he plans to call DW2, DW3 and DW4, each of whom will (if permitted) testify that he had consensual intercourse with V/AV on several occasions. Is this evidence admissible over a Rule 412 objection?

Answer:

It is excluded per Rule 412(a)(1) unless D can persuade the judge that their testimony falls within one of the exceptions set out in Rule 412(b)(1).

Question 7.

D serves pretrial notice that he plans to call DW2, DW3 and DW4, each of whom will (if permitted) testify that he told D that he had had sex several times with V/AV. How does this differ from the evidence in Q6? Is admissible over a Rule 412 objection?

Answer:

D may argue that this is not FRE 412 evidence at all: here, DW2, DW3 and DW4 have not testified that they *had* sex with V/AV; rather, that they *told D* they had sex with V/AV. Therefore, it is not offered to show anything about V/AV's actual prior sexual conduct, but only to show that, having heard this, it was reasonable for D to interpret V/AV's responses to D's advances as consent.[13]

---

13. And, this argument goes, their testimony is not offered to prove the truth of what they told D about the alleged victim, but only to show the impact of their statements on D's state of mind—even if they lied to D. Therefore, their statements to D do not consist of hearsay, either. See *A Student's Guide to Hearsay* § 2.31-§ 2.33 (5th ed. 2019).

FRE 412 does not directly address this situation, but the prosecutor has solid arguments against it. First, FRE 412 constitutes a statement of public policy that it is no longer acceptable for D to rely on what others say about V/AV in assessing whether V/AV consents to have sex with D. Since Rule 412 rejects that theory of relevance, the court should reject the testimony of DW2, DW3, and DW4, even though their testimony was carefully tailored to try to evade Rule 412.

Second, the prosecutor might argue that testimony by DW2, DW3, and DW4 is simply an attempt to sneak in evidence of V/AV's alleged reputation for promiscuity in the guise of indirect evidence of V/AV's specific sexual conduct.

Third, the evidence should be excluded by FRE 403. A jury might assume that DW2, DW3 and DW4 told D the truth. The prosecutor would be reluctant to ask them that on cross, since they might well lie about it. Thus, to rebut their testimony, the prosecutor would have to recall V/AV to deny their allegations, which would expose V/AV to cross-examination about those allegations—precisely what FRE 412 is designed to prevent.

For each and all of these reasons, the judge should exclude the testimony of DW2, DW3 and DW4.

B. Rule 412(b)(1): Exceptions to Exclusions in Criminal Cases

§ 9.12 The three exceptions

Rule 412(b)(1) creates three exceptions to the Rule 412(a)(1) ban on evidence of an alleged victim's prior sexual conduct:

> **(b) Exceptions.**
>
> **(1) Criminal Cases.** The court may admit the following evidence in a criminal case:
>
> (A) evidence of specific instances of a victim's sexual behavior, if offered to prove that someone other than the defendant was the source of semen, injury, or other physical evidence;
>
> (B) evidence of specific instances of a victim's sexual behavior with respect to the person accused of the sexual misconduct, if offered by the defendant to prove consent or if offered by the prosecutor; and
>
> (C) evidence whose exclusion would violate the defendant's constitutional rights.

Note that the rule says that "[t]he court *may* admit," not "shall admit." The judge has discretion to exclude evidence which fits into one of the 412(b)(1) exceptions, so long as excluding it does not deprive a defendant of the right to a fair trial.

1. Rule 412(b)(1)(A): biological evidence; "injury"

§ 9.13 Biological evidence

Rule 412(b)(1)(A) allows a defendant to offer "evidence of specific instances of a victim's sexual behavior, if offered to prove that someone other than the defendant was the source of semen, injury, or other physical evidence[.]" This section discusses evidence relating to semen and other biological evidence; the next section discusses evidence relating to "injury."

It is apparently standard investigative practice, when an alleged victim reports a rape or other sexual assault, to ask whether the alleged victim has had intercourse with anyone (other than D) within 72 hours of the alleged rape. Cases arise where the alleged victim says no, but DNA testing reveals biological evidence from D and a third person ("3P"). The prosecutor is entitled to admit the evidence relating to D, to corroborate V/AV's testimony that D had a sexual encounter with V/AV. This leaves D with no valid basis to offer evidence that someone else was "the source of semen ... or other physical evidence," since the evidence of D's DNA pinpoints D and no one else as the source of that DNA which the prosecutor has introduced into evidence.[14]

If the DNA reveals a third person's biological evidence but not D's, D is entitled to bring out that no biological evidence attributable to D was obtained from alleged victim, and that's all, unless D can successfully argue that the evidence should be admitted to show the source of "injury," see § 9.14, or per FRE 412(b)(1)(C), see § 9.18.

Evidence that the alleged victim has a venereal disease is not admissible unless the state alleges that the alleged victim caught that disease from the defendant, and the defendant did not have that disease prior to D's alleged sexual assault on V/AV.

§ 9.14 "Injury"; emotional trauma

i. Physical injury

FRE 412 and numerous other statutes authorize admission of prior sexual conduct evidence if sufficiently relevant to prove that someone other than the defendant

14. This assumes there is sufficient quantity of DNA to establish, to a sufficient degree of statistical certainty, that D was clearly a source of the biological evidence. Mixed samples can make that difficult sometimes.

was the source of the alleged victim's "injury." Bruises, abrasions, scratches and other evidence of physical abuse obviously come within the term "injury."

The injuries discussed most frequently in the case law are vaginal or anal injuries; lamentably, many of these cases involve children in their early teens or even younger. Whether evidence of the alleged victim's prior sexual behavior with others is admissible in such cases depends primarily on whether such evidence is truly probative on the question of who caused the injury. If the injury is unlikely to be the result of consensual sex, a judge should exclude evidence of the consensual encounter as lacking sufficient relevance to justify admitting it.

ii. Psychological trauma; "syndrome" evidence

This is an issue that you can ignore unless your professor spends time on it in class.

V/AV accuses D of sexual assault, and D asserts V/AV's consent as a defense. Often, in such cases, the prosecutor will offer testimony from V/AV's friends and relatives as to how V/AV's behavior and personality have changed since the alleged sexual assault, together with expert testimony (a) describing the symptoms of post-traumatic stress disorder (PTSD), (b) expressing the opinion that V/AV's changes in behavior are consistent with PTSD, and (c) specifying that being sexually assaulted is one of the events that can bring on PTSD. The inference, of course, is that it was D's sexual assault of V/AV that caused V/AV's PTSD.

In appropriate cases, this may entitle a defendant to offer evidence that a prior sexual assault on the alleged victim by someone else—or some other non-sexual trauma—was the actual event which triggered an alleged victim's psychological and emotional distress.

2. Rule 412(b)(1)(B): Prior sexual behavior with the accused

a. To prove consent

§ 9.15 Relevance

V/AV alleges that on May 10, D raped V/AV. D acknowledges that intercourse occurred, but insists that V/AV consented. D serves pretrial notice per FRE 412(b)(1)(B) that D wishes to testify—and perhaps offer other evidence as well—that D and V/AV had consensual sex on one or more occasions prior to May 10.

FRE 412(b)(1)(B) provides:

> **(b) Exceptions**
>
> **(1) Criminal Cases.** The court may admit the following evidence in a criminal case: ...

(B) evidence of specific instances of a victim's sexual behavior with respect to the person accused of the sexual misconduct, if offered by the defendant to prove consent; ...

Rule 412(b)(1)(B) recognizes that such evidence often has much greater probative value on the issue of consent than the "yes/yes" inference discussed in § 9.3. D's assertions, if true, indicate that V/AV had previously considered D attractive enough[15] to have sex with D, which may support either of two inferences: (a) that V/AV continued to have that attitude toward D on May 10, or (b) that, at least, D reasonably believed that V/AV continued to have that attitude toward D on May 10.

Often, of course, neither of these inferences is true. The prior consensual encounters (assuming they occurred) may have left V/AV unsatisfied. Or subsequent to the consensual encounters, D may have behaved badly toward V/AV. Or subsequent to the consensual encounters, V/AV may have learned information about D which rendered D unattractive to V/AV. Or V/AV might have started seeing someone else. Or on the occasion in question, D may have insisted on certain activities that V/AV found unpleasant, uncomfortable or painful. Or on May 10, V/AV simply may not have been in the mood. And V/AV's reactions to D's conduct on May 10 might have been so unequivocal that no reasonable person could have mistaken V/AV's unwillingness for consent. Or V/AV may have suffered physical injuries on May 10 that preclude any possibility of consent.

Note again that Rule 412(b)(1) says that the court "may admit" such evidence, rather than "must admit" it. The rule gives the judge discretion to weigh the probative value of the (alleged) prior consensual sex against the concerns that prompted the enactment of Rule 412.

§ 9.16 Factors in assessing admissibility

That a defendant (D) asserts the defense of consent does not automatically open the door to evidence of D's prior sexual relationship with the alleged victim. A court must still weigh the legitimate probative value of the evidence against the risk of unfair prejudice, embarrassment and harassment of the alleged victim, confusion of issues, etc. Courts have considered a variety of factors in exercising this discretion, including the nature of the previous relationship, the passage of time between the prior consensual sex and the alleged sexual assault, the similarity or dissimilarity between the prior sexual acts and the alleged assault, and the presence of physical evidence corroborating the alleged victim's testimony that the sexual encounter giving rise to the charges was violent and forced rather than consensual. Many of these

15. I use the word "attractive" here to include any and all aspects of D then known to V/AV, not merely physical attractiveness.

factors are legitimate, some may be less so; inevitably, the weight to be given to their presence or absence poses difficult questions of judgment.

Note: each of the following questions involves different people, even though I use the initials "D" and "V/AV" in each.

Question 1.

D and V/AV had dated[16] with some frequency during the spring and summer, on various occasions having dinner, going to a movie, visiting a museum, going bicycling, attending a ball game or a concert, etc. On August 10, after another such date, they went to D's apartment where, according to V/AV, D raped V/AV.

D acknowledges that they had intercourse that evening, but insists that V/AV consented, and wishes to testify that roughly half of his prior dates with V/AV ended with the two of them having consensual intercourse. V/AV denies this. Discuss the issues thus presented.

Answer:

Assuming D has filed a pretrial motion as required by FRE 412(c),[17] the judge should hold a hearing per Rule 412(c)(2). Even if V/AV testifies at the hearing that V/AV and D had never had consensual sex, in ruling on whether D's testimony is admissible, the judge must assume that D's testimony is true. See § 9.9. Given that assumption, the judge must permit D to testify as to D's version of the relationship prior to August 10, because to deprive D of that opportunity would deprive him of the right to a fair trial.

During the state's case-in-chief, the prosecutor can elicit testimony from V/AV describing V/AV's version of their relationship prior to August 10—that they had never engaged in consensual intercourse or, for that matter, they had not even kissed. On cross, D's attorney can challenge V/AV's testimony. After the state rests, D can testify as to D's version of the relationship prior to August 10. Each juror will

---

16. Regarding my use of the word "date": Half a century ago, it was common for two people to go out on "dates" as a way of getting acquainted—to dinner, a movie, a concert, a play, a hike or bike ride, a ball game, a museum, a party. Sometimes this was with a group of friends, sometimes the two would go alone. "Dating" someone was done to explore the possibility that the two might eventually become a couple, and it was considered acceptable for a person to "date" more than one person at a time. There was no implicit agreement that a "date" meant having sex at the end of the afternoon or evening. My wife and I married in 1968, so I am somewhat out of touch of how singles comingle and explore the possibility of entering relationships these days, but from various current definitions of "dating" I found online, I gather that the process I describe in this footnote is still in use today among some people looking for a relationship. Hence I use the word "dating" in that context, reassured that such use is not an anachronism, i.e., I do not thereby date myself.

17. When a rule requires a preliminary step such as a pretrial motion, if the stem of an essay question did not explicitly state that a party complied with the requirement, the answer should begin with, "Assuming [the offering party] has complied with the provisions of...."

weigh this conflict in D and V/AV's testimony in deciding who is telling the truth about August 10th.

Question 2.

V/AV claims that D raped V/AV on June 1. D claims that V/AV consented. Prior to trial, D files a motion seeking to call DW1 (defense witness # 1), who will, if permitted, testify that early in March of the same year, V/AV told DW1, "I would like to have sex with D and other men for money." Discuss the issues presented.

Answer:

Let's start with V/AV's alleged statement about "sex with other men" and "for money." Its only relevance is to show V/AV's sexual predisposition, which is banned by Rule 412(a)(2). The judge should order that DW1 not repeat those portions of V/AV's (alleged) statement.

The question then becomes: does V/AV's alleged statement of desire to have sex with D comprise "prior sexual behavior"? Probably—according to the Advisory Committee Note to the original version of the Rule, that phrase includes "fantasies or dreams." See § 9.6. And the Advisory Committee Note to the 1994 amendment makes it clear that V/AV's (alleged) statement about wanting to have sex with D would be presumptively admissible under the "consent" exception codified in FRE 412(b)(1)(B). Nevertheless, a judge might plausibly conclude that too much time elapsed since V/AV's statement to DW1 and June 1, and that V/AV's attitude toward sex with D in March was no longer very relevant as to V/AV's willingness of have sex with D nearly three months later.

b. Offered by the prosecutor

§ 9.17 Relevance

Rule 412(b)(1)(B) permits a prosecutor to offer evidence that on occasions prior to the alleged sexual assault, the alleged victim had consensual sex with D. Such evidence could be relevant to explain the alleged victim's ability to identify D as the rapist even though the alleged victim was unable to see the perpetrator.

3. Rule 412(b)(1)(C): "evidence whose exclusion would violate the defendant's constitutional rights"

§ 9.18 In general

Cases arise, not fitting within FRE 412(b)(1)(A) or FRE 412(b)(1)(B), in which excluding evidence of an alleged victim's prior sexual conduct would deprive a defendant to the right to a fair trial. FRE 412(b)(1)(C) is included in the Rule in recognition of this fact.

Cases applying FRE 412(b)(1)(C) generally fall into the following categories:

1. Evidence of the alleged victim's other sexual conduct to show bias or motive to lie.
2. Evidence of the alleged victim's other sexual conduct to show the circumstances immediately leading up to the alleged sexual assault.
3. Where the alleged victim alleges that the defendant forced the alleged victim to engage in an unusual, bizarre or degrading sexual activity, evidence that the alleged victim has frequently and voluntarily engaged in such activity in the past.
4. Evidence that the alleged victim has engaged in acts of prostitution.

a. To show bias or motive to lie

§ 9.19 Introduction

Often the greatest challenge in defending against a sexual assault charge is to present a plausible explanation to the jury why the alleged victim would falsely accuse defendant. Defendants frequently argue that the alleged victim's prior sexual conduct provides such a motive. Such cases fall into four basic patterns.

(1) The defendant asserts that the alleged victim consented to sex, then falsely claimed it was rape to persuade the alleged victim's spouse or lover that the alleged victim had not consented.

(2) The defendant denies engaging in sexual behavior with the alleged victim and claims the alleged victim falsely accused defendant in order to hide the fact that the alleged victim was having consensual sex with someone else.

(3) The defendant offers evidence of the alleged victim's prior sexual conduct to bolster a defense that the alleged victim is fabricating charges against defendant to avenge some real or imagined slight.

(4) The defendant asserts that the alleged victim agreed to have sex for money, then falsely claimed it was rape to avoid being charged with prostitution, or accuses the defendant with rape because the defendant refused, or was unable, to pay.

A defendant's assertion of "motive" or "bias" should not automatically strip the alleged victim of the protection of rape shield legislation. If the evidence is of insufficient probative value, it should be excluded. The Supreme Court has made it clear, however, that as a general rule, "cross-examination directed toward revealing possible biases, prejudices, or ulterior motives of the witness as they may relate directly to issues or personalities in the case at hand... is a proper and important function" of the Sixth Amendment rights to confront one's accusers and to present a defense.[18] And these rights guarantee, not merely the opportunity "to ask a witness *whether* he is biased," but also the right "to make a record from which to argue *why* he might have been biased" or motivated to testify falsely.[19]

Thus, rape shield legislation must in appropriate circumstances yield to a defendant's right to offer probative evidence of bias or motive to lie. Several state statutes explicitly recognize this constitutional requirement by including bias among the valid purposes for which evidence of the alleged victim's prior sexual conduct may be offered, and courts generally have acknowledged that, with or without such a provision, such evidence sometimes is constitutionally required to be admitted.

§ 9.20 To deny infidelity: *Olden v. Kentucky*

In a substantial number of cases, defendant concedes that the defendant had intercourse with the alleged victim, insists that it was consensual, and alleges that the alleged victim has falsely accused defendant of sexual assault to prevent the alleged victim's spouse or lover from realizing that the alleged victim had been unfaithful. In *Olden v. Kentucky*,[20] defendant, an African American, was convicted of sexually assaulting a White woman named Matthews. Matthews testified that after the assault, defendant and a friend drove her to the vicinity of the home of another African American named Russell. Russell circumstantially corroborated Matthews by testifying that he heard a noise, saw Matthews get out of defendant's friend's car, and that Matthews immediately told him that she had been raped by defendant and his friend. Defendant asserted the defense of consent.

At the time of the alleged rape, Matthews and Russell, although married to and living with other people, were apparently involved in an extramarital relationship; by the time of trial, they were living together. Defendant maintained that Matthews concocted the rape story to protect her relationship with Russell, who otherwise would have grown suspicious upon seeing her disembark from defendant's friend's car. To demonstrate Matthews' motive to lie, defendant sought to introduce evidence that Matthews and Russell were cohabiting. The trial court, however, granted

18. Davis v. Alaska 415 U.S. 308, 316-17 (1974). Bias may include a witness' self-interest or his favor, fear or dislike of another party or witness "which might lead the witness to slant, unconsciously or otherwise, his testimony in favor of or against another party." United States v. Abel 469 U.S. 45, 52 (1984). *Davis* is discussed in § 12.8–ii. *Abel* is discussed in § 12.7 & § 13.7–iii. (Neither case involves sexual assault or FRE 412.)

19. *Davis, supra* at 318. A defendant must be given the opportunity "to expose to the jury the facts from which jurors, as the sole triers of fact and credibility, could appropriately draw inferences relating to the reliability of the witness." *Id.*

20. 488 U.S. 227 (1988).

the prosecutor's motion in limine to keep all evidence of Matthews' and Russell's living arrangement from the jury.

A nearly unanimous Supreme Court reversed, ruling that it violates the Confrontation Clause to prevent a defendant from "engaging in otherwise appropriate cross-examination designed to show a prototypical form of bias on the part of the witness, and thereby to expose to the jury the facts from which jurors... could appropriately draw inferences relating to the reliability of [Matthews]." Evidence of Matthews and Russell's relationship might have given the jury "a significantly different impression of [Matthews'] credibility had [defense counsel] been permitted to pursue his proposed line of cross-examination."[21]

The Committee Note to the 1994 amendment of Rule 412 cites *Olden* as an example of evidence that satisfies Rule 412(b)(1)(C), and numerous courts have held that evidence of the alleged victim's sexual relationship with another man must be admitted where the evidence is relevant to suggest a motive to falsely accuse the defendant.[22]

Question 1.

V/AV, a college student, accused D, another student, of rape. D asserted that V/AV consented to intercourse, then charged rape for fear of V/AV's boyfriend BF's jealousy. To support this defense, D seeks to elicit testimony from other witnesses that on several prior occasions they heard BF accuse V/AV of cheating on him. Should the evidence be admitted over a rape shield objection?

Answer:

There are actually two different kinds of evidence being offered here: first, that V/AV and BF are (or were) in a sexual relationship; and second, the implication that V/AV may have cheated on BF in the past, i.e., that V/AV had a history of sexual promiscuity.

With regard to the nature of V/AV's relationship with BF, based on *Olden v. Kentucky*, the nature of V/AV'S relationship with BF is clearly an issue that D should be allowed to explore while cross-examining V/AV, and if V/AV denies that their relationship is sexual and D has otherwise admissible evidence to contradict that denial, D should be allowed to introduce such evidence during the defense case in chief.[23]

---

21. *Id.* at 231–32, quoting and citing Davis v. Alaska 415 U.S. 308, 316–17 (1974); Greene v. McElroy, 360 U.S. 474, 496 (1959); Delaware v. Van Arsdall, 475 U.S. 673, 680 (1986).

22. *Olden* is not, in fact, a "rape shield" case. Kentucky courts excluded evidence that Matthews and Reynolds were living together because the interracial nature of the relationship would have been "extremely prejudicial" to Matthews. It is clear, however, that the Supreme Court would have reversed Olden's conviction even if the state had relied on a rape-shield statute, rather than the state equivalent of FRE 403, to exclude the evidence.

23. For example, D might call witnesses to testify that V/AV had told others that the relationship with BF was sexual.

Some courts go half-way in cases like this, allowing the defendant to elicit that V/AV and BF were in a "romantic relationship" but prohibiting the defendant from asking, or offering evidence, that the relationship involved sexual intercourse.

With regard to BF's prior accusations, I think D has a plausible argument that this is not evidence of V/AV's "other sexual behavior" at all, because D is not offering it to prove that V/AV in fact cheated on BF in the past, but only to underscore why V/AV feared BF's reaction if BF learned that V/AV had consented to have sex with D. D's attorney could carefully word his or her questions to make it clear that the witness is only being asked about what BF said; not whether BF's accusations were true; and the judge could give a limiting instruction to the jury to that effect.[24] This does not completely protect V/AV from the inference of promiscuity, but, given the substantial relevance of BF's jealousy, to forbid D to offer evidence of that jealousy, in my opinion, would deprive him of a fair trial.

§ 9.21 Other issues relating to bias or motive to lie

On occasion, a defendant seeks to offer evidence of the alleged victim's other sexual behavior to show the alleged victim had a motive (other than denying infidelity) to falsely accuse him of rape. Such cases generally fall into one of the following categories.

(1) The defendant denies engaging in sexual behavior with the alleged victim and claims the alleged victim is falsely accusing him of rape to hide the fact that the alleged victim was having consensual sex with someone else. For example, a teenager might tell such a lie so V/AV's parents won't learn that V/AV has in fact been having sex.

(2) The defendant offers evidence of the alleged victim's prior sexual conduct to bolster a defense that the alleged victim is fabricating charges against him to avenge some real or imagined slight. For example: V/AV is living with foster parents, or with a parent and stepparent, or with a parent and that parent's partner. V/AV accuses D, the non-parent (or one of the foster parents), of sexual assault. D claims V/AV is falsely accusing D because D attempted to prevent V/AV from having sex with one or more of V/AV's acquaintances.

(3) The defendant asserts that the alleged victim agreed to have sex for money, then falsely claimed it was rape to avoid being charged with prostitution, or accuses the defendant with rape because the defendant refused, or was

24. In the case that is the basis for this problem, *Commonwealth v. Berkowitz*, 537 Pa. 143, 151, 641 A.2d 1161, 1165 (1994), the court held (wrongly, in my opinion) that the trial judge properly precluded Berkowitz from introducing the evidence.

unable, to pay. To corroborate this allegation, the defendant seeks to offer evidence that the alleged victim has worked as a prostitute in the past.

In handling questions based on any of these theories, keep in mind that so long as a jury could believe defendant's evidence of the alleged victim's prior sexual behavior and could believe defendant's evidence suggesting the alleged victim had a motive to lie, the judge, in assessing admissibility, must assume that evidence is true. Of these three situations, courts seem least willing to admit evidence of V/AV's prior acts of prostitution.

b. Other arguably "constitutionally required" circumstances

§ 9.22 Immediately surrounding circumstances

The alleged victim's conduct at or near the time immediately surrounding the alleged offense may be highly relevant on the issues of consent and credibility. The Advisory Committee Note to the 1994 amendment provides an example: "statements in which the victim has expressed an intent to have sex with the first person encountered on a particular occasion might not be excluded without violating the due process right of a sexual assault defendant seeking to prove consent." The Advisory Committee Note also observes that the Rule would not exclude evidence of sexual behavior that was "intrinsic" to the alleged rape.

Other circumstances might include: how the alleged victim was dressed on that occasion,[25] the manner in which the alleged victim danced, particularly with the defendant; and so on. Assessing the relevance of such evidence may pose a cultural or generational challenge: conduct that might seem overtly sexual and inviting to some people might, to others, be considered acceptable and normal conduct that does not implicitly indicate a willingness to have sex. If your professor gives you an essay question that involves such conduct, give it your best, honest answer, but then add, "On the other hand, other people might consider this to be [etc.]."

§ 9.23 "Pattern" vs. promiscuity

Although evidence of an alleged victim's prior sexual behavior is generally excluded, such evidence may have special relevance if it is sufficiently frequent, unusual, and similar to the defendant's version of the alleged victim's behavior on the occasion in question.

---

25. Although how a person dresses generally is not admissible to show his, her, or their sexual disposition, what that person was wearing on the occasion giving rise to the rape allegation might have factually specific relevance independent of the "disposition" inference.

The key questions are: (1) how unusual, idiosyncratic, kinky, abnormal, bizarre or disgusting[26] must the behavior be, (2) how many prior instances must be proved to establish a "common scheme" or "pattern," (3) how closely must the other instances resemble the (defendant's version of the) facts in the instant case, and (4) once the judge has assessed the legitimate probative value of the evidence, how is that value to be weighed against the risk of unfair prejudice to the state and embarrassment to the alleged victim?

Evidence that the alleged victim engaged in occasional, merely fungibly similar conduct does not satisfy the "pattern" exception. Some courts have held, however, that a defendant must be permitted to introduce evidence that the alleged victim had "a distinct pattern of past sexual conduct, involving the extortion of money by threat after acts of prostitution"[27]; to cross-examine the alleged victim concerning a pattern of consensual intercourse with men she barely knew in furtherance of her attempt to run away from home;[28] and to elicit an acknowledgment from the alleged victim that her addiction to crack cocaine had on numerous occasions caused her to engage in sex in exchange for crack.[29]

Where the alleged "pattern" does not involve a motive extrinsic to sexual activity such as money (extortion), a desire to escape an unpleasant home, or drugs, it is difficult to define the degree of similarity or abnormality required to qualify as a pattern. Logic suggests that the more unusual or inherently unlikely the defendant's version of events, the greater the probative value that the alleged victim engaged in similar conduct on other occasions. Wherever one draws the line, problems will arise.

My bet is that few law professors will quiz or examine students on this aspect of evidence law. (I never did.)

§ 9.24 Prior sexual assault allegations by V/AV

Where the defendant claims that the alleged victim consented or denies that sexual behavior in fact occurred, should the defendant be allowed to offer evidence that the alleged victim had on one or more other occasions accused someone else of sexual assault? This raises several issues.

26. Attentive readers have no doubt noted that the first two terms in this list of adjectives are value-neutral; thereafter, the list grows increasingly judgmental. The list was written thus to remind the reader of an issue that lurks near the surface in these cases: in assessing the legitimate probative value of the evidence and its risk of unfair prejudice, how (if at all) should a judge consider the extent to which the behavior in question violates contemporary social norms and mores—assuming it is in fact possible these days to define "contemporary social norms and mores"?

27. Winfield v. Commonwealth, 225 Va. 211, 301 S.E.2d 15, 20 (1983).

28. State v. Vaughn, 448 So. 2d 1260 (La. 1983) (reversing defendant's conviction).

29. Johnson v. State, 332 Md. 456, 473, 632 A.2d 152, 161 (1993).

1. Does Rule 412 exclude evidence that the alleged victim was the victim of sexual assault by someone else prior to the defendant's alleged sexual assault on the alleged victim? The consensus is that it does exclude such evidence, barring a special showing of relevance. Courts have admitted such evidence, for example, where the defendant makes a strong case that the prior assault so traumatized the alleged victim that the alleged victim confused the prior assault with her encounter with the defendant.
2. Evidence that the alleged victim had *falsely* accused someone of sexual assault on a prior occasion is highly relevant on the question whether the current charges against the defendant are also fabricated. The Advisory Committee Note to the 1994 amendment to FRE 412 comments, "Evidence offered to prove allegedly false prior claims by the victim is not barred by Rule 412."
3. There is uncertainty as to the quality of proof required to establish that the alleged victim made a prior false sexual assault complaint. Does it suffice to satisfy the *Huddleston*/FRE 104(b) "sufficient to support a finding" standard, or does a higher standard apply? (I think FRE 104(b) is the correct standard, but many disagree.)
4. Assuming defendant's evidence satisfies the required threshold, is its use restricted to cross-examination of the alleged victim, or may defendant also offer extrinsic evidence of the prior complaints and their falsity?[30]

If your professor gives a question relating to V/AV's prior sexual assault allegations, be particularly sure your answer demonstrates that you recognize each of these issues.

C. Rule 412(b)(2): Civil Cases

§ 9.25 In general

Rule 412 applies in civil cases pretty much like it does in criminal cases, with some exceptions:

Rule 412. Sex-Offense Cases: The Victim's Sexual Behavior or Predisposition

30. Defense counsel should argue that V/AV's prior false accusations of sexual assault have factually specific relevance to prove the alleged victim's conduct in this case is a lie, per FRE 404(b)(2), independent of the rape-shield purposes of FRE 412. A prosecutor may argue that the defense should be limited to cross-examination, per the restrictions imposed by FRE 608(b). That issue is discussed in § 13.3.

(a) Prohibited Uses. The following evidence is not admissible in a civil or criminal proceeding involving alleged sexual misconduct:

(1) evidence offered to prove that a victim engaged in other sexual behavior; or

(2) evidence offered to prove a victim's sexual predisposition.

(b) Exceptions.

...

(2) **Civil Cases.** In a civil case, the court may admit evidence offered to prove a victim's sexual behavior or sexual predisposition if its probative value substantially outweighs the danger of harm to any victim and of unfair prejudice to any party. The court may admit evidence of a victim's reputation only if the victim has placed it in controversy.

The Advisory Committee Note to the 1994 amendment explains the differences. First, the Rule employs a balancing test, rather than an assumption of exclusion, due to "the difficulty of foreseeing future developments in the law," such as suits alleging sexual harassment. Second, the Rule 412 balancing test shifts the burden. Unlike Rule 403, which places the burden on the party seeking to exclude relevant evidence, Rule 412(c) places that burden on the offering party. Third, that burden is much greater than the 403 burden: the offering party must persuade the judge that the probative value of the evidence *substantially* outweighs the negative risks. Finally, "the danger of harm to the victim," as well as risk of prejudice to a party, must be considered in assessing the negative risk involved in admitting the evidence.

Chapter 10

Rules 413–415: Similar Crimes and Acts in Sexual Assault Cases, Child Molestation Cases, and Civil Cases Involving Sexual Assault or Child Molestation

§ 10.1 Introduction

Rules 413–415 inspire substantial debate and criticism among evidence professors. The criticism focuses on the central feature of these provisions: *they explicitly and unashamedly endorse the propensity inference.* Although FRE 403 applies to evidence offered under these rules, to win exclusion, the defendant must point to some the risk of unfair prejudice *other than* the "bad person inference," because these rules permit a prosecutor or plaintiff to argue, in essence, "D did this to other people in the past; that shows that D did it this time to V/AV," and permit a jury to accept such reasoning.

§ 10.2 FRE 413

FRE 413 provides:

> **Rule 413. Similar Crimes in Sexual-Assault Cases**
>
> **(a) Permitted Uses.** In a criminal case in which a defendant is accused of a sexual assault, the court may admit evidence that the defendant committed any other sexual assault. The evidence may be considered on any matter to which it is relevant.

(b) **Disclosure to the Defendant.** If the prosecutor intends to offer this evidence, the prosecutor must disclose it to the defendant, including witnesses' statements or a summary of the expected testimony. The prosecutor must do so at least 15 days before trial or at a later time that the court allows for good cause.

(c) **Effect on Other Rules.** This rule does not limit the admission or consideration of evidence under any other rule.

(d) **Definition of "Sexual Assault."** In this rule and Rule 415, "sexual assault" means a crime under federal law or under state law (as "state" is defined in 18 U.S.C. § 513) involving:

(1) any conduct prohibited by 18 U.S.C. chapter 109A;

(2) contact, without consent, between any part of the defendant's body—or an object—and another person's genitals or anus;

(3) contact, without consent, between the defendant's genitals or anus and any part of another person's body;

(4) deriving sexual pleasure or gratification from inflicting death, bodily injury, or physical pain on another person; or

(5) an attempt or conspiracy to engage in conduct described in subparagraphs (1)–(4).

The primary purpose of the rule, as set out in FRE (a), is to endorse the use of the propensity inference in sexual assault prosecutions. In other words, the prosecutor is allowed to argue, "since D committed this other extrinsic sexual assault, it's likely D committed the sexual assault for which D is now on trial." The only requirements are:

(1) The defendant is now on trial for a "sexual assault."
(2) The extrinsic act also constituted a "sexual assault," as defined in subrule 413(d). Note that the conduct specified in FRE 412(d) must have been intentional, not accidental; an unintentionally misplaced hand or bump would not constitute a "sexual assault."

The prosecutor is not required to prove that the defendant was convicted of the prior sexual assault; all that is required is evidence "sufficient to support a finding" that the defendant committed an extrinsic "sexual assault." If D is charged with a sexual assault against V/AV and the prosecutor calls PW1 to testify that several years earlier D sexually assaulted PW1, PW1's testimony need not be corroborated to be admissible.

Rule 412(b) is self-explanatory.

§ 10.3 Rule 413(c) and other evidence rules

Subsection (c) is less than pellucid,[1] but in essence, it means that all other rules of evidence apply, so long as their application is consistent with Rule 413(a). So, for example, evidence that the defendant committed a prior, extrinsic sexual assault that would satisfy Rule 413(a) still has to be excluded if the only evidence available to the prosecutor about that extrinsic sexual assault is inadmissible hearsay.

FRE 403 applies to Rule 413 evidence, except that the propensity inference does not constitute "unfair prejudice." But some details of the other sexual assault may nonetheless raise issues of unfair prejudice. And other aspects of Rule 403—unnecessary presentation of cumulative evidence, confusion, waste of time—still apply.

§10.4 Questions

Questions 1–5

D is charged with the rape of V/AV, alleged to have been committed on February 1. When arrested, D acknowledged having sex with V/AV, but insisted that V/AV consented. (That intercourse occurred is strongly confirmed by DNA evidence. V/AV's consent remains D's defense throughout the case.)

At trial, V/AV testifies that on February 1, V/AV went, alone, to a local singles bar; that D initiated a conversation and bought V/AV a drink, then a second drink, then offered V/AV a ride home. D and V/AV walked to the door of V/AV's apartment; then D forced his way in and raped V/AV. D's attorney challenges this testimony on cross.

Question 1.

The prosecutor then calls PW1, who is of the same gender and roughly the same age as V/AV, who will testify that D did the same thing to PW1 six months earlier. PW1 never reported the matter to the police. Discuss the issues presented.

Answer:

First, did the prosecutor properly serve pretrial notice to D, per FRE 413(b)? If not, D has a plausible argument to exclude it.

Let's assume for the rest of this sequence that the prosecutor did serve pretrial notice of the evidence in Q1-4, and that D moved in limine (see § 2.2) to exclude the testimony and evidence offered in each of those questions.

---

1. "Pellucid" means "translucent," which means "allowing light, but not detailed shapes." In other words, to describe a statute whose meaning is only vaguely discernible, I used a word whose meaning is, for many people, only vaguely discernible. Which reminds me of one of my favorite t-shirts, which says, "Eschew obfuscation," which means "avoid being intentionally difficult to understand." Lawyers should, whenever possible, use words that are familiar to non-experts. Don't say that X "purloined" or "pilfered" or "unlawfully expropriated by force"; say "X stole."

PW1's testimony clearly violates FRE 404(b), but it falls within FRE 413(a), and therefore is admissible to suggest that since D raped PW1, it is more likely than it would be without the evidence that D raped V/AV, too. That PW1 never reported the matter goes to the weight the jury might give PW1's testimony, but not its admissibility. D's motion to exclude is denied.

Question 2.

The prosecutor calls PW2, who will, if permitted, testify that seven years ago, when PW2 and D were medical students, D accosted PW2 in a deserted hallway, forced PW2 into an empty hospital room, and fondled PW2's genitals despite PW2's protests and attempts to resist; the event ended when a custodian entered the room to clean it. Discuss the issues presented.

Answer:

PW2's testimony is admissible per Rule 413(a). True, the extrinsic sexual assault of PW2 occurred seven years prior to D's alleged rape of V/AV, and was a less serious crime than rape. These factors arguably diminish the probative value of the assault on PW2, but the permissible propensity inference is still quite strong. D's motion to exclude is denied.

Question 3.

PW3, another medical student at the time, will, if permitted, testify that the word among other medical students was, "If you ever find yourself alone with D, you'd better be ready to fight like hell, or else!" Discuss the issues presented.

Answer:

This evidence does not come within the FRE 413(a) inclusionary rule. That rule admits only "evidence that the defendant committed any other sexual assault"—in other words, it admits only specific extrinsic acts, not character (reputation or opinion) evidence. PW3 is offering testimony about D's reputation, not of a specific act committed by D. Thus, its admissibility depends upon FRE 404(a), which prohibits a prosecutor from offering character evidence about a defendant unless the defendant has first opened the door by offering evidence of his own good character. D's motion to exclude is granted.

Question 4.

The prosecutor offers in evidence a certified copy of an arrest report relating that in 2018, D was arrested and charged with attempted rape of PW4. If you have already covered hearsay, choose the correct answer from among the following:

(A) The arrest report is admissible over a Rule 404(b) objection per Rule 413(a), and is admissible over a hearsay objection per FRE 803(8)(A)(iii); therefore, the report is admissible.

(B) The arrest report would be admissible over a Rule 404(b) objection per Rule 413(a), but is hearsay and does not satisfy any hearsay exception; therefore, the report is inadmissible.

(C) The arrest report would be admissible over a hearsay objection per 803(8)(A)(iii), but does not satisfy Rule 413(a); therefore, the report is inadmissible per Rule 404(b).

(D) The arrest report does not satisfy Rule 413 and therefore is inadmissible over a Rule 404(b) objection, and is hearsay and does not satisfy any hearsay objection; therefore, the report is inadmissible on both grounds.

Answer:

The correct answer is (B). Why?

Suppose this was an essay question, not a multiple-choice question. In other words, suppose the call of the question was: "Discuss the issues thus presented." The answer would go as follows:

An attempted rape is included within the definition of "sexual assault," see FRE 413(d)(5), so if PW4 appeared in court, PW4's testimony would qualify under Rule 413(a). Still, D's attorney might plausibly object that since the judge has already admitted testimony by PW1 and PW2, PW4's testimony has little additional probative value and therefore constitutes needless presentation of cumulative evidence per FRE 403.

But the prosecutor has not called PW4 as a witness; instead, the prosecutor is offering a document which alleges that D attempted to rape PW4. That document is being offered as proof of what the document says, i.e., it is offered as evidence that D attempted to rape PW4, therefore it is inadmissible hearsay; and its admission would also violate D's rights under the Sixth Amendment Confrontation Clause.[2] D's motion to exclude is granted.

Comment: Assuming you have already covered hearsay, even though you know the report is hearsay and does not satisfy any exception, you should still include in your answer (1) that the underlying facts (attempted rape) satisfy Ruled 413(a) but (2) that the judge could nevertheless exclude it as cumulative under Rule 403. Simply answering, "Exclude as inadmissible hearsay" would only earn you partial credit for your answer. Remember: your goal in answering an essay question is not merely to reach the right conclusion, but to demonstrate how brilliantly your evidence professor has taught you to recognize all the issues presented in a question.

2. See Fishman, *A Student's Guide to Hearsay* (5th ed. 2019) §§ 2.1–2.8, concerning the definition of hearsay, and §§ 9.43 et seq., concerning the public reports exception to the hearsay rule, which does not admit a police report over a hearsay objection—whether the report is "certified" or not. Concerning the Confrontation Clause, see generally *id.*, Chapter 6.

Question 5.

The judge rules that PW1 and PW2 will be permitted to testify. In response, D's attorney serves notice that D proposes to call DW1, DW2, DW3 and DW4. Each will, if permitted, testify that during the 12 months preceding February 1, he himself met V/AV at a party or in a bar, took V/AV to V/AV's home, and had consensual sex with V/AV. Discuss the issues presented.

Answer:

This evidence is excluded by Rule 412(a): evidence that V/AV had consensual sex with DW1, DW2, DW3 and DW4 is not admissible to show that V/AV is predisposed to have consensual sex with people V/AV has just met.

"But wait," D's attorney argues, "that is fundamentally unfair. If the prosecutor is allowed to offer evidence of my client's alleged prior sexual misconduct under Rule 413(a), it violates my client's constitutional rights to be denied the right to offer evidence of V/AV's sexual misconduct! It violates Rule 412(b)(1)(C)!"

This argument may seem plausible at first glance, but it is not.

First of all, that V/AV allegedly had four casual sexual liaisons with strangers over the course of a year is not so bizarre or unusual as to fit within the "pattern" rubric discussed in § 9.23. Thus, the proffered testimony by DW1-DW4 does not itself satisfy FRE 412(b)(1)(C).

Second, and more fundamentally, defense counsel's argument—"If the prosecutor can do it to D, it's only fair that I can do the same thing to V/AV"—is based on a false equivalency, because D's alleged extrinsic acts, as described by PW1 and PW2, and V/AV's alleged extrinsic acts, as described by DW1-DW4, are in no way morally or legally equivalent. V/AV's liaisons with DW1-DW4 (assuming their testimony is true) were choices V/AV had a legal right to make, even if some might consider them unwise or unsafe or unsavory. By contrast, D's conduct as alleged by PW1 constitutes a violent felony—among the worst that one person can commit against another; and his conduct as alleged by PW2 is also illegal—and might have ended with rape, had he not been interrupted—and certainly demonstrates D's predisposition to commit sexual assaults.

Question 6.

You represent D (age 32), who is accused of raping V/AV, who is 22 years old. V/AV will testify that after passing out from excessive drinking, V/AV awoke as D was raping V/AV. D claims V/AV was conscious and was a willing participant. The prosecutor has served you notice that, in addition to V/AV, she intends to call PW, who will testify that, 7 years earlier, when PW was 13 years old, PW got drunk, passed out at a party, and awoke to find defendant raping PW. What should you do?

Answer:

I would make a pro forma argument to exclude PW's testimony completely, but the judge will overrule that per Rule 413(a).

I would also object to testimony that PW was only 13 at the time D allegedly committed the rape. That, I would argue, would be massively prejudicial while adding no legitimate probative value to the current case against D, since V/AV was 22 when D had sex with V/AV.

The point of this question is to remind you that even though the prior sexual assault presumptively "may be considered on any matter to which it is relevant," Rule 403 may still be a basis to exclude at least some details about the alleged prior assault.

§ 10.5 Rules 414 and 415

These rules, which involve criminal and civil actions for sexual abuse of a child, follow the same pattern as rule 413.

Chapter 11

Witnesses and Examination, FRE 601, 602, 611; Introduction to Impeachment; and Roadmaps to FRE 404–406, 412–415, and 608–609

A. Witnesses and Examination: FRE 601, 602, 611

1. Competency and Personal Knowledge: Rules 601–602

§ 11.1 Rule 601: competency to testify

FRE 601 provides:

> **601. Competency to Testify in General**
>
> Every person is competent to be a witness unless these rules provide otherwise. But in a civil case, state law governs the witness's competency regarding a claim or defense for which state law supplies the rule of decision.

FRE 601 begins by stating: "Every person is competent to be a witness unless these rules provide otherwise."[1] The Advisory Committee Note to the Rule under-

1. The phrase "these rules" refers to the entire Federal Rules of Evidence. Rules that speak to whether a witness is legally barred from testifying include Rules 605 (a judge who is presiding over

scores this proposition: "No mental or moral qualifications for testifying as a witness are specified.... A witness wholly without capacity is difficult to imagine. The question is one particularly suited to the jury as one of weight and credibility, subject to judicial authority to review the sufficiency of the evidence." Thus, the rule eliminates several common-law grounds for disqualifying certain people from testifying (which the law labeled as legally "incompetent" to testify).

Although the law strongly assumes that every witness is competent, a party may still challenge a witness's competence to testify—most often, because the witness is a very young child, or suffers from a mental disease or defect or emotional trauma, or was under the influence of drugs when the events in question occurred, or is under the influence while testifying. Except in the most extreme cases, evidence showing a lack of (or diminished) capacity goes to the weight of the witness's testimony, but not its admissibility.

Evidence that W1 suffered from a mental disease or defect or emotional trauma when the events in question occurred, or suffers from such a condition when he or she is testifying, is not automatically admissible to challenge the accuracy of W1's testimony. Counsel must first offer evidence (such as expert studies or testimony) that W1's condition is likely to have affected W1's ability to perceive, remember or narrate accurately.

§ 11.2 Rule 602: the "personal knowledge" requirement

FRE 602 provides:

> **Rule 602. Need for Personal Knowledge**
>
> A witness may testify to a matter only if evidence is introduced sufficient to support a finding that the witness has personal knowledge of the matter. Evidence to prove personal knowledge may consist of the witness' s own testimony. This rule does not apply to a witness's expert testimony under Rule 703.

FRE 602, which is based on many of the same considerations as is the hearsay rule, is basically straight-forward: witness W should be permitted to testify about an event or condition only if W had personal knowledge of that event or condition—i.e., only if W perceived or experienced it first-hand. Before eliciting W's testimony about an event, therefore, an attorney must "lay a foundation" by establishing that W was present and perceived the event or condition. Thus, before asking W,

---

a trial cannot be a witness at the trial); 606(a) (a juror cannot testify before other jurors at the trial in which he or she is a juror); 606(b) (concerning when a juror can testify at a post-judgment motion to set aside a verdict); and certain uncodified rules governing legal privileges. This book does not cover these rules; nor does it cover Rules 603 and 604.

"What happened at the intersection of Eighteenth and Vine[2] at 3 p.m. on August 1," you would first ask, "Where were you at about 3 p.m. on August 1? Did you see something unusual in that intersection at that time? Tell the jury what you saw."

FRE 602 does not require that a witness have personal knowledge of an ultimate fact of consequence; it only requires personal knowledge of a relevant, admissible fact. A server in a restaurant who did not see which vehicle ran a red light nevertheless can testify, "I served the defendant a gin and tonic before dinner, wine with dinner and a brandy afterward."

FRE 602 does not impose the personal knowledge requirement on expert witnesses, although of course, the expert should be allowed to testify only if the party calling the witness elicits testimony that the expert in fact has a valid factual basis on which to base his or her opinion.

§ 11.3 Questions

Question 1.

D is on trial for burglary. The prosecutor intends to call the victim, V, who will, if permitted, identify D as the burglar even though, as V conceded at a preliminary hearing, he was able to see the burglar's face for "maybe a second or so before the guy turned and ran out of the house," and that the burglar was standing in a shadow during that "second or so." D objects, arguing that V lacks first-hand knowledge of the burglar's appearance, and therefore, should not be allowed to identify D as the burglar. Discuss the issues presented.

Answer:

Objection overruled. Granted, V did not observe the burglar under ideal conditions, and eyewitness identification testimony is often flawed; but those aspects go to the weight the jury chooses to give to V's testimony, not its admissibility.

Question 2.

P sues D for personal injuries received in an automobile collision between P's car and D's pickup truck. P was traveling south on N-S Avenue and D was heading east on E-W Road. At trial, P calls PW1 who proposes to testify as follows: "I was standing near the northwest corner of the intersection of N-S and E-W when I saw D's pickup run the red light on E-W Road."

2. The intersection of Eighteenth and Vine Streets in Kansas City, Missouri, is recognized as an historical point of origin of jazz music. (This is distinct from the song "Kansas City," which glorifies the intersection of Twelfth Street and Vine—an intersection which, according to various websites, does not actually exist. It is also distinct from the intersection of Hollywood and Vine, which does exist, but in a galaxy far, far away from the world most of us inhabit.)

D objects and asks the trial judge for the opportunity to ask one question on voir dire.[3] The judge grants the request, and D elicits the following:

Q. PW1, were you in any position to personally observe the light in question?

A. Well, actually, a tree branch blocked my view of the light.

If D renews the objection that W1 lacks personal knowledge, how should the trial judge rule?

Answer:

Objection sustained. PW1 has admitted he lacked personal knowledge of which vehicle ran the red light.

Question 3.

How might P secure admissibility of PW1's testimony, despite his answer to D's question?

Answer:

Q PW1, what did you actually see at that time and place?

A I saw traffic proceeding both ways on E-W Road. Then all the traffic on E-W Road stopped, and vehicles on N-S Avenue started entering the intersection in both directions, when suddenly D's pickup truck entered the intersection heading east on E-W Road and collided with P's car which was heading south on N-S Avenue.

This testimony clearly is admissible, because PW1 has adequately established that he has personal knowledge of these facts—from which, of course, the jury can logically conclude that D ran the red light.

Question 4.

P calls PW2 who was standing next to HDL.[4] P asks:

Q Did you see the light?

A No.

Q Did you hear anyone say something about the light?

A Yes.

3. In this context, "voir dire" means "a limited mini-cross-examination in the middle of direct examination, testing whether the witness has an adequate factual foundation to testify."

4. "HDL" is my abbreviation for "hearsay declarant," i.e., a person whose "out-of-court" statement is being offered into evidence.

Q What did you hear?

A I heard HDL shout "Oh, no, the pickup is running the red light!"

How should the trial judge rule on D's objection that PW2 lacked personal knowledge?

Answer:

Objection overruled. Although PW2 lacked personal knowledge of who ran the light, W2 did have personal knowledge of what HDL said.

Question 5.

What objection could D have made to PW2's testimony about HDL's statement? How is the judge likely to have ruled on such an objection?

Answer:

D could have objected that HDL's statement was hearsay: it was HDL's out-of-court statement, which P is offering in evidence, via W2's testimony, to prove the truth of the matter asserted in HDL's statement—i.e., to prove that D ran the red light.[5]

But the judge should overrule the objection, because HDL's statement clearly appears to be an excited utterance, and is therefore admissible per FRE 803(2).[6]

Question 6.

Suppose PW3, a lawyer in good standing, saw the collision, in which P was seriously injured. P retains PW3 to represent him in a civil action for damages against D. Under the FRE, is PW3 competent to be a witness?

Answer:

Yes. There is no provision in the FRE that bans an attorney from testifying at a trial in which he or she represents a party.

Question 7.

Is there any other body of law or authority regulating whether a person should be both attorney of record and also a witness in a case?

Answer:

Yes. ABA Model Rules of Professional Conduct 3.7, and its predecessor, Model Disciplinary Rule 5-102, each makes it unprofessional conduct for an attorney to try a case when the attorney knows that he or she will have to testify about significant contested issues in the case.

5. See Clifford S. Fishman, *A Student's Guide to Hearsay* (5th ed. 2019), Chapter 2.

6. See Clifford S. Fishman, *A Student's Guide to Hearsay* (5th ed. 2019), § 8.2 to § 8.3.

B. Method and Order of Interrogation: Rule 611

§ 11.4 Overview

The next several sections very briefly outline some preliminary rules governing cross-examination and impeachment of a witness.

§ 11.5 Counsel's role

Question 1.

You represent Drum, the defendant in a personal injury action brought by Piccolo. Piccolo's first witness is Woodwind. What is your primary responsibility while Woodwind is testifying on direct examination? What FRE provision most closely regulates what you should do, and how, and when?

Answer:

You must listen carefully to each question Piccolo asks Woodwind and analyze whether it calls for an answer to which you can object. If so, you must make an immediate tactical decision whether to object or not.[7] If you do object, you must be prepared to specify the rule or rules you think the question violates, and to argue your point if the judge is willing to hear argument.

And you must listen to the answers, to determine if the answer is objectionable; make a tactical decision whether to object or not; be prepared to specify the rule or rules you think the answer violates, and to argue your point if the judge is willing to hear argument.

Thus, the FRE provision most directly applicable to your role as Drum's attorney is FRE 103(a):

Rule 103. Rulings on Evidence

> **(a) Preserving a Claim of Error.** A party may claim error in a ruling to admit or exclude evidence only if the error affects a substantial right of the party and:
>
> (1) if the ruling admits evidence, a party, on the record:

7. As law students, your job is not to make tactical decisions; it is to demonstrate to your professor how brilliantly he or she has taught you evidence law. Thus, it is probably a good idea to assert every plausible objection that can be made, even if, in some scenarios, you doubt an actual attorney would do so.

(A) timely objects or moves to strike; and

(B) states the specific ground, unless it was apparent from the context; or

(2) if the ruling excludes evidence, a party informs the court of its substance by an offer of proof, unless the substance was apparent from the context.

Waiting until you hear the answer before objecting is risky, because if the question clearly called for an answer that would be objectionable, a judge might conclude that failure to object in a timely fashion waived the right to object, per Rule 103(a)(A). I offer no opinion as to whether your professor (or the bar exam) will test you on this concept.

In addition to deciding whether to object, you should begin to plan your cross-examination of the witness, both as to substance—what aspects of Woodwind's testimony should you challenge, which aspects should you leave alone (at least at first), and style—should you be polite and gentle, or aggressive and antagonistic?

When I was a trial lawyer a century or so ago, the tensest part of a trial was when my opponent was conducting direct examination of his or her witnesses.

Your professor (or casebook) may provide you with a list of the most common objections. Here is the list I gave my students:

> Objections as to the form of a question. These objections are appropriate when an attorney believes that the wording of a question or the procedure being used by the offering party is improper.
>
> Argumentative
> Assumes facts not in evidence
> Compound question
> Question (on cross-examination) exceeds the scope of direct examination
> Insufficient foundation (e.g., to introduce an exhibit)
> Leading question (on direct examination)
> Calls for a narrative
>
> Objections to the answer called for by the question. These objections are appropriate when the adverse party contends that the answer violates or would violate some substantive rule of evidence.
>
> Calls for a legal conclusion
> Calls for hearsay
> Impermissible impeachment (specify precise reasons)
> Irrelevant

Calls for privileged communication
Reply not responsive to the question
Unfairly prejudicial (specify the nature of the unfair prejudice)
Witness lacks first-hand knowledge
Witness not qualified to express expert opinion

These lists are not exhaustive. And, whenever possible, the lawyer making the objection should cite the specific rule of evidence the objector thinks the question or answer violates.

§ 11.6 Examining witnesses: Rule 611

FRE 611 provides:

Rule 611. Mode and Order of Examining Witnesses and Presenting Evidence

(a) **Control by the Court; Purposes.** The court should exercise reasonable control over the mode and order of examining witnesses and presenting evidence so as to:

(1) make those procedures effective for determining the truth;

(2) avoid wasting time; and

(3) protect witnesses from harassment or undue embarrassment.

(b) **Scope of Cross-Examination.** Cross-examination should not go beyond the subject matter of the direct examination and matters affecting the witness's credibility. The court may allow inquiry into additional matters as if on direct examination. [I explain what this means in § 11.8.]

(c) **Leading Questions.** Leading questions should not be used on direct examination except as necessary to develop the witness's testimony. Ordinarily, the court should allow leading questions:

(1) on cross-examination; and

(2) when a party calls a hostile witness, an adverse party, or a witness identified with an adverse party.

Each major subdivision of the rule is discussed in the following sections.

§ 11.7 Rule 611(a)(3): "protect witnesses from harassment or undue embarrassment"

Rule 611(a) gives the trial judge "reasonable control" over how testimony is elicited from witnesses, in order to further the three aspirational goals set out in the rule.

With regard to cross-examination and impeachment, Rule 611(a)(3) is particularly significant. Being required to testify can be upsetting and embarrassing; particularly so when the questions are asked by an attorney seeking to persuade a jury not to believe or accept the witness's testimony, a situation that arises most often on cross-examination. The attorney who calls witness W for direct examination and hopes the jury will accept W's testimony as true owes it to W as well as the client to protect W from mistreatment and embarrassment to the extent possible. An attorney should not object that a line of questioning is "prejudicial" to W—unless W is also a party to the case. "Unfair prejudice," as Rule 403 uses the phrase, refers only to unfair prejudice to the party. Rather, the attorney relying on W's testimony should cite Rule 611(a)(3) when objecting to the other attorney's treatment of the witness.

That being said, the judge's authority is limited. If the information the impeaching attorney seeks to elicit has sufficient relevance in the outcome of a case, unduly restricting cross-examination or other impeachment can be reversible error.

§ 11.8 Rule 611(b): scope of cross-examination

Cross-examination serves a variety of functions. It permits the adverse party to elicit information that was omitted during direct examination; it is opposing counsel's first opportunity to probe for weaknesses in the witness's direct testimony; and it is also the first opportunity to attack the witness's character for truthfulness.

The law has taken two different approaches to the proper scope of cross-examination. One view holds that the adverse party may cross-examine the witness about any matter that is relevant to the lawsuit. The other view is that cross-examination should be limited to facts and details elicited on direct, and matters reasonably related to what was elicited on direct.

The Advisory Committee that drafted the rules urged the broad approach, but Congress disagreed. Rule 611(b) provides:

> **(b) Scope of Cross-Examination.** Cross-examination should not go beyond the subject matter of the direct examination and matters affecting the witness's credibility. The court may allow inquiry into additional matters as if on direct examination.

Clearly, the rule takes the narrower approach;[8] but federal courts have interpreted "the subject matter of the direct examination" to include matters reasonably related to what was covered on direct. If W testifies "I saw [or otherwise perceived]" something, adverse counsel can cross-examine to test W's witness's ability to perceive, remember and accurately narrate what W saw or heard; and, at least where the tes-

8. I'll address the final sentence of the rule later in this section.

timony favors one party and disfavors another, counsel can cross-examine W to explore possible reasons why W might be biased or have a reason to lie.

The difference between the two approaches is illustrated by the following example. On March 1, P was injured when scaffolding fell on him. P was rushed to the nearest hospital emergency room, where P was examined and treated by Dr. X. P returned to Dr. X on March 4 and 7. Dr. X seemed unimpressed by P's complaints of continuing pain and disability, however, so on March 10, P consulted Dr. Y, who has treated P ever since.

P sues C, the contractor whose scaffolding fell on P. At trial, P wants to call Dr. X to testify to P's condition on March 1, immediately after the injury, but does *not* want to elicit testimony from Dr. X concerning Dr. X's examination or diagnosis of P on March 4 and 7; rather, P plans to rely exclusively on Dr. Y's testimony to prove the seriousness of P's injury and prolonged pain and suffering. C, on the other hand, plans to elicit testimony from Dr. X concerning his examination of P, in an effort to persuade the jury that P's claim for pain and disability is grossly exaggerated.

Under the broad Advisory Committee "any matter that is relevant" approach, after P conducted direct examination of Dr. X concerning March 1, C would have been permitted to cross-examine Dr. X, not only about March 1, but also about the examinations Dr. X conducted on March 4 and 7, because those examinations are "relevant to an issue in the case." Under Rule 611(b) as revised by Congress however, C will be permitted to cross-examine Dr. X only concerning "the subject matter of the direct examination"—i.e., Dr. X's examination and treatment of P on March 1. As is almost always the case, while conducting this cross-examination, C is entitled to ask leading questions.

This does *not* mean that C is prohibited from eliciting testimony concerning March 4 and 7 from Dr. X. C *may* do so, but, as a rule, not until after P rests and it is C's turn to present its own case. At that time, C may call Dr. X as a defense witness and elicit such testimony from Dr. X on direct examination.

In short, the rule permits each litigant to tailor its case as it sees fit (within reasonable limits, of course).

The disadvantage to Rule 611(b) as it is written is that witnesses such as Dr. X in the previous example are sometimes required to appear more than once during the same trial. This can result in considerable inconvenience for the witness. The last sentence of Rule 611(b) affords the trial judge discretion to alter the ordinary sequence in appropriate circumstances.

Suppose, for example, Dr. X had planned to leave on vacation the day after testifying as a witness for P, and was anxious to avoid having to stay in town for three or four extra days until P rested and the defense had its chance to call witnesses. Under these circumstances, the testimony of Dr. X might proceed in the following sequence:

a. Direct examination of Dr. X by P concerning March 1. (Leading questions would not be permitted, barring unusual circumstances, such as a judicial finding that Dr. X is "hostile" to P.)

b. Cross-examination of Dr. X by C concerning Dr. X's perception, memory and choice of words to describe the events of March 1, and concerning her character for truthfulness.[9] During cross, leading questions may be used.

c. With permission of the court, C could then elicit testimony from Dr. X concerning March 4 and March 7; but in questioning about these matters, which are beyond the scope of the direct examination, C would have to proceed, as the last sentence in Rule 611(b) provides, "as if on direct examination"—i.e., *without* using leading questions.

d. Once C has finished questioning Dr. X, P has an opportunity to conduct redirect examination of Dr. X concerning March 1, during which (unless the judge concludes that Dr. X is "hostile" toward P) P would not be permitted to ask leading questions, and to conduct cross-examination of Dr. X concerning March 4 and March 7—during which P *would* be permitted to ask leading questions

These notes should not leave you with the impression that cross-examination is narrowly limited to a rehash of what the witness said on direct. So long as it is reasonably connected to the subject matter of direct examination, or to the witness's character for truthfulness, cross-examination may explore a wide variety of subjects.

§ 11.9 Rule 611(c): leading questions

Rule 611(c) provides:

> **(c) Leading Questions.** Leading questions should not be used on direct examination except as necessary to develop the witness's testimony. Ordinarily, the court should allow leading questions:
>
> (1) on cross-examination; and
>
> (2) when a party calls a hostile witness, an adverse party, or a witness identified with an adverse party.

A leading question is one which contains the information the attorney seeks to have the witness testify to, and is worded in a way that clearly suggests that the

9. It is unlikely that C would have any reason to challenge Dr. X's character for truthfulness. I mention it here because a cross-examiner is entitled to ask such questions of almost any witness, assuming the cross-examiner has information about the witness that satisfies FRE 608(b) or FRE 609.

attorney thinks is the "right answer." The classic example of a leading question is one which begins, "Isn't it a fact that," or an equivalent phrase ("It is true, is it not, that," etc.).

You are likely to come across statements such as "A leading question is one that can be answered 'yes' or 'no.'" That statement is true to the extent that many leading questions are yes-no questions. But not all yes-no questions are leading questions. Suppose, for example, a contested issue is whether Winston Smith attended a particular meeting in Room 101. I call witness O'Brien. After he gives name, address and occupation, examination continues:

Q Let's talk about April 6. Do you recall what the weather was like that day?

A Yes. It was bright and cold.

Q Where were you at 1 p.m.?

A I was at a meeting in Room 101, 1984 Orwell Drive.

Q Prior to that date, were you acquainted with a man named Winston Smith?

A Yes, he and I had met on several occasions prior to that date.

Q Did you see Smith at the meeting that day?[10]

A Yes.

None of these questions—including the last one, which is clearly a yes/no question—is leading. (If the final question had been worded, "You saw Smith at that meeting, right?" it would be leading.)

§ 11.10 "Ordinarily, the court should allow leading questions on cross-examination"

"Ordinarily," the rule states, "the court should allow leading questions ... on cross-examination." FRE 611(c)(1). But sometimes a judge should not allow it.

Question 1.

P files a personal injury claim against D Company following a collision between P's car and D's truck, driven by X. At trial, P calls X as his first witness. X is sworn, and direct examination proceeds as follows.

Q By whom were you employed on [the date in question]?

10. "It was a bright, cold day in April and the clocks were striking thirteen." That is the first sentence in George Orwell's classic dystopian novel *1984*. Winston Smith is the antagonist; O'Brien is his nemesis; and Room 101 is where Smith is tortured.

A D Company.

Q Were you working that day?

A Yes.

Q Doing what?

A Driving the company truck.

Q I have no further questions.

On cross-examination, after a desultory question or two concerning the scope of X's duties for D, D's attorney asks:

Q Mr. X, isn't it a fact that P's car ran a red light and collided with you on [the date in question]?

Is this question proper? Select the correct answer or answers from among the following.

(A) The question is proper.

(B) The question is impermissible because it is leading.

(C) The question is improper because it is beyond the scope of direct examination.

(D) The question is improper because it does not relate to the witness's credibility.

Answer:

Given the four options, the correct answer is (A).

The question ("Isn't it a fact that...") is clearly a leading question. But P called X, D's employee, as a witness. Technically, therefore, D's attorney is conducting cross-examination, and leading questions are permitted on cross-examination, so option (B) is incorrect.

On direct examination, P brought out that X was driving the D Company truck that day. D's question about what happened while X was driving that day clearly relates to what P elicited from X on direct, and is therefore within the proper scope of cross-examination. Thus, option (C) is incorrect. And while Rule 611(b) permits questions relating to a witness's credibility on cross-examination, that is not the only subject permissible on cross-examination. Therefore, option (D) is incorrect.

But I would not ask this question on a quiz or exam, because although a judge *could* allow D to ask leading questions while "cross-examining" X, the judge should *not* allow it. This is not "ordinary" cross-examination. After all, the central issue in the trial is whether (as P claims) X's reckless or negligent driving caused the collision. Barring unusual circumstances, D and X are really on the same side: if P had not called X as a witness, D certainly would have, to deny P's accusation.

Assuming X's testimony will be favorable to D, D's questioning of X is not "ordinary" cross-examination; it is actually direct examination of D's main witness in the middle of P's case. So the judge might allow D to question X about what happened that day, but insist that D do so only by asking non-leading questions, the way Rule 611(b) gives the judge discretion to allow a party to go beyond the scope of cross-examination discussed in the previous section.

§ 11.11 When leading questions are allowable on direct examination

As a rule, leading questions are not permitted on direct examination, but there are exceptions. The first exception arises, per Rule 611(c), when leading questions are "necessary to develop the witness's testimony." This situation arises, for example, where the witness is a young child or of limited intelligence, or for some other reason is unable to testify in a narrative form.

The other situations are set out in Rule 611(c)(2): "when a party calls a hostile witness, an adverse party, or a witness identified with an adverse party."

The first situation—the "hostile witness"—arises when a party calls HW to testify, but as direct examination proceeds, it becomes clear that HW is willfully resisting giving the answers that the attorney is seeking to elicit. An attorney confronting such a witness in essence asks the judge to classify the witness as hostile and therefore allow the attorney to proceed with leading questions.

The easiest of these three situations is the second: when a witness calls an adverse party. This situation arises only in civil cases.[11] If the plaintiff calls the defendant as a witness, it is likely that the defendant will resist giving testimony helpful to the plaintiff; allowing leading questions is probably the only way the plaintiff's attorney will be able to elicit all the information the attorney thinks the defendant has. The same is true if the defendant calls the plaintiff to testify.

The third situation is closely related to the second. If plaintiff is suing a corporation and calls a corporate officer as a witness, for example, the witness may resist providing information that will help the plaintiff. Similarly, in a criminal trial, if the prosecutor calls two police officers who participated in the arrest and the defendant calls a third officer, it may quickly become clear that the third officer is providing as

11. In criminal cases, the parties are the government or the state on one side, and the defendant on the other. The defense cannot call "the Government" (or the State or the Commonwealth or the People—whatever label a state gives the prosecution) as a witness, because "the Government" (or State, etc.) is not a person who can testify. The complainant or victim in a criminal case is not a party. The prosecutor cannot call the defendant as a witness, because doing so would violate the defendant's Fifth Amendment privilege against self-incrimination.

little information about events as he or she can manage. In such cases, the judge can authorize the attorney to ask leading questions on direct.

Perhaps the most memorable exchange involving a hostile witness occurs in the movie *My Cousin Vinny.*[12] Vinny Gambini, a young lawyer from Brooklyn, N.Y., is defending his cousin on a murder charge in rural Alabama. (Needless to say, his brash manners do not endear him to the judge.) During the defense case, Gambini calls his fiancée, Mona Lisa Vito, as an expert witness regarding automobiles. Unfortunately, the course of true love between them recently had not run smoothly, and she basically refuses to help at all. Whereupon the following exchange takes place.

VINNY GAMBINI:	Your Honor, may I have permission to treat Ms. Vito as a hostile witness?
MONA LISA VITO:	You think I'm hostile now, wait 'til you see me tonight.
JUDGE CHAMBERLAIN HALLER:	Do you two know each other?
VINNY GAMBINI:	Yeah, she's my fiancée.
JUDGE CHAMBERLAIN HALLER:	Well, that would certainly explain the hostility.

C. Introduction to Impeachment

§ 11.12 Witness "credibility"

You will see frequent discussions in case law and legal literature about impeaching (or rehabilitating) a witness's "credibility." Unfortunately, the use of the word "credibility" can cause confusion in this context, because "credibility" can mean two somewhat different things.

The first meaning focuses on impeaching witness W's *testimony*: did W accurately perceive, remember, and narrate the events about which W testified?

12. If you haven't seen this movie, put it at the very top of your list of must-sees. It is brilliantly written, the acting is superb, and it is hysterically funny. But that's secondary. More important and most impressive: it is one of the few movie or tv depictions of a trial that I can watch without wanting to throw a shoe through the screen, because everything that happens in the courtroom complies with the rules of evidence and criminal procedure. You can learn a lot from this movie about evidence and how to try a case.

My other favorite courtroom drama is *Anatomy of a Murder.* It, too, is true to how cases are tried. For many years I showed it to my criminal law students when we studied the insanity defense.

The second way in which the phrase "impeaching credibility" is used focuses on the witness's *character for truthfulness*. The rules and principles governing each differ substantially, so it is important not to confuse or conflate the two.

Rule 607 provides that a party may impeach that party's own witness on direct or redirect. Rules 608 and 609 regulate how an attorney may attempt to impeach a witness's character for truthfulness, which occurs when the impeaching attorney attempts to convince the jury: "Witness W's character for truthfulness is bad; therefore, W's word is simply not worthy of belief; therefore, you should not trust W's testimony in this trial." This type of impeachment is covered in Chapter 13.

Once a witness's character for truthfulness has been impeached, the attorney relying on that witness's testimony is permitted to offer evidence rebutting the impeachment and bolstering the witness's character for truthfulness.

§ 11.13 Impeaching W's testimony; impeaching W's character for truthfulness

i. Impeaching W's testimony

Impeaching W's testimony consists of one or more of the following:

1. Impeach the *testimony*, by casting doubt on the accuracy of W's *perception, memory, or narration*. No specific rule governs such impeachment; as the Advisory Committee Note to FRE 601 observes, "matters bearing upon the perception, memory, and narration of witnesses" are "highly relevant to credibility and require no special treatment [within the Federal Rules]." This type of impeachment is examined in § 12.4 to § 12.6 and § 12.10 to § 12.11.
2. Impeach the *testimony*, by showing that the witness has a *bias* for or against one of the litigants, or has some other motive (consciously or subconsciously) to shade his/her testimony to favor one side over the other. No specific rule governs such impeachment; as the Advisory Committee Note to Rule 601 observes, "[i]nterest in the outcome of the litigation [is] of course highly relevant to credibility and require[s] no special treatment" within the Federal Rules. See § 12.7 to § 12.9.
3. Impeach the *testimony*, by offering extrinsic evidence that *contradicts* testimony that the witness has given at the trial. See § 12.10 to § 12.11.
4. Impeach the *testimony*, by showing that on a *prior* occasion the witness made one or more statements that are *inconsistent* with the testimony the witness has given at trial. Such impeachment is governed by FRE 613 & 801(d)(1)(A), although use of prior statements may involve several other rules as well, including FRE 106, 612, 801(d)(1)(B), and 803(5). See § 12.12 to § 12.14.

ii. Impeaching W's character for truthfulness

Here, the impeaching attorney is not directly challenging W's testimony; rather, the effort is to show that W has lied often in the past, or is considered an untruthful person by others, or both—and that therefore the factfinder (jury or judge) should not believe W's testimony on that ground.

Impeaching W's *character for truthfulness* is regulated by FRE 608 & 609.[13] Rule 608(a) allows an attorney to offer reputation or opinion evidence that a witness has a poor character for truthfulness. Rules 608(b) and 609 permit the impeaching attorney to offer evidence—or at least ask W questions that suggest—that W lied on other, unrelated occasions, or has been convicted of certain types of crimes, to support the inference that W's testimony in this trial is not worthy of belief. This type of impeachment covered in Chapter 13.

iii. They are not treated equally

Because the purpose of impeachment is to assist the factfinder in evaluating a witness's testimony, impeachment that focuses directly on the testimony is more relevant than evidence that attacks W's character for truthfulness. Impeachment that falls into any of the subcategories of impeaching *testimony* is therefore considered more relevant and less subject to abuse than impeachment that focuses primarily upon the character of the witness. Moreover, attacks on a witness's character are almost always unpleasant, often embarrassing and sometimes quite nasty.

For these reasons, the law governing impeaching a witness's *testimony* is quite permissive; by contrast, impeachment of a witness's *character* is carefully restricted.

iv. Impeachment across the categories

Impeaching evidence often "fits" into more than one of the categories listed above. If an attorney offers evidence that W is a drug addict—on the theory that drug addicts cannot be trusted to tell the truth—this constitutes an attack on the witness' character (which would not be permitted, as you will see in Chapter 13, because it fails to satisfy Rules 608 or 609). On the other hand, evidence that W was high on drugs when W perceived the event in question, or is high on drugs while W is testifying, would be admitted. Even though such evidence is to some extent an attack on the witness' character and therefore is apparently subject to the restrictive provisions of FRE 608–609, it has a much more compelling relevancy because it also

---

13. FRE 404(a), you may recall, directs that evidence of a person's character, or of a trait of his character, is not admissible as evidence that he acted in conformity therewith on the occasion in question, subject to certain exceptions. Rule 404(a)(2) lists three exceptions that apply only in criminal cases. Rule 404(a)(3), however, is not limited to criminal cases; it applies to the character of a <u>witness</u>—any witness in any case (civil as well as criminal). But FRE 404(a)(3) does not articulate any substantive rule; rather, it basically says, "See FRE 607–609." FRE 607 provides that a party may impeach his or her own witness on direct or redirect. FRE 608 and 609 regulate how an attorney may attempt to impeach a witness's character for truthfulness.

impeaches W's ability to perceive, remember or accurately communicate the events or situations that W testified about. Evidence that is relevant to impeach perception, memory, communication, or sincerity (bias) therefore need *not* satisfy Rules 608–609.

§ 11.14 Impeachment and rehabilitation: when and how

An attorney's first opportunity to impeach witness W1 is while W1 is testifying, during cross-examination or, if a party is impeaching its own witness, on direct or redirect examination. The impeaching attorney may ask questions designed to challenge W1's perception, memory, communication; to reveal potential bias; to expose prior inconsistent statements; to attack W1's character for truthfulness; or all of the above. Various rules govern what may be asked about and how questions must be worded.

After W1's testimony is complete, an attorney can also call a different witness (W2) to impeach W1's testimony, or to impeach W1's character for truthfulness, or both. Once W1's testimony or character for truthfulness have been attacked, the other side may rehabilitate or bolster W1's testimony in a variety of ways, depending on the nature of the impeachment. Impeaching and rehabilitating testimony is covered in Chapter 12; impeaching and rehabilitating a witness's character for truthfulness is covered in Chapter 13.

§ 11.15 "Good-faith basis": what is it, when is it required

An attorney cross-examining W should not ask certain types of questions unless the attorney has a good-faith basis for the question. We first addressed the "good-faith basis" issue in § 6.16, with regard to cross-examining a character witness per FRE 405(a)(2nd sentence). Here we address it with regard to cross-examination generally.

The basic rule is this: An attorney must have a good-faith basis to ask an accusatorily-worded question or a non-accusatory question which asserts a fact, but does not require a good-faith basis to ask a neutrally-worded question seeking information.

<u>Question 1.</u>

In lawsuit Penguin v. Dolphin, Dolphin calls DW1, who testifies that he and Penguin were among ten people who attended a June 1st dinner party held in a local restaurant, and that he heard Penguin make a statement that is extremely helpful to Dolphin's case.[14] Penguin's attorney now cross-examines DW1. Which of these questions require a good-faith basis; which do not?

---

14. If you have covered hearsay already, you know that, when offered by Dolphin against Penguin, DW1's testimony about Penguin's statement is admissible over a hearsay objection per FRE

a. Did you consume any alcohol before or after dinner that evening? [Assuming the witness answers "Yes":] When, what kind, and how much?

b. You drank quite a few alcoholic beverages before and during dinner that night—that's a fact, isn't it?

c. Who was sitting near you at the table that night, and what did you talk about with them?

d. A very attractive young woman was sitting to your right—correct?

e. And you were paying much more attention to her than to what people were saying at the other end of the table, isn't that a fact?

Answer:

Questions a and c do not require a good-faith basis, because each is neutrally worded—neither question asserts a fact in the form of a question.

Questions b, d and e do require a good-faith basis, because each contains an assertion.

A good-faith basis for a factual assertion in a question can arise in a variety of circumstances. As a general rule, a good-faith basis exists if the attorney has received information (whether directly or indirectly) that someone who claimed first-hand knowledge asserted that fact. This might arise in several different ways.

(1) If one witness testifies at trial to certain facts, that testimony gives an attorney a good-faith basis to assert that fact in a question. Suppose, for example, that earlier in the trial, Z testified that the room was so crowded and noisy that unless you were within maybe one or two feet of a person, it was often impossible to make out what they were saying. This gives the attorney a good-faith basis to ask W, "It was incredibly noisy in the room that night, wasn't it? Wasn't it very difficult to hear what someone saying unless you were quite close to that person?"

(2) But a good-faith basis can come from information that was not admitted at the trial and could not be admitted. Suppose, for example, when Dolphin's attorney's investigator (D-Inv) interviewed people who had attended the party, one of the guests (G1) told D-Inv, "I was sitting several feet away from W, so I can't tell you much myself about him, but G2 was sitting on his left and he told me after the party that W was pretty sloshed and spent the entire dinner chatting up an attractive woman sitting to his right." Even if D-Inv was unable to interview G2 (or the woman), G1's statement to D-Inv gives the attorney a good-faith basis to ask questions a, c and d.[15]

801(d)(2)(A). See generally *A Student's Guide to Hearsay* §§ 5.1 to 5.11.

15. If G2 testified at the trial, he could describe what he noticed about W's behavior at the dinner party. But if G2 does not testify, neither G1 nor D-Inv would be allowed to testify at trial as to what G2 allegedly told G1, because G2's statement to G1 would be hearsay and what G1 told D-Inv

If challenged by the other attorney to show a good-faith basis for these questions, the attorney can tell the judge about D-Inv's report. But as a general rule, in questioning W in the jury's presence, the impeaching attorney cannot refer specifically or generally to D-Inv, G1 or G2. Thus, Dolphin's attorney cannot ask a question such as, "According to G2, who was a guest at the party, you were paying all your attention to the attractive woman sitting on your right. That's true, isn't it?"

(3) A good-faith basis can also come from something the attorney read—a letter, an email, a blog post, a Facebook entry, a newspaper article, etc., as long as it is plausible to believe that the person who wrote the item either had first-hand knowledge of the fact (such as G2) or learned the fact from someone who did (such as G1).

(4) An attorney can also have a good-faith basis to assert an alleged fact in a question which is supported circumstantially by other facts. Suppose D is on trial for burglary: he is accused of breaking into a bar late at night and stealing its cash register. Later that morning, police interviewed G, who told them that earlier that morning, he saw a man a few miles from the bar, parked at the side of a road, trying to break open a cash register. Two days later, police showed G a photo of D, and G identified D as the man he saw. At trial, G testifies about seeing the man and identifies D as the man.

At the time G told the police about seeing the man, G himself was on probation after being convicted of a burglary.[16] On cross-examination, D's attorney asks:

Q1 You were on probation from a burglary conviction when the police questioned you: correct?

A Yes.

Q2 I'll bet that made you pretty nervous, didn't it?

A Not particularly.

Q3 Really? Weren't you afraid they would suspect you of being the burglar—being on probation already for burglary?

A Why should I be? It wasn't me that broke into the bar.

Q4 And isn't it also true that when they showed you D's picture, you said that D was the man you saw, so the police would focus on him and not investigate you any further?

A No, D was the guy I saw![17]

---

would be double hearsay, and does not appear to satisfy any hearsay objection. See generally *A Student's Guide to Hearsay* (5th ed. 2019).

16. This hypothetical is based on *Alaska v. Davis*, discussed in § 12.8.

17. Tactically, it might be wise to stop at Q3, or even Q2. Those questions, and G's answers, are enough to give D's attorney the basis to argue during summation that G made a hasty identification of D's photo as a way of deflecting suspicion from himself. Asking Q4 just gives G the opportunity to deny the inference that D's attorney wants to create.

Each of these questions asserts a fact; most of the questions are at least somewhat accusatory. The only actual, proven fact in the entire sequence is the first—that G was on probation from a burglary conviction when he gave information to the police. G has denied each assertion after the first. Yet the attorney has a good-faith basis for the entire line of questioning, because each question after the first one can logically be inferred from the fact that, when questioned about the bar burglary, G himself was on probation from a prior burglary conviction.

Given G's answers to these questions, you might think: the attorney has accomplished nothing, because G denied all of the accusations explicit in the questions. But these questions may have raised doubts in jurors' minds despite G's answers. And in closing argument, D's attorney can still use his theory—that G was eager to tell the police what they wanted to hear, to deflect suspicion from himself—in urging the jury not to rely on G's identification of D prior to and at trial. Moreover, while G was answering these questions, jurors were watching and listening. G's facial expressions, body language and tone of voice during this cross-examination are likely to influence whether the jury believes G's testimony.

§ 11.16 "Intrinsic" and "extrinsic" wording; "intrinsic" and "extrinsic" impeachment

A full understanding of the rules governing impeachment requires an understanding of the differences between "intrinsically" and "extrinsically" worded questions, and between "intrinsic" and "extrinsic" impeachment.

Recall from § 6.19 that a question is worded *intrinsically* if it asks the witness, in essence, "Is this a fact," or "did you do [see, hear] this," without explicitly invoking an outside source of information in the question. A question is worded *extrinsically* if it does explicitly invoke or name an outside source of information.

Asking *intrinsically worded questions*, which is often referred to as "*intrinsic impeachment* of a witness," is generally permissible, assuming the subject-matter of the question is not objectionable.

Extrinsically worded questions generally are not permissible, unless the question satisfies a specialized rule—e.g., cross-examining a character witness per FRE 405(a)(2), see § 6.20 & § 6.21, supra; or cross-examining a witness about a prior inconsistent statement per FRE 613(a) or FRE 801(d)(1)(A), see § 12.13 & § 12:14.

Extrinsic impeaching evidence. Extrinsic impeachment occurs when an attorney produces a source of evidence other than W1 to introduce the impeaching information. The impeaching attorney can do this in either of two ways. (1) The attorney calls another witness (W2) to impeach W1's testimony, see Chapter 12; or who impeaches W1's character for truthfulness per FRE 608(a), see § 13.30 & § 13.31. (2) The attorney introduces evidence—e.g., a document or a voice or video recording—that impeaches W1's testimony (Chapter 12), or impeaches W1's character for truthfulness by introducing documentary proof, per FRE 609, that W1 has been convicted of a crime, see § 13.10 et seq.

The law governing the admissibility of extrinsic impeachment varies depending on what is to be impeached. (Sometimes extrinsic impeaching evidence is not permitted, period. We saw examples of this in § 6.22 with regard to FRE 405(a)(2); we will see it again in § 13.3 regarding FRE 608(b).)

§ 11.17 Questions

These questions are designed to illustrate (a) when an attorney needs a good-faith basis to ask a question; (b) the differences between intrinsically and extrinsically worded questions; and (c) what constitutes extrinsic impeachment.[18]

Question 1.

A 2 p.m. on May 1, cars driven by Dodge and Plymouth collided in an intersection. In the resultant lawsuit, Plymouth calls PW1, who testifies, "I saw Dodge run a red light just before Plymouth and Dodge collided." Cross-examining PW1, Dodge's attorney asks:

Q1 Were you wearing your eyeglasses when you saw the collision?

Is this question worded intrinsically, or extrinsically?

Answer:

It is intrinsically worded, because no source of information other than (extrinsic to) the witness is mentioned or referred to.

Question 2.

Does Dodge's attorney need a good-faith basis to ask this question?

Answer:

No. It does not accuse PW1 of wrongdoing and asserts no fact; it merely asks, in neutral language, whether or not PW1 was wearing PW1's eyeglasses at the time.

Question 3.

Suppose instead the attorney had asked:

Q3 "You weren't wearing your glasses when the cars collided, were you?"

(a) Is this worded intrinsically or extrinsically? (b) Would Dodge's attorney need a good-faith basis to ask it?

---

18. The last four footnotes in this section refer to the rules and principles governing specific types of impeachment, and whether the impeachment in each question is permissible or not. If you are reading this section for the first time, it's probably best to ignore those footnotes until you have read and digested Chapters 12 and 13.

Answer:

(a) It is worded intrinsically, because it does not explicitly invoke or name any source of information.

(b) It does require a good-faith basis, because the question asserts a fact—that PW1 was not wearing eyeglasses when he/she saw the collision. An attorney is permitted to ask about a fact (Q1) without a good-faith basis, but needs a good-faith basis to assert a fact in the form of a question.

Question 4.

Suppose PW1 answers Q1 by saying, "Yes, I was wearing my glasses when I saw the collision." Cross-examination continues:

Q4 Well, suppose I told you that DW1 [who has not yet testified, but who had described what he saw to D-Inv, Dodge's attorney's investigator] says you weren't wearing your glasses when the collision occurred. What would you say to that?

Is this question worded intrinsically or extrinsically?

Answer:

This question is worded extrinsically, because it explicitly invokes or mentions a source of information (DW1) other than PW1, the witness who is now testifying. In essence, therefore, Dodge's attorney is offering multiple hearsay[19] in evidence in violation of the rule against hearsay.

Question 5.

Prior to trial, DW2 told D-Inv, "I had lunch with PW1 that day–I'm pretty sure it was May 1, although it could have been on the second—no, I'm pretty sure it was May first. Anyhow, we met at Café Jabberwock. I remember that at lunch PW1 had trouble reading the menu and I had to point him toward the men's room because he couldn't read the sign across the room. I wondered why he wasn't wearing his glasses, but I felt awkward about asking him why, so I didn't ask. Anyway, we left the restaurant at about 5 minutes to two; I headed downtown and he headed uptown."

How, if at all, can Dodge's lawyer use this information to question PW1?

Answer:

Dodge's lawyer can ask:

Q5 It's true, isn't it, that you had lunch on May 1st until just before two p.m. at Café Jabberwock, and you weren't wearing your glasses at lunch, either?"

---

19. It is multiple hearsay: DW1 told someone (let's assume DW1 told it to D-Inv, the defense attorney's investigator), who told it to D's attorney, who is now telling the jury about it in the form of a question to PW1. (This is as good a place as any to remind you that I have also written *A Student's Guide to Hearsay* (5th ed. 2019).)

This question is entirely proper.

(a) The question contains an assertion, but DW2's statement to D-Inv gives Dodge's attorney a good-faith basis to assert that fact in a question. True, DW2 wasn't certain whether the lunch was on May 1st (the date of the accident) or May 2nd, but a good-faith basis can exist without absolute certainty that the alleged fact is indeed true.

(b) The question is worded intrinsically, because it asks PW1 whether a certain assertion is true without specifying who provided the underlying information. The jury might assume that someone must have provided Dodge's attorney with the information on which the question is based, and indeed, we know that the attorney's source is DW2, but the question is intrinsically worded because Dodge's attorney did not explicitly name DW2 as the extrinsic source of the information.

Question 6.

After Plymouth rests and it is Dodge's turn to call witnesses, Dodge's attorney calls DW1 to testify. After eliciting testimony that DW1 heard (but did not see) the collision and its immediate aftermath, the attorney asks:

Q6a What did you do when you heard the collision?

A I turned around to see what had happened and saw the two cars crunched together.

Q6b Did you see anyone else in the immediate vicinity?

A Yes, I saw PW1.

Q6c Did you notice whether PW1 did anything immediately after the collision?

A Yes. He reached into his pocket and put on a pair of glasses.

Q6d He was not wearing glasses until after collision?

A That's right.

(a) Are these questions worded intrinsically or extrinsically? (b) Is this intrinsic impeachment, or extrinsic impeachment?

Answer:

(a) These questions are worded intrinsically, because the only source of information is DW1, who is now testifying.

(b) DW1's testimony constitutes extrinsic impeachment of PW1's testimony (see Q4) that he (PW1) was wearing his glasses when he saw the collision.[20]

20. As you will see in § 12:10 & § 12:11, DW1's testimony is proper. Extrinsic impeachment that relates to a witness' perception memory, narration or bias is permissible, subject to judicial

Question 7.

Let's backtrack: for this question, we are still in Plymouth's case-in-chief, and Dodge's attorney is still cross-examining PW1. Dodge's attorney asks:

Q7. The day after the collision, didn't you tell DW3 that you were not wearing your glasses when the cars collided?

(a) Is this question worded intrinsically, or extrinsically?

Answer:

This question, like Q4, is worded extrinsically, because it explicitly invokes a source of information (DW3) other than the witness (PW1) who is being cross-examined.[21]

Question 8.

Suppose PW1 denies telling DW3 that he was not wearing his classes when the two cars collided. After Plymouth rests, Dodge calls DW3, and asks:

Q The day after the collision, did you have a conversation with PW1 about the collision?

A Yes.

Q What did PW1 tell you?

A He told me he was not wearing his glasses when he saw the collision; he only put them on afterward, when he walked over to see if anyone was hurt.

(a) Are these questions worded intrinsically, or extrinsically? (b) Does this constitute intrinsic or extrinsic impeachment of W1?

Answer:

(a) These questions are extrinsically worded, because they explicitly invoke a source of information (PW1) other than DW3, the witness now testifying.

(b) DW3's testimony constitutes extrinsic impeachment of PW1's testimony.[22]

---

discretion if the relevance of the impeaching evidence (or the testimony being impeached) is marginal, and subject also to the discretion afforded the trial judge by Rule 403 and 611(a)(3). And unlike Q4, there is no hearsay involved here: DW1 is on the witness stand testifying about what he saw, and Plymouth's attorney will have an opportunity to cross-examine—and attempt to impeach—DW1. But don't worry about that now. In fact, for now, ignore this footnote.

21. But it is a proper question, assuming there is a good-faith basis for it (see § 11.15, *supra*), because Rule 613(b)—which we have not covered yet—permits this particular kind of extrinsically worded question regarding a statement PW1 allegedly made that is inconsistent with the testimony PW1 has just given at trial. We will cover Rule 613 and related rules in § 12.13 & § 12.14. (For now, ignore this footnote, too.)

22. But this is proper, as you will see in § 12:13, *infra*, because Rule 613(b) (which we have not yet covered) allows this kind of extrinsic impeachment.

§ 11.18 Asking a witness to compare her testimony to another witness's

Here's a cross-examination issue that arises with some frequency. Let's say in a criminal case, prosecution witness PW1 testified that she saw defendant near the scene of the crime near the time of the crime. After the prosecutor rests, the defendant testifies on direct that he was not where PW1 claims he was. On cross, the prosecutor asks, "In other words, you are saying that PW1 was lying when she testified two days ago?" The overwhelming majority of courts hold that this is *improper* cross-examination. A witness should not be required to characterize the testimony of another witness as lying, first, because it seeks to usurp the jury's role as sole determiner of witness credibility, and second, because it is misleading: the disparity between PW1's testimony and D's could be an honest mistake, not a lie.

Suppose, instead, the prosecutor asks: "In other words, you are saying that PW1's testimony is incorrect; that she was mistaken when she said he saw you there that night?" Many courts consider this a perfectly acceptable question. Asking a witness whether a previous witness who gave conflicting testimony is "mistaken" highlights the objective conflict without requiring the witness to accuse the prior witness of lying.

§ 11.19 Bolstering a witness's testimony; rehabilitation

Often the outcome of litigation will depend upon which party's witnesses the jury accepts as the more credible. Naturally, therefore, a litigant might, if permitted, offer evidence that his or her key witnesses are keen-sighted individuals, blessed with photographic memories, without a biased bone in their bodies, who have always described the event in question consistent with their testimony at trial, and who are persons of sterling character. If such evidence were generally admitted, the only sure result is that litigation would take even longer than it now does. Hence, as a rule, a party is *not* permitted to offer evidence bolstering a witness's ability to perceive, remember or communicate accurately, nor to bolster the witness's character for truthfulness.

Once a particular aspect of a witness' testimony has been impeached, however, a litigant may, subject to the trial judge's discretion, offer evidence rebutting the impeachment. The categories of impeachment outlined in § 11.13 and discussed in Chapters 12 and 13 *infra* are important here, because a party should be permitted to rehabilitate a witness only on a "category-by-category" basis. In the *Plymouth v. Dodge* collision case, for example, if Dodge's attorney called DW1 to testify that PW1 was not wearing his glasses when the two cars collided (thereby impeaching PW1's ability to have perceived the event in question), during Plymouth's rebuttal case, Plymouth would be permitted to call PW2 to testify that PW1 *was* wearing his glasses when the cars collided, thereby rebutting the impeachment and rehabilitating the accuracy of PW1's testimony. DW3's testimony does *not*, on the other hand, entitle Plymouth to elicit testimony as to PW1's good character for truthfulness, because DW1's testimony did not impeach PW1's character for truthfulness.

D. Road Maps for FRE 404, 405, 406, 412–415, 608, and 609

1. In general

§ 11.20 Overview

In Chapters 4–10, we worked our way through FRE 404–406 and 412–415. When we add impeachment to the mix, things get a bit more complicated.

Chapter 12 covers impeaching witness W's testimony, which challenges W's perception, memory, narration, bias or motive to lie; and then covers rehabilitating W's testimony if it has been impeached (or to put it differently, rebutting the impeachment). This process is governed mostly by general relevance principles, i.e., by Rules 401–403. Only one aspect of impeaching testimony is covered by specific rules: the use of a prior statement by W which is inconsistent with the testimony W has given at trial. That process is governed by FRE 613 and FRE 801(d)(1)(A). Another rule, FRE 801(d)(1)(B), regulates the use of W's prior consistent statements to rehabilitate testimony that was impeached. Those rules are covered in depth in *A Student's Guide to Hearsay*, but will be summarized briefly at the end of Chapter 12.

Chapter 13 covers impeaching W's character for truthfulness, and rehabilitating W's character for truthfulness if it has been impeached.

Even though (with that one exception) there are no specific rules governing impeachment (and post-impeachment rehabilitation) of W's *testimony*, applying Rules 401–403 to that process has its complications. And FRE 608 and 609, which govern impeaching (and subsequent rehabilitation) of W's character for truthfulness, actually contain seven separate provisions, each of which contain technical requirements and raise tactical issues. The evidence regulated by Rules 608 and 609 in many ways resembles what we already covered regarding Rules 404–406 and 412–415. And sometimes, of course, an offer of evidence will implicate rules in both Article IV and Article VI. And sometimes impeaching W's testimony also implicates Rules 404–406, 412–415, and 607–609.

As I said, things get a bit more complicated.

§ 11.21 The over-all context: review and explanation

Your first challenge, in working through the maze of rules and issues covered in Chapters 4 through 13, is to figure out what rules you can eliminate, and which ones you have to consider.

§ 11.22 divides all of these rules (and non-ruled aspects of impeachment) into two categories—character (reputation and opinion) testimony and evidence of "other acts." You've seen shorter versions of this list in prior chapters, but the list in § 11.22 is comprehensive. It includes all of the rules we have covered and will cover regarding character, extrinsic acts, habit and impeachment. Once again, rules in the left-hand column deal with character evidence—i.e., reputation or opinion testimony about a person's character or a trait of his character. Rules in the right column deal with questions about or evidence of extrinsic acts.

But remember that when deciding what rules are worth discussing, there is an important step to take *before* looking at the chart. First, you have to analyze the facts and the substantive (i.e., non-evidence law) issues of a case or question. Your analysis has to include:

1. <u>What are the elements</u> of the crime, cause of action and/or defense in the case being tried? Although some cases or problems or exam questions present issues involving evidence law without regard to the underlying legal issues, in most cases, you will not be able to figure out what rule to apply in resolving an evidence issue until you understand the factual and legal issues at stake in the lawsuit. When reading a court opinion, find the passage(s) in which the court spells out the black-letter law and/or the factual issues that underlie the lawsuit.

Regarding the law, in a criminal case, the court will either quote or summarize the statute defining the crime and relevant case law applying that statute; or the court will do so regarding the defense; or (depending on the issues the court is deciding), the law defining both the crime and the defense. In a civil case, the court may quote or cite a statute, a Restatement provision or caselaw which spells out the elements of the claim or defense. (I am not referring here to principles of evidence law. We'll get to that shortly.) In a casebook problem or quiz or exam question, the stem of the question will usually provide the information you need.[23] To repeat: often you cannot successfully apply evidence law until you know the substantive-law issues before the court.

2. <u>Who is the evidence about?</u> A litigant offers evidence about "X" that arguably does not relate directly to the events at issue in the case. Make sure you know what

23. I say "generally will provide" because there are exceptions. For example, in formulating a question, your professor may assume that an upper-class law student knows the elements of a negligence claim or a breach of contract claim. And on the MBE, a question may test your knowledge of both substantive law and evidence law.

X's role is in the lawsuit. Usually X is the defendant, or the victim or alleged victim, or the plaintiff, or a witness.[24] Often X plays more than one role in the case: when a defendant, victim, complainant or plaintiff testifies, we have to apply (or consider applying) several different sets of rules, to determine the admissibility of the evidence (or the propriety of a question put to a witness). Identifying who the evidence is about—and what role or roles that person plays in the trial—are essential in figuring out which rule or group of rules to apply.

3. Why is the offering party seeking to ask that question or elicit that testimony or introduce that evidence? In other words, what is the offering party's theory of relevance? To figure that out, you have to be able to identify what I call the "litigation situation" that exists during the trial when the question is asked or the testimony or other evidence is offered. Litigation situations are spelled out in §§ 11.23 to § 11.31.

24. Sometimes X is none of these—X may be an alleged coconspirator, for example, or a hearsay declarant, or anyone else whose conduct or character is relevant to the case.

§ 11.22 Rules 404–406, 412–415, 608–609 & impeachment generally: your master list

Here is the master chart containing every provision about character, extrinsic acts, habit, and impeachment that we have already covered or will cover in Chapters 5–13.

Reputation or opinion testimony	Evidence or questions about specific acts
404(a)(unwritten sent.), CEE 404(a)(1) general prohibition 404(a)(2)(A) (about D) 404(a)(2)(B) (by D about V/AV) 404(a)(2)(B)(i) (by P about V/AV) 404(a)(2)(B)(ii) (by P about D)	401–403 (PMNB) 404(b) (about anyone) 405(a)(2nd sentence) (XX CW re D, or XX CW re V/AV) 405(b), CEE
405(a)(1) (re D or V/AV)	406 (about anyone)
406 (about anyone)	412(a)(1) (about V/AV in sex off. case) 412(b)(1)(A) (re V/AV in sex off. case) 412(b)(1)(B) (re V/AV in sex off. case) 412(b)(1)(C) (re V/AV in sex off. case) 413–415 (about D in sex off. case)
412(a)(2) (about V/AV in sex off. case)	607 (any party can impeach W's testimony or character for truthfulness)
607 (a party can call W1 and then call W2 to impeach W1's char.tru per 608(a))	608(b)(1) (impeach W's char.untru) 608(b)(2) (rehab W's char.tru)
608(a) (about a prior W at the trial): * 608(a)(1) to attack W1's char.untru.; or * 608(a)(2), to defend W1's char.tru., but only if W1's char.tru. was first attacked via FRE 608(a), 608(b), or 609.	609 (impeach W's char.untru) 613, 801(d)(1)(A) (PIS) 801(d)(1)(B) (PCS to rebut 613, 801(d)(1)(A) or PMNB impeachment)

Abbreviations:

CEE	Character as an essential element of a crime, cause of action or defense.
Char.tru	Character for truthfulness
Char.untru	Character for untruthfulness
CW	character witness
D	Defendant
PCS	prior consistent statement
PIS	prior inconsistent statement
PMNB	perception, memory, narration, bias/motive-to-lie
V	Victim
V/AV	Victim or alleged victim
Sex off.	Sexual offense
W	Witness
XX	Cross-examination

2. Litigation situations

§ 11.23 Litigation situations: what they are and how to use them

The chart in § 11.22 is useful to help narrow the list of rules that you might be called upon to apply in analyzing a case or answering a problem or question, but even after you have eliminated the rules in one of the columns, you are still left with a dozen or more rules to consider. Whether a given rule applies depends on the kind of case being tried, who the evidence is about, and why it is being offered.

I have broken down what happens during a trial into the following eight "litigation situations," listed in the order in which I have covered them so far and in which I will cover them in Chapters 12 and 13. Each of the next eight sections of this chapter describes the litigation situation and lists the rules which can (or cannot) apply to each.

Here is the list:

Litigation situation A: civil litigation: character as essential element. § 11.24.

Litigation situation B: civil litigation generally. § 11.25.

Litigation situation C: criminal defendant's case-in-chief. § 11.26.

Litigation situation D: cross-examining a character witness. § 11.27.

Litigation situation E: prosecutor's case-in-chief. § 11.28.

Litigation situation F: any case, any witness, any party: cross-examining W about him/herself (or direct-examining W about him/herself, to "reduce the sting"). § 11.29.

Litigation situation G: prosecutor's rebuttal case. § 11.30.

Litigation situation H: any case, any party, any witness: calling W2 to testify about W1. § 11.31.

In using this list and the following eight sections, keep the following in mind.

1. As always, rules governing reputation and opinion testimony are in the left column; rules governing specific act evidence (or questions about someone's specific, extrinsic acts) are in the right column. Once you have identified a litigation situation that fits your case or problem, you can automatically eliminate the rules in either the left or right column, depending on the form of evidence the case or problem entails.
2. An offer of evidence may involve more than one litigation situation. After you have found one litigation situation that fits the case or problem, continue through the rest of the litigation situations to see if the case fits any of the

others as well. Evidence that would be admitted by a rule in one litigation situation may be excluded by a rule listed under another applicable litigation situation, and vice versa.

3. If a rule listed under a litigation situation has a ~~line through it,~~ that means an attorney cannot use that rule to admit the evidence or ask a question about it. (Keep in mind, though, that the same evidence or question may be proper under a different rule.)
4. But the converse is not true. The absence of a line through a rule number does not mean that the evidence is necessarily admissible under that rule. It means you have to consider whether the evidence in fact satisfies that rule. For example, you will see Rule 404(b) listed in the right column under several of the litigation situations. That means you have to analyze (a) whether the evidence being offered is intrinsic or extrinsic to the key facts and issues in the case, and, if extrinsic, (b) decide whether the evidence is excluded per Rule 404(b)(1) because its relevance relies primarily or exclusively on the propensity ("bad-person" or "good-person") inference, or whether the evidence has fasprelipi. Similarly, if Rule 609 (covered in Chapter 13) is listed, you have to analyze several issues in deciding whether the evidence satisfies that rule. And so on.

A few other comments may be appropriate.

First: why do I put these litigation situation charts in between coverage of the Article IV rules and the coverage of impeachment? Wouldn't it be more logical to put them at the very beginning or the very end? Answer: More logical, yes; but based on 40+ years of teaching this material, I think this placement is more useful to students. It seems to work better to first tackle rules 404–406 and 412–413—which, heaven knows, are complex and challenging enough—without mixing in references to the law governing impeachment in general. But once students have a grounding in the Article IV rules we have studied, it becomes useful to give you a larger structure to see how the rules we have already covered fit with the rules we will cover in the next two chapters.

In other words, litigation situations A through E review what we've already covered. Litigation situations F through H preview what we will cover in Chapters 12 and 13. (Sections in Chapters 12 and 13 include cross-references to the appropriate litigation situations, so you can preview the appropriate litigation situation chart(s) before reading a particular section of Chapters 12 or 13, and review the chart afterward.)

Second, there is always the risk of "paralysis by analysis": some students might conclude that I've given you so many charts and lists and ways to organize these rules that you are getting lost in them. I hope not, but if so, just ignore all references to litigation situations in this book for the time being. At some point it will be useful to you to integrate all this material, but do so in whatever manner and sequence works best for you.

§ 11.24 Litigation situation A: civil litigation: character as essential element

As Chapter 5 makes clear, an aspect of a person's character is an "essential element" (CEE) in only a few kinds of civil litigation: child custody, negligent entrustment, and (some) defamation cases, and regarding the damages in wrongful death and personal injury actions.[25] In such cases, these are the rules:

Character (reputation and opinion testimony)	Evidence or questions relating to specific acts
404(a)(1), 405(a)(1)	404(b) does not apply here; see 405(b)
406	405(a)(2nd sentence) 405(b)
	406

§ 11.25 Litigation situation B: civil litigation generally

The general rule is that unless someone's character is an essential element of a claim or defense, a civil litigant is not permitted to offer reputation or opinion evidence in a civil case as a basis to infer how a person behaved on a particular occasion. Nor may a party offer evidence of a person's unrelated specific conduct, in order to show he or she had a propensity to act that way and therefore did act that way on the occasion in question. But evidence of that person's specific acts may be admissible where those acts have factually specific relevance independent of the propensity inference ("fasprelipi"). A civil litigant can also offer evidence of that person's habit, per FRE 406.

Character (reputation and opinion testimony)	Evidence or questions relating to specific acts
404(a), 405(a)(1st sentence) forbid such evidence to support a propensity inference	404(b)(1) forbids such evidence to support a propensity inference
406	404(b)(2) admits evidence with fasprelipi
	406

25. There may be others, but these are the main CEE categories.

§ 11.26 Litigation situation C: criminal defendant's case-in-chief

As set out in Chapter 6, a criminal defendant is permitted to offer reputation or opinion testimony about (a) his or her own character, or (b) the victim or alleged victim's behavior, or (c) both. The left column lists the rules that govern the admissibility of such evidence.

With regard to evidence offered during the defense case-in-chief about a person's specific acts, Rules 404(b)(1) and 404(b)(2) apply the same way they do in any other litigation situation. In sexual assault cases, Rule 412(b)(1) applies where a defendant offers specific act evidence about the victim or alleged victim.

Character (reputation and opinion testimony)	Evidence or questions relating to specific acts
404(a)(2)(A): D calls CW about D	404(b)(1) forbids such evidence to support a propensity inference
404(a)(2)(B): D calls CW about V/AV	404(b)(2): D can offer such evidence with fasprelipi about himself, a gov't witness, or another person
405(a)(1) governs forms of permissible rep. or op. testimony	412(b)(1): re V/AV in sex-offense cases
412(a)(2): neither party can offer rep. or op. testimony about V/AV in sex offense prosecution	

Abbreviations:

Fasprelipi	Factually specific relevance independent of the propensity inference
CW	Character witness
Rep. or op.	Reputation or opinion
V/AV	Victim or alleged victim

This litigation situation chart does not include defense fact witnesses, i.e., witnesses who testify to the actual events in a case. For example, it does not include a witness who might provide the defendant with an alibi, or who contradicts the prosecutor's witnesses as to whether the defendant engaged in the conduct that constituted the crime, or who might support a defendant's self-defense claim or testify favorably about a defendant's state of mind. This chart focuses only on a defendant's use of reputation or opinion testimony about him/herself, or about the alleged victim, and reminds you that defendants, as well as prosecutors, can offer evidence which satisfies FRE 404(b)(2) and its equivalent in sex-offense cases, FRE 412(b)(1).

Usually, of course, when a defendant calls a witness, it is with the expectation that the witness will give favorable testimony—such as favorable character evidence. Other situations may arise. For example, a defendant may call a police officer during the defense case-in-chief and proceed to cross-examine him in an effort to bring out favorable information, and, in the process, attempt to impeach the officer's answers, in which case litigation situation F is the one to consult.

§ 11.27 Litigation situation D: cross-examining a character witness

This situation arises only in (a) a criminal case where the defense has called a character witness to give favorable reputation or opinion testimony about him/herself (litigation situation C); or (b) a criminal case where the defense has called a character witness to give negative reputation or opinion testimony about the victim or alleged victim (also litigation situation C); or (c) in a civil case where X's character is an essential element of a claim or defense (litigation situation A).

Character (reputation and opinion testimony)	Evidence or questions relating to specific acts
	405(a)(2nd sentence) about D (extrinsic wording ok) 405(a)(2nd sentence) about V/AV (extrinsic wording ok)

Abbreviations:
V/AV — Victim or alleged victim

Rule 405(a) permits cross-examination of a character witness, regarding the person about whom the witness has testified. See § 6.14 to § 6.24.

§ 11.28 Litigation situation E: prosecutor's case-in-chief

Character (reputation and opinion testimony)	Evidence or questions relating to specific acts
404(a)(2)(C), 405(a)(1) (only in homicide cases where D's opening statement alleges that the victim was the initial aggressor)	404(b) - frequently! 413–415 (sex offense cases)

Regarding Rules 404(a)(2)(C) and 405(a)(1), remember that the prosecutor is not permitted to open the door to evidence of either the defendant's character or the victim or alleged victim's character. § 6.13 sets out ways in which a defendant may open the door to the prosecutor's use of character evidence during the prosecution's case-in-chief.

§11.29 Litigation situation F: any case, any witness, any party: cross-examining W about him/herself (or direct-examining W about him/herself, to "reduce the sting")

Character (reputation and opinion testimony)	Evidence or questions relating to specific acts
	401–403 perception, memory, narration, bias
	613, 801(d)(1(A) (prior inconsistent Statements)
	801(d)(1)(B) (prior consistent statement, to rebut 613/801(d)(1)(A) or 401-PMNB impeachment)
	608(b) (intrinsic wording only?*)
	609 (use of word "convicted" ok)
	404(b)
	412(b) (by D about V/AV in sex offense cases)
	413–415 (about D in sex offense case)

Abbreviations:

PMNB	Perception, memory, narration, bias
V/AV	Victim or alleged victim

*Some courts permit extrinsic wording, others don't. See § 13.5.

The first group—Rules 401–403, 613, 801(d)(1)(A), 608(b), 609—are rules generally invoked in cross-examination. But a party may "impeach" its own witness, to reduce the sting. For example, in a criminal case, defense counsel calls the defendant (D) to testify, knowing that the judge will allow the prosecutor to use D's prior convictions to impeach D. Counsel therefore brings out the convictions during direct examination, in the hopes that doing so will "reduce the sting" of the impeachment. See § 13.24.

The second group—404(b), 412, 413–415—are rules usually invoked in a party's case-in-chief, but can also be invoked while cross-examining an opponent's witness, particularly if the witness's testimony on direct opened the door to evidence that otherwise would have been inadmissible.

§ 11.30 Litigation situation G: prosecutor's rebuttal case

Character (reputation and opinion testimony)	Evidence or questions relating to specific acts
If defendant has opened the door in litigation situation C: 404(a)(2)(A)(ii) 404(a)(2)(B)(i) 404(a)(2)(B)(ii) 404(a)(2)(C)	404(b) 413–415 (sex offense cases)
406	406

If the defense has called character witnesses, the prosecutor may do likewise in rebuttal; and sometimes the defense case will open the door to rebuttal evidence invoking Rule 404(b) or 413–415 that would not have been admissible during the prosecution's case-in-chief.

§ 11.31 Litigation situation H: any case, any party, any witness: calling W2 to testify about W1 (extrinsic impeachment and rehabilitation)

This section lists the rules that govern when a party calls W2 either to extrinsically impeach W1's testimony or to rehabilitate W1.

<u>Character (reputation and opinion testimony)</u>
406 (opinion only)
Bias
608(a)(1) (to attack W1's char.untru)
608(a)(2) (defend W1's char.tru if it has been attacked)

<u>Evidence or questions relating to specific acts—extrinsic evidence is admissible unless otherwise noted</u>
404(b)
406
608(a)(1)
608(a)(2)
608(b) (W2 cannot testify negatively about W1's alleged untruthful acts if the only relevance is to attack W1's Char.Tru.)
Evidence of bias—extrinsic evidence is admissible
Impeach or rehab W1's PMNB
<u>"Specific contradiction/impeachment" on collateral matters—see §12:11.</u>
613/801(d)(1)(A) (PIS)
801(d)(1)(B) (PCS to rebut impeachment)

<u>Abbreviations:</u>

Char.tru	character for truthfulness
Char.untru	character for untruthfulness
PCS	Prior consistent statement
PIS	Prior inconsistent statement
PMNB	Perception, memory, narration, bias/motive to lie

Chapter 12

Impeaching and Rehabilitating Testimony

A. Introduction

§ 12.1 Overview

Witness W's testimony is relevant only if the factfinder is satisfied that W accurately perceived, remembered, and communicated the events or situations about which W is testifying, and is also satisfied that W is sincerely attempting to testify accurately, rather than consciously or subconsciously shading the truth to favor one litigant over the other. See § 1.7. Therefore, any party adversely affected by that testimony—including the party that called W to testify[1]—has the right to attempt to impeach W, that is, to ask W questions and introduce evidence that casts doubt on whether the jury should accept W's testimony as accurate or true.

§ 12.2 Impeaching testimony: categories

W's testimony can be impeached in four different ways.

1. Impeach W's testimony by casting doubt on the accuracy of W's perception, memory, or narration. No specific rule governs such impeachment; as the Advisory Committee Note to Rule 601 observes, "matters bearing upon the perception, memory, and narration of witnesses" are "highly relevant to credibility [i.e., the accuracy of W's testimony] and require no special treatment [within the Federal Rules]."

2. Impeach W's testimony by showing that the witness has a bias for or against one of the litigants, or has some other motive (consciously or subconsciously) to shade his/her testimony to favor one side over the other. No specific rule governs such impeachment; as the Advisory Committee Note to FRE 601 observes, "[i]nterest in the outcome of the litigation [is] of course highly relevant to credibility and require[s] no special treatment" within the Federal Rules.

3. Impeach W's testimony, by showing that on a prior occasion, the witness made one or more statements that are inconsistent with the testimony the witness has given at trial. Such impeachment is governed by FRE 613 & FRE 801(d)(1)(A), although use of prior statements may involve several other rules as well, including FRE 106, FRE 612, FRE 801(d)(1)(B), and FRE 803(5).

4. Impeach W's testimony by offering extrinsic evidence that contradicts testimony that the witness has given at the trial.

These categories are not rigid, and the same evidence might impeach different aspects of W's testimony. But they are important, first, to help you analyze the relevance of questions that are asked or evidence that is offered to impeach W's testimo-

1. See FRE 607.

ny.[2] Second, the categories of impeachment also define what kind of rehabilitative evidence the other party can offer; as a rule, a party can rehabilitate only those aspects of W's testimony that have been impeached. For example, in lawsuit *P v. D*, evidence that W is biased against P—because of P's race or nationality or religion or sexual identity or educational level or financial status—can be rebutted by evidence suggesting that W is not biased in that way; but it does not open the door to testimony praising W's acute eyesight or keen memory.

§ 12.3 Impeaching testimony: when and how

An attorney's first opportunity to impeach W is while W is testifying, during cross-examination or, if a party is impeaching its own witness, on direct or redirect examination. The impeaching attorney may ask questions designed to challenge W's perception, memory, narration; to reveal W's potential bias; and to expose W's prior inconsistent statements.[3] After witness W1 has left the stand, an attorney has additional opportunities to impeach W1's testimony, for example by calling other witnesses who will testify negatively about W1's perception, memory, narration, or bias; to testify about W1's prior statements; or to contradict specific aspects of W1's testimony. In evaluating the purpose and admissibility of impeaching questions and evidence, it would be worthwhile to periodically review the material in § 11.14 to § 11.18.

B. Impeaching the Testimony: Perception, Memory, Narration

---

§ 12.4 Overview

Witness W has testified on direct as to things W did, saw and heard (and, less often, felt, smelled or tasted); and, perhaps, W's state of mind at particular times in the past. The probative value of W's testimony therefore depends (among other things) on how accurately W perceived these matters, how well W remembers them, and whether W's narration of them from the witness stand accurately communicates these matters to the jury. An attorney seeking to impeach W's testimony is entitled to ask W intrinsically worded questions that challenge these aspects of W's testimony, and—during cross-examination of W, or later in the trial—to introduce extrinsic evidence impeaching W's perception, memory and narration.

---

2. They are also useful to keep in mind as you prepare to cross-examine a witness in a law school exercise—or in a courtroom.

3. The impeaching attorney can also attack W's character for truthfulness. This is covered in Chapter 13.

The impeachment discussed in the next several sections arises in litigation situation F, § 11.29, and litigation situation H, § 11.31.

§ 12.5 Impeaching perception and memory

As to each of the following questions, consider:

a. What is the purpose for the question?

b. Is the question worded intrinsically, or extrinsically?

c. Is this intrinsic or extrinsic impeachment?

d. Does the question require a good-faith basis?

e. Is there any objection Charger can interpose, and if so, how should the trial judge rule on the objection?

Questions 1–5

Fury filed a personal injury action against Charger for damages arising out of a collision between their cars at an intersection on the evening of June 5. Fury's complaint alleges that Charger was driving while intoxicated and negligently drove through a red light, causing the collision. After Fury presents his case and rests, Charger calls CW1 for direct examination.

Q. What did you do on the evening of June 5, 2021?

A. I went to a dinner party at Smith's house.

Q. Did you go alone?

A. No, I went with Charger.

Q. After the party, did you leave alone or with Charger?

A. With Charger. He offered to drive me home.

Q. Was Charger intoxicated that night?

A. Not at all. He had, I think it was two glasses of wine all evening.

On cross-examination of CW1, Fury intends to ask the following series of questions.

Question 1.

Q. Did you drink any alcohol that evening?

a. What is the purpose for the question?

b. Is the question worded intrinsically, or extrinsically?

c. Is this intrinsic or extrinsic impeachment?

d. Does the question require a good-faith basis?

e. Is there any objection Charger can interpose, and if so, how should the trial judge rule on the objection?

Answer:

a. The purpose of the question is inquire whether CW1 drank any alcohol, because if so, that might have had a negative impact on CW1's ability to perceive and remember what happened at or after the party. And if Fury's attorney already has information that CW1 had drunk alcohol, she hopes to elicit that information from CW1.

b. It is worded intrinsically, because the question does not name or refer specifically to any outside source of information.

c. It is intrinsic impeachment—CW1 is the only source of information involved in the question.

d. It does not require a good-faith basis, because the question neither accuses CW1 of anything, nor asserts a fact in the form of a question.

e. The question is unobjectionable.

Question 2.

Cross-examination continues:

Q. Isn't it a fact that Charger had at least five martinis at the party on June 5?

a. What is the purpose for the question?

b. Is the question worded intrinsically, or extrinsically?

c. Is this intrinsic or extrinsic impeachment?

d. Does the question require a good-faith basis?

e. Is there any objection Charger can interpose, and if so, how should the trial judge rule on the objection?

Answer:

a. The purpose is to suggest that Charger was drunk when he drove from the party that night.

b. The question is worded intrinsically; it asserts no explicit outside source of information (even though the specificity of the question implies that Fury's attorney did have an outside source of information).

c. This is intrinsic impeachment—the only source of information explicitly invoked by the question is CW1.

d. The question asserts a fact (that Charger had 5 martinis); therefore, it requires a good-faith basis.

e. Charger can ask the judge (in a bench conference) to ask Fury's attorney if she has a good-faith basis for the question; otherwise, there is no legitimate basis to object.

Question 3.

Cross-examination of CW1 continues:

Q. What was served at the party?

A. Beef stroganoff.

a. What is the purpose for the question?

b. Is the question worded intrinsically, or extrinsically?

c. Is this intrinsic or extrinsic impeachment?

d. Does the question require a good-faith basis?

e. Is there any objection Charger can interpose, and if so, how should the trial judge rule on the objection?

Answer:

a. The purpose is to explore how much CW1 remembers about that evening besides the facts he testified to on direct.

b. This question is worded intrinsically.

c. This is intrinsic impeachment.

d. No good-faith basis is required, since the question does not contain any assertion of fact.

e. Charger could object that the question is irrelevant, but a judge should allow it, since it does test CW1's memory of the evening. If CW1 testifies that he did not remember what the main course was, that might cast doubt on the accuracy of what he claims he can remember. This Q&A consumes minuscule time, and there is no risk it will distract the jury from the important issues in the case.

Question 4.

Cross-examination of CW1 continues:

Q. Is it not a fact that at one point in your life you were confined in St. Elizabeth's Hospital for treatment of a manic-depressive disorder?

a. What is the purpose for the question?

b. Is the question worded intrinsically, or extrinsically?

c. Is this intrinsic or extrinsic impeachment?

d. Does the question require a good-faith basis?

e. Is there any objection Charger can interpose, and if so, how should the trial judge rule on the objection?

Answer:

a. The purpose of the question is to suggest CW1 lacks the mental capacity or competency to perceive, remember and accurately relate what happened at the party and afterward.

b. I think this is extrinsically worded, because it implicitly asserts that mental health experts came to the conclusion that CW1 needed to be "confined" in a hospital. (The equivalent intrinsically worded question would be along the lines of, "Did you commit yourself to the hospital for treatment?")

c. The question does not involve calling anyone else to testify, nor does it involve offering a document into evidence, so I'd classify it as intrinsic impeachment.

d. The question requires a good-faith basis because it contains an assertion of fact—i.e., that CW1 was "confined" for treatment.

e. The question is objectionable because of its dubious relevance. First, assuming CW1 was in fact confined for treatment, that is relevant only if Fury can produce acceptable expert authority that CW1's specific condition—manic-depressive disorder—has a negative impact on a person's ability to perceive, remember and describe the events in question. Second, even assuming Fury can produce such evidence, before ascertaining its relevance, we would have to know whether CW1's manic-depressive disorder was fairly recent. If it happened several years ago, without a recurrence, it tells very little about CW1's current capacity to perceive, remember and describe the events on the night of the party.

In the real world, these issues should be explored at a pretrial motion in limine. Unless Fury's attorney can persuade the judge of the relevance of the information, she should be precluded from asking the question.

Question 5.

Charger completes presenting the defense case and rests. On rebuttal, Fury calls FRW1,[4] who testifies that he knows both Charger and CW1, and that he attended the Smith dinner party. Direct examination continues:

Q. Where were you sitting at Smith's dinner party?

A. I was sitting next to CW1.

Q. Did you notice whether CW1 was drinking that night?

A. Yes, I did. He had four, maybe five martinis; by the end of the evening, he was pretty sloshed.

a. What is the purpose for the question?

4. "Fury rebuttal witness 1."

b. Is the question worded intrinsically, or extrinsically?

c. Is this intrinsic or extrinsic impeachment?

d. Does the question require a good-faith basis?

e. Is there any objection Charger can interpose, and if so, how should the trial judge rule on the objection?

Answer:

a. This question (and answer) has two purposes: is intended to impeach CW1's testimony by contradicting what he said in Question 1, and to support the inference that CW1 was too intoxicated to perceive or remember much of what went on at the party.

b. The question and answer are intrinsic—neither the question nor the answer invoked any source of information other than FRW1.

c. This is extrinsic impeachment—Fury called FRW1 to contradict CW1's testimony and cast doubts on CW1's ability to perceive and remember what happened at the party.

d. The question does not require a good-faith basis, because it contained no assertion of fact; it merely asked what FRW1 saw.

e. Charger has no basis to object.

Question 6.

In an unrelated personal injury case arising out of an automobile collision of cars driven by Park and Drab at the intersection of Fifth and Main Streets at 7:30 p.m. on the evening of July 1, Park calls PW1 as her first witness. After PW1 testifies to his name, address and occupation, direct examination continues:

Q. Did you see anything unusual occur at about 7:30 p.m. on the evening of July 1st?

A. Yes. I was coming out of my church and I saw Drab go right through the red light and collide with Park's car.

Park presents the rest of her evidence, and rests. During Drab's case-in-chief, DW1 is called; if permitted, DW1 will testify:

Q. Do you know PW1?

A. Yes.

Q. Did you happen to see PW1 at about 7:30 p.m. on the evening of July 1st?

A. As a matter of fact, I did.

Q. Where was he?

A. I saw him coming out of the pool hall.

Q. Pool hall?

A. Yup.

Q. You're sure it wasn't a church you saw him coming out of?

A. Quite sure.

a. What is the purpose of this testimony?

b. Is the question worded intrinsically or extrinsically?

c. Does it require a good-faith basis?

d. Is this evidence intrinsic impeachment or extrinsic impeachment?

e. Is there any plausible objection Park can interpose, and if so, how should the trial judge rule on the objection?

<u>Answer:</u>

a. The purpose of this testimony is to impeach PW1 by contradicting his testimony that he was coming out of the church.
b. The question is worded intrinsically, because it invokes no source of information except DW1, the witness now testifying.
c. This testimony is extrinsic impeachment of PW1, since the source of the information is DW1, not PW1.
d. The question contains no assertion of fact, and therefore does not require a good-faith basis.
e. This may constitute extrinsic impeachment on a collateral matter. Is it important whether PW1 was exiting a church or a pool hall? Yes, if the pool hall was much further from the intersection than the church, or if for some other reason a person would have a better view of the intersection from the church door than from the entrance to the pool hall. Otherwise, does this testimony serve any purpose other than, perhaps, to embarrass PW1?

Some might argue that the distinction between pool hall and church is significant because it is more likely that a person might drink alcohol in a pool hall than a church. Let's assume that this is true. That still should not influence the evidentiary ruling here, because a jury should not make assumptions about a particular witness based on such generalizations.

§ 12.6 Impeaching a witness's narration

The English language—every human language, probably—is a marvelous thing. But it is often annoyingly imprecise. Words and expressions often have more than one meaning—even, sometimes, contradictory meanings. Such words are "contranyms." Consider the word "sanction," which can mean either a threatened punishment for violating a law or rule; or official permission or approval of an action. "Cleave" can mean to separate and discard; or to cling to. "Clip" can mean to separate and discard, or to save and bind together. "Dust" can mean "to clear away", or to add (a "dusting of sugar" on a baked good). "Left" can mean "what or who remains", or "who departed." "Hold up" can mean to support or bolster; it can also mean to impede. "Oversight" can mean exercising supervision or failing to notice ("it was an unfortunate oversight").

"Yeah, right," depending on how it is said, can mean enthusiastic approval or total disbelief. Likewise, "Big deal!" and "Are you happy now?" And even "May I help you?"—which can either mean, "May I help you" or "You don't belong here and if you are smart you will leave right now."

Sometimes two words can be both synonyms and antonyms. Consider "sight" and "vision," both of which mean something perceived by the eyes. But saying "She was a vision" has a very different meaning than "She was a sight!"

For a humorous take on the various meanings of a common three-letter word, see https://www.youtube.com/watch/RAGcDi0DRtU.[5]

Moreover, a word's meaning may vary widely depending on who is using it. The adjective "moderate" can be a compliment, or an insult. "Tall" may have a very different meaning to someone who is 5'2" than it does to someone who is, say, 5'11". "Heavy" and "skinny" are thoroughly subjective assessments. What is the difference between being "skinny" versus "thin" versus "lanky" versus "svelte"? Although each has a different meaning, different people might use each of these terms if asked to describe someone, because the answer is in the eye of the beholder.

Age is another area in which people use the language rather subjectively.[6]

The occasional need for—and utility of—cross-examining and impeaching a witness's means of expression is wonderfully illustrated in the classic 1936 movie, *Mr. Deeds Goes to Town.* Longfellow Deeds (Gary Cooper), who owns a small business in rural Vermont, unexpectedly inherits a huge fortune, and decides to give the money away to poor people. Other members of the family, determined to get the money for themselves, try to have him declared mentally incompetent. At a competency hearing, they call two elderly sisters, who testify that they are Longfellow's neighbors and have known him all their lives and are very fond of him, but that he is, sadly, completely "pixilated"—i.e., he acts as if he were kidnapped by pixies. Damning testimony indeed—until, on gentle cross-examination by Mr. Deeds, it turns out that the

---

5. I accept no responsibility for (and receive no commission from) whatever annoying ad you will be subjected to before the video plays.

6. For example, the preferred term for anyone over the age of 70 is "mature," even though, in movie classifications, "mature" often means "juvenile regardless of age."

sisters firmly believe that *everyone* in the town (except themselves) is pixilated—and so, say the sisters, are the attorneys for the greedy relatives, and even the judge.

Suppose W, describing his or her encounter with X, testifies that X had a "threatening, angry" look on his face. That conveys a certain image to the jury. Suppose it turns out that, to W, anyone who is not smiling thereby looks "threatening and angry." Or, even worse, suppose W frequently uses those words to describe pretty much every member of X's race or ethnic group. That might well alter a jury's assessment of X's facial expression, conduct and intent.

In sum: if a witness uses a word that can have more than one meaning, an impeaching attorney can legitimately question the witness to clarify what is meant.

C. Impeaching the Testimony: Bias; Motive to Lie

---

§ 12.7 In general

In *U.S. v. Abel*, 469 U.S. 45 (1984), the Court defined "bias" as follows:

> Bias is a term used in the "common law of evidence" to describe the relationship between a party and a witness which might lead the witness to slant, unconsciously or otherwise, his testimony in favor of or against a party. Bias may be induced by a witness' like, dislike, or fear of a party, or by the witness' self-interest. Proof of bias is almost always relevant because the jury, as finder of fact and weigher of credibility, has historically been entitled to assess all evidence which might bear on the accuracy and truth of a witness' testimony. The "common law of evidence" allowed the showing of bias by extrinsic evidence, while requiring the cross-examiner to "take the answer of the witness" with respect to less favored forms of impeachment.

Abel, 469 U.S. at 52.

"Motive to lie" is quite similar to "bias"; in fact, "bias" is an example of a motive to lie. But witness W may have a motive to lie even though W does not care who wins or loses the lawsuit. Suppose, for example, W and Y were together at 11 p.m. on April 10th. On April 13th, Y was accused of committing a crime at 11 p.m. on April 10th in a location several miles away. When arrested, Y confidently told police that W would vouch for Y's whereabouts at 11 p.m., on the 10th, but when approached by the police, W denied being with Y, fearful of how W's spouse (or partner or parent, as the case may be) would react if W acknowledged being with Y at that time of night. At trial, the prosecutor has a police officer testify that Y claimed to be with

W at 11 p.m. on April 10th, then calls W, who again denies having been with Y that night.[7] In such an instance, W does not have a bias for or against either the prosecutor or Y; indeed, W's sympathies may be with Y. Still, W has a motive to lie to protect W's own "self-interest"[8]—i.e., W's relationship with W's spouse, partner or parent. In such a case, evidence of prior conduct by W that aroused the suspicions or ire of W's spouse, partner or parents would be relevant to show W's motive to deny having been with Y at 11 p.m. on April 10th.[9]

Bias or motive to lie is highly relevant in any litigation situation, civil or criminal.

The Supreme Court has handed down several decisions relating to the use of bias or motive to lie to impeach a witness's testimony. Five merit mention here: *Abel*; *Davis v. Alaska*, 415 U.S. 308 (1974); *Giglio v. U.S.*, 405 U.S. 150 (1972); *Wearry v. Cain*, 577 US 385 (2016); and *Olden v. Kentucky*, 488 U.S. 277 (1988).

In in *Abel*, the Court held that a prosecutor's right to show a defense witness's bias in favor of the defendant was so fundamental to the fact-finding process that it allowed the introduction of evidence which another evidence rule—FRE 608(b)—otherwise would have excluded. See the next chapter, § 13.7.

In *Davis* and *Olden*, the Court held that a defendant's right to show that a prosecution witness had a motive to lie was so fundamental to a fair trial that it trumped an evidence rule that otherwise would have precluded the impeachment. *Olden* so held with regard to Rule 403 and, by implication, Rule 412. See § 9.20.

In *Giglio* and *Wearry*, the Court held that the prosecution's failure to inform the defense about a prosecution witness's bias or motive to lie violated the defendant's right to due process of law.

Giglio, Wearry and *Davis* are described in the next section.

§ 12.8 *Giglio v. U.S.; Wearry v. Cain; Davis v. Alaska*

i. Giglio v. U.S.; Wearry v. Cain

Giglio was convicted of passing forged money orders. Taliento, Giglio's alleged coconspirator, was the government's key witness. While Giglio's appeal was pending, defense counsel discovered that a federal prosecutor had made an "informal" promise to Taliento, that if Taliento testified against Giglio, Taliento would not be prosecuted. When cross-examined at trial, Taliento denied that any such promise had been made, and the federal prosecutor stressed that "fact" in closing argu-

7. Evidence that a defendant asserted a false alibi—and in this hypothetical, the prosecutor reasonably believes that is what Y has done—is relevant as suggestive of guilt.

8. The Supreme Court referred to "the witness' self-interests" in the second sentence of the passage from Abel quoted *supra*.

9. Showing that W had a motive to lie would not completely undo the damage that W's false testimony did to Y's defense, but it might at least diminish the damage somewhat.

ment.[10] The Court held that by failing to inform Giglio's attorney of the promise to Taliento, which the attorney could have used to impeach Taliento, the government violated Giglio's right to due process of law as guaranteed by the Fifth Amendment. *Giglio v. U.S.*, 405 U.S. 150 (1972).

Similarly, consider *Wearry v. Cain*, 577 U.S. 385 (2016). In the state's opening argument at Wearry's murder trial, the prosecutor told the jury that a man named Brown would give important testimony, and that although Brown "is doing 15 years on a drug charge right now, [he] hasn't asked for a thing." During Brown's testimony, Brown testified that he had "agreed to testify against Wearry, not for any prosecutorial favor, but solely because his sister knew the victim's sister." In closing argument, the State reiterated that Brown "has no deal on the table" and was testifying because the victim's "family deserves to know." *Id.* at 387. After Wearry's conviction, the defense discovered that "the State had failed to disclose that, contrary to the prosecution's assertions at trial, Brown had twice sought a deal to reduce his existing sentence in exchange for testifying against Wearry, and the police told Brown that they would "'talk to the D.A. if he told the truth.'" *Id.* at 390. The Court held that this and other failures by the state to reveal exculpatory evidence required reversal and a new trial.

Giglio and *Wearry* are both based on the "*Brady* doctrine": in *Brady v. Maryland*, 373 USA 83 (1963), the Supreme Court held that "[T]he suppression by the prosecution of evidence favorable to an accused upon request violates due process where the evidence is material either to guilt or to punishment, irrespective of the good faith or bad faith of the prosecution." *Id.* at 87.

ii. Davis v. Alaska

Davis was charged with burglary for stealing a safe from a bar. The next day, Green, age 16, identified Davis as the man he saw with the safe several hours after it was stolen.[11] At the time, Green was on probation from a juvenile court delinquency adjudication for burglarizing two cabins, and was still on probation when Green again identified Davis at Davis' trial. Davis' attorney sought to cross-examine Green about whether Green might have hastily identified the defendant when the police first interviewed him, for fear that otherwise the police might suspect that he was the burglar, thereby jeopardizing his probation. The trial court, relying on an Alaska statute protecting the confidentiality of juvenile court adjudications, refused to allow any reference to Green's adjudication or probation.

---

10. The prosecutor who made the promise was not authorized to do so, and did not inform the prosecutor who tried Giglio that he had made this promise to Taliento. The Court properly held that this made no difference: the government is responsible for the conduct of its agents, and the good faith conduct of the trial prosecutor could not shield the government from the misconduct of the prosecutor who made the promise and then failed to disclose it.

11. The state's case was not solely based on Green's testimony; other evidence also incriminated Davis.

The Supreme Court, per Chief Justice Burger, reversed Davis' conviction. The Sixth Amendment right to confront one's accuser, the Court emphasized, included the right to cross-examine the prosecution's witness in an attempt to prove his prejudice or bias. Although defense counsel had been permitted at trial to ask Green *whether* he feared that the police might suspect him, counsel had not been permitted bring out the underlying reason *why* Green might feel that way. This, the Court held, prevented the defense from exposing the jury to information it needed to make a properly informed decision regarding the credibility of Green's testimony. The Court acknowledged the state's legitimate interest in protecting the anonymity of juvenile offenders, but held this interest "cannot require yielding of so vital a constitutional right as the effective cross-examination for bias of an adverse witness." *Davis v. Alaska,* 415 U.S. 308, 315 (1974). "Confrontation," Chief Justice Burger wrote, "means more than being allowed to confront the witness physically. Our cases construing the [confrontation] clause hold that a primary interest secured by it is the right of cross-examination...." *Id.*

Note that Davis's attorney had no direct evidence or proof that Green's identification of Davis was motivated by concern over Green's own situation or status on probation. The best counsel could have done was to ask Green about his probationary status and whether that prompted him to make a hasty identification or tell the police what he thought they wanted to hear. Presumably, if Green had been asked, he would have denied that this was so. Nevertheless, the Supreme Court held that the *possibility* that Green was thus motivated was enough to give Davis's attorney a good-faith basis to argue to the jury that Green's identification of Davis was untrustworthy, and that denying the attorney the opportunity to introduce the evidence that supported that argument deprived Davis of his Sixth and Fourteenth Amendment rights to confront and cross-examine Green, despite the state law designed to protect juveniles from being impeached with juvenile court adjudications.

§ 12.9 Questions

Question 1.

P, who is Black, sues polices officers D1 and D2, who are White, and the police department, for unlawful and unreasonable use of force in arresting P during a Black Lives Matter protest against police violence. P calls PW who testifies that P was protesting peacefully but was struck several times by D1 and D2. On cross-examination, a defense attorney asks:

Q: It is true, is it not, that three years ago you were accepted as a cadet for the police department, but were dismissed from the police academy for failure to complete required assignments?

Is this question proper? If so, and if PW denies that this is true, could a defendant offer evidence to establish these facts, during the defense case-in-chief?

Answer:

This question would not be proper impeachment to challenge PW's perception, memory or narration (§§ 12.4–12.6); nor would it be permissible to attack W's character for truthfulness (Chapter 13). But it is proper in this case, because it suggests that PW resents having been kicked out of the police academy and therefore has a bias against the police department in general. This is litigation situation F: cross-examining a witness about him/herself. See § 11.29.

Suppose PW denies that he was dismissed from the police academy, claiming instead that he quit for personal reasons. During the defense case-in-chief, defendants could call police academy officials and introduce academy documents to prove that PW was dismissed from the academy. (That would be litigation situation H. See § 11.31.) In fact, even if the defense did not cross-examine PW about this, the defense still could have offered such extrinsic evidence to show PW's alleged bias against the police department.

Question 2.

In the same suit, the defense calls DW, who testifies that P threw several rocks at the police before D1 and D2, using only reasonable force, subdued him. P's lawyer has learned that the church where DW worships has no Black congregants; the neighborhood where DW lives contains no Black families; and the country club DW belongs to has no Black members. How, if at all, may P's attorney use this information to impeach DW?

Answer:

This evidence is relevant to suggest that DW, consciously or not, has a bias against Blacks, and therefore that DW is either lying, or subconsciously slanting his testimony to favor the (White) police officer defendants. Therefore, P's attorney can question DW about these matters on cross-examination (litigation situation F); or could wait until the defense rests, and then offer extrinsic evidence of these facts during P's rebuttal case—by calling the minister, pastor or priest of the church, several of DW's neighbors, and the membership chairman of the country club (litigation situation H).

Of course, it does not necessarily follow from these facts that DW is biased. But a rational jury could consider this evidence as suggestive of bias, and discount DW's description of events accordingly.

Question 3.

D, your client, is on trial for robbing an all-night supermarket at 11:30 p.m. on May 31, 2021. His physical appearance matches the description of the robber, but because the perpetrator wore a mask, none of the store employees or customers who were present during the robbery can make a positive identification. One Government witness, W, has testified, however, that she saw your client less than two blocks from the supermarket at about 11:20 that same evening, not yet wearing a mask; further, W testified that your client was wearing clothing of the same general type that store employees say the robber wore. W testified that she is positive it was your client she saw, because she has known your client for several years.

As W completes direct examination, court recesses for lunch. During the recess, your client informs you that W's testimony is true: he was indeed within a few blocks of the supermarket shortly before the robbery, and was dressed as W described him. Further, W has in fact known your client for several years; a few years ago, she had an affair with YMB, your client's younger, married brother, and became pregnant; your client helped YMB persuade W to keep the matter a secret and to abort the child. Since then, W has become active in the Right to Life movement, and is engaged to marry the local chapter chairman.

Your client wants you to use this information on cross-examination to impeach W. May you? Should you? Must you? Would it make any difference whether your client admits his guilt to you, or insists that he is innocent? Assuming he insists he is innocent, would it make any difference whether you believe or disbelieve his protestations of innocence?

Answer:

As a matter of law, you have the right to impeach W, because your client's information demonstrates that W has a reason to resent him and to seek revenge against him, and therefore a motive to lie: to punish him for persuading her to commit what she now considers a terrible sin.[12] And this is so even though you know that W's testimony is truthful. Your job as defense attorney is not to assure that only truthful evidence is admitted against your client; it is to probe the state's case for weaknesses that might undercut the state's case. It might well constitute ineffective assistance of counsel for a defense attorney to refuse to cross-examine a state witness merely because the attorney is satisfied that the witness is telling the truth.

Would it be tactically wise to cross-examine W about her affair and pregnancy and abortion? That's a significant gamble. When the jury in this case was chosen, presumably, no one had a clue that abortion might become an issue,[13] so no ques-

12. Putting aside that we know W's testimony is truthful, we might reasonably question whether it would be rational for someone in W's situation to lie under oath to get back at Y. But—and you may have already noticed this from time to time—people do not always respond logically or rationally in emotionally-fraught situations.

13. Actually, the prosecutor might in fact know. When the prosecutor interviewed W prior to trial, he or she presumably asked W, "How were you and D acquainted? What was the nature of your relationship?" If W answered that question truthfully, the prosecutor would know that W may regard D with resentment, anger, perhaps even hatred. But until the prosecutor called W as a witness, neither D nor D's attorney had any idea she would testify; in fact, D's attorney did not

tions were asked of potential jurors about whether they would be prejudiced against someone who persuaded a woman to have an abortion.

Tactical considerations aside, how can an attorney justify, in his or her own conscience, the idea of forcing W to publicly relive an excruciating experience in order to impeach testimony that the attorney knows is truthful? Answer: Practicing law—in civil or criminal matters, whether or not litigation is involved—will often present an attorney with difficult moral or ethical choices.[14]

D. Impeaching the Testimony: Extrinsic Impeachment By Contradiction; Impeachment On "Collateral" Matters

§ 12.10 In general

W1 testifies to certain facts at trial. Later, the adverse party seeks to call W2 who will contradict W1's testimony as to one or more of the facts W1 asserted in his testimony (litigation situation H; see § 11.31). W2's testimony therefore constitutes extrinsic impeachment of W1's testimony. Should W2's testimony be admitted?

The answer depends primarily on three factors.

1. First, what is the relevance of W1's testimony that W2 will contradict? The more central that fact is to the outcome of the lawsuit, the greater the tendency to allow it. If the testimony to be impeached is only collaterally or tangentially relevant to important issues, a judge has discretion to disallow it.
2. If extrinsic impeachment involves a collateral fact, which party elicited the collateral fact in the first place—the party relying on W1's testimony, or the party seeking to impeach that testimony?
3. Would permitting the impeachment violate some other rule of evidence, and if so, does that require precluding the impeachment?

The following questions[15] illustrate the law's basic approach.

---

even know that W existed. Remember that, unlike the wide-open discovery available to litigants in civil litigation, in federal courts and in most states, as a rule, neither side is required to reveal the identity of their witnesses until each witness is called during trial.

14. This scenario is the plot of an as yet unfinished novel I am writing.

15. Most of the following questions, anyhow.

§ 12.11 "Collateral impeachment" rule; "specific impeachment" or "specific contradiction" exception

A "collateral fact" is a fact that is only indirectly or tangentially relevant to the important issues in the trial. The general rule is that if witness W1 testifies to a collateral fact, the impeaching attorney should be permitted to ask an intrinsically worded question or two about that fact,[16] but should not be permitted to dwell on it unduly. Nor should the impeaching attorney be permitted to introduce extrinsic evidence (e.g., by later calling W2 to contradict W1's testimony) on the collateral matter.[17] There are two reasons for this rule. First, allowing extrinsic impeachment on a collateral matter would waste time; second, it might distract the jury from the important issues it will be required to resolve.

Suppose, for example, an important issue at a trial is whether P made a certain statement at a business meeting in the building at 1984 Orwell Avenue at 1 p.m. on April 7th. D calls W1 to testify that she attended the meeting and heard P make the statement. At some point during W1's testimony, she testifies that the weather that afternoon was cold and sunny.[18] Once D rests, should P's attorney, in rebuttal, be allowed to offer extrinsic evidence that it was cloudy that afternoon?[19]

Unless the weather at that time and place plays an important role in the lawsuit, the answer should be: no. If the only relevance of the impeaching evidence is to suggest, "Since W1 misremembered what the weather was like, she also probably misremembered what P said," the judge should exclude the contradictory testimony.

If the impeaching attorney him/herself elicited the collateral fact, the "no intrinsic impeachment" rule is fairly absolute: an attorney should not be allowed to elicit testimony from W1 on a collateral matter and then call W2 to contradict W1's testimony about that matter.[20]

---

16. If the questions are worded assertively, the impeaching attorney must have a good-faith basis. See § 11:15.

17. Other forms of extrinsic impeachment—such as offering a document which contradicts W1's testimony—are also banned by the rule. But since the most frequently used method to extrinsically impeach W1 is by calling W2 to give contradictory testimony, I'm using that scenario in this discussion.

18. "It was a bright, cold day in April, and the clocks were striking thirteen." This is first sentence of George Orwell's novel *1984*. In that simple, seemingly mundane sentence, Orwell informs readers that they are about to enter a world that differs from the one they habit in strange and perhaps even sinister ways.

19. Such evidence might take several forms. P could offer the National Weather Service record of the weather in that immediate area. Or P could call witnesses to testify that they remember the weather that day, and that it was overcast. Or P could introduce authenticated photographs taken near that building at around 10 a.m., which demonstrate that the sky was gray and there were no shadows on the ground.

20. Nor offer other extrinsic evidence, either. See notes 16 and 18.

But if W1 testifies about a collateral fact on direct examination, or gratuitously volunteers such testimony in a non-responsive answer on cross, the situation is a bit more complicated. If it would give one party an unfair advantage to allow that assertion of fact to stand unchallenged, or if it opens the door to an issue previously off-limits, the judge has discretion to permit the impeaching attorney to offer evidence that contradicts what W1 said. This is sometimes known as the "specific contradiction" rule, or an application of the "specific impeachment" rule.

That does not mean that the judge should allow the impeaching attorney to go to extremes. The judge must exercise discretion, per FRE 403 and state equivalents, as to how much and what kind of extrinsic evidence to allow.

This issue crops up from time to time,[21] particularly in the realm of character evidence, when a defendant, while testifying, foolishly opens the door to the issue of his or her own character (see § 6.13). A defense attorney sometimes also does so, by asking witnesses inadvisable questions on direct or cross-examination

The following questions illustrate some of these issues.[22]

Questions 1–3

D is charged with robbery on March 3. PW1, the state's first witness, testifies that at 10 p.m., after spending an hour or so in a bar that evening, after he left the bar, he was struck from behind and knocked down; that someone pushed a metal object to the back of his neck and said, "If you turn around or get up I'll shoot you"; and that his assailant then stole his wallet. PW1 also testified that he lay on the sidewalk for a minute or two before he got up, and never saw his assailant.

Next, the state calls PW2, who testifies that about five minutes after 10 that evening, he heard sirens coming from the vicinity of the bar, went to check out what was going on, and learned about the robbery. PW2 further testifies that he had seen D a block away from the bar at about 5 minutes before 10, and recognized him because D and PW2 went to high school together.

Question 1.

On cross-examination, D's attorney asks, "This man you claim was D—what was he wearing?" PW2 replies, "D was wearing light grey sweatpants and a dark long-sleeve sweatshirt." The attorney also asks PW2 whether PW2 noticed what movie was playing in the theater next to the bar. PW2 testifies, "It was a movie called *All is True*. I didn't see the movie, but I remember the name on the theater sign."

---

21. But if it does not "crop up" in your evidence class or casebook, it is probably safe to read this section purely for your own enjoyment, and not worry about it being on the exam.

22. Well, most of the questions, anyway.

After the prosecutor rests,[23] the defendant calls DW1, who will (if permitted) testify that she was with defendant until about 9:45 that evening, and that the defendant was wearing dark jeans and a denim jacket.

The prosecutor objects that DW1's testimony should be excluded because it tends to impeach PW2 on a collateral matter. "What the defendant was wearing isn't important, Your Honor; what's important is whether or not he was the person that PW2 saw near the scene and near the time of the crime." How should defense counsel respond; how should the judge rule?

Answer:

DW1's testimony constitutes extrinsic impeachment of PW2's testimony by contradicting PW1's testimony (litigation situation H, § 11.31).

Defense counsel argues that if DW1's testimony is accurate, the man PW2 saw wearing what PW2 described could not have been the defendant; thus, the discrepancy goes directly to the accuracy of PW2's identification of the defendant as the man he saw.

The judge should agree, overrule the objection, and allow DW1 to testify.

Question 2.

Defense counsel also calls DW2, who lives in the neighborhood and who will, if permitted, testify that *All is True* had completed its run on March 1st, that all signs about that movie had been removed, and that on the 3rd, the theater was showing a movie called *Maiden*.

The prosecutor objects that DW2's testimony should be excluded because it tends to impeach PW2 on a collateral matter. "This isn't a trial about movies; it's about who assaulted and robbed PW1!" How should defense counsel respond; how should the judge rule?

Answer:

Defense counsel argues: "Your honor, the issue is how well PW2 noticed and remembers the events of that evening. Showing he was wrong about the movie that was playing right next to the crime scene casts doubts about how well he remembers everything else he claims to remember from that night."

This argument is a pretty good attempt to make bricks out of broccoli,[24] but it fails, because the underlying factoid being impeached—what movie was showing—has

23. Let's assume the prosecutor had more evidence than just the testimony of PW1 and PW2; otherwise, the judge would have dismissed the case when, after the prosecutor rested, the defense moved for a directed verdict (or for a judgment of acquittal, which is what a motion for a directed verdict is sometimes called in criminal cases). See § 2.12.

24. "Make bricks out of broccoli" is a Googlenope, i.e., a phrase which, according to an Internet search, has never before appeared in print. The term "googlenope," and the hobby of inventing them, was coined by reporter and humor columnist Gene Weingarten.

no real connection to the crime, yet may distract the jury from the important aspect of PW2's testimony, which is PW2's identification of D as the man he saw near the scene of, and shortly before, the crime.[25]

Question 3.

"OK, prof, what's with the two movies you mentioned? What are they about, and are they worth seeing?"

Answer:

I was hoping you'd ask.

All is True is a poignant, moving movie about Shakespeare's final years, after he left London and returned to his family in Stratford-on-Avon. Kenneth Branagh plays Shakespeare, and Judy Dench plays his wife. The entire cast is superb. You don't have to be a Shakespeare buff to enjoy it.

Maiden is a documentary about the first-ever all-women crew that competed in an around-the-world yacht race. It is a superbly produced combination of actual footage of the race and interviews with the participants two decades later.

I highly recommend both—but maybe not until after you've taken (and, hopefully, aced) your evidence exam.

Question 4.

D, who is 21 years old, is charged with felonious assault. His defense: mistaken identity. He testifies on direct that he was nowhere near the assault when it happened, then adds, "I detest violence. Violence is for losers!"

On cross, the prosecutor seeks to bring out that two years earlier, while attending a college football game, D started a fight with fans who were rooting for the other team, was arrested, and pleaded guilty to several counts of misdemeanor assault. Should the prosecutor be allowed to do so?

Answer:

Normally, the answer would be: no. Cross-examining a defendant generally is litigation situation F, § 11.29. The applicable rules are FRE 404(b) and FRE 609(a).

---

25. For example, if the judge allows DW2 to testify, then after the defense rests, the prosecutor, in rebuttal, might call two witnesses, PWx and PWy, each of whom will testify that it was *All is True* that was playing on March 3—thereby extrinsically impeaching DW2. And then the defendant might call additional witnesses to testify that, no, it was *Maiden,* to extrinsically impeach the testimony of PWx and PWy, who contradicted DW1. And then ... well, you get the idea. (You may wonder: couldn't one of the parties just call the theater manager and have her testify about what movie was showing? Good thinking, but it wouldn't work in this case, because the theater went out of business as a result of the Covid-19 pandemic, and no one can find the theater manager or the theater's records.)

D is on trial for assault; evidence that the defendant committed other assaults on other occasions is relevant only to show a propensity for assaultive conduct, and would be barred by FRE 404(b)(1). See § 7.2. And since the convictions were for misdemeanors and not felonies, they would not be admissible per FRE 609, either. See § 13.10.

But by testifying on direct that he "detest[s] violence," D has opened the door to the prior assault in two ways. First, the judge should allow the prosecutor to cross-examine D about his prior assault convictions via the doctrine of specific contradiction. Second, D has expressed an opinion of his own good character, so the case is now also litigation situation D (§ 11.27): FRE 405(a)(2nd sentence) directs that the judge "may allow"—in this case, in my opinion, should allow—the prosecutor to cross-examine D about his prior acts of violence. See § 6.14 to § 6.23.[26]

And if D is brazen enough to deny the prior assaults, the prosecutor should be permitted to bring out that D pleaded guilty to the assaults. The prosecutor cannot cite FRE 405(a)(2nd sentence), which only allows "inquiry" into a defendant's relevant prior conduct. But the doctrine of specific contradiction gives the judge discretion to permit a party to extrinsically contradict a prior witness's testimony, even if on a collateral matter, if the witness (or the party relying on the witness) would otherwise gain an unfair advantage by asserting the collateral matter.

Question 5.

Suppose D does not testify on direct as described in Question 4. Instead, on cross-examination, the prosecutor asks D, "What is your attitude about violence and fighting in general?" D answers, "I detest violence. Only losers start fights." Can the prosecutor question D about the football game fights?

Answer:

No. A party cannot deliberately elicit testimony on a collateral matter on cross-examination and then offer evidence to impeach that answer. This is particularly so where, as here, the evidence the prosecutor wants to present is banned by another rule, FRE 404(b)(1).

Question 6.

But wait a minute. Isn't that exactly what the defense attorney did in Q1? It was defense counsel who elicited PW2's testimony about what the man was wearing, and it was also the defense attorney who called DW1 to contradict PW2's testimony!

Answer:

Yes, Question 5 resembles what the defense attorney did in Question 1, but no, it's not the same. What defense counsel brought out in Q1 was not a collateral matter;

---

26. Of course, the form of cross-examination would have to differ somewhat from normal Rule 405(a)(2nd sentence) cross-examination. It would be comical to require the prosecutor to ask D, "Have you heard" or "Did you know" about the football game assaults and D's guilty pleas.

it went directly to the accuracy of PW2's identification of the man he saw near the scene shortly before the crime. When the testimony to be impeached by contradiction has direct relevance to the ultimate facts to be resolved (in this case, whether PW2's identification of defendant near the scene near the time of the crime was accurate), it doesn't matter who elicited the testimony to be impeached.

Questions 7–8

Fury filed a personal injury action against Charger for damages arising out of a collision between their cars at an intersection on the evening of June 5.[27] Fury's complaint alleges that Charger was driving while intoxicated and negligently drove through a red light, causing the collision. After Fury presents his case and rests, Charger calls CW1 for direct examination. CW1 testifies that he was with Charger at a dinner party that night, and that Charger was not intoxicated.

Question 7.

On cross-examination, among other questions, Fury's attorney also asks CW1:

Q. What was served at the party?

A. Beef Stroganoff.

a. What is the purpose for the question?

b. Is the question worded intrinsically, or extrinsically?

c. Is this intrinsic or extrinsic impeachment?

d. Does the question require a good-faith basis?

e. Is there any objection Charger can interpose, and if so, how should the trial judge rule on the objection?

Answer:

a. The purpose is to explore how much CW1 remembers about that evening besides the facts he testified to on direct.
b. This question is worded intrinsically.
c. It is intrinsic impeachment: it neither names nor evokes any source of information other than CW1.
d. No good-faith basis is required, since the question does not contain any assertion of fact.
e. Charger could object that the question is irrelevant, but a judge should allow it, since it does test CW1's memory of the evening. If CW1 testifies that he did not remember what the main course was, that might cast doubt on the accuracy of what he claims he can remember.

27. For previous questions based on this same scenario, see § 12.5.

Question 8.

Fury's attorney might ask additional questions: "What was the host wearing? What was the hostess wearing? Where were you sitting? Who was sitting to your left? What did he/she have to drink that evening? Who was sitting to your right? What did he/she have to drink that evening? Who was sitting across the table from you? What did he/she have to drink that evening?"

Assume CW1 does not remember what the Smiths were wearing and is able to name one or two of the people, but with regard to what they drank, his answers will be: "I don't remember."

a. What is the purpose for these questions?

b. Are these questions worded intrinsically, or extrinsically?

c. Is this intrinsic or extrinsic impeachment?

d. Do these questions require a good-faith basis?

e. Is there any objection Charger can interpose, and if so, how should the trial judge rule on the objection?

Answer:

a. In general, the purpose is to highlight more things that CW1 cannot remember about the party. In particular, these questions suggest that it is unlikely that CW1 could remember so clearly what Charger had to drink, when he could not remember what others drank that night.
b. These are all intrinsically worded questions.
c. This is intrinsic, not extrinsic, impeachment.
d. No good-faith basis is required.
e. The same objection: irrelevant. But this is not a valid objection: these are all reasonable questions testing CW1's memory about what happened that evening. Rather, Charger's attorney should object that this is excessive cross-examination about a collateral matter. At some point, the judge should tell Fury's attorney, "Enough is enough, move on to something else."

Question 9.

Assuming the judge permits this cross-examination, how might Charger's attorney respond?

Answer:

On redirect examination, Charger's attorney will take CW1 through the following Q&A:[28]

28. It is always risky to ask a witness a question to which you do not know the answer. But an experienced trial attorney would have anticipated that Fury's attorney would ask all these questions.

Q On cross-examination, FA [Fury's attorney] asked you a series of questions—who was sitting to your left, to your right, across the table; and how much each of them had to drink that night. Do you recall those questions?

A Yes.

Q And you answered that you didn't remember what those people had to drink. Correct?

A Yes.

Q So how is it that you remember how much Charger had to drink?

A I had no particular reason to notice or remember what other people were drinking. But early on during the evening, Charger offered me a ride home, so I kept an eye on what he was drinking—I don't accept rides from people who are intoxicated! And when we left the party, he showed no signs of being intoxicated. He was steady on his feet, his speech was clear, he didn't seem distracted or noticeably "up" or "down."

Besides, there is no reason why I should remember what anyone else was drinking that night. But once Fury ran the stop sign and collided with us, I knew it would be important to remember that Charger had, at most, two glasses of wine over the whole two-and-a half hours we were at the Smiths'.[29]

Question 10.

Charger rests. As a rebuttal witness, Fury calls FRW1, who was also a guest at the party. If permitted, Fury will ask FRW1 what the main course was at the Smiths' party on June 5, and FRW1 will answer, "Beef Wellington."

a. What is the purpose for the question and answer?

b. Is the question worded intrinsically, or extrinsically?

c. Is this intrinsic or extrinsic impeachment?

d. Does the question require a good-faith basis?

e. Is there any objection Charger can interpose, and if so, how should the trial judge rule on the objection?

Answer:

a. The question (and FRW1's answer) are intended to contradict CW1's testimony in Q7, thereby casting doubts on CW1's ability to remember other events or aspects of the dinner party.

Accordingly, Charger's attorney (or the attorney's investigator) would have asked the same questions while interviewing CW1 prior to trial—perhaps even prior to CW1's pretrial deposition.

29. Come to think of it, Charger's attorney probably should have elicited this testimony from CW1 on direct examination.

b. The question is worded intrinsically.

c. This is extrinsic impeachment of CW1, because FRW1, not CW1, is the source of information.

d. No good-faith basis is required.

e. Charger should object that this constitutes impermissible extrinsic impeachment on a collateral matter. The judge should sustain the objection: whether the main course was beef Wellington or beef Stroganoff simply is not important enough to waste the court's time and could distract the jury from the important factual issues it was empaneled to resolve.[30]

The same objection, and ruling, would apply if Fury called other guests to contradict CW1's testimony about who was sitting near him and how much those guests had to drink that night: such testimony would be extrinsic impeachment on collateral matters.

E. Prior Statements by the Witness

§ 12.12 The hearsay issue

In lawsuit *P v. D*, D calls W. During direct examination, D asks:

Q Did you have a conversation with HDL?[31]

A Yes.

Q What did HDL say?

P's attorney should immediately object that the question calls for a hearsay response.[32]

Whenever a witness (W) is called to the stand to testify about anything anybody ("HDL") said or wrote (other than while HDL was testifying at this trial or hearing), the first issue you must address is whether HDL's statement is relevant, and if so, how.

30. Beef Wellington is often prepared with a wine sauce, but I doubt that even a generous helping of beef Wellington would contain enough alcohol to affect a person's ability to perceive or remember.

31. HDL is my abbreviation for "hearsay declarant." FRE 801(b) defines "declarant" as "the person who made the statement."

32. In the real world, there are circumstances when P's attorney would not object. But in law school, this sort of Q&A is designed to test whether you recognize the hearsay issue, so you should always discuss whether DL's statement is hearsay, barring specific circumstances in which your professor tells you not to.

Once you have defined how the statement is relevant, then, you must (in addition to any other issues presented), determine whether that prior statement is hearsay.

FRE 801(c) defines hearsay:

> **(c) Hearsay.** "Hearsay" means a prior statement—one the declarant does not make while testifying at the current trial or hearing—that a party offers in evidence to prove the truth of the matter asserted by the declarant.

A Student's Guide to Hearsay devotes an entire chapter—36 pages— to unpacking this definition, but here's a quick summary: if the relevance of what HDL said depends on whether the factfinder accepts that statement as both truthful and accurate, then the statement is hearsay, and P's hearsay objection must be sustained, and the statement must be excluded, unless D persuades the judge that the statement satisfies a hearsay exception. But if the statement is relevant for a non-hearsay purpose—that is, if it is relevant regardless of whether the trier of fact believes that HDL spoke truthfully or accurately—then HDL's statement is not hearsay, and therefore is admissible over a hearsay objection.[33]

If you haven't studied hearsay yet, the idea that a statement might be relevant even if it is untrue may seem confounding and confusing. Here are some examples.

1. Suppose relatives of N bring an action to have him committed to an institution because he is mentally incompetent. At the hearing, a police officer testifies that N was standing in the middle of a major intersection, shouting that all traffic must stop immediately. When he approached N and requested N to identify himself, N shouted, "I am Emperor Napoleon Bonaparte! Kneel before your Emperor, peasant, or you will go to straight to the Bastille!" N's statement is relevant because it is *not* true—N clearly is not Napoleon, and the fact that N believed that he was is proof of his derangement. Therefore, his statement, "I am Emperor Napoleon Bonaparte," is not hearsay, because its relevance does not depend on its truth.

2. A key issue in a trial is whether HDL was still alive at 7 p.m. on a particular evening. W testifies that a few minutes after 7, she came upon HDL lying on the ground. She touched HDL on the shoulder and asked, "Sir, are you alive?" HDL replied, "Yes." Here, HDL's statement is clearly true and accurate. But is it hearsay? The answer, actually, is: no, because what HDL said doesn't matter; the fact that he was able to say *anything* is what's important. His saying "Yes" to W's question is no more probative on whether he was alive than if he had answered, "'Twas brillig, and the slithy toves did gyre and gimble in the wabe," or "I had one grunch, but the eggplant over there," or "ting, tang, walla-walla bing-bang."[34] Thus, under the circumstances, HDL's "Yes" is not hearsay.

---

33. It still might be excluded on other grounds; here we are only discussing the hearsay issue.

34. In case you are curious, the first quoted phrase is from "Jabberwocky," a poem in Lewis Carroll's *Through the Looking Glass,* a sequel to *Alice in Wonderland*; the second is a phrase that

If you are still mystified (or even if you are not), might I gently suggest that a book about hearsay, written by a wise retired law professor for law students, might come in handy? —Nah, that would be blatant self-promotion.

1. Prior inconsistent statements[35]

§ 12.13 Prior inconsistent *unsworn* statements: FRE 613

Philly was injured when a bus operated by the Dallas Bus Company collided with his car at the intersection of Broadway and 48th Street. At trial, Dallas calls DW1 as a witness. Direct examination proceeds as follows:

> Q: Did you see what happened that day?
>
> A: Absolutely. I was standing right there. The light turned red for the eastbound traffic on 48th Street and green for the north-south traffic on Broadway. Suddenly this car on 48th went through the red light into the intersection and got hit by the bus heading south on Broadway.
>
> Q: The bus had the green light?
>
> A: The bus had the green light. Absolutely. I saw it all.

This may sound pretty convincing to the jury; but on cross examination by Philly's attorney, the following exchange occurs:

> Q: I believe you testified on direct that you saw the entire accident?
>
> A: Absolutely.
>
> Q: No question about that in your mind?
>
> A: Like I said, I saw it all.
>
> Q: Do you remember speaking to Police Officer Renko shortly after the collision?
>
> A: Yeah, there was cops there.
>
> Q: And you spoke to Officer Renko about the collision?
>
> A: Absolutely.

---

appeared in several issues of Mad Magazine; and the third is a line from "The Witch Doctor," a 1950's song that was number one on the Billboard Top 100 for three weeks.

35. For more thorough coverage, see *A Student's Guide to Hearsay* (5th ed. 2019) § 4.1 to § 4.13, pp. 59–68.

Q: Did you tell Officer Renko, quote, "The bus went barreling through the red light and hit the car like a tank," unquote?

DALLAS'S LAWYER: Objection! Hearsay.

Dallas has a valid objection, because if Philly offers DW1's out-of-court statement to Officer Renko to prove that the bus ran the red light, the statement is hearsay.[36] But DW1's statement to Renko has another, more limited use. Even if the jury cannot consider it as evidence that the bus ran the red light, it is relevant in helping the jury assess how much weight or credibility it should give to DW1's in-court testimony that the bus had the green light. The inconsistency between the two statements undermines (impeaches) the accuracy of DW1's direct testimony.

The law has long permitted a party to use a witness' prior inconsistent statement to impeach that witness' testimony, even when, as here, the statement is inadmissible hearsay if offered as substantive evidence. FRE 613 implicitly acknowledges this common law principle:

Rule 613. Witness's Prior Statement

(a) Showing or Disclosing the Statement During Examination. When examining a witness about the witness's prior statement, the party need not show it or disclose its contents to the witness. But the party must, on request, show it or disclose its contents to an adverse party's attorney.

(b) Extrinsic Evidence of a Prior Inconsistent Statement. Extrinsic evidence of a witness's prior inconsistent statement is admissible only if the witness is given an opportunity to explain or deny the statement and an adverse party is given an opportunity to question the witness about it, or if justice so requires. This subdivision (b) does not apply to an opposing party's statement under Rule 801(d)(2).

Note that the rule does not explicitly say "If a witness had previously made a statement that is inconsistent with the testimony the witness has just given, that prior statement is admissible to impeach the witness's testimony." Rather, the rule simply assumes this is the case, and codifies a few procedural rules governing admissibility of a witness's prior statement.

An attorney can use witness W1's prior inconsistent statement at two different stages of the trial. First, the impeaching attorney can cross-examine W1 about the statement, as Philly's attorney did to DW1 in the Q&A set forth above. See litigation situation F, § 11.29.

36. Under the FRE, even though DW1 is now testifying, his own out-of-court statement, if offered to prove the truth of what he said in that statement, would be hearsay.

FRE 613(b) permits the impeaching attorney to wait until it is his or her turn to call witnesses, then call a second witness (here, Renko) to testify that DW1 made the prior inconsistent statement. See litigation situation H, § 11.31. Under this second option, instead of cross-examining DW1 about his statement to Officer Renko, P could have waited until D rested, and then, in rebuttal, called Renko to testify that DW1 told him that the bus ran the red light.[37]

Sometimes an attorney can employ both options. For example, if P's attorney cross-examines DW1 about the statement and DW1 denies he said it, in rebuttal, P could call Renko to testify that DW1 in fact made the statement.

A statement is admissible under FRE 613 if three conditions are satisfied:

1. The declarant is testifying (or has already testified) at the current trial or hearing about events that are relevant to the trial.
2. The prior statement is inconsistent with what declarant has testified to. The prior statement need not be the polar opposite of the testimony. For example, if DW1 had told Renko, "I'm pretty sure the bus had the green light, but I'm not positive," this is inconsistent enough with DW1's direct testimony ("The bus had the green light. Absolutely. I saw it all") to cast doubt on the reliability of DW1's testimony, and therefore satisfies the FRE 613 "inconsistent" requirement.
3. Except in unusual circumstances, at some point in the trial (usually, during cross-examination or redirect examination of the declarant), each party's attorney must have an opportunity to question the declarant about the inconsistent statement.

Cross-examination of DW1 continues:

DALLAS'S LAWYER: Objection! Hearsay!

PHILLY'S LAWYER: Your honor, Rule 613—prior inconsistent statement.

COURT: Overruled.

Q: Did you say that to Officer Renko?

A: Uhhh . . .

Q: Well, did you?

A: Uh, I may have.

Q: You "may have"? Did you say that, or not?

A: I guess so.

---

37. This is sometimes called "sandbagging." Secondary meanings of the verb "sandbag" include "to hit or stun with a sandbag," such as, "the robber hit the victim with a sandbag," and "to trap another poker player by checking a strong hand and then raising if the other player bets."

Q: You "guess so"?

A: I gue—yeah. I did say that.

Q: "Absolutely"?

A: Yeah.

Q: So now you're telling us that it was the bus that ran the red light?

A: No, no. It happened just like I said before: the bus had the green light.

Q: Let me make sure I have this straight. Today you say the bus had the green light, even though back then, five minutes after the collision, you told Officer Renko that the bus ran the red light?

A: Yeah.

Question

What should Dallas's attorney do at this point?

Answer:

Request, per FRE 105, that the judge instruct the jury that they can consider DW1's statement to Renko ("red light") only in assessing how much weight to give to DW1's testimony that the bus had the green light; they cannot consider DW1's statement as substantive evidence that the bus ran the red light.

§ 12.14 Prior inconsistent *sworn* statements: FRE 801(d)(1)(A)[38]

Suppose DW1's prior statement was made, not to Officer Renko on the street shortly after the collision, but several months later, during a pretrial deposition. In that case, FRE 801(d)(1)(A) comes into play:

> **(d) Statements That Are Not Hearsay.** A statement that meets the following conditions is not hearsay:
>
> **(1) A Declarant-Witness's Prior Statement.** The declarant testifies and is subject to cross-examination about a prior statement, and the statement:
>
> (A) is inconsistent with the declarant's testimony and was given under penalty of perjury at a trial, hearing, or other proceeding or in a deposition;...

38. For more extensive coverage, see *A Student's Guide to Hearsay* (5th ed. 2019) § 4.8 to § 4.13.

To satisfy FRE 801(d)(1)(A), the party offering the statement has to persuade the judge that four conditions are satisfied:

1. The declarant is testifying (or has testified) at the current trial or hearing about events that are relevant to the trial.
2. The prior statement is inconsistent with what declarant has just testified to.
3. At some point in the trial, each party's attorney must have an opportunity to cross-examine the declarant concerning the prior statement.
4. The prior statement was made while the declarant was "under penalty of perjury [in other words, under oath] at a trial, hearing, or other proceeding or in a deposition."

Note that to satisfy FRE 801(d)(1)(A), a statement must meet the requirements for FRE 613, and must also satisfy a fourth requirement: it must have been made while the declarant was "under penalty of perjury [in other words, under oath] at a trial, hearing, or other proceeding or in a deposition." If the prior statement satisfies Rule 801(d)(1)(A), then, unlike a statement that satisfies only Rule 613, it is admissible over a hearsay objection as substantive evidence, to prove the truth of the matter asserted in the statement. If DW1's statement in § 12.13, *supra*, had been made at a pretrial deposition, then the statement would be admissible, not only to impeach DW1's in-court testimony that the bus had the green light, but also as substantive evidence that the bus ran the red light. Moreover, Dallas's attorney would not be entitled to a limiting instruction. Instead, the judge might instruct the jury:

> DW1 has told two conflicting versions of what happened. At a deposition a few months ago, DW1 testified that the bus ran the red light. Today DW1 testified the bus had the green light. You can believe whichever one you choose; or, if you think they cancel each other out, you can ignore DW1's testimony on this point altogether.

2. Prior consistent statements[39]

§ 12.15 Overview

The mere fact that, prior to trial, HDL/W[40] made a statement consistent with what HDL/W testifies to during the trial is no reason to admit the prior statement. The

39. For more thorough coverage, see *A Student's Guide to Hearsay* (5th ed. 2019) § 4.14 to § 4.25, pp. 69–75.

40. HDL/W: a hearsay declarant (i.e., a person whose hearsay statement has been or now is being offered in evidence) who is now testifying at the trial or hearing.

fact that HDL/W has told the same basic story numerous times in the past does not add all that much to HDL/W's testimony. Moreover, the prior statements usually are hearsay. There is no general exception to the hearsay definition or hearsay rule covering prior consistent statements. Thus, if a proper objection is made, a witness's prior consistent statement is inadmissible unless it is relevant for a non-hearsay purpose or unless it satisfies a hearsay exception.

Question 1.

In the bus-automobile collision litigation, DW2 told Officer Renko at the scene that the bus had the green light when it entered the intersection. That night he told his cousin about it. The next day he said the same thing to several colleagues at work. A month or so later, he told the same story to investigators for the lawyers in the case. Several months later, at a deposition, he said the same thing again.

At trial, DW2 is asked:

Q. Did you see what happened?

A. Yes. The light changed, so traffic going north and south on Broadway had the green. The bus pulled into the intersection. Then this car sped eastbound into the intersection along 48th Street, right into the path of the bus.

Q. So which vehicle had the green light?

A. The bus, for sure.

Is there anything objectionable about this testimony?

Answer:

No. DW2 is testifying about what he saw.

Question 2.

Continuing on direct, Dallas's lawyer asks:

Q Before testifying here today, did you ever tell anyone else that the bus had the green light?"

Philly objects: hearsay. Ruling?

Answer:

Objection sustained. There is no general "prior consistent statement" provision in Article VIII of the Federal Rules of Evidence. Nor are any of DW2's prior statements in this case likely to qualify under other exceptions to the hearsay definition or rule.

§ 12.16 FRE 801(d)(1)(B)

Effective December 1, 2014, FRE 801(d)(1)(B) provides:

> **(d) Statements That Are Not Hearsay.** A statement that meets the following conditions is not hearsay:
>
> **(1) A Declarant-Witness's Prior Statement.** The declarant testifies and is subject to cross-examination about a prior statement, and the statement: . . .
>
> . . .
>
> (B) is consistent with the declarant's testimony and is offered:
>
> (i) to rebut an express or implied charge that the declarant recently fabricated it or acted from a recent improper influence or motive in so testifying; or
>
> (ii) to rehabilitate the declarant's credibility as a witness when attacked on another ground; . . .

FRE 801(d)(1)(B) creates two special categories of prior consistent statements that are *not* hearsay.

FRE 801(d)(1)(B)(i) directs that a statement is not hearsay if it is relevant "to rebut an express or implied charge" that the declarant "recently fabricated" his testimony, or has shaped his testimony as a result of "a recent improper influence or motive."

FRE 801(d)(1)(B)(ii) categorizes as nonhearsay a statement which is relevant "to rehabilitate the declarant's credibility as a witness when attacked on another ground" besides the grounds of "recent fabrication or improper motive or influence." (The phrase "credibility as a witness" probably refers primarily to an attack on the witness's testimony, rather than his or her character for truthfulness.)

A prior consistent statement that falls into either of these two categories is not considered hearsay—even though it fits the FRE 801(c) definition of hearsay—and therefore is admissible to prove the truth of the matter asserted in the statement.

Here is the basic scenario. At trial, HDL/W testifies on direct to certain facts. On cross-examination (or later in the trial), the attorney for the adverse party attacks W's "credibility as a witness." If, prior to trial, the witness made a statement that is consistent with his direct testimony, that prior consistent statement is admissible as non-hearsay—but only if the prior statement, and the circumstances in which W made the statement, are sufficiently relevant to rebut the attack on W's "credibility."

At common law, the statement could be admitted, but only to rebut the impeachment, but not to prove the truth of the matter asserted in the statement. This required the judge to give a limiting instruction to the jury that often was practically meaningless or confusing or both. In essence, Rule 801(d)(1)(B) eliminates the need for the limiting instruction.

§ 12.17 FRE 801(d)(1)(B)(i): "to rebut an express or implied charge. . ."

To utilize FRE 801(d)(1)(B)(i), the party offering HDL/W's prior consistent statement must persuade the judge that four conditions are satisfied:

1. "The declarant testifies [at the current proceeding] and is subject to cross-examination about the prior statement." In other words, either HDL/W must now be on the witness stand, and can be questioned (on direct, cross, or redirect) about the statement; or, HDL/W has already testified at the current trial or proceeding, and can be recalled so a party can question HDL/W about the statement.
2. The prior statement is consistent with what HDL/W has testified to at trial.
3. At some point in the current trial or proceeding, an attorney has impeached HDL/W by explicitly or implicitly accusing HDL/W of having recently fabricated his or her testimony, or of allowing his/her testimony to be affected by a "recent improper influence or motive."
4. The prior statement is relevant to rebut the accusation.

Rationale: A prior consistent statement that rebuts an accusation of recent fabrication or improper motivation is relevant in helping the factfinder decide whether to believe the testimony despite the accusation.

Unlike FRE 801(d)(1)(A), an 801(d)(1)(B)(i) statement need not have been made while under oath and need not have been made in a formal setting. A statement to a police officer, private investigator, attorney, bartender, barber, radio talk show host, or anyone else can qualify. So can a statement posted on social media.

The most frequent issues that arise in applying FRE 801(d)(1)(B)(i) are the third and fourth requirements. To elaborate:

3. Did the impeaching attorney explicitly or implicitly accuse HDL/W1 of "recently fabricat[ing his or her testimony]," or explicitly or implicitly accuse HDL/W of testifying as he or she did because of "a recent improper influence or motive"?
4. Was the prior consistent statement made *before* the alleged fabrication or improper influence or motive occurred? In Tome v. United States, 513 U.S. 150 (1995), the Supreme Court held that only consistent statements that were made before the alleged motive or fabrication arose can satisfy FRE 801(d)(1)(B)(i).

Back to *Philly v. Dallas*. DW2 testified that the bus had the green light. On cross, Philly asks questions challenging the accuracy of DW2's direct testimony. After Dallas rests, Philly calls PWX to further impeach DW2's testimony. In rebuttal, Dallas, hoping to persuade the jury to believe DW2 despite Philly's efforts at impeachment, wants to bring out the fact that DW2 made one or more statements prior to trial consistent with what DW2 testified to on direct.

Dallas may do so under FRE 801(d)(1)(B)(i) only if (a) Philly's impeachment of DW2 explicitly or implicitly accused DW2 of fabricating his/her testimony, or accused DW2 of allowing his/her testimony to be affected by "a recent improper influence or motive" such as friendship, a bribe, or bias or prejudice; and (b) the statement was made before DW2 allegedly "fabricated" the version of events he/she testified to, or before the improper motive or influence arose.

If, instead, Philly's impeachment of DW2 merely tried to show that DW2's testimony is simply inaccurate, or that the jury shouldn't believe DW2 because DW2 is not a truthful person, Dallas will not be able to use Rule 801(d)(1)(B)(i) to introduce DW2's prior statements.

§ 12.18 Questions

Question 1.

In *Philly v. Dallas*, after DW2 testifies that the bus had the green light, Philly's attorney cross-examines DW2 as follows.

> Q. How did you happen to be at that intersection at one o'clock when the collision occurred?
>
> A. I had just finished having lunch at a place up the block.
>
> Q. Do you remember the name of the restaurant?
>
> A. Uhhhh . . .
>
> Q. It was the "Bar None," wasn't it?
>
> A. Yeah.
>
> Q. And you'd been there that morning since they opened, hadn't you?
>
> A. Yeah.
>
> Q. You'd been drinking all morning and afternoon?
>
> A. I guess. Yes, I was.
>
> Q. So that by 1 p.m. you were quite intoxicated?
>
> A. I was feelin' pretty good, but I wasn't drunk or nothin'.

On redirect, Dallas's attorney wants to bring out the fact that at about 1:20 that afternoon, DW2 told Officer Renko that the bus had the green light. P objects: hearsay. D responds: Rule 801(d)(1)(B)(i). Ruling?

Answer:

Objection sustained. Philly's cross-examination implicitly accused DW2 of being drunk (and therefore, presumably, in no shape to accurately perceive or remember how the collision occurred); but that is not an expressed or implied accusation of recent fabrication or improper influence or motive. ("Under the influence of alcohol" is not the kind of "improper influence" the rule is concerned with.)

Question 2.

Suppose, instead, Philly's cross-examination of DW2 is as follows.

Q. You just testified that you saw the car enter the intersection against the red light?

A. That's right.

Q. Do you recall being interviewed by PI, an investigator for my law firm, about a month after the collision?

A. Yes.

Q. Didn't you tell PI that you didn't really see what caused the collision?

Does this constitute accusing W2 of "recent fabrication"?

Answer:

Perhaps. Philly's cross alleges that DW2 made a prior inconsistent statement. Whether this implicitly accuses DW2 of "recently fabricating" his current testimony depends on the underlying circumstances. But as a general rule, merely bringing out a prior inconsistent statement does not constitute an accusation of recent fabrication or improper motive. Rather, it suggests that DW2's memory of the event has gotten fuzzy since he spoke to PI. Ergo, Dallas cannot rely on FRE 801(d)(1)(B)(i) to introduce DW2's consistent statement to Officer Renko shortly after the collision.

Question 3.

Suppose, instead, Philly's cross-examination of DW2 is as follows:

Q. You testified on direct that the bus had the green light.

A. That's right.

Q. Why did you testify that way?

A. 'Cause that's the way it happened.

Q. That's the only reason?

A. Yes.

Q. I see.—Oh, by the way, do you happen to be personally acquainted with the person who was driving that bus?

A. Yes—

Q. And that acquaintanceship is more than just casual, I believe.

A. We're engaged to be married.

Q. The driver of the bus is your fiancée?

A. That's right.

On redirect, Dallas asks DW2:

Q Five minutes or so after the collision, did you give a statement about what you saw to Police officer Renko?

Both sides had deposed DW2 and Renko prior to trial. Philly knows that DW2 will (if permitted) answer that DW2 told Renko that the bus had the green light. Philly therefore objects that the question calls for hearsay. Dallas responds: "Rule 801(d)(1)(B)(i)." Ruling?

<u>Answer:</u>

It depends.

Philly's cross-examination of DW2 implicitly accused DW2 of testifying the way he/she did to protect his fiancée. (Even love is an "improper influence or motive" if it prompts someone to lie under oath.) There is nothing improper with this cross-examination, but it does open the door to a prior consistent statement by DW2—but only if DW2 made that prior consistent statement *before* the alleged improper motive arose. Dallas has offered no evidence that DW2's statement to Renko was made before that motive arose. Therefore, Dallas has failed to satisfy that requirement of FRE 801(d)(1)(B)(i).

<u>Question 4.</u>

On redirect, DW2 testifies that he met the bus driver for the first time at a party several months after the collision. Then Dallas's attorney calls Officer Renko as a witness:

Q: On the day of the collision, did you interview a witness named W2?

A: I did.

Q: Did W2 tell you what he saw?

A: Yes. He said—

P'S ATTORNEY: Objection! Hearsay!

D'S ATTORNEY: 801(1)(d)(1)(B)(i), Your Honor.

Ruling?

Answer:

Objection overruled. Assuming the judge believes DW2's testimony that at the time he made the statement to Renko, he had not even met the bus driver, DW2's statement to Renko satisfies each of the Rule 801(d)(1)(B)(i) requirements:

(1) DW2 has testified at the trial and can be recalled for more cross-examination about the statement.

(2) DW2's statement to Renko is consistent with his trial testimony.

(3) The cross-examination in Question 3 implicitly accused DW2 of testifying as did to protect the person DW2 plans to marry.

(4) DW2's statement to Renko rebuts this implicit accusation, because DW2 made the statement before DW2 and the bus driver even met, let alone became engaged to be married.

Question 5.

Suppose instead DW2 had already been engaged to the bus driver at the time of the collision. Would DW2's statement to Renko still have adequate "rebuttal value"?

Answer:

No, because DW2 would have had the same "improper motive" the day of the accident as he did at trial (unless, at the time he made the statement to Renko, he did not yet know that his fiancee was driving that particular bus).

Question 6.

Suppose DW2 and the bus driver were casual acquaintances prior to the collision, but had not dated. What then?

Answer:

Does being casually acquainted with someone create a motive to lie to protect that person from being found at fault for causing a collision? If so, the statement is not admissible per FRE 801(d)(1)(B)(i). If not, it is admissible per that rule. This is probably a case where the judge has discretion to decide either way.

§ 12.19 FRE 801(d)(1)(B)(ii): prior consistent statements to rebut other attacks on the declarant's "credibility"

As of December 1, 2014, FRE 801(d)(1)(B) now includes rule 801(d)(1)(B)(ii):

> **(d) Statements That Are Not Hearsay.** A statement that meets the following conditions is not hearsay:
>
> **(1) A Declarant-Witness's Prior Statement.** The declarant testifies and is subject to cross-examination about a prior statement, and the statement:...

> (B) is consistent with the declarant's testimony and is offered:
>
> . . .
>
> (ii) to rehabilitate the declarant's credibility as a witness when attacked on another ground;...

The addition of this sub-rule considerably expands the kinds of prior consistent statements that are admissible as substantive evidence. The Advisory Committee Note to FRE 801(d)(1)(B)(ii) offers, as examples, "consistent statements that are probative to explain what otherwise appears to be an inconsistency in the witness's testimony," and "consistent statements that would be probative to rebut a charge of faulty memory."

Such statements, if probative to rebut such impeachment, are now admissible as substantive evidence, not for some limited purpose. Therefore, the adverse party is not entitled to a limiting instruction.

The Advisory Committee Note emphasizes that the new rule "does not allow impermissible bolstering of a witness." In other words, HDL/W's prior statements consistent with his testimony are still generally inadmissible, unless they have special relevance to rebut certain types of impeachment. The Note also emphasizes that "the trial court has ample discretion to exclude prior consistent statements that are cumulative accounts of an event."

In sum: a HDL/W's prior consistent statement is admissible under Rule 801(d)(1)(B)(ii) "only if [it] properly rehabilitates a witness whose credibility has been attacked," and only if it survives a Rule 403 objection (such as "needless presentation of cumulative evidence")—assuming the adverse party makes the objection.

§ 12.20 Questions: "Rocky v. Apollo"

On March 1, Rocky and Apollo argued with each other and eventually started fighting. Both sustained injuries, and each sued the other, claiming self-defense and alleging that the other started it. The characters in our drama are:

Apollo
Albert, Apollo's lawyer
Angst, Albert's investigator
Aardvark, a witness who testifies for Apollo
Rocky
Rose, Rocky's lawyer
Rueful, Rose's investigator
Rabbit, a witness who testifies for Rocky

Question 1.

The case goes to trial in December. Aardvark testifies as a witness for Apollo that Rocky threw the first punch. Prior to trial, Aardvark made two statements about the fight:

1. On March 8, Aardvark gave Rueful, Rose's investigator, a signed statement that Apollo threw the first punch.
2. On June 1, Aardvark told Angst, Albert's investigator, that Rocky threw the first punch.

On cross-examination, Rose, Rocky's attorney, wants to introduce the March 8th signed statement that Aardvark gave Rueful, i.e., that Apollo threw the first punch. How should Rose go about it?

Answer:

Rose should ask that the statement be marked as an exhibit for identification (let's call it exhibit 3). After it is marked, Rose should show it to Aardvark and ask whether Aardvark recognizes it and whether it has Aardvark's signature on the bottom. Assuming Aardvark acknowledges the signature, Rose should offer it in evidence.

Question 2.

Albert, Apollo's attorney, objects: hearsay! How should Rose respond?

Answer:

FRE 613(b): exhibit 3 is extrinsic evidence of Aardvark's prior inconsistent statement. See § 12.13. Objection overruled.

Question 3.

What should Albert do next?

Answer:

Request a limiting instruction: Aardvark's written statement (Rocky's exhibit 3) is admissible only to impeach Aardvark's testimony that Rocky threw the first punch; it is not admissible as evidence that Apollo threw the first punch.

Question 4.

Why isn't Aardvark's statement admissible per FRE 801(d)(2)(B)(ii), which holds that a witness's prior statement offered to rebut impeachment is not hearsay—and that therefore no limiting instruction need be given?

Answer:

Aardvark's statement to Rueful is not a FRE 801(d)(2)(B)(ii) statement. It is not consistent with her testimony on direct—FRE 801(d)(2)(B)(ii) only covers a witness's prior statement that is consistent with the witness's trial testimony. Rather, Aardvark's statement to Rueful is *inconsistent* with Aardvark's testimony, and therefore is admissible only per Rule 613. Rule 613 statements are admissible only to impeach a witness's trial testimony, not as substantive evidence.

Question 5.

Continuing on cross-examination, Rose, Rocky's attorney, suggests that Aardvark's memory of the fight must have been better on March 8, when Aardvark signed the statement for Rueful, than it is now, at trial in December, 9 months later. Aardvark nevertheless insists that Rocky threw the first punch.

On redirect, Albert asks Aardvark:

Q. Did you have a conversation on June 1 about this fight with Angst, my investigator?

A. Yes, I did.

Q. And what did you tell Angst about what happened?

Rose objects: hearsay. Is Aardvark's statement to Angst admissible per FRE 801(d)(1)(B)(i)?

Answer:

No. Rose's impeachment of Aardvark challenged the accuracy of her memory, but did not, directly or indirectly, accuse Aardvark of a deliberate, recent fabrication.

Question 6.

Is Aardvark's statement to Angst admissible per Rule 801(d)(1)(B)(ii)?

Answer:

No, because it is not really relevant to rebut Rose's suggestion that Aardvark's memory of the fight was better on March 8 than it is now, in December, when Aardvark is testifying. Why? Because Aardvark's statement to Angst on June 1 does not really rebut Rose's impeachment of Aardvark. Aardvark's prior statement consistent with Aardvark's direct testimony was made on June 1, almost three months after Aardvark's prior inconsistent statement to Rueful—plenty of time for Aardvark's memory about the fight to have become faulty.

General reminder: when a professor puts dates in an exam question, they are almost always important facts. Look for ways that the dates help define or resolve issues in the question.

Question 7.

Rabbit also made two statements about the fight:

1. On April 1, Rabbit gave a signed statement to Rueful, Rocky's investigator, that Apollo threw the first punch.
2. On May 10, he told Angst, Apollo's investigator, that Rocky threw the first punch.

Rabbit testifies for Rocky that Apollo threw the first punch.

On cross, Albert seeks to introduce Rabbit's May 10th statement to Angst that Rocky, not Apollo, started the fight. May Albert do so?

Answer:

Yes. What Rabbit told Angst is a prior inconsistent statement, i.e., inconsistent with Rabbit's testimony on direct. Therefore, it is admissible, per FRE 613, to impeach Rabbit's trial testimony that Apollo started the fight. But that statement satisfies no hearsay exception. Therefore Rose, Rocky's attorney, should ask the judge to instruct the jury that what Rabbit told Angst is admissible only to impeach Rabbit's direct testimony; it is not admissible, and they should not consider it, as evidence that Rocky started the fight.

Question 8.

Angst proceeds to challenge Rabbit: "Wasn't your memory clearer and fresher back on May 10, than it is now, 7 months later?" Rabbit insists he remembers clearly that Apollo started the fight.

On redirect, Rose asks Rabbit:

Q. Did you have a conversation on April 1 about this fight with Rueful, my investigator?

A. Yes, I did.

Q. And what did you tell Rueful?

Angst objects: hearsay. Is Rabbit's statement to Rueful admissible per FRE 801(d)(1)(B)(i)?

Answer:

No. Angst's impeachment of Rabbit challenged the accuracy of his memory, but did not, directly or indirectly, accuse Rabbit of a deliberate, recent fabrication.

Question 9.

Is Rabbit's statement to Rueful admissible per Rule 801(d)(1)(B)(ii)?

Answer:

Yes. Rabbit's prior consistent statement to Rueful (that Apollo started the fight) was made on April 1, forty days before he gave his (inconsistent) statement to Rueful accusing Rocky. Therefore (unlike Aardvark's statement in Question 5), it is relevant to rebut the implication that Rabbit now has a faulty memory.

Question 10.

After the judge allows Rose to elicit Rabbit's April 1 statement to Rueful, Albert, Apollo's lawyer, asks the judge to instruct the jury that Rabbit's statement to Rueful is admissible only to rebut Albert's impeachment of Rabbit, but is not admissible as proof that Apollo started the fight. Should the judge give the instruction?

Answer:

No. Rule 801(d)(1)(B)(ii) is an exception to the hearsay definition; therefore, it is admissible, over a hearsay objection, as substantive evidence that Rocky started the fight, not merely to rebut the impeachment.

Chapter 13

Impeaching and Rehabilitating the Character of the Witness: Rules 608–609

§13.1 In general; Rule 610

i. In general

In the previous chapter, we looked at how the law governs impeaching and rehabilitating witness W1's *testimony*. This chapter examines how the law regulates impeaching W1's *character for truthfulness*, and how, if one party has attacked W's character for truthfulness, the other party can offer evidence rebutting that attack.

Such an attack can take three forms: (1) cross-examining W1 about W1's prior untruthful acts, which is regulated by FRE 608(b); (2) cross-examining W1 about W1's prior convictions, which is regulated by FRE 609; and (3) offering negative reputation or opinion testimony about W1's character for truthfulness, which is regulated by FRE 608(a).

(1) The law recognizes that information about prior untruthful acts is relevant, because if W1 has committed other untruthful acts—if W1 has lied or deceived or defrauded or cheated on other occasions—it is arguably more probable than it would be without that evidence, that W1 lied or deliberately shaded his testimony in order to favor one party or disfavor the other, or to paint himself in a more favorable light than the facts truly permit. Hence FRE 608(b).

(2) The law recognizes that if W1 has previously been convicted of certain types of crimes, this is relevant, because if W1 has committed such crimes—thereby violating important norms of acceptable behavior—it is arguably more probable than it would be without that evidence, that W1 is also willing to lie under oath—therefore violating another important norm of acceptable behavior. Hence FRE 608(a).

(3) Similarly, if W1's reputation in a particular community is that W1 lies or cheats or deceives frequently, or if witness W2, who knows W1 well, is of the opinion that W1's word cannot be trusted, that testimony makes it more probable than it would be without the evidence that W1's testimony in this case cannot be trusted. Therefore, FRE 608(a) permits an impeaching attorney to call a witness to give such testimony about W1.

In the previous chapter, we saw that the law gives the impeaching attorney considerable leeway in impeaching W1's *testimony*. By contrast, FRE 608 and 609 narrowly limit how an attorney can attempt to impeach W1's *character for truthfulness*. The law does so for two reasons. First, a witness's character for truthfulness or untruthfulness is generally less relevant than evidence that directly challenges the accuracy of W1's testimony. Second, attacking a witness's character for truthfulness makes testifying even more unpleasant than usual.

Once W1's character for truthfulness has been attacked by one or more of the methods permitted in FRE 608 and 609, the party who hopes the jury will believe W1's testimony can, if it chooses to, attempt to rehabilitate or bolster W1's character for truthfulness by offering favorable reputation or opinion testimony about that aspect of W1's character, per FRE 608(a).[1]

A brief word about vocabulary: Rule 608 refers to "character for truthfulness or untruthfulness." "Untruthfulness" is simply the opposite, or absence, of truthfulness. Perhaps the rule uses both terms to avoid quibbles as to how negative reputation or opinion testimony must be worded. There is no real difference between testimony that W1's reputation for truthfulness is poor and testimony that W1's reputation is that he is an untruthful person.

Nor is a witness restricted to using the terms "truthful," "truthfulness," "untruthful" and "untruthfulness." Courts have held that (assuming a proper foundation is

1. If the impeaching attorney calls W2 to give negative reputation or opinion evidence about W1 per FRE 608(a), Rule 608(b)(2) offers another way to bolster W1's credibility. It is used so rarely that it is hardly worth mentioning, but I cover that rule in § 13.33.

laid) W2 may describe W1 as a "consummate liar" or a "wily and deceptive person," and more colorful language would probably also be permitted.

ii. Religious beliefs or opinions: FRE 610

Before studying Rules 608 and 609, it is worthwhile to look at FRE 610, which also addresses, in a way, an issue that some might think affects a witness's character for truthfulness. FRE 610 provides:

> **Rule 610. Religious Beliefs or Opinions**
>
> Evidence of a witness's religious beliefs or opinions is not admissible to attack or support the witness's credibility.

This rule is straightforward enough. P sues D. On direct examination, P calls W, a particularly important witness in P's case. In an attempt to persuade the jury to place special trust and reliance in W's truthfulness, P asks W: "What is your religion? How does your religion regard the importance of telling the truth? What does your religion say about someone who lies? Do you follow your religion's doctrine when it comes to testifying under oath?" Rule 610 precludes such questions. In fact, it precludes any attorney from asking W anything at all about W's religious beliefs or affiliation (or lack of such beliefs or affiliation), if the only relevance of such questioning would be to impeach or bolster W's character for truthfulness. It also precludes an attorney from offering extrinsic evidence relating to religious beliefs or affiliation to impeach or bolster W's character for truthfulness.

Rule 610 does *not* preclude eliciting evidence about W's religious affiliation if that fact is relevant in some other, more direct way. Suppose CSM (a church, synagogue or mosque) sues, or is sued by, XYZ Corp., a company with which CSM had done business. CSM calls W, who testifies to certain events that are relevant to the suit. On cross, or by extrinsic evidence, or both, XYZ could certainly elicit the fact that W is a member of CSM, because that fact is relevant to suggest that W is consciously or subconsciously spinning the facts to favor CSM. But neither CSM nor XYZ could offer evidence of CSM's religious doctrines about the importance of testifying truthfully, nor about W's beliefs in that regard.

A. Cross-Examining W1 about Him/Herself: FRE 608(b)(1) and FRE 609

1. Rule 608(b)(1)

§ 13.2 The rule

Generally, the first opportunity to impeach the character of a witness is while the witness is on the witness stand. This is litigation situation F (§ 11.29): cross-examining W about W's prior untruthful acts. The impeaching attorney may seek to ask W1 about prior unsavory acts the witness allegedly committed. Rule 608(b)(1), which governs such cross-examination, reads as follows:

> Rule 608. A Witness's Character for Truthfulness or Untruthfulness
>
> . . .
>
> (b) Specific Instances of Conduct. Except for a criminal conviction under Rule 609, extrinsic evidence is not admissible to prove specific instances of a witness's conduct in order to attack or support the witness's character for truthfulness. But the court may, on cross-examination, allow them to be inquired into if they are probative of the character for truthfulness or untruthfulness of:
>
> (1) the witness; or
>
> (2) another witness whose character the witness being cross-examined has testified about.[2]
>
> By testifying on another matter, a witness does not waive any privilege against self-incrimination for testimony that relates only to the witness's character for truthfulness.

The rule thus codifies two important principles.

1. If the only relevance about a "specific instance of a witness's conduct" is to attack his character for truthfulness, the impeaching attorney cannot introduce "extrinsic evidence" of that conduct. The only exception to this rule is evidence of a conviction that satisfies FRE 609.[3]

2. Let's ignore FRE 608(b)(2) for now; we will cover it in § 13.32.

3. However, if evidence of "a specific instance of a witness's conduct" is relevant and admissible for some other purpose under a different rule—such as FRE 404(b)(2) or FRE 412(b) or FRE 413

2. But the trial judge "may allow" the impeaching attorney to "inquire into," i.e., ask the witness about, one or more "specific instances of [the] witness's conduct" if each instance is "probative of the [witness's] character for... untruthfulness...."

This gives rise to several issues:

1. What kinds of "specific instances of ... conduct" are considered relevant to attack the witness's "character for truthfulness"?
2. How must such questions be worded?
3. How may the impeaching attorney respond, if the witness falsely denies having engaged in a particular instance of conduct about which the witness was questioned on cross-examination?
4. How much discretion does the trial judge have to permit or forbid such cross-examination?
5. If a party's witness has had his character for truthfulness impeached in this way, what can that party do to rebut the impeachment?

Such cross-examination falls within litigation situation F, § 11.29.

The final sentence of Rule 608(b) is designed to protect a witness's Fifth Amendment privilege against self-incrimination. Suppose, in a criminal or civil trial (it doesn't matter), a party calls W1 to testify about certain events—say, who ran a red light in a traffic collision case. As it happens, W1 is currently being investigated for, or is currently under indictment for, engaging in securities fraud—conduct which satisfies the "probative of character for ... untruthfulness" requirement in FRE 608(b)(1) (see § 13.4). On cross, the other party can ask W1 properly worded questions about the securities fraud, but W1 may (and even if he is innocent, probably should) assert his Fifth Amendment privilege and refuse to answer. Assuming this occurs in the jury's presence, the jury is likely to draw a highly negative inference about W1.

The situation described in the previous paragraph arises most often when defendant D, who is on trial for one crime or set of crimes, testifies, and on cross, the prosecutor wants to question D about an unrelated crime for which D is currently under indictment or being investigated. To force D to "plead the Fifth" in front of a jury is so highly prejudicial that the law essentially forbids asking a defendant questions which would require the defendant to do so.

---

or FRE 406—then the assumption is that the evidence should be admissible for that other purpose, unless FRE 403 or some other rule (e.g., hearsay, or an evidentiary privilege) requires exclusion.

§ 13.3 The ban on extrinsic evidence

P and D entered into a contract in which D was to deliver certain materials to P on a strict schedule. The contract contained a clause giving P the right to cancel the contract if a delivery was late, and spelling out the damages P was entitled to if D failed to comply with the schedule. D was late with the second delivery; P canceled the contract and sued D to enforce the damages clause.

During D's case-in-chief, SA, D's sales agent, testified that X, P's purchasing agent, promised that P would not enforce the damages contract if circumstances beyond D's control prevented a timely delivery. (D's failure was due to a strike against another company in the supply chain and complications arising out of a landslide that destroyed the main road to D's facility.) In rebuttal, P calls X as a witness. X testifies that he made no such promise, and in fact insists that he stressed to SA that the contract did not include an escape clause for circumstances beyond D's control.

X's character for truthfulness, it turns out, is wretched. D's attorney has accumulated the following evidence:

1. Seven years ago, X was fired from a prior job for submitting false expense account claims, including travel expenses for a trip he never took, and theater tickets supposedly purchased to entertain a potential customer, when in fact he took FGF, his then-girlfriend. FGF and the supposed customer are both willing to testify to these facts; so is the personnel director of the company that fired X when he learned of this.
2. FGF will testify that she agreed to move in with X because he assured her he was single when, in fact, he was married but separated from his wife and two young children.
3. CB will testify that four years ago, he purchased a car from X which X claimed to own, when it turned out the car belonged to FGF.
4. Two years ago, X made several purchases with a stolen credit card. D's attorney has lined up documentary proof and witnesses to clearly establish these facts.
5. Six months before X was hired by P, X took out a car loan from a bank. To obtain a loan, he had to submit a statement of outstanding debts. X's statement asserted that he had no outstanding debts, when in fact he owed $6,000 in back rent. P's attorney has lined up witnesses and documentary evidence to prove these facts.

Each of these "specific instances" of X's conduct involves lying or deception or deceit or fraud. Each, therefore, demonstrates X's character for untruthfulness. As such, each is an instance of X's conduct that comes within the ambit of Rule 608(b). How much of this evidence may P's attorney introduce, to attack X's character for truthfulness?

None of it. None of these five examples of X's character for untruthfulness has anything to do with the contract between P and D; none of the incidents go directly to whether X made the promises and representations that D, SA's sales agent, claims X did. Since their only relevance is to attack X's character for truthfulness, all this evidence is extrinsic to the key factual issues in the case; hence, none of it is admissible.

Why? Because such evidence could prolong trials extensively. It would take a lot of courtroom time for D to call all those witnesses and introduce all those documents, and of course P's attorney would be entitled to cross-examine and impeach each witness. Moreover, once D rested, P would be entitled to call witnesses to rebut the witnesses and documents that D used to impeach X. For example, D might call several people who were friendly with X and FGF when they were living together, all of whom would testify that FGF was well aware, when she moved in with X, that X was married and had two young children. And so on.

Thus, Rule 608(b) does not permit an impeaching attorney to offer extrinsic evidence of "specific instances" of a witness's conduct, if the only relevance of those instances is to attack X's character for truthfulness or show X's character for untruthfulness. The rule does permit the impeaching attorney to "inquire into" these instances on cross-examination.

Section 13.4 discusses what kinds of conduct come within Rule 608(b) questioning. Section 13.5 discusses how such questions can be worded (i.e., how the impeaching attorney may "inquire into" the witness's prior untruthful conduct). Section 13.6 discusses what the impeaching attorney can do if witness W denies having engaged in the conduct he was cross-examined about per FRE 608(b).

§ 13.4 What kind of conduct comes within Rule 608(b)?

Rule 608(b) directs that, to attack witness W's character for untruthfulness, the court may allow an impeaching attorney to cross examine W about "specific instances of [W's] conduct" so long as each instance is "probative of [W's] character for truthfulness or untruthfulness." What does "probative of [W's] character for truthfulness or untruthfulness" mean? Section 13.3 provides several examples. The following discussion illustrates the matter further.

L, a lawyer who was admitted to the bar seven years ago, is on trial for attempting to bribe a juror in a contract case that was tried last year. He has taken the stand and has just completed direct examination, during which he denied bribing, or even contacting, any jurors. You, the prosecutor (PA), are about to cross-examine L. You have learned:

1. Five years ago, after having three or four alcoholic beverages, he was forced to leave a bar because he was disturbing other customers; after the bar closed, he smashed its door and window with a baseball bat. He was arrested for

destruction of property; the charges were dropped when he paid to replace the door and window and agreed to attend anger management classes.

2. Three years ago, L was appointed to be the administrator of the estate of Missy Havisham, a woman who had died a few weeks earlier. L unlawfully diverted funds from the estate into his own bank account, and filed false statements with the court in attempt to cover up what he had done. He did so on nine separate occasions before his scheme was discovered. The matter was reported to the state bar's Committee on Professional Misconduct. After a hearing, the state bar association suspended him from the practice of law for a year.
3. Six months ago, demonstrators met at the state capital to support a hotly contested legislative proposal. L was photographed at a demonstration wearing a brown shirt with swastikas on each arm,[4] until leaders of the protest demanded that he remove the swastikas.

You have documentary evidence of each of these incidents, and witnesses lined up eager to testify about them if called.

Question 1.

On cross-examination, what use (if any) can you make of the bar-smashing incident?

Answer:

None. You are not entitled to refer to it in any way.

Why? First, to state the obvious, the bar-smashing incident has no direct relevance to whether L attempted to bribe a juror in an unrelated case four years later (for which he is now on trial). Therefore, the only relevance the bar-smashing has is to attack L's character.

The bar-smashing certainly does suggest negative aspects about L's character—that he drinks too much, has anger-management problems, and that he may resort to violence when frustrated or embarrassed. Based on this incident, I would not want him as a neighbor—or as a lawyer, either.[5]

---

4. In the 1920s, as Adolph Hitler strove to bring the Nazi party to power in Germany, he was assisted by a militia called the "Brownshirts" after the uniform they wore. The swastika (also called the "crooked cross") was the symbol of the Nazi Party and became the official emblem of Germany after Hitler and the Nazi Party came to power.

5. This may strike some of you as unduly harsh: "It's not fair to judge a person based on only one incident in his or her life. Suppose this was very atypical of his conduct? Suppose he had just suffered a major blow—loss of a loved one, a crushing professional setback or the like?" I agree. We should be wary of judging a person based solely on what might have been a single, isolated instance. But if the only fact you knew about someone

But smashing a bar's door and window, though strongly suggestive of significant lapses in his character, do not directly implicate his *character for truthfulness*. Therefore, Rule 608(b) precludes P from using it to cross-examine L.

Question 2.

On cross-examination, what use (if any) can you make of the swastika incident?

Answer:

None. You are not entitled to refer to it in any way.

Someone who wears Nazi symbols at a political event proclaims himself or herself as a racist and bigot of the worst order.[6] Personally, I would not believe anything L said about anything. But wearing swastikas is not in-and-of-itself untruthful behavior—it does not involve lying or deception. (L is not trying to hide his hateful bigotry; he is advertising it.) Therefore, it is not within the scope of Rule 608(b)(1), and must not be referred to while cross-examining L in this case.

As these two questions illustrate, there is a wide range of behavior which, although antisocial, evil and, often, illegal, nevertheless cannot be asked about per Rule 608(b). Acts of violence are not probative of character for untruthfulness. Drug or alcohol abuse is not a subject for valid 608(b)(1) questioning.

Certain forms of theft-related crimes do involve "a dishonest act or false statement": Forgery. Fraud. Using a stolen credit card. Writing a check on a closed-out account or on an account knowing there are insufficient funds to cover the check now and for the foreseeable future. On the other hand, robbery is not an act which involves lying or fraud or deceit or deception. Nor are pickpocketing or shoplifting.[7] Nor is burglary.

Question 3.

On cross-examination, what use (if any) can you make of the misappropriation of estate funds, the false reports, and the punishment of suspension imposed upon him by the state bar?

---

was this one instance, I suspect you would hesitate to enter into a close personal or professional relationship with that person.

6. This is sad, because the swastika has a long and benign history. According to Wikipedia, "It is used as a symbol of divinity and spirituality in Indian religions, including Hinduism, Buddhism and Jainism. In the Western world, it was a symbol of auspiciousness and good luck until the 1930s," when the Nazis appropriated it. "The swastika continues to be used as a symbol of good luck and prosperity in Hindu, Buddhist and Jain countries such as Nepal, India, Mongolia, China and Japan. It is also commonly used in Hindu marriage ceremonies."

7. Some courts hold that all forms of theft are Rule 608(b) "dishonest acts." Your professor will probably tell you what approach to take on the issue.

Answer:

Misappropriating funds and filing false reports come squarely within Rule 608(b)(1), because each involves untruthful conduct. Depositing estate funds in his own bank is untruthful, because it is inherently deceptive. And filing false statements with the court is by definition an effort to deceive—i.e., a lie. Therefore, each misappropriation, and each false report, is a specific act which is, as Rule 608(b)(1) puts it, "probative of the character for truthfulness or untruthfulness of" L, in his capacity as a witness for himself.

Here's how I might cross-examine L:

Q Mr. L, three years ago, you were retained to be the executor of the estate of Missy Havisham, is that correct?

Q That meant you were responsible to collect money coming to the estate, pay bills, and make sure that the estate's assets would be preserved for her adopted daughter Estella, her only heir. True?

Q And you had a legal duty to file regular reports with the probate court specifying income and payments, is that also true?

Q On [specify date] did you receive a check from [specify who issued the check] for the estate in the amount of [specify amount]?

Q You were duty bound, were you not, to deposit that in the estate's bank account?

Q In fact, you deposited it in your own personal account instead, didn't you?

Q And it is also true, isn't it, that when you filed a report with the probate court on [specify date], you deliberately omitted any mention of that check for [specify amount], to hide the fact that you were stealing from the estate?

I would then ask the same series of questions about the second check, and so on, until the judge interrupted me:

J Mr. PA, wrap this line of questioning up.

PA Yes, Your Honor. I have one more question, if I may.

J One more, and that's it.

Q Mr. L, is it not a fact that on nine separate occasions, you received checks for the Havisham estate, totaling [the aggregate sum], and diverted them into your own bank account, and deliberately filed false reports with the probate court to hide your thefts?

Note that this entire line of questioning is worded intrinsically: "Did you do these dishonest, untruthful things?" None of these questions explicitly or indirectly refers to any outside source of information.

Question 4.

Can PA, the impeaching attorney, introduce proof that L was investigated by the state bar, which concluded that he had engaged in professional misconduct and suspended him from practice for a year?

Answer:

No. Offering documentary proof that he stole money and filed false reports would be offering "extrinsic evidence." Rule 608(b) is quite specific: "Except for a criminal conviction under Rule 609, extrinsic evidence is not admissible to prove specific instances of a witness's conduct in order to attack... the witness's character for truthfulness." And while there are similarities between a bar disciplinary hearing and a criminal trial, a finding of professional wrongdoing by the state bar is not a "criminal conviction under Rule 609."

Good-faith basis requirement. Rule 608(b) is also subject to the good-faith requirement: an attorney can ask witness W about W's prior conduct per FRE 608(b)(1) only if the attorney has a good-faith basis for the question. The attorney doesn't need airtight proof that W committed the "specific act" the attorney wants to ask W about, but if challenged, the attorney must convince the judge that a good-faith basis exists that W in fact committed that act. (The challenge, and the attorney's response, should be conducted out of the jury's hearing.) The good-faith requirement regarding 608(b)(1) cross-examination of W about him/herself follows the same pattern as the good-faith requirement regarding cross-examining a character witness about a defendant's prior "relevant" conduct, per FRE 405(a)(2nd sentence). See § 6.16.

§ 13.5 Must FRE 608(b)(1) questions be worded intrinsically; or is extrinsic wording okay?

Perhaps you noticed that in cross-examining L in Q3 in § 13.4, PA never mentioned the state bar proceeding and never used the word "suspended." PA never asked a question such as:

> Q It is a fact, is it not, that you were brought before the state bar committee on professional misconduct for doing all this, and were suspended from practicing law for a full year as punishment?

The word "suspended" makes this an extrinsically worded question. The word "suspended" is clearly extrinsic: the question itself informs the jury that someone else (in this case, the state bar) came to the conclusion that L misappropriated funds and submitted untrue documents to a court. (See § 6.19 for a list of words which would make a question "extrinsically worded.") Would it be proper to ask such a question ("were you suspended") during Rule 608(b)(1) cross-examination?

Some courts say yes, others say no.

I agree with the courts that rule that FRE 608(b)(1) precludes the use of extrinsically worded questions when cross-examining a witness about his alleged prior acts of untruthfulness or deceit.[8] Nor, in an "intrinsic questions only" jurisdiction, is the impeaching attorney allowed to refer to, or hint at, any negative effects that falsehood may have had on the witness's life.

Other courts, though, hold that it is permissible to ask L, "And in fact, sir, as a result, you were suspended from the practice of law for one year. Yes or no?"

As to which is the right approach, if your professor doesn't discuss the issue, there is probably no need for you to worry about it. If your professor does discuss the issue, consult Fishman Rule of Evidence 001, in §1 of the Preface, on page vii.

Question 1.

L's diversion of estate income into his own account was first discovered by a diligent court clerk. How did the clerk react upon first discovering the theft?

Answer:

The clerk exclaimed, "What the Dickens!" (If you don't get it, Google "Miss Havisham.")

§13.6 Response to a denial

During your cross-examination of L in §13.4, when you asked L whether he deposited that check in his own account and deliberately withheld including any reference to that check when he filed a report with the court, suppose he answered, "No, that's not true. I never did that!" What then?

You still cannot introduce the extrinsic evidence—the check, records from the estate account or from L's own account. You still cannot introduce the state bar report concluding that L did these things, nor the fact that the bar suspended L from practice for a year. The law says you must "take the answer," which is an opaque legalism meaning, "you can't introduce evidence which would prove that he is lying."[9]

8. The Advisory Committee Note to the 2003 amendment to the rule also endorses this approach, but this endorsement is less authoritative than might first appear. See *U.S. v. Dawson*, 434 F.3d 956 (7th Cir. 2006) (Posner, J.).

9. Why? Isn't this "impeachment by contradiction"? Yes, but L's misdeeds regarding the Havisham estate are only collateral matters in the bribing-a-juror trial. A judge has discretion to permit extrinsic impeachment-by-contradiction evidence on a collateral matter only if the testimony being contradicted was brought out on direct examination or was gratuitously volunteered in a non-responsive answer on cross. See § 12.10 & 12.11.

But the law does allow the impeaching attorney—subject to the trial judge's discretion—to "press the witness for a truthful answer."

The most direct way to "press" L "for a truthful answer," if the jurisdiction permits extrinsically worded questions, is to ask:

Q "Mr. L, in [specify year], isn't it a fact that you were investigated for this behavior by the State Bar's Committee on Professional Misconduct?

Q Is it not also a fact that that agency conducted a full hearing, at which you were entitled to be represented by a lawyer?

Q And is it not also a fact that at the end of that hearing, the Committee concluded you had done these things, and suspended you from the practice of law for a full year?

In a jurisdiction that does not permit extrinsically worded questions, you could do the following:

PA Your honor, may I have these documents marked as prosecution exhibits one, two, three and four for identification? (Let's say Exhibit 1 is the largest check L misappropriated; exhibit 2, a statement from L's bank showing a deposit of that amount into his personal account; exhibit 3, a statement from the estate's account, demonstrating that no such deposit was made to that account; and exhibit 4, a certified copy of the Report of the State Bar Committee on Professional Misconduct.)

J Proceed.

PA hands the documents to the court clerk, who labels them accordingly.

PA May I show them to the witness?

J You may. (The prosecutor does so.)

PA Mr. L: I ask you to examine state exhibits 1–4 for identification.

Have you read them over, sir?

L I've looked at them.

PA I ask you again: it is true, is it not, that on [date] you received a check payable to the Havisham estate; that instead of depositing that check in the estate's bank account, you deposited it in your own; and that you filed a report with the probate court, and that you deliberately omitted that check from your report of estate assets?

This procedure invokes FRE 612, which allows an attorney to show a document to a witness to "refresh the witness's recollection." That rule is probably invoked more often when a friendly witness has forgotten an important detail during direct examination; here, PA is pretending to "refresh" L's memory about thefts from the Havisham estate and L's subsequent suspension.[10]

If L repeats his answer—"No, that is not true!"—PA takes the paper back from him, shaking his or her head as-much-in-sorrow-as-in-anger, and quickly shifts gears to question L about something else. Because—in a jurisdiction that does not allow extrinsically worded questions during Rule 608(b) cross-examination—this, if the judge allows you to go this far, is the absolute most you can do in questioning L about his misappropriations and false reports.

Note that the jury does not know what documents you showed to L. Note further that the jury has heard no actual evidence that L did anything wrong in handling the Havisham estate: in essence, what the jury has actually heard is, "Did you steal from the estate and file false reports to the court?" "No, I did not." Therefore, the prosecutor must not make any reference whatsoever to any of this in his closing argument to the jury.

Nevertheless, this entire procedure—the questions, showing the documents, etc.—will likely leave the jury with the impression that L must have done something wrong regarding the estate, or else the judge would not have allowed the prosecutor to make such a big thing about it. And that is precisely why FRE 608(b) allows it: to enable the impeaching attorney to create that impression.

If this sounds too absurd to be the law, re-read § 4.1.

§ 13.7 FRE 608(b)(1) and FRE 404–405; bias; *U.S. v. Abel*

When different rules of evidence closely resemble one another, it is a challenge to determine whether one, or the other, or both, or neither, governs a particular offer of evidence or question on direct or cross-examination. Moreover, evidence or questions of a certain type may be excluded or limited by one rule or if offered for one purpose, but may be admitted or allowed under another rule or if offered for a different purpose. This section discusses the relationship between FRE 608(b)(1) and FRE 404–405, and between FRE 608(b)(1) and the common law principles governing impeachment to show bias.[11]

i. FRE 608(b)(1) and FRE 404(a)–405(a)

Rules 404(a)–405(a)(2nd sentence) and Rule 608(b)(1) relate to the admissibility of evidence of a person's extrinsic acts. They differ, however, in several significant respects. The interplay between Rule 608(b)(1) and Rule 405(a) can cause confusion. It need not, so long as a few rules are kept in mind.

---

10. For a more detailed discussion of FRE 612, see *A Student's Guide to Hearsay* (5th ed. 2019), §§ 9.2–9.5.

11. Issues comparing Rules 608(b)(1) and 609 are discussed in § 13.22.

1. Any party, in any kind of trial, may (subject to trial-judge discretion), per FRE 608(b)(1), impeach any witness (including a party who testifies). This entitles the impeaching attorney to ask W1 questions[12] which seek to show that W1, at some time in the past, engaged in conduct "probative of [W1's] character for... untruthfulness." (This is litigation situation F, § 11.29.)

2. In a *criminal* trial, a defendant (X) can call a character witness ("CW") per FRE 404(a)(2)(A) to testify favorably about a pertinent trait of defendant X's character. (This is litigation situation C, § 11.26.)

3. The prosecutor, cross-examining CW, may:

a. Impeach CW's character for truthfulness, by asking CW questions about *him/herself* pursuant to Rule 608(b) (and per FRE 609(a), if CW has been convicted of a Rule 609(a) crime, see § 13.10, *infra*). (This is litigation situation F, § 11.29). And—

b. Impeach CW's testimony about X, pursuant to the second sentence of Rule 405(a), by asking CW *intrinsically or extrinsically* worded questions about alleged prior acts by X that are inconsistent with the supposed good character of X: "Have you heard [or "Did you know] that in 2020 X was arrested for/charged with/accused of..." While the prosecutor may ask CW such questions, the prosecutor may not offer substantive evidence to prove that X in fact had been arrested/charged/accused, nor that X had in fact done the thing he had been arrested (etc.) for. (See litigation situation D, § 11.27.)

ii. FRE 608(b)(1) and FRE 404(b)(2)

FRE 608(b)(1) allows an attorney (subject to trial-judge discretion) to attack witness W's character for truthfulness by questioning W about W's prior acts involving dishonesty and false statement, but does not allow the impeaching attorney to offer extrinsic evidence to prove that W committed those acts. But where that extrinsic evidence is admissible per FRE 404(b)(2), admissibility under that rule trumps the inadmissibility under Rule 608(b)(1).

Suppose, for example, D is charged with selling what appeared to be a Nikon camera, but was in fact a cheap counterfeit doctored to look like a Nikon. Four years earlier, D was arrested for selling what appeared to be a Rolex watch but was in fact a cheap counterfeit imitation. In the watch case, D claimed he thought it was real, that he himself had been duped by someone else, and repaid the purchaser, and the charges were dropped.

Prior to the current (camera) trial, the prosecutor informed the defense, per FRE 404(b)(3), that it planned to offer evidence relating to the fake Rolex case during the

12. Some jurisdictions insist that the questions must be worded intrinsically; others permit extrinsic wording. See § 13.5, *supra*.

state's case-in-chief. (This is litigation situation E. See § 11.28.) D's attorney moved in limine to exclude that evidence, and indicated to the judge that the defense in the camera case would be a straight-forward denial: it must have been someone else, not D, who sold the phony camera. Based on this assurance and the general principle that a fungibly similar extrinsic act is not admissible to prove identity (see § 7.16), the judge denied the prosecutor's motion to introduce evidence of the fake Rolex incident during the state's case-in-chief.

It turned out that the state's evidence identifying D as the camera-seller was much stronger than D's attorney anticipated,[13] so after the state rested, defense counsel switched to a mens rea defense: D took the stand, admitted that he had sold the camera saying it was a Nikon, but claimed he himself had been deceived by the person from whom he bought it.[14]

Question 1.

The prosecutor now asks the judge to reconsider the earlier ruling on the fake Rolex incident. What is the prosecutor's theory; how should the judge rule?

Answer:

The judge's ruling excluding the watch incident during the state's case-in-chief was based on defense counsel's assurance that the defense would be mistaken identity. But now things are different in two respects. First, the defense is not mistaken identity; it is mental state. Second, D is now a witness.

Which litigation situation are we in? Go through the entire list: § 11.23–11.31. From their titles, only two litigation situations could possibly apply: litigation situation C, § 11.26, criminal defendant's case-in-chief, and litigation situation F, § 11.29, which applies whenever any witness in any case is being cross-examined.

---

13. In most jurisdictions, in criminal cases, neither party is required to inform the other of who its witnesses will be. (There are exceptions to this rule, but none of the exceptions would apply to this case.)

14. Judges understand that what happens during a trial sometimes requires defense counsel to shift gears like this. Many defense attorneys avoid telling the jury what the defense will be until after the prosecutor presents the state's case. In this hypothetical, the judge and prosecutor know that the defense has changed, but the jury probably doesn't.

You might wonder: doesn't a switch like this involve some degree of dishonesty by defense counsel? Most often, no, it doesn't. Suppose prior to trial, D told his lawyer that he did sell the camera, but thought it was genuine. Given the watch incident, the attorney would be highly skeptical about how this defense would play before a jury, and hoped the state's case identifying D as the camera seller was weak enough to avoid having to call D as a witness. Even knowing it was D who sold the camera, D's lawyer has an obligation to D to challenge the strength of the state's evidence identifying D as the seller. But if the state's case identifying D as the seller is strong, D's lawyer may legitimately decide that there is no choice but to go with the "I didn't know it was a phony" defense—even though the lawyer doubts D's claim of ignorance—in the hopes that the jury might buy it. (Besides, whether to testify is ultimately a defendant's choice, not the lawyer's.)

But litigation situation C does not actually apply here, because the rules listed there all involve evidence that the defense might offer. Here, though, the defense isn't offering evidence; rather, the defendant is being cross-examined—litigation situation F. The prosecutor wants to cross-examine D about a prior specific act.

We can skip the first rules and principles listed in litigation situation F, because questioning D about the Rolex case doesn't attack D's perception, memory, narration or motive to lie about the facts in the camera case being tried.

We can eliminate FRE 613 and FRE 801(d)(1), because D has not testified about the Rolex case on direct, so there is no testimony about it to impeach.

Next, we come to FRE 608(b) and 609. We can eliminate 609, because D was not convicted of anything in the Rolex incident.

FRE 608(b), by contrast, is very much in play, because selling counterfeit watches most definitely involves dishonesty and false statements. Rule 608(b) entitles the prosecutor to cross-examine D about a the fake Rolex incident, but cannot introduce evidence to prove that D in fact sold a fake Rolex.

But is 608(b) the only rule that applies to this case?

Look at the final grouping of rules in litigation situation F. Eliminate 412–413, because this is not a sex offense case. What's left? FRE 404(b).

The judge quite reasonably applied FRE 404(b)(1) to preclude the prosecutor from using the fake watch incident as evidence that it was D, not someone else, who sold the fake Nikon for which D is now in trial. But now the defense is conceding identity and conduct, and is defending on mental state. Prior similar acts that would be inadmissible to prove identity or conduct often are admissible per FRE 404(b)(2) to prove mental state. See § 7.24, § 7.26 & § 7.28.

Question 2.

On cross-examination, the prosecutor will, if permitted, ask:

Q It is a fact, is it not, that four years ago you sold a man what you said was Rolex watch. True?

A Yes.

Q Was it a Rolex watch?

A No. It turned out that it was a cheap imitation.

Q Which you knew at the time, right?

A Knew what?

Q Isn't it a fact that when you sold that quote Rolex watch unquote four years ago, you knew it was a fake?

A No, I thought it was real. I paid a lot of money for that watch!

Q Just like, in this case, you knew the camera was fake, too, right?

A No! I thought it was a real Nikon.

Is there any basis on which D's attorney can object?

Answer:

No. This is proper FRE 608(b) cross-examination.

Question 3.

After the defense presents the rest of its case, in rebuttal, the prosecutor calls WB, the watch-buyer in the fake Rolex incident, who will, if permitted, testify:

> ... I told D I was skeptical—Rolex watches generally sell for more than twice what he was asking. He told me that the company would be releasing a newer model soon and wanted to get rid of its existing inventory quickly. He said he bought this watch directly from the Rolex distribution warehouse on 27th Street.

D's attorney objects that this is impermissible extrinsic evidence of a prior untruthful act, which is inadmissible per FRE 608(b). Is counsel right? How should the prosecutor respond, how should the judge rule?

Answer:

Defense counsel is correct: WB's testimony constitutes extrinsic evidence of a prior untruthful act—a prior act that occurred four years ago, and which had no direct connection to the phony Nikon sale for which D is now on trial. Therefore, the prosecutor cannot rely on FRE 608(b) to justify WB's testimony.

But extrinsic evidence *is* admissible per FRE 404(b)(2). And since D's defense is now mental state—"I thought the camera was real"—evidence that on a prior occasion D sold a cheap imitation of an expensive item, knowing it was a counterfeit, is admissible to show "absence of mistake" on this occasion regarding the bogus Nikon. And WB's testimony—that D claimed he had purchased the fake Rolex "directly from the Rolex distribution warehouse"—establishes that D knowingly lied about where he had obtained the supposed Rolex.

The bottom line: if FRE 608(b) says certain evidence is inadmissible and FRE 404(b)(2) says it is admissible, the evidence is admissible, subject to trial judge discretion, unless banned by some other rule, such as FRE 403.

iii. FRE 608(b)(first sentence) and bias or motive to lie: *U.S. v. Abel*

The same is true when FRE 608(b)'s ban on extrinsic proof conflicts with extrinsic act evidence which, although relevant to show someone's character for untruthfulness, is also relevant to show that person's bias or motive to lie: the latter rule of admissibility trumps the former's rule of exclusion. The Supreme Court so held in *U.S. v. Abel*, 469 U.S. 45 (1984). Abel and two confederates were indicted for bank robbery. The codefendants pleaded guilty, and one of them, Ehle, testified against Abel. To impeach Ehle, defendant called another witness, Mills, who testified that Ehle had falsely incriminated Abel in order to receive favorable treatment from the Government. To impeach Mills, the prosecutor questioned him on cross-examination as to his membership in a secret prison organization that required its members to lie, steal or kill on behalf of another member. *Id.* at 47–48. After Mills denied any knowledge of the organization, the prosecutor, in rebuttal, recalled Ehle to testify that he, the defendant and Mills were all members of the organization.

The Supreme Court, per Chief Justice Rehnquist, unanimously upheld admitting Ehle's rebuttal testimony concerning Mills's and Abel's membership in the gang. Such testimony, the Court held, was sufficiently probative of Mills's possible bias towards Abel to warrant its admission into evidence. *Id.* at 49, 54. The Court rejected the defendant's contention that the district court abused its discretion under FRE 403 in permitting Ehle to describe of the organization's beliefs and practices, which, defendant argued, "inflamed" and unduly prejudiced the jury against him. It also rejected defendant's claim that the trial court should have cut off testimony after the prosecutor had elicited that Mills knew Abel and belonged to an organization with him. "This argument ignores the fact that the type of organization in which a witness and a party share membership may be relevant to show bias.... The attributes of the [organization]—a secret prison sect sworn to perjury and self-protection—bore directly not only on the *fact* of bias but also on the *source* and *strength* of Mills' bias." *Id.* at 54.

The Court noted that the district court took steps to limit the prejudicial effect of contested evidence. The trial judge instructed the prosecutor and Ehle not to use the organization's name ("Aryan Brotherhood"), and sustained Abel's objections to the prosecutor's questions to Ehle concerning the punishment meted out to unfaithful members (death). Moreover, the judge offered to give a limiting instruction concerning the use the jury could make of Ehle's testimony. *Id.* at 54. Thus, while the trial court could not prevent all prejudice, it successfully averted any undue prejudice to the defendant.

<u>Question 4.</u>

When the prosecutor recalled Ehle in rebuttal to impeach Mills' denial that he, Abel and Ehle were members of the "secret prisoner organization," which litigation situation(s) did that implicate?

<u>Answer:</u>

At most, two: <u>litigation situation G</u>, the prosecutor's rebuttal case, § 11.30; and <u>litigation situation H</u>, calling W2 to impeach W1, § 11.31. <u>Litigation situation G</u> refers primarily to rebutting evidence of a defendant's good character—clearly not the situation here. But this scenario fits squarely into litigation situation H: Ehle has been recalled to rebut and impeach Mills's denial. The right column explicitly acknowledges that FRE 608(b) does not permit W2 (here, Ehle) to extrinsically impeach W1's (Mills's) character for truthfulness. But extrinsic evidence is admissible to show a prior witness's (Mills's) bias or motive to lie, unless banned by another rule (such as FRE 403).

§ 13.8 Questions

Question 1.

In the prosecution of Attorney L for attempting to bribe a juror (see § 13.4 & § 13.6), after the government presents its case and rests, L's first witness is LCW (L's character witness), who will, if permitted, testify that "I've known L for years, and I am convinced that he is an honest, honorable, law-abiding man." What litigation situation does this problem involve? What rule governs the admissibility of this testimony?

Answer:

This is litigation situation C, § 11.26: in a criminal trial, the defense calls a character witness. The applicable rules are FRE 404(a)(2)(A) and FRE 405(a)(1st sentence). Since the traits of being "honest, honorable and law-abiding" are "pertinent" to rebut an accusation of attempting to bribe a juror, this testimony satisfies that rule. Assuming LCW's testimony establishes an adequate foundation (see § 6.9), it is admissible.

Question 2.

The judge permits LCW to testify. On cross, the prosecutor asks: "Had you heard that L was suspended from practice from the State Bar three years ago, for stealing money from a client and filing false documents with the probate court?"

What litigation situation does this problem involve; what rule applies; is the question worded intrinsically or extrinsically; is the question proper?

Answer:

This is litigation situation D, § 11.27: cross-examining character witness LCW to test LCW's knowledge of the defendant's prior behavior, per FRE 405(a)(2nd sentence). See § 6.14 & § 6.15. That rule permits the impeaching attorney to ask a character witness about "relevant" instances of the defendant's conduct. LCW testified to L's "honesty"; stealing and lying are "relevant" to rebut LCW's testimony about L's "honesty."

The use of the phrase "suspended from practice by the State Bar" is clearly extrinsic. But extrinsically worded questions are clearly permitted during FRE 405(a)(2nd sentence) cross-examination. See § 6.19.

The question is proper.

Question 3.

Why isn't this also a Rule 608(b)(1) situation?

Answer:

Because this is only litigation situation D. PA, the prosecuting attorney, is cross-examining LCW about L's prior untruthful acts, per FRE 405(a)(2nd sentence). FRE 608(b)(1) applies only when the impeaching attorney is cross-examining witness W about W's own prior untruthful acts or other aspects of W's circumstances. (*See* litigation situation F, § 11.29.) Defendant L has not testified (not yet, anyhow), so FRE 608(b)(1) does not come into play yet.

Question 4

LCW replies, "No, I never heard that." May the prosecutor introduce documents to prove that L was in fact suspended?

Answer:

No. Although FRE 405(a)(2nd sentence) permits an attorney cross-examining a character witness to ask the character witness extrinsically worded questions about the defendant's prior "relevant" behavior, the attorney cannot introduce extrinsic evidence that proves the defendant in fact committed that behavior. See § 6.22.

Question 5.

The prosecutor next asks: "Did you know that five years ago, L was forced to leave a bar because he was disturbing other customers; and later that night he was arrested for smashing the bar's door and window with a baseball bat?"

What litigation situation does this problem involve; what rule applies; is the question worded intrinsically or extrinsically; is the question proper?

Answer:

This is still litigation situation D—cross-examining a character witness about what the character witness knows or had heard about the defendant, whose character the witness, LCW, had praised.

If LCW had only testified about L's "honesty," this question would be improper, because "honesty" relates to how one deals with money (particularly other people's money), and may also be used to describe someone who is truthful. But LCW made the mistake of describing L as "honorable and law-abiding."[15] Law-abiding people don't smash bar windows and doors, so that incident is "relevant" (as FRE 405(a) (2nd sentence) puts it) to challenge the accuracy of LCW's assessment of L's character. See § 6.15. FRE 405(a)(2nd sentence) directs that the judge "may allow" cross-examination about the bar incident, but has discretion to preclude such questioning.

15. Maybe the mistake was L's lawyer's, for failing to instruct LCW what to say and what to avoid saying. Or maybe LCW just got carried away and went too far.

The question is worded extrinsically ("arrested"), but this is permissible per FRE 405(a)(2)(2nd sentence). See § 6.19.

Question 6.

Next, the prosecutor asks LCW, "It's true is it not, that L owes you $3,000?"

What litigation situation does this fall into? What rule applies? Is the question worded intrinsically or extrinsically? Is the question proper?

Answer:

This question has nothing to do with anyone's character. Rather, this is falls into litigation situation F, § 11.29: cross-examining witness LCW about himself. It is relevant because it shows LCW's personal interest in the outcome of the case: LCW may be testifying for L because he realizes that if L is convicted and goes to jail or loses his license to practice law, L probably won't be able to repay LCW. In fact, if LCW answers yes, the prosecutor's next questions will be:

> Q You are aware, I assume, that if L is convicted, he may well lose his license to practice law; and if that happens, it is unlikely that he will be able to repay you?[16]

L has a legitimate objection to this question, not because of its subject-matter, but because it is a compound question: i.e., it is really two questions. First, is LCW aware that if L is convicted, he may lose his license? Second, if LCW answers that he is aware of that possibility, was LCW conscious of the impact that would likely have on L's ability to repay the loan?

In fact, the prosecutor knew the question was improper as to form, but asked the question this way anyway, to make sure that the jury understood how the consequences of a conviction would go against LCW's personal interest.[17] If the judge sustains the objection, the prosecutor asks,

> Q Had it occurred to you, before I just mentioned it, that if L is convicted, there is a distinct possibility that he will lose his license to practice law?

If LCW says "No, that had not occurred to me," the prosecutor's next question is, "Really!? It didn't occur to you that bribing a juror is an extremely serious crime that

16. For tactical reasons, the prosecutor might avoid mentioning the possibility that L could (should!) receive a prison sentence.

17. How do I know what the prosecutor was thinking? Because I'm the one writing this scenario; and because I was a trial lawyer for eight years before ascending to the ivory tower of legal education. A lawyer should take care not to violate rules of evidence in a wholesale fashion, because doing so might create reversible error in the case, and will also damage the lawyer's reputation among the bench and bar. But bending a minor rule here and there—and knowing when doing so is more-or-less permissible, and when to avoid doing so—is part of a trial lawyer's arsenal.

could have very serious consequences?" If LCW insists that he had been ignorant of that possibility, the prosecutor asks, her incredulity obvious in her intonation and facial expression, "And so I assume that it also never occurred to you that helping LCW beat this case was your best chance to have his loan to you repaid?" If LCW insists that the thought had never crossed his mind, the prosecutor should look at the jury, shrug and roll his eyes, say "Really!" again, and move on to something else.[18]

<u>Question 7.</u>

Next, the prosecutor asks LCW:

> Q When you were a senior in college, you put on your resume that you were in the top twenty percent of your class, when in reality you were in the 24th percentile, isn't that true?

What litigation situation is involved here? What rule applies? Is the question worded intrinsically or extrinsically? Is the question proper?

<u>Answer:</u>

This is again <u>litigation situation F</u> (§ 11.29): cross-examining LCW about himself. The applicable rule is FRE 608(b). The question is worded intrinsically—it simply asks, "did you do this untruthful thing," without naming any outside source or suggesting negative consequences. The question is proper, assuming a good-faith basis, because lying on a resume is an act of untruthfulness.

But should the judge allow it? Perhaps not. First, I'd like to know how long ago LCW circulated this resume. Did LCW just graduate from college last year, or was that six, eight, twelve years ago? Second, as misstatements on a resume go, this one is rather minor.[19] Third, LCW's testimony is not all that important—juries tend not to be overly impressed with character testimony anyway, unless the character witness is a person of very substantial standing. Fourth, the prosecutor has already impeached LCW's testimony rather significantly.

<u>Question 8.</u>

L takes the stand and denies having any contact with the juror, let alone trying to bribe him. On cross-examination, the prosecutor asks:

18. Indulge in this kind of mugging to the jury only if you are confident you can pull it off naturally, without seeming rehearsed and pre-planned. (But plan it in advance and rehearse it in the mirror first.)

19. You should not include untrue assertions in your resume, because you never know when someone might discover the lie and use it against you. Still, there are fibs, and there are whoppers. In my 42+ years as a law professor, I've seen a few resumes that could be nominated for a Pulitzer Prize in fiction.

Q Mr. L, three years ago, the state bar suspended you from the practice of law because you stole money from the Havisham estate and filed false reports with the probate court to hide what you are doing. That's a fact, is it not?

What litigation situation does fall into? What rule applies? Is the question worded intrinsically or extrinsically? Is the question proper?

Answer:

This is litigation situation F (§ 11.29): cross-examining a witness about him/herself. The applicable rule is FRE 608(b)(1), and the subject matter satisfies the rule, since stealing funds that were entrusted to L for another, and filing false reports, are clearly evidence of untruthful behavior. The question is worded extrinsically ("suspended by the state bar"). Some jurisdictions permit extrinsically worded questions per FRE 608(b); some do not. See § 13.5.

§ 13.9 "The court may allow": the scope of judicial discretion

FRE 608(b)(1) provides that "the court ... may, on cross-examination, allow ... specific instances of a witness's conduct ... to be inquired into if they are probative of the character for ... untruthfulness." The phrase "may allow" gives the trial judge a degree of discretion as to whether to permit Rule 608(b)(1) impeachment.

But this discretion is not absolute. A judge cannot simply state, "I don't allow Rule 608(b) cross-examination in my courtroom." Rather, it permits the judge to impose reasonable limits on the degree and extent of such cross-examination. (The judge did so in § 13.4, Q3, by limiting the prosecutor's cross-examination of L about the nine checks L deposited into his own account instead of the Havisham estate's account.)

A judge should consider several factors in deciding whether, and to what extent, to permit such cross-examination.

First: the importance of witness W's testimony. The greater the importance of the testimony, the more important it is to allow the impeaching attorney reasonable latitude to impeach. This is particularly true with regard to prosecution witnesses in a criminal case. If the judge unduly restricts defense counsel's cross-examination of an important prosecution witness, an appellate court may conclude that this denied the defendant his Sixth Amendment right to confront the witness. But it also violates FRE 608(b) to preclude a prosecutor or a civil litigant from a reasonable opportunity to cross-examine a witness.

On the other hand, if W's testimony relates solely to facts which are uncontested and both sides agree that W's testimony is truthful and accurate, the judge might reasonably rule that there is no reason to allow any Rule 608(b) impeachment of W.[20]

20. See also § 13.8, question 7 (cross-examination of LCW about his class rank in college).

Second: the degree to which a particular instance demonstrates a character for untruthfulness. A minor fib—"Sorry I'm late, there was a tie-up at an intersection" instead of "Sorry I'm late, I was doing a cross-word and lost track of time"—has much less impeaching value than, say, the lies and deceptions by salesman X in §13.3.

Third: the availability of other impeachment material. If W's *testimony* has already been thoroughly impeached, it is less important to also impeach W's character for truthfulness.

Fourth: needless presentation of cumulative evidence, per FRE 403. For example, in §13.3, a judge might reasonably limit P's attorney to cross-examining X about, say, only two or three of the incidents in X's past.

2. Rule 609

a. In general

§13.10 The rule

FRE 609 provides:

Rule 609. Impeachment by Evidence of a Criminal Conviction

(a) **In General.** The following rules apply to attacking a witness's character for truthfulness by evidence of a criminal conviction:

(1) for a crime that, in the convicting jurisdiction, was punishable by death or by imprisonment for more than one year, the evidence:

(A) must be admitted, subject to Rule 403, in a civil case or in a criminal case in which the witness is not a defendant; and

(B) must be admitted in a criminal case in which the witness is a defendant, if the probative value of the evidence outweighs its prejudicial effect to that defendant; and

(2) for any crime regardless of the punishment, the evidence must be admitted if the court can readily determine that establishing the elements of the crime required proving—or the witness's admitting—a dishonest act or false statement.

(b) Limit on Using the Evidence After 10 Years. This subdivision (b) applies if more than 10 years have passed since the witness's conviction or release from confinement for it, whichever is later. Evidence of the conviction is admissible only if:

(1) its probative value, supported by specific facts and circumstances, substantially outweighs its prejudicial effect; and

(2) the proponent gives an adverse party reasonable written notice of the intent to use it so that the party has a fair opportunity to contest its use.

(c) Effect of a Pardon, Annulment, or Certificate of Rehabilitation. Evidence of a conviction is not admissible if:

(1) the conviction has been the subject of a pardon, annulment, certificate of rehabilitation, or other equivalent procedure based on a finding that the person has been rehabilitated, and the person has not been convicted of a later crime punishable by death or by imprisonment for more than one year; or

(2) the conviction has been the subject of a pardon, annulment, or other equivalent procedure based on a finding of innocence.

(d) Juvenile Adjudications. Evidence of a juvenile adjudication is admissible under this rule only if:

(1) it is offered in a criminal case;

(2) the adjudication was of a witness other than the defendant;

(3) an adult's conviction for that offense would be admissible to attack the adult's credibility; and

(4) admitting the evidence is necessary to fairly determine guilt or innocence.

(e) Pendency of an Appeal. A conviction that satisfies this rule is admissible even if an appeal is pending. Evidence of the pendency is also admissible.

This rule applies only in litigation situation F.

Our primary focus will be on FRE 609(a), with some attention devoted to the other sections of FRE 609.

FRE 609(a) is an exception to FRE 608(b). Rule 608(b) imposes a number of restrictions on questions a litigant may ask a witness about the witness's prior conduct in order to impeach that witness's character for truthfulness: (1) the witness's prior conduct must have been "probative of untruthfulness," and (2) the impeaching attorney can only "inquire" about the conduct on cross-examination, but cannot introduce extrinsic evidence of the conduct. (3) Nor, according to some courts, can the impeaching attorney word a 608(b)(1) question extrinsically.

Where the subject matter of the impeaching information is a criminal conviction that satisfies FRE 609(a), however, we are free of these restrictions. The impeaching attorney can ask about conduct that is not particularly probative of truthfulness or untruthfulness, so long as that conduct resulted in a conviction as specified in Rule

609(a). The word "convicted" may be included in the question: "Are you the Mary Doe who was convicted on March 9, 2021, in Santa Fe, New Mexico, of the crime of...." Moreover, if the witness denies having been convicted, the impeaching attorney is entitled to introduce extrinsic proof that the witness was in fact convicted.[21]

The key questions in applying Rule 609(a) are (1) which convictions can be used for impeachment purposes, which cannot, (2) who (in the context of the trial) is the witness whose character for truthfulness is being impeached, and (3) how much discretion does the trial judge have in deciding whether or not to permit the impeachment? Resolving these issues was not easy—at least seven separate versions of the Rule were proposed at one time or another. During my 40+ years teaching evidence, I stressed the importance of each rule's legislative history, but regarding Rule 609, I told my students *not* to read the various committee reports; doing so would be a waste of time.

b. "Impeachable convictions": FRE 609(a)

§ 13.11 Overview

A conviction is a conviction for purposes of Rule 609, whether it occurred after a trial, or via a plea of guilty, or a plea of nolo contendere.

As it now is worded, Rule 609(a) creates three separate situations for the use of a prior conviction to impeach a witness's character for truthfulness. To begin with the simplest and end with the most complex: (1) Rule 609(a)(2) convictions; (2) Rule 609(a)(1) convictions, where the witness being impeached is anyone in any litigation except the defendant in a criminal case; and (3) Rule 609(a)(1) convictions, where the witness being impeached is the defendant in a criminal case.

Only convictions which satisfy either FRE 609(a)(1) or 609(a)(2) may be used to impeach a witness's character for truthfulness. I'll spell out the details of those two provisions shortly, but one clear directive that emerges is this: if a witness was convicted of a *misdemeanor* (i.e., punishable by a maximum of a year or less) which is *not* a crime involving "a dishonest act or false statement," an attorney cannot use that conviction to impeach the witness's character for truthfulness.

§ 13.12 FRE 609(a)(2) convictions

i. "The evidence must be admitted"

Rule 609(a)(2) directs that if the crime was one involving "a dishonest act or false statement," then "the evidence must be admitted," i.e., the judge has no discretion, but must permit the impeachment; and this is so whether the crime is a felony or a

21. In fact, although most of the time, the conviction is used while cross-examining the witness, the rule does not require it be done then. An attorney could wait until later in the trial to do so. But this is rare, and you can assume that FRE 609 is used only while cross-examining W, unless your professor mentions this wrinkle.

misdemeanor, and whether the person being impeached is the defendant in a criminal case. A party cannot invoke FRE 403 to preclude impeaching a witness with a Rule 609(a)(2) conviction.

Take a most extreme case: D is on trial for mail fraud. According to the government, D organized and ran the conspiracy that committed the fraud. At trial, D testifies and claims he was an innocent dupe. Unfortunately for him, D was previous convicted of participating in a rather different kind of mail fraud, in which his involvement was comparatively minor. If the prosecutor sought to offer evidence of the latter (extrinsic) mail fraud per FRE 404(b)(2), the judge might well exclude it per FRE 404(b)(1) or because the risk of unfair prejudice substantially outweighed its legitimate probative value. See generally Chapter 7. But since the previous matter resulted in a mail fraud conviction, the judge must permit the impeachment, despite the risk that the jury will consider the prior case as evidence of D's propensity to commit mail frauds.

ii. Defining Rule 609(a)(2) crimes: the elements of the impeaching crime

What crimes involve "a dishonest act or false statement"? The Conference Report specifies that the phrase is used to mean "crimes such as perjury or subornation of perjury, false statement, criminal fraud, embezzlement, or false pretense, or any other offense in the nature of *crimen falsi*, the commission of which involves some element of deceit, untruthfulness, or falsification bearing on the accused's propensity to testify truthfully." One way to tell if a crime qualifies as a Rule 609(a)(2) crime, therefore, is to examine the definition (elements) of the crime that the witness had been convicted of. If the definition includes a "dishonest act or false statement": impeachment must be permitted pursuant to Rule 609(a)(2). Such crimes include perjury, false swearing, mail fraud, wire fraud, bank fraud, credit card fraud and any other kind of fraud. Forgery involves a false statement, because the forger seeks to create a false impression as to who wrote or signed a document (or took a photograph or painted a painting, etc.). Bigamy is also a crime that inherently involves deception: the defendant deceived his or her second "spouse," and also deceived the officiant (judge, clergyperson, etc.), who performed what the officiant believed was a lawful and legally binding wedding.[22]

iii. Defining Rule 609(a)(2) crimes: how it was committed[23]

May a crime be considered one involving "a dishonest act or false statement" for purposes of Rule 609(a)(2) even if deception, fraud, or some other form of false statement is not an *element* of the crime? Suppose a witness had been convicted of

---

22. If the officiant used the traditional mantra—"Should anyone present know of any reason that this couple should not be joined in holy matrimony, speak now or forever hold your peace," the bigamist's silence constitutes yet another deception and fraud.

23. The issue discussed in this subsection is a comparatively arcane one. If your professor does not focus on it in class, it is unlikely he or she will test you on it.

a felony that does not include a dishonest act or false statement within its definition, but a dishonest act or false statement was used in its commission· For example, D, now a defendant in a criminal case, was indicted five years ago for forgery and grand larceny: she forged her employer's name on a business check and cashed it. She was allowed to plead guilty to grand larceny; the forgery charge was dropped. Grand larceny is not, on its face, a "crimen falsi": the crime is defined as stealing property worth more than certain amount, whether by purse-snatching, stealing an auto, embezzlement, or whatever. Under the facts of this case, however, D committed the prior grand larceny in a way that clearly involved a false statement. Accordingly, the prosecutor will want to cross-examine D about the conviction, under Rule 609(a)(2), and about the underlying facts, 608(b).

In December 2006, Rule 609(a)(2) was amended to include such crimes, "if the court can readily determine that establishing the elements of the crime required proving—or the witness's admitting—a dishonest act or false statement." As to the meaning of the phrase "can readily determine," the Advisory Committee Note explains:

> Where the deceitful nature of the crime is not apparent from the statute and the face of the judgment—as, for example, where the conviction simply records a finding of guilt for a statutory offense that does not reference deceit expressly—a proponent may offer information such as an indictment, a statement of admitted facts, or jury instructions to show that the witness was necessarily convicted of a crime of a dishonest act or false statement. ... But the amendment does not contemplate a "mini-trial" in which the court plumbs the record of the previous proceeding to determine whether the crime was in the nature of *crimen falsi.*

§ 13.13 Rule 609(a)(1): "felonies"

Rule 609(a)(1) provides that, subject to the trial judge's discretion, an attorney may impeach a witness with a conviction for a crime that is *not* one involving "a dishonest act or false statement," if the maximum punishment for that crime could have been at least a year-and-a-day. Such crimes are generally called "felonies," and that's the term I will use here.

What matters is *not* the sentence the witness actually received, but the maximum sentence under the statute he or she *could have* received. If the statutory maximum sentence is, say, two years, but under applicable sentencing guidelines, the maximum sentence is six months, and the judge sentenced the witness to probation, that is still a "felony" as defined in FRE 609(a)(1).

How to tell whether a *crime is a 609(a)(1) felony or not.* How do you know whether a particular conviction was for a felony? In the real world, you'd look up the statutory definition of the crime the witness was convicted of, and ascertain what maximum sentence the witness theoretically could have received. It is unlikely your professor will expect you to do so on a quiz or exam; he or she may provide you with a list of crimes that are felonies. Otherwise, you have to determine whether a particular crime is a "felony" for FRE 609(a)(1) purposes, first check the following list; if the crime is not on the list, then consult the paragraph immediately after the list.

The following crimes are always felonies:

Any degree of homicide except misdemeanor manslaughter
Any crime with "grand" in its title, e.g., grand larceny, grand theft
Any crime with "felonious" in its title, e.g., felonious assault
Any "assault with intent to…" (kill, rape, maim, etc.)
Assault with a deadly weapon
Burglary
Arson
Robbery
Kidnapping
Escape from a penal institution
Rape, sexual assault
Sale (or distribution) of a controlled substance
Possession of a controlled substance with intent to sell (or distribute)
Possession of a firearm by someone previously convicted of a felony
Inciting a riot
In most jurisdictions, an attempt, solicitation, or conspiracy to commit any of these crimes is also likely to be a felony

This list does not include a wide range of crimes that may be felonies or misdemeanors, depending on how a particular jurisdiction defines them or distinguishes between them. Larceny, for example, may be a felony or a misdemeanor, depending on how it is committed or the value of the property stolen. The same is true for receiving or possessing stolen property. Criminal mischief (or destruction of property) may be a misdemeanor or felony depending on the kind of property or the dollar value of the property damaged. Simple possession of drugs may be a felony or misdemeanor, depending on the type and quantity the defendant was convicted of possessing. Conspiracy may be a felony or misdemeanor, depending on the crime the suspects are accused of conspiring to commit.

In an essay question, if you are uncertain whether the crime is a 609(a)(1) felony, write your answer in the alternative. Begin a paragraph thus: "Assuming this qualifies as a FRE 609(a)(1) felony,…" Then discuss the conviction's probative value as it relates to witness W's character for truthfulness or untruthfulness. Next, apply the appropriate probative-value-vs-risk-of-unfair-prejudice standard (609(a)(1)(A) or 609(a)(1)(B), which are discussed in the next two sections). Then, in a separate paragraph, say, "If this is a misdemeanor conviction, it cannot be used to impeach W's character for truthfulness."[24]

§ 13.14 FRE 609(a)(1)(A): felonies—impeaching most witnesses

If a witness was previously convicted of a felony which involved a dishonest act or false statement, FRE 609(a)(2) governs the case, rather than FRE 609(a)(1), and the judge must permit the impeachment. Rule 609(a)(1) regulates the use of a conviction to impeach a witness if the felony was *not* one which involved a dishonest act or false statement.

Rule 609(a)(1)(A) provides that, subject to the usual balancing test of Rule 403, a litigant may impeach any witness by bringing out (usually during cross-examination) that the witness has been convicted of a felony not "involving a dishonest act or false statement." If W was convicted of felonious assault for breaking someone's shoulder blade during an argument about a parking space; or of selling cocaine; or of breaking into a store looking for something to steal; or of sexual assault—all of them serious crimes, but none of which involve a "dishonest act or false statement"—the law says that this conviction *may* be used (subject to FRE 403) to impeach that witness's character for truthfulness.

You may reasonably wonder, why? In essence, the theory underlying FRE 609(a)(1)(A) is this: societies exist only because its members agree to abide by certain rules. Every society has its do's and don't's, some written, some implicit, some enforced, some winked at. Only conduct which seriously undermines the social good, however, is categorized as a felony (i.e., as a crime punishable by imprisonment for more than a year). Someone who has been convicted of a felony therefore has demonstrated that he did not consider himself bound to obey even the minimum standards we impose on ourselves. Evidence that the witness refused to obey so important a rule of conduct, the reasoning goes, is highly relevant in evaluating whether the witness is also willing to flout another rule of conduct, the rule saying a person must not lie under oath.

You may agree or disagree with this reasoning, but the *law* accepts it, and codifies it in FRE 609(a)(1)(A). That rule articulates a strong assumption that a prior felony conviction *is* highly relevant as to a witness's character for truthfulness.

Still, admissibility of evidence of a witness's prior felony conviction is subject to judicial discretion per FRE 403. Sometimes a judge can legitimately exercise discretion to exclude the conviction altogether—where, for example, the witness testifies to uncontested facts, and does so without any apparent intent of favoring one side or

---

24. Remember, though: if the crime involved "dishonesty or false statement," i.e., if it was a Rule 609(a)(2) crime, the judge must allow the impeachment, even if the crime was a misdemeanor.

the other. If a witness has been convicted of several felonies, the judge may limit the number the impeaching attorney may refer to. Sometimes the exercise of discretion justifies tailoring what the jury should be allowed to hear about the conviction.

Keep in mind that the "unfair prejudice" clause of FRE 403 is generally understood to mean unfair prejudice to a party in the lawsuit—not to a witness who is not a party. A judge's authority to restrict or preclude impeachment to protect a witness from embarrassment or harassment comes, not from FRE 403, but from FRE 611(a)(3), discussed in § 11.7.

§ 13.15 FRE 609(a)(1)(B): felonies—impeaching a criminal defendant

If the witness to be impeached is the defendant in a criminal case, however, Rule 609(a)(1)(B) creates a somewhat different balancing test. A felony conviction may be used to impeach the defendant only "if the probative value of the evidence [on the limited question of the defendant's character for truthfulness] *outweighs its prejudicial effect to that defendant....*" Whereas FRE 609(a)(1)(A), relying on the Rule 403 standard, states a strong assumption *in favor* of allowing the impeachment of every other kind of witness, FRE 609(a)(1)(B) creates a slight assumption *against* allowing the impeachment of a criminal defendant.

§ 13.16 Judicial discretion: factors to consider

What factors should a judge consider in assessing the probative character-for-untruthfulness-value of a Rule 609(a) conviction? And what additional factors should a judge consider, where the witness being impeached is the defendant in a criminal case?

In *Jackson v. State*, 340 Md 705, 668 A2d 8 (1995), Maryland's highest court enunciated five factors—perhaps to be known hereafter as the "*Jackson* Five"?[25]—that a judge should consider in deciding whether to permit impeachment by prior conviction: (1) the impeachment value of the crime; (2) how recently or long ago the prior conviction occurred, and the witness's subsequent history; (3) the similarity between the past crime and the crime for which defendant is currently on trial; (4) the importance of defendant's testimony to the defense; and (5) the centrality of the defendant's credibility. *Id.* Other courts have enunciated similar or identical lists of factors.

---

25. In case you didn't get the reference, "The Jackson Five" was a singing group comprised of five siblings: (1) Michael, the "king of pop," who went on to become the Lord of Neverland; (2) his sister Janet, who went on to become Miss Wardrobe Malfunction of 2003; and their brothers, (3) Andrew, who went on to be President; (4) Phil, who went on to become a spectacularly successful basketball coach; and (5) Stonewall, who joined the military, started out extremely well, but then was accidently shot and killed by his own men.

The first two factors apply to the use of a Rule 609(a)(1) conviction of any witness. The other factors, however, apply only when the witness is the defendant in a criminal case.

The first factor—the impeachment "value" of the prior conviction—depends on what the conviction tells the jury about the witness's character for truthfulness. Crimes of violence generally are thought to have comparatively less probative value in weighing credibility, but may still be admitted after balancing the other factors. In contrast, it is often argued that crimes that by their nature imply some dishonesty, such as theft, have greater impeachment value and are significantly more likely to be admissible. And some have argued that while crimes committed impulsively have little truthfulness-impeaching value, crimes that were thought out and planned in advance have somewhat greater impeachment value, albeit not so much as a crime which involved a dishonest act or false statement.

Unless your professor specifies how to handle this issue, if an essay question requires you to discuss it, the best approach is the "some say this, some say that" format. Doing so shows your professor that you noticed the issue and are aware that there is no clear-cut law consensus, and demonstrates that you know how argue both sides. As to your conclusion—again, assuming your professor has not specified what he or she is looking for—remember that, for most witnesses, FRE 609(a)(1)(A) creates a strong assumption of admissibility, but if the witness being impeached is the defendant in a criminal case, FRE 609(a)(1)(B) creates a slight assumption against admissibility.

The second factor—how long ago the witness was convicted, and his or her subsequent history—is pretty straightforward. The older the conviction (in the curious way FRE 609(b) counts time, see § 13.26), the less probative value it has with regard to the witness's character for truthfulness when the witness testifies—assuming, that is, the witness has stayed out of trouble since that conviction. Suppose, though, witness W was released from prison eight years ago after serving ten months for auto theft, but, as W takes the stand to testify, there are 3 separate charges pending against W: on one occasion, a purse snatch; a month later, drug possession; two months after that, a misdemeanor assault. Under most circumstances, the impeaching attorney would not be permitted to question W about any of them on cross-examination, since none involve Rule 609(a) convictions or untruthful conduct.[26] But the judge could take them into consideration in deciding whether to allow the impeaching attorney to cross-examine W about W's eight-year-old conviction for grand larceny auto.

---

26. In at least one situation, these pending charges could be used to cross-examine W: if W is testifying for the state, even though the pending charges would not satisfy Rules 608(b) or 609, the impeaching attorney could cross-examine W about those charges—and in fact could offer extrinsic evidence that the charges are pending—to show that W has a motive to lie, i.e., to suggest that W was testifying for the government in the hopes of receiving leniency from the state regarding those charges. See § 13.7–iii.

The third factor—the similarity between the crime a defendant is now on trial for, and the 609(a)(1) impeachment felony—is also straightforward: the greater the similarity, the greater risk the jury will rely on the conviction to show defendant's propensity to commit this type of crime, despite an instruction by the judge not to use the conviction in that manner.[27] But this does not automatically preclude impeachment.

The fourth and fifth factors—the importance of defendant's testimony and the importance of his or her credibility—seem either to say the same thing, or to cancel each other out. If the defendant's testimony is particularly important to the defense, which argues in favor of letting him testify without the risk of impeachment, then his credibility becomes a central issue in the case,[28] which argues in favor of permitting the impeachment. Accordingly, some courts reject the latter two *Jackson* factors altogether. Here, too: follow your professor's lead in how to handle the issue.

A sixth general factor should be added: sometimes the particular circumstances of a case would make it unfair to preclude the prosecutor from using a defendant's prior felony conviction to impeach him or her. Suppose, for example, a key issue is who is telling the truth—W, the state's main witness, or D, the defendant—both of whom have previously been convicted of FRE 609(a)(1) felonies. When W testifies, D's lawyer impeaches W's character for truthfulness by bringing out W's convictions. Now D is about to testify. If the judge precludes the prosecutor from impeaching D with D's prior convictions, the jury will be left with a very inaccurate impression that W is a frequent criminal, but that D has never committed a crime. A judge might not buy this argument, but the prosecutor should certainly make it.

§ 13.17 Impeaching a criminal defendant: judicial instruction

If a judge permits such impeachment, defense counsel should ask the judge to give a limiting instruction to explain how they may, and how they must not, consider the prior conviction in evaluating the evidence. The following—the First Circuit's *Pattern Jury Instruction, Criminal Cases*, Instruction no. 2.04—is typical:

> You have heard evidence that [defendant] was convicted of a crime. You may consider that evidence in deciding, as you do with any witness, how much weight to give [defendant's] testimony. The fact that [defendant] was previously convicted of another crime does not mean that he/she committed the crime for which he/she is now on trial. You must not use that prior conviction as proof of the crime charged in this case.

---

27. How the judge should instruct the jury is discussed in § 13.17.

28. In my experience, once the defendant testifies in a criminal case, the jury's assessment of the defendant's credibility often becomes the central, dominant factor in their deliberation.

The judge would give a similar instruction regarding a prior conviction for a 609(a)(2) crime involving a dishonest act or false statement.

Is such an instruction worth the time and breath it takes the judge to give it? In the real world, there is no way to know. In law school, though, your professor is probably expecting (or at least hoping) his or her students will remember to include this in a class discussion or an essay answer. See § 2 of the preface.

§ 13.18 Questions

Question 1.

Iosef Djugashvili is on trial for participating in a two-man armed robbery committed in Moscow, Idaho. The government's main witness against him is Lev Bronstein, who was arrested a few weeks after the robbery. Bronstein told the authorities that Djugashvili was his partner in crime, has pleaded guilty, and is testifying against Djugashvili as part of a plea bargain.

Bronstein has previous convictions for perjury, selling heroin (twice), possession of an explosive device, shoplifting, submitting a false affidavit (a misdemeanor) and disorderly conduct. Djugashvili's attorney seeks to impeach Bronstein with each of these convictions. What litigation situation or situations are involved here? What is the applicable rule? If the prosecutor objects to the impeachment, how should the judge rule?

Answer:

This is litigation situation F (§ 11.29): cross-examining a witness (Bronstein) about his own past acts. Since all the incidents mentioned in the question were convictions, the appropriate rule is FRE 609(a).

The judge must allow defense counsel to impeach Bronstein with the convictions for perjury and for submitting a false affidavit (even though the latter is a misdemeanor), because they are FRE 609(a)(2) crimes involving a false statement.

At the other extreme, disorderly conduct is probably a low-level misdemeanor, and shoplifting is also probably a misdemeanor (depending on the value of the property Bronstein was convicted of stealing), and neither involves lying or deceit, so the judge must not permit their use for impeachment.[29]

As to the other crimes, which are felonies but do not involve dishonesty or false statement, admissibility is governed by FRE 609(a)(1)(A), since Bronstein is not the defendant in this trial. The judge certainly has discretion to permit Djugashvili's

29. Some people argue that shoplifting should be regarded a crime of deception. After all, the thief takes store merchandise, conceals it on his/her person, and walks out of the store hoping to deceive store personnel into thinking he doesn't have anything from the store. I am not particularly impressed by this argument, but if your evidence prof is, apply Fishman Rule of Evidence 001.

attorney to impeach Bronstein with the explosive device conviction (assuming it is a felony), and the two felony drug convictions as well. After all, Bronstein is a key witness in the government's case; an appellate court might hold that to preclude the defense from using these convictions deprived Djugashvili of his right to confront and cross-examine Bronstein.

On the other hand, that's five convictions; the judge might reasonably conclude that allowing defense counsel to use all five would constitute needless presentation of cumulative evidence (FRE 403), and allow defense counsel to use only three or four, not all five.

Question 2.

Djugashvili asserts mistaken identity and alibi as his defense. He calls Vladimir as a defense witness, and Vladimir testifies that he and Djugashvili were together in Sebastapol, California, at the time the Moscow robbery was committed. On cross-examination of Vladimir, the prosecutor wants to inquire about Vladimir's conviction seven years ago for felonious assault. Djugashvili's attorney objects that this is improper impeachment. What standard should the judge apply in deciding the motion?

(a) The judge must permit the impeachment of Vladimir.

(b) The judge must permit the impeachment of Vladimir unless the risk of unfair prejudice substantially outweighs the conviction's probative value.

(c) The judge must permit the impeachment of Vladimir if the probative value of the conviction outweighs the risk of unfair prejudice.

(d) The judge must rule that the prosecutor is barred from using the conviction to impeach Vladimir.[30]

Before selecting one of the options, which litigation situation or situations are involved here, and what rules apply?

Answer:

This is litigation situation F: cross-examining a witness about his own conduct.

The correct option is (b). Vladimir is a defense witness, but he is not the defendant. Felonious assault is a felony, so this situation fits within FRE 609(a)(1)(A), which directs that a prior felony conviction "must be admitted, subject to Rule 403 ... in a criminal case in which the witness is not a defendant." FRE 403 directs that relevant evidence should be admitted unless "its probative value is substantially outweighed by a danger of ... unfair prejudice...."

30. If you are unfamiliar with the format of this question, in the not-to-distant future, you will become quite familiar with it: it is the kind of question asked on the Multistate Bar Exam.

Option (a) is wrong, because felonious assault is not a Rule 609(a)(2) crime involving a dishonest act or false statement.

Option (c) is wrong, because that is the standard set out in Rule 609(a)(1)(B) where the witness being impeached is the defendant in a criminal case.

Option (d) is wrong, because that option applies only if the crime was a misdemeanor not involving a dishonest act or false statement.

<u>Question 3.</u>

Should the judge allow the impeachment of Vladimir?

<u>Answer:</u>

Yes.[31]

Felonious assault is not usually a crime considered highly probative of a character for untruthfulness, but it is not irrelevant for that purpose either. The conviction was seven years old, which reduces its probative value somewhat regarding Vladimir's character for truthfulness or untruthfulness, but if Vladimir did time on that conviction, the length of his confinement gets subtracted from the 7 years. (See FRE 609(b), discussed in § 13.26.)

There is a risk of unfair prejudice to Djugashvili—a jury might hold it against him that he hangs out with someone with a felony conviction.[32] But it is not likely that a jury would decide to convict Djugashvili for that reason.

<u>Question 4.</u>

At the same trial, Djugashvili testifies that he was in Sebastopol with Vladimir when the Moscow bank robbery was committed. On cross-examination, the prosecutor wants to inquire about Djugashvili's conviction six years ago for arson, for which he was sentenced to 10 months' imprisonment, served sixth months and was then released on parole. Djugashvili's attorney objects that this is improper impeachment.

What standard should the judge apply in deciding the motion?

(a) The judge must permit the impeachment of Djugashvili.

(b) The judge must permit the impeachment of Djugashvili unless the risk of unfair prejudice substantially outweighs the conviction's probative value.

(c) The judge must permit the impeachment of Djugashvili if the probative value of the conviction outweighs the risk of unfair prejudice.

---

31. Reasonable people could disagree, I suppose, but my sense is that the vast majority of courts would allow the impeachment.

32. Moral of story: advise your clients that if they know in advance that they might be falsely accused of committing a crime, they should make a point not to hang out with people who have felony convictions, because they tend to be poor alibi witnesses.

(d) The judge must rule that the prosecutor is barred from using the conviction to impeach Djugashvili.

Answer:

The correct answer is (c). Here the witness being impeached by a prior felony conviction is the defendant in a criminal case, so the applicable rule is FRE 609(a)(1)(B). Arson does not involve a dishonest act or false statement (unless the arson was part of a scheme to collect on a fire insurance policy), but it is a felony. (See the list in § 13.13.) Remember that a crime's classification as a felony depends on the maximum penalty a convicted person could receive under the statute, not on the sentence he or she in fact received.

Option (a) is wrong, because arson is not a crime involving a dishonest act or false statement.

Option (b) is wrong, because that is the standard set out in FRE 609(a)(1)(A), which applies to any witness in any kind of litigation *except* the defendant in a criminal case. Here the witness being impeached is the defendant.

Option (d) would be correct if arson was a misdemeanor, but arson is a felony.

Question 5.

By what name are Ioseph Djugashvili and Lev Bronstein better known?

Answer:

Joseph Stalin and Leon Trotsky.

§ 13.19 Permitted information about the crime; response

When a prior conviction is being used to impeach a witness's character for truthfulness, federal courts generally permit the impeaching attorney to bring out the name of the crime the witness was convicted of; the time and place of the conviction; and the sentence imposed. Other details cannot be elicited. For example, if a defendant is on trial for aggravated assault for attacking the victim with a knife, a judge may permit the prosecutor to elicit that the defendant has a previous conviction for aggravated assault, but it would be error—potential reversible error—to elicit that the prior assault was also committed a knife.

Where the witness being impeached is the defendant in a criminal case, in at least some circuits, the judge has discretion to limit the prosecutor to what is known as the "mere fact" approach: rather than specifying the nature of the crime, the prosecutor is allowed to ask only whether the defendant was convicted of "a crime punishable by more than a year" or "a crime involving dishonesty or false statement," plus the time and place of the conviction, and the sentence.

Courts generally allow the attorney relying on the witness to elicit from the witness on redirect a brief explanation or effort at mitigation. Assume, for example, in

State v. Valjean, after Valjean testifies on direct, Javert, the prosecutor, is allowed to impeach Valjean on cross that a few years earlier, Valjean was convicted of attempted burglary. On redirect, defense counsel asks:

Q. Mr. Valjean, on cross-examination, Mr. Javert asked you about your conviction for burglary. Please tell us the circumstances surrounding that conviction.

A. My sister's child was starving and we had no money for food. I broke the window of a house to steal a loaf of bread.

Similarly, the attorney relying on the witness's testimony may bring out that the conviction was by a guilty plea, rather than a conviction after a trial. In turn, the impeaching attorney may seek to impeach or contradict the explanation or mitigation, although a judge might well preclude this as too collateral to the key issues at trial.

Question 1.

Years later, Valjean adopted a young girl. What was her name?

Answer:

Cosette.[33]

c. Rule 609(a) and other rules

§ 13.20 Overview

The interplay between Rule 609 and other provisions of the FRE merits careful attention. The next few sections illustrate some of the complexities that can arise.

§ 13.21 Rules 609(a) and 103(b)

FRE 103(b), governing objections, states:

> **(b) Not Needing to Renew an Objection or Offer of Proof.** Once the court rules definitively on the record—either before or at trial—a party need not renew an objection or offer of proof to preserve a claim of error for appeal.

Suppose, in lawsuit *X v. Y*, X brought a motion in limine to preclude Y from using witness W's prior conviction to impeach W. Assume the judge ruled against X. It is up to the party that lost the motion in limine (here: X) to ask the judge whether that

33. These events—Valjean's conviction and his subsequent de facto adoption of Cosette—play a significant role in Victor Hugo's novel, *Les Miserables.*

ruling was "definitive" or only provisional. If the judge said the ruling was "definitive," X would not have to renew the motion at trial in order to appeal the judge's ruling. But if the judge's in limine ruling was provisional, X would have to renew the motion to preclude when Y called W as a witness.

Keep in mind that a judge might reverse even a "definitive" ruling depending on what happens at trial. See § 2.2. Suppose, for example, in *State v. D*, prior to trial, the judge ruled "definitively" that a prosecutor could not use the defendant's prior conviction for impeachment purposes. When D's attorney calls D to the stand, D gratuitously asserts, "I've never been convicted of any crime." Or suppose on cross, the prosecutor asks D "How well did you know X," and D responds, "I've never been convicted of any crime!"—a non-responsive answer which the prosecutor did not elicit. The purpose of the judge's pretrial ruling was to protect the defendant from the risk of unfair prejudice; the defendant is now using it as a license to lie. The judge should, and in all likelihood would, reverse his or her "definitive" pretrial ruling in "a New York second"—to impeach the false testimony the defendant just gave.

§ 13.22 Rules 609(a) and 608(b)

Where a witness had engaged in conduct "probative of ... untruthfulness" (Rule 608(b)) which resulted in a conviction, an impeaching attorney may, if permitted by the judge, ask intrinsically worded questions concerning the details of the affair, as well as bring out the fact of the conviction itself. For example, in § 13.4, suppose attorney L had been convicted of stealing funds from the Havisham estate. When L testifies at his juror-bribing trial, on cross-examination, the prosecutor, per Rule 608(b)(1), can ask:

Q Mr. L, three years ago you were retained to be the executor of the estate of Missy Havisham, is that correct?

Q That meant you were responsible to collect money coming to the estate, pay bills, and make sure that the estate's assets would be preserved for her adopted daughter Estella, her only heir. True?

Q And you had a legal duty to file regular reports with the probate court specifying income and payments, is that also true?

Q On [specify date] did you receive a check from [specify who issued the check] for the estate in the amount of [specify amount]?

Q You were duty bound, were you not, to deposit that in the estate's bank account?

Q In fact, you deposited it in your own personal account instead, didn't you?

Q And it is also true, isn't it, that when you filed a report with the probate court on [specify date], you deliberately omitted any mention of that check for [specify amount], to hide the fact that you were stealing from the estate?

This series of questions would not be allowed per FRE 609(a), but the judge may allow it per Rule 608(b)(1). Then, regardless of whether L answers "yes" or "no" to these questions, the prosecutor asks:

Q And is it not a fact, sir, that on [date], in [specify the county], as a result of these acts, you were convicted of the crimes of embezzlement and knowingly filing false reports with the probate court?

Because these crimes involve dishonest acts and false statements, the judge must permit this question per Rule 609(a)(2). If L denies he was convicted, the prosecutor can offer a certified copy of the judgment of conviction into evidence.

On request, the judge must instruct the jury that the jury could consider L's handling of the Havisham estate, and his conviction, solely in deciding how much weight to give to L's testimony, but could not consider it as evidence of L's guilt or innocence of the witness-bribing charge.

§ 13.23 Rules 609(a) and 404(b)(2)

Recall that FRE 404(b)(2) permits a litigant to prove that a person engaged in particular conduct in the past, when such evidence is relevant for a purpose other than the forbidden "bad (or good) person inference." Suppose that conduct resulted in a Rule 609(a)(1) conviction. For what purpose or purposes could the impeaching attorney use that evidence?

Question 1:

Last January, Heathcliff, Lockwood and the Bronte sisters traveled together from the U.S. to Colombia and back again. U.S. ICE[34] officials noticed that Lockwood seemed extremely nervous and uncomfortable, so they detained and questioned Lockwood. Lockwood admitted that he had swallowed several balloons containing high-purity cocaine. He consented to take a laxative and excreted the balloons, which contained several ounces of the drug.

Lockwood's attorney worked out a deal: Lockwood pleaded guilty and testified for the government that Heathcliff had planned and paid for the trip, the real purpose of which was to smuggle cocaine back into the U.S. Originally the women were supposed to swallow the balloons to get the cocaine into the U.S., but when they balked, Heathcliff persuaded Lockwood to do so instead.

34. Immigration and Customs Enforcement, a branch of the U.S. Department of Homeland Security.

Heathcliff is charged with smuggling cocaine into the U.S., and of conspiring with Lockwood to do so. (Let's call this the "Heathcliff-Lockwood case.") At trial, Heathcliff's attorney tells the jury in her opening statement that Heathcliff and Lockwood and the sisters went to Colombia to vacation together, that Heathcliff had nothing to do with the cocaine, and that Lockwood's accusation is a lie he told to get a break in his own case.

Six years earlier, Heathcliff went to Colombia with a man named Edgar; when they returned to the U.S., ICE officials found several ounces of cocaine in Edgar's underwear. Edgar pleaded guilty and testified at Heathcliff's trial that Heathcliff paid him $1,000 to smuggle the drugs into the U.S. Heathcliff was convicted of conspiring to import cocaine into the United States and sentenced to three years' imprisonment. We'll call this the "Heathcliff-Edgar case."

Prior to trial, in the Heathcliff-Lockwood case, Heathcliff's attorney moved in limine to preclude the prosecutor from introducing evidence of the Edgar incident or the conviction. The judge reserved judgment. The prosecutor now plans to call Edgar as a witness to testify about his trip with Heathcliff, and to offer evidence of Heathcliff's conviction that resulted.

What litigation situation or situations are involved/implicated? What rules must be considered? How should the judge rule?

Answer:

This is litigation situation E (§ 11.28): the prosecutor's case-in-chief. The only rule that need be considered—aside from FRE 403, which is almost always potentially in play—is FRE 404(b). (I used a slightly different version of the facts in § 7.25, Question 2, and explained that a judge could quite plausibly rule either way. It might be a good idea to re-read my answer to that question.)

You might wonder: isn't it also litigation situation F (§ 11.29)? After all, the prosecutor wants to offer evidence that Heathcliff was convicted in the Heathcliff-Edgar case. But litigation situation F arises only when an impeaching attorney seeks to question a witness about the witness's *own* prior specific acts. Here the prosecutor is offering Edgar's testimony, and Heathcliff's conviction, during the government's case in chief; Heathcliff is not a witness.

Let's assume the judge rules that the prosecutor may call Edgar and elicit his testimony.

Question 2.

In addition to Edgar's testimony, the prosecutor also wants to offer Heathcliff's conviction in the Heathcliff-Edgar case into evidence. Is it within the judge's discretion to allow this and, if so, for what purpose or purposes? Choose the correct answer:

(a) The conviction is admissible as evidence that Heathcliff conspired with Edgar to smuggle cocaine six years ago, and to impeach Heathcliff's character for truthfulness.

(b) The conviction is admissible as evidence that Heathcliff conspired with Edgar to smuggle cocaine six years ago but is not admissible to impeach Heathcliff's character for truthfulness.

(c) The conviction is admissible to impeach Heathcliff's character for truthfulness, but is not admissible as evidence that Heathcliff conspired with Edgar to smuggle cocaine six years ago.

(d) The conviction is not admissible as evidence that Heathcliff conspired with Edgar to smuggle cocaine six years ago, and is also not admissible to impeach Heathcliff's character for truthfulness.

Answer:

The correct answer is (b). The conviction—just like Edgar's testimony—is admissible per FRE 404(b)(2), as substantive evidence that Heathcliff conspired with Edgar in that case.[35] But Heathcliff's conviction in the Heathcliff-Edgar case is not admissible to impeach Heathcliff's character for truthfulness, because Heathcliff is not the witness; Edgar is. Heathcliff hasn't testified (yet, anyhow)—we are still in the prosecution's case-in-chief—so Heathcliff's character for truthfulness is not (yet) an issue in the case.

Question 3.

Suppose instead the trial judge ruled that the prosecutor could not introduce either Edgar's testimony or Heathcliff's conviction during the state's case-in-chief in the Heathcliff-Lockwood trial. The prosecutor presents its evidence in the Heathcliff-Lockwood case (without any reference to the Heathcliff-Edgar case) and rests.

During the defense case, Heathcliff takes the stand and testifies that he and Lockwood went to Colombia to "party" with the Bronte sisters and do some sightseeing. He testified that Lockwood's testimony—that Heathcliff brought the sisters to Colombia so they would swallow the balloons and bring the cocaine into the U.S.—was a lie. On cross-examination, Heathcliff acknowledges that he paid everyone's travel expenses, and that there were plenty of places in the U.S. where the four of them could have "partied" together for a whole lot less money. At the end of cross-examination, the prosecutor asks:

Q: So why Colombia, as opposed to anywhere else?

A: It's a beautiful country. And I wanted to practice my Spanish.

---

35. Using the Heathcliff-Edgar conviction as substantive evidence invokes FRE 803(22), set out in § 13.28.

Q: No other reason?

A: No other reason.

Q: Your honor, may we approach the bench?

J: I have a better idea. [Addressing the jury:] Ladies and gentlemen, the prosecutor and defense attorney and I have some business to discuss. So let's give you a longer lunch period. Please be back in the courtroom by 1 p.m.

After the jury leaves, the prosecutor asks the judge to reconsider her ruling banning evidence of the Heathcliff-Edgar case. What litigation situation or situations are implicated here? What rule or rules apply?

Answer:

Litigation situation F applies while Healthcliff is still being cross-examined. The relevant rules are FRE 609(a)(1)(B) and FRE 404(b).

Question 4.

Assuming the judge decides to revoke her in limine ruling, does it make any difference whether the judge allows the prosecutor to use the conviction while cross-examining Heathcliff per Rule 609 vs. Rule 404(b)(2)?

Answer:

Yes. If the judge allows use under Rule 609, the prosecutor can introduce into evidence only the name of the crime, when and where Heathcliff was convicted, and the sentence he received. See § 13.19. That is because, if evidence of a conviction is admitted per Rule 609(a), it is only the *fact* of the conviction (plus date, location and sentence) that is admitted, and solely to impeach the witness's character for truthfulness.

But if the judge allows the prosecutor to use the Heathcliff-Edgar case per Rule 404(b)(2), neither of those restrictions apply. The prosecutor can cross-examine Heathcliff as follows about the underling facts:

Q1: Mr. Heathcliff, do you recall going to Colombia six years ago with a man named Edgar?

A: Yes.

Q2: Where in Colombia did you go?

A: Medellin.

Q3: Same city as your trip with Mr. Lockwood and the Bronte sisters?

A: Um, yes

Q4: Isn't it a fact that the reason for that trip six years ago was to obtain cocaine and smuggle it back into the United States?

It almost doesn't matter whether Heathcliff admits this, or denies it, because either way, the prosecutor's cross-examination will continue:

> Q5: In fact, didn't you obtain [specify weight] of [specify purity] of cocaine while you were in Medellin?
>
> Q6: Is it not a fact that you paid Edgar $1,000 to secrete that cocaine in his underwear to smuggle it into the U.S.?
>
> Q7: And in fact, on [date], in [location of court], you were convicted, were you not, of conspiring with Mr. Edgar to smuggle that cocaine into the U.S.?[36]
>
> Q8: Please inform the jury of the sentence you received.

If the prosecutor is permitted to use the conviction as substantive evidence per FRE 404(b)(2), and not merely to impeach Heathcliff's testimony, Heathcliff is not entitled to the kind of limiting instruction set out in § 13.17. Rather, the instruction will be of the kind set out in § 7.14–iv.

If Heathcliff denies being convicted (which would be a remarkably stupid thing to do), the prosecutor can offer documentary proof of the conviction.[37]

If Heathcliff admits that his prior trip to Medellin was to obtain cocaine and that he was convicted for that crime, the prosecutor has pretty much maxed out on the Edgar incident, and the judge would probably preclude the prosecutor from calling Edgar to testify in the prosecutor's rebuttal case. But if Heathcliff acknowledges that he was convicted but insists that he was innocent in that case, the judge might well allow the prosecutor to call Edgar as a witness in the prosecutor's rebuttal case.[38]

d. Other Rule 609 issues

§ 13.24 "Reducing the sting"

An attorney calls W to testify. W gives testimony highly favorable to the attorney's client. Nevertheless, the attorney impeaches W by questioning W about W's prior FRE 609 convictions. What's going on? Why would an attorney impeach a favorable witness?

---

36. Note: using the Heathcliff-Edgar conviction this way invokes FRE 803(22)(C), set out in § 13.28.

37. This proof would include fingerprints and photographs taken of Heathcliff when he arrived at prison, to assure the jury that it was indeed the defendant, and not someone else named Heathcliff, who was convicted and sentenced in that case.

38. Litigation situation G (§ 11.30) and litigation situation H (§ 11.31) will apply if, after the defense rests, the prosecutor calls Edgar as a witness during the prosecutor's rebuttal case. The rule governing Edgar's testimony would still be FRE 404(b).

It's a matter of trial tactics. If you know that your opponent will be able to impeach W—with W's prior convictions or with other unsavory information—it is often better for you to bring out such negative matters on direct. Doing so, the theory goes, "reduces the sting": the hope is that the information will have less of an impact if the party relying on the witness brings it out on direct, than if the other side elicits it for the first time on cross-examination.

I used this tactic from time to time as a prosecutor—usually, when I called an informer as a witness. I knew defense counsel would bring out my informer's prior convictions, so I did it first.[39] In fact, sometimes I informed the jury that I would call a witness with a record during jury selection or in my opening statement. Then, in summation, I remind the jury: "I did not try to hide Mr. W's record from you. You have a right to know about that, in deciding whether to believe his testimony."

§ 13.25 Should the defendant testify?— Defense counsel's quandary

This section discusses constitutional and tactical issues a defense attorney must consider in deciding whether to call the defendant to testify.[40] That is often the biggest tactical decision that defense counsel has to make. This section discusses some of the legal and tactical issues that arise in connection with that decision.[41]

A defendant is under no constitutional obligation to testify, and the judge will (if requested) tell the jury to draw no inferences against the defendant if he or she exercises the Fifth Amendment privilege to remain silent. Most experienced trial attorneys and judges agree, however, that most juries expect to hear from the defendant and will be disappointed and skeptical if defendant does not testify. On the other hand, if the defendant does take the stand, his testimony and credibility can become the dominant factor in the jury's deliberation.

The decision whether to call the defendant is even more difficult where the defendant has prior convictions which can be used to impeach the defendant. Knowing whether the trial judge will permit or preclude such impeachment would resolve at least one major uncertainty. Thus, it is logical for defense counsel to bring a motion in limine prior to calling the defendant as a witness, seeking a ruling whether, if the

39. Defense counsel is still entitled to question the informer about those convictions, but the jury may wonder: "Why is counsel wasting our time? We heard all that already."

40. Actually, it is the defendant's decision, not the lawyer's: if the defendant insists on testifying, defense counsel has no right to forbid it. Defendants sometimes insist on testifying despite counsel's strenuous objections. When that happens, a wise defense counsel will put on the record (out of the jury's hearing, of course) that the defendant is testifying "against the advice of counsel." This protects the lawyer's reputation with the judge and opposing counsel, and protects against a post-conviction charge by the defendant that it was the lawyer's decision—and ineffective assistance of counsel—to have the defendant testify.

41. If your professor doesn't discuss this in class, it is probably safe to skip this section.

defendant testifies, the judge will permit the prosecutor to impeach the defendant per FRE 609(a)(1)(B) with prior convictions.[42]

A judge is not required to make a definitive ruling. Suppose, though, the judge rules that he or she will allow the impeachment, and the defense attorney decides that in that case, the defendant should not testify. May defendant appeal his conviction on the ground that the judge's allegedly erroneous in limine ruling had the effect of preventing defendant from exercising his right to testify in his own defense?

In *Luce v. United States,* 469 U.S. 38 (1984), the Supreme Court, per Chief Justice Burger, unanimously held that under those circumstances, the defendant could not base an appeal on the trial judge's in limine ruling. Whether it is error to permit a prosecutor to impeach a testifying defendant with his convictions, the Court held, is a "subtle evidentiary question" which cannot be decided "outside a factual context." This context includes "the precise nature of the defendant's testimony, which is unknowable when, as here, the defendant does not testify." Moreover, if the defendant does not testify, "the reviewing court also has no way of knowing whether the Government would have sought to impeach with the prior conviction."[43] Additionally, "Because an accused's decision whether to testify seldom turns on the resolution of one factor, a reviewing court cannot assume that the adverse ruling motivated a defendant's decision not to testify." Finally, where the defendant does not testify, it is impossible to judge whether a ruling which persuaded him not to testify was only harmless error. The Court therefore held that "to raise and preserve for review the claim of improper impeachment with a prior conviction, a defendant must testify."

Luce also makes it clear that the judge need not rule on the motion in limine until after the defendant has completed direct examination.

Luce left unanswered a closely related question. Suppose the judge rules in limine that the prosecutor will be permitted to use defendant's convictions to impeach if the defendant testifies. Defense counsel, when calling her client as a witness, brings out the convictions herself.

Why would she do that? In the hopes that doing so would reduce the sting.[44] Moreover, bringing it out on direct examination also gives the defense counsel the

42. Keep in mind that if the defendant had been convicted of a Rule 609(a)(2) crime involving a dishonest act or false statement, the judge must permit the impeachment (See § 13.12)—unless the conviction is more than ten years old, as time is measured by Rule 609(b) (see § 13.26).

43. Right. And we have "no way of knowing" whether the sun will rise in the east or west tomorrow morning.

44. See § 13.24. Doing so also enables defense counsel, during summation, to remind the jury: "My client did not try to hide his previous conviction from you. You have a right to know that about him, so we brought it out ourselves." Since the litigation over admissibility of the conviction takes place before trial or out of the jury's presence, the jury does not know that defense counsel tried to prevent the conviction from being mentioned. Counsel's inconsistency—some might even call it duplicity—may seem disturbing, or even shocking, but in the context of a trial, it is quite acceptable

opportunity to ask an additional question or two to spin the facts in as favorable (or at least, less unfavorable) light as possible. See § 13.19.

The question is: If defense counsel uses this tactic, may defendant nevertheless appeal the judge's ruling in limine; or by bringing out the convictions on direct, does the defense waive the issue?

In *Ohler v. U.S.*, 529 U.S. 753 (2000), the Supreme Court, dividing 5–4, held that "reducing the sting" waives the issue on appeal. As defendant drove a van from Mexico into California, a customs inspector, noticing that someone had tampered with the van's interior panels, searched the van and found 81 pounds of marijuana. The trial judge ruled in limine that, if defendant testified, the Government could impeach her with her four-year-earlier felony conviction for possession of methamphetamine. When she took the stand, her attorney brought out the prior conviction on direct before eliciting her defense that she did not know the marijuana had been hidden in the van. Chief Justice Rehnquist, joined by Justices O'Connor, Scalia, Kennedy and Thomas, viewed the question as a straightforward application of the "commonsense principle" that a party cannot object to evidence that it itself has introduced. The Court acknowledged that the situation presents the defense with a difficult tactical choice, but observed that making difficult tactical decisions is inherent in the trial process. The majority considered the case a logical extension of the *Luce* decision, pointing out that by bringing the convictions out on direct, the defense precluded the trial court from reversing its in limine ruling and deprived the prosecution of the tactical option to forego impeaching to reduce the likelihood of giving defendant a viable issue on appeal.

Dissenting, Justice Souter, joined by Justices Stevens, Ginsburg and Breyer, argued that the situation in *Ohler* differed considerably from that in *Luce:* in *Luce*, an appellate court could only speculate as to what the defendant would testify to and whether the prosecutor would impeach or forgo, while in *Ohler*, the record was complete. The majority's "commonsense principle" was inapt, the dissent protested, because that principle applied only if a party *voluntarily* introduced the evidence or did so while maintaining inconsistent positions. Finally, the dissent argued, forcing the defense to forgo the tactical choice of "reducing the string" does not enhance the legitimate probative value of the prior conviction on the issue of the defendant's credibility, while creating a significant and unfair risk that the jury will further discount his credibility by assuming that the defendant tried to hide the conviction from the jury. From the dissenting Justices' perspective, that this assumption is accurate in no way reduces its unfairness.

The bottom line, then, is this: by bringing out the defendant's conviction on direct examination, defense counsel in essence waives the defendant's right to appeal the

---

to take one approach in arguing a legal question to a judge, and a totally different approach when arguing facts to a jury. Doing so fits comfortably within the concept of "zealous representation."

judge's denial of the defendant's motion in limine to preclude the prosecutor from using the conviction to impeach the defendant's character for truthfulness.

§ 13.26 Time limit: FRE 609(b)

Rule 609(b) provides:

> **Rule 609. Impeachment by Evidence of a Criminal Conviction**
>
> ...
>
> **(b) Limit on Using the Evidence After 10 Years.** This subdivision (b) applies if more than 10 years have passed since the witness's conviction or release from confinement for it, whichever is later. Evidence of the conviction is admissible only if:
>
> (1) its probative value, supported by specific facts and circumstances, substantially outweighs its prejudicial effect; and
>
> (2) the proponent gives an adverse party reasonable written notice of the intent to use it so that the party has a fair opportunity to contest its use.

Rule 609(b) provides that a conviction more than ten years old (as defined by the rule) is admissible to impeach a witness "only if [the probative value of the conviction on the witness's character for truthfulness], supported by specific facts and circumstances, substantially outweighs its prejudicial effect," and the adverse party is given reasonable written advance notice. It is obvious from this language that Congress intended to create a strong assumption *against* admissibility of more-than-10-year-old convictions. The strength of this negative assumption can be best appreciated by comparing Rule 609(b) to other provisions governing the appropriate balance between relevance and prejudice generally and with regard to impeachment.

1. Rule 609(a)(2) directs that crimes involving a dishonest act or false statement are admissible to impeach the character for truthfulness of any witness (including the defendant in a criminal case), regardless of how great the risk of unfair prejudice may be.
2. Rule 609(a)(1)(A) directs that a felony conviction must be admitted to impeach any witness (except the defendant in a criminal case) unless, per FRE 403, its probative value as to the witness's character of truthfulness is substantially outweighed by the danger of unfair prejudice to a party in the lawsuit. Thus, Rule 609(a)(1)(A) establishes a strong assumption in favor of permitting the impeachment.
3. Rule 609(a)(1)(B) permits a prosecutor to use a defendant's prior felony conviction to impeach the defendant only if the probative value of the conviction

as to the defendant's character for truthfulness outweighs the risk of unfair prejudice: there is a slight assumption against permitting the impeachment.

Once a ten-year period has run, by contrast, Rule 609(b) erects a substantial assumption *against* admissibility regardless of who the witness is and regardless of the nature of the crime. Indeed, the Senate Judiciary Committee Report expresses the expectation that "convictions over ten years old will be admitted very rarely and only in exceptional circumstances."[45] The factors to be considered by the trial judge in assessing probative value and prejudicial impact are similar to those discussed in § 13.16, *supra*. Given the assumption against admissibility, it is probably even more important with regard to Rule 609(b) than with Rule 609(a)(1) for the trial judge to conduct an on-the-record hearing, and to enunciate his or her reasons for permitting a more-than-ten-year-old conviction to be used.

A potentially troublesome issue under Rule 609(b) is how to measure the ten-year period—i.e., the date that marks the beginning of the ten-year period. (This is another of those issues that you can probably ignore unless your professor makes a point of covering it.)[46]

Assuming witness W was not incarcerated following W's conviction, there are two possible beginning points: the date W had pleaded or was found guilty, and the date (often several weeks or months later) when W was sentenced. If a prison sentence was imposed, on the other hand, the rule is fairly explicit: the ten-year period begins on the date W was "released from confinement."

Thus, if W was convicted fifteen years ago, served six years and then was paroled, the ten-year period begins to run on the date W was released on parole—nine years ago. For purposes of Rule 609(b), the fifteen-year-ago conviction is considered to be only nine years old. Suppose, two years after being released, W was re-incarcerated for violation of parole, remained in prison for two years, and then was again paroled five years ago. In that case, presumably, the conviction is considered to be only five years old for purposes of Rule 609(b).[47]

45. My reading of the case law indicates that judges permit such impeachment perhaps a bit more often than Congress intended. Then again, the government often has no incentive to appeal trial judge decisions precluding the use of post-time limit convictions.

46. But it is still worth reading the footnote at the end of this section.

47. There are, of course, other potential variations. Suppose the defendant was sentenced 20 years ago to a five-year sentence, but the judge allowed the defendant to remain at liberty for two additional months to "put his affairs in order." Two months later, the defendant failed to surrender, and stayed "on the lam" for another eight years before surrendering, and once incarcerated, he "maxed out"—served the full five years before being released. Even though he was sentenced 20 years ago, he did not begin to serve time until twelve years ago, and was not released until seven years ago, so for purposes of Rule 609(b), his 20-year-old conviction is only seven years old. But suppose the reason for the 8-year hiatus between his report-to-prison date and his surrender was that, while flying back to be imprisoned, his plane crashed, he washed up on an uninhabited island in the Pacific and remained there with only a volleyball for company, before being rescued. Or

§ 13.27 Rules 609(c), 609(d) and 609(e)

These provisions are basically self-explanatory. Unless your professor stresses them, it's probably enough to know in general that:

> Rule 609(c) in essence cancels a conviction, for Rule 609(a) purposes, if the witness has been pardoned or the conviction was annulled or lifted upon a finding of rehabilitation or innocence.
>
> Rule 609(d) prohibits or restricts a juvenile adjudication of a Rule 609(a) crime to be used to impeach the character for truthfulness of a witness who testifies in a civil case. In a criminal case, such a juvenile adjudication cannot be used to impeach a now-adult defendant's character for truthfulness. Such an adjudication can be used against other witnesses in criminal cases only where such impeachment is necessary to reach a fair verdict.
>
> Rule 609(e) mandates that a Rule 609(a) conviction may be used to impeach a witness even if that conviction is currently on appeal, but the party relying on the impeached witness may introduce evidence that the case is on appeal.

§ 13.28 Other evidentiary uses of a conviction; FRE 803(22)

A person's (X's) conviction of a crime can be relevant on either of two theories. The first is simply to prove that X was in fact convicted of that crime. FRE 609 is an example of such a use: the fact of X's conviction is offered in evidence, as a factor which the jury may consider in judging X's character for truthfulness.

But it is worth noting that, depending on circumstances, X's conviction might be offered in evidence to prove the facts underlying the conviction—to prove that X engaged in the conduct, with the mens rea, that satisfies the definition of the crime. If offered for this purpose, the conviction is hearsay: it is a statement by the jury in that case that they were convinced beyond a reasonable doubt that those facts are true. Many convictions, however, are admissible for that purpose over a hearsay objection, per FRE 803(22), which provides as follows:

> **Rule 803 Exceptions to the Rule Against Hearsay**
>
> The following are not excluded by the rule against hearsay, regardless of whether the declarant is available as a witness:...
>
> (22) **Judgment of a Previous Conviction.** Evidence of a final judgment of conviction if:

---

suppose he accepted an invitation by sentient beings from another solar system to visit them for a week, only to discover that, because he traveled there and back at the speed of light, per Einstein's theory of special relativity, more than eight years had elapsed on earth. Or suppose....

(A) the judgment was entered after a trial or guilty plea, but not a nolo contendere plea;

(B) the conviction was for a crime punishable by death or by imprisonment for more than a year;

(C) the evidence is admitted to prove any fact essential to the judgment; and

(D) when offered by the prosecutor in a criminal case for a purpose other than impeachment, the judgment was against the defendant.

The pendency of an appeal may be shown but does not affect admissibility.

Here's how the rule works. Suppose F was indicted for robbing a liquor store at gunpoint at 12th and Elm at 11 p.m. on June 1, 2020. To find F guilty, the jury must conclude (1) that F was in the liquor store at 12th and Elm at 11 p.m. on June 1, (2) that she had a gun, and (3) that she used the gun to force W1, the store clerk, to empty the register and give her the money. All three points are, as Rule 803(22)(C) puts it, "facts essential to sustain the judgment" that F committed that liquor store robbery.

Suppose in 2022 plaintiff files a lawsuit against F—or against someone else!—and for some reason needs to offer evidence of one of the "numbered" facts in the previous paragraph. One way plaintiff can do so is to offer evidence of F's robbery conviction. Even though that conviction is hearsay, so long as that conviction satisfies the requirements of FRE 803(22), the conviction is admissible. Such a conviction is considered highly reliable, because we expect that someone would fight criminal charges that are untrue, and because the prosecutor's burden of proof in a criminal case is so heavy (guilt must be established beyond a reasonable doubt).

Note that only convictions are admissible to prove "any fact essential to sustain the judgment." Acquittals, by contrast, are not admissible in subsequent litigation as proof that the criminal defendant did not do what he was charged with. This is because an acquittal is not a finding that the defendant is innocent of the charge; it is only a finding that a reasonable doubt exists as to the defendant's guilt.

For a more detailed discussion of this provision, see *A Student's Guide to Hearsay* §10.13 (5th ed. 2019).[48]

§13.29 Questions

In the following problems, first determine the litigation situation or situations the problem involves; then determine which rule(s) apply and whether the question is proper.

---

48. In some circumstances, the prior conviction is treated as conclusive under the doctrine of res judicata, either as a bar or as collateral estoppel. This use of prior convictions is not covered in the Federal Rules of Evidence; it is governed by constitutional principles that have nothing to do with hearsay.

Question 1.

Purdue is on trial for possession of oxycontin with intent to distribute. The prosecuting attorney has certified documentary evidence of Purdue's prior misdemeanor conviction for possession of cocaine five years earlier. During the government's case-in-chief, the prosecutor offers the certified document. Discuss the issues thus presented.

Answer:

This is litigation situation E (§ 11.28): prosecutor's case-in-chief. The only rule in the right column that applies is FRE 404(b). The misdemeanor possession conviction has minimal relevance—if he possessed a small amount of cocaine five years earlier, I suppose that makes it slightly more likely than it would be without that evidence that he possessed oxycontin this time with intent to distribute it. But this relevance is based solely on the propensity inference banned by FRE 404(b)(1). The judge should sustain Purdue's Rule 404(b)(1) objection.

Since the word "conviction" is most closely associated (in this context) with Rule 609, if confronted with a quiz or exam question like this, your answer should probably include something like: "Rule 609 is not in play here because that rule only governs impeaching a witness, and Purdue has not testified."

Question 2.

During the defense case-in-chief, Purdue took the stand to deny possession of the oxycontin. On cross-examination, the prosecutor asks, "Were you convicted five years ago for the misdemeanor of possession of cocaine?" Discuss the issues thus presented.

Answer:

Now we are in litigation situation F (§ 11.29): cross-examining W about W's prior conduct. The applicable rules are 404(b), 608(b) and 609.

Regarding Rule 404(b): the situation is no different, really, than it was in Question 1, when the prosecutor tried to offer evidence of Purdue's misdemeanor cocaine possession during the state's case-in-chief. It is still only weakly relevant, and that relevance is via the propensity inference banned by FRE 404(b)(1). If, however, Purdue foolishly testified on direct examination that he has never had anything to do with unlawful drugs, or blurted out that assertion on cross even though the prosecutor did not refer to it, the judge might allow the prosecutor to impeach Purdue's testimony under the doctrine of specific contradiction. See § 12.10 & § 12.11.

Rule 608(b) does not permit any use of the cocaine conviction to impeach Purdue's character for truthfulness, because that is not conduct indicative of a poor character for truthfulness.

Rule 609 does not permit its use to impeach, because misdemeanor possession of a controlled substance does not satisfy Rule 609(a).

Conclusion: the prosecutor cannot use the cocaine conviction for any purpose, unless the defendant opened the door during direct or cross.

Question 3.

Continuing to cross-examine Purdue, the prosecutor asks, "Were you convicted three years ago for the misdemeanor of petty larceny?" Discuss the issues thus presented.

Answer:

Petty larceny is not a felony, so it does not come within FRE 609(a)(1). It still may be used to impeach Purdue's character for truthfulness, but only if the manner in which the larceny was committed involved dishonesty, deception, or a false statement, per FRE 609(a)(2). The burden is on the prosecutor to establish that it was. See § 13.12–iii.

Questions 4–9

Five years ago, Lily was convicted of two counts of selling heroin to an undercover police agent, a crime for which the maximum penalty was ten years. She was sentenced to, and served, nine months, and was released. Now she is on trial for selling fifteen tinfoil packets containing cocaine to a police informer for $300 last February first.

Question 4.

Prior to trial, Lily's attorney thinks it may be necessary to call Lily to testify, but fears the negative impact of impeachment. Discuss the issues presented. (Note: This question requires you to apply the material covered in § 13.25. If your professor did not cover that subject, feel free to skip this question.)

Answer:

Lily's attorney should bring a pretrial motion in limine, asking the judge to preclude the prosecutor from using the prior conviction to impeach Lily if she testifies.

The prosecutor should of course oppose the motion, not only on the merits ("Your Honor, if the defendant testifies, it is important that the jury have an adequate basis to assess her credibility"), but because it is too early for the judge to make an informed decision ("Your Honor, you'll be in a much better position to assess the probative value and risk of unfair prejudice after you've heard all the evidence").

For the rest of this sequence, assume the judge refuses to rule on Lily's motion.

Question 5.

At trial, the informer testifies that he purchased the cocaine from Lily in an apartment on East Fifth Street at 2 p.m. last February 1. On cross-examination, Lily's attorney plans to impeach the informer by questioning him about his several prior drug felony convictions. Discuss the issues presented.

Answer:

This is litigation situation F (§11.29). Because the informer's convictions are for felonies, the applicable rule is FRE 609(a)(1)(A), which directs that a judge "must" allow the impeachment," subject to FRE 403. The prosecutor should not move in limine to ask the judge to preclude defense counsel from using the convictions to impeach the informer. To preclude such impeachment would violate the defendant's right, guaranteed by the Sixth Amendment, to cross-examine his accuser. At most, the judge might limit the number of convictions about which the defense can cross-examine: "Counselor, choose your three favorites."

In fact, the prosecutor would probably begin his or her direct examination of the informer by eliciting testimony about the informer's convictions, to "reduce the sting." See §13.24.

Question 6.

After cross-examination of the informer concludes, the prosecutor calls a Drug Enforcement Agency agent, who testifies that on last February 1, at about 1:50 p.m., he searched the informer to ascertain that he had no drugs on him, gave the informer $360, and watched the informer enter the apartment building on East Fifth Street. The agent further testifies that he saw the informer emerge from the building at about 2:05 p.m., at which time the informer handed him fifteen tinfoil packets of cocaine and $60 change. On cross-examination, the agent concedes that he has no first-hand knowledge where or from whom the informer purchased the drugs. Next, the government chemist testifies that she analyzed the contents of the fifteen packets, and that each packet contained cocaine. The government then rests. (Assume all this was properly admitted.)

The first defense witness is Lily's husband. He testifies that he and Lily lived on West Twelfth Street; that Lily was home, sick in bed on last February 1; and that he remembers the date because he had to stay home from work that day to nurse her. Lily's next witness is a friend of the family, who testifies that "I had heard that Lily wasn't feeling too well, so I phoned her at home—on her landline phone—sometime between 2:00 and 2:30 that afternoon to see how she was getting on."

Lily's attorney now must decide whether to call Lily as a witness. What should she do before making that decision?

Answer:

Defense counsel asks, "Your Honor, may I approach the bench?" The judge (who knows what Lily's attorney has in mind) states: "Both attorneys, approach the bench." The judge then turns to the jury. "Ladies and gentlemen, I have to discuss a few matters with the lawyers." The judge then has two basic options: send the jury out of the courtroom (either to the jury room or to lunch), or turn on the white noise machine so the jury cannot hear what the attorneys and judge say to each other.

Once the judge has assured that the jury cannot overhear the discussion, Lily's attorney says, "Your Honor, I now have to decide whether to put Lily on the stand to deny these charges. I thereby move that the court preclude the prosecutor from using her prior conviction to impeach her."

In her argument, Lily's attorney should stress the following.

(a) Rule 609(a)(1)(B) directs that a defendant's prior conviction must be admitted to impeach the defendant's character for truthfulness only if its probative value as to the defendant's character for truthfulness outweighs the risk of unfair prejudice. In other words, the rule begins with an assumption against admissibility.

(Note how I have worded this. I have cited the precise provision—Rule 609(a)(1)(B). I have quoted the text of that provision, but have inserted the phase "as to the defendant's character for truthfulness," to remind the judge—as you should, in an essay answer, to make it clear to the professor that you understand—that in Rule 609, the phrase "probative value" refers only to the conviction's probative value regarding the defendant's character for truthfulness or untruthfulness, *not* to its probative value as to whether the defendant is guilty of the heroin sales she is now charged with.)

(b) Selling drugs five years ago tells us very little, really, about her current character for truthfulness. It is her only conviction. It was a single, isolated mistake. She's been out trouble since then. She's married.

(Here, defense counsel is marshaling available facts to suggest that a five-year-old conviction sheds little light on her current character for truthfulness.)

(c) She's on trial for selling drugs. Her prior conviction is for selling drugs. Despite a limiting instruction, it is inevitable that the jury—subconsciously if not deliberately—will use that fact to conclude that she has a propensity to sell drugs. This reinforces Rule 609(a)(1)(B)'s assumption of inadmissibility because the risk of unfair prejudice substantially outweighs the limited probative value that conviction has on her character for truthfulness.

(Here, defense counsel clearly articulates her ultimate argument for inadmissibility, spelling out the risk of unfair prejudice and paraphrasing the balancing test that rule 609(a)(1)(B) directs the judge to apply.)

The prosecutor counter-argues:

(a) Lily hasn't really been "out of trouble" for five years; she was released from prison only four years and two months ago.

(b) Her conviction wasn't for a "single, isolated mistake"; she sold drugs twice, not once.

(c) Selling drugs is not an impulsive act; it is an act the seller must think about and plan in advance—particularly when, as here, the defendant did it more than once. Her willingness to deliberately sell drugs is revealing about her probable willingness to lie under oath.

(d) In the context of this case, precluding the impeachment would be significantly unfair to the state. After all, defense counsel impeached the informer, my key witness, with his prior drug convictions. If I am precluded from impeaching Lily, the jury will naturally assume she is as pure as the driven snow—an assumption which is as inaccurate as it is unfair. Therefore, her conviction has considerable probative value regarding her character for truthfulness.

The judge could rule either way without fear of being reversed

Comment: This answer (omitting the "stage-setting" paragraph about approaching the bench and the parenthetical comments I inserted at certain points) is roughly 400 words long. It demonstrates how to inform a professor that you know what the applicable rule says, you know what it means, and you know how each side on an issue would marshal the facts and apply the law to those facts in a way most favorable to that side. But if the question is worth only, say, three points or so, you probably won't have time to write out so elaborate an answer.

<u>Question 7.</u>

Assume the judge denies Lily's motion, and rules that he will allow the impeachment—or refuses to rule until after Lily testifies on direct. Her attorney nevertheless decides to call her as a witness. On direct examination, defense counsel asks: "You were convicted five years ago, were you not, on two counts of distributing heroin?" Discuss the issues presented.

<u>Answer:</u>

Lily's attorney is bringing out Lily's conviction on direct, hoping to "reduce the sting," i.e., lessen the impact the conviction will have on the jury. By doing so, however, she in essence is waiving the right to appeal the judge's denial of her motion to preclude the impeachment. (See § 13.25.)

<u>Question 8.</u>

Assume that Lily has testified in her own behalf but that her attorney did not ask her the question proposed in the previous problem. On cross, the prosecutor asks:

Q Are you the same Ms. Lily who was convicted on [specify date] in [specify state, county, etc.] of two counts of distributing heroin?

A Yes, that's true.

Q And what sentence did you receive in that case?

Discuss the issues presented.

Answer:

The question is proper. Once Lily answers it, her attorney should ask the judge to give a limiting instruction. See § 13.17.

Question 9.

The prosecutor next asks:

Q What quantity of heroin was involved in each count?

Q How much money was involved in each transaction?

Q What was your defense in that case?[49]

Discuss the issues presented.

Answer:

These questions are generally considered improper, because they go beyond the basic facts—the date, location and general nature of the conviction—that are relevant to impeach a witness or defendant's character for truthfulness. See § 13.19.

B. Calling W2 to Impeach or Rehabilitate W1's Character for Truthfulness

---

1. Rule 608(a): impeachment

§ 13.30 The rule

Another means of impeaching the *character* of a witness is to call a second witness to testify negatively about the previous witness. (See litigation situation H, § 11.31.) For example: DW1 testifies for D during D's case-in-chief (and is cross-examined). D rests. P, in rebuttal, may call PW to attack DW1's character. Rule 608(a) governs this form of impeachment. This aspect of the rule reads as follows:

> **Rule 608. A Witness's Character for Truthfulness or Untruthfulness**
>
> **(a) Reputation or Opinion Evidence.** A witness's credibility may be attacked [or supported] by testimony about the witness's reputation for having a character for truthfulness or untruthfulness, or by testimony in

49. Assuming she was convicted after trial rather than by guilty plea.

> the form of an opinion about that character. [But evidence of truthful character is admissible only after the witness's character for truthfulness has been attacked.][50]

Thus, Rule 608(a) provides that the credibility of witness W1 may be attacked by *reputation or opinion testimony relating to W1's character for truthfulness.* But W1's character for truthfulness is the only aspect of W1's character that P can attack via PW's testimony.

§ 13.31 Questions

Note: if your professor does not cover FRE 608(a), ignore these questions.

Question 1.

At 2:30 a.m. on January 1, P, a pedestrian, was struck by a car driven by D. P sues for personal injuries. P presents his evidence, including witnesses who testify that D appeared to be intoxicated immediately after his car struck P. P offers evidence as to injuries and damages, and rests.

D's first witness is DW1, who testifies that she and D attended the same New Year's Eve party and that D was sober throughout the evening until the party broke up at about 2:15 a.m. On cross-examination, DW1 testified that she, too, was sober that night. D presents the rest of his case and rests.

In rebuttal, P calls PRW (plaintiff rebuttal witness). PRW testifies that he saw DW1 consume several alcoholic beverages that night, and that by the time the party broke up, DW1 was "pretty much out of it—slurring her words, not making much sense."

In other words, PRW has been called to testify about DW1, which puts us in litigation situation H (§ 11.31). Because PRW is testifying about DW1's specific conduct that New Year's Eve, we look at the right column. What rule or principle applies?

Answer:

PRW's testimony is directly relevant to impeach DW1's capacity to have perceived and remembered what happened at the party, and in particular, whether DW1 accurately perceived and remembers D's condition by the time the party ended. The only specific rule required is FRE 401: PRW's testimony is relevant to help the jury decide how much weight they should give to DW1's testimony. PRW's testimony is admissible.

Question 2.

P's direct examination of rebuttal witness PRW continues:

---

50. The words "or supported," and the second sentence of the rule, have been set in brackets because we are ignoring those aspects of the rule for now.

Q. Are you familiar with DW1's reputation in the community for sobriety?

A. Yes, I am.

Q. What is the reputation?

A. DW1's reputation is that she is a lush.

Is this testimony proper?

Answer:

We are still in litigation situation H, but because PRW is now offering reputation or opinion testimony, we look to the left column. Two rules govern the use of reputation evidence to attack a person's character: 404(a) and 608(a). If the testimony satisfies either rule, it is admissible; if not, it must be excluded.

Examine Rule 404(a):

Rule 404. Character Evidence; Crimes or Other Acts

(a) **Character Evidence.**

(1) **Prohibited Uses.** Evidence of a person's character or character trait is not admissible to prove that on a particular occasion the person acted in accordance with the character or trait.

(2) **Exceptions for a Defendant or Victim in a Criminal Case.** The following exceptions apply in a criminal case:

(A) a defendant may offer evidence of the defendant's pertinent trait, and if the evidence is admitted, the prosecutor may offer evidence to rebut it;

(B) subject to the limitations in Rule 412, a defendant may offer evidence of an alleged victim's pertinent trait, and if the evidence is admitted, the prosecutor may:

(i) offer evidence to rebut it; and

(ii) offer evidence of the defendant's same trait; and

(C) in a homicide case, the prosecutor may offer evidence of the alleged victim's trait of peacefulness to rebut evidence that the victim was the first aggressor.

(3) **Exceptions for a Witness.** Evidence of a witness's character may be admitted under Rules 607, 608, and 609.

This is not a case in which anyone's character is an essential element of a claim or defense, so the "unwritten sentence" of Rule 404(a) (see § 5.2) does not apply. Therefore, per Rule 404(a)(2) and (3), reputation or opinion testimony is admissible in only three circumstances. Since this is not a criminal case, the two exceptions set out in Rule 404(a)(2) do not apply, and Rule 404(a)(3) simply refers us to Rules 607–609.

Of Rules 607–609, only 608(a) speaks to reputation or opinion evidence about a *witness's* character. Rule 608(a) clearly states that reputation or opinion evidence about the character of a witness is admissible *only* if the evidence refers to the witness' character for truthfulness or untruthfulness. The second part of PRW's testimony, however, did not attack DW1's character for truthfulness; it attacked DW1's character for sobriety. Hence, PRW's testimony does not "fit" within Rule 608(a), and is therefore inadmissible.

Suppose instead PRW had been asked about DW1's reputation in the community for "truthfulness and veracity," and PRW had replied, "Her reputation is that of someone who will lie whenever she feels like it." Since this testimony *does* "fit" within Rule 608(a)(1st sentence), it *is* admissible, assuming PRW has established an adequate foundation. (The foundation requirements for a Rule 608(a) character witness are the same as those for a Rule 404(a) character witness, as set out in § 6.8 and § 6.9.)

<u>Question 3.</u>

Suppose instead this was a criminal case: D is charged with driving under the influence, and for aggravated assault, for recklessly injuring P with a dangerous instrument (D's car). At trial, D calls DW1, who testifies that D was sober that night. DW1 further testifies that she was sober that night, too.

In rebuttal, may the prosecutor elicit PRW's testimony about DW1's character for non-sobriety?

<u>Answer:</u>

Clearly not with regard to FRE 608(a), which restricts reputation or opinion testimony about a witness to testimony relating to that witness's character for truthfulness.[51]

Is PRW's testimony about DW1's character for sobriety admissible per FRE 404(a)(2)?

No. FRE 404(a)(2)(A) allows a defendant in a criminal case to offer reputation or opinion testimony about a pertinent trait of <u>defendant</u>'s character. FRE 404(a)(2)(B) allows a defendant to offer reputation or opinion testimony about a pertinent trait of the alleged <u>victim</u>'s character. But DW1 is neither the defendant, nor the alleged victim; DW1 is only a witness.

51. It may be that people who often get drunk tend to lie more often than people who do not drink to excess. (I have not researched the issue.) Even if that is true, Rule 608(a)'s mandate is clear: the only character trait that the rule permits an attorney to ask PRW about regarding DW1 is DW1's character for truthfulness.

Question 4.

Suppose, in the criminal case, after DW1 testifies that D was sober at 2:15 a.m., D's attorney asks:

Q Are you familiar with D's reputation for sobriety in the community?

A Yes. It is excellent. Everyone says he is very moderate in his drinking; I've never heard anyone say they saw D drinking too much or being under the influence.

Q And are you familiar with D's reputation for truthfulness and veracity?

A Yes. He's regarded as a straight shooter. If he says something is so, you can take it to the bank.[52]

Is this admissible?

Answer:

Now we are in litigation situation C (§ 11.26): D, charged with a crime, is eliciting character testimony from DW1 about D's own character. Such evidence is governed by FRE 404(a)(2)(A) and FRE 405(a)(1st sentence), which permit a criminal defendant to offer reputation or opinion testimony about a "pertinent trait" of his own character.

Is character for sobriety "pertinent" to defend against an accusation of driving under the influence?

Yes, clearly it is: a "sober" person is less likely to drive under the influence. The first Q&A is admissible per Rules 404(a)(2)(A) and 405(a)(1st sentence).

Is character for truthfulness "pertinent" to defend against an accusation of driving under the influence?

No. Therefore, the second Q&A does not satisfy Rules 404(a)(2)(A) and 405(a)(1st sentence).

Well, what about Rule 608(a)? Is the second Q&A admissible under that rule?

No. Rule 608(a) only permits reputation or opinion testimony about a *witness's* character for truthfulness. D has not testified at the trial; therefore, Rule 608(a) does not apply to him.

Question 5.

Go back a few steps. DW1 has testified that D was sober that night. In rebuttal, PRW testifies per Rule 608(a) that DW1 has a poor reputation for truthfulness. In D's rebuttal, D calls DW2 to testify that PRW's character for truthfulness is poor. Is this admissible?

52. In case you are unfamiliar with these idioms, they are ways of saying "D doesn't lie."

Answer:

Once again, this is litigation situation H (§ 11.31). The judge may allow it. In this context, PRW is "W1"; by testifying, he automatically puts his own character for truthfulness in issue, and D may call DW2 to attack it with negative testimony about PRW's character for truthfulness. And in turn, P could call PRW2, to give negative reputation or opinion testimony about DW2's character for testimony. But Rule 403 gives the judge discretion to tell the lawyers to stop acting like name-calling school children and disallow any further permutations of this sequence.

2. Rehabilitating a previous witness's character for truthfulness

§ 13.32 Rehabilitating W1 by cross-examining W2: Rule 608(b)(2)

This provision is invoked very, very rarely, and unless your professor covers it, you can safely ignore this provision and this section of the book (although the footnote contains a good example of Mark Twain's humor).

If P attacks W1's credibility by calling W2, who gives negative reputation or opinion testimony about W1's character for truthfulness per Rule 608(a)(1st sentence), D may seek to rehabilitate W1 by cross-examining W2 about W1. Rule 608(b)(2) governs such cross-examination. It provides:

> **(b) Specific Instances of Conduct....** [E]xtrinsic evidence is not admissible to prove specific instances of a witness's [W1's] conduct in order to... support [W1's] witness's character for truthfulness. But the court may, on cross-examination, allow them to be inquired into if they are probative of the character for truthfulness... of:
>
> (2) another witness [W1] whose character the witness being cross-examined [W2] has testified about.

In other words, the attorney seeking to rehabilitate W1 can ask W2 intrinsically worded questions about whether W2 had heard about truthful things W1 has done in his life.

For example, suppose Hamilton is on trial for, let's say, conspiring to corruptly influence the outcome of an election in New York State. Washington [W1] testifies as a fact witness in favor of Hamilton. In rebuttal, the prosecutor calls Genet [W2], who testifies, per FRE 608(a)(1st sentence), that Washington has a very poor reputation in the community for truth. On cross, FRE 608(b)(2) allows Hamilton's attorney to ask Genet:

Q Did you know that when Washington's father asked him what happened to the family cherry tree, Washington responded, "Father, I cannot tell a lie. It was me. I chopped it down with my little hatchet." Did you know that?[53]

I cannot recall ever seeing a case in which this rule was invoked.

§ 13.33 Rehabilitating W1 by calling W3: Rule 608(a)(2nd sentence)

This is litigation situation H (§ 11.31)—calling a later witness (W3) to testify about a previous witness (W1).

Rule 608(a) provides a method to rehabilitate W1's character for truthfulness after that character has been attacked: It is to call another witness—let's call that witness W3—to give favorable character testimony about W1's character for truthfulness. This aspect of Rule 608(a) reads as follows:

> **Rule 608. A Witness's Character for Truthfulness or Untruthfulness**
>
> **(a) Reputation or Opinion Evidence.** A witness's [W1's] credibility may be... supported by testimony [from W3] about the witness's [W1's] reputation for having a character for truthfulness... or by testimony in the form of [W3's] opinion about that character [of W1]. [2nd sentence:] But evidence of [W1's] truthful character is admissible only after [W1's] character for truthfulness has been attacked.

This rule is invoked occasionally—more often, at least, than FRE 608(b)(2)—but if your professor ignores it, you should skip this section.

This raises several questions: first, what constitutes an "attack" on witness W1's "character for truthfulness"? Second, what is the required foundation for W3's testimony? Third, what limitations are placed on W3's testimony? Fourth, how can the other side's attorney cross-examine W3?

i. What constitutes an attack on W1's character for truthfulness?

Rule 608(a)(2) provides that witness W1's character may be rehabilitated "only after [W1's] character for truthfulness has been attacked." As we have seen, the primary methods of attacking a witness's character for truthfulness are:

53. This story about our nation's president's childhood was invented by his first biographer, Mason Lock (Parson) Weems. But consider Mark Twain's view of the story: "[Washington] was ignorant of the commonest accomplishments of youth. He could not even lie." Mark Twain, "Brief Biographical Sketch of George Washington," *The Celebrated Jumping Frog of Calaveras County, and Other Sketches* (1867).

(1) Cross-examination of W1 about W1's alleged prior untruthful or dishonest acts, per Rule 608(b)(1st sentence).

(2) Cross-examination of W1 about W1's prior convictions, pursuant to Rule 609.

(3) Calling a witness (W2), per Rule 608(a)(1st sentence), to give negative reputation or opinion testimony about W1's character for truthfulness.

If a party in a lawsuit has done any of these things to attack W1's character for truthfulness, the party relying on W1's testimony can invoke Rule 608(a)(2nd sentence), by calling W3 to give favorable reputation or opinion testimony about W1's character for truthfulness.

It is important to understand that impeachment of W1's testimony, by showing bias or prior inconsistent statements, or challenging W1's ability to perceive, remember, or accurately narrate, is *not* generally considered an attack on W1's *character for truthfulness,* and therefore does not open the door to W3's favorable testimony about W1's character for truthfulness. But sometimes the distinction between impeaching W1's testimony and impeaching W1's character for truthfulness pretty much amounts to the same thing. If an impeaching attorney implies that W1 is biased or has testified inconsistent with prior statements because he has been bribed, for example, a judge might properly consider this as an attack W1's character for truthfulness, and permit rehabilitation.

ii. Foundation for W3's testimony

Before W3 can give favorable reputation or opinion testimony about W1's character for truthfulness, W3 must first establish sufficient familiarity for his or her testimony. If W3 is to testify as to W1's reputation for truthfulness and veracity in a particular community, for example, W3 must first testify that he knows W1 and has had occasion to discuss W1's character for truthfulness with others in the community, etc. If W3 seeks to give his own opinion of W1's character for truthfulness, W3 must first explain how well and how long he knows W1. If this sounds familiar, it should: the same requirements exist when a litigant seeks to call a reputation or opinion witness pursuant to Rules 404–405. See § 6.8 & § 6.9.

iii. Limits on W3's direct testimony

After the attorney seeking to rehabilitate W1 elicits the foundational testimony from W3, the next question he or she asks W3 should explicitly specify W1's character for truthfulness: "And what is W1's reputation for truthfulness?" or "And what is your opinion of W1's character for truthfulness?" W3's answer should consist of one short sentence: "In my opinion, she is an honest, truthful person." "Everyone says that you can rely on her word."[54] Etc.

---

54. Compare this character endorsement: "Barring that natural expression of villainy which we all have, the man looked honest enough." Mark Twain, "A Mysterious Visit", *Buffalo Express*, 19

iv. Cross-examining W3

Assume in a criminal case D called DW1 as a witness. On cross-examination, P asked intrinsically worded questions, per FRE 608(b), concerning whether DW1 forged a colleague's paycheck four years ago. Because DW1 is an important witness to D, D decided to attempt to rehabilitate DW1 by calling DW3,[55] who testifies that in his opinion, DW1 is an honest, truthful person. On cross-examination of DW3, P asks: "Have you heard [or: did you know] that DW1 was arrested four years ago for forging a co-worker's paycheck?"

Although the wording of Rule 608(b)(2) is not a model of clarity, the intent appears to allow such cross-examination. Again, the parallel between cross examination of a Rule 608(a) character witness, and cross-examination of a Rule 404- 405 character witness, is obvious. (Well, maybe not "obvious"; nothing about character evidence is "obvious.") Using the litigation situation chart will help you determine which rules (608 or 404–405) apply in any particular situation.

§ 13.34 Questions

Question 1.

Disc is on trial for murdering Vinyl. In her opening statement, Disc's attorney tells the jury that the killing was a "tragic accident": Disc was showing Vinyl a new handgun, and it slipped out of Disc's hand, discharging a bullet that killed Vinyl. During the government's case-in-chief, the prosecutor calls PW1, a taxi driver, who testifies that she drove Disc and Vinyl to Disc's home on the evening the fatal shot was fired. On cross, D's attorney asks PW1: "It's true, is it not, that you were convicted four years ago of selling a Zoloft capsule to an undercover officer, and received a suspended sentence?" Discuss the issues thus presented.

Answer:

This is litigation situation F (§ 11.29): cross-examining a witness about him/herself. Of the rules listed, the only ones that could possibly apply are FRE 608(b) and FRE 609. 608(b) is a non-starter, because selling a Zoloft capsule is not an act suggestive of untruthfulness. The word "conviction" in the question triggers FRE 609(a). Sale of a controlled substance is a felony, so the crime qualifies, even though PW1 was not imprisoned—it is the potential sentence, not the actual sentence, that determines whether a crime is a felony.

Rule 609(a)(1)(A) says the conviction "must be allowed, subject to Rule 403." In this case, the judge should not allow the question, because PW1's testimony is relevant only to put both Disc and Vinyl in Disc's home—a fact which Disc does not contest.

March 1870. Anthologized in *Mark Twain's Sketches, New and Old* (1875).

55. There is no DW2 in this scenario. I'm calling the rehabilitation witness "DW3" because I've used W3 as the label for rehabilitation witnesses throughout these sections.

So (barring unusual circumstances), PW1's character for truthfulness is irrelevant in this case, because both sides agree that PW1's testimony in this case is true.

Question 2.

After the prosecutor rests, Disc calls DW1 as his first witness. DW1 testifies that he was present when Vinyl was shot and killed. Asked on direct, "How did this tragedy occur," DW1 replies, "Disc and Vinyl are—were—both gun enthusiasts, and Disc was showing Vinyl a replica Colt 45, when Disc sneezed so hard the gun slipped out of Disc's hand; it hit a table and discharged, killing Vinyl."

On cross-examination, the prosecutor asks:

Q1. Do you consider Disc to be a peaceful, non-violent man?

A. Yes.

Q2. Did you know that five years ago in [specify location], Disc was convicted of felonious assault for beating two teenagers with a baseball bat, and was sentenced to 2 years?

Discuss the issues presented.

Answer:

This question appears to implicate litigation situation D (§11.27), cross-examining a character witness per Rule 405(a)(2nd sentence). But does it?

No. Disc did not call DW1 as a character witness; DW1's direct testimony was strictly about how the fatal bullet came to be fired. Rule 404(a)(2)(A) directs that only the defendant can open the door to reputation or opinion testimony about the defendant's character. The prosecutor's Q1 clearly violates that rule.

The split second after DW1 answered said "Yes" in answer to Q1, Disc's attorney should call out, "Your Honor, may we approach the bench," and, at the bench, ask the judge to instruct the prosecutor that she cannot cross-examine DW1 per rule 405(a)(2nd sentence), since it was improper for the prosecutor to open the door in the first place.

You might wonder: shouldn't Disc's attorney object immediately after the prosecutor asks Q1, before DW1 answers it?

In this particular situation, doing so would be tactically unwise. Think about it: the prosecutor asks a defense witness about the defendant's character for peacefulness, and the defense attorney objects? The jury naturally would wonder, why is the defense attorney objecting? What is D's attorney trying to hide? The only way to avoid giving that impression is to let DW1 answer and then cut off the prosecutor before the prosecutor starts asking Rule 405(a)(2nd sentence) questions about Disc's prior conduct.

Question 3.

Next, Disc calls DW2 who will, if permitted, testify that "D's reputation for truthfulness in the community is very good." Discuss the issues thus presented.

Answer:

This is litigation situation C: defendant's case-in-chief. See § 11.26. Since Disc is calling a character witness, the appropriate rules are FRE 404(a)(2)(A) and 405(a) (1st sentence).

DW2's testimony is not admissible. D is on trial for murder; DW2 proposes to testify about Disc's reputation for truthfulness. Truthfulness is not a "pertinent" trait in a murder trial. See § 6.6.

Nor can Disc cite Rule 608(a), which admits testimony about prior witness's character for truthfulness, if that character has been attacked. Since Disc has not testified (not yet, at any rate), Rule 608(a) is inapplicable.

Question 4.

Disc testifies that the killing of Vinyl was an accident. During cross-examination, Disc acknowledges that he and Vinyl were business competitors and that, at the time of the fatal encounter, their companies were competing for a major contract. After Disc leaves the stand, Disc's attorney recalls DW2, who will, if permitted, testify as per the previous question. Discuss the issues thus presented.

Answer:

We are still in the defendant's case-in-chief, which involves litigation situation C, § 11.26; and DW2 is now being called to give reputation testimony about a previous witness (Disc), which puts us in litigation situation H, § 11.31. Thus, we have to consider whether DW2's testimony is now admissible per either FRE 404(a)(2)(A) (litigation situation C) or FRE 608(a) (litigation situation H).

FRE 404(a)(2)(A): DW2's testimony is still inadmissible per this rule, because Disc's character for truthfulness is not "pertinent" to defend against a charge of murder.

FRE 608(a): Since Disc has now testified, this rule is now in play. But if the prosecutor's cross-examination of Disc is limited to what is described in the stem of Question 4, then the prosecutor did not open the door to DW2's testimony. That cross-examination attacked Disc's testimony, by suggesting that Disc had a financial motive to kill Vinyl, but that does not attack Disc's general character for truthfulness.

Remember that most courts read Rule 608(a) as categorizing only three types of impeachment as an attack on a witness's character for truthfulness: (1) cross-examining the witness (here: Disc) about his or her prior untruthful acts, per FRE 608(b); (2) cross-examining the witness about his or her prior convictions, per FRE 609; or (3) calling a witness to give negative reputation or opinion testimony about Disc's character for truthfulness. Since the prosecutor has done none of these things to Disc, the prosecutor did not open the door to DW2's testimony about Disc's character for truthfulness per Rule 608(a).[56]

Question 5.

Next, Disc calls DW3, who will testify that "Disc's reputation for peacefulness in the community is very good." Discuss the issues thus presented.

Answer:

We are still in the defendant's case-in-chief, which involves litigation situation C; and DW3 is now being called to give reputation testimony about a previous witness (Disc), which puts us in litigation situation H. Thus, we have to consider whether DW3's testimony is now admissible per either FRE 404(a)(2)(A) (litigation situation C) or FRE 608(a) (litigation situation H).

We can dispose of Rule 608(a) quite quickly, because that rule admits reputation or opinion testimony only if that testimony relates to a prior witness's character for truthfulness or untruthfulness. DW3's testimony relates to Disc's peacefulness, and therefore does not satisfy FRE 608(a).

But (assuming Disc's attorney first elicited from DW3 the foundation necessary to support DW3's testimony (see § 6.8)), DW3's testimony does satisfy FRE 404(a)(2)(A). Disc is charged with murder; peacefulness is clearly a "pertinent" trait of character (§ 6.6), because peacefulness is inconsistent with murder. DW3's testimony is admissible.

Question 6.

On cross-examination of DW3, the prosecutor asks:

> Q Did you know that five years ago in [specify location], Disc was convicted of felonious assault for beating two teenagers with a baseball bat, and was sentenced to 2 years?

Discuss the issues presented.

Answer:

We are now in litigation situation D (§ 11.27): the prosecutor is cross-examining a character witness. The applicable rule is FRE 405(a)(2nd sentence): "On cross-examination of the character witness, the court may allow an inquiry into relevant specific instances of the person's conduct." Here, "the person" (about whom DW3 testified on direct) is Disc.

56. Some judges and scholars argue that if a defendant in criminal case testifies and the prosecutor cross-examines him or her at all, the defendant should be permitted to call a witness to testify about the defendant's character for truthfulness per Rule 608(a)(2nd sentence). If your professor takes this position, see Fishman Rule of Evidence 001.

Cross-examination of a character witness per Rule 405(a)(2nd sentence) raises four issues: (1) the nature of the conduct; (2) whether the prosecutor has a good-faith basis for the question; (3) whether the incident being asked about was known, or at least knowable, to the community or the character witness; and (4) the wording of the question. See § 6.14 to § 6.20.

1. Assaulting someone with a baseball bat is, as rule 405(a)(2nd sentence) requires, "relevant" to challenge the accuracy of Disc's supposed good character for peacefulness.
2. If Disc was convicted of assaulting the teenager, it is clear that the prosecutor has a good-faith basis for the question.
3. It is probably a general rule that a criminal conviction is either known or knowable by the community DW3 testified about.
4. "Have you heard" and "Did you know" are both acceptable ways to ask a Rule 405(a)(2nd sentence) question, and extrinsic wording ("convicted") is permissible when cross-examining a character witness.

The question is proper.

<u>Question 7.</u>

DW3 replies, "No, I never heard anything like that!" The prosecutor has documents in her case folder proving Disc's assault, the teenager's injuries, and Disc's conviction and sentence. Moreover, the assault victims are waiting just outside the courtroom, eager to testify against Disc. How may the prosecutor use those documents and these witnesses?

<u>Answer:</u>

The prosecutor is not permitted to use them, nor pursue the issue further in any way. See § 6.22.

<u>Question 8.</u>

Once DW3 has answered the prosecutor's question, what should Disc's attorney do?

<u>Answer:</u>

Ask the judge to give an explanatory instruction. See § 6.23.

<u>Question 9.</u>

The defense rests. In rebuttal, the prosecutor calls PW3 who will testify: "D's reputation in this community is that he is an immoral person who is prone to violence." Discuss the issues thus presented.

<u>Answer:</u>

This is <u>litigation situation G</u> (§ 11.30): the prosecutor's rebuttal case. Because DW3 gave reputation or opinion testimony about Disc's character for peacefulness, per

FRE 404(a)(2)(A), that same rule permits the prosecutor to call a witness to rebut DW3's testimony. And we are also in litigation situation H (§ 11.31): since Disc has testified, the prosecutor can call DW3 to testify about Disc's character for truthfulness, per Rule 608(a). Is PW3's testimony admissible under these rules?

Regarding Rule 404(a)(2)(A), the answer is—yes, and no. DW3 gave favorable testimony about Disc's character for peacefulness; assuming the prosecutor has elicited testimony from PW3 to establish the proper foundation, PW3's testimony about Disc's reputation for violence is proper rebuttal. But PW3 went beyond that; PW3 also offered reputation testimony that Disc is "an immoral person." That is much broader than the character trait about which DW3 testified; it is, therefore, improper rebuttal.

Regarding Rule 608(a), PW3's testimony is not admissible. Since Disc testified as a witness, Rule 608(a) entitles the prosecutor to call a witness to give negative reputation or opinion testimony about Disc's character for (un)truthfulness; PW3's testimony about Disc's reputation for "immorality" does not satisfy Rule 608(a). (If PW3 had testified that "Disc's reputation is that he is a liar," or "in my opinion, Disc will lie whenever he thinks he can get away with it," that testimony would have been admissible per Rule 608(a)—assuming in each case that the prosecutor first elicited the necessary foundation testimony.)

PW3 therefore can testify, "D's reputation in this community is that he is prone to violence."[57]

§ 13.35 More questions

The following is a take-home quiz I gave in the spring of 2000, followed by the model answer I distributed to the class after I graded it.[58] (I gave this quiz before I had developed the "litigation situation" approach.)

---

57. "Prone" is a homonym—a word with two distinct and apparently unrelated meanings. As used here, it means "likely to or liable to suffer from, do, or experience something, typically something regrettable or unwelcome." But it can also mean "lying flat, especially face downward." "He was prone to be prone when he should have been standing up."

58. I gave three to five take-home quizzes each semester, which counted for 15–25% of the final grade. Class size generally ranged between 30 and 65 students. I imposed word limits for two reasons. First, it required students to think and analyze before answering, by making it impossible to answer each question by copying everything they had in their notes—the "I'll repeat back everything the prof said and leave it up to the prof to find what he's looking for" approach. Second, it saved my eyesight and sanity, and afforded me at least some time during the semester to devote to my wife, our daughters (and more recently, our grandkids), my synagogue and the Washington Nationals.

The point value assigned to each question approximates what it would be worth if it was a question on the final exam. A perfect "score" on this quiz would total 42 points. This quiz was worth 8 points toward the final. I awarded points based on a curve: students received, say, between 4–8 points depending on where their total for the quiz fell on the curve.

Facts:

¶ 1. At 3 a.m., a woman called 911 and reported that a man about 5'10" tall wearing a light-colored nylon windbreaker and dark jeans was trying to open the door to a store at 2704 Randolph Road. Police Officers P01 and P02 arrived at the store about three minutes later. The store door was locked, and no one was there. Cruising the area in their marked patrol car, five minutes later, the officers saw X, a man fitting the description, walking on the 3100 block of Randolph. As X saw the car, he made a furtive throwing motion toward the small lawn in front of 3113 Randolph.

¶ 2. P01 stopped X while P02 quickly scanned the lawn with her flashlight. In addition to a bit of debris here and there, she saw a dark nylon pouch. Opening it, she found screwdrivers and wires and thin metal rods of several sizes, and a plastic hotel credit card-like room key.

¶ 3. X denies having anything to do with the pouch or its contents.

¶ 4. W, the woman who called 911, is willing to testify that X looks like the man she saw trying to open the door at 2704 Randolph, but she cannot be sure.

¶ 5. The prosecutor therefore decided not to charge X with attempted burglary. Instead, X is charged with possession of burglar tools. That crime is defined as follows:

> Possession of burglar tools. A person is guilty of possession of burglar tools if he or she possesses any implement or device that can be used to gain unlawful entry into a fixed premises, automobile or locked container, with the intent to so use that implement or device.

¶ 6. Seven years earlier, N, a neighbor of X, caught X attempting to sneak out of N's house late at night with N's television set. X was arrested for burglary; he was given probation before judgment, and the charges were ultimately dismissed.

¶ 7. Four years ago, X was convicted of possession of cocaine with intent to distribute, and served nine months of a one-year sentence.

¶ 8. Three years ago, X was arrested for forging an employer's check. He signed a confession and made restitution, and the charges were dropped.

Question 1. At trial, the prosecutor calls W. X's attorney objects that her testimony violates rules 401, 404(b) and 403. Discuss the issues thus presented.
Points: 7 Maximum length: 250 words

Question 2. Is there any way the prosecutor can use the information described in ¶ 6 during the state' case-in-chief? Discuss the issues presented.
Points: 12 Maximum length: 250 words

Question 3. After the state rests, X takes the stand and denies being near the store that night or knowing anything about the pouch found by P02. On cross-examination, may the prosecutor use the information in ¶ 6, and if so, how may the question be worded? (Assume the judge sustained defense counsel's objection in question 2.)
Points: 3 Maximum length: 75 words

Question 4. On cross, may the prosecutor use the information in ¶ 7 and if so, how may the question be worded?
Points: 5 Maximum length: 150 words

Question 5. On cross, may the prosecutor use the information in ¶ 8 and if so, how may the question be worded?
Points: 5 Maximum length: 125 words

Question 6. Defense counsel calls CW, a character witness, who testifies that he lived in the same neighborhood with X for the last ten years, and that in his opinion, X is a "very honest" man. Assume this testimony is unobjectionable. On cross, may the prosecutor use the information in ¶ 6, and if so, how may the question be worded? (Assume the judge sustained defense counsel's objection in question 2.)
Points: 4 Maximum length: 125 words

Question 7. Ditto Q6, re the information in ¶ 7.
Points: 3 Maximum length: 75 words

Question 8. Ditto Q6, re the information in ¶ 8.
Points: 3 Maximum length: 75 words

Model Answer: General comment 1:

A few students answered the exam as if X was charged with attempted burglary. This aggravated me no end, because ¶ 5 of the fact pattern very explicitly stated that the defendant was *not* charged with attempted burglary, and explained why. I realize, of course, that to some students, aggravating a professor has a certain amount of entertainment value; but doing so on a quiz or exam has a side effect: it tends to depress that student's grade. Such was the case here, because assuming that X was charged with attempted burglary caused those students to miss several issues.

I mention this here, not to berate those students, all of whom, I am sure, have gone on to successful careers. I mention this here because I am quite sure that some law students who are using this book made the same mistake in answering this quiz.

Please read the facts of a quiz or exam question carefully!

General comment 2:

"Burglary" and "robbery" are not synonyms. They are very different crimes. If you don't believe me, go back and ask whoever taught you criminal law last year. A few answers discussed whether the evidence could be admitted at defendant's trial for "robbery" and the like. I didn't subtract points for this terminological inexactitude (a phrase coined by Winston Churchill, by the way), but here's a general piece of advice: learn to use legal terms precisely and correctly.

Now, back to the Questions.

Question 1. At trial, the prosecutor calls W. X's attorney objects that her testimony violates rules 401, 404(b) and 403. Discuss the issues thus presented.
Points: 7 Maximum length: 250 words

Answer:

> 401: W's testimony supports the inference that X was the man she saw attempting to burglarize the store, which in turn "has [a] tendency" to make it more probable than it would be without the evidence that X possessed the items found near X on the lawn, and possessed them with intent to use them to enter the store unlawfully. Overruled.
>
> 404(b): the attempted burglary is part of the same sequence of events. Therefore, it is not an "extrinsic" act, and is not covered by FRE 404(b).
>
> 403: The jury can evaluate this evidence (including W's uncertainty) without risk of undue prejudice.
>
> (102 words)

Comments:

1. This is litigation situation E: prosecutor's case in chief (§ 11.28). It is specific act evidence, which eliminates the left column, and the only rule in the right column that arguably applies here is FRE 404(b).
2. Although my model answer says this is not a Rule 404(b) case at all, I gave full credit to answers saying that the evidence satisfied FRE 404(b) because what W saw at the store was inextricably intertwined with the seizure of the burglar tools; ditto that it demonstrated the intent with which X possessed the items in the pouch.
3. X was not charged with attempted burglary because the evidence was too weak (given W's uncertainty that the man she saw was X) to convict him of it beyond a reasonable doubt. This does not preclude the use of W's testimony, however, because her testimony suffices to satisfy the *Huddleston* standard (see § 7.11)—a rational jury could conclude, based on all the evidence, that X was the person W saw at the door to the store.

Question 2. Is there any way the prosecutor can use the information described in ¶ 6 during the state's case-in-chief? Discuss the issues presented.
Points: 12 Maximum length: 400 words

Answer:

X objects that the ¶6 burglary should be excluded per FRE 404(b)(1); the prosecutor argues it should be admitted per FRE 404(b)(2).

Purpose/Issue: The prosecutor argues the issue is intent: why did X possess the items in the pouch? Both crimes —burglary seven years ago, possession of burglar's tools with intent now—have the same mens rea, and therefore have sufficient fungible similarity to give the seven-year-old burglary sufficient factually significant relevance to overcome a rule 404(b)(1) objection.

Defense counsel argues the issue is conduct: did X possess the pouch? Fungible similarity is relevant to show conduct only via the forbidden 404(b)(1) propensity inference. Defense counsel also argues that 7 years makes the burglary of marginal relevance even on intent.

Need: Intent is a contested issue. (But so is conduct.)

How to prove: The prosecutor can prove X committed the ¶6 burglary by calling N to testify as to what he saw. (P could not offer the arrest report, which would be inadmissible hearsay.) N's testimony satisfies the *Huddleston* standard; that X was not prosecuted is no bar to admissibility of the evidence.

Fasprelipi: Although the evidence has some non-propensity relevance on the issue of intent, the risk that the jury will rely on the "bad person inference" on the issue of conduct is far too great. I would exclude.

(220 words)

Comment:

This is still litigation situation E, and 404(b) is the only rule that could possibly apply.

I accepted "identity" rather than "conduct" as the defendant's argument, although really there is no doubt who the police officers claim threw the tools; here, the issue is conduct (did the defendant possess them).

Students who misread the question and thought that X was on trial for attempting to burglarize the store missed the whole "intent" issue.

Although I would exclude, some courts might admit, so either conclusion received full credit, assuming the answer properly recognized and analyzed the issues.

Question 3. After the state rests, X takes the stand and denies being near the store that night or knowing anything about the pouch found by P02. On cross, may the prosecutor use the information in ¶6, and if so, how may the question be worded? (Assume the judge sustained defense counsel's objection in question 2.)
Points: 3 Maximum length: 75 words

Answer:

Burglary is not 608(b) material, because breaking into a house or store and stealing something is not particularly probative of truthfulness or untruthfulness. Therefore, the prosecutor cannot use the information while cross-examining X. And X's testimony does not strengthen the prosecutor's FRE 404(b) argument, since X is denying conduct (and identity), not intent.

52 words

Comment:

This is litigation situation F (§ 11.29): cross-examining a witness about his/her own prior acts. Rules 404(b) and 608(b) are the only rules listed there that could apply here.

The sentence, "Assume the judge sustained defense counsel's objection in question 2," tells you not to rehash what you've already discussed in question 2. And nothing in X's testimony on direct permits the prosecutor to revisit the 404(b) issues discussed therein.

Question 4. On cross, may the prosecutor use the information in ¶ 7 and if so, how may the question be worded?

Points: 5 Maximum length: 150 words

Answer:

If X *could have received more than* a *year,* the crime is a 609(a)(1)(B) felony despite the lesser sentence. Subject to the special trial judge's discretion when the witness being impeached is a criminal defendant, the prosecutor may ask: "You were convicted in 1996, were you not, of the crime of possession of cocaine with intent to distribute? And did you not receive a 1-year sentence?"

69 words

Comment:

When a question asks, "How may the question be worded," I don't want you to answer "extrinsically" or "intrinsically," I want you to tell me the actual words the cross-examiner would use in asking the question.

Under FRE 609, the extrinsic word "convicted" is entirely permissible.

Question 5. On cross, may the prosecutor use the information in ¶ 8, and if so, how may the question be worded?

Points: 5 Maximum length: 125 words

Answer:

Forgery is 608(b) material, so the prosecutor can ask, intrinsically, "Isn't it a fact that you forged an employer's check on [specify date]?" But the prosecutor cannot offer the confession in evidence: that would be violate 608(b)'s rule against extrinsic evidence. (41 words)

Comment:

This is litigation situation F, § 11.29. FRE 608(b) is the only rule listed in that section that is worth discussing.

I'm not sure if you could ask, "... and didn't you sign a confession," but I gave credit for the answer.

Question 6. Defense counsel calls CW, a character witness, who testifies that he lived in the same neighborhood with X for the last ten years, and that in his opinion, X is a "very honest" man. Assume this testimony is unobjectionable. On cross-examination, may the prosecutor use the information in ¶ 6, and if so, how may the question be worded? (Assume the judge sustained defense counsel's objection in question 2.)

Points: 4 Maximum length: 125 words

Answer:

Rule 405(a)(2nd sentence): is burglary pertinent to challenge "honest" character? Clearly: if "honesty" is a pertinent trait to rebut a burglary-related charge, a prior burglary is "relevant" to challenge "honest" character. Wording: "Did you know that X was arrested for burglary seven years ago?" Extrinsic wording is permissible when cross-examining a character witness per 405(a)(2nd sent.). (56 words)

Comment:

This is litigation situation D (§ 11.27): cross-examining a character witness, which implicates rule 405(a)(2nd sentence). Likewise, questions 7 and 8.

Question 7. Ditto Q6, re the information in ¶ 7.
Points: 3 Maximum length: 75 words

Answer:

Rule 405(a)(2nd sentence): Drug possession probably is not "pertinent" to rebut character for "honesty." If it was pertinent, the question would be worded: "Did you know that D was convicted of PWID..." (32 words)

Question 8. Ditto Q6, re the information in ¶ 8.
Points: 3 Maximum length: 75 words

Answer:

R 405(a)(2nd sentence). This is relevant to rebut testimony about X's "honest" character. "Did you know that X was arrested for forgery in 1998?" Extrinsic wording ("arrested") is permitted under Rule 405(a)(2nd sentence). (32 words)

Chapter 14

FRE 407: Subsequent Remedial Measures

A. Overview

§14.1 FRE 407

i. The rule

FRE 407 provides:

> **Rule 407. Subsequent Remedial Measures**
>
> When measures are taken that would have made an earlier injury or harm less likely to occur, evidence of the subsequent measures is not admissible to prove:
>
> - negligence;
> - culpable conduct;
> - a defect in a product or its design; or
> - a need for a warning or instruction.
>
> But the court may admit this evidence for another purpose, such as impeachment or—if disputed—proving ownership, control, or the feasibility of precautionary measures.

This rule is unusual because it applies exclusively in civil, not criminal, litigation and benefits only defendants in civil litigation.

The first sentence of Rule 407 excludes evidence of repairs or other safety precautions taken after a harm-or-injury-causing event, if such evidence is offered to prove that defendant was "negligent" or "culpable" for not having taken such precautions before the event.

Example: It snows overnight, and the next morning, Homeowner (HO) shovels his sidewalk. An hour later a pedestrian ("Ped-1"), walking on the sidewalk in front of Homeowner's house, slips on a patch of ice and falls, suffering injuries. Shortly thereafter, Homeowner spreads salt on the sidewalk. Ped-1 sues Homeowner, alleging that Homeowner negligently failed to take reasonable precautions to make the sidewalk safe for people walking on the sidewalk. At trial, Ped-1 calls a witness W1, who testifies, "I saw Homeowner put salt down shortly after Ped-1 fell." Homeowner objects, citing Rule 407. Ruling?

Objection sustained. Putting salt down after Ped-1 fell was, in the words of Rule 407, a "measure [that was]... taken that would have made [Ped-1's fall and injury] less likely... to occur[.]" The rule mandates that evidence of this "remedial measure" by Homeowner after Ped-1's injury "is not admissible to prove" that Homeowner was negligent in not putting down salt *before* Ped-1 fell.

Let's be clear about what the rule permits as well as what it prohibits. Ped-1 is still entitled to argue that HO *should* have put salt down before Ped-1 fell, and to argue that HO was negligent in failing to do so; but, per FRE 407, Ped-1 cannot introduce evidence that HO did so after Ped-1's injury, to support Ped-1's claim that HO was negligent in not doing so earlier.

The first sentence of Rule 407 excludes evidence of post-event "precautionary [i.e., remedial] measures" in a variety of other contexts. See § 14.2.

The second sentence provides that evidence of subsequent remedial measures is not excluded by Rule 407 if that evidence is offered for a legitimate purpose *other* than to prove negligence or fault.[1] See §§ 14.14 to 14.19. In some jurisdictions, the "other purpose" provision has been interpreted so broadly that it has virtually nullified the first sentence altogether. See § 14.17 & § 14.18.

ii. Justifications for the rule

The rule is motivated by several concerns. First, as the Advisory Committee Note explains, the rule is based on "a social policy of encouraging people to take, or at least not discouraging them from taking, steps in furtherance of added safety." In the context of Ped-1 vs. HO, assume that HO, seeing Ped-1 slip and fall on the sidewalk, would think, "Whoa! I didn't realize the sidewalk had gotten so icy. I should probably go out and put salt on the icy spots; otherwise, someone else might slip and fall and get hurt, too. But wait!—if I do, Ped-1 can use that against me if he sues me. So it's best I do nothing." FRE 407 reassures HO not to worry about Ped-1 using that evidence against him.

But does the rule truly promote the "social policy" cited in the ACN? And, how likely is it that HO would think along the lines suggested in the previous paragraph? Second, assuming HO had those thoughts, how likely is it that HO is aware that FRE 407 exists, so as to overcome HO's reluctance to put down salt after Ped-1 fell?

Such concerns are even less relevant when the defendant is a large corporation that produces products or provides services to numerous consumers. See § 14.3, *infra*.

Two more realistic justifications have been cited, however, to support the rule. The first is that a jury may weigh the evidence of the "subsequent remedial measure" too heavily. The fact that D took steps after the event to improve the quality and safety of its premises, product or service may seem to the jury as a tacit admission by D that D was at fault for not doing so beforehand. That may be quite unfair: the fact that D improves its premises, product or service with experience does not automatically mean D was negligent for failing to do so earlier.

1. But evidence offered for "another purpose" is still subject to other objections—e.g., relevance, Rule 403, hearsay, etc.

Another argument cited in favor of the rule is that it just doesn't seem fair, somehow, to "punish" a defendant for "doing the right thing" by making its location or product or service safer or better.

iii. "Event"

In the next several sections, I use the word "event" to mean the incident that caused (or allegedly caused) plaintiff's injury or harm. That word may seem cold and heartless when applied to someone's death or permanent disablement or the destruction of someone's home or livelihood, but the use of such a bland, generic term makes it somewhat less cumbersome to discuss the application of FRE 407 to what defendant did after the "event."

iv. Caveat reader

This is an area of the law—not the only one, needless to say—in which courts in some jurisdictions are known (plaintiffs' attorneys would say "notorious") for interpreting the rule broadly to afford maximum protection to defendants; and courts in other jurisdictions are known (defense attorneys would say "notorious") for interpreting the rule narrowly, to allow plaintiffs to offer evidence of the defendant's subsequent remedial measure under the widest possible circumstances. So if results from one case to the next sometimes seem inconsistent, it may well be because they *are* inconsistent.

§ 14.2 Types of evidence excluded

FRE 407 lists four purposes for which subsequent remedial measures should not be admitted: to prove "negligence; culpable conduct; a defect in a product or its design; or a need for a warning or instruction." You learned what "negligence" means in your Tort course. "Culpable conduct" is discussed in § 14.4. Concerning the phrase "a defect in a product or its design," see § 14.3. The phrase "a need for a warning or instruction" is self-explanatory.

FRE 407 has been cited most often in personal injury wrongful death cases, but courts have excluded evidence of subsequent remedial measures in a variety of other factual situations, including litigation relating to property damage, suits between corporations, etc.

Examples of Exclusion. Courts have relied upon FRE 407 to exclude evidence of post-accident changes including:

> *Design changes.* Courts have excluded such evidence in cases involving motor vehicles, manufacturing and construction materials, and various other products.

Operating instructions. Cases include post-accident supplementation or revision of owner's manuals and instructions on how to use motor vehicles and other consumer products, and on how to use or maintain industrial equipment.

Drugs and medicines: package inserts, etc. Several courts have relied upon the rule to exclude evidence of revised and upgraded inserts and warnings that were issued subsequent to plaintiff's use of the drug in question. In addition, a state court has applied the rule to exclude evidence that a manufacturer withdrew a product from the market altogether.

Roads, signs, etc. Courts have excluded evidence that after a car crash, governments have improved road conditions, increased the number and visibility of traffic signals, warning signs, etc.

Rules and procedures; personnel actions. Courts have excluded evidence that, after an event, a business, or an organization, or a government agency, or some other entity changed its rules or policies; instituted training programs to educate employees about avoiding discrimination or harassment; or disciplined personnel who engaged in such conduct.

§ 14.3 Products liability litigation: "defect in a product or design"

P uses a product manufactured by D Corp. Something goes wrong, and P suffers harm of some kind. P sues, alleging a defect in the product caused the harm. In a strict products liability claim, P need show only (a) there was a defect in the product or its design (b) which caused P's damages. P need not show that D Corp. was negligent in allowing the defect to exist.

Until 1997, federal courts were divided as to whether FRE 407 ought to apply in strict products liability litigation. Those against allowing product liability defendants to invoke the rule reasoned that a company that mass-produces a product which is directly or indirectly used by the general public already has powerful motives to improve that product's safety. A competitive marketplace is a powerful incentive to do so—not to mention the risks of massive class action suits, awards of punitive damages, and reputation-destroying bad publicity if a company stubbornly refuses to take corrective action once a safety risk is discovered. FRE 407 serves no valid public policy in such cases, the argument goes, while depriving injured parties of valuable evidence to prove that a defect in fact existed in the defendant's product.

The 1997 amendment to FRE 407, which inserted the phrase "a defect in a product or its design," resolved this conflict: a mass producer of consumer or other products may assert the rule to exclude evidence of a subsequent remedial measure, just as a landlord, storekeeper or any other defendant can.

§ 14.4 "Culpable conduct"

"Culpable conduct" is a bit of a catch-all—in essence it means, "any blameworthy conduct which causes harm for which the causer can be held responsible." It applies, for example, when an entity (corporation, organization, government agency) is sued for discriminating against P on an improper basis.

Suppose, for example, P sues her employer for sex discrimination, alleging she was denied a promotion (which instead went to a younger man) because she is a woman. D's defense: P was denied the promotion because she lacked the interpersonal skills for the job. To rebut this defense, P's attorney offers evidence that P was in fact promoted a few months later, the next time an opening to the higher position occurred. In *Lust v. Sealy, Inc.*, 383 F.3d 580 (7th Cir. 2004), Judge Posner observed that evidence of P's subsequent promotion is precisely the sort that FRE 407 would exclude, even though this case, unlike the typical FRE 407 case, involved an intentional rather than an unintentional tort.[2]

§ 14.5 Conduct not protected by the rule

D allegedly damaged P's property, and P sues. D has no basis to object if P offers evidence that P made repairs to undo the damage or hired someone else to do so.

Similarly, if D makes repairs to plaintiff's property, such conduct is admissible as a basis to infer a tacit admission of fault by D for having caused the original damage. The rule protects D only with regard to improvements D made to its own premises, product, procedures, personnel, etc.[3]

§ 14.6 Issues presented

Plaintiff offers evidence that at some point Defendant took steps to change or improve its premises, product, service, etc. Defendant objects that the evidence is barred by FRE 407. Plaintiff responds that FRE 407 does not apply in the first place, or if it did, the evidence falls within the "other purpose" clause of the second sentence. Such a case raises the following issues.

(1) Who can invoke the rule? See § 14.7 and § 14.8.

(2) Was the measure in question truly "*remedial*"? That depends on what the defendant did. See § 14.9 and § 14.10.

---

2. D failed to object, so the issue was waived.

3. But if D made repairs to P's property in an attempt to persuade P to settle the dispute and avoid litigation, those repairs might be excludable per FRE 408, covered in Chapter 15.

(3) Was the measure in question taken *after* the event causing plaintiff's "injury or harm"? If not, Rule 407 does not apply and cannot be used to exclude the evidence. See § 14.11 and § 14.12.

(4) *The second sentence of Rule 407* provides that evidence of a subsequent remedial measure is not excluded under the rule if that evidence is offered "for another purpose [i.e., other than to prove negligence or fault], such as impeachment or—if disputed—ownership, control, or feasibility of precautionary measures." How does one determine whether the evidence is truly being offered for such an "other purpose," and whether issues such as control, feasibility, etc. are in fact "disputed"? See § 14.13 to § 14.17 and § 14.19.

(5) Under what circumstances may such evidence be used for impeachment? See § 14.18 to § 14.19.

B. Requirements

---

1. Who can invoke the rule

§ 14.7 In general

The purpose underlying FRE 407 is to protect a defendant who has taken remedial measures after an "event," from having those measures used against the defendant at trial as proof that defendant should be held liable to plaintiff for damages plaintiff claims to have suffered as a result of that "event." See § 14.1–ii. Logically, therefore, the rule can be invoked only by a person or entity who (a) made or took the remedial measure, and (b) is a party to the current litigation.

But as the Reporter's Comment on the 2011 "restyling" of the rule points out, some courts also apply it, in at least some situations, to alterations or improvements made by a non-party. For example, what if a distributor of a product made an alteration that would have made the injury less likely to occur, but the plaintiff is suing the manufacturer, not the distributor. Some courts would admit the distributor's post-event alteration against the manufacturer; others would not.

If your professor does not address this issue in class, it is probably safe to assume you will not be called upon to address it in class, on a quiz or on an exam. If your prof does discuss this issue in class, take careful notes and apply whatever approach the professor dictates.

<u>Question 1.</u>

Assume the following sequence of events.

(1) Two companies—Mfg1 and Mfg2—manufacture competing products, each of which can be used to quickly freeze or quickly thaw various substances.

(2) P1 is injured while using Mfg1's product.

(3) Mfg1 changes its product to reduce the likelihood of a recurrence.

(4) P2 is injured while using Mfg2's product.

In *P2 v. Mfg2*, P2 calls employees of Mfg1 to testify about the improvements it made in its product. This is relevant, P2 argues, as evidence that Mfg2's failure to make such improvements *before P2 was injured* is proof that Mfg2's product was defective when P2 used it.

Mfg1 and Mfg2 both object to the testimony, citing rule 407. How should the judge rule?

Answer:

The judge should deny both motions.

Mfg1's objection should be denied, because it is not a party in the current trial. Witnesses and non-parties generally cannot object to evidence (or to being questioned) unless the question calls for information protected by a legally recognized privilege (such as the privilege against self-incrimination or the attorney-client privilege or one of the marital evidentiary privileges).

Mfg2's FRE 407 objections should be denied, because although it is the defendant in the current trial, it was not the entity that made the change and played no part in the manufacture or distribution of the device which caused P1's harm.

Question 2.

Are there other objections that Mfg2 could make?

Answer:

Yes. The fact that Mfg1's product competed with Mfg2's does not mean that their products are the same. They might be made of different materials; they might be made by very different processes. Suppose, for example, P1 was injured while using Mfg1's product to quickly freeze certain chemical solutions, and P2's use of Mfg2's product to heat a very different substance caused a fire. If P2 is unable to show substantial similarity in the products and in how P2 and P1 used each, and that the injury or harm each suffered were of the same nature, Mfg1's subsequent remedial measure—intended to prevent other users from suffering injury that P1 suffered—may have little relevance as to whether the same remedy would have made P2's injury or harm using Mfg2's product less likely.

And if there were both similarities and differences between P1's "event" and P2's "event"? In such a case, P2 would want to call witnesses (including experts) to testify that the two events were substantially similar, to enable P2 to argue to the jury that the jury should rely on the similarities to consider Mfg1's remedial measure relevant against Mfg2. Naturally, Mfg2 would want to call witnesses to testify that the situations were so different that Mfg1's remedial measure has no relevance in P2's case. The result might prolong the trial considerably and distract and confuse the jury, and on that basis, the judge could exclude the evidence per FRE 403.

Here's another twist. Suppose, in *P1 v. Mfg1*, Mfg1 conceded that its product caused P1's injuries; its defense focuses on whether P1's injuries were as severe as P1 claimed. In its case-in-chief, Mfg1 offers evidence that immediately after P1's injury, it took remedial action—suspended sales, issued a recall, and installed improvements. Such evidence might be relevant to undercut efforts by P1's attorney to paint Mfg1 as cold and uncaring and interested only in money, in order to rebut a claim for punitive damages; and if the trial was widely covered in the media, it might even result in favorable publicity. FRE 407 would not preclude Mfg1 from offering such evidence, since only the party who took the remedial action can invoke the rule.

But if Mfg1 introduces evidence of its post-event remedial measures, presumably, this entitles P1 to argue that by making post-event improvements, it was tacitly acknowledging that it was negligent for not making those improvements early enough to prevent plaintiff's "event."

§14.8 Government-mandated recalls, repairs, etc.

Courts are divided on the question whether a remedial measure mandated by a government agency, such as a product recall, falls within or outside the exclusionary principle. The argument against allowing defendants to exclude such government-mandated remedial measures is this: if compliance with a government directive is required by law, courts need not fear that admitting such evidence will discourage a defendant from making improvements or repairs. And because such compliance is mandatory, there is no inference that by taking the remedial step after plaintiff's injury, the defendant is tacitly admitting that it was negligent, or its product or service was defective when the plaintiff was injured.

The counter-argument, particularly with regard to product recalls, is that the recall process depends on manufacturers' reporting complaints and negative inferences to the government agency in the first place, so stripping defendants of the protection of FRE 407 in essence punishes them indirectly for complying with the reporting requirement.

As in all things relating to evidence this semester, follow your professor's lead on how to handle such cases.

2. "Remedial"

§ 14.9 In general

FRE 407 excludes evidence of a subsequent measure only if the measure was in fact intended, and likely, to remedy the dangerous condition, i.e., to make the event which damaged or injured plaintiff, less likely to recur. It provides no basis to exclude evidence of signs warning of potential dangers that were changed for reasons of aesthetics rather than safety; nor of measures that would not have made a similar accident less likely to recur; nor that defendant repeated the same procedures that caused plaintiff's accident, in order to test whether those procedures were safe; nor that defendant merely restored the situation to the status quo that had existed prior to plaintiff's injury.

Suppose, for example, a car failed to make a turn on a twisty, curvy county road and crashed through the wooden guardrail to the ravine below. Plaintiffs sue the county, alleging that the guardrail was inadequate to prevent this. Evidence that a day, week or month later the county installed the same kind of guard rail would not be considered remedial, because it would not make a similar mishap less likely.

§ 14.10 Investigative reports

Evidence of a post-event investigation by defendant, not connected with a remedial measure, should be admitted over an FRE 407 objection. But what about an investigative report which leads to remedial measures? Is the report admissible, or not?

Police, responding to a disturbance call, seriously injured P, a person involved in the disturbance. The Chief of Police immediately assigned a special panel to investigate what happened. The panel issued a report concluding that, viewed narrowly, the use of force by PO1 and PO2 might have been justified, but that they and other officers mishandled the situation by allowing it to escalate to the point where that degree of force was required to subdue P. The investigative panel recommended that the ranking officer on the scene be reprimanded and demoted, and that the department institute training for all officers on how to better handle such situations. The department follows the recommendations.

P sues the Police Department and several of the officers for assault, personal injuries, and excessive use of force in violation of Fourth Amendment right against unreasonable searches and seizures. Prior to trial, the defendants, citing FRE 407, move in limine to preclude P from offering the report or the subsequent measures in evidence. How should the judge rule?

The subsequent measures—disciplining the ranking officer and retraining the entire department in handling such matters—should be excluded. Clearly they were instituted after P's event. Clearly, they were intended to make similar events less likely to recur.

But the report itself remedied nothing. Therefore, arguably, it should be admitted into evidence against the department.

On the other hand, implementing additional safety precautions often requires extensive time and effort, including an investigation to determine what went wrong, a report detailing the results of the investigation, follow-up tests and studies, plans, and so on. The policies underlying FRE 407 apply with equal logic to the preliminary steps as they do to the actual implementation.

Courts are divided on whether such reports are admissible over a FRE 407 objection.[4]

3. The "subsequent" requirement

§ 14.11 In general

The Advisory Committee Note to a 1997 amendment to the rule specifies that "the rule applies only to changes made *after the occurrence that produced the damages giving rise to the action.*" (Emphasis added.) The sequence in which the events occur is essential in determining whether FRE 407 applies to exclude evidence, or not. Consider the following scenarios.

(1) In 2018, Piper purchased a product manufactured by D Corp. In 2019, the product malfunctioned, causing damage to Piper's home. In 2020, D Corp began making a newer version of the product which replaced a component that had an unexpectedly high failure rate. In Piper's suit against D Corp, D Corp can object per FRE 407 if Piper offers evidence of the new-and-improved model that D Corp began selling in 2020, because that improvement was made after the damage to Piper's home.

(2) In 2018, Pepper purchased the same product. In 2020, D Corp began making a newer version which replaced a component that had an unexpectedly high failure rate. In 2021, the 2018 model in Pepper's house malfunctioned, causing damage to Piper's home. At Pepper's trial against D Corp, D Corp cannot raise an FRE 407 objection when Pepper offers evidence of the new-and-improved model that D Corp began selling in 2020, because that "remedial measure" was made before, not after, the "event"—the product's failure—that is the basis for Pepper's lawsuit.

In essence, D Corp is deprived of the protection of the rule because the device installed in Pepper's house lasted two years longer before malfunctioning than the one installed in Piper's. Is there any logical, equitable reason that justifies the different results—other than, they are mandated by the language of the rule?

---

4. The report would be admissible over a hearsay objection as a statement by the opposing party or an agent of an opposing party per FRE 801(d)(2)(C), see C. Fishman, *A Student's Guide to Hearsay* § 5.19 to § 5.21; per FRE 801(d)(2)(D), see *id.*, § 5.23 to § 5.28; if the defendant was a private entity, also possibly as a business record, per FRE 803(6), see *id.*, § 9.20 to § 9.35; and if the defendant was a government agency, as a public record per FRE 803(8)(A)(iii), see *id.* § 9.46 to § 9.48. But the report would still be excluded per FRE 407, if it is considered to be part of the remedial measures.

Or, from the other perspective, Piper is deprived of highly relevant evidence because the device installed in his home malfunctioned two years before the one in Pepper's house.

§ 14.12 No causal relationship need be shown between the event and the remedial measure

To invoke the protection of the rule, defendant need not show that it improved its product, procedures or location *because* of the event which injured plaintiff. Defendant need not even show that it was aware of the injury or harm to plaintiff. Defendant need only show that, sometime after plaintiff was injured, defendant did something to make its product, premises, procedure or service safer. That is enough to secure exclusion of that remedial measure, unless the plaintiff persuades the judge that the case falls within the second sentence of the rule.

C. The "Other Purpose" clause

§ 14.13 In general

The second sentence of FRE 407 reads:

> But the court may admit this evidence for another purpose, such as impeachment or—if disputed—proving ownership, control, or the feasibility of precautionary measures.

The use of the phrase "precautionary measures" is in essence synonymous with "subsequent remedial measures," i.e., measures which, if taken earlier as a precaution against injury or damage, would have made the plaintiff's injury or damage less likely.

The following sections discuss the issues which have arisen in applying this sentence.

§ 14.14 Ownership or control

If a defendant denies that it had ownership or control over the item, location or activity which caused plaintiff's injury or loss, evidence that that defendant subsequently took remedial measures to prevent a similar mishap is admissible to rebut that defense.

§ 14.15 Feasibility

A plaintiff alleging that D was negligent is required to prove that D breached a duty of care. Negligence, Black's Law Dictionary (11th ed. 2019). One way of doing so is to prove that, prior to P's injury, D should have done "X" to make its product or premises safer. To prove that D was negligent in failing to have done "X," however, P must prove that it would have been "feasible" for D to have done "X." Similarly, a products liability plaintiff must show that D's product was defective in design or manufacture, which often requires P to prove that D could and should have done "X" to improve the product's safety. Here too, therefore, P must prove the feasibility of "X."

The second sentence of FRE 407 provides: "[T]he court may admit [evidence that defendant made a subsequent remedial measure] for another purpose, such as...—if disputed—proving... the feasibility of precautionary measures." Applying this language requires defining two terms. First, what does "feasibility" mean? Second, what constitutes "disputing" feasibility? Note, too, that the provision says "the court *may* admit" the evidence. The word "may" indicates the court has discretion to admit or not. What are the parameters of that discretion?

§ 14.16 Defining "feasibility"

The primary meaning of "feasibility" is "capable of being done." If D claims it did not take "precautionary measure" X because it was not possible to do so, evidence that D subsequently did take precautionary measure X "may" be admitted to rebut D's claim that doing so was not feasible.

A secondary meaning relates to the "ultimate utility and success [of a measure] in its intended performance." Thus, if D concedes that he could have taken measure "X" prior to P's injury but asserts, "I did not do X because X would not make my [product or premises] any safer," many courts hold that D has "disputed the feasibility" of "X," thereby opening the door to evidence that after P's injury, D in fact did "X."

§ 14.17 "Disputing" feasibility

What constitutes "disputing" feasibility? Courts differ widely. Some apparently hold that a defendant "disputes" the feasibility of other "precautionary measures" unless it stipulates that such measures were available. Other courts hold that a defendant does not dispute feasibility unless, in its pleadings or during the trial, it explicitly claims that such measures were not feasible.

Assume P was injured in 2019 when the cover of a pressure cooker, manufactured by D in 2012, blew off. P sued, alleging that the product was defective because it lacked a locking device and safety valve that would have prevented the accident. To prevail, P must prove that it was feasible for D to include such a device on the cooker. In 2021, D began marketing a newer model which include a locking device and safety vale.

If D does not "dispute" P's allegation that it was technologically and economically feasible to include such a device, the rule precludes P from proving that D in fact incorporated such devices shortly after D's injury. P is still free to offer other proof of feasibility, including, for example, evidence that competing companies were marketing comparable pressure cookers in 2012 that included locking devices. Moreover, P could argue to the jury that D had not contested the feasibility of such a design.

If, on the other hand, D claims that such a design was not feasible when it manufactured the cooker in question, the feasibility exception permits P to overcome D's subsequent measures objection, because D has "disputed" the feasibility of such a design. (The judge retains discretion to exclude the evidence on relevance or FRE 403 grounds. For example, evidence that D added a locking device and safety valve to pressure cookers it manufactured in 2021 might not be particularly relevant on the question of whether it was feasible to do so in 2012.)

Suppose D's attorney, DATT, is careful in drafting D's pleadings, on DATT's opening statement to the jury, and in the questions DATT asks D's witnesses, to avoid directly or even inferentially disputing that it was feasible for D to have taken measure "X," but that a witness for D nonetheless testifies in a way that denies feasibility. Should this open the door?

That brings us to the next issue: the "impeachment" exception to FRE 407.

§ 14.18 Impeachment

The most frequent use of subsequent remedial measures evidence is to impeach the testimony of defense witnesses. A number of courts have expressed concern that the impeachment exception threatens to swallow the rule or may be used as a subterfuge to prove negligence or culpability.

The need and justification for such impeachment is clear when defendant opens the door by creating a false impression that the product or location in question has been used safely without change since plaintiff's injury, when in fact, precautionary measure "Z" was added to the product or location after P's injury or damage.

It is also proper to admit evidence of a defendant's post-injury remedial measure to impeach excessively assertive testimony by defense experts. Thus, in products liability actions, plaintiffs have been permitted to offer such evidence to impeach testimony that the defendant's product was the safest of its kind available on the market, that a particular hazard had been designed out of the product at the time it was sold to plaintiff's employer, or that there was no need to alert consumers to the risks involved because those risks were both slight and common knowledge. Similarly, in suits alleging that defendant negligently maintained an unsafe premises, evidence of subsequent precautions has been admitted to impeach testimony that it was counterproductive to install safety measures, or that defendant had done "everything necessary" to assure safety, or that defendant had exercised all reasonable care, or that the existence of a hazardous condition was so plainly visible that it was unnecessary to post a warning sign. These decisions demonstrate that counsel should caution defense witnesses not to over-state the quality or safety of the defendant's premises, products, etc.

In deciding whether to permit the evidence of a subsequent remedial measure to impeach, a court should also consider the vigor with which the defendant has maintained the assertion to be impeached. It may be entirely fair to admit the evidence to impeach the testimony of several defense expert witnesses, but to exclude the evidence if offered to impeach the testimony of a fact witness who is not testifying as an expert. Consider a Fifth Circuit decision, *Baker v. Canadian National/Illinois Cent. R.R.*, 536 F.3d 357, 366–67 (5th Cir. 2008). A train hit a truck at a crossing. Defendant maintained that the crossing was safe without lights or gates, and plaintiff was negligent in failing to see the train approaching the crossing. The locomotive engineer testified (presumably on cross-examination by plaintiff, although the opinion does not specify who elicited it) that in his opinion, the crossing was safer *without* lights or gates. Nevertheless, the trial judge refused to permit plaintiff to impeach this testimony with evidence that, two years later, the railroad put up lights and gates at the crossing. The Fifth Circuit, emphasizing that the engineer had been called by the defendant as a fact witness, not an expert, concluded that it was no abuse of discretion for the trial judge to rule that the engineer's personal opinion about lights and gates did not open the door to evidence about the subsequent installation of lights and gates at the crossing.

The situation described in the prior paragraph is analogous to an aspect of character evidence we saw in § 6.13: If the defendant in a criminal trial calls a witness (FW) to testify about specific facts in the case, the prosecutor cannot on cross-examination question FW about the defendant's reputation or FW's opinion of the defendant's character, and then impeach that testimony per FRE 405(a)(2nd sentence).

But some courts may reject the Fifth Circuit's approach in *Baker*, and permit plaintiffs' lawyers to goad or trick defense witnesses into overstating the safety of the defendant's product, premises, etc., and then allow plaintiff to introduce evidence of the defendant's subsequent remedial measure to contradict and impeach that testimony.

§ 14.19 Questions

Question 1.

P and H were guests in D's motel. H left to run an errand; sometime later, P heard a knock on the door and asked, "Who is it?" The response: "It's me." Thinking it was

H, P opened the door; an intruder forced his way in and assaulted P. P sued D, alleging that the hotel failed to provide acceptable safety from intruders. D testified that he had done "everything necessary" to assure the safety of its patrons, and had not installed chains and peepholes in the doors because it had been advised by experts that to do so would be counterproductive by giving guests a false sense of security.

Plaintiff thereupon offered evidence that that defendant subsequently installed peepholes and chains. Should the judge admit that evidence?

Answer:

The trial judge excluded the evidence; the Eighth Circuit held that doing so was reversible error. D's testimony disputed the feasibility (i.e., the utility) of peepholes and chains; therefore, P was entitled to prove that after the assault, D installed them. *Anderson v. Malloy*, 700 F.2d 1208, 1214 (8th Cir. 1983).

Question 2.

P was injured when he drove off a winding road, and sued, claiming that the township was negligent because the single "winding road" sign and the lack of a posted speed limit failed to give adequate notice of road conditions. The township called two witnesses, one a county official and one a township official, both of whom testified that the single "winding road" sign in existence at the time of the accident was adequate. To impeach this testimony, plaintiff sought to prove that after P's accident, those two officials were responsible for posting additional signs. Should the judge admit the evidence?

Answer:

Illinois' Supreme Court held that the evidence would not be admissible, because the relevance of the subsequent signage, even if offered to impeach, was still based on the forbidden inference that the township was negligent in failing to post additional signs prior to P's accident. *Herzog v. Lexington Township*, 167 Ill. 2d 288, 301–02, 657 N.E.2d 926, 212 Ill. Dec. 581 (1995). Permitting impeachment in such circumstances, the court added, "would swallow the general rule." *Id.* The court emphasized that the township's witnesses "never made any exaggerated claims regarding the safety of the roadway or disputed that placing the additional signs on this roadway was possible. Defendant's witnesses only testified that the single, winding road sign was adequate and that traffic was capable of moving safely through the turns. Thus, plaintiff was not entitled to impeach this testimony with evidence of the additional signs defendant placed on the roadway after the accident."

Question 3.

On June 1, P fell on a staircase in landlord D's building. Two weeks later, a work crew put better lighting in the stairwell and a new surface on the steps. In response to P's personal injury suit alleging that the staircase was unsafe, D filed an answer that contained a general denial of P's allegations. During the presentation of D's case-in-chief, DW, D's resident manager, testified on direct examination that the staircase was in good condition on June 1 and fully complied with building code requirements. The following occurs on cross-examination:

Q You didn't pay very close attention to the upkeep of that staircase, did you?

A Yes, I did.

Q In fact, there was a great deal more that could have been done to make sure that staircase was safe, isn't that true?

Suppose you represented D, and anticipated that P's attorney would ask a question along these lines. How would you have prepared DW to answer the second question?

Answer:

A Those stairs complied with the building code and were in good condition on June 1st. It was a safe staircase to walk on.

If you are paying attention, you've noticed that DW did not actually answer the question. Guess what: P's lawyer noticed that, too.

Question 4.

Cross-examination continues:

Q That's not what I asked. I asked, "In fact, there was a great deal more that could have been done to make sure that staircase was safe, isn't that true?"

A Sure, yes, that's true.

Does this answer dispute the feasibility of making the staircase safer?

Answer:

No, it concedes the feasibility of additional precautionary measures.

Question 5.

Cross continues:

Q3 For example, you could have improved the lighting and put a new, no-slip surface on the steps. Right?

Is this question objectionable? If not, how would you have prepared DW to answer this question?

Answer:

It is not objectionable. You (D's attorney) and DW and P's attorney and the judge all know that two weeks after P fell, D did precisely that. But P is not offering evidence that D did so; P is merely asking whether it had been feasible for D to have done so before P fell.

DW should answer: "Yes, sir, we could have done those things, but that staircase complied with the building code and was safe to walk on." P's attorney might request that the judge strike the second part of the answer (beginning with "but"), and the judge might grant the motion. P's attorney might ask the judge to admonish DW to answer the question and not volunteer more information.

Chapter 15

FRE 408: Compromises, Offers, and Related Conduct

A. A First Look

§15.1 The rule and its purpose

FRE 408 reads as follows:

Rule 408. Compromise Offers and Negotiations

(a) Prohibited Uses. Evidence of the following is not admissible—on behalf of any party—either to prove or disprove the validity or amount of a disputed claim or to impeach by a prior inconsistent statement or a contradiction:

(1) furnishing, promising, or offering—or accepting, promising to accept, or offering to accept—a valuable consideration in compromising or attempting to compromise the claim; and

(2) conduct or a statement made during compromise negotiations about the claim—except when offered in a criminal case and when the negotiations related to a claim by a public office in the exercise of its regulatory, investigative, or enforcement authority.

(b) Exceptions. The court may admit this evidence for another purpose, such as proving a witness's bias or prejudice, negating a contention of undue delay, or proving an effort to obstruct a criminal investigation or prosecution.[1]

FRE 408(a)(1) codifies the common-law rule. The Advisory Committee Note to the original draft of the rule explains:

> [E]xclusion may be based on two grounds. (1) The evidence is irrelevant, since the offer may be motivated by a desire for peace rather than from any concession of weakness of position. The validity of this position will vary as the amount of the offer varies in relation to the size of the claim and may also be influenced by other circumstances. (2) A more consistently impressive ground is promotion of the public policy favoring the compromise and settlement of disputes.[2]

Regarding the first basis for exclusion (irrelevance), the rule recognizes that a potential litigant might be willing to compromise a claim even if it is convinced that it would win in court. Potential defendant X might offer a settlement to potential plaintiff Y because X wants to maintain a good relationship with Y, or because it would cost X more time and energy and money to win a lawsuit than it would to pay Y a modest settlement. For the same reasons, Y might be motivated to accept X's offer, even if Y is convinced that it would win more if it went to court.

The note adds that the rule covers, not only offers to compromise, but also "completed compromises when offered against a party thereto. This latter situation will not, of course, ordinarily occur except when a party to the present litigation has compromised with a third person."[3] That issue is discussed in § 15.6 & § 15.8.

1. FRE 408, eff. Dec. 1, 2011.
2. ACN to original draft of FRE 408.
3. ACN to original draft of FRE 408.

FRE 408(a)(2) excludes "conduct or a statement made during compromise negotiations about the claim...." This represents a considerable expansion to the common law rule. See §15.7.

§15.2 Overview

Cars driven by P and D collide in an intersection, and P sues, seeking compensation for damage to his automobile plus $350,000 for medical expenses, pain and suffering. D, through her attorney, approaches P's attorneys and offers to pay for the car repairs and $5,000 to cover medical expenses, and add an extra $10,000 to compensate P for his pain, if P will drop the suit. P rejects this offer.

At trial, one of P's attorneys takes the stand and seeks to testify that D offered to settle P's claim. D objects, citing FRE 408. Ruling?

Objection sustained; the testimony is inadmissible. This situation is squarely covered by Rule 408(a)(1): that D offered to settle the lawsuit is *not* admissible as evidence suggesting that D was at fault. To permit such evidence would interfere significantly with attempts to settle lawsuits before trial.

The same result would apply if it had been P who approached D: P's willingness to settle his $350,000 lawsuit for, say, $50,000 would not be admissible at trial if offered by D to suggest that P's pain and suffering was "worth" only one seventh what P was suing for. Unlike FRE 407, which protects only defendants in civil litigation, FRE 408 protects any party in a civil case, assuming the requirements of the rule are satisfied and the case does not fall into an exception to the rule.

Suppose, instead, there had been four people in P's car; all four sue D, alleging D's negligence caused the collision. D (or D's insurance company, which for purposes of FRE 408 are considered to be one-and-the-same) is able to settle with three of the claimants, but P refuses to accept anything less than $350,000 for pain and suffering. At trial, P seeks to prove that D paid P's fellow passengers $37,500 each to compensate them for their injuries. P obviously hopes that the jury will reason: "D wouldn't have paid the other claims unless she knew that the accident was her fault." D objects to the evidence, citing Rule 408. Ruling?

The objection *should* be sustained. This situation, too, appears to be clearly within the scope of Rule 408(a)(1). D would have been reluctant to settle with the other three passengers[4] if the fact that she did so could be used by P as evidence that the collision was D's fault. Rule 408 excludes the evidence because admitting it would discourage litigants from compromising or settling lawsuits. (See the first paragraph of the original Advisory Committee Note.) (But some disagree with this reading of the rule. See §15.8, *infra*.)

4. In reality, it was probably D's insurance company, not D herself, that settled with the other three plaintiffs. But that does not alter the application of FRE 408.

Similarly, where P sues D1 and D2 and settles with D1, D2 should not be allowed to offer the P-D1 settlement in evidence to suggest that D1 was the sole cause of P's injuries. (But, again, see § 15.8, *infra*.)

The previous seven paragraphs give you an informal introduction to FRE 408 in the context of a single case. Now let's discuss it in more general terms.

In civil litigation, *X v. Y*, Y offers evidence of a compromise offer made by X, or a "statement" or "conduct" by X. The evidence has some relevance tending to show that Y, not X, deserves to win the lawsuit. X objects that the evidence is banned by FRE 408 because it was made or done in an effort to avoid a trial on the dispute between X and Y. In deciding whether to grant or overrule the objection, the judge (i.e., you) must consider the following issues.

1. ***"Standing" to invoke the rule.*** Who can invoke the rule to exclude evidence? See § 15.3.

The party (X) seeking to invoke Rule 408 to exclude the evidence must satisfy the judge on the next three issues by a preponderance of the evidence. (See § 2.5.) If X fails to do so, the evidence is admissible over a Rule 408 objection.

2. ***Context.*** Was X's statement or conduct merely gratuitous? Was it made during *business* negotiations? Was it made during an entity's internal grievance process? If it falls into any of these categories, it is admissible over X's FRE 408 objections. FRE 408 excludes only statements or conduct which were made in an attempt to prevent or settle a lawsuit. See § 15.4.
3. ***Dispute.*** At the time the statement was made, there must have been a dispute between the parties, either as to the validity of one party's claim against the other, or as to the amount of the claim, or as to both. A statement by the defendant acknowledging both the validity and amount of the plaintiff's claim would not be excluded by the rule. See § 15.5.
4. **"Compromise" or "offer"; "conduct" and "statements."** FRE 408(a)(1) excludes evidence that X compromised a dispute with Y, or offered a compromise to Y, or promised to accept a particular offer. FRE 408(a)(2) likewise excludes "*conduct and statements*" made during compromise negotiations. Both these clauses seem straightforward, but there are grey areas. See § 15.6 & § 15.7.

Assuming X satisfies the judge as to issues 2, 3, and 4, the judge may also have to resolve one or more of the following issues.

5. ***Third parties and other lawsuits.*** A dispute has arisen among the circuits whether FRE 408 excludes evidence of a defendant's settlement with another plaintiff. The same dispute exists as to the admissibility of "conduct and statements" from one suit, when offered in evidence in a different case. See § 15.8.

6. ***"Otherwise discoverable."*** X cannot use FRE 408 to render inadmissible, evidence that Y would have been entitled to discover and use anyway. See § 15.9.
7. ***Party's own statement.*** The rule generally precludes a party from offering evidence of its own efforts to compromise or settle. See § 15.10.
8. ***Impeachment by prior inconsistent statement or contradiction.*** The rule generally precludes using a party's compromise-related conduct or statements for these purposes. See § 15.11.
9. ***Admissibility in criminal cases.*** X engages in conduct or makes statements in an effort to prevent or settle civil litigation with Y. Later on, X is charged with a crime relating to the underlying facts in the X-Y dispute. In *U.S. v. X*, can the prosecutor use X's compromise-related conduct or statement as evidence in X's criminal trial? See § 15.12.
10. Does the rule apply to **plea bargaining**? See § 15.13.
11. ***"Permitted purposes."*** FRE 408(b) directs: "The court may admit this evidence for another purpose. . . ." See § 15.14 & § 15.16. The "other purpose" that is invoked most frequently is "proving a witness's bias or prejudice of a witness." See § 15.15.

§ 15.3 Standing to invoke the rule

The purpose of the rule is to protect a party from having its settlement of a dispute, or its attempt to settle it, used against it to "prove or disprove" that party's claim or defense. Arguably, therefore, the rule protects only a person or entity who was (a) a party to the earlier compromise or attempted compromise, and also (b) a party at the trial in which the evidence is offered.

But some courts disagree.

Assume a dispute arises among three parties: Pickle, Dill and Gherkin. Pickle sues Dill; Dill interpleads Gherkin. Gherkin pays Dill to settle that suit. Pickle's suit against Dill goes to trial. At the trial *Pickle v. Dill*, Dill wants to offer evidence that Gherkin paid money to Dill to settle Dill's claim. The evidence is relevant, let us assume, to suggest that Pickle's injury or loss was Gherkin's fault, not Dill's. Pickle and Gherkin both object, citing FRE 408.

The judge should not allow Gherkin to object, because (as the ACN to Rule 408 puts it), Gherkin is not "a party to the present litigation."[5] As a general rule, someone who is not a party to a case being tried cannot object to evidence offered by any party in that litigation, unless the information falls into an evidentiary privilege (e.g., the attorney-client privilege, the spousal communication privilege, etc.).

---

5. Therefore, the evidence is not being used (to quote the rule) "either to prove or disprove the validity or amount of a disputed claim" by or against Gherkin.

But Pickle *is* a party to the current trial, and objects because Dill is using its settlement with Gherkin as evidence to prove the invalidity of Pickle's claim against Dill. Here is where it is less clear. It is plausible to argue that Pickle should not be allowed to object, either, because Pickle was not a party to the compromise. But some courts hold that Pickle can object, because the rule, as written, arguably applies whenever a compromise or compromise offer is offered to prove or disprove the validity of a claim, and here, Dill is offering the Dill-Gherkin compromise to disprove the validity of Pickle's claim against Dill.

Should Pickle, who was not a party to the Dill-Gherkin settlement, nevertheless be permitted to object to Dill's evidence about that settlement? If your professor does not address the issue in class, seek clarification on the point after class.[6]

B. Factual Issues

§ 15.4 Context

FRE 408(a)(2) does not exclude all potentially disserving statements or conduct by a litigant. It does not exclude statements made during contract negotiations or business negotiations, nor statements or conduct that were made during an existing pre-litigation dispute-resolving process. The rule excludes only statements or conduct "made during compromise negotiations about the claim." To exclude the evidence, it is not necessary that a party has already filed a lawsuit, but the party seeking to exclude the evidence must persuade the judge by a preponderance of the evidence that the statement or conduct was made for the purpose of preventing a lawsuit.

<u>Question 1.</u>

ABC Publishing Company markets a book containing the work of a prominent author, recently deceased. A competitor, the DEF Company, writes a letter to ABC's president, claiming that DEF owns the copyright to the work. Prex, ABC's president, writes back, saying: "We were going through a management change back when we supposedly signed a contract with the author to do this book, so it's possible we let

6. By now, I suspect you have learned that professors are not always able to answer any and all questions that might arise. It never bothered me; I'd respond, "Good question, I'm not sure, I'll check it out." The next time the class met, I'd tell the class what the answer was; or that "some say yes, some say no"; or that "the answer is so arcane and hypertechnical that it's not worth class time and I won't ask that question on the exam, but if you are really that interested, see me after class and I'll show you how to research it." Occasionally a student was "really that interested"; I recruited a few excellent research assistants that way. But some profs might not enjoy having to answer "I don't know" in class, so an after-class office visit or email might be a more tactful way of asking.

things slip between the cracks. Why don't we both make the best of it and go fifty-fifty on expenses and profits?"

After further communications back and forth, however, DEF insists that it owns the sole rights to the book, and sues.

Prior to trial, both sides bring a motion in limine, asking the judge to rule on whether DEF will be permitted to introduce Prex's letter as evidence. Naturally, ABC wants the judge to rule that the letter is inadmissible per FRE 408; DEF wants the judge to rule that it is admissible over a FRE 408 objection. How should each party argue the case; how should the judge rule?

Answer:

DEF's argument is simple: there was nothing in its letter to ABC threatening or even hinting at a lawsuit. Nor was there any reference to that possibility in Prex's response. Rather, DEF argues, Prex was proposing a joint business deal. Therefore FRE 408 does not apply, and Prex's letter should be admissible as a tacit admission that it lacked the right to publish the book.

ABC's argument is also plausible, but weaker: "Of course I was worried about a lawsuit," Prex will testify at the hearing on the motion in limine. "That's why I wrote the letter—to try to head off a lawsuit before DEF filed one!" DEF's response: "Oh, yeah? Then why didn't you say so in your letter?"

There is no right or wrong answer here: it depends on whether Prex's testimony persuades the judge by a preponderance that the letter was motivated to some significant extent by a desire to prevent and avoid litigation. The judge could quite legitimately decide the issue either way.

Question 2.

What could Prex have included in the letter to pretty much guarantee that it would be inadmissible if DEF filed suit against ABC?

Answer:

Suppose the letter had been worded:

> We were going through a management change back when we supposedly signed a contract with the author to do this book, so it's possible we let things slip between the cracks. The last thing ABC wants is to get involved in a lawsuit, and I'm sure you feel the same way. Why don't we both make the best of it and go fifty-fifty on expenses and profits?

Do you understand why this letter would clearly be inadmissible per FRE 408? If not, compare it to the text of the letter in Question 1.

Question 3.

Why do you suppose that ABC's president did not word his letter as per Question 2?

Answer:

There are two possibilities.

(1) Prex wrote the letter without consulting the company's lawyer.

Or:

(2) Prex did consult the company's lawyers, who failed to insist that the letter include the extra sentence.

Question 4.

P worked for D Co. for eight years. Four times during that period—during the second, third, fourth and sixth year—P applied for promotions to the next level pay grade—a $5,000 per year increase. Each time, the promotion was given instead to someone who was younger and (in P's opinion) less experienced and less qualified.

D Co.'s employee handbook directs: "If you believe you have been treated unfairly in a personnel matter, you should file a complaint with our Human Resources Department (HRD), which will look into the matter." In year 8, P filed a complaint with HRD, alleging age discrimination, seeking an immediate promotion and a $5,000 per year raise dating back to year 2, the first time he was passed over for promotion—i.e., an additional $35,000 in back pay.

HRD sends P the following response:

> We have investigated your complaint and conclude that it has merit. You definitely should have received the promotion two years ago. On behalf of the company, we apologize for our failure to adhere to our commitment not to improperly discriminate against any employee. You are hereby promoted to the next pay grade, retroactive to the date you should have received that promotion and the higher salary. This entitles you to a retroactive pay increase of $5,000 for each year since you were denied that promotion, or a total of $10,000.
>
> We gave serious consideration to your three earlier promotion applications. We acknowledge that there is some support for those claims as well, but conclude that the weight of the evidence is that the decision to promote the other candidate on each of those occasions was based on valid considerations. However, as evidence of our good faith, we are raising your retroactive pay from $10,000 to $15,000.

Unsatisfied, P sues anyway. Prior to trial, D Co. brings a motion in limine to preclude P from introducing evidence of D's response to P's HRD complaint. Ruling?

Answer:

Motion to exclude denied.

When P filed the complaint with HRD, P was not asserting a "claim," as that term is used in FRE 408. P had not filed a lawsuit; P had not threatened to file a lawsuit. Rather, P followed D Co.'s employee handbook to seek redress for unfair treatment. And nothing in the DHR response suggests that its decision is a compromise offer to head off a lawsuit. Thus, FRE 408 does not apply. HRD's decision and the memo are admissible against D Co.

§ 15.5 "Disputed claim"

FRE 408 applies only when a "disputed claim" exists. The Advisory Committee Note to the original text of the rule explains: "The policy considerations which underlie the rule do not come into play when the effort is to induce a creditor to settle an admittedly due amount for a lesser sum. Hence the rule requires that the claim be disputed as to either validity or amount."[7]

Question 1.

D, a plumber, installed a new water heater in P's home. A few weeks later, while P and his family were away for the weekend, the water heater sprung a leak and did substantial water damage to the house.[8] P sent D an angry letter alleging that it cost $40,000 to repair the damage, and threatened to sue D for that amount unless D paid him.

D responded by denying the leak was her fault, but offered to install a new water heater free of charge. P rejected this offer, and the case went to trial. P wants to testify about D's offer; D objects, citing FRE 408. Ruling?

Answer:

Objection sustained. D was responding to P's threat to sue, and disputed the validity of P's claim. The most realistic way to interpret D's offer was an effort to persuade P not to sue D. Thus, the offer is protected by FRE 408, and therefore is inadmissible.

Question 2.

Suppose instead D responded, "It looks like we goofed pretty bad, but $40,000 seems excessive. I'll pay you $12,000 to settle the matter."

P rejects the offer. Prior to trial, D brings a motion in limine, asking the court to rule that D's response to P is inadmissible per FRE 408. How should the judge rule?

---

7. ACN to 1975 draft of FRE 408.

8. If you own or rent a private home and all the occupants go away for several days, it is a good idea to shut off the water supply before you leave.

Answer:

Motion granted. D conceded the validity of P's claim, but disputed the amount. Therefore, per FRE 408(a), D's compromise offer is inadmissible in its entirety.

Question 3.

Suppose, instead, prior to trial, P and D entered into a full written settlement of the dispute: D agreed to pay P $24,000 in twelve equal installments. After the first payment, however, D refused to make any further payments. P brought a civil action against D to recover the $22,000 balance.

P takes the stand to testify about the settlement. D objects on the basis of Rule 408. How should the trial judge rule on D's objection?

Answer:

Objection overruled. There is no dispute as to the validity of P's claim, or the amount: in the settlement, P and D each agreed that P had a valid claim and that $24,000 was the agreed-upon amount. Moreover, P is not offering the settlement agreement to prove that D caused damage to P's home; P is seeking to enforce a contract—i.e., the settlement agreement. Therefore FRE 408 does not apply, and the contract (settlement) is admissible.

Question 4.

Pursuant to a contract, P delivered certain items to D. When D refused to pay, P sued for $50,000, the amount specified in the contract. D responds: "It was a misjudgment on our part to have signed the contract at that price in the first place; it violated our internal policy on such matters. In accordance with that policy, we will pay you $25,000." P rejects the offer. Prior to trial, P brings a motion in limine, seeking a ruling that D's response is admissible. D objects that the response should be excluded per FRE 408(a)(1). Ruling?

Answer:

Objection overruled. D's response concedes both that it is obliged to pay P and that, per the contract, it owes P $50,000. (The fact that that amount allegedly violated D's "internal policies" in no way invalidates the contract.) Because D did not dispute either the validity of P's claim, or the amount, D's response is not protected by the rule; the response is admissible.

§ 15.6 Compromises and offers to compromise

FRE 408 excludes evidence that in a dispute between P and D, either party (let's say D) offered or agreed to settle a dispute rather than go to trial—assuming that evidence is offered, at a trial, to prove or disprove P's claim or D's defense in that dispute.

In Y1 (year one), D and P sign a contract requiring D to supply certain chemicals to P, which P uses in the manufacture of True Love cosmetics.. But for some reason, True Love was lumpy, and therefore unsellable. P alleges that this occurred because the chemicals provided by D were defective. P sues.

D denies that its chemicals were defective, but proposes a compromise to settle the dispute. If P rejects D's offer, can P offer evidence of D's compromise proposal as evidence that D's materials were at fault? No. FRE 408 bars the evidence.

Suppose P accepts the settlement. Thereafter, D assures P that it has improved its quality control process, and in Y2, P and D again sign a contract in which D supplies those chemicals. But once again, True Love came out lumpy,[9] and in the meantime, another company successfully marketed a product that did what True Love was designed to do, and P had to terminate the True Love line at a substantial loss. P threatens to sue D.

D makes the same compromise offer for Y2 as it did for Y1. This time P rejects the offer—its losses in Y2, it insists, are far greater than its losses in Y1. P submits a counterproposal, for an amount far greater than D proposed, albeit, say, 25% less than the amount for which it is suing. D rejects P's counterproposal.

Neither party, over the other's objection, can offer either D's Y2 compromise offer, nor P's Y2 counterproposal. D cannot offer evidence that it made an offer, nor that P made a counterproposal. P cannot offer evidence that D made an offer, or that it made a counterproposal.[10]

Prior to trial, D also moves in limine to preclude P from offering evidence of the Y1 settlement in which D paid damages to P. Should the judge grant or deny the motion?

Logic says: yes, grant the motion! After all, P is trying to use D's settlement payment to P regarding Y1 to prove that since D's chemicals were flawed in Y1, they were probably still flawed in Y2—i.e., to prove the validity of P's current, Y2 claim against D.

But some argue that the rule should not apply, because the Y1 claim that was settled is a different claim than the Y2 claim that is about to be tried. See § 15.8.

Which approach is the right one? Whichever one your professor says. (If your professor does not discuss the issue, ether ask the professor about it after class, or assume that the issue will not be on the exam.)

§ 15.7 "Conduct or statements made during compromise negotiations"

M and L have a lengthy and mutually beneficial relationship—it could be parent-child, sibling-sibling, friend-friend, mentor-mentee. Then M does something

9. In other words, the course of True Love never did run smooth.

10. That assumes that the evidence does not fall into the exception clause.

wrong—deliberately or accidentally or thoughtlessly—that upsets L so deeply that the nature of the relationship may change forever; perhaps, in fact, there is a clear possibility that L may terminate the relationship completely.

At some point in our lives, every one of us has been M. At some point in our lives, every one of us has been L.

If M hopes to save the relationship and restore it to its prior status, what is the first, essential, fundamental thing M must do?

M must say, "I'm sorry. I'm sorry I hurt you. I never should have done that."[11]

It may not work immediately; it may work only partially; it may not work at all. But without it, the damage to the relationship could be substantial and perhaps permanent.

What is true in human relationships generally is often true in litigation as well—even litigation involving large, impersonal entities like corporations (which, ultimately, act through their human agents). If someone's inattentive driving caused a collision which injured X or disrupted X's life in a significant way; if a contractor did a poor job making repairs or improvements on Y's home; if Company B was late in delivering supplies to Company E, thereby causing E to miss a deadline and incur costly penalties; in each case, those who suffered as a result—X; Y; Company E's personnel—are likely to feel offended, wronged, and angry. These are natural and understandable human reactions, but they are not very conducive to avoiding or settling a lawsuit. An apology and acknowledgment of fault by the inattentive driver, or by the contractor, or by Company B personnel would help to ease X's or Y's or E's agents' anger and resentment and might make them more willing to consider settling rather than seeking vengeance in the courtroom.

Re-read the first paragraph in the section. Put yourself in L's situation. Which approach by L is more likely to ameliorate your sense of hurt and betrayal?

"I'm sorry. It was wrong of me to do that. I hurt you and I'm sorry."

Or:

"Speaking conditionally and solely for the purposes of trying to put our relationship back on track, let's assume it was wrong for me to do what I did."

The first, of course. The second is absurd—if anything, it would likely intensify the anger and hurt. Yet, prior to the enactment of FRE 408, the common law rule did not protect "conduct or statements" made as part of an effort to compromise

11. A fairly extensive body of scholarship exists as to what else M should say, and when. For example, when, if ever, should M ask: "Please forgive me?" Some urge that M should say that immediately; according to others, it is unwise to ask for forgiveness without having earned it. All agree that M should *not* say, "I'm sorry you were hurt," because that's not an acknowledgment of fault or wrongdoing, and therefore is not really an apology at all; in fact, it may reasonably be interpreted as "It's too bad you are so thin-skinned as to take offense and make a 'federal case' out if it."

unless they were made along the lines of the second option. Thus, if the errant driver or contractor or a company B official said something like the first version, that statement would have been admissible at trial. Only statements like the second, couched in careful, lawyerly terminology, would be protected by the common-law predecessor of Rule 408. Lawyers presumably were aware of the distinction, but non-lawyers generally were not, and a non-lawyer who admitted fault and apologized in a sincere effort to encourage the injured party to accept a compromise might discover that he or she gave the other side valuable evidence against him or her.

FRE 408(a)(2) is a substantial expansion of the common law rule: it excludes *any* "conduct or statement" a litigant or potential litigant made "during compromise negotiations about the claim";[12] there is no need to cloak the statement or conduct with phrases such as "speaking conditionally and without prejudice to my right to object if you offer what I am about to say in evidence. . . ."

Question 1.

Bloch Construction Incorporated (BCI) contracted to build a 40-room motel for Norman Bates. When construction was complete, Bates refused to make the final payments because of alleged defects in the building and furnishings. Their lawyers exchanged letters, threatening to sue and counter-sue. In an attempt to settle the dispute, BCI hired A. Perkins, an architect, who studied the alleged defects Bates complained about and submitted a report, confirming Bates' complaints about some defects and rejecting others. BCI submitted the report to Bates and offered to make the changes suggested in the report. Bates still refused to make the final payment, and BCI sued.

At trial, Bates attempts to introduce the report as proof of many of the defects he complained about.

BCI objects per FRE 408. How should the judge rule?

Answer:

Objection sustained. Hiring an independent architect to inspect and report was "conduct ... during compromise negotiations about the claim," per FRE 408(a)(2). Perkins' report constitutes "statements" made during negotiations. And BCI's offer to make all the repairs listed in Perkins' report constitutes offering a compromise to resolve the dispute.[13]

---

12. We will cover the "except ... in a criminal case" clause in § 15.12.

13. In the case on which this problem is based, the judge sustained the objection. The Fifth Circuit affirmed, concluding that the report "was a tool used in an unsuccessful settlement attempt," and therefore was excluded under the "conduct or statement" provision of Rule 408. *Ramada Development Co. v. Rauch,* 644 F.2d 1097 (5th Cir. 1981). (At the time, the rule was worded differently than the current version, but in essence, the court held that the report was properly excluded per language which is now codified as FRE 408(a)(2).)

C. Other Legal Issues

§ 15.8 Third parties and other lawsuits

A dispute has arisen among the circuits whether FRE 408 excludes evidence of a defendant's settlement with another plaintiff. In pertinent part, the rule reads:

> Evidence of the following is not admissible—on behalf of any party—either to prove or disprove the validity or amount of a disputed claim ... (1) furnishing, or offering—or accepting, promising to accept, or offering to accept—a valuable consideration in compromising or attempting to compromise the claim....

The rule can be read to apply only to evidence of compromise offered to prove liability for or the amount of the *claim that was compromised,* not the validity or amount of someone else's claim. *See Zurich Am. Ins. Co. v. Watts Indus., Inc.*, 417 F.3d 682, 688-90 (7th Cir. 2005), and cases cited therein.

The other (and in my opinion, the better) view is that the rule should protect, i.e., exclude a defendant's settlement of another plaintiff's claim; otherwise, a defendant may be unwilling to settle with P1, for fear that P2 can use this settlement as proof that defendant is also liable to P2. It is difficult to reconcile admitting such evidence with the language of FRE 408, its purpose, or the Advisory Committee Note.

The same dispute exists as to the admissibility of "conduct and statements" from one suit, when offered in evidence in a different case.

Which approach should you take? Consult Fishman Rule of Evidence 001, § 1 of the preface.

<u>Question 1.</u>

A bus and a car collide at an intersection. Some passengers on the bus (the "BPs") suffer minor injuries; sadly, a passenger in the car is seriously injured. Evidence suggests that the cause of the accident is that the car's brakes failed, but the car's driver (CD) and his passenger (CP) dispute this, claiming the bus driver's inattentiveness caused the collision. CD, who also owned the car, was uninsured and has no significant assets—in other words, suing CD would be fruitless, since CD would not be able to pay any judgment against him. So, everyone—CD, CP, and all the injured BPs—all sue the bus company.

The bus company passengers are seeking fairly small amounts of money—so little, that it would cost the company more to litigate their claims and win than to pay them what they are seeking. On the other hand, the car driver (CD) is suing for $50,000, and his passenger (CP) is suing for $500,000 for medical expenses, loss of livelihood, pain and suffering, etc. Firmly convinced that the collision was the car driver's fault, the company plans to go to trial on their claims.

Should the bus company settle the bus passengers' claims?

Answer:

It depends on how that jurisdiction interprets FRE 408. If it applies the rule narrowly, so as not to apply to third-party suits, the bus company probably should not settle the BPs claims, because if it did settle the BP claims, then CD and CP will be able to introduce that fact, as evidence that it was the bus driver, and not CD or his vehicle, who caused the collision. On the other hand, if the jurisdiction interprets FRE 408 broadly, to apply to third-party suits, it would be safe for the bus company to pay the BPs' modest claims, because the company's Rule 408 objection will be sustained in the *CD & CP v. Bus Company* suit.

Question 2.

The federal government brought an action against several chemical and petroleum companies to require them to clean up two related toxic waste sites. As to site 1, D1 commissioned a special study, which it submitted to D2, D3 and D4 in an attempt to persuade them to avoid litigation and accept what D1 believed was a fair settlement. In the study, D1 acknowledged that it was partially responsible for the toxic waste that had been discarded on site 1.

In litigation over the second site, D2 offered D1's site 1 study, which was relevant in establishing D1's partial responsibility there, too. D1 objected, citing FRE 408(a). How should the judge rule?

Answer:

Here, too, it depends on how narrowly or broadly the court construes the rule.

The narrow reading restricts the application of Rule 408 to the precise "claim" in which the compromise, conduct or statement was made. Under this view, Rule 408 applies only to an attempt to use the site 1 study in the lawsuit regarding site 1. Therefore, the D1 site 1 study would be admissible against D1 in the site 2 litigation.

The broader view is that a Rule 408(a) compromise, conduct or statement made with regard to one claim is excluded in evidence not only in litigation involving that claim, but in additional litigation involving other claims as well, at least where (as here) excluding the compromise, conduct or statement made in regard to prior litigation would serve to further the underlying purpose of FRE 408—i.e., so long as it would encourage the effort to settle a "disputed claim" without a trial. Under this approach, D1's motion to exclude the study at the site 2 trial should be granted, because D1 probably would not have distributed the site 1 study if it knew that it could be used against D1 in the site 2 litigation.[14]

§ 15.9 "Otherwise discoverable"

Prior to the 2006 amendment, FRE 408 stated explicitly that the rule did not require exclusion of evidence that is "otherwise discoverable." In other words, a party could not make information or documents inadmissible by offering them to the other side during negotiations, if the other side would have been able to obtain that information or those documents anyway during pretrial discovery.

The "otherwise discoverable" clause was deleted by the 2006 amendment, not to change the law, but because, the Committee concluded, the language was "superfluous." Thus, material disclosed during compromise negotiations that would be "otherwise discoverable" is still admissible over a Rule 408 objection.

§ 15.10 A party's own compromise, offer, conduct, or statement

Most often, in lawsuit *X v. Y*, X is trying to introduce evidence of Y's offer, conduct or statement against Y. But FRE 408 also excludes the evidence where X is trying to introduce evidence of its own compromise, offer, conduct, or statement, because if X introduces such evidence, Y might have to respond at trial by introducing evidence of its own offer, conduct or statement. X should not be permitted to force Y to do what FRE 408 precludes X from doing directly. The Advisory Committee Note to the 2006 amendment specifies: "the Rule, by definition, protects both parties from having the fact of negotiation disclosed to the jury."

§ 15.11 Impeachment by prior inconsistent statement or contradiction

FRE 408(a) directs that evidence that comes within FRE 408(a)(1) and FRE 408(a)(2) is not admissible "to impeach by a prior inconsistent statement or a contradiction." Here's an example.

> ¶ 1. Building owner B hired contractor C to update the building's HVAC[15] system and equipment. When the work was complete, it was necessary to

14. This question is based on *Lyondell Chemical Co. v. Occidental Chemical Corp.*, 608 F.3d 284, 294–300 (5th Cir. 2010). The judge admitted D1's site 1 report against D1 in the site 2 litigation. The Fifth Circuit held that this violated FRE 408(a)(2), and remanded the case for further proceedings.

15. Heating, ventilation, and air conditioning.

turn off the water system of the building overnight. This was not done, and the building suffered water damage. The next morning when C arrived at his office, he heard a voicemail from B informing him of this and threatening to sue.

¶ 2. C summoned PM, C's project manager on the B building job. PM told C, "I tried to turn off the water system when we wrapped up at 6:30 last night, but BS, B's building superintendent, told me not to; that he would turn the water system off before he left the building. I told him three times, and he said, 'yeah, yeah, I heard you the first time.' I even sent him an email at 6:45, and he answered back that he would do it!" PM showed C the email exchange.

¶ 3. Based on this, the odds are pretty good that C would win the case if B actually sued. But B owned several other large commercial buildings, and C hoped that B would hire C to work on them, as well. An added complication: BS, B's building superintendent, was B's son-in-law. Telling B that it was B's own son-in-law's fault probably would not prompt B to give more work to C. "OK, here's what we'll do. I'll call B and calm him down. You're gonna say you should have made sure the water was off—that's not true. You and I know it was BS's fault. But sometimes taking the blame for something that's not our fault can be good for business; at least, let's give it a try."

¶ 4. C called B and said, "We can work this out; let's straighten this out, neither of us wants to get involved in a lawsuit, OK? PM's got something to tell you." PM said, "I should have made sure the water was turned off before I left the building last night." C then said, "I'll send my water damage guy over right now to make things right by you." B grumbled but said, "OK, let's see."

¶ 5. WDG, C's water damage guy, reported back that it would cost about $6,000 to repair the damage. C said "Ouch," but told WDG, "Do it now!"

¶ 6. A day or so after WDG finished the work, C called B. "OK, we've fixed the damage. How's this: you sign off on the job we did, and we'll give you a 10% discount on parts and appliances on the next job we do for you."

¶ 7. Unfortunately, it didn't work. "Sign off on the job? You're dreaming," B replied, "the flood damaged the whole building electrical system. Replace it, or I'll see you in court!"

¶ 8. C asked WDG, "What about B's building's electrical system?"

¶ 9. "Oh, it needs replacing, all right," WDG told C, "but that's because it's about 35 years old. The water never got into the electrical system; B is just trying to gouge us."

¶ 10. C told B that C was not responsible for the condition of the building's electrical system. B made good his threat to sue.

Question 1.

Prior to trial, each side brings a motion in limine, asking the judge to rule on whether B could testify that the day after the damage, PM, C's project manager, told B, "I should have made sure the water was turned off before I left the building last night." (¶ 4.) How should the judge rule?

Answer:

Clearly this was "a statement made during compromise negotiations"—P had already threatened to sue, and C stressed his desire to avoid a lawsuit. Therefore, PM's statement is inadmissible per FRE 408(a)(2). (We haven't gotten to the "impeach" clause in FRE 408(a) yet.)

Question 2.

Both parties also bring a motion in limine seeking a ruling whether B can introduce evidence that C made repairs to the water damage in B's building. How should the judge rule?

Answer:

Making the repairs was clearly "conduct made during compromise negotiations" (see ¶ 4 and ¶ 6), and therefore is inadmissible per FRE 408(a)(2). (We still haven't gotten to the "impeach" clause in FRE 408(a) yet.)

Question 3.

After B presents his case and rests, C calls PM as a witness. PM testifies that he was C's project manager on the HVAC job on B's building; that the work was done properly; and that to assure that the new system worked properly, it was necessary to turn off the water in the building overnight. He further testifies:

> I tried to turn off the water system when we wrapped up at 6:30 that night, but BS, B's building superintendent told me not to; that he would turn the water system off before he left the building. I told him three times, and he said, "yeah, yeah, I heard you the first time." I even sent him an email at 6:45, and he answered back that he would do it!

C then introduces the email exchange into evidence. Assume this evidence was properly admitted. On cross, B's attorney seeks to ask:

> Isn't it true that the next day, you told B, and I quote, "*I*"—[meaning you, Mr. PM]—quote—"I should have made sure the water was turned off before I left the building last night." Unquote. Didn't you say that to B the next day?

Should B's attorney be permitted to ask this question?

Answer:

At first glance, the question seems entirely proper. PM has just testified that it was not his fault that the water wasn't turned off, which is clearly inconsistent with what he told B over the phone (¶ 4). Impeaching PM with PM's prior inconsistent statement is explicitly permitted by FRE 613. See § 12.13.[16]

But this is precisely what the "impeach" clause of FRE 408(a) prohibits: "Evidence of ... [a statement] is not admissible to impeach by a prior inconsistent statement...." The Advisory Committee Note to the 2006 amendment explains: "The amendment prohibits the use of statements made in settlement negotiations when offered to impeach by prior inconsistent statement or through contradiction. Such broad impeachment would tend to swallow the exclusionary rule and would impair the public policy of promoting settlements." Thus, the FRE 408(a) exclusionary rule precludes what FRE 613 would otherwise permit.

Question 4.

B also seeks to impeach PM's denial of fault by introducing evidence that C made repairs to the water damage at C's expense—an example of impeachment by contradiction (because the repairs C made tend to contradict PM's denial of fault). Is this admissible over a FRE 408(a) objection?

Answer:

No. C made those repairs as part of an effort to persuade B not to sue. Therefore, it falls squarely within the same impeachment prohibition of FRE 408(a).

§ 15.12 Admissibility of compromise-related evidence in criminal cases

Applying the rule as originally enacted in 1975, courts divided as to whether a civil litigant's offer or acceptance of a compromise, or statements or conduct during compromise negotiations, should be admitted if one of the litigants is subsequently prosecuted for the same conduct that gave rise to the civil lawsuit. Needless to say, if I represent a client and there is any possibility that my client's compromise-oriented conduct or statements might later be used by a prosecutor to convict my client of a crime, my advice would be: "Let me handle the compromise negotiations. *You* should say nothing and do nothing—no apologies, no admission of fault—to nudge the other side to settle; the risk is too great."

And I'd be reluctant to advise my client to settle, if that settlement might be used to convict my client of a crime.

The 2006 amendment to the rule clears up the uncertainty. It divides FRE 408-related evidence into three categories.

16. In fact, since PM is C's employee, his statement to B would be admitted, over a hearsay objection, not only to impeach his testimony, but as substantive evidence per FRE 801(d)(2)(C) and FRE 801(d)(2)(D). See *A Student's Guide to Hearsay,* § 5.29 to § 5.21 and § 5.23 to § 5.24.

1. <u>Compromise offers; responses to offers; completed compromises.</u> FRE 408(a) creates a blanket prohibition: evidence that a party to a civil dispute made or responded or agreed to a compromise offer is not admissible in a criminal trial to prove that that party's conduct in creating the dispute was a crime. Why? First, because accepting a compromise in a civil dispute is often only minimally relevant if offered to prove guilt of a crime. Second, as the Advisory Committee Note so wisely put it, "'A target of a potential criminal investigation may be unwilling to settle civil claims against him if by doing so he increases the risk of prosecution and conviction.'"[17]

2. <u>Conduct and statements made during compromise negotiations: disputes between private parties.</u> If all the parties to a civil dispute are individuals or non-government entities, FRE 408(b) establishes the same rule for conduct and statements as it does for compromise offers: such evidence is not admissible to prove that a person's conduct in the events leading up to the dispute were criminal. There are two reasons for this rule: first, to encourage parties to a dispute to say and do things that may lead to a compromise. Second, it protects unsophisticated people involved in a civil dispute from witlessly incriminating themselves while trying to settle the civil dispute.

3. <u>Conduct and statements made during compromise negotiations: disputes between a private party and a government agency.</u> The "except" clause in FRE 408(b) directs that X's statements or conduct made during compromise negotiations with a government agency *can* be used against X if X is later charged with committing a crime with regard to the underlying dispute. To paraphrase the Advisory Committee Note, when X is speaking to any government agency, what X says can be used against X in a criminal trial.

<u>Question 1.</u>

XYZ hired PQR to do a major construction project. PQR subcontracted the scaffolding work to D. Several weeks into the contract, part of the scaffolding gave way. Fortunately, no one was injured, but work on the project was delayed considerably, and XYZ threatened to sue.

On June 1, D sat down with agents for PQR and XYZ in an attempt to avoid a lawsuit. During this conference, D said, "Look, we all know the fault was mine. I miscalculated what the job required."

On August 1, Inv, an investigator from the U.S. Occupational Safety and Health Administration (OSHA), approached D. Inv informed D that OSHA was contemplating bringing a lawsuit against D for endangering the men and women who

---

17. ACN to the 2006 amendment to FRE 408, 4th ¶. (Modesty precludes me from identifying the source the ACN quoted.)

worked on or around the scaffolding. D told Inv pretty much what he'd said to PQR and XYZ back on June 1.

Two years later, D was indicted for mail fraud. The indictment charges that D knowingly mailed invoices to PQR which significantly, and deliberately, overstated the amount of labor and materials that D devoted to the scaffolding.

At D's criminal trial for mail fraud, the government seeks to introduce D's June 1 statement to PQR and XYZ, and D's August 1 statement to Inv. Choose the correct answer:

(a) The June 1 and August 1 statements are both admissible over a Rule 408 objection.

(b) The June 1 statement is admissible over a Rule 408 objection, but the August 1 statement is not.

(c) The August 1 statement is admissible over a Rule 408 objection, but the June 1 statement is not.

(d) Neither the June 1 nor the August 1 statement is admissible over a Rule 408 objection.

Answer:

The correct answer is (c).

D's statements to PQR and XYZ fall within FRE 408(a)(2). The stem of the question tells you "the meeting was held in an attempt to avoid a lawsuit," and neither PQR nor XYZ are government agencies. Therefore, the June 1 statement is inadmissible in the mail fraud prosecution against D. That eliminates options (a) and (b).

But D's statement on August 1 to Inv, OSHA's investigator, comes within the "except" clause of FRE 408(a)(1): it was made "in negotiations related to a claim by public office [OSHA] in the exercise of its regulatory, investigative or enforcement authority." Therefore, D's statement to Inv is admissible. That eliminates option (d). Option (c) is the correct answer.

Question 2.

Continuing the sequence of events set out in the first question, on September 1, D agreed to a compromise settlement of PQR's and XYZ's claims against him.

At D's trial for mail fraud, can the government introduce D's September 1 settlement of PQR's and XYZ's against D?

Answer:

No. FRE 408(a) enacts an absolute ban against the government using evidence of a compromise or offer to compromise as proof that D engaged in criminal conduct involving the claim that was compromised.

Question 3.

On October 1, D entered a consent decree with OSHA in which D acknowledged failing to build safe scaffolding, and forfeited the right to bid on federal government contracts for three years.

At D's trial for mail fraud, can the government introduce D's October 1 consent decree with OSHA?

Answer:

No. FRE 408(a) enacts an absolute ban against the government using evidence of a compromise or offer to compromise as proof that D engaged in criminal conduct involving the claim that was compromised—even if that compromise (or compromise negotiations) was with a government agency.

The bottom line is this. Nothing D said or did with regard to PQR or XYZ is admissible in the criminal case against D. The fact that D entered into a consent decree with OSHA (in other words, settled the OSHA case) is not admissible in the criminal case against D. But D's statement to Inv is admissible against D in the criminal case.

§ 15.13 Rule 408 and plea bargaining

Questions sometimes arise whether FRE 408 applies to plea-bargaining, i.e., to "settling" a criminal case without a trial. The simple answer is that Rule 408 does not apply to plea-bargaining. See § 16.5.

D. Permitted Purposes: FRE 408(b)

---

§ 15.14 FRE 408(b)

FRE 408(b) provides:

> **(b) Exceptions.** The court may admit this evidence for another purpose, such as proving a witness's bias or prejudice, negating a contention of undue delay, or proving an effort to obstruct a criminal investigation or prosecution.

Potential uses include: impeaching a witness's testimony to show bias or prejudice; proving that a party served notice of a claim in a timely fashion; "negating a contention of undue delay"; and "proving an effort to obstruct a criminal investigation or prosecution."

§ 15.15 "Showing a witness's bias or prejudice"

FRE 408(b) permits evidence of a compromise, or statements or conduct made during compromise negotiations, to "show[] a witness's bias or prejudice." The prior settlement may be relevant to show a witness's bias for a party, or bias against a party. Here is an example.

McShain (P) purchased an airplane manufactured by Cessna. After the plane was serviced by Butler Aviation, its landing gear gave way. P sued Cessna, alleging defective design, seeking the cost of repairs and consequential and punitive damages. Cessna joined Butler as a third-party defendant, alleging that faulty servicing by Butler, not the plane's design, caused the mishap. Prior to trial, plaintiff released Butler from any liability regarding the accident in exchange for $10 and the right to engage W, an employee of Butler's sister corporation, as a consultant and witness. When W testified for plaintiff at trial, Cessna, over plaintiff's objection, was permitted to impeach W by introducing the terms of plaintiff's settlement with Butler to show W's bias in favor of plaintiff. The Fifth Circuit, observing that "[t]he fact that a sister corporation of [W's] employer had been released from liability in exchange for [W's] testimony cast doubt upon [W's] impartiality," upheld the trial judge's conclusion that neither Rule 408 nor Rule 403 required exclusion. *John McShain, Inc. v Cessna Aircraft Co.*, 563 F.2d 632 (3d Cir. 1977).

Here's another example:

P was badly scalded when hot liquid spewed from a BMW's radiator, and sued BMW, alleging defective design in the radiator cap. At trial, he called three witnesses—PW1, PW2 and PW3—to testify that the same thing happened to each of them. To impeach those witnesses, BMW sought to introduce evidence that each of them sued BMW and settled, to show their bias and disgruntlement against BMW because each had to settle for much less than he originally sought. The Sixth Circuit held that this evidence was properly admitted to show the witnesses' bias against BMW. *Croskey v. BMW of North America, Inc.*, 532 F.3d 511, 519 (6th Cir. 2008).

§ 15.16 Other purposes; questions

<u>Notice.</u> Often a plaintiff must prove that it gave the defendant notice of a complaint or claim by a certain date. A communication from plaintiff, or an acknowledgment by the defendant that it received such a complaint or claim, should be admitted for that limited purpose, even if the wording of the communication (from plaintiff to defendant or from defendant to plaintiff) suggests a willingness to settle the matter without litigation.[18]

---

18. Where feasible, the judge might redact out the references to compromise or settlement.

Avoid jury confusion. Plaintiff sues four defendants, alleging that they each, individually and collectively, caused loss or injury, and seeking damages of, say, $1,000,000. D2, D3 and D4 each settle with plaintiff, who then goes to trial against D1. D1's defense, naturally enough, is: "It was these three other guys—D2, D3, and D4—it was their fault, not mine." Naturally, the jury will wonder: why is Plaintiff suing only D1? Many courts have held that the trial judge has discretion to inform the jury that D2, D3 and D4 have each settled with P—but not inform them of the amount of the settlement; and to remind the jury their job is to decide whether D1 also should be held liable for P's loss or injury, and if so, what portion of that loss should be attributed to D1, without speculating how much P has already received from D2, D3, and D4.

FRE 408(b) cites a few additional "other purposes," but they are, I hope, self-explanatory.

A reminder: if evidence satisfies the "other purpose" clause of FRE 408(b), that means it is admissible over an objection based on FRE 408(a). It still may be excluded, however, if it is barred by another rule—if it is inadmissible hearsay, for example, or if it falls within an evidentiary privilege, or if its legitimate probative value for a valid Rule 408(b) purpose is substantially outweighed by the risk of unfair prejudice to one of the parties, etc.

Question 1.

Doctor MD prescribed medication to patient P. P filled the prescription at a CVS pharmacy. Although P suffered a side-effect from the medication, P continued to take it and suffered a permanent disability as a result. P sued CVS, alleging Rx, its pharmacist, failed to warn P to stop taking the medication if P experienced that particular side-effect. At trial, CVS defends on two bases: (1) Rx, the pharmacist, testifies that he did in fact warn P. (2) Even if Rx failed to inform P, P would not have heeded the warning.

In support of this second defense, CVS called MD, who testified that she did warn P to stop taking the medication immediately if P suffered that side effect. (After all, the pharmacy reasons, since P ignored MD's warning, P also would have ignored any warning Rx might have given, too.)

On cross-examination, P wants to bring out that P had originally sued MD as well as CVS, alleging that MD also failed to warn him, and MD (actually, MD's malpractice insurance company) paid P a certain amount of money to settle P's claim. Should the judge allow the cross-examination?

Answer:

MD testified at trial against P. This evidence is clearly relevant to show MD's bias against P: no one likes being sued and having to settle the suit (even if an insurance company, rather than MD herself, paid money to P). On the other hand, there is the risk that the jury might assume that the settlement between MD and P was a tacit admission by MD that MD had failed to warn P—which might prompt the jury to reject CVS's second defense—a use forbidden by FRE 408(a)(1).

In the case on which this problem is based, the trial judge allowed the cross-examination, but did not permit P to elicit the amount of the settlement. The trial judge also instructed the jury that it could consider the fact of the settlement in assessing the credibility of MD's testimony, but could not consider it on the issue of the pharmacy's liability to P. The appellate court approved.[19] See § 15.15.

Question 2.

In the litigation between publishers ABC and DEF (§ 15.4 Question 1), while letters and emails were going back and forth between the companies, DEF at one point wrote to ABC, "We had big plans for that book, and your publishing it has made a big hole in our anticipated profits for the year. Unless you make us whole, we will take you to court!" In response, ABC replied, "We really hope we can resolve this problem without a lawsuit. We will pay to DEF all of ABC's after-cost profits." As part of this offer, ABC voluntarily sends to DEF an accounting of its costs, gross sales, and net profits. DEF, however, is convinced that it would have been able to make a much higher profit on the book it had planned to publish; it therefore rejects the compromise offer, and sues. When DEF offers ABC's accounting of costs, gross sales and net profits in evidence, ABC objects, saying the information and records should be excluded under FRE 408. Result?

Answer:

Objection overruled. Once DEF filed a suit, all of that information would have been discoverable to DEF per the Federal Rules of Civil Procedure anyway. ABC cannot shield that information or those documents from DEF by giving them to DEF during compromise negotiations. See § 15.9.

Question 3.

"But wait a minute, Prof. Remember the hotel question in § 15.7? You told us that the architecture report that BCI (the builder) commissioned was *not* admissible, because Bloch gave the report to plaintiff Bates to try to persuade Bates to compromise and avoid litigation. Now you are telling us that ABC's financial records *are* admissible, even though ABC gave them to DEF to try to persuade DEF to compromise and avoid litigation. Aren't the two results inconsistent?"

---

19. Cottam v. CVS Pharmacy, 436 Mass. 316, 764 N.E.2d 814 (2002). The case was decided based on common law principles (Massachusetts had not yet adopted its FRE-based evidence rules), but it neatly demonstrates how the "impeach for bias or prejudice" aspect of FRE 408(b) might apply. (Note: as a general rule, pharmacies are not liable for a failure to warn a customer about a medication's potential side-effects, but the court held that under the circumstances of the case, if Rx did in fact fail to warn, P (Cottam) would have a viable claim against CVS.)

Answer:

The results in the two cases may seem inconsistent, but actually no, they are not. The BCI report in § 15.7 is protected by FRE 408(a)—not because BCI gave it to Bates, but because the report was *created* as part of a compromise effort. It would not have existed at all, but for BCI's desire to try to persuade Bates to accept a compromise. That is why it is inadmissible over an FRE 408(a) objection. By contrast, the records ABC voluntarily gave to DEF—its normal records of expenditures, income, projections, etc.—were records ABC routinely made and kept, independent of the dispute between the two companies. If ABC had not turned them over voluntarily, ABC would have been required to do so during pretrial discovery. Therefore, they are not protected by the rule, and are admissible against ABC at trial.

Chapter 16

Other Relevance Issues

§ 16.1 Introduction

Relevance issues can arise in so many contexts that no one book can cover them all. This chapter quickly summarizes three for which the FRE codifies a rule (FRE 409, 410 and 411), and then discusses a grab-bag of others.

A. Offers to Pay Medical and Similar Expenses: FRE 409

---

§ 16.2 The rule; purpose and scope

FRE 409 provides:

> **Rule 409. Offers to Pay Medical and Similar Expenses**
>
> Evidence of furnishing, promising to pay, or offering to pay medical, hospital, or similar expenses resulting from an injury is not admissible to prove liability for the injury.

The Advisory Committee Note to the rule explains: "the reason often given [for excluding such evidence is] that such payment or offer is usually made from humane impulses and not from an admission of liability, and that to hold otherwise would tend to discourage assistance to the injured person."[1] The rule is likely to be invoked only by the defendant in a personal injury suit.

The following issues may arise in applying FRE 409.

1. The rule covers only offers regarding "medical, hospital or similar expenses resulting from an injury." It does not cover offers to pay for repairs to property, lost wages, etc.
2. Unlike FRE 408, the defendant need not show that the offer was made in an effort to prevent or terminate litigation.

---

1. ACN to FRE 409, quoting Annot., 20 A.L.R.2d 291, 293.

3. Unlike FRE 408, the rule does not exclude other "factual statements" that the defendant made when he or she offered to pay plaintiff's "medical, hospital or similar expenses."
4. Admissibility for other purposes. If plaintiff's attorney can come up with a plausible theory of relevance other than to suggest liability for the injury, well, good for her! But defendant could still oppose the evidence per Rule 403: the risk that the jury would improperly use the offer as proof of negligence or wrongdoing anyway.

§ 16.3 Questions

Question 1.

P, riding a bicycle, collides with motorist D's car. P fell and cried out in pain. D immediately phoned for an ambulance. P said, "What are you doing? I don't have insurance! I can't pay for an ambulance or a hospital!" D replied, "Don't worry about that, I'll pay for the ambulance and the hospital." D followed the ambulance to the hospital and in fact paid P's ambulance and hospital bills. Subsequently P sues D, alleging that the collision was D's fault, and offers evidence that D offered to, and did, pay the ambulance and hospital bills. D objects, citing FRE 409. Ruling?

Answer:

Objection sustained. That D paid those expenses is relevant only to suggest that, by doing so, D tacitly admitted that the collision was D's fault. FRE 409 excludes such payment, or an offer or promise to make such payment, if the evidence is "to prove [D's] liability for the injury."

Question 2.

Suppose instead D said: "I'm sorry, I'm sorry, it's all my fault. I'll pay the ambulance and the hospital bills and I'll buy you a new bicycle." D objects, citing FRE 408 and 409. Ruling?

Answer:

The judge should overrule D's FRE 408 objection. There is nothing in the facts that suggest D's statement was motivated by a desire to avoid litigation. Even if D testifies that that's what motivated his statement, the judge should probably rule that the far more likely explanation is that D spoke out of remorse and guilt, and that Rule 408 does not apply.

With regard to FRE 409: that rule excludes, "I'll pay for the ambulance and the hospital bills." But it does not exclude the rest of what D said. Thus, P is entitled to testify that D said, "I'm sorry, I'm sorry, it's all my fault. I'll buy you a new bicycle."

D might now argue that the bicycle reference is so misleading out of context that, per FRE 403, its unfair prejudice to him outweighs the legitimate probative value.

If the judge rules against D (i.e., if the judge rules that "I'll buy you a new bicycle" is admissible), D might well decide to withdraw the FRE 409 objection and let the whole statement in.

Question 3.

Suppose P and D disagree about what D said. D's version: "All I said was, I would pay for the ambulance and the hospital." But P insists that D said, "I'm sorry, I'm sorry, it's all my fault. I'll pay the ambulance and the hospital bills and I'll buy you a new bicycle."

Answer:

D's FRE 408 objection is still overruled, since neither version establishes that D's purpose at that moment was to avoid litigation.

Whether D actually said "I'm sorry, it was all my fault" is simply a factual issue for the jury to resolve. P will testify that D said it; after P rests, D will testify that he did not say it. Once the judge concludes that FRE 408 does not apply, there is no basis for the judge to exclude it. But D can exclude the offer to pay for the ambulance and hospital, and (as per Question 2), ask the judge to exclude the bicycle offer per FRE 403.

B. Pleas, Plea Discussions, and Related Statements: FRE 410

§ 16.4 Plea bargaining: an introduction

If D wants to plead guilty to all of the charges against D, D has an absolute right to do so: D does not need permission from the prosecutor or the judge. And D can do so even if D's attorney strenuously objects.

But even if there is a strong case against D, D has a certain amount of leverage: by pleading guilty, D is saving the government the expense and effort of taking the case to trial and the uncertainty as to outcome. (Juries sometimes render strange verdicts.[2]) Therefore it is common practice for the prosecutor to offer concessions to D to encourage D to give up the right to a trial. And many judges will give D a

2. In one of my first jury trials as a prosecutor, a jury acquitted the defendant of selling drugs. Dismayed, after the judge discharged the jury, I asked the foreman why they had a reasonable doubt. "Oh, we all knew he was guilty," the foreman replied, "there were no doubts about that. But you didn't *prove* it." Now stunned as well as dismayed, I reported this to my bureau chief. His advice: "Don't worry about it; you tried the case well. You probably just had too many PhDs on the jury." Thereafter I challenged (i.e., excluded) potential jurors with PhDs whenever I could, and won most of the rest of the cases I tried.

lighter sentence after a guilty plea than D would have received if D was convicted after a trial.

In most if not all American jurisdictions, the vast majority of criminal cases are disposed of without a trial. Some cases get dismissed because the prosecutor or judge concludes that there is insufficient admissible evidence or because the defendant has completed a pre-conviction diversion program. But most cases are disposed of by a plea bargain. Prosecutors and defendants (via their attorneys) plea bargain for the same reasons that civil litigants settle civil cases: to avoid the expense, uncertainty and risk of a total loss at trial. The criminal justice system relies on the process, because (except perhaps in a very few sparsely populated counties), there simply are not enough courtrooms, judges or lawyers to try every criminal case.

Plea bargaining is a complex subject, which may be covered in some detail in the second level criminal procedure course.[3] I'm giving you more background about it than you will need for your evidence course because it is really quite interesting and is a subject that every attorney should be somewhat familiar with.

The term "plea bargaining" is used to describe several related but not identical types of negotiations.

1. ***"Charge bargaining."*** The defendant agrees to plead guilty to a particular charge; in exchange, the prosecutor agrees to dismiss, or not to file, other charges. A defendant charged with two robberies, for example, might plead guilty to one, while the prosecutor dismisses the other; or a defendant charged with assault in the first degree might be offered a plea to assault in the second or third degree—less serious charges which carry less severe penalties than assault in the first.[4] A charge of distributing a controlled substance might be bargained down to the lesser count of possession with intent to distribute. And so on.
2. ***"Recommendation bargaining."*** This resembles charge bargaining, with the additional feature that, as part of the bargain, the prosecutor promises to recommend (or promises not to recommend) a particular sentence.
3. ***"Sentence bargaining."*** In this variation, prosecutor and defense attorney tell the judge, "We've agreed, subject to the court's approval, that *D* will plead guilty to *X*, and receive a sentence of *Y*." The judge may defer accepting the bargain until he or she has examined the pre-sentence report. In effect, this

3. Typically, the first crim pro law school course covers how the state can gather evidence against the defendant—i.e., the constitutional and statutory rules regulating search, seizure, arrest, interrogation, lineups, etc. The second crim pro course, often referred to "bail to jail," focuses on what happens in a criminal case after a defendant is arrested and charged.

4. Assaults are usually divided into degrees depending on various factors: the victim's injuries, whether a weapon was used, whether the assault was gang-related, whether it constituted a hate crime, whether the victim came within certain categories (e.g., a child, an elderly person, etc.).

means that if the judge concludes that justice requires a stiffer sentence than the prosecutor has agreed to, D may withdraw his or her plea.

4. ***"Cooperation bargaining."*** Sometimes the plea bargain includes a promise by the defendant to cooperate in some way with the authorities—to inform against former associates, to testify in an upcoming trial, etc. In exchange, the prosecution promises to reduce the charges, accept a plea to a lesser charge, and/or to inform the sentencing judge of D's cooperation.

But there is no one universal approach to plea bargaining. The laws vary from jurisdiction to jurisdiction. So do practices and customs. Within the same state, a district attorney in one county may have a very different approach than the district attorney in a neighboring county. Even within the same county, one judge's attitude toward plea bargaining may differ substantially from another judge's. Some judges lean hard on prosecutors and defense attorneys to plead out as many cases as possible; others simply leave it to the parties. Some judges pretty much rubber-stamp any agreement the parties reach; others are more inclined to resist.

§ 16.5 FRE 410

FRE 410 provides:

Rule 410. Pleas, Plea Discussions, and Related Statements

(a) **Prohibited Uses.** In a civil or criminal case, evidence of the following is not admissible against the defendant who made the plea or participated in the plea discussions:

(1) a guilty plea that was later withdrawn;

(2) a nolo contendere plea;[5]

(3) a statement made during a proceeding on either of those pleas under Federal Rule of Criminal Procedure 11 or a comparable state procedure;[6] or

(4) a statement made during plea discussions with an attorney for the prosecuting authority if the discussions did not result in a guilty plea or they resulted in a later-withdrawn guilty plea.

---

5. Nolo pleas are explained in § 16.6.

6. Fed. R. Crim. Proc. 11 governs the process whereby a defendant pleads guilty. It is often referred to as the "plea allocution." During the allocution, defendant is informed on the record of all the rights he would have if he went to trial, including a trial by jury, the right to have defense counsel cross-examine the prosecutor's witnesses, the right to call witnesses in defense, the right to testify or not testify, and so on. Then the defendant admits the facts that establish his or her guilt of the crime specified in the bargain.

(b) Exceptions. The court may admit a statement described in Rule 410(a)(3) or (4):

(1) in any proceeding in which another statement made during the same plea or plea discussions has been introduced, if in fairness the statements ought to be considered together; or

(2) in a criminal proceeding for perjury or false statement, if the defendant made the statement under oath, on the record, and with counsel present.

At first glance, FRE 410 appears to be the criminal law equivalent of FRE 408. Rule 408 assures that in a civil case, all the parties can engage in settlement discussions, confident that if no settlement is reached, nothing that either party said or did during the negotiations can be used against that party if the case ultimately goes to trial. Rule 410 does the same thing regarding plea bargaining, right?

Wrong. First glances are often misleading.

Question 1.

D is charged with assault in the first degree (shorthand: "assault one"), a class B felony that carries a maximum potential penalty of 25 years. Prior to trial, D (or, more likely, D's attorney) tells the prosecutor that D is willing to plead guilty to assault in the third degree ("assault three"), which carries a maximum of seven years. The prosecutor rejects the offer. At trial, the prosecutor offers evidence of D's willingness to plead to assault three. The offer is relevant because it constitutes an acknowledgment by D that D in fact committed the assault. Is D's offer admissible?

Answer:

No. FRE 410(a)(4) clearly excludes all evidence of D's offer.

Question 2.

Now turn the situation around. Suppose it is the prosecutor, not the defendant, who makes the offer:[7] D can plead guilty to assault three if D agrees in advance that the sentence will be seven years. D rejects the deal. At trial, D's attorney seeks to introduce the prosecutor's offer in evidence, to support the argument that, at worst, the jury should convict D only of assault three, rather than assault one—and to suggest that the defendant must be innocent, to reject such an attractive plea offer. The prosecutor objects per FRE 410. Ruling?

7. Usually it is the prosecutor, not the defendant, who initiates the plea-bargaining process by making an offer. Many prosecutors' offices have a standard plea policy—for example, barring unusual circumstances, a defendant will be permitted to plead to a crime "one step down" from what the defendant is charged with. If D is charged with a Class B felony, for example, the standard offer would be a plea to a lesser-included Class C felony.

Answer:

Objection overruled. FRE 410 protects only the *defendant* in the plea-bargaining context. Rule 410(a) clearly states that "evidence of the following is not admissible *against the defendant....*"

Question 3.

Rule 410 doesn't protect the prosecutor from having a plea offer used as evidence against the state? Really??!?

Answer:

Really.

Question 4.

That doesn't make sense. Well, then, what about Rule 408. That protects both sides of the bargaining process, right? So that's what protects the prosecutor from having the plea offer used against the state. Right?

Answer:

Yes, FRE 408 protects both sides of the bargaining process; but no, it does not protect a prosecutor. Rule 408 speaks explicitly about settling a "claim." The word "claim" in this context is a term of art referring to civil, not criminal cases.

Question 5.

But there must be some rule that precludes a defense attorney from offering evidence of a prosecutor's plea offer, right?

Answer:

Right: FRE 403.

Anyone familiar with the criminal justice system knows that plea bargaining is a common and constant part of the process. That a prosecutor offered a plea bargain in a particular case is usually only minimally relevant regarding the defendant's guilt, or the degree of defendant's guilt (such as an offer of a plea to assault two or assault three in a case charging assault one). If the judge allowed a defense attorney to offer evidence of a prosecutor's plea offer, the judge would have to allow the prosecutor to offer evidence to explain why its plea offer in this case did *not* indicate that the state thought its case was weak or that D had only committed assault three and not assault one. This would interrupt the trial with a mini-seminar about plea bargaining and therefore trigger the FRE 403 risks of prolonging the trial and distracting the jury from the facts it was empaneled to decide. A judge who allowed defense attorneys to offer evidence of a prosecutor's plea offers would swiftly find him/herself assigned for life to traffic court.

And guess what? If Attorney X made it practice to offer such evidence, prosecutors might stop making plea offers to Attorney X's clients. Word would get around quickly in the criminal milieu: unless you absolutely want to go to trial, stay away from Attorney X, because the DAs won't give X's clients plea offers. Pretty soon Attorney X would become an unemployed attorney, at least with regard to criminal cases.

§ 16.6 Nolo contendere pleas

FRE 410(a)(2) refers to a plea of nolo contendere, so here's a brief explanation.

A defendant who pleads *guilty* is required to acknowledge, during the on-the-record plea allocution, that he or she committed the crime to which he or she is pleading guilty. In a nolo contendere plea, the defendant refuses to admit guilt, but acquiesces in the entry of a judgment of conviction for that crime. The sentencing options are identical regardless whether the defendant pled guilty or entered a nolo plea, but there are ways in which a nolo plea is less burdensome to a defendant. Unless your evidence professor specifically covers those matters, you can safely ignore the reference to nolo pleas. (The ins and outs of nolo pleas are generally covered in a criminal procedure course.)

§ 16.7 Scope of the rule; exceptions

i. Scope of the rule: in theory, and in reality

FRE 410 is fairly comprehensive in what it excludes. If D pleads guilty but then withdraws the plea, the fact that he at first pled guilty (i.e., admitted his guilt) is inadmissible against him in any civil or criminal case. FRE 410(a)(1). The same is true with what regard to what D said during his plea allocution: such statements are also inadmissible against him in any civil or criminal case. FRE 410(a)(3).

There is, however, one tiny little glitch in this protection: federal prosecutors generally require a defendant to agree to waive most of these protections as part of a plea bargain. In reality, the system works something like this:

At some point after D has been arrested and arraigned, either defendant D (or D's attorney) or the prosecutor is likely to raise the possibility of a plea bargain. The prosecutor agrees that, if no plea agreement is reached and D goes to trial, what D said during plea discussions will not be used by the government against D during its case-in-chief. But the prosecutor informs D (and D's attorney) that the government will refuse to enter plea negotiations unless D agrees, in writing to the following:

(1) If a plea agreement is reached and D pleads guilty pursuant to the bargain, but then withdraws his/her guilty plea and goes to trial,

the government *can* use what D said during plea negotiations against D, during the government's case-in-chief, as evidence of D's guilt.

(2) If no plea is reached and the case goes to trial, if D testifies, the government can use those statements to impeach D's trial testimony.

(3) If D's cooperation with law enforcement authorities is part of the plea agreement, and D fails to perform as promised, the government can revoke the plea, take the case to trial, and use D's plea negotiation statements against D during its case-in-chief.

In essence, the government tells D: "If you want to discuss a plea bargain with us, you first have to waive most of the protections built into FRE 410 (and Fed. R. Crim. Pro. 11). No waiver, no plea offer." In *U.S. v. Mezzanatto,* the Supreme Court held that it is permissible for a prosecutor to require such waivers as a precondition to plea bargaining.[8]

But in answering questions about FRE 410, you should ignore reality and apply the rule as written—unless your evidence professor covers *Mezzanatto* and related issues and decisions.

ii. The exceptions

FRE 410(b) codifies two situations in which statements *are* admissible, even if they were made during a formal plea allocution (FRE 410(a)(3)) or during plea negotiations with a prosecutor (FRE 410(a)(4)):

> **(b) Exceptions.** The court may admit a statement described in Rule 410(a) (3) or (4):
>
> **(1)** any in any proceeding in which another statement made during the same plea or plea discussions has been introduced, if in fairness the statements ought to be considered together; or
>
> **(2)** in a criminal proceeding for perjury or false statement, if the defendant made the statement under oath, on the record, and with counsel present.

The exception codified in FRE 410(b)(1) is the equivalent of FRE 106. The exception codified in FRE 410(b)(2) applies only to statements that the defendant made

8. In *U.S. v. Mezzanatto,* 513 U.S. 196 (1995), the Supreme Court upheld the enforceability of a bargain which specified that if the defendant did not plead guilty or pled and then withdrew his plea and the defendant testified at trial, the prosecutor could impeach that testimony with any inconsistent statements the defendant had made during the course of plea bargaining. Since then, the government has gone further. Example: as part of a plea bargain, federal prosecutors sometimes require the defendant to stipulate that if he withdraws his plea for any reason, the government may use the defendant's in-court, on-the-record admission of guilt as evidence of guilt during the government's case-in-chief—thereby effectively abrogating FRE 410(a)(3).

in court, on the record, under oath, with his attorney present. It would apply if the defendant is now being prosecuted for lying during the plea allocution, or is now being prosecuted for making a statement in some other proceeding that is inconsistent with what he or she said during the plea allocution which is now being offered in evidence. My advice: ignore the provisions of FRE 410(b) in your evidence class unless your professor makes a point of stressing it.

§ 16.8 Question

Question.

Detectives Marple and Spade arrest *X* for participating in a shooting that resulted in a death.

After giving *X* his *Miranda* warnings, they tell *X* his best chance to help himself is probably "right now," by telling them who the other shooter was. *X* asks, "What am I going to be charged with?" The detectives reply, "Anywhere from first degree murder down to voluntary manslaughter, depending on circumstances." "What do I have to do to get it down to manslaughter?" "That's up to the D.A.," Marple responds, "but if you tell us who your partner was, we'll definitely let the D.A. know how much you helped." *X* responds, "OK, my partner was *Y*."

Shortly before arraignment, *X* asks the prosecutor the same question. The prosecutor says, "Let's not talk about that right now."

Based on *X*'s tip, the detectives gather evidence identifying *Y* as the other shooter. *X* and *Y* are both indicted for murder 1.

A week or so later, *X*'s attorney approaches the prosecutor and says, "My guy is still willing to cop a plea to manslaughter." "The only way I'll give him manslaughter," the prosecutor responds, "is if he testifies against *Y*. Otherwise, he can plead to murder 2, or go to trial." "Hey," defense counsel objects, "That wasn't part of his deal with the cops!"

"What deal?" the prosecutor asks. "All they promised him is that they would tell me that he gave up the other shooter. Okay, they told me. They kept their part of the deal. Your guy wants manslaughter, he's got to testify against *Y*. Otherwise, it's murder 2 or a trial."

Prior to trial, the prosecutor serves notice on *X* that he plans to offer into evidence, (a) *X*'s statement to Detectives Marple and Spade, and (b) the arraignment prosecutor's testimony that *X* offered to plead guilty to manslaughter. *X*'s attorney moves to exclude both statements, citing Rule 410. Choose the correct answer:

(a) Both statements are admissible.

(b) Neither statement is admissible.

(c) The statement to the detectives is admissible; the statement to the prosecutor is not.

(d) The statement to the prosecutor is admissible; the statement to the detectives is not.

Answer:

(c) is the correct answer.

The provision governing this question is FRE 410(a)(4). This problem does not involve an actual plea that was withdrawn, so FRE 410(a)(1) does not apply. It does not involve a nolo contendere plea, so FRE 410(a)(2) does not apply. And FRE 410(a)(3) applies only if there is a formal guilty plea allocution in court, which did not occur in this case.

FRE 410(a)(4) covers statements made by a defendant in a plea-bargaining context that are made *"with an attorney for the prosecuting authority."* Marple and Spade are not attorneys; they are detectives, conducting a custodial interrogation of an arrested murder suspect. The clause *"with an attorney for the prosecuting authority"* was inserted into the rule to assure that statements elicited during custodial interrogation would not be excluded by FRE 410, even if the defendant quite explicitly was seeking to cut a deal.

Thus, *X*'s statement to the detectives is admissible; his statement to the prosecutor is not.

C. Liability Insurance: FRE 411

§ 16.9 Overview

Does the fact that a party was insured against certain types of damage or loss have any real relevance as to who was at fault? I suppose, theoretically: "Because party X had insurance to over this kind of event, he probably was not as careful as he should have been." Or "Because party Y did not have insurance to cover this sort of event, she probably was extra careful and therefore it probably wasn't her fault that the event occurred."

But there is little empirical data that supports these inferences. So what is the actual "relevance" of evidence that either or both parties were insured?

Plaintiff sues defendant. The jury hears that the plaintiff is insured, and decides, "Since plaintiff is insured, let his insurance company pay for the damage; even if it was the defendant's fault, there's no reason why plaintiff should recover from the defendant, too."

Or:

The jury hears that the defendant is insured, and decides, "Even if the defendant wasn't at fault, let's find for the plaintiff, who really needs the money to compensate him for his loss. The defendant won't be out-of-pocket; let her insurance company pay." Or the jury might decide to be extra-generous to the plaintiff; after all, it is the insurance company, not the defendant, who will have to pay.

Such reasoning is understandable, but of course, it is also entirely improper. A jury's job is not to decide who can best afford to bear a financial loss; it is to decide which of the parties (if either) was at fault, and what amount of damages (if any) that party should be required to pay to the other. Thus, the rule basically bans evidence that a party was or was not insured. Of course, jurors may nevertheless assume that either or all parties carry insurance, but at least they won't hear evidence to confirm or contradict that assumption.

§ 16.10 Rule 411

FRE 411 provides:

> **Rule 411. Liability Insurance**
>
> Evidence that a person was or was not insured against liability is not admissible to prove whether the person acted negligently or otherwise wrongfully. But the court may admit this evidence for another purpose, such as proving a witness's bias or prejudice or proving agency, ownership, or control.

The first sentence of the rule declares the basic inadmissibility of evidence that a person was, or was not, insured against liability, if offered to prove or disprove negligence or other wrongdoing. This includes all kinds of insurance: auto insurance against collision or personal injury; business insurance against certain kinds of losses; homeowner insurance against fire, flood, injuries to guests; and so on.

The second sentence gives the judge discretion to admit evidence of insurance or its lack if that evidence is relevant for a purpose other than to support the inference of negligence or other wrongdoing. It cites specific other purposes as examples. In deciding whether to admit the evidence for such another purpose, the judge must apply FRE 403.[9]

<u>Question.</u>

P's 11-year-old son was playing in an area that had been unoccupied and unused for several years. The boy fell into an unmarked pit and was badly injured. P sued D on her son's behalf, alleging that D owned the land and that the failure to put a fence

9. The judge must also apply any other applicable rule, e.g., the rule against hearsay, rules governing authentication, etc.

or warning signs around the pit constituted a lack of due care and created a dangerous situation which D should have foreseen. D defends by asserting he no longer owned the land when P's son fell.

P wishes to introduce evidence that D paid the premiums on a liability insurance policy covering that land (albeit in an amount far less than P was suing for) during and even after the date of her son's injury. D objects that the evidence should be excluded per FRE 411 and 403. How should the judge rule?

Answer:

Rule 411 does not exclude this evidence, because P is not offering the insurance information as proof that D was negligent, but to show that, despite D's assertion that D no longer owned the land when P's son fell, D still owned it or had a degree of control over it. D's premium payments are clearly relevant for this other purpose.

Thus, the evidence is relevant on a permissible purpose, but creates a risk that the jury might improperly use the evidence to award damages even if D was not responsible for the land anymore. In assessing whether the relevance of the evidence to show ownership or control is substantially outweighed by the risk of unfair prejudice—the jury might decide, "a kid is hurt, who cares who owned the land, let's give the kid some of the insurance company's money, it can afford it"—the judge must consider three factors.

1. The importance of the issue for which the evidence is offered. Here, whether D still owned the land (or, at least, was responsible for its safety) is a crucial issue—if P fails to satisfy her burden of production on that issue, the judge will dismiss the case; if P fails to persuade the jury on that issue, the jury should find for D.
2. The availability of other evidence available to P to show D's continued ownership or control. For example, suppose several credible witnesses have or will testify that D continued to refer to the land as his, even well after the supposed sale; that D periodically advertised the land for sale after he allegedly sold it; and that D continued to pay real estate taxes on it. The judge might quite reasonably conclude that the additional probative value of the insurance information to prove ownership or control is substantially outweighed by the Rule 403 risk, and therefore exclude the insurance evidence. But if P lacked other significant credible evidence on the issue, the probative value of the insurance evidence is much more substantial, despite the risk of unfair prejudice to D.
3. The availability and presumed effectiveness of a limiting instruction. This is always a wild card. Nobody can predict with any degree of certainty what a jury will do with a given piece of evidence or whether it will understand or will follow the judge's instruction on how it should and should not use the evidence.

D. Similar Happenings

§ 16.11 Introduction

This subchapter deals with the admissibility of evidence concerning events somewhat similar but not directly related to the events that are the subject-matter of the case currently on trial. We will look at how the law evaluates such evidence in four factual settings:

1. In a personal injury or property damage action, defendant seeks to introduce evidence that plaintiff has brought several similar lawsuits in the past.
2. Conversely, in a personal injury or product liability action, plaintiff seeks to introduce evidence that other individuals suffered similar injuries or ill-effects while on defendant's property or after using defendant's product.
3. In a suit that focuses upon how a particular clause of a contract is to be construed, one of the litigants offers evidence of how similar prior contracts had been construed by parties to those prior contracts.
4. In an action (such as a condemnation proceeding) to determine the value of a piece of real estate, litigants often offer evidence of the sale price of other parcels of real estate, so the factfinder can use this information in calculating the value of the property that is the focus of the current litigation.

1. Prior suits by plaintiff

§ 16.12 Other personal injury or similar claims by plaintiff

P brings suit against D, claiming that D's negligence or other wrongful conduct caused P's injuries. D seeks to introduce evidence that P has brought several similar lawsuits in the past. Such evidence arguably may be relevant on several theories.

i. To suggest plaintiff is "accident-prone"

Evidence that P has frequently suffered various injuries in the past is, arguably, relevant to show that P's own clumsiness or negligence was probably the cause of those other injuries, and probably this one as well. (Another way of putting it: "P is such a klutz, it must be P's own fault.") Courts generally reject this theory as unduly prejudicial to the plaintiff. Indeed, such evidence appears to be banned by FRE 404(b)(1): "Prohibited Uses. Evidence of a crime, wrong, or other act is not admissible to prove a person's character in order to show that on a particular occasion the person acted in accordance with the character." In other words, evidence that P's inattention or clumsiness might have caused P's own previous mishaps is not admissible to show that is what happened in the current case.

ii. Plaintiff is "claim-conscious"

The defense argues that plaintiff's prior claims demonstrate that P exaggerates every little mishap or bump into a lawsuit. This, too, seems to fall within the ban of FRE 404(b)(1).

iii. To show that the current claim is fraudulent

This theory of relevance is consistent with several of the permitted "other purposes" permitted in FRE 404(b)(2), particularly absence of accident; intent; and common scheme or plan. Thus, a court should apply the five-step process set out in § 7.8 to § 7.14:

(1) Purpose: to show that the current lawsuit is fraudulent.

(2) Need for the evidence. What else does D have to support this defense?

(3) Proof that P's prior personal injury claims are fraudulent. Most courts hold that the mere fact that plaintiff has brought numerous prior personal injury lawsuits is not of itself sufficient to support the inference that the prior suits were fraudulent (and, by inference, so is this one). Rather, as to each prior claim D hopes to introduce, D must at least offer evidence sufficient to support a finding that that prior claim was fraudulent.

(4) Fasprelipi. The judge must assess whether the evidence indeed has factually specific relevance to show absence of accident, plan, etc., independent of the propensity inference. (See generally § 7.22 to § 7.33.) Let's assume that the evidence satisfies this requirement.

(5) FRE 403 and FRE 105. Assuming P objects per FRE 403, the judge must assess the legitimate probative value of the evidence that a prior claim was fraudulent, against the risk that the jury will give the evidence more weight than it is worth. If the latter substantially outweighs the relevance of the former, the evidence should be excluded. In making this assessment, the stronger the evidence that the prior claim was fraudulent, the more likely the judge will admit the evidence as circumstantial proof that this claim is fraudulent as well.

iv. The injury or disability plaintiff blames on defendant was actually the result of a prior mishap

Here, the evidence may be irrelevant as to whether the defendant was negligent or at fault in causing the plaintiff's fall (or other event). But such evidence may have considerable relevance on the issue of damages—if defendant can provide specific evidence connecting a prior injury to the condition or disability for which plaintiff is now suing. Often this will require expert testimony.

v. Similar claims other than personal injuries

The issues discussed in this section can also apply if P has filed numerous food poisoning claims against restaurants, or has filed several different law suits claiming that P suffered significant side-effect reactions to various medications, etc.

§ 16.13 Prior property damage suits—fires, etc.

Some people seem to be born under a bad sign: houses or other buildings they occupy tend to burn down. And by some strange coincidence, in each case, the building was heavily insured. At some point, an insurance company refuses to pay out on a policy; when P sues, the company will defend on the ground that P deliberately set the fire to collect on the insurance policy. The company will offer evidence of the prior fires to support that defense.

P should object to such evidence per FRE 404(b) and FRE 403, and the court should analyze the evidence accordingly.

Let's assume that as to at least one prior fire, there is credible evidence (such as a fire marshal's report or expert testimony) that that prior fire was set, rather than being an accident. There is no direct evidence as to who may have set it, but P had heavily insured the property sometime before the fire. Is that enough to allow the insurance company to introduce evidence of that other fire? And how many such prior fires must there be before the doctrine of chances (see § 7.31) kicks in?

Reasonable people disagree.

2. Prior claims against defendant

§ 16.14 Similar accidents or mishaps on defendant's property or premises

P is injured while on D's property or premises and sues, alleging that D negligently allowed a dangerous condition to exist and that the condition caused P's injuries. At trial, P offers evidence that other individuals also suffered, or almost suffered, injuries at the same location. Is such evidence admissible?

The answer depends upon a variety of factors: the purpose for which the evidence is offered, the extent to which that issue is truly contested, how persuasively the plaintiff can prove that the other incidents occurred, the probative value of such evidence with regard to the purpose for which it is offered, and the risk of unfair prejudice. If this list of factors has a familiar ring to it, it should: it is the same analysis originally suggested with regard to Rule 404(b).

We don't apply FRE 404(b) here, because the evidence does not concern the character or activities of an individual, and the issues in prior mishap cases are different than in FRE 404(b) litigation. Still, the outline is basically the same.

i. Purpose

Evidence that others were injured, or almost injured, on D's property or premises may be relevant on three theories: to prove that a dangerous condition existed; to prove that the dangerous condition caused P's injuries; and to prove that, prior to P's injuries, D had notice of the dangerous condition in time to have taken corrective action that would have prevented P's injury.[10]

ii. Need for the evidence

Any one or more of those purposes may be a contested issue in P's suit against D, depending on the facts and pleadings in the case.

iii. Proof of the other mishap

If a prior mishap is offered to prove notice, it suffices to show that D received notice of the complaint or allegation about the prior mishap. But the mere fact that someone complained or alleged he or she was injured (or almost injured), if offered to prove the danger existed, is hearsay; unless it fits into a hearsay exception, a complaint itself is not admissible to prove that the condition existed. Direct proof, such as testimony of someone who witnessed the danger and prior injury or near-injury, is generally required.

iv. Measuring relevance

The relevance of the prior mishap depends primarily on the similarity between the prior mishap and the occasion causing P's injury or loss. The degree of similarity required is greater if offered to prove the dangerous condition or causation, on one hand, than to show notice, on the other.

v. FRE 403

By now you are quite familiar with how to apply FRE 403. If you need a refresher, review Chapter 3. (Even if you don't think you need a refresher, it's not a bad idea to review Chapter 3 from time to time.)

§ 16.15 Structural defects and dangers

Questions

On a sunny July afternoon in 2021 in Winterfell, Maine, P, an elderly woman, tripped and fell on the sidewalk in front of the XYZ store, and broke her hip. That stretch of sidewalk had been put down in July of 2018. P sued the town, alleging that the sidewalk was uneven and rough, and that this caused her to fall. P testifies about what happened and the injuries, pain, and losses she suffered as a result. An ambulance attendant who took P to a nearby hospital testified that there was nothing on the sidewalk—no mud, no wet leaves, etc.—where P fell.

---

10. If P is the first to suffer such an injury, D may offer the absence of prior accidents or mishaps to rebut P's claim that a dangerous condition existed, or that the condition caused P's injury, or that D had notice of the danger.

Question 1.

Next, P calls PW1, who lived on that block, to testify that the condition of the sidewalk in front of the XYZ store in July, 2021, was pretty much the same as it was when the sidewalk was installed back in 2018. TA, the town's attorney, objects that this is irrelevant. How should P respond?

Answer:

The easiest response is to ask the judge to admit the testimony as conditionally relevant per FRE 104(b). (See § 1.13.)

Assume the judge does so.

Question 2.

PW2 will testify that at about 7 a.m. in early January of 2019, he slipped and fell on the same stretch of sidewalk. TA objects that the evidence is irrelevant. How should the judge rule?

Answer:

It depends to some extent on what PW2's testimony is being offered to prove. If offered to prove that the town had notice of the dangerous condition, PW2's testimony should be excluded, because PW2 has not testified that he notified anyone in the town government about the incident, nor publicized it in a way that would likely be heard by town officials.

If PW2's testimony is offered to prove that that stretch of sidewalk was dangerous and/or that this dangerous condition caused P's fall, the judge should still exclude PW2's testimony, because P failed to show sufficient similarities between PW2's mishap, and P's.

Question 3.

In what ways are the two incidents dissimilar, and why are the differences important?

Answer:

They are different in time of year and time of day. P tripped and fell on a sunny afternoon in July; PW2 slipped and fell at 7 a.m. on a January morning.

Why are these differences important?

Because it was bright and sunny when P fell, and it was dark when PW2 slipped and fell. Thus, the condition was inherently more dangerous when PW2 fell, than when P fell.

How do we know that it was dark when PW2 fell? Because Maine is pretty far north, and the sun probably wasn't up yet by 7 a.m. on a January morning. I know, because I checked: according to Google, in early January, the sun doesn't rise in Kennebunkport, Maine, in January until about 7:10 a.m.[11]

Question 4.

"Wait a minute, Prof," you may be thinking, "did you really expect us to do research about sunrise times in Maine just to answer this question?"

Answer:

No; and if this was a quiz or exam question, you wouldn't be able to even if you wanted to. But the facts tell you that these events occurred in a town in Maine, and PW2's fall was at 7 a.m. early in January. I assume you know enough about the seasons and our planet to know that except on the equator, in winter, the sun rises later and sets earlier than the rest of the year.[12] And I assume you know enough about earth science to know that and that the further north you go, the less daylight there is in the winter and the more daylight there is in the summer, and Maine is further north than any other state except Alaska.[13] So you had enough information to at least mention the possibility that it still might have been dark at 7 a.m. in January.

Remember: a law professor rarely includes facts in an exam question unless he or she has a reason. One of your challenges in answering a law school exam question (particularly an essay question) is to figure out why the prof included each fact in the question.[14]

Question 5.

How else are these differences in time of year and time of day significant?

Answer:

We know from the ambulance attendant's testimony that the sidewalk was dry and clear on the day that P fell and broke her hip that sunny afternoon in July 2021. But in Maine, in winter, there is a good chance that there was snow or ice on the sidewalk. Note, too, that PW2 "*slipped* and fell," which suggests that it was something on the sidewalk, rather than the sidewalk itself, that caused P's fall.

Remember: the relevance of PW2's fall depends on whether the circumstances of PW2's fall were sufficiently similar to those involving P's fall. P has the burden of establishing sufficient similarity. P's attorney failed to elicit from PW2 whether the sidewalk was clear and dry when he "slipped."

11. I chose Kennebunkport because the case on which this problem is based is *Simon v. Town of Kennebunkport, Me.*, 417 A.2d 982 (1980).

12. This effect is less dramatic the closer you are to the equator, but this effect is still noticeable even in the southern tip of Florida.

13. And if you didn't know this before, you know it now.

14. Sometimes I included facts in a quiz or exam question only because they supported some historical or artistic reference that amused me. But when I did that, I'd add a footnote: "Do not consider or discuss this fact in your answer."

Question 6.

P calls PW3, the town clerk, who testifies—perhaps reluctantly—that between August 2018 and August 2021, the town received nine complaints from people alleging that they fell or almost fell on that stretch of sidewalk. Discuss the issues presented.

Answer:

A complaint is inadmissible hearsay if offered to show that the condition complained about in fact existed; nor is it admissible to show that the condition caused P's injury. But if other evidence has been introduced sufficient to support a finding that the condition existed—and P's own testimony satisfies that requirement—evidence of complaints is admissible to prove that the town had notice of the defect long enough prior to P's fall to have taken corrective action that would have made P's fall much less likely.

But this is true only with regard to complaints received before P's trip-and-fall in July 2021. Any complaints that the town received after P fell would be irrelevant to show that the town had notice of the condition prior to P's fall.

The judge should admit PW3's testimony about the complaints the town received prior to P's fall, but exclude testimony about complaints that were made after P's fall. The judge should instruct the jury per FRE 105 that it cannot use the clerk's testimony as evidence that a dangerous condition existed, but if other evidence satisfies them by a preponderance of the evidence that this stretch of sidewalk was dangerous, they could use the clerk's testimony about the complaints in deciding whether the town had notice of the danger prior to P's fall.[15]

Question 7.

Finally, P calls PW4, the proprietor of the store closest to the sidewalk where P fell. PW4 will testify, "Every year since 2018 when they put in the sidewalk, I've seen dozens of people fall or almost fall on that stretch of sidewalk. Got so bad I put a sign up inside the store telling people to be careful about the sidewalk." Discuss the issues presented.

Answer:

PW4's testimony might be objectionable as too broad, because it includes incidents (such as PW2's) where the circumstances differed considerably from those in P's fall. If TA objects, or even if he doesn't, P's attorney should ask as a follow-up question, something along these lines.

"Let's narrow it down. During daylight hours, when it was not raining or snowing or terribly windy, when there was no ice or snow or mud or wet leaves or the like

15. The judge would not be required to give such an instruction unless TA requested it, but the judge could do so without a request.

on the sidewalk—did you see people trip and fall or almost fall there?" PW4 will, if permitted, answer, "A-yup. Yung uns, old-timers. Mainers, Flatlanders.[16] Couple times a week."

This testimony should be admitted as evidence that the sidewalk was dangerous and that its dangerous condition caused P's fall.

Note: In an actual case, P would probably call PW4 before calling PW2 or PW3. I put her last in the sequence because doing so made it easier to isolate the issues presented by PW2 and PW3.

Question 8.

Back in Question 1, the judge admitted PW1's testimony per FRE 104(b). Has P satisfied that condition, i.e., has P established that PW1's testimony is in fact relevant?

Answer:

Yes. PW4's testimony—that people frequently fell or almost fell at that stretch of sidewalk during the three years since the sidewalk was installed—is relevant only if the sidewalk was more or less in the same condition on those previous occasions as it was when P fell. Thus, PW1's testimony helped lay the foundation for PW4's testimony.

Note: the kind of "structural" defect—the uneven sidewalk—discussed in this section need not be a man-made structure. Suppose, for example, a large dead tree hangs over a path and bench in a park. On June 10, a large branch fell off the tree and struck P, causing serious injuries. In a lawsuit against the town that maintained the park, P wants to offer evidence that other branches from that tree had fallen on or near the path and bench, and within a day or so on those prior occasions, park personnel collected the pieces of branch that had fallen and cleared the bench and the path. On one such previous occasion, a person was badly scratched by a falling branch.

Those prior branch-falls would be relevant to prove that failure to take down the tree allowed a dangerous condition to exist, and that the town had notice of the situation and failed to take preventive action.

§ 16.16 Temporary and recurring situations; "slip and fall" cases

The previous section focused on long-term structural defects or natural dangers in the location in question. "Similar accident evidence" is also an issue where plaintiff claims to have been injured because defendant negligently allowed a temporary or transitory dangerous situation on its property. This situation arises most often

16. According to Google, Maine natives refer to themselves as "Mainers"; someone from anywhere else is a "flatlander."

when a plaintiff, who claims to have injured himself slipping on something on the floor of defendant's business premises, offers evidence that similar matter was on the floor on other occasions. Such evidence is arguably relevant on at least two theories.

First, to establish negligence in such cases, a plaintiff must generally prove that defendant had notice of the transitory condition. Evidence that the condition had occurred on numerous occasions in the past helps establish that defendant had actual or constructive notice of its probable recurrence.

Second, evidence that foreign matter was on the floor on numerous other occasions makes it more likely that such matter was on the floor at the time of, and caused, plaintiff's injury. Courts are not of one mind as to whether such evidence is admissible for this purpose. Some courts admit such evidence, explicitly or implicitly accepting its relevance to show that the store did not have adequate inspection procedures to avoid such a problem. Other courts, emphasizing the transitory nature of the condition, bar such evidence.

§ 16.17 Allegedly defective products or harmful substances

In products liability actions, it is common for a plaintiff to offer evidence that other people who used the defendant's product also suffered injuries or negative side effects as a result. The most frequent use of this evidence arises regarding products mass-produced for use by the general public—automobiles, cosmetics, medications, etc. But it also can arise in cases involving workplace accidents, in suits against the manufacturer of tools, machinery and substances used on the job.

Once again, the key is whether the "other" mishaps are similar enough to what the plaintiff alleges happened in his or her case. Keep in mind that the party seeking to offer the other-mishaps evidence has the burden of establishing sufficient similarity.

Suppose, for example, P claims that the brakes on his 2020 Saab sedan failed, causing the car to crash, injuring P. P plans to call witness PW5 to testify that his 2018 Saab pickup truck's brakes failed, causing a collision. D moves in limine to exclude that evidence, pointing out that a pickup truck is very different from a sedan. Should the judge exclude it?

It depends. If the braking system on the 2018 pickup was the same as that in the 2020 sedan, and the circumstances in which the brakes in each vehicle allegedly failed were pretty much the same, the judge might quite reasonably deny the motion and allow PW5 to testify. But if the pickup braking system was substantially different from the sedan's, or if P's crash occurred on a dry, well-maintained highway and PW5's collision occurred on an icy curvy poorly maintained back road, a judge would probably conclude that the two incidents were so different that the brake failure in PW5's pickup had little relevance in showing that the brakes in P's 2020 sedan were defective. In that case, the judge should exclude PW5's testimony.

Another example: in 2010, P, while at work, was exposed to a Nontox, a chemical manufactured by D Corp. In 2020, P developed a particular form of cancer (let's call it type A cancer), and sued D Corp., alleging that her exposure to Nontox caused her cancer. To bolster her claim that Nontox caused her cancer, P seeks to offer evidence that AV (another victim) 1, AV2 and AV3 were also exposed to Nontox at their places of work and later developed cancer. If Nontox caused cancer in AV1, AV2 and AV3, P argues, it is likely that it also caused P's cancer.

Admissibility depends on whether the similarities between P's case and any or all of the others were substantial enough. Suppose, for example, P was exposed to Nontox fumes for short periods of time for a few days. By contrast, AV1, AV2 and AV3 worked with it in liquid form for several hours a day over a multi-month period, occasionally having some splash on their bodies, and within five years of exposure, each developed type B cancer. The substantial differences between the facts in P's case and those involving AV1, AV2, and AV3 argue against allowing P to introduce testimony about AV1, AV2 and AV3.

Keep in mind, also, that the evidence of the other incidents must satisfy other requirements for admissibility. Such incidents cannot be proven by evidence which is inadmissible hearsay, or by documents which have not been properly authenticated. If expert testimony is required to establish the connection between the other cases and P's, testimony would be excluded if the witness P calls to make the connection lacks qualifications to give expert testimony on the subject.

3. Miscellany

§ 16.18 Other contracts

In litigation that focuses on how a particular clause of a contract should be construed, it is not unusual for a litigant to offer evidence of how similar contracts were construed by the parties to those contracts. Supplier S1 agreed to supply certain devices to Buyer (B). Suppose, in litigation between S1 and B over breach of contract, S1 is offering evidence about how other, similar contracts have been interpreted; B objects that the evidence is insufficiently relevant.[17]

1. <u>S1 offers evidence that S1 and B had encountered similar circumstances in previous contracts between them</u>. S1 further offers evidence of how B had interpreted the same clause in previous contracts between S1 and B; as evidence that the same clause should be interpreted the same way this time.

---

17. In such cases, it doesn't matter whether S1 is the plaintiff and B is the defendant, or vice versa; either might offer such evidence.

Courts generally hold that such evidence is admissible: B's approach to the contract clause in previous dealings with S1 is highly relevant as to how the parties intended that clause to be interpreted this time.

2. S1 offers evidence that B had similar contracts with suppliers S2 and S3, and that B interpreted the same clause with S2 and S3 the same way S1 seeks to have that clause interpreted this time.

As a general rule, courts do not admit such evidence. B's relationship with S2 or S3 might differ substantially from the S1-B relationship. Maybe B interprets the clause more generously for S2 because S2 has done the same for B regarding different contract clauses; or perhaps a few years ago, when B was having difficulty financially, S2 allowed B to delay paying S2 for a year, and out of gratitude, B is willing to interpret a clause in the B-S2 contract in a way quite favorable to S2. And maybe B interprets the clause with leniency for S3 because S3's CEO is B's CFO's SIL.[18]

The basic point is that there are lots of reasons why B might interpret the same clause differently with different companies. If the judge admitted the evidence, B should be entitled to offer evidence explaining why it did so—and why a jury should not automatically assume that S1 was entitled to the same leniency. Given the dubious relevance of the B-S2 and B-S3 cases, the better approach is to exclude the evidence.

3. S1 offers evidence of similar contracts it had with other buyers, and how those buyers interpreted the same clause.

Courts generally reject such evidence, reasonably holding that how other companies interpreted a particular clause in a contract should not be admissible against B.

4. S1 offers evidence of how the industry as a whole interprets that clause.

If S1 can establish that there is an industry-wide understanding as to the meaning and application of a particular clause in contracts of this kind, courts generally do admit such evidence. S1 can attempt to show this by offering evidence of generally accepted written business standards and practices; or by expert testimony; or by testimony from several people who are active in that industry.

Keep in mind that the four approaches outlined in this section are generalizations. Some jurisdictions may deviate from this pattern; or the particular facts of a case might justify a different result than what I've outlined here.

---

18. CEO: chief executive officer, i.e., the Alpha male or female who runs S3. CFO: chief financial officer. SIL: son-in-law.

§ 16.19 Other land sales

In an action (such as a condemnation proceeding) to determine the value of a parcel of real estate,[19] litigants often offer evidence of the sale price of other parcels of real estate as a basis to infer what the fair market value is of the property that is the focus of the current litigation. Say, for example, a city and an owner are battling over how much the city should be required to pay the owner for Oak Grove, a 50-acre parcel of land. The city offers evidence that during the past few years, three other parcels sold on the open market—Skunk Hollow, Rockfall Valley, and Webfoot Swamp—and the amounts each sold for.

The relevance of such other sales depends on a variety of factors: (1) How recently or long ago the other sales occurred. (2) Whether intervening events since those sales might have raised or lowered the value of Oak Grove compared to those other sales. (3) The size of the other properties compared to Oak Grove. (4) The desirability of Oak Grove's location compared to the other sales. (5) Whether Oak Grove or the others already had electric and sewer lines in place. (6) Whether each has or had existing structures that were usable or which had to be removed. (7) The aesthetic aspects of each parcel. And so on. To be relevant, less similarity need be shown if the value-comparing is done by an expert witness; greater similarity must be shown before the other sales may be introduced for the purposes of enabling the jury to make its own comparison.

19. A "condemnation proceeding" is typically one in which a government agency uses the power of eminent domain to acquire property from an owner to use it for the public good—for example, to build a highway or create a park or a school or hospital. The owner, however reluctantly, can be forced to cede the land to the government agency, but must receive fair market value for it.

Afterword

Here is the list from § P.8, telling you where to find each hidden or not-so-hidden reference and, where needed, an explanation.

The cosmic significance of 9:37 p.m., October 30, 2019. § 1.2.

Don't it make that brown eye blue? No, it don't. § 1.2.

Why it is good to have a friend with a short attention span who knows nothing about the law. § 1.9.

"Could this be magic" is the title of a doo-wop love song recorded by the Dubs in the 1950s. It is available on YouTube. § 1.9 and § 1.11.

Blake Shelton's 2004 hit song "Some Beach." § 1.12.

Twenties questions. § 1.12. The section title is a takeoff on an old radio and TV show, "20 Questions." The defendant is Jackson Zwanzig. Andrew Jackson is on the $20 bill; Zwanzig is the German word for twenty. Zwanzig's alibi witness is named "Venti," which is twenty in Italian, and a large cup of coffee at Starbucks.

Holodecks. § 2.3.

Professional advice: where not to interview a client. § 2.7.

Professional advice: where not to discuss a case. § 2.31.

Tissues and country and western music. § 3.11.

A business model you should *not* recommend to a client. § 3.11.

Judy Garland and L. Frank Baum. § 4.1. Baum wrote the Wizard of Oz books, on which the movie is based. Judy Garland played Dorothy.

Sir William S. Gilbert (HMS Pinafore). § 5.2 note 2.

What do Oliver Wendell Holmes, Eleanor Roosevelt, Linus Van Pelt, and Confucius have in common? § 5.2 note 3.

Charles Lutwidge Dodgson. § 6.2. Dodgson was a 19th-century British mathematician, scholar, teacher, photographer, inventor, and a deacon in the Anglican church. His best known publications are *Curiosa Mathematica, Part I: A New Theory of Parallels; Curiosa Mathematica, Part II: Pillow Problems*; and *The Principles of Parliamentary Representation.* Oh—Dodgson also wrote *Alice in Wonderland* and *Through the Looking Glass*, using the pen name "Lewis Carroll."

Lin-Manuel Miranda. §6:11 note 2. Miranda is the author, composer and star of the Broadway smash hit, *Hamilton*. (His first musical, *In the Heights*, won the 2008 Tony award for best musical.)

When history buffs and lovers of Shakespeare make poor jurors. §6.11 note 2.

Professor Fishman favorably compares himself to one of the greatest writers and statesmen in world history. §6.14.

Shar-peis. §6.18.

Dog poop. §6.20.

The official definition of "elderly." §6.22.

Dog poop. §6.22.

Professor Fishman favorably compares himself to the Bible. §6.22.

A defensive tackle for the Dallas Cowboys. §6.27.

Sainthood in everyday life. §7.4.

What Rudolph does the rest of the year. §7.5 note 10.

What "kemosabe" means in various Native American languages. §7.20.

Charles Dickens, §7.20 Question 8 ("What the Dickens"). All of the named participants are characters in a Dickens novel, albeit with one gender switch. If you don't know which one, there is a clue in footnote 7.

Taking three wickets from three consecutive balls. Or else, an octopus. §7.23.

Weather, in the Heights. §7.25. The characters are all taken from Emily Bronte's 1847 novel, *Wuthering Heights*. (Her sister Charlotte wrote *Jane Eyre*.) Neither, so far as I know, ever visited Colombia. (Or Columbia University, either, at least not while I was a student at the law school.)

A particularly bad way to pick up some extra cash fast. §7.25 note 4.

Professor Fishman's pre-law school employment history. §8.3.

Professor Fishman's efforts to insure domestic tranquility. §8.9.

Eschewing pellucidity. §10.03.

What Hollywood and Kansas City, Missouri, have in common. §11.2.

Ors well that ends well. (Or: the weather in April.) §11.9.

The professor channels his inner Roger Ebert. §11.11.

Longfellow Deeds and the pixies; or the professor again channels his inner Roger Ebert. §12.6.

Roger Ebert, 3.0. § 12.12.

What do a Jabberwock, Mad Magazine and a witch doctor have in common? § 12.12.

The difference between beef wellington and beef stroganoff. § 12.11.

What the Dickens? § 13.04. Miss Havisham and Estella are characters in Dickens' novel, *Great Expectations.*

Pulitzer Prize for fiction. § 13.08.

A-B-C, easy as 1-2-3-4-5. § 13.16.

We don't care how miserable you feel, Victor: you go first. § 13.18.

Volleyball and Einstein's theory of special relativity. § 13.26.

What to do before you go on vacation. § 15.5 note 2.

The prof quotes the Bard (but doesn't use quotation marks). § 15.6.

How not to apologize. § 15.7.

"Just when you thought it was safe to get back in the shower." § 15.7. Names are taken from Robert Bloch's novel *Psycho.* Norman Bates is the proprietor of the Bates Motel. The shower scene in the 1960 movie, portraying a brutal murder, was shocking in its time, even though it actually showed no violence or nudity at all. Directed by Alfred Hitchcock, it is considered by many to be among the best psychological horror movies ever made.

Albert King (not the basketball player), Jimi Hendrix, Pat Travers, Cream. Each of them has recorded Albert King's classic blues song, "Born Under a Bad Sign." § 16.13.

"Sunrise, sunset; sunrise, sunset; swiftly fly the days..." § 16.16.

When would someone from, say, the Rockies, be referred to as a "Flatlander"? § 16.15.

Index

References are to sections, not page numbers.